THE NOBEL
SCIENTISTS

THE NOBEL SCIENTISTS

A BIOGRAPHICAL ENCYCLOPEDIA

GEORGE THOMAS KURIAN

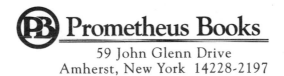 Prometheus Books

59 John Glenn Drive
Amherst, New York 14228-2197

Published 2002 by Prometheus Books

Inquiries should be addressed to
Prometheus Books
59 John Glenn Drive
Amherst, New York 14228–2197
VOICE: 716–691–0133, ext. 207
FAX: 716–564–2711
WWW.PROMETHEUSBOOKS.COM

06 05 04 03 02   5 4 3 2 1

Library of Congress Cataloging-in-Publication Data

Kurian, George Thomas.
    The Nobel scientists : a biographical encyclopedia / George Thomas Kurian.
        p. cm.
    Includes bibliographical references and index.
    ISBN 1–57392–927–1 (alk. paper)
    1. Scientists—Biography—Dictionaries. 2. Science—Awards. 3. Nobel Prizes.
I. Title.

Q141 .K78 2001
509.2'2—dc21
[B]   2001048473

Printed in the United States of America on acid-free paper

CONTENTS

CONTENTS

PHYSICS

CONTENTS

CONTENTS

PHYSIOLOGY OR MEDICINE

CONTENTS

CONTENTS

PREFACE

The Nobel Scientists: A Biographical Encyclopedia is a biographical reference that celebrates one hundred years of the Nobel Prize in 2001. It contains the profiles of 466 scientists and chronicles their lives and achievements in, as far as possible, simple, nontechnical language. Each laureate receives a separate entry, even when the prize was awarded in a given year to two or three persons. This may mean some overlap, but makes each entry self-contained.

Among intellectual and scientific institutions in the modern world, the Nobel Prize occupies a unique position. It is the accolade par excellence for accomplishments in six fields and it confers on its winners the crown of ultimate achievement. Begun in 1900, it has honored over 700 individuals, of whom more than 450 were scientists. The emphasis on science was a direct legacy of Alfred Nobel, who himself was a child of the nineteenth century. It reflected the great hopes that his generation placed on the ability of science and scientists to usher in a brave new world of limitless possibilities. This dream was achieved in the sense of creating a world where the mysteries of matter and the world were, if not solved, at least clarified, and many dread diseases that afflicted mankind for centuries were, if not eliminated, at least controlled. In only very rare instances in human history has the dream of one man to create a better world been so fruitful and so inspiring.

Nobel Prize winners form one of the most exclusive clubs in the world. The scientific prizes have been more or less uncontroversial and often widely applauded. This is because the Nobel Prize Committee itself is a highly respected body and its selection norms and procedures are among the most rigorous in the world. They involve nominations from distinguished captains of erudition and professional associations throughout the world. Nominations of candidates can be made only on invitation. Between 200 and 250 nominations are received every year by the Nobel selection bodies for science. In many cases, the same candidate is nominated by more than one nominator. Some candidates are proposed over and over again for many years before they are selected. The only criterion adopted by the selection committee is that laid down by Alfred Nobel himself—the discoveries should "confer the greatest benefit on mankind." According to the statutes, no more than three persons can be awarded the Nobel Prize in any one field in any one year, and this seriously limits the number of laureates. The Nobel Foundation itself is not involved in proposing candidates or evaluating their work or the final selections, but it arranges the Nobel Prize ceremonies and also administers the Nobel Symposia. A second reason why the prize is so prestigious is that it is one of the first truly international prizes to be awarded in the twentieth century. Citizens from over thirty nations have received the prizes in science. Because of the statutory limitations on the number of winners in any one year, many great discoveries have not received an award and big science projects involving many teams of workers are often ignored. The turbulence of the twentieth century is reflected in the history of the Nobel Prizes. The two world wars resulted in a hiatus in the awards between 1914 and 1918 and between 1939 and 1945. Nazi Germany prohibited the award of the prizes to its citizens during the latter part of the 1930s.

The Nobel Scientists is organized in three sections: Chemistry, Physics, and Physiology or Medicine. In each section, the names are presented chronologically.

The Nobel Scientists is a rich tableau of the lives of the many geniuses whose lives have changed the very nature of knowledge in the twentieth century.

CHEMISTRY

VAN'T HOFF, JACOBUS HENRICUS

Prize: Chemistry, 1901. *Born*: August 30, 1852; Rotterdam, Netherlands. *Died:* March 1, 1911; Berlin, Germany. *Nationality*: Dutch. *Education*: Polytechnic School, Netherlands, technology diploma, 1871; University of Utrecht, Netherlands, doctorate, 1874. *Career*: Veterinary College, Utrecht, Netherlands, Professor, 1876–77; University of Amsterdam, Netherlands, Professor, 1877–78; University of Leipzig, Germany, Professor, 1878–96; University of Berlin, Germany, Professor, 1896–1911. *Other Awards*: Davy Medal, 1893; Chevalier de la Legion d'Honneur, 1894; Helmholtz Medal, Prussian Academy of Sciences, 1911.

Citation: "In recognition of the extraordinary services he has rendered by the discovery of the laws of chemical dynamics and osmotic pressure in solutions."

Life Work: Van't Hoff's views on asymmetrical carbon atoms is the foundation of modern stereochemistry or the study of the three-dimensional structure of molecules. In 1884 Van't Hoff applied the principles of thermodynamics to formulate the concept of mobile equibilrium resulting from variations in temperature. He also introduced the now familiar double arrow symbol to denote revsersible reactions. He showed that the osmotic pressure of dilute solutions varies with concentration and temperature and thus obeys the thermodynamic laws governing gases.

Publications: *La Chimie dans l'Espace.* (Rotterdam: P. M. Bazendijk, 1875). *Ansichten Uber die Organische Chemie.* 2 vols. (Braunschweis, Germany: F. Viewes, 1878–81). *Etudes de Dynamique Chimique* (Amsterdam: F. Muller & Co., 1884). *Lois de l'Equilibre Chimique dans l'Etate Dilue, Gazeux on Dissous* (Stockholm: P. A. Norstedt, 1886). *Vorlesunsen uber Theoretischen und Physikalischen Chemie.* 3 vols. (Braunschweig, Germany: F. Vieweg und Sohn, 1898–1900).

Bibliography: E. Cohen, *Jacobus Henricus Van't Hoff. Sein Leben und Werken* (Leipzig, Germany: Akademische Verlags-gesellschaft, 1912).

FISCHER, EMIL HERMANN

Prize: Chemistry, 1902. *Born:* October 9, 1852; Euskirchen, Germany. *Died:* July 15, 1919; Berlin, Germany. *Nationality:* German. *Education:* University of Bonn, Germany, B.S., 1871; University of Strasbourg, France, Ph.D., 1874. *Career:* University of Munich, Germany, Professor, 1875–82; University of Erlangen, Germany, Professor, 1882–85; University of Wurzberg, Germany, Professor, 1885–92; University of Berlin, Germany, Professor, 1892–1919. *Other Awards:* Davy Medal, 1890; Hoffman Medal, German Chemical Society, 1906; Elliot Cresson Gold Medal, Franklin Institute, Philadelphia, Pennsylvania, 1913.

Citation: "In recognition of the extraordinary services he has rendered by his work on sugar and purine syntheses."

Life Work: Fischer's discovery of the hydrozine derivatives proved to be a brilliant solution to the problem of artificially reproducing sugars and other compounds. Fischer greatly expanded the science of biochemistry by elucidating basic chemical structures, clarifying structural relationships within chemical groups, and synthesizing new variations and configurations of organic substances. A practical aspect of his research was the development of laboratory principles that were applicable in the technological production of synthetic chemicals and foodstuffs. Furthermore, his method of synthesizing glucosides added to the knowledge of vegetable physiology.

Publications: *Anleitung zur Darstellung Organischer Praparate* (Wurzberg, Germany: Verlag der Stahel'schen kgl. Hof-und Universitäts-Buch und Kunstbandlung, 1893). *Untersuchungen uber Aminosauren, Polypeptide, und Proteine, 1899–1906* (Berlin: Springer, 1906). *Untersuchungen in der Puringrupp, 1882–1906* (Berlin: Springer, 1907). *Untersuchungen uber Triphenylmethanfarbstoffe, Hydrazine, und Indole* (Berlin: Springer, 1924).

Bibliography: *Aus Meinem Leben* (Berlin: Verlang Julius Springer, 1921). Martin Onslow Forster, "Emil Fischer Memorial Lecture," *Journal of the Chemical Society* 117 (1920): 1157–1201. Kurt Hoesch, *Emil Fischer, Stein Leben und Sein Werk* (Berlin: Verlag Chemie, 1921).

ARRHENIUS, SVANTE AUGUST

Prize: Chemistry, 1903. *Born:* February 19, 1859; Wijk, Sweden. *Died:* October 2, 1927; Stockholm, Sweden. *Nationality:* Swedish. *Education:* University of Uppsala, Sweden, B.S., 1878; University of Uppsala, Sweden, Ph.D., 1884. *Career:* University of Uppsala, Sweden, Professor, 1884–91; University of Stockholm, Sweden, Professor and Administrator, 1891–1905; Nobel Institute for Physical Chemistry, Sweden, Director, 1905–27. *Other Awards:* Davy Medal, Royal Society, 1902; Willard Gibbs Medal, United States, 1911; Faraday Medal, 1914.

Citation: "In recognition of the extraordinary services he has rendered to the advancement of chemistry by his electrolytic theory of dissociation."

Life Work: Arrhenius's work on ions gave a quantitative basis to electrochemistry, thus allowing it to be treated mathematically. Throughout his life Arrhenius continued his work on electrolytic dissociation and osmotic pressure. (Osmotic pressure is a measure of the effort of two different solutions to equalize their concentrations when separated by a semipermeable membrane). Arrhenius also investigated many aspects of physics, such as ball lightning, solar radiation, climatic changes, and physicohemical theories of volcanic actions. In 1901 he confirmed James Clark Maxwell's hypothesis that cosmic radiation exerts pressure on particles. Arrhenius used this phenomenon to explain the aurora borealis and solar corona.

Publications: *Lehrbuch der Elektrochemie* (Leipzig, Germany: Quandt & Handell, 1901); *Textbook on Electrochemistry,* trans. John McCrae (New York: Longmans Green & Co., 1902). *Theorien der Chemie* (Leipzig, Germany: Akademische Verlagsegesellschaft, 1906); *Theories of Chemistry.* trans. T. Slater Price (New York: Longmans Green & Co., 1907). *The World in the Making: Evolution of the Universe* (New York: Harper & Brothers, 1908). *The Silliman Lectures and Theories of Solutions* (New Haven, Conn.: Yale University Press, 1912). *The Quantitative Laws in Biological Chemistry.* (London: G. Bell & Sons, 1915).

Bibliography: I. Solovev, *Svante Arrhenius, 1859–1927* (Moscow, Russia: Nauka, 1990). "Svante August Arrhenius," *Zeitschrift fur Physikalische Chemie* 69 (1909): 5–20. *Svenst Biografiskt Lexikon* (Stockholm: Albert Bonniers Forlag, 1920), vol. 2, pp. 287–301.

RAMSAY, SIR WILLIAM

Prize: Chemistry, 1904. *Born:* October 2, 1852; Glasgow, Scotland. *Died:* July 23, 1916; High Wycombe, England. *Nationality:* Scottish. *Education:* University of Tübingen, Germany, Ph.D., 1872. *Career:* Anderson College, Glasgow, Scotland, Professor, 1872–74; University of Glasgow, Scotland, Professor, 1874–80; Bristol University, England, Professor, 1880–87; University of London, England, Professor, 1887–1913. *Other Awards:* Davy Medal, Royal Society, 1895; Hodgkins Prize, Smithsonian Institution, 1895; French Academy of Scientists Prize, 1895; Knighthood, 1902; A. W. Hoffman Medal, German Chemical Society, 1903; Prussian Order of Merit; Commander of the Crown of Italy.

Citation: "In recognition of his services in the discovery of the inert gaseous elements in air, and his determination of their place in the periodic system."

Life Work: Ramsay discovered fives gases that possessed the properties expected of a new class of elements and thus added a new group to the periodic table. The first was argon (from Greek, inert), which he produced by removing nitrogen and oxygen from air. Next he discovered helium, another inert gas, by heating certain minerals. Using a device that could chill and liquefy a large sample of argon, Ramsey identified krypton and neon (from Greek, hidden and new, respectively), and lastly he discovered xenon (Greek, stranger). His discovery of an entirely new group of elements was something utterly unique in the annals of chemistry.

Publications: *The Gases of the Atmosphere: The History of Their Discovery* (New York: Macmillan, 1896). *Modern Chemistry: Theoretical* (London: J. Dent, 1900). *Modern Chemistry: Systematic* (London: J. Dent, 1900). *Introduction to the Study of Physical Chemistry* (London: Joseph Black, 1904). *Essays Biographical and Chemical* (London: A. Constable & Co., 1908). *Elements and Electrons* (New York: Harper, 1912).

Bibliography: Morris W. Travers, *A Life of William Ramsay* (London: Edward Arnold, 1956).

BAEYER, JOHANN FRIEDRICH WILHELM ADOLF VON

Prize: Chemistry, 1905. *Born:* October 31, 1835; Berlin, Germany. *Died:* August 20, 1917; Starnberg, Bavaria, Germany. *Nationality:* German. *Education:* University of Berlin, Germany, Ph.D., 1858. *Career:* Kekule Laboratory, Heidelberg, Germany, Researcher, 1858–60; Trade Academy, Berlin, Germany, Professor, 1860–66; University of Berlin, Germany, Professor, 1866–69; War Academy, Germany, Professor, 1869–72; University of Strausberg, Germany, Professor, 1872–75; University of Munich, Germany, Professor, 1875–1913. *Other Awards:* Davy Medal, Royal Society, 1881.

Citation: "In recognition of his services in the advancement of organic chemistry and the chemical industry, through his work on organic dyes and hydroaromatic compounds."

Life Work: In 1870 Baeyer synthesized indigo for the first time and later isolated several important dye substances, particularly eosin pigments, which he also synthesized. The research into dyes led Beyer to study Benzene, a hydrocarbon molecule in which six carbon atoms are arranged around a ring. He developed his strain theory according to which the bonds between the carbon atoms are stressed or strained by the presence of other atoms in the molecule and that this stressing determines not only the shape of the molecule but also its stability. He also found that the structure of a group of aromatic benzene compounds called the hydroaromatics was transitional between the ring-based types and those without the ring structure, known as aliphatic hydrocarbons. His later work led to discoveries about the role of quadrivalent and basic oxygen.

Publications: *Adolph von Baeyer's Gesammelte Werke (Collected Works)*, 2 vols. (Brunswick, Germany: F. Viewig und Sohn, 1905).

Bibliography: *Dictionary of Scientific Biography* (New York: Scribner's, 1970), vol. 2, pp. 389–91. H. Rupe, *Adolf von Baeyer als Lehrer und Forscher* (Stuttgart, Germany: F. Enke, 1932).

MOISSAN, FERDINAND FREDERICK HENRI

Prize: Chemistry, 1906. *Born:* September 28, 1852; Paris, France. *Died:* February 20, 1907; Paris, France. *Nationality:* French. *Education:* University of Paris, France, baccalaureate, 1874; University of Paris, France, licence, 1877; University of Paris, France, docteur es sciences physiques, 1880. *Career:* École Supérieure de Pharmacie, France, Professor, 1879–83, 1886–1900; University of Sorbonne, France, Professor, 1900–1907. *Other Awards:* Lacaze Prize, Academy of Sciences, 1887; Davy Medal, Royal Society, 1896; Hoffman Medal, German Chemical Society, 1903.

Citation: "In recognition of the great services rendered by him in his investigation and isolation of the element fluorine, and for the adoption in the service of science of the electric furnace called after him."

Life Work: In 1886 Moissan prepared free fluorine by using an electrolyte of dry potassium and fluoride dissolved in anhydrous hydrofluoric acid with platinum iridium electrodes at very low temperatures. His studies eventually led to the discovery of carbon tetrafluoride, methyl, ethyl, isobutyl fluorides, and sulfuryl fluoride. Fluorine is used in the separation of uranium 235 from uranium 238. He also studied metal fluorides of platinum, alkaline earths, silver and manganese and the nonmetallic iodine pentafluoride and nitryl fluoride. Moissan improved the techniques used to extract the element boron. In his effort to separate crystalline diamonds, he designed an electric arc furnace capable of heating substances to 3500°C. With this device Moissan became the founder of high-temperature chemistry particularly by melting and vaporizing of materials that had been hitherto considered nonvolatile, such as zirconium, molybdenum, manganese, chromium, thorium, tungsten, platinum, uranium, titanium, and vanadium. He also prepared silicon carbide, or carborundum.

Publications: *Le Four Electrique* (Paris: G. Steinheil, 1897). *Le Fluor et ses Composes* (Paris: G. Steinheil, 1900). *Le Chimie Minerale, ses Relations avec les Autres Sciences* (Paris: G. Steinheil, 1904). *Traite de Chimie Minerale* (Paris: Masson, 1904–1906).

Bibliography: Paul Lebeau, "Henri Moissan," *Bulletin de la Société Chimique de France* 3, 4th series (1908): 1–38.

BUCHNER, EDUARD

Prize: Chemistry, 1907. *Born:* May 20, 1860; Munich, Germany. *Died:* August 13, 1917; Focsani, Romania. *Nationality:* German. *Education:* University of Munich, Germany, Ph.D., 1888. *Career:* University of Munich, Germany, Professor, 1889–93; University of Kiel, Germany, Professor, 1893–96; University of Tübingen, Germany, Professor, 1896–98; Agricultural College, Berlin, Germany, Professor, 1898–1908; University of Breslau, Germany, Professor, 1908–11; University of Wurzburg, Germany, Professor, 1911–17.

Citation: "For his biochemical researches and his discovery of cell-free fermentation."

Life Work: Buchner's research into fermentation yielded the discovery of the active agent in the process, an enzyme called xymase. No one before him had isolated the agent of fermentation or produced the process from nonliving substances. Buchner found the active agent by obtaining pure samples of the inner fluid of yeast cells. Buchner pulverized yeast cells in a pestle with a mixture of sand and diatomaceous earth. When squeezed through canvas under pressure, the cellular material yielded its fluid contents. When Buchner tried to preserve the fluid by adding a concentrated solution of sucrose, carbon dioxide was released.

Publications: *Die Zymassegarung* (*Zymosis*), with H. Buchner and M. Hahn (Munich: R. Oldenbourg, 1903).

Bibliography: *Dictionary of Scientific Biography* (New York: Scribner's, 1970), vol. 2, pp. 560–63.

RUTHERFORD, SIR ERNEST

Prize: Chemistry, 1908. *Born:* August 30, 1871; Spring Grove, New Zealand. *Died:* October 19, 1937; Cambridge, England. *Nationality:* British. *Education:* Canterbury College, New Zealand, B.A., 1892; Canterbury College, New Zealand, M.A., 1893; Canterbury College, New Zealand, B.Sc., 1894. *Career:* McGill University, Canada, Professor, 1898–1907; Victoria University, England, Professor, 1907–19; Cambridge University, England, Professor, 1919–37. *Other Awards:* Rumford Medal, Royal Society, 1904; Bressa Prize, 1910; Knighthood, 1914; Copley Medal, Royal Society, 1922; Order of Merit, 1925; Albert Medal, Royal Society of Arts, 1928; Faraday Medal, 1930.

Citation: "For his investigations into the disintegration of the elements, and the chemistry of radioactive substances."

Life Work: In 1896, working at the Cavendish Laboratory, Rutherford discovered the electron, an atomic particle with a negative electrical charge. Along with J. J. Thompson, he proposed that as X rays pass through a gas, they disrupt its atoms, releasing equal number of positively and negatively charged particles called ions. At McGill University in Montreal, he began an important series of experiments on radiation produced by the element uranium. He discovered two forms of radiation, alpha and beta. He next found that radioactive thorium, radium, and actinium emitted a gaseous radioactive product called emanation. He also discovered that every radioactive element decreases in radioactivity over a certain period of time, suggesting that all radioactive elements belonged to a single atomic family. In 1902 he and Frederick Soddy announced the disintegration theory of radioactivity, according to which radioactivity occurs when an atom expels a small portion of itself at an enormous velocity, the loss transforming the atom from one chemical element to another. In 1903 he proved that alpha particles are positively charged. Because these particles have a measurable mass, their ejection from the atom is crucial in transforming a radioactive element into another element at a predictable rate.

Publications: *Radioactivity* (Cambridge: Cambridge University Press, 1904). *Radioactive Transformations* (London: A. Constable, 1906). *Radioactive Substances and Their Radiations* (Cambridge: Cambridge University Press, 1913). *Radiations from Radioactive Substances*, with J. Chadwick and C. D. Ellis (Cambridge: Cambridge University Press, 1930). *The Newer Alchemy* (New York: Macmillan, 1937). *Collected Papers of Lord Rutherford of Nelson*, 3 vols. (New York: Interscience Publishers, 1962–65).

Bibliography: *Dictionary of Scientific Biography* (New York: Scribner's, 1975), vol. 12, pp. 25–36. Norman Feather, *Lord Rutherford* (London: Blackie and Son, Ltd., 1940). *Obituary Notices of the Royal Society of London* (Cambridge: Royal Society, 1938), vol. 2, pp. 395–423.

CHEMISTRY | **1909**

OSTWALD, FRIEDRICH WILHELM

Prize: Chemistry, 1909. *Born:* September 2, 1853; Riga, Latvia. *Died:* April 4, 1932; Grossbothen, Germany. *Nationality:* Latvian; later German citizen. *Education:* University of Dorpat, Latvia, baccalaureate, 1875; University of Dorpat, Latvia, M.A., 1876; University of Dorpat, Latvia, Ph.D., 1878. *Career:* Riga Polytechnic Institute, Latvia, Professor, 1881–87; University of Leipzig, Germany, Professor, 1887–1906. *Other Awards:* Faraday Medal, Royal Society, 1904.

Citation: "In recognition of his work on catalysis and for his investigations into the fundamental principles governing chemical equilibria and rates of reaction."

Life Work: Ostwald was associated with Svante Arrhenius in developing the ionization theory that molecules dissociated into stable, electrically charged particles when dissolved in polar solvents such as water. The theory was a good explanation for the many chemical reaactions that are catalyzed by weak acids or bases. Ostwald showed that when chemical equilibrium exists, the presence of a catalyst speeds up the reaction both forward and backward by an equal amount. He also demonstrated that a system moving from a less stable to a more stable state does so by degrees and does not always move to the more stable state, a behavior now called Ostwald's Law of Stages. He also developed the Ostwald process for synthesizing ammonia from hydrogen. After 1906, he devoted himself to color research and color harmony.

Publications: *Lehrbuch der Allgemeinen Chemie* (Leipzig, Germany: Engleman, 1891–1902). *Handund Hilfsbuch zur Ausfuhrung Physikochemischer Messungen* (Leipzig, Germany: W. Englemann, 1893). "Uber Physikochemische Messmethoden," *Zeitschrift fur Physikalische Chemie* 17 (1895): 427–45. *Grundlinien der Anorganischen Chemie* (Leipzig, Germany: W. Englemann, 1900). "Uber Katalyse." *Verhandlungen der Gesellschaft Deutsch Naturforscher und Arzte* 73 (1901): 184–201.

Bibliography: *Dictionary of Scientific Biography* (New York: Scribner's, 1978), vol. 15, pp. 455–69. *Lebenslinien*, 3 vols. (Berlin: Klasing and Co., 1926–27). Gretee Ostwald, *Wilhelm Ostwald, Mein Vater* (Stuttgart, Germany: Berliner Union, 1953).

WALLACH, OTTO

Prize: Chemistry, 1910. *Born:* March 27, 1847; Königsberg, Germany. *Died:* February 26, 1931; Göttingen, Germany. *Nationality:* German. *Education:* University of Göttingen, Germany, Ph.D., 1869. *Career:* Aktiengesellschaft fur Anilinfabrikation, Germany, Researcher, 1871–73; University of Bonn, Germany, Professor, 1873–89; University of Göttingen, Germany, Professor, 1889–1915. *Other Awards:* Davy Medal, 1912; German Royal Order of the Crown, 1915.

Citation: "In recognition of his services to organic chemistry and the chemical industry by his pioneer work in the field of alicyclic compounds."

Life Work: Wallach studied essential oils, also known as ethereal oils because of their tendency to change rapidly. He began with terpenes, so named because some are present in turpentine. By 1887 Wallach demonstrated that turpenes involved only eight substances, and he cataloged the reactions that converted one terpene to another as well as the reactions that produced their chemical derivatives. He classified turpenes as a special class of alicyclic compounds or open-chain molecules.

Publications: "Zur Kentniss de Terpene und Atherischen Oele IV," *Justus Liebigs Annalen der Chemie* 238 (1887): 78–89. "Zur Constitutionsbestimmung des Terpineols," *Berichte der Deutschen Chemischen Gesellschaft* 28 (1895): 1773–77. *Die Terpene und Campher* (Leipzig, Germany: Veit, 1909).

Bibliography: *Dictionary of Scientific Biography* (New York: Scribner's, 1979), vol. 14, pp. 141–42. William S. Partridge and Ernest R. Schierz, "Otto Wallach: The First Organizer of the Terpenes," *Journal of Chemical Education* 24 (1947): 106–108.

CURIE, MARIE (SKLODOWSKA, MARIA)

Prize: Chemistry, 1911; Physics, 1903. *Born:* November 7, 1867; Warsaw, Poland. *Died:* July 4, 1934; Sancellemoz, France. *Nationality:* Polish; later French citizen. *Education:* University of Paris–Sorbonne, France, licence es sciences physiques, 1893; University of Paris–Sorbonne, France, licence es sciences mathematiques, 1894; University of Paris–Sorbonne, France, Ph.D., 1904. *Career:* Governess, 1885–91; École Normale Supérieur, Sevres, France, Professor, 1900; University of Sorbonne, France, Professor, 1904–34. *Other Awards:* Bertholet Medal, Académie des Sciences, 1902; Gegner Prize, 1902; Davy Medal, Royal Society, 1903; Elliott Cresson Medal, 1909.

Citations: Chemistry, 1911: "In recognition of her services to the advancement of chemistry by the discovery of the elements radium and polonium, by the isolation of radium and the study of the nature and compounds of this remarkable element." Physics, 1903: "In recognition of the extraordinary services they have rendered by their joint researches on the radiation phenomena discovered by Professor Henri Becquerel" (with Pierre Curie).

Life Work: Beginning in 1898 Curie began to study Becquerel radiation, which she later named radioactivity, seeking to ascertain whether any other substances besides uranium compounds emitted radiation. She made the discovery that pitchblende, a mineral ore, emits four times as much radiation as uranium. Using acids and hydrogen sulfide, Marie and her husband, Pierre, separated pitchblende into its known constituents. In July and December 1898 they announced the discovery of two previously undetected elements in pitchblende: polonium (after Marie's native country, Poland) and radium. In 1902 the Curies isolated one-tenth of a gram of radium chloride from several tons of pitchblende. (They were unable to isolate polonium, which was produced by the disintegration of radium.) Marie found the atomic weight of radium to be 225. She succeeded in preparing pure radium in 1910 and thereby established the status of radium as an element and radiology as a new branch of science. Marie Curie was the first woman to win a Nobel Prize and the first person to receive two Nobel Prizes.

Publications: *Recherches sur les Substances Radioactives* (Paris: Gauthier-Villars, 1904). *Traite de Radioactivite*, 2 vols. (Paris: Gauthier-Villars, 1910). "Les Mesures en Radioactivite et l'Etalon du Radium," *Journal de Physique* 2 (1912): 715. *Oeuvres de Marie Sklodowska-Curie* (Warsaw: Panstwowie Widawnictwo Naukowe, 1954).

Bibliography: Eugene Cotton, *Les Curies* (Paris: Seghers, 1963). Eve Curie, *Madame Curie* (Paris: Gallimard, 1939). *Dictionary of Scientific Biography* (New York: Scribner's, 1971), vol. 3, pp. 497–503.

GRIGNARD, FRANÇOIS AUGUSTE VICTOR

Prize: Chemistry, 1912. *Born:* May 6, 1871; Gherbourg, France. *Died:* December 13, 1935; Lyons, France. *Nationality:* French. *Education:* University of Lyons, France, licence es sciences mathematiques, 1893; University of Lyons, France, Licencie es sciences physiques, 1898; University of Lyons, France, Docteur es Sciences, 1901. *Career:* University of Lyons, France, Professor, 1894–1905; University of Besançon, France, Professor, 1905–1906; University of Lyons, France, Professor, 1906–1909; University of Nancy, France, Professor, 1909–20; University of Lyons, France, Professor, 1920–32. *Other Awards:* Cahours Prize (Institute de France), 1901, 1902; Bertholet Medal, 1902; Prix Jecker, 1905; Lavoisier Medal, 1912.

Citation: "For the discovery of the so-called Grignard reagent, which in recent years has greatly advanced the progress of organic chemistry."

Life Work: Grignard began investigating a technique in which a metal is used to transfer organic material from one organic material to another. Compounds that result from the union of the metal with one or more organic radicals are known as organometallic compounds. Following the lead of British scientists Edward Frankland and James Wanklyn Grignard heated manganese together with organic substances in the presence of anhydrous ether. The Grignard reaction has been used to produce a wide range of organic compounds.

Publications: "Sur Quelques Nouvelles Combinasions Organometalliques du Magnesium et Leur Application a des Syntheses d'Alcohols et d'Hydrocarbures," *Comptes Rendus de l'Académie des Sciences* 126 (1898): 1322. "Sur les Combinasions Organomagnesiennes Mixtes et Leur Application a des Syntheses d'Acides, d'Alcohols, et d'Hydrocarbures," *Annales de l'Université de Lyon* 6 (1901): 1–116. *Traite de Chimie Organique* (Paris: Masson, 1935–59).

Bibliography: *Dictionary of Scientific Biography* (New York: Scribner's, 1972), vol. 5, pp. 540–41. "Victor Grignard," *Journal of the American Chemical Society* 59 (1937): 17–19.

SABATIER, PAUL

Prize: Chemistry, 1912. *Born:* November 5, 1854; Carcasone, France. *Died:* August 14, 1941; Toulouse, France. *Nationality:* French. *Education:* École Normale Supérieure, France, Agrege in Physical Sciences, 1877; Collège de France, Doctor of Science, 1880. *Career:* Lycée de Nimes, France, Professor, 1877–78; Collège de France, Professor, 1878–80; University of Bordeaux, France, Professor, 1880–82; University of Toulouse, France, Professor, 1882–1929. *Other Awards:* Prix La Caze, Academy of Sciences, 1897; Prix Jecker, Academy of Sciences, 1905; Davy Medal, Royal Society, 1915; Royal Medal, Royal Society, 1918; Special Award, American Chemical Society, 1926; Franklin Medal, Franklin Institute of Philadelphia, 1933; Commander, Legion d'Honneur.

Citation: "For his method of hydrogenating organic compounds in the presence of finely disintegrated metals whereby the progress of organic chemistry has been greatly advanced in recent years."

Life Work: In the 1890s Sabatier began work on organic chemistry, especially the catalytic processes involved in hydrogenation, through which unsaturated organic compounds became saturated. By 1896 he had effected the chemical union or fixing of nitrogen peoxide on copper, cobalt, and nickel. Next he repeated the experiment by passing gaseous ethylene over slivers of nickel. He observed intense incandescence, deposits of pure carbon forming on the nickel and a buildup of ethane, a fully hydrogen-saturated compound. Saturated hydrocarbons and important intermediaries in the production of pharmaceuticals, perfumes, detergents, edible fats, and other commercial products. In 1897, in collaboration with the Abbe Jean-Baptiste Senderens, he initiated over thirty years of research and refinement of the chemical theory involved. He elaborated on his hypothesis in *La Catalyse en Chimie Organique*, considered a fundamental work in organic catalysis.

Publications: *Leçons Elementaires de Chimie Agricole* [*Elementary Lessons in Agricultural Chemistry*] (Paris: G. Masson, 1890). *La Catalyse en Chimie Organique* [*Catalysis in Organic Chemistry*] (Paris: Beranger, 1913). "How I Have Been Led to the Direct Hydrogenation Method by Metallic Catalysts," *Industrial and Engineering Chemistry* 18 (October 1926): 1005–1008.

Bibliography: *Biographical Memoirs of the Fellows of the Royal Society* (London: Royal Society, 1942–44), vol. 4, pp. 63–66. *Dictionary of Scientific Biography* (New York: Scribner's, 1975), vol. 12, pp. 46–47. "Paul Sabatier, 1854–1941," *Nature* 174 (November 6, 1954): 859–60.

WERNER, ALFRED

Prize: Chemistry, 1913. *Born:* December 12, 1866; Mulhausen, France. *Died:* November 15, 1919; Zürich, Switzerland. *Nationality:* French. *Education:* Zürich Polytechnikum, Switzerland, baccalaureate, 1889; University of Zürich, Switzerland, doctorate, 1890. *Career:* Zürich Polytechnikum, Switzerland, Professor, 1889–91; Collège de France, 1891–92; Zürich Polytechnikum, Switzerland, Professor, 1893–1919. *Other Awards:* Leblanc Medal, Société Chimique; Officer de l'Instruction Publique, Société Chimique.

Citation: "In recognition of his work on the linkage of atoms in molecules by which he has thrown new light on earlier investigations and opened up new fields of research especially in inorganic chemistry."

Life Work: In his 1891 paper "Contribution to the Theory of Affinity and Valence," Werner explained the nature of the chemical bonds of inorganic molecular compounds. He defined affinity as "a force issuing from the center of the atom, uniformly attractive in all directions, whose geometrical expression is therefore not a given number of guiding lines but a spherical surface. Two years later, in "A Contribution to the Construction of Inorganic Compounds," he proposed his Coordination Theory, according to which single atoms act as central nuclei in inorganic molecular compounds. Around these central atoms, a definite number of other atoms or molecules are arranged in a simple geometrical octahedron. Werner called the number of atoms grouped around the central nucleus the coordination number and the sharing of a pair of electrons contributed by one molecule or atom to another as the coordination bond. His synthesis in 1911 of more than forty optically active molecules without carbon atoms proved the validity of his theories.

Publications: "Bietrage Zur Theorie der Affinitat und Valenz," *Vierteljahrsschrift der Naturforschenden Gesellschaft in Zürich* 36 (1891): 129–69. *Lehrbuch der Stereochemie* [*Textbook of Stereo-Chemistry*] (Jena, Germany: G. Fischer, 1904). *Neuere Anschauungen auf dem Gebiete der Anorganischen Chemie* (Brunswick, Germany: Viewig and Son, 1905).

Bibliography: *Dictionary of Scientific Biography* (New York: Scribner's, 1976), vol. 14, pp. 264–72. G. B. Kaufmann, *Alfred Werner, Founder of Coordination Chemistry* (New York: Springer-Verlag, 1966).

RICHARDS, THEODORE WILLIAM

Prize: Chemistry, 1914. *Born:* January 31, 1868; Germantown, Pennsylvania. *Died:* April 2, 1928; Cambridge, Massachusetts. *Nationality:* American. *Education:* Haverford College, Pennsylvania, S.B., 1885; Harvard University, Massachusetts, A.B., 1886;

Harvard University, Massachusetts, A.M., Ph.D., 1888. *Career:* Harvard University, Massachusetts, Professor, 1894–1928. *Other Awards:* Davy Medal, Royal Society, 1910; Faraday Medal, Chemical Society, 1911; Willard Gibbs Medal, American Chemical Society, 1912; Franklin Medal, Franklin Institute of Philadelphia, 1916; Lavoisier Medal, Paris, 1922; Le Blanc Medal, Paris, 1922.

Citation: "In recognition of his accurate determinations of the atomic weight of a large number of chemical elements."

Life Work: Beginning 1886 Richards determined the atomic weights more than thirty elements, twenty-one of which he himself established. To increase the precision of his measurements, he devised several new instruments, including a calorimeter and a nephelometer, which permits visual determination of the concentration or size of particles in a solution. He showed that contrary to accepted theory, atomic weight was not the basis of the chemical order. He also confirmed the existence of isotopes, or atoms of the same element with different atomic weights. In addition, Richards worked on equilibrium, electrochemistry, and chemical thermodynamics. His work on the thermodynamics of elements at low temperatures anticipated the Third Law of Thermodynamics, developed in 1905 by Walther Nernst.

Publications: "The Relative Values of the Atomic Weights of Hydrogen and Oxygen," with J. Cooke Jr., *Proceedings of the American Academy of Arts and Sciences* 23 (1887): 149. "A Revision of the Atomic Weights of Sodium and Chlorine," with R. C. Wells, *Journal of the American Chemical Society* 27 (1905): 459. "The Atomic Weight of Lead of Radioactive Origin," *Journal of the American Chemical Society* 36 (1914): 1329.

Bibliography: *Dictionary of Scientific Biography* (New York: Scribner's, 1975), vol. 11, pp. 416–18. "Theodore William Richards Memorial Lecture," *Journal of the American Chemical Society* (1930): 1930–68.

WILLSTÄTTER, RICHARD MARTIN

Prize: Chemistry, 1915. *Born:* August 13, 1872; Karlsruhe, Germany. *Died:* August 3, 1942; Locarno, Switzerland. *Nationality:* German. *Education:* University of Munich, Germany, Ph.D., 1894. *Career:* University of Munich, Germany, Professor, 1896–1905; Federal Institute of Technology, Germany, Professor, 1905–12; University of Berlin, Germany, Professor and Administrator, 1912–16; University of Munich, Germany, Professor, 1916–25. *Other Awards:* Davy Medal, 1932; Gibbs Medal, 1933.

Citation: "For his researches on plant pigments, especially chlorophyll."

Life Work: In Zürich, Willstatter began his studies on chlorophyll, an important component in photosynthesis, the process by which sugar, starch and oxygen are produced from carbon dioxide and water through the action of light on green plants. He demonstrated that chlorophyll has one basic structure: it is a tetrapyrrole, or a compound with four pyrrole rings, bound through a central manganese atom. He also proved that although it has one structure, it has two nearly identical forms, *a* and *b*. Continuing his research in Berlin from 1912, he established that most of the red, blue, and purple pigments of plants consist of anthocyanins or compounds that can be extracted from plants by means of alcohol, ether or water. He found that most flower colors are produced by only three anthocyanins.

Publications: *Untersuchungen uber Chlorophyll*, with Arthur Stoll (Berlin: J. Springer, 1913). *Untersuchungen uber die Assimilation der Kohlensaure*, with Arthur Stoll (Berlin: J. Springer, 1918). *Untersuchngen uber Enzyme*, 2 vols. (Berlin: J. Springer, 1928).

Bibliography: *Aus Meinem Leyben* (Weinheim, Germany: Verlag Chemie, 1948). *Dictionary of Scientific Biography* (New York: Scribner's, 1976), vol. 14, pp. 411–12.

HABER, FRITZ

Prize: Chemistry, 1918. *Born:* December 9, 1868; Breslau, Germany. *Died:* January 29, 1934; Basel, Switzerland. *Nationality:* German. *Education:* Technische Hochschule, Germany, Ph.D., 1891. *Career:* University of Jena, Germany, Researcher, 1892–94; Technische Hochschule, Karlsruhe, Germany, Professor, 1894–1911; Kaiser Wilhelm Institute, Dahlem, Germany, Director, 1911–33. *Other Awards:* Rumford Medal, Royal Society, 1932.

Citation: "For the synthesis of ammonia from its elements."

Life Work: Beginning 1905, Haber worked on the production of ammonia which, in turn, could be further processed into nitrates. He combined atmospheric nitrogen with hydrogen at very low temperatures and at very high pressure. He discovered that substituting osmium and uranium for the standard iron catalyst increased the yield of ammonia substantially. He increased the efficiency of this method still further by using the heat produced by the union of the gases to sustain the reaction. Perfected by Carl Bosch, the Haber-Bosch method is the basis of large-scale ammonia production worldwide.

Publications: *Experimentelle Untersuchungen uber Zertsetzgung und Verbrennung von Kohlenwasserstoffen* (Munich: R. Oldenbourg, 1896). *Grundriss der Technischen Elektrochemie auf Theoretischer Grundlage* (Munich: R. Oldenbourg, 1898). *Thermodynamik Technisher Gasreaktionen Vorlesungen* (Munich: R. Oldenbourg, 1905). "Processes for the Preparation of Ammonia," with R. Le Rossignol, U.S. Patent 971,501, 1910. "Production of Synthetic Ammonia," with K. Bosch and A. Mittasch, U.S. Patent 1,149,510, 1915.

Bibliography: *Dictionary of Scientific Biography* (New York: Scribner's, 1972), vol. 5, pp. 620–23. Morris Goran, *The Story of Fritz Haber* (Norman: University of Oklahoma Press, 1967). D. Stoltzenberg, *Fritz Haber* (New York: VCH, 1994).

NERNST, WALTHER HERMANN

Prize: Chemistry, 1920. *Born:* June 25, 1864; Briesen, Germany. *Died:* November 18, 1941; Muskau, Germany. *Nationality:* German. *Education:* University of Wurzburg, Germany, Ph.D., 1887. *Career:* University of Leipzig, Germany, Researcher, 1887–90; University of Göttingen, Germany, Professor, 1890–1904; University of Berlin, Germany, 1904–33.

Citation: "In recognition of his work in thermochemistry."

Life Work: Beginning in 1889, Nernst investigated the behavior of electrolytes (solutions of electrically charged particles, or ions) in the presence of electric currents and developed a fundamental law, known as the Nernst Equation, which describes the relation between electromotive force or voltage and ionic concentration. The equation makes it possible to predict the maximum work potential that an electrochemical reaction can generate when only simple properties of pressure and temperature are known. It thus linked thermodynamic and electrochemical theory involving very dilute solutions. Between 1890 and 1891 Nernst investigated substances that, when dissolved in liquids, do not mix with each other. He developed the Nernst Distribution Equation to describe the activity of these substances as a function of concentration. By applying Amedeo Avogadro's hypothesis (that the number of integral molecules in any gas is always the same for equal volumes) as well as the thermodynamic law of energy conservation, Nernst strengthened the foundations of physical chemistry. In 1905 at Berlin, Nernst proposed his heat theorem, now known as the Third Law of Thermodynamics, which makes it possible tp use thermal data to calculate chemical equilibria. In 1912 Nernst expressed his heat theorem as the basic unattainability of absolute zero. The physical activities of substances tend to vanish at absolute zero temperatures. The fields of cryogenics and solid-state physics depend on this law.

Publications: *Theoretische Chemie vom Standpunkte der Avogadroschen Regel und der Thermodynamik* (Göttingen, Germany: F. Enke, 1893); *Theoretical Chemistry from the Standpoint of Avogadro's Rule and Thermodynamics,* trans. Prof. Charles Skeele Palmer (New York: Macmillan and Co., 1895). *Einfuhrung in die Mathematische Behandlung der Naturwissenschaften-Kurzgefasstes Lehrbuch der Differential-und Integralrechnung mit Besonderer Berucksichtigung der Chemie* (Munich: Dr. E. Wolff, 1895). *Experimental and Theoretical Applications of Thermodynamics to Chemistry* (New York: C. Scribner's Sons, 1907). *Die Theoretischen und Experimentellen Grundlagen des Neuen Warmesatzes* (Halle-Salle, Germany: W. Knapp, 1918). *Das Weltgebaude im Lichte der Neueren Forschung* (Berlin: Julius Springer, 1921).

Bibliography: Max Bodenstein, "Walther Nernst," *Berichte der Deutschen Chemischen Gesellschaft* 75 (1942): 79–104. *Dictionary of Scientific Biography* (New York: Scribner's, 1978), vol. 15, pp. 432–53. Kurt Mendelsohn, *The World of Walther Nernst. The Rise and Fall of German Science, 1864–1941* (New York: Macmillan, 1973).

SODDY, FREDERICK

Prize: Chemistry, 1921. *Born:* September 2, 1877; Eastbourne, Sussex, England. *Died:* September 22, 1956; Brighton, England. *Nationality:* British. *Education:* Oxford University, England, B.A., 1898; Oxford University, England, M.A., 1910. *Career:* McGill University, Canada, Researcher, 1900–1902; University of London, England, Researcher, 1903–1904; University of Glasgow, Scotland, Professor, 1904–14; Aberdeen University, Scotland, Professor, 1914–19; Oxford University, England, Professor, 1919–36. *Other Awards:* Cannizzaro Prize, Academia dei Lincei, Rome, 1913.

Citation: "For his contributions to our knowledge of the chemistry of radioactive substances, and his investigations into the origin and nature of isotopes."

Life Work: Beginning in 1904, Soddy investigated the properties of radioactive elements that cannot be separated from each other by chemical means. In 1910 he established that elements of different atomic weight, both radioactive and nonradioactive, may possess identical chemical properties. In 1913 he proposed the concept of isotopes, which occupy the same place in the periodic table as their element but have different atomic weights. Soddy's Displacement Law states that the emission of an alpha particle transforms an element into an isotope of an element two places lower in the periodic table, while the emission of a beta particle causes the element to move one place higher in the table. With this theory it is possible to deduce the decay sequences of many radioactive elements and to identify related elements. In 1920 he predicted that isotopes could be used to determine the geological age of rocks and fossils from the known rates of radioactive decay.

Publications: *Radio-Activity: An Elementary Treatise from the Standpoint of the Disintegration Theory* (London: Electrician Printing and Publishing, 1904). *The Interpretation of Radium* (London: J. Murray, 1908). *The Chemistry of the Radio-Elements* (London: Longmans, Green, 1911–14). *Science and Life* (London: J. Murray, 1920).

Bibliography: *Biographical Memoirs of the Fellows of the Royal Society* (London: Royal Society, 1957), vol. 3, pp. 203–16. *Dictionary of Scientific Biography* (New York: Scribner's, 1981), vol. 12, pp. 504–509. Muriel Howorth, *Pioneer Research on the Atom, Rutherford and Soddy in a Glorious Chapter of Science, the Life of Frederick Soddy* (London: New World Publications, 1958). George G. Kaufman, *Frederick Soddy: Early Pioneer in Radiochemistry* (London: Reidel, 1986).

ASTON, FRANCIS WILLIAM

Prize: Chemistry, 1922. *Born:* September 1, 1877; Harborne, Birmingham, England. *Died:* November 20, 1945; Cambridge, England. *Nationality:* British. *Education:* Malvern College, England, B.S., 1893; Cambridge University, England, B.A., 1912.

Career: British Brewery, Chemist, 1900–1903; University of Birmingham, England, Researcher, 1903–1909; Cambridge University, England, Researcher, 1909–14; Royal Aircraft Establishment, England, Researcher, 1914–18; Cambridge University, England, Researcher, 1919–45. *Other Awards:* Mackenzie Davidson Medal, Roentgen Society, 1920; Hughes Medal, Royal Society, 1922; John Scott Medal, Franklin Institute, 1923; Paterno Medal, 1923; Royal Medal, Royal Society, 1938; Duddell Medal, Physical Society, 1941.

Citation: "For his discovery, by means of his mass spectrograph, of isotopes, in a large number of non-radioactive elements, and for his enunciation of the whole-number rule."

Life Work: Aston's familiarity with cathode rays and positive rays enabled him to conduct experiments on the boundary between physics and chemistry. To weight the products of distillation, he invented a quartz microbalance sensitive to one-billionth of a gram. In 1919 he constructed the mass spectrograph, which accelerated positively charged ions through an electric field using a strong magnetic field to focus them on to a photographic plate. Because heavy atoms are deflected somewhat less than light atoms, particles of different mass are separated to produce a mass spectrum. The patterns formed as particles strike the photographic plate enabled Aston to deduce their mass and relative quantity and thus prove that all elements are mixtures of isotopes. Aston went on to formulate the whole number rule which states that atomic weight is always a whole number and that fractional weights are due to the presence of isotopes.

Publications: "Constitution of Atmospheric Neon," *Philosophical Magazine* 39 (1920): 449–55. "The Mass Spectra of Chemical Elements," *Philosophical Magazine* 40 (1920): 628–34. *Isotopes* (London: E. Arnold and Co., 1922). *Structural Units of the Material Universe* (London: Oxford University Press, 1925). *Mass-Spectra and Isotopes* (London: Arnold, 1933). "Masses of Some Light Atoms Measured by Means of a New Mass Spectrometer," *Nature* 137 (1936): 357–58.

Bibliography: *Dictionary of Scientific Biography* (New York: Scribner's, 1970), vol. 1, pp. 320–22. *Obituary Notices of Fellows of the Royal Society* (Cambridge: Royal Society, 1945–48), vol. 5, pp. 635–51.

PREGL, FRITZ

Prize: Chemistry, 1923. *Born:* September 3, 1859; Laibach, Austria. *Died:* December 13, 1930; Graz, Austria. *Nationality:* Austrian. *Education:* University of Graz, Austria, M.D., 1894. *Career:* University of Graz, Austria, Professor, 1893–1907; Medico-Chemical Institute, Graz, Austria, Forensic Chemist, 1907–10; University of Innsbruck, Austria, Professor, 1910–13; University of Graz, Austria, Professor, 1913–30. *Other Awards:* Lieben Prize, Imperial Academy of Science, Vienna, Austria, 1914.

Citation: "For his invention of the method of micro-analysis of organic substances."

Life Work: During his investigation into bile acids and protein chemistry, Pregl developed improved analytical techniques and microbalances that were accurate to within one-thousandth of a milligram. Pregl's studies involved organic molecules, which contain chiefly carbon, hydrogen, and oxygen, often with traces of nitrogen sulfur, phosphorus, and other elements. Their analysis began with the conversion of all carbon to carbon to carbon dioxide and all hydrogen to water. To avoid contamination of the samples, he developed a special filter that retained everything but carbon dioxide and water. Pregl devised microanalytic methods for the study of common organic groups, as the halogen, carboxyls and methyls. By 1915 he applied his methods to analyze 3 milligrams within an hour. His methods are particularly valuable in the analysis of complex biomedical compounds.

Publications: *Die Quantitative Organische Mikroanalyse* [*Quantitative Organic Microanalysis*] (Berlin: J. Springer, 1917).

Bibliography: *Dictionary of Scientific Biography* (New York: Scribner's, 1975), vol. 11, pp. 128–29. "Fritz Pregl," *Berichte der Deutschen Chemischen Gesellschaft* 64A (1931): 113.

ZSIGMONDY, RICHARD ADOLF

Prize: Chemistry, 1925. *Born:* April 1, 1865; Vienna, Austria. *Died:* September 24, 1929; Göttingen, Germany. *Nationality:* Austrian; later German resident. *Education:* University of Munich, Germany, Ph.D., 1890. *Career:* University of Berlin, Germany, Researcher, 1891–92; Technische Hochschule, Graz, Austria, Professor, 1893–97; Schott und Genossen, Jena, Germany, Researcher, 1897–1900; Personal Researcher, 1900–1907; University of Göttingen, Germany, Professor and Administrator, 1907–19.

Citation: "For his demonstration of the heterogenous nature of colloid solutions and for the methods he used, which have since become fundamental in modern colloid chemistry."

Life Work: Zsigmondy devised a number of hybrid techniques to determine the nature of colloids or substances in which extremely fine particles are stably dispersed in a fluid medium. To observe the particles he developed the ultramicroscope in 1903. It employs a perpendicular illumination. By improving the technology of what is known as darkfield illumination, Zsigmondy was able to view particles as small as 10 millimicrons (ten-millionths of a millimeter). Further refinements produced the immersion ultramicroscope which revealed particles of 4 millimicrons. His investigations led Zsigmondy to study the dynamics of colloids. He proved that particles of gold in a colloid are electrically negative and the resulting mutual repulsion accounts for their stability. The addition of salts to the solloid provides centers of electrical attraction around which the gold begins to aggregate until the particles precipitate out of the colloidal suspension.

Publications: *Zur Erkenntnis der Kolloide* [*Colloids and the Ultramicroscope*] (Jena, Germany: G. Fischer, 1905). *Kolloidchemie: ein Lehrbuch* [*The Chemistry of Colloids*] (Leipzig, Germany: Otto Spamer, 1912). *Das Kolloid Gold* [*Colloidal Gold*], with P. A. Thiessen (Leipzig, Germany: Akademische Verlagsgesellschaft, 1925).

Bibliography: *Asimov's Biographical Encyclopedia of Science and Technology* (Garden City, N.Y.: Doubleday, 1982), pp. 603–604. *Dictionary of Scientific Biography* (New York: Scribner's, 1976), vol. 14, pp. 632–34.

SVEDBERG, THEODOR H. E.

Prize: Chemistry, 1926. *Born:* August 30, 1884; Flerang, Valbo, Sweden. *Died:* February 25, 1971; Orebro, Sweden. *Nationality:* Swedish. *Education:* University of Uppsala, Sweden, B.S., 1905; University of Uppsala, Sweden, Ph.D., 1907. *Career:* University of Uppsala, Sweden, Professor, 1912–49; Gustaf Werner Institute of Nuclear Chemistry, Sweden, Director, 1949–67. *Other Awards:* Scheele Award, Royal Swedish Academy of Sciences, 1907, 1916; Oscar II Reward, University of Uppsala, Sweden, 1908; Edlund Award, Royal Swedish Academy of Sciences, 1909; Bergstedt Reward, Royal Society of Sciences, Sweden, 1910; Wallmark Award, Royal Swedish Academy of Sciences, 1910; Bjorken Prize, 1913, 1923, 1926; Berzelius Medal, 1941; Medal, City of Uppsala, Sweden, 1948; Franklin Medal, Franklin Institute, 1949; Gustaf Adolf Medal, 1964.

Citation: "For his work on disperse systems."

Life Work: Svedberg is best known for his investigations into the physical properties of colloids. He demonstrated that the colloidal particles would be hastened in an increased gravitational field produced by a high-field centrifuge. In 1923 he began the construction of an optical centrifuge in which particle sedimentation could be followed photographically. By designing a wedge-shaped holding cell and by placing the rotor holding the cell in a hydrogen atmosphere, Svedberg obtained a convection-free sedimentation. Svedberg discovered that proteins could also be made to settle out of solution. He established that the molecules of proteins are of one size only in contrast to the molecules of metal colloids that occur in many different sizes. Moreover, the rate of sedimentation of proteins gave a direct measure of the size of a molecule, thus proving that proteins have well-defined molecular weights and shapes. Svedberg's researches made the centrifuge a central tool of biochemical research. He spent much of his later life improving the design of the centrifuge until he constructed one capable of 120,000 revolutions per minute.

Publications: *Die Methoden zur Herstellung Kolloider Losungen Anorganischer Stoffe* (Dresden, Germany: T. Steinkopff, 1909). *Die Existenz der Molekule* (Leipzig, Germany: Academische Verlagsgesselschaft, 1912). *Colloid Chemistry* (New York: Chemical Catalog Company, 1924). *The Ultracentrifuge,* with K. O. Pedersen (Oxford: Clarendon Press, 1940). "The Osmotic Balance," with I. Jullander, *Nature* 153

(1944): 523. "The Cellulose Molecule. Physical-Chemical Studies," *Journal of Physical and Colloid Chemistry* 51 (1947): 1–18.

Bibliography: *Biographical Memoirs of the Fellows of the Royal Society* (Cambridge: Royal Society, 1972), vol. 18, pp. 595–627. *Dictionary of Scientific Biography* (New York: Scribner's, 1976), vol. 13, pp. 158–64.

WIELAND, HEINRICH OTTO

Prize: Chemistry, 1927. *Born:* June 4, 1877; Pforzheim, Germany. *Died:* August 5, 1957; Starnberg, Germany. *Nationality:* German. *Education:* University of Munich, Germany, Ph.D., 1901. *Career:* University of Munich, Germany, Professor, 1901–13; Technische Hochschule, Munich, Germany, Professor, 1913–21; University of Freiburg, Germany, Professor, 1925–50. *Other Awards:* Lavoisier Medal, France, 1938; Ordre Pour le Mérite, 1952; Otto Hahn Prize, 1955.

Citation: "For his investigations of the constitution of the bile acids and related substances."

Life Work: Wieland's field of investigation was organic nitrogen compounds, particularly the mechanism of the addition of nitrogen oxides to carbon-carbon double bonds and the nitration of aromatic hydrocarbons. He demonstrated the sequence of reactions and intermediate compounds in the synthesis of fulminic acid from ethanol, nitric acid and mercury. His analysis of the color reactions of hydrazines led to the discovery of the first known nitrogen free radicals. He unified the disciplines of organic chemistry and biochemistry with his dehydrogenation theory based on the activation of hydrogen. He interpreted the oxidation of many organic and inorganic compounds as dehydrogenations and demonstrated dehyderogenations in living cells as in the conversion of acetates to succinic acid in oxygen-depleted yeast cells. His Nobel Prize was in recognition of his solution to one of the most difficult problems in organic chemistry, his production from bile a saturated acid that can be regarded as the mother substance of the bile acids. His demonstration that cholic acid, deoxycholic acid and lithocholic acid could be converted to cholanic acid showed that these bile acids have the same carbon skeleton and differ only in the number of attached hydroxyl groups.

Publications: *Die Hydrazine* (Stuttgart, Germany: F. Enke, 1913). "Die Chemie der Gallensauren," *Zeitschrift fur Angewandte Chemie und Zentralblate fur Technische Chemie* 42 (1929): 421–24. "Recent Researches on Biological Oxidation," *Journal of the Chemical Society* (1931): 1055–64. *On the Mechanism of Oxidation* (New Haven, Conn.: Yale University Press, 1932).

Bibliography: "Autobiography," *Nachrichten aus Chemie und Technik* (1955): 222–23. *Dictionary of Scientific Biography* (New York: Scribner's, 1976), vol. 14, pp. 334–35. Gulbrand Lunde, "The 1927 and 1928 Nobel Chemistry Prize Winners, Wieland and Windaus," *Journal of Chemical Education* 7 (1930): 763–71.

WINDAUS, ADOLF OTTO REINHOLD

Prize: Chemistry, 1928. *Born:* December 25, 1876; Berlin Germany. *Died:* June 9, 1959; Göttingen, Germany. *Nationality:* German. *Education:* University of Berlin, Germany, medical license, 1897; University Freiburg, Germany, Dr. phil., 1900. *Career:* University of Berlin, Germany, Researcher, 1900–1901; University of Freiburg, Germany, Professor, 1901–13; Innsbruck University, Austria, Professor, 1913–15; University of Göttingen, Germany, Professor, 1915–44. *Other Awards:* Pasteur Medal, 1938; Goethe Medal, 1941; Grand Order of Merit, 1951; Order Pour le Merite, 1952; Grand Order of Merit with Star, 1956.

Citation: "For the services rendered through his research into the constitution of the sterols and their connection with the vitamins."

Life Work: Windaus began his career with a study of cholesterol which he believed was closely associated with sterol. His investigations led him to vitamin D, which was the provitamin of vitamin D. A pure vitamin called vitamin D2, or Calciferol, was produced by irradiating fungus sterol known as ergosterol. He further showed that another compound, 7-hydrocholesterol, was a provitamin called vitamin D3. The term vitamin D1was reserved for the original mixture of calciferol and other sterols. In collaboration with Franz Knoop, Windhaus studied the reactions of sugars with ammonia, attempting to convert carbohydrates into amino acids. The resulting products turned out to be derivatives of imidazole, compounds containing rings of three carbons and two nitrogen molecules. Analysis of these substances produced the amino acid histidine and the compound histamine, a dilator of blood vessels.

Publications: "Die Konstitution des Cholesterins," *Nachricten Gesellschaft d. Wissenschaften* (Göttingen, Germany: 1919). "Anwendungen der Spannungstheorie," *Nachrichten Gesellschaft d. Wissenschaften* (Göttingen, Germany: 1921). "Ultra-violet Bestrahlung von Ergasterin," with others, *Nachrichten Gesellschaft d. Wissenschaften, Göttingen* (1929): 45 59. "Chemistry of Irradiated Ergosterol," *Proceedings of the Royal Society* B 108 (1931): 568–75.

Bibliography: Adolf Butenandt, *Proceedings of the Chemical Society* (1961): 131–38. *Dictionary of Scientific Biography* (New York: Scribner's, 1976), vol. 14, pp. 443–46.

EULER-CHELPIN, HANS KARL AUGUST SIMON VON

Prize: Chemistry, 1929. *Born:* February 15, 1873; Augsburg, Germany. *Died:* November 6, 1964; Stockholm, Sweden. *Nationality:* German; later Swedish citizen. *Education:* University of Munich, Germany, doctorate, 1895. *Career:* Researcher, 1895–1906; University of Stockholm, Sweden, Professor, 1906–41. *Other Awards:* Lindblom Prize, Germany, 1898; Grand Cross for Federal Services with Star, Germany, 1959.

Citation: "For their investigations on the fermentation of sugar and fermentative enzymes" (with Arthur Harden).

Life Work: Euler-Chelpin's field of investigation was the chemistry of enzymes that serve as catalysts in living cells for specific biochemical reactions. He was especially interested in the role that enzymes play in fermentation. He showed that for an enzyme to perform its function it first had to become attached to the molecule, or substrate, it would act upon. He proceeded to identify each of these substrates at each step of the process by introducing metal atoms into the fermenting solutions. In the process, two molecules of hexoise and two molecules of phosphate combine to form alcohol, carbon dioxide, water and a phosphorus-containing compound called zymodiphosphate.The two hexose fragments that split from the sugar molecule are neither complete nor equal. One is more energy rich than the other and the phosphate is attached to the less energetic fragment. He also described the chemical nature of the nonprotein constituent of zymase, called cozymase. By determining its molecular weight, he established cozymase contains fragments of sugar, phosphoric acid and a crystalline chemical called purine. He also proved that cozymase is a constituent of the enzymes that regulate the cell's hydrogen-transferring activity and thus affect respiration.

Publications: *Chemie der Hefe und der Alkoholischen Garung*, with Paul Lindner (Leipzig, Germany: Akademische Verlagsgesellschaft, 1915). *Chemie der Enzyme* (Munich: J. F. Bergman, 1920–27). *Biokatalysatoren* (Stuttgart, Germany: F. Enke, 1930). *Biochemie der Tumoren*, with Bol Skarzynski (Stuttgart, Germany: Enke, 1942).

Bibliography: *Dictionary of Scientific Biography* (New York: Scribner's, 1971), vol. 4, pp. 485–86. "Hans von Euler-Chelpin," *Bayerische Akademie der Wissenschaften, Jahrbuch* (1965): 206–12.

HARDEN, SIR ARTHUR

Prize: Chemistry, 1929. *Born:* October 12, 1865; Manchester, England. *Died:* June 17, 1940; Bourne End, England. *Nationality:* British. *Education:* University of Manchester, England, B.S., 1885; University of Erlangen, Germany, Ph.D., 1888. *Career:* University of Manchester, England, Researcher, 1888–97; British Institute of Preventive Medicine, Professor, 1897–1930. *Other Awards:* Knighthood, 1926; Davy Medal, Royal Society, 1935.

Citation: "For their investigations on the fermentation of sugar and fermentative enzymes" (with Hans von Euler-Chelpin).

Life Work: Harden's field of investigation was fermentation caused by the action of certain bacteria.When he filtered zymase under high pressure through porous porcelain impregnated with gelatin, he discovered that zymase consisted of two components, one of which passed through the filter and the other did not. The first component was zymase, made of protein, and the second was cozymase, which was not a protein. Both needed to be present to function effectively. In 1905 Harden made his second major discovery, that fermentation requires the presence of phosphate, which is a combination of one molecule of phosphorus and four of oxygen. Harden concluded that phosphate molecules joined with the sugar molecules to enable enzymes to produce fermentation. Furthermore, he found that the phosphate broke free from the products of fermentation at the conclusion of a complex series of reactions. Harden's work on the role of phosphate in fermentation formed the basis of intermediary metabolism, or the study of compounds formed during chemical reactions in living tissues.

Publications: *An Elementary Course of Practical Organic Chemistry*, with F. C. Garrett (London: Longmans, Green, 1897). *Inorganic Chemistry for Advanced Students*, with H. E. Roscoe (London: Macmillan and Co., 1899). "The Alcoholic Ferment of Yeast Juice," with W. J. Young, *Proceedings of the Royal Society* 77B (1907): 405–20. *Alcoholic Fermentations* (London: Longmans, Green, and Company, 1911).

Bibliography: *Dictionary of Scientific Biography* (New York: Scribner's, 1972), vol. 6, pp. 110–12. *Obituary Notices of Fellows of the Royal Society* (Cambridge: Royal Society, 1942–44), vol. 4, pp. 3–14. Ida Smedley-Maclean, "Arthur Harden (1865–1940)," *Biochemical Journal* 35 (1941): 1071–81.

FISCHER, HANS

Prize: Chemistry, 1930. **Born:** July 27, 1881; Hochst-am-Main, Germany. **Died:** March 31, 1945; Munich, Germany. **Nationality:** German. **Education:** University of Marburg, Germany, doctorate, 1904; University of Munich, Germany, M.D., 1908. **Career:** University of Berlin, Germany, Researcher, 1908–10; University of Munich, Germany, Professor, 1910–16; University of Innsbruck, Austria, Professor, 1916–18; University of Vienna, Austria, Professor, 1918–21; Technische Hochschule, Germany, Professor, 1921–45. **Other Awards:** Liebig Memorial Medal, 1929; Davy Medal, Royal Society, 1937.

Citation: "For his researches into the constitution of haemin and chlorophyll and especially for his synthesis of haemin."

Life Work: Fischer's field of investigation was naturally occurring pigments consisting of simple compounds called pyrroles, made of four carbon atoms and one nitrogen atom arranged in a ring. Four pyrrole nuclei are linked in a ring structure called porphyrin. In naturally occurring pigments such as bilirubin and hemin, the porphyrin groups have different arrangements with many structural variations or isomers, each of which exhibits widely differing chemical properties. In his investigations, Fischer built and split the larger molecules and studied thousands of pyrrole combinations to discover the characteristics of each combination. In 1929 he synthesized hemin.

Publications: *Die Chemie des Pyrrols*, 3 vols., with H. Orth (Leipzig, Germany: Akademische Verlagsgesellschaft, 1934–40). *Vorlesungen uber Organische Chemie.* 2 vols. (Munich: P. Beleg, 1950).

Bibliography: *Biographical Dictionary of Scientists* (New York: John Wiley, 1982), p. 181. *Dictionary of Scientific Biography* (New York: Scribner's, 1978), vol. 15, pp. 157–58.

BERGIUS, FRIEDRICH KARL RUDOLPH

Prize: Chemistry, 1931. *Born:* October 11, 1884; Goldschmieden, Germany. *Died:* March 30, 1949; Buenos Aires, Argentina. *Nationality:* German. *Education:* University of Leipzig, Germany, Ph.D., 1907. *Career:* Technical University, Hanover, Germany, Professor, 1909–14; Goldschmidt Company, Essen, Germany, Research Director, 1914–45; Argentine Ministry of Industries, Researcher, 1946–49. *Other Awards:* Liebig Medal, Germany.

Citation: "In recognition of their contributions to the invention and development of chemical high pressure methods" (with Carl Bosch).

Life Work: Bergius's fields of investigation were the transformation of heavy oils and oil residues into lighter oils and gasoline and the effects of high pressure and high temperature on wood and peat in the formation of coal. Because viscous types of petroleum possessed less hydrogen than lighter types he added hydrogen to petroleum to replace hydrogen lost during refining to increase gasoline yield. In 1913 he produced a liquid hydrocarbon by forcing hydrogen into lignitic coal. Between 1922 and 1925 he developed the industrial apparatus for the coal hydrogenation process.

Publications: *Die Anwendung Hoher Drucke bei Chemischen Vorgangen und Eine Nachbildung des Entstehungsprozesses der Steinkohle* (Halle, Germany: W. Knapp, 1913). "Die Verflussigung der Kohle," *Zeitschrift des vereins Deutscher Ingenieure* 69 (1926). "Gewinnung von Alkohol and Glucose aus Holz," *Chemical Age* (*London*) 29 (1933): 481–83.

Bibliography: *Dictionary of Scientific Biography* (New York: Scribner's, 1970), vol. 2, pp. 3–4. A. Stranges, "Friedrich Bergius and the Rise of the German Synthetic Fuel Industry," *ISIS* 75 (December 1984): 643–67.

BOSCH, CARL

Prize: Chemistry, 1931. *Born:* August 27, 1874; Cologne, Germany. *Died:* April 26, 1940; Heidelberg, Germany. *Nationality:* German. *Education:* University of Leipzig, Germany, Ph.D., 1898. *Career:* Badische Anilin-und Sodafabrik, Germany, Researcher and Administrator, 1899–1925; I. G. Farben Industrie, Researcher and Administrator, 1925–40. *Other Awards:* Liebig Medal, Germany; Bunsen Medal, Germany; Siemens Ring, Germany; Exner Medal, Austria; Carl Lueg Medal, Germany.

Citation: "In recognition of their contributions to the invention and development of chemical high pressure methods" (with Friedrich Bergius).

Life Work: Bosch's field of investigation was nitrogen fixation for synthesizing ammonia from atmospheric nitrogen and hydrogen. Bosch developed equipment for this purpose capable of withstanding high pressure and high temperatures and also cheap, effective, and abundant catalysts. In the construction of a reaction chamber he built a double-walled container with a thin annular space between the two walls. When hydrogen and nitrogen reacted within the inner cylinder, a mixture of cold hydrogen gas and nitrogen gas was forced into the annular region. The inner wall, made of low-carbon chrome steel, was protected from the high pressure while the outer wall made of carbon steel, was protected from the high temperature. Bosch synthesized methanol in 1923 by reacting carbon monoxide and hydrogen under high pressure in the presence of a catalyst.

Publications: "Verfahren zur Herstellung von Ammoniak aus Seinen Elementen mit Hilfe von Katalysatoren," *Chemisches Zentralblatt* (1913): 195. "Stickstoff in Wihtschaft und Technik," *Naturwissenschaften* 8 (1920): 867–68. "Probleme Grosstechnischer Hydrierung-Verfahren," *Chemische Fabrik* 7 (1934): 1–10.

Bibliography: "Carl Bosch, 1874–1940," *Chemische Berichte* 90 (1957): 19–39. *Dictionary of Scientific Biography* (New York: Scribner's, 1970), vol. 2, pp. 323–24.

LANGMUIR, IRVING

Prize: Chemistry, 1932. *Born:* January 31, 1881; Brooklyn, New York. *Died:* August 16, 1957; Falmouth, Massachusetts. *Nationality:* American. *Education:* Columbia University, New York, B.S., 1903; University of Göttingen, Germany, Ph.D., 1906. *Career:* Stevens Institute of Technology, Hoboken, New Jersey, Professor, 1906–1909; General Electric Research Laboratory, Schenectady, New York, Researcher and Administrator, 1909–50. *Other Awards:* Hughes Medal, Royal Society, 1918; Rumford Medal, 1920; Nichols Medal, American Chemical Society, 1920; Gibbs Medal, 1930; Franklin Medal, 1934; Faraday Medal, Chemical Society, 1938; Faraday Medal, Institute of Electrical Engineers, 1943; John Carty Medal, National Academy of Sciences, 1950.

Citation: "For his discoveries and investigations in surface chemistry."

Life Work: Langmuir's field of investigation was the characteristics of various gases. He invented the nitrogen-filled lightbulb that was brighter than any yet made. His interest in vacuums led to his invention of the mercury pump used in the manufacture of vacuum tubes. He discovered the electron-emitting powers of thoria, an oxide of thorium. This led him to investigate surface phenomena, or the molecular activity occurring in a thin film, or surface. He described the chemical behavior of surfaces in terms of six forces: Coulomb forces, forces between dipoles, valence forces, attractive van der Waals forces, repulsive forces, and electron pressures. His investigations of atomic structure yielded a theory describing chemical valence as the effect of electrons filling up electron shells, or orbits, surrounding the atomic nuclei. He studied of the properties of electronic discharge in gases between 1923 and 1931. He coined the term plasma for ionized gas, developed the concept of electron temperature, and devised a method for measuring both electron temperature and ion density with a special electrode called the Langmuir Probe.

Publications: *The Collected Works of Irving Langmuir* (New York: Pergamon Press, 1962).

Bibliography: *Dictionary of American Biography* (New York: Scribner's, 1980), suppl. 6, pp. 363–65. Leonard Reich, "I. Langmuir and the Pursuit of Science and Technology in the Corporate Environment," *Technology and Culture* 24 (1983): 199–221. Albert Rosenfeld, *The Quintessence of Irving Langmuir*, vol. 12 of *Collected Works* (New York: Pergamon Press, 1962).

UREY, HAROLD CLAYTON

Prize: Chemistry, 1934. *Born:* April 29, 1893; Walkerton, Indiana. *Died:* January 5, 1981; La Jolla, California. *Nationality:* American. *Education:* University of Montana, B.S., 1917; University of California, Ph.D., 1923. *Career:* University of Copenhagen, Denmark, Researcher, 1923–24; John Hopkins University, Maryland, Professor, 1924–29; Columbia University, New York, Professor and Administrator, 1929–42; Manhattan Project, United States, Director of War Research, 1940–45; University of Chicago, Illinois, Professor, 1945–58; University of California, San Diego, Professor, 1958–70. *Other Awards:* Gibbs Medal, American Chemical Society, 1934; Davy Medal, Royal Society, 1940; Franklin Medal, Franklin Institute, Pennsylvania, 1943; Medal for Merit, 1946; Distinguished Service Award, Phi Beta Kappa, 1950; Cordoza Award, 1954; Priestley Award, Dickinson College, Pennsylvania, 1955; Hamilton Award, Columbia University, New York, 1961; Remsen Award, 1963; Medal, University of Paris, 1964; National Medal of Science for Astronomy, 1964; Achievement Award, American Academy, 1966; Gold Medal, Royal Astronomical Society, 1966; Leonard Medal, Meteoritical Society, 1969; Day Award, Geological Society of America, 1969; Chemical Pioneer Award, American Institute of Chemists, 1969; Linus Pauling Award, Oregon State University, 1970; Johann Kepler Medal, American Society for the Advancement of Science, 1971; Gold Medal, American Institute of Chemists, 1972; Priestley Medal, American Chemical Society, 1973; Exceptional Scientific Achievement Award, NASA, 1973; Knight of Malta, 1973; Headliner Award, San Diego Press Club, 1974; Goldschmidt Medal, Geochemical Society, 1975.

Citation: "For his discovery of heavy hydrogen."

Life Work: Urey's initial field of investigation was the isolation of a hydrogen isotope. He calculated the probable line spectra of an isotope twice as heavy as ordinary hydrogen. He analyzed the spectra for hydrogen gas and detected the calculated lines and thus confirmed the isotope's existence. He named this second lightest atom deuterium. Deuterium offered a convenient model for physicists and chemists studying nuclear particle interactions. It was also useful in the production of heavy water, which moderates nuclear fission reactions and its fusion with tritium fuels thermonuclear reactions in hydrogen bombs. Urey is also recognized as the father of cosmochemistry. In one 1956 study he explained the origins and relative natural abundance of elements and isotopes in the universe. His paleontological investigations led to the invention of a thermometer that calculated past cimatic changes by measuring oxygen isotopes in fossils.

Publications: *Atoms, Molecules and Quanta*, with A. E. Ruark (New York: McGraw-Hill, 1930). *The Planets: Their Origin and Development* (New Haven, Conn.: Yale University Press, 1952). *Production of Heavy Water*, with others (New York: McGraw-Hill, 1955). *Reprints* (LaJolla: University of California, San Diego, 1990). *Some Cosmochemical Problems* (University Park: Pennsylvania State University Press, 1963).

Bibliography: *Current Biography Yearbook* (New York: H. W. Wilson, 1960), pp. 441–42. *New York Times*, January 7, 1981, p. 1.

JOLIOT, FRÉDÉRIC

Prize: Chemistry, 1935. *Born:* March 19, 1900; Paris, France. *Died:* August 14, 1958; Paris, France. *Nationality:* French. *Education:* École de Physique et de Chimie Industrielle, France, engineering degree, 1923; École de Physique et de Chimie Industrielle, France, licence es science, 1927; University of Paris, France, docteur es sciences, 1930. *Career:* Radium Institute, Paris, France, Researcher, 1925–31; Caisse Nationale des Sciences, Researcher, 1931–37; Collège de France, Professor, 1937–44; Centre National de la Recherche Scientifiques, Director, 1944–46; Atomic Energy Commission, France, Commissioner, 1946–50; University of Paris, France, Professor and Researcher, 1956–58. *Other Awards:* Henri Wilde Prize, France, 1933; Marquet Prize, France, 1934; Barnard Gold Medal, Columbia University, 1940.

Citation: "In recognition of their synthesis of new radioactive elements" (with Irène Joliot-Curie).

Life Work: Frédéric Joliot and Irène Joliot-Curie, working on experiments in which alpha particles bombard boron or aluminum, discovered that some of the aluminum and boron in their exposed samples had been transmuted into new radioactive chemical elements. Aluminum, absorbing the two protons and two neutrons of the alpha particle, had been transformed into radioactive phosphorus, while the boron had become a radioactive isotope of nitrogen. They proceeded to prepare a large number of new radioactive elements.

Publications: *Oeuvres Scientifiques Completes* (Paris: Presses Universitaires de France, 1961).

Bibliography: *Current Biography Yearbook* (New York: H. W. Wilson, 1946), pp. 294–96. *Dictionary of Scientific Biography* (New York: Scribner's, 1973), vol. 7, pp. 151–57. Maurice Goldsmith, *Frédéric Joliot-Currie, A Biography* (London: Laurence and Wishart, 1976).

JOLIOT-CURIE, IRÈNE

Prize: Chemistry, 1935. *Born:* September 12, 1897; Paris, France. *Died:* March 17, 1956; Paris, France. *Nationality:* French. *Education:* Collège Sevigne, France, baccalaureat, 1914; University of Paris, France, licentiate, 1920; University of Paris, France, Sc.D., 1925. *Career:* Curie Laboratory, Paris, France, Researcher, 1921–35; Caisse Nationale de la Recherche, Researcher, 1935–36; University of Paris and Radium Institute, France, Researcher, 1937–56. *Other Awards:* Henri Wilde Prize, France, 1933; Marquet Prize, France, 1934; Barnard Gold Medal, Columbia University, New York, 1940.

Citation: "In recognition of their synthesis of new radioactive elements" (with Frédéric Joliot).

Life Work: See Joliot, Frédéric, p. 39.

Publications: *Oeuvres Scientifiques Completes* (Paris: Presses Universitaires de France, 1961).

Bibliography: *Current Biography Yearbook* (New York: H. W. Wilson, 1940), pp. 435–36. Robin McKown, *She Lived for Science: Irène Joliot-Curie* (New York: Messner, 1961). Ethlie Ann Vare, *Mothers of Invention* (New York: Morrow, 1988), pp. 143–48.

DEBYE, PETRUS JOSEPHUS WILHELMUS

Prize: Chemistry, 1936. *Born:* March 24, 1884; Maastricht, Netherlands. *Died:* November 2, 1966; Ithaca, New York. *Nationality:* Dutch; later American citizen. *Education:* Aachen Institute of Technology, Germany, electrical technology degree, 1905; University of Munich, Germany, Ph.D., 1908. *Career:* Aachen Technological Institute, Germany, Researcher, 1905–1906; University of Munich, Germany, Researcher, 1906–10; University of Zürich, Switzerland, Professor, 1910–12; University of Utrecht, Netherlands, Professor, 1912–14; University of Göttingen, Germany, Professor, 1914–20; University of Zürich, Switzerland, Professor, 1920–27; University of Leipzig, Germany, Professor, 1927–34; University of Berlin, Germany, Professor, 1934–39; Cornell University, New York, Professor, 1939–52. *Other Awards:* Rumford Medal, Royal Society; Franklin Medal, Philadelphia, Pennsylvania; Faraday Medal; Lorentz Medal, Royal Netherlands Academy; Willard Gibbs Medal, 1949; Max Planck Medal, West German Physical Society, 1950; Kendall Award, 1957; Nichols Medal, 1961; Priestley Medal, American Chemical Society, 1963; American Physics Society High-Polymer Physics Prize, Ford Motor Company, 1965; Madison Marshall Award, American Chemical Society, 1965; National Medal of Science, 1965.

Citation: "For his contributions to our knowledge of molecular structure through his investigations on dipole moments and on the diffraction of X-rays and electrons in gases."

Life Work: Debye's field of investigation was the structure of molecules, especially the distribution of electrical charges in atoms and molecules. His studies in polarity (the positive-to-negative orientation of such charges) led to the discovery that the dipole moment (the differences between the degree of polarity) of a molecule and that of its component atoms can clarify their relative positions when chemically combined. Debye revised Einstein's quantum theory of specific heat (the amount of energy needed to raise the temperature of a substance by 1° C) and developed a formula for calculating the associated temperature, now called the Debye temperature. His molecular studies led him to demonstrate an association between the diffraction patterns and thermal movements of atoms in crystals. Working with Paul Scherrer in 1916, he devised the Debye-Scherrer method, which proved that even in a powder of small or imperfect crystals, enough crystals would be so aligned that X-ray diffraction studies could elucidate molecular structure. His contributions to the study of electrolytes include the 1923 Debye-Huckel Theory (with Erich Huckel), which mathematically calculates the ionic intensities of electrolytic solutions.

Publications: *The Dipole Moment and Chemical Structure* (London: Blakiston, 1932). "Energy Absorption in Dielectrics with Polar Molecules," *Faraday Society* 30 (1934): 679–84. *Collected Papers* (New York: Interscience, 1954).

Bibliography: Mansel Davies, *Journal of Chemical Education* 45 (1968): 467–73. *Dictionary of Scientific Biography* (New York: Scribner's, 1971), vol. 3, pp. 617–21.

HAWORTH, SIR WALTER NORMAN

Prize: Chemistry, 1937. *Born:* March 19, 1883; Chorley, Lancashire, England. *Died:* March 19, 1950; Birmingham, England. *Nationality:* British. *Education:* University of Manchester, England, baccalaureate, 1906; University of Göttingen, Germany, Ph.D., 1910; University of Manchester, England, D.Sc., 1911. *Career:* University of London, England, Professor, 1911–12; University of St. Andrews, Scotland, Professor, 1912–20; University of Durham, England, Professor, 1920–25; University of Birmingham, England, Professor and Administrator, 1925–48. *Other Awards:* Longstaff Medal, 1933; Davy Medal, 1934; Royal Medal, 1942; Knighthood, 1947.

Citation: "For his investigations on carbohydrates and vitamin C."

Life Work: Haworth's field of investigation was carbohydrates, especially the structure of monosaccharides (simple sugars) and oligosaccharides, the somewhat more complex sugars. In 1925 he proposed that glucose was composed of six atoms attached to one another in a ring. At the same time, he began to study hexuronic acid found in the adrenal glands of animals. In 1932 Haworth established that this carbohydrate consists of six carbon, eight hydrogen, and six oxygen atoms, arranged in a five-sided ring with three short branches. Because of its antiscorbutic properties Haworth renamed it ascorbic acid, or vitamin C, thus becoming the first person to synthesize a vitamin.

Publications: *The Constitution of Sugars* (London: E. Arnold & Company, 1929). "The Constitution of Some Carbohydrates," *Chemische Berichte* (1932): 43–65. "Synthesis of Asorbic Acid," with E. L. Hirst *Chemistry and Industry* (1933): 2790–2806. "Starch," *Journal of the Chemical Society* (1946): 543–49. "The Structure, Function and Synthesis of Polysaccharides," *Proceedings of the Royal Society* (1946): 1–9.

Bibliography: *Dictionary of Scientific Biography* (New York: Scribner's, 1972), vol. 6, pp. 184–85. "Walter Norman Haworth," *Journal of the Chemical Society* (1951): 2790–2806.

KARRER, PAUL

Prize: Chemistry, 1937. *Born:* April 21, 1889; Moscow, Russia. *Died:* June 18, 1971; Zürich, Switzerland. *Nationality:* Russian; later Swiss citizen. *Education:* University of Zürich, Switzerland, doctorate, 1911. *Career:* University of Zürich, Switzerland, Researcher, 1911–12; Georg Speyer Haus, Frankfurt-am-Main, Germany, Researcher and Administrator, 1918–59. *Other Awards:* Marcel Benoist Prize, Switzerland, 1923; Cannizzaro Prize, Italy, 1935; Officier de la Legion d'Honneur, 1954.

Citation: "For his investigations on carotenoids, flavins and vitamins A and B2."

Life Work: Karrer's field of investigation was stereochemistry, the spatial arrangement of atoms into molecules. In 1927 he began a study of anthocyanins, group of pigments found in red and blue flowers. He determined the structure of beta-carotene, a constituent of carrots and crocin, a yellow pigment found in the crocus. His study of beta-carotene led him to isolated vitamin A and establish its molecular structure. He found that vitamin A consists of twenty carbon atoms, thirty hydrogen atoms, and one oxygen atom in a six-sided closed ring, with three small molecules attached at two points and a long zigzag chain at a third point. Karrer was the first scientist to describe the molecular structure of a vitamin. In 1935 he synthesized riboflavin, or vitamin B, and determined its formula and molecular structure. In 1938 Karrer synthesized vitamin E, followed by vitamin K. In 1942 he determined the structure of NAD, nicotinomide adenine dinucleotide, an enzymatic substance that regulates the transfer of hydrogen between molecules within cells and thereby produces cellular energy.

Publications: *Einfuhrung in die Chemie der Polymeren Kohlehydrate, ein Grundiss der Chemie der Starke, des Glykogen, der Zellulose und Anderer Polysaccharide* (Leipzig, Germany: Akademische Verlagsgesellschaft, 1925). *Lehrbuch der Organischen Chemie* (Leipzig, Germany: Thieme, 1928). *Die Carotenoids*, with E. Jucker (Basel, Switzerland: Birkhauser, 1948).

Bibliography: *Biographical Memoirs of the Fellows of the Royal Society* (London: Royal Society, 1978), vol. 24, pp. 244–321. *Dictionary of Scientific Biography* (New York: Scribner's, 1978), vol. 15, pp. 257–58.

KUHN, RICHARD

Prize: Chemistry, 1938. *Born:* December 3, 1900; Vienna, Austria. *Died:* August 1, 1967; Heidelberg, Germany. *Nationality:* Austrian; later German citizen. *Education:* University of Munich, Germany, Ph.D., 1922. *Other Awards:* Pour le Mérite für Wissenschaften und Kunste, 1958.

Citation: "For his work on carotenoids and vitamins."

Life Work: Kuhn's field of investigation was the chemistry of organic compounds as related to their function in biological systems. He began with enzymes or proteins that accelerate the rates at which chemical reactions occur in cells. Kuhn was interested in the configuration of atoms in organic molecules, especially conjugated double bonds, a molecular structure in which doubly bonded and singly bonded carbon atoms alternate with one another. He focused on carotenoids, biological pigments found in living cells, and carotene, the pigment found in carrots. Using chromotography, he found three compounds in carotene: beta-carotene, which bends with light; alpha-carotene, which does not; and gamma-carotene. Kuhn proved that beta-carotene is a precursor to vitamin A. Kuhn continued to work on members of the water-soluble vitamin B group. He isolated and synthesized riboflavin or vitamin B2 and adermin, or vitamin B6. Later in life Kuhn worked to identify para-aminobenzoic acid, a compound used in synthesizing anesthetics and pantothenic acid, important in hemoglobin formation and the release of energy from carbohydrates.

Publications: "Materials of Living Nature," *Naturwissenschaften* 25 (1937): 225–31. "Fertilizing Gamones and Sex-Determining Substances (Termones) in Plants and Animals," *Angewandte* 53 (1940): 1–6. "Carotene Dyes," with H. Bielig, German Patent 719845 (March 26, 1942). "Vitamins and Medicines," *Die Chemie* 55 (1942): 1–6.

Bibliography: *Biographical Encyclopedia of Scientists* (New York: Facts on File, 1981), p. 455. *Dictionary of Scientific Biography* (New York: Scribner's, 1973), vol. 7, pp. 517–18. G. Oberkoflker, *Richard Kuhn* (Innsbruck, Austria: Das Archiv, 1992).

BUTENANDT, ADOLF FRIEDRICH JOHANN

Prize: Chemistry, 1939. *Born:* March 24, 1903; Bremer-haven-Lehe, Germany. *Died:* January 18, 1995; Munich, Germany. *Nationality:* German. *Education:* University of Göttingen, Germany, Ph.D., 1927. *Career:* Schering Corporation, Germany, Researcher, 1927–31; University of Göttingen, Germany, Professor, 1931–33; Technische Hochschule, Danzig, Germany, Professor, 1933–36; Kaiser-Wilhelm Institute for Biochemistry, Berlin, Germany, Director, 1936–45; Max-Planck Institute for Biochemistry, Germany, Professor and Administrator, 1945–85. *Other Awards:* Von Harnack Medal, 1973, 1983.

Citation: "For his work on sex hormones."

Life Work: Butenandt's field of investigation was sex hormones. In 1929 he isolated a female sex hormone in pure crystalline form, called folliculin, later renamed estrone. The hormone is an estrogen that feminizes the human body and promotes growth of the lining of the uterus. In 1931 he turned his attention to the isolation and chemical identification of a male sex hormone called androsterone, synthesized and secreted by the Leydig cells of the testes. Next he analyzed the chemical structure of the estrogenic hormones estrone and estriol, and their relationship to sterols. He proved that the female sex hormones and sterols (especially cholesterol and the bile acids) were related chemically. Cholesterol was later shown to be a precursor to the male and female sex hormones. By 1934 Butenandt isolated crystalline progesterone, a hormone that prepares the lining of the uterus for the implantation of the fertilized ovum. In 1935 he synthesized testosterone from its biochemical precursor. Butenandt also discovered the biochemical pathways of interconversion of male and female sex hormones, which are chemically related by their common sterol nucleus. Male sex hormonal activity is governed by a double bond between the fourth and fifth carbon atoms of the four-ring sterol nucleus, and female sex hormonal activity by a double bond between the first and second carbon atoms. During the war years Butenandt studied the genetic regulation of eye pigment biosynthesis in insects. These eye pigments, called omochromes, belonged to a new class of biological compounds. In 1953 he and a colleague Peter Karlson isolated the first crystalline insect hormone, called ecdysone, a derivative of cholesterol.

Publications: *Untersuchungen uber das Weibliche Sexualhormon (Follikel-oder Brunsthormon)* (Berlin: Weidmannsche Buchhandlung, 1931). *Die Biologische Chemie im Dienste der Volkagesundheit* (Berlin: W. de Gruyter, 1941). *Uber die Biochemische analyse einer Gen-Wirkkette der Pigmentbildung bei Insekten* (Debrecen, Hungary: Tisza Istvan-Tudomanyegyetemi Nyomda, 1943). *Zur Feinstruktur des Tabakmosaik-Virus* (Berlin: Akademie der Wissenschaften, W. de Gruyter, 1944).

Bibliography: "Adolf Butenandt," *Journal of Chemical Education* 26 (February 1949): 91. *Asimov's Biographical Encyclopedia of Science and Technology.* (Garden City, N.Y.: Doubleday, 1982), p. 792. O. Karlson, *Adolf Butenandt* (Stuttgart, Germany: Wissenschaftliche Verlagsgesselschaft, 1990).

RUZICKA, LEOPOLD STEPHEN

Prize: Chemistry, 1939. *Born:* September 13, 1887; Vukovar, Yugoslavia. *Died:* September 26, 1976; Zürich, Switzerland. *Nationality:* Yugoslavian; later Swiss citizen. *Education:* Technische Hochschule, Germany, Dr. Ing., 1910. *Career:* Federal Institute of Technology, Zürich, Switzerland, Professor, 1923–26; University of Utrecht, Netherlands, Professor, 1926–29; Federal Institute of Technology, Zürich, Switzerland, Professor, 1929–57.

Citation: "For his work on polymethylenes and higher terpenes."

Life Work: Ruzicka's field of investigation was terpines, organic compounds found in the oils of plants and ketones. He and his colleagues elucidated the structures of complex terpines and other large-ring hydrocarbons. In 1916 he began researching natural odoriferous compounds, which culminated in the discovery that the molecules of muskone and civetone, important to the perfume industry, contain rings of fifteen and seventeen carbon atoms, respectively. Prior to his work, rings with more than eight atoms were thought to be unstable, if they did exist. By 1933/34, Ruzicka was able to offer the first complete proof of the consitution of a sex hormone and accomplish the first artificial production of a sex hormone. His patent for the preparation of testosterone from cholesterol earned him a fortune as well as international acclaim.

Publications: *Uber den Bau der Organischen Materie; Antrittarede Gehalten am 10* (Utrecht, Netherlands: Aula der Reichsuniversitat, 1926). *Uber Konstitution und Zusammenhange in der Sesquiterpenreihe* (Berlin: Gebruder Borntraeger, 1928). *Conferenze di Chimica Organica, Tenute Nell'Instituto Chimico dell'Universita di Roma* (Rome: Academia Nazionale dei Lincei, 1951). "The Isoprene Rule and the Biogenesis of Terpenic Compounds," *Experimentia* 9 (1953): 357–65.

Bibliography: *Asimov's Biographical Encyclopedia of Science and Technology* (Garden City, N.Y.: Doubleday, 1982), p. 712. *Biographical Memoirs of the Fellows of the Royal Society* (London: Royal Society, 1980), vol. 26, pp. 411–501. "Dr. Leopold Ruzicka Dies in Switzerland at Age 89; Won Nobel in Chemistry," *New York Times*, September 27, 1976, p. 34.

HEVESY, GEORG KARL VON (HEVESY, GEORGE CHARLES DE)

Prize: Chemistry, 1943. *Born:* August 1, 1885; Budapest, Hungary. *Died:* July 5, 1966; Freiburg, Germany. *Nationality:* Hungarian; later German resident, Danish resident, and Swedish citizen. *Education:* University of Freiburg, Germany, Ph.D., 1908. *Career:* Technical High School, Zürich, Switzerland, Teacher, 1908–10; Austrian-Hungarian Government Worker, 1910–12; University of Budapest, Hungary, Professor, 1912–20; Institute of Theoretical Physics, Copenhagen, Denmark, Researcher, 1920–26; University of Freiburg, Germany, Professor, 1926–34; Institute of Theoretical Physics, Copenhagen, Denmark, Researcher, 1934–43; University of Stockholm, Sweden, Professor, 1943–55. *Other Awards:* Canizzaro Prize, Academy of Sciences, Rome, 1929; Copley Medal, 1949; Faraday Medal, 1950; Bailey Medal, 1951; Sylvanus Thompson Medal, 1955; Atoms for Peace Award, United Nations, 1959; Niels Bohr Medal, 1961; Rosenberger Medal, University of Chicago, 1961.

Citation: "For his work on the use of isotopes as tracers in the study of chemical processes."

Life Work: Hevesy's most important work began in 1911 in the Manchester laboratory of Ernest Rutherford where he worked on the separation of radium D from a sample of lead. In fact, radium D was a radioactive isotope of lead and could not be chemically separated from it. Hevesy therefore suggested that radium D could be added to lead as a detectable marker or label. The behavior of lead in chemical reactions could then be followed by measuring radioactive emissions. He also proved that radium D was an isotope of lead. Beginning in 1920, working at the Bohr Institute in Copenhagen, Hevesy began separating isotopes of mercury and chrlorine Working with Dick Coster, Hevesy identified the new element hafnium. At Freiburg he worked on the analysis of minerals by the characteristic X rays they emit when bombarded by a powerful X-ray beam. He was also involved in biological research using heavy water as a tracer. His radioactive tracers developed into one of the most widely used techniques for the investigation of living systems.

Publications: *Adventurers in Radioisotope Research: The Collected Papers of George Hevesy* (New York: Pergamon Press, 1952).

Bibliography: *Current Biography Yearbook* (New York: H. W. Wilson, 1959), pp. 186–88. *Dictionary of Scientific Biography* (New York: Scribner's, 1972), vol. 6, pp. 365–67. Hilde Levi, *George de Hevesy* (Stockholm: Hilger, 1985).

HAHN, OTTO

Prize: Chemistry, 1944. *Born:* March 8, 1879; Frankfurt-am-Main, Germany. *Died:* July 28, 1968; Göttingen, Germany. *Nationality:* German. *Education:* University of Marburg, Germany, Ph.D., 1901. *Career:* University of Berlin, Germany, Professor, 1907–33; Kaiser Wilhelm Institute of Chemistry, Germany, Professor, 1928–45; Max Planck Society for the Advancement of Science, Germany, President, 1946–60. *Other Awards:* Grand Cross of the Order of Merit, Germany, 1959; Fermi Award, United States Atomic Energy Commission, 1966.

Citation: "For his discovery of the fission of heavy nuclei."

Life Work: Working in London in 1904, Hahn discovered a new radioactive species of the element thorium which he called radiothorium. Over the next ten years, he discovered thorium C, now called polonium 214, with a half-life of about one-third of a millionth of a second, and identified several previously unknown radioactive products, including rubidium. After World War I Hahn discovered uranium Z, the first example of an isomer of radioactive atoms. Hahn's most important work was done in the 1930s when, with Lise Meitner, he made one of the most important discoveries of the century—namely, nuclear fission. In 1938 Hahn bombarded uranium with slow neutrons and detected some strange new half-lives. At that time it was believed that nuclear transmutations always involved the emission of either an alpha particle (helium nucleus) or a beta particle (electron) and that the change could take place only between elements separated by no more than two places in the periodic table. Hahn assumed that the uranium had changed into radium, but found that in fact it had changed into barium, which was far down the periodic table. The heavy uranium nucleus had split into two lighter ones. It was soon recognized that the process, now named nuclear fission, released large amounts of energy in a chain reaction.

Publications: *Applied Radiochemistry* (Ithaca, N.Y.: Cornell University Press, 1936). *New Atoms, Progress and Some Memories: A Collection of Papers* (New York: Elsevier, 1950).

Bibliography: *Dictionary of Scientific Biography* (New York: Scribner's, 1972), vol. 6, pp. 14–17. K. Hoffman, *Schuld und Verantwortung* (Berlin, Germany: Springer-Verlag, 1993). *Otto Hahn: A Scientific Autobiography* (New York: Scribner's, 1966).

VIRTANEN, ARTTURI ILMARI

Prize: Chemistry, 1945. *Born:* January 15, 1895; Helsinki, Finland. *Died:* November 11, 1973; Helsinki, Finland. *Nationality:* Finnish. *Education:* University of Helsinki, Finland, M.Sc., 1916; University of Helsinki, Finland, Ph.D., 1919. *Career:* Central Laboratory of Industry, Finland, Researcher, 1916–17; Government Butter and Cheese Control Station, Finland, Researcher, 1919; Finnish Cooperative Dairies Association, Researcher, 1919–24; University of Helsinki, Finland, Professor, 1924–48; Academy of Finland, President, 1948–63. *Other Awards:* Friesland Prize, Netherlands, 1967; Atwater Prize, 1968; Siegfried Thannhauser Medal, 1969; Gold Medal, Germany, 1971; Gold Medal and Prize, Spain, 1972; Uovo d'oro, Italy, 1973.

Citation: "For his research and inventions in agricultural and nutrition chemistry, especially for his fodder preservation method."

Life Work: Virtanen is best known for his AIV (after his initials) method of fodder preservation. He studied the process of fermentation that occurs in stored green fodder and determined that acidifying the fodder to a pH level slightly under 4 would halt the deterioration of the forage. Tests showed that the acidified fodder not only kept well but also continued to be satisfactory in taste and nutrition. This discovery was particularly important for countries with long winters, as it ensured a constant supply of feed regardless of the time of harvest. Virtanen did additional research on leguminous, nitrogen-fixing plants; the chemical composition of higher plants; and the methods by which plants synthesize vitamins.

Publications: *Cattle, Fodder and Human Nutrition: With Special Reference to Biological Nitrogen Fixation* (Cambridge: Cambridge University Press, 1938). *Kirjakauppojen Liiketalous ja Kannattavuus, 1952* (Helsinki: Liiketalous tieteellinen Tutkimuslaitos, 1954). *On Nitrogen Metabolism in Milking Cows* (Helsinki: Suomalainen Tiedeakatemia, 1968). *Fundamental Studies of Organic Compounds in Plants, Especially Vegetables and Fodder Plants, and Their Enzymic and Chemical Splitting Products Which Often Have Physiological Effects, in Order to Improve the Utilization Potential for Their Products, Final Report* (Helsinki: Biochemical Research Institute, 1969).

Bibliography: *Biographical Encyclopedia of Scientists* (New York: Facts on File, 1981), p. 812. *Dictionary of Scientific Biography* (New York: Scribner's, 1976), vol. 14, pp. 454–56.

NORTHROP, JOHN HOWARD

Prize: Chemistry, 1946. *Born:* July 5, 1891; Yonkers, New York. *Died:* May 27, 1987; Wickenberg, Arizona. *Nationality:* American. *Education:* Columbia University, New York, B.S., 1912; Columbia University, New York, M.A., 1913; Columbia University, New York, Ph.D., 1915. *Career:* Rockefeller Institute, New York, Professor, 1916–62; University of California, Berkeley, Professor, 1949–62. *Other Awards:* Stevens Prize, Columbia University, 1931; Daniel Giraud Elliot Medal, National Academy of Sciences, 1939; Certificate of Merit, United States, 1948; Alexander Hamilton Award, Columbia University, 1961.

Citation: "For their preparation of enzymes and virus proteins in a pure form" (with Wendell M. Stanley).

Life Work: Northrop's major efforts dealt with the crystallization of a number of enzymes and the proof of their protein nature. The techniques he developed were used in his laboratory to isolate pepsin, trypsin, chymotripsin, ribonuclease, and deoxyribonuclease. He worked later with isolation and characterization of a bacterial virus and also studied temperature effects on life span. In 1939 Northrop became the first to isolate a bacterial virus and the following year he crystallized diphtheria antitoxin.

Publications: "Crystalline Pepsin," *Science* 69 (1929): 580. "Crystalline Pepsin. I. Isolation and Tests of Purity," *Journal of General Physiology* 13 (1930): 739–66. "The Isolation of Crystalline Pepsin and Trypsin," *Scientific Monthly* 35 (1932): 333–40. "Concentration and Partial Purification of Bacteriophage," *Science* 84 (1936): 90–91. *Crystalline Enzymes*, with others (New York: Columbia University Press, 1939).

Bibliography: *Biographical Encyclopedia of Scientists* (New York: Facts on File, 1981), pp. 599–600. *Current Biography Yearbook* (New York: H. W. Wilson, 1947), pp. 472–74. *The Excitement and Fascination of Science.* (Palo Alto, Calif.: Annual Reviews), vol. 1, pp. 355–44. *New York Times* Biographical Service, July 16, 1987, p. 693.

STANLEY, WENDELL MEREDITH

Prize: Chemistry, 1946. *Born:* August 16, 1904; Ridgeville, Indiana. *Died:* June 15, 1971; Salamanca, Spain. *Nationality:* American. *Education:* Earlham College, Indiana, B.S., 1926; University of Illinois, M.A., 1927; University of Illinois, Ph.D., 1929. *Career:* University of Illinois, Professor, 1929–30; University of Munich, Germany, Researcher, 1930–31; Rockefeller Institute, New York, Professor, 1931–48; University of California, Professor and Administrator, 1948–71. *Other Awards:* American Association for the Advancement of Science Prize, 1937; Isaac Adler Award, Harvard University, Massachusetts, 1938; Rosenburger Medal, University of Chicago, Illinois, 1938; Scott Award, Philadelphia, Pennsylvania, 1938; Gold Medal, American Institute of New York, 1941; Copernician Citation, 1943; Nichols Medal, American Chemical Society, 1946; Gibbs Medal, American Chemical Society, 1947; Franklin Medal, Franklin Institute, 1948; Certificate of Merit, United States, 1948; Modern Medicine Award, 1958; Distinguished Service Medal, American Cancer Society, 1963; Scientific Achievement Award, American Medical Association, 1966.

Citation: "For their preparation of enzymes and virus proteins in a pure form" (with John H. Northrop).

Life Work: Stanley's initial field of investigation was th tobacco mosaic virus, which he proved consists essentially of protein. Since that discovery more than three hundred different viruses have been identified, including those that cause smallpox, yellow fever, dengue fever, poliomyelitis, measles, mumps, pneumonia, and the common cold.

Publications: "Chemical Studies on the Virus of Tobacco Mosaic. VI. The Isolation from Diseased Turkish Tobacco Plants of a Crystalline Protein Possessing the Properties of Tobacco-Mosaic Virus," *Phytopathology* 26 (1936): 305–20. "The Isolation of a Crystalline Protein Possessing the Properties of Ancuba-Mosaic Virus," *Journal of Bacteriology* 31 (1936): 52–53. "The Isolation of Crystalline Tobacco Mosaic Virus Protein from Diseased Tomato Plants," with H. S. Loring, *Science* 83 (1936): 85.

Bibliography: *Asimov's Biographical Encyclopedia of Science and Technology* (Garden City, N.Y.: Doubleday, 1982), pp. 801–802. *Current Biography Yearbook* (New York: H. W. Wilson, 1947), pp. 604–607. *National Cyclopedia of American Biography* (Clifton, N.J.: James T. White, 1977), vol. 57, pp. 161–63.

SUMNER, JAMES BATCHELLER

Prize: Chemistry, 1946. *Born:* November 19, 1887; Canton, Massachusetts. *Died:* August 12, 1955; Buffalo, New York. *Nationality:* American. *Education:* Harvard University, Massachusetts, B.A., 1910; Harvard University, Massachusetts, M.A., 1913; Harvard University, Massachusetts, Ph.D., 1914. *Career:* Cornell University, New York, Professor, 1914–55. *Other Awards:* Scheele Medal, Sweden, 1937.

Citation: "For his discovery that enzymes can be crystallized."

Life Work: Sumner's field of investigation was enzymes. Experimenting with urease, a plant enzyme involved in the decomposition of urea, he produced microscopic crystals that proved to be protein. He later crystallized the enzymes pepsin and trypsin.

Publications: "The Isolation and Crystallization of the Enzyme Urease," *Journal of Biological Chemistry* 69 (1926): 435–41. *Textbook of Biological Chemistry* (New York: Macmillan Company, 1927). "Crystalline Catalase," *Journal of Biological Chemistry* 121 (1937): 417–24. *Chemistry and Methods of Enzymes* (New York: Academic Press, 1943). *The Enzymes, Chemistry and Mechanism of Action*, with K. Myrback, 2 vols. (New York: Academic Press, 1950–52).

Bibliography: *Biographical Memoirs of the National Academy of Sciences* (Washington, D.C.; National Academy of Sciences, 1958), vol. 31, pp. 376–96. *Current Biography Yearbook* (New York: H. W. Wilson, 1947), pp. 620–22. *Dictionary of Scientific Biography* (New York: Scribner's, 1976), vol. 13, pp. 152–53.

ROBINSON, SIR ROBERT

Prize: Chemistry, 1947. *Born:* September 13, 1886; Chesterfield, Derbyshire, England. *Died:* February 8, 1975; Great Missenden, Buckinghamshire, England. *Nationality:* British. *Education:* University of Manchester, England, baccalaureate, 1906; University of Manchester, England, D.Sc., 1910. *Career:* University of Sydney, Australia, Professor, 1912–15; University of Liverpool, England, Professor, 1915–20; British Dyestuffs Corporation, Director of Research, 1920; University of St. Andrews, Scotland, Professor, 1921; University of Manchester, England, Professor, 1922–28; University of London, England, Professor, 1928–30; Oxford University, England, Professor, 1930–55. *Other Awards:* Davy Medal, 1930; Royal Medal, 1932; Knighthood, 1939; Copley Medal, 1942; Franklin Institute, 1947.

Citation: "For his investigations on plant products of biological importance, especially the alkaloids."

Life Work: Robinson's field of investigation was alkaloids containing isoquinoline, a two-ring carbon and nitrogen structure found in plants, including quinine, cocaine, atropine, morphine, and opium. His synthesis of papaverine, hydrastine, narcotine, and tripinone led him to believe that these chemical substances are synthesized in a similar way by plants. His theory of alkaloid biogenesis was later confirmed by radioactive tracer studies of reactions in living plants. In his laboratory he synthesized many pigments including anthocyanin (blue-red) and anthoxanthin (yellow). He contributed a qualitative electronic theory of chemical reactions concerning the distribution of electrons and partial valences in aromatic carbon compounds. Investigating steroid hormones, he prepared the female hormone estrone and three synthetic estrogens.

Publications: "A Synthesis of Tropinone," *Journal of the Chemical Society* 111 (1917): 762–68. "A Theory of the Mechanism of the Phytochemical Synthesis of Certain Alkaloids," *Journal of the Chemical Society* 111 (1917): 876–99. "An Electrochemical Theory of the Mechanism of Organic Reactions," *Inst. Internat. Chim. Solvay Conseil Chim 4e Conseil, Brussels* (1932): 423–50.

Bibliography: *Biographical Memoirs of the Fellows of the Royal Society* (London: Royal Society, 1976), pp. 415–527. *Memoirs of a Minor Prophet* (New York: Elsevier, 1976). T. Williams, *Robert Robinson, Chemist Extraordinary* (Oxford, England: Clarendon Press, 1990).

TISELIUS, ARNE WILHELM KAURIN

Prize: Chemistry, 1948. *Born:* August 10, 1902; Stockholm, Sweden. *Died:* October 29, 1971; Stockholm, Sweden. *Nationality:* Swedish. *Education:* University of Uppsala, Sweden, M.A., 1924; University of Uppsala, Sweden, Ph.D., 1930. *Career:* University of Uppsala, Sweden, Researcher and Professor, 1925–68. *Other Awards:* Bergstedt Prize, Royal Swedish Scientific Society, 1926; Paterno Medal, 1954; Hoffman Medal, 1955; Franklin Medal, 1956; Mookerjee Medal, 1959; Karrer Medal, 1961; Messel Medal, 1962.

Citation: Tiselius: "For his research on electrophoresis and adsorption analysis, especially for his discoveries concerning the complex nature of the serum proteins."

Life Work: Tiselius's field of investigation was electrophoresis, the movement of electrically charged molecules in a solution to which an electric field has been applied. He succeeded in accurately measuring the diffusion of water molecules in zeolite crystals. With a sensitive electrophoretic apparatus he analyzed blood serum to show that the serum protein known as globulin actually consists of three types, alpha, beta and gamma. In the 1940s and 1950s he turned to another modes of separation of molecular constituents: partition and gel filtration, chromatography or adsorption analysis, utilizing the principle of adsorption.

Publications: "A New Method for Determination of the Mobility of Proteins," with T. Svedberg, *Journal of the American Chemical Society* 48 (September 1926): 2272–78. "The Moving Boundary Method of Studying the Electrophoresis of Proteins," *Nova Acta Regiae Societatis Scientarium Upsaliensis* 7, 4th series (1930): 100–107. "Adsorption and Diffusion in Zeolite Crystals," *Journal of Physical Chemistry* 40 (February 1936): 223–32. "A New Apparatus for Electrophoretic Analysis of Colloidal Mixtures," *Transactions of the Faraday Society* 33 (1937): 524–31. "Electrophoresis of Serum Globulin II. Electrophoretic Analysis of Normal and Immune Sera," *Biochemical Journal* 31 (July 1937): 1464–77. "Separation and Fractionation of Macromolecules and Particles," with J. Parath and P. A. Albertsson, *Science* 141 (July 1963): 13–20.

Bibliography: *Biographical Memoirs of the Fellows of the Royal Society* (London: Royal Society, 1974), vol. 20, pp. 401–28. *Current Biography Yearbook* (New York: H. W. Wilson, 1949), pp. 603–604. *Dictionary of Scientific Biography* (New York: Scribner's, 1976), vol. 13, pp. 418–22. *The Excitement and Fascination of Science* (Palo Alto, Calif.: Annual Reviews, Inc., 1978), vol. 2, pp. 549–72.

GIAUQUE, WILLIAM FRANCIS

Prize: Chemistry, 1949. *Born:* May 12, 1895; Niagara Falls, Ontario, Canada. *Died:* March 29, 1982; Berkeley, California. *Nationality:* American. *Education:* University of California, B.S., 1920; University of California, Ph.D., 1922. *Career:* University of California, Berkeley, Professor, 1922–62. *Other Awards:* Pacific Division Prize, American Association for the Advancement of Science, 1929; Medal, Chandler Foundation, Columbia University, New York, 1936; Elliot Cresson Medal, Franklin Institute, 1937; Gibbs Medal, American Chemical Society, 1951; Lewis Medal, 1956.

Citation: "For his contributions in the field of chemical thermodynamics, particularly concerning the behaviour of substances at extremely low temperatures."

Life Work: Giauque's field of investigation was the properties and behavior of matter at extremely low temperatures involving the laws of thermodynamics. In 1924 Giauque suggested an experimental method that would permit temperatures below 1°K based on a phenomenon known as adiabatic demagnetization. An adiabatic system is one in which heat is neither gained nor lost, as in paramagnetic substances such as rare earth. Using gadolinium sulfate, Giauque finally achieved a temperature of 0.25°K. To measure temperatures below this limit, Giauque devised a thermometer that employed the electrical resistance properties of amorphous carbon. Giauque compared the entropy values obtained by this method with spectroscopic data and identified two hitherto unknown oxygen isotopes, 17 and 18. Discovery of these isotopes led to the recalibration of atomic weight scales, which until then had used oxygen-16.

Publications: "Thermodynamic Treatment of Certain Magnetic Effects: A Proposed Method of Producing Temperatures Considerably Below 1° Absolute," *Journal of the American Chemical Society* 49 (1927): 1864–70. "Temperatures Below 1° Absolute," *Industrial and Engineering Chemistry* 28 (1936): 743–45.

Bibliography: *The Annual Obituary, 1982* (New York: St. Martin's Press, 1983), pp. 143–45. *Current Biography Yearbook* (New York: H. W. Wilson, 1950), pp. 170–72.

ALDER, KURT

Prize: Chemistry, 1950. *Born:* July 10, 1902; Konigshuette, Germany. *Died:* June 20, 1958; Cologne, Germany. *Nationality:* German. *Education:* University of Kiel, Germany, Ph.D., 1926. *Career:* University of Kiel, Germany, Professor, 1930–36; I. G. Farben Industrie, Administrator, 1936–40; University of Cologne, Germany, Professor and Administrator, 1940–59. *Other Awards:* Emil Fischer Memorial Medal, Association of German Chemists, 1938.

Citation: "For their discovery and development of the diene synthesis" (with Otto Diels).

Life Work: Alder's field of investigation was diene synthesis, which became a basic chemical tool enabling scientists to study many previously inaccessible types of organic reactions and which laid the foundations of polymer chemistry. A diene is a molecule with a base structure consisting of a four-carbon chain in which two double bonds are separated by a single bond. At room temperature it will combine with a philodiene molecule to form a new, stable six-carbon ring molecule. His research led to the discovery of synthetic rubber which is produced by joining butadiene to philodienes, such as styrene. He also applied diene synthesis to unveil the chemical compositions of D vitamins and terpenes.

Publications: "Synthesen in der Hydroaromatischen Reihe. I. Mitteilung, Anlagerungen von 'Di-en'—ko-hlenwasserstoffen," with O. Diels, *Annalen die Chemie* 460 (1928): 98–122. "Die Methode der Dien-Synthese," in *Handbuch der Biologischen Arbeitsmethoden* (Berlin: Urban and Schwartzenburg, 1933), vol. 2, pp. 31–71. *Neuere Methoden der Praeparativen Organischen Chemie* (Berlin: Verlag Chemie, 1943). "Uber den Sterischen Verlauf von Dien-Synthesen mit Acyclischen Dienen. Die Allgemeine Sterische Formel," *Annalen die Chemie* 571 (1951): 157–66.

Bibliography: *Dictionary of Scientific Biography* (New York: Scribner's, 1970), vol. 1, pp. 105–106. M. Guenzl-Schumacher, "Kurt Alder," *Chemikerzeitung* 82 (1958): 489–90.

DIELS, OTTO PAUL HERMANN

Prize: Chemistry, 1950. *Born:* January 23, 1876; Hamburg, Germany. *Died:* March 7, 1954; Kiel, Germany. *Nationality:* German. *Education:* University of Berlin, Germany, Ph.D., 1899. *Career:* University of Berlin, Germany, Professor, 1899–1916; University of Kiel, Germany, Professor and Administrator, 1916–48. *Other Awards:* Gold Medal, St. Louis Exposition, Missouri, 1906; Adolf von Baeyer Memorial Medal, Society of German Chemists, 1931.

Citation: "For their discovery and development of the diene synthesis" (with Kurt Alder).

Life Work: Diels's field of investigation was the structure of cholesterol. Through dehydration, he converted cholesterol into cholesterone, a ketone. He dehydrated cholesterol by mixing selenium, a method later applied to produce polyunsaturated oils. With Kurt Alder, he was one of the discoverers of diene synthesis. By means of this method a large number of compounds of complex structure can easily be produced. Diels continued to study Diels-Alder reactions and their applications throughout his career. He also isolated, earlier in his career, carbon suboxide, and developed a method for removing hydrogen from steroids using selenium.

Publications: "Uber das Kohlensuboxyd I," with B. Wolf, *Berichte der Deutschen Chemischen Gesellschaft* 39 (1906): 689. *Einfuhrung in die Organische Chemie* (Leipzig, Germany: Weinheim, 1907). "Synthesen in der Hydroaromatischen Reihe. I. Mitteilung, Anlagerungen von'si-en-'kohlenwasserstoffen," with K. Alder, *Annalen die Chemie* 460 (1927): 98–122.

Bibliography: *Dictionary of Scientific Biography* (New York: Scribner's, 1971), vol. 4, pp. 90–92. S. Olsen, "Otto Diels," *Chemische Berichte* 95 (1962): 5–46.

McMILLAN, EDWIN MATTISON

Prize: Chemistry, 1951. *Born:* September 12, 1907; Redondo Beach, California. *Died:* September 7, 1991; El Cerrito, California. *Nationality:* American. *Education:* California Institute of Technology, B.S., 1928; California Institute of Technology, M.S., 1929; Princeton University, New Jersey, Ph.D., 1932. *Career:* University of California, Berkeley, Professor, 1932–73. *Other Awards:* Research Corporation Scientific Award, 1951; Atoms for Peace Award, 1963; Alumni Distinguished Service Award, California Institute of Technology, 1966; Centennial Citation, University of California, Berkeley, 1968.

Citation: "For their discoveries in the chemistry of the transuranium elements" (with Glenn T. Seaborg).

Life Work: McMillan used the cyclotron to conduct studies on the effects of neutrons on uranium. In 1940 he found that some of the uranium nuclei bombarded with neutrons did not undergo fission, but instead decayed, forming a new element with 93 protons and electrons. This element, named neptunium, was the first transuranium element to be synthesized. In 1945 McMillan proposed a solution to the theoretical limits of the cyclotron by devising the synchrocyclotron (also independently suggested by the Russian scientist Vladimir Veksler) in which the fixed frequency of the cyclotron was abandoned. The variable frequency of the synchrocyclotron could be adjusted to correspond to the relativistic mass gain of the accelerating particles. In this way accelerators could be built that were forty times more powerful than the cyclotron. McMillan was involved also in the wartime work on radar, sonar, and the atomic bomb, and devised the theory of phase stability used in the construction of high-energy atom-smashing equipment.

Publications: "The Synchrotron—A Proposed High-Energy Particle Accelerator," *Physical Review* 68 (September 1945): 143–44. *Lecture Series in Nuclear Physics* (Washington, D.C.: United States Government Printing Office, 1947). "Production of Mesons by X rays," with J. Peterson and R. White, *Science* 110 (1949): 579–83.

Bibliography: *Current Biography Yearbook* (New York: H. W. Wilson, 1952), pp. 382–84. *National Cyclopedia of American Biography* (New York: J. T. White, 1952), vol. H, pp. 236–37. *New York Times* Biographical Service, September 9, 1991, p. 941.

SEABORG, GLENN THEODORE

Prize: Chemistry, 1951. *Born:* April 19, 1912; Ishpeming, Michigan. *Died:* February 25, 1999; Berkeley, California. *Nationality:* American. *Education:* University of California, Los Angeles, A.B., 1934; University of California, Ph.D., 1937. *Career:* University of California, Berkeley, Professor and Administrator, 1937–1999. *Other Awards:* Award in Pure Chemistry, 1947; Perkin Medal, 1957; Enrico Fermi Award,

United States Atomic Energy Commission, 1959; Priestley Memorial Award, 1960; Franklin Medal, 1963; Charles Lathrop Parsons Award, 1964; Chemistry Pioneer Award, 1968; Gold Medal Award, 1973; Arches of Science Award, 1968; John R. Kuebler Award, Alpha Chi Sigma, 1978; Priestley Medal, American Chemical Society, 1979; Henry DeWolf Smyth Award, American Nuclear Society, 1982; Actinide Award, 1984; Bush Award, 1988; National Medal of Science, 1991.

Citation: "For their discoveries in the chemistry of the transuranium elements" (with Edwin M. McMillan).

Life Work: Seaborg's field of investigation was the chemistry of elements. In 1941 Seaborg and a number of colleagues found that through beta decay neptunium formed an element with the atomic number 94. They named the new element plutonium. When bombarded with slow neutrons, the isotope plutonium 239 underwent fission with the release of neutrons. They also discovered the fissionable uranium 233 isotope which had the potential for serving as the explosive ingredient of a nuclear bomb. As a member of the Manhattan Project, Seaborg pioneered a novel ultramicrochemical analysis for handling small amounts of radioactive material. By 1944 Seaborg had achieved large-scale separation of plutonium from uranium. After the war, Seaborg resumed his work on the chemistry of transuranium elements and discovered elements 95 and 96 as well as additional members of a new actinide series: berkelium (97), californium (98), einsteinium (99), fermium (100), mendelevium (101) and nobelium (102).

Publications: *The Chemistry of the Actinide Elements*, with Joseph J. Katz (New York: Wiley, 1958). *The Transuranium Elements* (New Haven, Conn.: Yale University Press, 1958). *Education and the Atom*, with Daniel M. Wilkes (New York: McGraw-Hill, 1964). *Man and Atom*, with William R. Corliss (New York: E. P. Dutton, 1971). *Nuclear Milestones* (San Francisco, Calif.: W. H. Freeman, 1972). *Transuranium Elements: Products of Modern Alchemy*, with others (New York: Academic Press, 1978).

Bibliography: *Asimov's Biographical Encyclopedia of Science and Technology* (Garden City, N.Y.: Doubleday, 1982), pp. 842–43. *Biographical Encyclopedia of Scientists* (New York: Facts on File, 1981), pp. 721–22. *Current Biography Yearbook* (New York: H. W. Wilson, 1961), pp. 413–15.

MARTIN, ARCHER JOHN PORTER

Prize: Chemistry, 1952. *Born:* March 1, 1910; London, England. *Nationality:* British. *Education:* Cambridge University, England, B.A., 1932; Cambridge University, England, M.A., 1935; Cambridge University, England, Ph.D., 1936. *Career:* Cambridge University, England, Researcher, 1933–38; Wool Industries Research Association, Leeds, England, Researcher, 1938–46; Boots Pure Drug Company, Nottingham, England, Researcher, 1946–48; Medical Research Council, England, Researcher, 1948–52; National Institute for Medical Research, London, England, Researcher, 1952–56; Consultant, England, 1956–59; Abbotsbury Laboratories, England, Director,

1959–70; Wellcome Foundation, England, Consultant, 1970–73; University of Houston, Texas, Professor, 1974–79. *Other Awards:* Berzelius Gold Medal, Swedish Medical Society, 1951; John Scott Award, 1958; John Price Wetherill Medal, 1959; Franklin Institute Medal, 1959; Leverhulme Medal, 1963; Kolthoff Medal, 1969; Callendar Medal, 1971; Achievement Award, The Worshipful Company of Scientific Instrument Makers, 1972; Randolf Major Medal, 1979; Fritz Pregl Medal, 1985.

Citation: "For their invention of partition chromatography" (with R. L. M. Synge).

Life Work: Martin's field of investigation was chromotography for separating closely related chemical compounds. Initially, he collaborated with R. L. M. Synge on the separation of amino acids applying the principle of countercurrent distribution to a technique known as column chromotography which had been devised by the Russian scientist Michael Tsvet. This analytical technique was named partition chromatography because it depended on the chemical partition of the solute between the two solvents used in the column. Unlike column chromotography, partition chromotography allows a wide choice of solvents and packing materials. In 1938 Martin and Synge found that cellulose was a good water-holding medium. This discovery led them to the invention in 1944 of paper chromotography, in which paper is used as the supporting material. Two-dimensional paper chromotography gave even further separation and allowed the analysis of complex mixtures at low cost. Paper chromotography was rapidly adopted in all branches of chemistry and led to important discoveries about rare earths, polysaccharides, vaccines and antibiotics.

Publications: "A New Form of Chromatography Employing Two Liquid Phases," with R. Synge, *Biochemical Journal* 35 (1941): 1358–68. "Identification of Lower Peptides in Complex Mixtures," with R. Consden and A. Gordon, *Biochemical Journal* (February 1947): 595–96. "Separation of the C12-C13 Fatty Acids by Reversed-Phase Partition Chromatography," with G. Howard, *Biochemical Journal* (May 1950): 532–38.

Bibliography: W. A. Campbell and N. N. Greenwood, *Contemporary British Chemists* (London: Taylor and Francis, 1971). *Current Biography Yearbook* (New York: H. W. Wilson, 1953), pp. 417–19.

SYNGE, RICHARD LAURENCE MILLINGTON

Prize: Chemistry, 1952. *Born:* October 28, 1914; Liverpool, England. *Died:* August 18, 1994; Norwich, England. *Nationality:* British. *Education:* Cambridge University, England, baccalaureate, 1936; Cambridge University, England, Ph.D., 1941. *Career:* Wool Industries Research Association, Leeds, England, Researcher, 1941–43; Lister Institute of Preventive Medicine, London, England, Researcher, 1943–48; Rowett Research Institute, Aberdeen, Scotland, Researcher and Administrator, 1948–67; Food Research Institute, Researcher, Norwich, England, 1967–76; University of East Anglia, England, Professor, 1967–84. *Other Awards:* John Price Wetherill Medal, Franklin Institute, 1959.

Citation: "For their invention of partition chromatography" (with A. J. P. Martin).

Life Work: Synge worked with A. J. P. Martin on improvements to the technique of chromotography. Their work resulted in the invention of partition chromotography and, later, two-dimensional paper chromotography. In this method, a drop of the substance to be analyzed is placed near the end of a sheet of filter paper, which is then inserted into a closed vessel containing a saturated solution of water dissolved in the transport solvent. As the transport solvent migrates by capillary action along the paper, the components of the mixture are carried at different rates. With the aid of this technique Synge determined the amino acid composition of the antibiotic gramicidin S. Later in life, Synge investigated amino acid and peptide absorption on charcoal and the purification of intermediates in protein metabolism.

Publications: "A New Form of Chromatography Empolying Two Liquid Phases," with A. Martin, *Biochemical Journal* 35 (1941): 1358–68. *Science in Society* (London: Edward Arnold, 1969).

Bibliography: *A Biographical Encyclopedia of Scientists* (New York: Facts on File, 1981), p. 769. *Current Biography Yearbook* (New York: H. W. Wilson, 1953), pp. 611–12.

STAUDINGER, HERMANN

Prize: Chemistry, 1953. *Born:* March 23, 1881; Worms, Germany. *Died:* September 8, 1965; Freiburg-im-Breisgau, Germany. *Nationality:* German. *Education:* University of Halle, Germany, Ph.D., 1907. *Career:* Technische Hochschule, Karlsruhe, Germany, Professor, 1907–12; Federal Technical Institute, Zürich, Switzerland, Professor, 1912–26; University of Freiburg, Germany, Professor and Administrator, 1926–56. *Other Awards:* Emil Fisher Medal, 1930; Le Blanc Medal, 1931; Cannizzaro Prize, Reale Academia Nazionale dei Lincei, Rome, Italy, 1933.

Citation: "For his discoveries in the field of macromolecular chemistry."

Life Work: During World War I, Staudinger invented synthetic substitutes for pepper, atropine, and coffee. After the war, he turned to the study of natural rubber. He countered the prevailing view, known as the micellar theory, that natural rubber was not a single molecule, but a loose aggregate of rings, each consisting of two or more isoprene units. Staudinger argued that the natural rubber molecule was a true stable molecule (which he named macromolecule) composed of a chain of isoprene units held together by primary bonds and containing thousands of atoms. Staudinger later developed his idea into macromoleular theory of polymers, long chain-shaped molecules composed of scores of small units. He showed that the viscosity of a polymer is directly proportional to its molecular weight.

Publications: *Die Keene* [*Ketenes*] (Stuttgart, Germany: Enke, 1912). *Anleitung zur Organischen Qualitativen Analyse* [*Introduction to Organic Qualitative Analysis*].

(Berlin: Springer, 1923). *Die Hochmolekularen Organischen Verbindungen, Kautschuk und Cellulose* [*The High-Molecular Organic Compounds, Rubber and Cellulose*] (Berlin: Springer, 1932). *Organische Kolloid Chemie* [*Organic Colloid Chemistry*] (Braunschweig, Germany: Vieweg, 1940). *Makromolekulare Chemie und Biologie* [*Macromolecular Chemistry and Biology*] (Basel. Switzerland: Wepf and Co., 1947).

Bibliography: *Arbeitserrinnerungen* [*Working Memoirs*] (Heidelberg, Germany: A. Huthig, 1961). *Dictionary of Scientific Biography* (New York: Scribner's, 1976), vol. 13, pp. 1–4.

PAULING, LINUS CARL

Prize: Chemistry, 1954. *Born:* February 28, 1901; Portland, Oregon. *Died:* August 9, 1994; Big Sur, California. *Nationality:* American. *Education:* Oregon State College, B.Sc., 1922; California Institute of Technology, Ph.D., 1925. *Career:* Oregon State College, Corvallis, Teacher, 1919–20; California Institute of Technology, Professor, 1925–64; Center for Study of Democratic Institutions, Professor, 1964–67; University of California, San Diego, Professor, 1967–69; Stanford University, California, Professor, 1969–74. *Other Awards:* Langmuir Prize, American Chemical Society, 1931; Nichols Medal, 1941; Davy Medal, Royal Society, 1947; Medal for Merit, 1948; Pasteur Medal, Biochemical Society of France, 1952; Addis Medal, National Nephrosis Federation, 1955; Phillips Memorial Award, American College of Physicians, 1956; Avogadro Medal, Italian Academy of Science 1956; Fermat Medal, 1957; Sabatier Medal, 1957; International Grotius Medal, 1957; Order of Merit, Republic of Italy, 1965; Medal, Academy of Rumanian People's Republic, 1965; Linus Pauling Medal, 1966; Silver Medal, Institute of France, 1966; Supreme Peace Sponsor, World Fellowship of Religion, 1966; Martin Luther King Jr. Medal, 1972; National Medal of Science, 1974; Priestley Medal, 1984; American Chemical Society Award in Chemical Education, 1787; Bush Award, 1989; Tolman Medal, 1991.

Citation: "For his research into the nature of the chemical bond and its application to the elucidation of the structure of complex substances."

Life Work: Pauling's field of investigation was the nature of chemical bonding. In 1928 he published his resonance, or hybridization, theory, which was based on the quantum mechanical concept of electron orbitals. It stated that the bonds between the six carbon atoms in benzene were hybrids, intermediate in character between single and double bonds. In 1934 he turned his attention to the biochemistry of proteins and formulated a theory of protein structure and function. In 1942 Pauling and his colleagues succeeded in altering the chemical structure of certain blood proteins known as globulins, and produced the first synthetic antibodies. Pauling established that the three-dimensional structures of an antigen and its antibody are complementary, thus accounting for the formation of antigen-antibody complexes. Working on sickle-cell anemia in 1949, Pauling found that the sickling of a red cell was caused by a genetic defect in the globin, or protein, portion of the cell's hemoglobin. In 1951 he and R. B. Corey published the first complete description of the molecular structure of proteins, a major advance in biochemistry. Later in life Pauling formulated a theory of orthomolecular medicine that stressed the importance of vitamins and amino acids. Linus Pauling was the first person to receive two unshared Nobel Prizes in two different fields.

Publications: *Introduction to Quantum Mechanics*, with E. B. Wilson Jr. (New York: McGraw-Hill, 1935). *The Nature of the Chemical Bond* (Ithaca, N.Y.: Cornell University Press, 1939). *No More War!* (New York: Dodd, Mead, 1958). *The Architecture of Molecules*, with R. Hayward (San Francisco, Calif.: W. H. Freeman, 1964). *Vitamin C and the Common Cold* (San Francisco, Calif.: W. H. Freeman, 1970).

Bibliography: *Current Biography Yearbook* (New York: H. W. Wilson, 1964), pp. 339–42. *The Excitement and Fascination of Science* (Palo Alto, Calif.: Annual Reviews, 1965, 1990), vol. 1, pp. 347–60; vol. 3, part 1, pp. 541–49. *The Roots of Molecular Medicine: A Tribute to Linus Pauling* (New York: W. H. Freeman, 1986). A. Serafini, *Linus Pauling* (New York: Paragon House, 1991). F. M. White, *Linus Pauling: Scientist and Crusader* (New York: Walker and Co., 1980).

DU VIGNEAUD, VINCENT

Prize: Chemistry, 1955. *Born:* May 18, 1901; Chicago, Illinois. *Died:* December 11, 1978; White Plains, New York. *Nationality:* American. *Education:* University of Illinois, B.Sc., 1923; University of Illinois, M.Sc., 1924; University of Rochester, New York, Ph.D., 1927. *Career:* DuPont Laboratory, Delaware, Researcher, 1924; Philadelphia General Hospital, Pennsylvania, Researcher, 1924–25; University of Rochester, New York, Researcher, 1925–27; Johns Hopkins University, Maryland, Researcher, 1927–28; University of Illinois, Professor, 1929–32; George Washington University, Washington, D.C., Professor, 1932–38; Cornell University, New York, Professor, 1938–75. *Other Awards:* Hildebrand Award, Washington Chemical Society, 1936; Mead-Johnson Vitamin B Complex Award, American Institute of Nutrition, 1942; Nichols Medal, New York Section, American Chemical Society, 1945; Borden Award, American Association of American Medical Colleges; Lasker Award, American Public Health Association, 1948; Award of Merit for War Research, 1948; Osborne and Mendel Award, 1953; John Scott Medal and Award, American Pharmaceutical Manufactuerers' Association, 1954; Passano Foundation Award, 1955; Willard Gibbs Medal, American Chemical Society, 1956.

Citation: "For his work on biochemically important sulphur compounds, especially for the first synthesis of a polypeptide hormone."

Life Work: Du Vigneaud's field of investigation was insulin. He synthesized peptides containing cystine and tested them in bioassay systems for insulin activity. In 1936 he synthesized glutathione, a tripeptide containing the amino acids cystine, glycine, and glutamic acid. In 1937 he presented conclusive evidence that cystine accounts for the entire sulfur content of insulin. Working at Cornell, du Vigneaud isolated, purified, and synthesized the hormones oxytocin (which stimulates the contraction of the uterus at the time of birth and causes ejection of milk from the female mammary glands) and vasopressin (which stimulated the constriction of peripheral blood vessels and promotes reabsorption of water by the kidney). He also isolated biotin, a coenzyme involved in cellular respiration and synthesized penicillin. Du Vigneaud prepared the first crystalline oxytocin, the first in vitro synthesis of a polypeptide hormone.

Publications: *A Trail of Research in Sulphur Chemistry and the Metabolism and Related Fields* (Ithaca, N.Y.: Cornell University Press, 1952). "Tritiation of Oxytocin by the Wilzbach Method and the Synthesis of Oxytocin from Tritium-Labeled Leucine," with others, *Journal of the American Chemical Society* 84 (1962): 409–13. "The Hormones of the Posterior Pituitary Gland with Special Reference to Their Milk-Ejecting Ability," *Bulletin of the New York Academy of Medicine* 41 (1965): 802–803.

Bibliography: *Biographical Encyclopedia of Scientists* (New York: Facts on File, 1981), p. 222. *Current Biography Yearbook* (New York: H. W. Wilson, 1956), pp. 160–62. *New York Times* Biographical Service, August 27, 1994, p. 1252.

HINSHELWOOD, SIR CYRIL NORMAN

Prize: Chemistry, 1956. *Born:* June 19, 1897; London, England. *Died:* October 9, 1967; London, England. *Nationality:* British. *Education:* Oxford University, England, B.A., 1920; Oxford University, England, M.A., 1924. *Career:* Oxford University, England, Professor, 1921–64. *Other Awards:* Lavoisier Medal, Société Chimique de France, 1935; Davy Medal, Royal Society, 1943; Royal Medal, Royal Society, 1947; Longstaff Medal, Chemical Society, 1948; Knighthood, 1948; Guldberg Medal, University of Oslo, 1952; Faraday Medal, Chemical Society, 1953; Order of the Republic, Italy, 1956.

Citation: "For their researches into the mechanism of chemical reactions" (with Nikolay N. Semenov).

Life Work: Hinshelwood's field of investigation was the chemistry of explosives. Following work on the explosive decomposition of solids, he examined gas-phase decomposition reactions. He conceived the idea of a quasi-unimolecular reaction which enabled him to predict the relationship between collisional activation and deactivation. In 1927 Hinshelwood began a detailed study of the reaction between hydrogen and oxygen gases using the concept of chain or branched chain reactions that Nikolay Semenov had applied to the oxidation of phosphorus. He explained explosive reactions in terms of a branching chain-reaction mechanism in which the reaction proceeds very slowly over a certain pressure range and quicly becomes explosive beyond this range. In the early 1930s Hinshelwood became interested in the kinetics of reactions in solutions. In 1937 he initiated studies on the reactions of bacterial cells, which remained his main focus for the rest of his life. He developed a general theory for enzyme reactions in bacteria and investigated their behavior when exposed to new sources of nutrients or inhibiting agents.

Publications: *Kinetics of Chemical Change in Gaseous Systems* (Oxford: Clarendon Press, 1926). *Thermodynamics for Students of Chemistry* (London: Methuen, 1926). *The Reaction Between Hydrogen and Oxygen*, with A. T. Williamson (Oxford: Clarendon Press, 1934). *The Chemical Kinetics of the Bacterial Cell* (London: Clarendon Press, 1947). *The Structure of Physical Chemistry* (Oxford: Clarendon Press, 1951). *Growth, Function and Regulation in Bacterial Cells*, with A. C. R. Dean (Oxford: Clarendon Press, 1966).

Bibliography: *Current Biography Yearbook* (New York: H. W. Wilson, 1957), pp. 259–60. *Dictionary of Scientific Biography* (New York: Scribner's, 1972), vol. 6, pp. 404–405.

SEMENOV, NIKOLAY NIKOLAEVICH

Prize: Chemistry, 1956. *Born:* April 16, 1896; Saratov, Russia. *Died:* September 25, 1986; Moscow, USSR. *Nationality:* Russian. *Education:* Leningrad State University, USSR, graduate, 1917. *Career:* Leningrad Poly-Technical Institute, USSR, Professor, 1920–31; Institute of Chemical Physics of the Academy of Sciences, USSR, Director, 1932–86. *Other Awards:* Stalin Prize; Order of the Red Banner of Labor; Order of Lenin (seven times); Lomonosov Gold Medal, USSR.

Citation: "For their researches into the mechanism of chemical reactions" (with Cyril N. Hinshelwood).

Life Work: Semenov's field of investigation was the ionization of gases, especially metal and salt vapors. Another of his interests was the study of electric fields and electric phenomena in gases and solids. He investigated the passage of electric current through gases as well as the breakdown of electrically inert solids induced by electric currents. This, in turn, stimulated Semenov to make his first important contribution to the science of combustion, a thermal theory of gaseous explosions. According to this theory, under certain conditions, the heat generated in a chemical reaction will not have time to dissipate before it raises the temperature of the reactants, causing the reaction to speed up and produce more heat, resulting in an explosion. This led Semenov to investigate chain reactions, which are a series of self-propagating steps in a chemical reactions that, once started, continue in domino fashion. In 1934 Semenov showed that many chemical reactions, including polymerization, proceed by means of a branched-chain mechanism. This chain-reaction model has immense practical importance and led directly to improvements in the efficiency of internal combustion engines. Semenov was the first Soviet citizen living in his homeland to win the Nobel Prize.

Publications: *Chain Reactions*, trans. Prof. Frenkel and Judviga Smidt-Chernysheff (Oxford: Clarendon Press, 1935). *Chemical Kinetics and Chain Reactions*, trans. Prof.

Frenkel and Judviga Smidt-Chernysheff (Oxford: Clarendon Press, 1935). *Some Problems of Chemical Kinetics and Reactivity*, trans. Michel Boudart (Princeton, N.J.: Princeton University Press, 1958–59).

Bibliography: *Biographical Memoirs of the Fellows of the Royal Society* (London: Royal Society, 1990), vol. 36, p. 527. *Current Biography Yearbook* (New York: H. W. Wilson, 1957), pp. 498–500. *New York Times*, November 2, 1956, p. 1.

TODD, LORD ALEXANDER ROBERTUS

Prize: Chemistry, 1957. *Born:* October 2, 1907; Glasgow, Scotland. *Died:* January 10, 1997; Cambridge, England. *Nationality:* British. *Education:* Glasgow University, Scotland, baccalaureate, 1928; University of Frankfurt, Germany, Ph.D., 1931; Oxford University, England, Ph.D., 1933. *Career:* Edinburgh University, Scotland, Researcher, 1934–36; Lister Institute for Preventive Medicine, England, Researcher, 1936–38; Manchester University, England, Professor, 1938–44; Cambridge University, England, Professor, 1944–78. *Other Awards:* Lavoisier Medal, French Chemical Society, 1948; Davy Medal, Royal Society, 1949; Knighthood, 1954; Royal Medal, 1955; Cannizzaro Medal, Italian Chemical Society, 1958; Longstaff Medal, Chemical Society of London, 1963; Copley Medal, Royal Society, 1970; Ordre Pour Le Merite, Federal Republic of Germany, 1973; Second Class Order of Rising Sun, Japan, 1978; Lomonosov Gold Medal, USSR, 1979; Hanbury Medal, 1986.

Citation: "For his work on nucleotides and nucleotide co-enzymes."

Life Work: Todd's field of investigation was studies on vitamins E (tocopherol), B12, and B1 (thiamine). He succeeded in synthesizing thiamine in crystalline form. He also studied the active principle from cannabis, extracting the compound cannabinol from cannabis resin. In 1942 he began to study nucleic acids and nucleotide coenzymes. He also synthesized two important nucleotides, flavin adenine dinucleotide (FAD), and the energy-rich compounds adenosine triphosphate (ATP) and adenosine diphosphate (ADP). He synthesized all the pruine and pyimidine bases of nucleic acids (DNA and RNA) and established their structures.

Publications: "Chemical Structure and Properties of Tocopherol (Vitamin E). I. Chemistry," *Soc. Chem. Ind., Food Group* (April 1939): 3–8. "Vitamins of the B Group," *Journal of the chemical Society* (1941): 427–32. "Synthesis in the Study of Nucleotides," *Journal of the Chemical Society* (1946): 647–53. "Synthesis of Nucleotides," *Bull. Soc. Chem. France* (1948): 933–38. "A Hundred Years of Organic Chemistry," *Advancement of Science* 8 (1952): 393–96. *Perspectives in Organic Chemistry* (New York: Interscience, 1956).

Bibliography: *Current Biography Yearbook* (New York: H. W. Wilson, 1958), pp. 437–39. *A Time to Remember: The Autobiography of a Chemist* (Cambridge, England: Cambridge University Press, 1983).

SANGER, FREDERICK

Prize: Chemistry, 1958; Chemistry, 1980. *Born:* August 13, 1918; Rendcomb, England. *Nationality:* British. *Education:* Cambridge University, England, B.A., 1940; Cambridge University, England, Ph.D., 1943. *Career:* Cambridge University, England, Professor, 1944–. *Other Awards:* Corday-Morgan Medal and Prize, Chemical Society, 1951; Gairdner Foundation Annual Award, 1971, 1979; William Bate Hardy Prize, Cambridge Philosophical Society, 1976; Copley Medal, Royal Society, 1977; Wheland Award, 1978; Horwitz Prize, 1979; Lasker Award, 1979.

Citation: 1958: "For his work on the structure of proteins, especially that of insulin." 1980: "For their contributions concerning the determination of base sequences in nucleic acids" (with Walter Gilbert).

Life Work: Sanger established the complete amino acid sequence of the protein bovine insulin. This was one of the first protein structures thus identified. Sanger's work was a breakthrough in the field of molecular biology by proving conclusively that proteins consist of amino acids joined into chains by peptide bonds. He established that a protein is a specific chemical substance and that each position in the chain is occupied by a given amino acid. In the late 1950s the direction of Sanger's research turned toward sequencing DNA, the chemical molecule that specifies the amino acid sequence of proteins and ribonucleic acid. By 1977 Sanger had obtained the complete sequence of the bacterial virus Phi X174 which is composed of more than fifty-four hundred DNA bases.

Publications: "The Free Amino Groups of Insulin," *Biochemical Journal* 39 (1945): 507–15. "The Amino-Acid Sequence in the Glycyl Chain of Insulin. The Identification of Lower Peptides from Partial Hydrolysates," with E. O. P. Thompson, *Biochemical Journal* 53 (1953): 353–66. "DNA Sequencing with Chain-Terminating Inhibitors," with A. R. Coulson and S. Nicklen, *Proceedings of the National Academy of Sciences, USA* 74 (1977): 5463–67. "Nucleotide Sequence of Bacteriophage Phi X174 DNA," with others, *Nature (London)* 265 (1977): 687–95.

Bibliography: *Current Biography Yearbook* (New York: H. W. Wilson, 1981), pp. 354–56. A. Silverstein, *Frederick Sanger* (New York: Day, 1969).

HEYROVSKY, JAROSLAV

Prize: Chemistry, 1959. *Born:* December 20, 1890; Prague, Czechoslovakia. *Died:* March 27, 1967; Prague, Czechoslovakia. *Nationality:* Czechoslovakian. *Education:* University of London, England, B.Sc., 1913; Charles University, Czechoslovakia, Ph.D., 1918; Charles University, Czechoslovakia, D.Sc., 1921. *Career:* University of London, England, Professor, 1913–14; Charles University, Prague, Czechoslovakia, Professor and Administrator, 1919–54; Institute of Physical Chemistry, Prague,

Czechoslovakia, Director, 1926–54; Central Polarographic Institute, Prague, Czechoslovakia, Director, 1950–63. *Other Awards:* First State Prize, Czechoslovakia, 1951; Order of the Czechoslovak Republic, 1955.

Citation: "For his discovery and development of the polarographic methods of analysis."

Life Work: Heyrovsky's field of investigation was the analysis of chemical solutions. His main legacy is the polarograph, one of the most versatile of all analytical techniques. It works on the principle that in electrolysis the ions are discharged at an electrode, and if the electrode is small, the current may be limited by the rate of movement of ions to the electrode surface. In polarography, the electrode is a small drop of mercury. The voltage is increased slowly and the current plotted against the voltage. The current increases in steps, each corresponding to a particular type of positive ion in the solution. The height of the steps indicates the concentration of the ion.

Publications: "Electrolysis with a Dropping Mercury Cathode, Park I. Deposition of Alkali and Alkaline Earth Metals," *Philosophical Magazine* 45 (1923): 303–14. "Researches with the Dropping Mercury Cathode, Part II. The Polarograph," with M. Shikata, *Recueil des Travaux Chimiques des Pays-Bas* 44 (1925): 496–98. *A Polarographic Study of the Electrokinetic Phenomena of Adsorption, Electroreduction and Overpotential Displayed at the Dropping mercury Cathode* (Paris: Hermann, 1934). *Polarographie: Theoretische Grundlagen, Praktische Ausfuhrung und Anwedungen der Elektrolyse mit der Tropfenden Quecksilberelektrode* (Vienna: Springer, 1941). *Bibliography of Publications Dealing with the Polarographic Method*, 5 vols. (Prague: Nakladatelstvi Ceskoslovenske akademie ved, 1960–1964).

Bibliography: *Current Biography Yearbook* (New York: H. W. Wilson, 1961), pp. 202–204. *Dictionary of Scientific Biography* (New York: Scribner's, 1975), vol. 6, pp. 370–76. J. Koryta, *Jaroslav Heyrovsky* (Prague: Melantrich, 1990).

LIBBY, WILLARD FRANK

Prize: Chemistry, 1960. *Born:* December 17, 1908; Grand Valley, Colorado. *Died:* September 8, 1980; Los Angeles, California. *Nationality:* American. *Education:* University of California, B.S., 1931; University of California, Ph.D., 1933. *Career:* University of California, Berkeley, Professor, 1933–45; University of Chicago, Illinois, Professor, 1945–54; United States Atomic Energy Commission, 1954–59; University of California, Los Angeles, Professor and Administrator, 1959–80. *Other Awards:* Research Corporation Award, 1951; Chandler Medal, Columbia University, 1954; Remsen Memorial Lecture Award, 1955; Bicentennial Lecture Award, City College of New York, 1956; Nuclear Applications in Chemistry Award, 1956; Cresson Medal, Franklin Institute, 1957; Willard Gibbs Medal, 1958; Priestley Memorial Ward, Dickinson College, 1959; Albert Einstein Medal Award, 1959; Day Medal, Geological Society of America, 1961; Gold Medal, American Institute of Chemists, 1970; Lehman Award, New York Academy of Science, 1971.

Citation: Libby: "For his method to use carbon-14 for age determination in archaeology, geology, geophysics, and other branches of science."

Life Work: Libby's field of investigation was dating techniques. Libby found that when cosmic rays strike atoms in the upper atmosphere they create showers of neutrons and convert atmospheric nitrogen into radioactive carbon which is rapidly oxidized to carbon and is absorbed by plants through photosynthesis. Any organism eating these plants would also incorporate the radioactive carbon atoms. The radioactive carbon is generated at a constant rate and once included remains forever in the molecule. All living things have a constant level of radioactivity that decreases after death. Since the half-life of carbon-14 is 5,730 years, it is possible to determine the time elapsed since death. To test his radiocarbon dating hypothesis Libby built a geiger counter. Cosmic ray interactions in the upper atmosphere also produce small amounts of tritium, a radioactive isotope of hydrogen, with one proton and two neutrons and a half-life of twelve years. Using tritium concentrations as a tracer, Libby analyzed the earth's hydrologic systems.

Publications: "Stability of Uranium and Thorium for Natural Fission," *Physical Review* 55 (1939): 1269. *Radiocarbon Dating* (Chicago: University of Chicago Press, 1952). "Chemistry and the Peaceful Uses of the Atom," *Chemical and Engineering News* 35 (1957): 14–17.

Bibliography: *Current Biography Yearbook* (New York: H. W. Wilson, 1954), pp. 406–407. *The Excitement and Fascination of Science* (Palo Alto, Calif.: Annual Reviews, 1965), vol. 1, pp. 241–46. *New York Times*, September 10, 1980, p. D23.

CALVIN, MELVIN

Prize: Chemistry, 1961. *Born:* April 8, 1911; St. Paul, Minnesota. *Date:* January 8, 1997; Berkeley, California. *Nationality:* American. *Education:* Michigan College of Mining and Technology, B.S., 1931; University of Minnesota, Ph.D., 1935. *Career:* University of Manchester, England, Researcher, 1935–37; University of California, Berkeley, Professor, 1937–80. *Other Awards:* Davy Medal, Royal Society, 1964; Priestley Medal, American Chemical Society, 1978; Gold Medal, American Institute of Chemists, 1979; Lynen Medal, 1983; Hendricks Medal, 1983; Calvin Medal, 1985; National Medal of Science, 1989; Ericsson Award, 1991.

Citation: "For his research on the carbon dioxide assimilation in plants."

Life Work: Calvin's field of investigation was photosynthesis. Using carbon-14 radiocarbon-dating and paper chromotography he determined that carbon dioxide first reacts with ribulose diphosphate, a five-carbon compound to form phosphoglyceric acid which, in a series of reactions, becomes fructose-6-phosphate and glucose-6-phosphate. The steps in the conversion of carbon dioxide to carbohydrates is called the Calvin Cycle, and it takes place in chloroplasts, highly organized subcellular bodies in plants and algal cells. It contains the dark reactions of photosynthesis driven by the high-energy compounds ATP (adenosine triphosphate) and NADPH (reduced nicoti-namide adenine dinucleotide phosphate) generated in "light" reactions, in which light is absorbed by chlorophyll molecules. Using radioactive isotopes, Calvin also traced the path of oxygen in photosynthesis

Publications: "The Path of Carbon in Photosynthesis," *Science* 107 (1948): 476. *The Path of Carbon in Photosynthesis*, with J. A. Bassham (Englewood Cliffs, N.J.: Prentice-Hall, 1957)."Quantum Conversion in Photosynthesis," *Journal of Theoretical Biology* 1 (1961): 258. *Photosynthesis of Carbon Compounds* (New York: W. A. Benjamin, 1962).

Bibliography: *Asimov's Biographical Encyclopedia of Science and Technology* (Garden City, N.Y.: Doubleday, 1982), p. 837. *Current Biography Yearbook* (New York: H. W. Wilson, 1962), pp. 68–70. *Following the Trail of Light* (Washington, D.C.: American Chemical Society, 1992).

KENDREW, SIR JOHN COWDERY

Prize: Chemistry, 1962. *Born:* March 24, 1917; Oxford, England. *Died:* August 23, 1997; Cambridge, England. *Nationality:* British. *Education:* Cambridge University, England, B.A., 1939; Cambridge University, England, M.A., 1943; Cambridge University, England, Ph.D., 1949; Cambridge University, England, D.Sc., 1962. *Career:* British Military Service, 1939–46; Cambridge University, England, Researcher and Professor, 1947–74; European Molecular Biology Laboratory, Heidelberg, Germany, Director, 1975–82. *Other Awards:* Royal Medal, Royal Society, 1965; Knighthood, 1974; Order of the Madara Horsemen, Bulgaria, 1980.

Citation: "For their studies of the structures of globular proteins" (with Max Perutz).

Life Work: Kendrew's field of investigation was crystalline structure of proteins, especially the muscle protein myoglobin, using the technique of X-ray crystallography. His work received an impetus in 1953 when his colleague Max Perutz discovered that the introduction of mercury atoms into the hemoglobin crystals altered the diffraction patterns produced by X rays. Kendrew modified this new method and four years later built up a rough model of the three-dimensional structure of myoglobin. By 1959 he had greatly clarified the structure by being able to distinguish objects with a width of only two angstroms (two ten-billionths of a meter) and could pinpoint most of the atoms.

Publications: "The Crystal Structure of Horse Myoglobin," *Haemoglobin (Symposium on Conference at Cambridge in Memory of Joseph Barcoft)* (June 1948): 131–49. "The Crystal Structure of Horse Metmyoglobin I. General Features: The Arrangement of the Polypeptide Chains," *Proceedings of the Royal Society (London)* A201 (1950): 62–89. "A Three-Dimensional Model of the Myoglobin Molecule Obtained by X-ray Analysis," with others, *Nature* 181 (1958): 666. "The Molecular Structures of Myoglobin and Hemoglobin," *New Perspectives in Biology, Proceedings of the Symposium, Rehovoth, Israel* (1963): 18–27.

Bibliography: *Biographical Encyclopedia of Scientists* (New York: Facts on File, 1981), p. 434. *Current Biography Yearbook* (New York: H. W. Wilson, 1963), pp. 215–17. *Thinkers of the Twentieth Century* (Detroit, Mich.: Gale Research Company, 1983), pp. 292–93.

PERUTZ, MAX FERDINAND

Prize: Chemistry, 1962. *Born:* May 19, 1914; Vienna, Austria. *Nationality:* Austrian; later British citizen. *Education:* Cambridge University, England, Ph.D., 1940. *Career:* Cambridge University, England, Researcher and Professor, 1939–79. *Other Awards:* Royal Medal, Royal Society, 1971; Copley Medal, Royal Society, 1979.

Citation: "For their studies of the structures of globular proteins" (with John C. Kendrew).

Life Work: Perutz's field of investigation the three-dimensional structure of hemoglobin by applying the fundamental X-ray crystallographic technique known as isomorphous heavy-ion replacement. In this method heavy metal atoms, such as mercury or gold, are incorporated into the molecule under study. This alters the diffraction patterns, making it easier to compute the positions of atoms in the molecule. By 1959 he had shown hemoglobin to be composed of four chains, together making a tetrahedral structure, with four home groups near the molecule's surface. Further refining his model of the hemoglobin molecule Perutz showed how its structure transported in the blood.

Publications: *Proteins and Nucleic Acids: Structure and Function* (New York: Elsevier, 1962). *Haemoglobin and Myoglobin*, with G. Fermi, Atlas of Molecular Structures in Biology Series, no. 2 (New York: Oxford University Press, 1981).

Bibliography: *Biographical Encyclopedia of Scientists* (New York: Facts on File, 1981). *Current Biography Yearbook* (New York: H. W. Wilson, 1963), pp. 324–26. *Is Science Necessary?* (Oxford, England: Oxford University Press, 1991).

NATTA, GIULIO

Prize: Chemistry, 1963. *Born:* February 26, 1903; Imperia, Italy. *Died:* May 1, 1979; Bergamo, Italy. *Nationality:* Italian. *Education:* Polytechnic Institute, Italy, Ph.D., 1924. *Career:* Polytechnic Institute, Milan, Italy, Professor, 1924–33; University of Pavia, Italy, Professor and Administrator, 1933–35; University of Rome, Italy, Professor and Administrator, 1935–37; Polytechnic Institute, Turin, Italy, Professor and Administrator, 1937–74. *Other Awards:* Gold Medal, Milan, Italy, 1960; Gold Medal, President of Italy, 1961; Gold Medal, Synthetic Rubber Industry, 1961; Stas Medal, Belgian Chemical Society, 1962; Gold Medal, Society of Plastic Engineers, New York, 1963:

Perrin Medal, French Chemical Physical Society, 1963; Perkin Gold Medal, English Society of Dyers and Colourists, 1963; John Scott Award, Philadelphia, Pennsylvania, 1964; Lomonosov Gold Medal, Academy of Sciences, USSR, 1969.

Citation: "For their discoveries in the field of the chemistry and technology of high polymers" (with Karl Ziegler).

Life Work: Natta's field of investigation was catalytic syntheses of such important chemicals as methanol, butadiene, formaldehyde and butyraldehyde. Building on Karl Ziegler's work on polymer catalysis, Natta investigated the reaction mechanisms of polymerizations. Next Natta turned his attention to propylene, a by-product of petroleum refining, and discovered a method to polymerize it catalytically. Natta carried further X-ray and electron diffraction studies of the new polypropylene to determine its molecular structure. The result showed stereoregular polymers, macromolecules with extraordinarily regular atomic spatial relationships. They are distinguished by the remarkable fact that all the side chains of each monomer unit were arrayed on the same side of the molecule rather than being randomly oriented as in regular plastics. Called isotactic (same-side) polypropylene, the new material could be case or extruded into solid objects, spun into fibers, and spread into films, as clear as cellophane. His further research led to the discovery of polystyrene and polybutadiene.

Publications: "The Kinetics of the Stereospecific Polymerization of A-Olefins," with I. Pasquon, *Advances in Catalysis* 11 (1959): 1–66. "Organometallic Complexes As Catalysts in Ionic Polymerization," with G. Mazzanti, *Tetrahedron* 8 (1960): 86–100. "Precisely Constructed Polymers," *Scientific American* 205 (August 1961): 33–41. "Alternating Copolymer of Dimethylketene with Acetone," with G. F. Pregaglia and M. Binaghi, *Macromolecular Syntheses* 4 (1972): 73–75. *Polymerization Reactions*, with others (New York: Springer, 1975). *Structure and Behavior of 3-Dimensional Molecules. An Introduction to Stereochemistry*, with Mario Farino (Weinheim, Germany: Verlag Chemie, 1976).

Bibliography: *Current Biography Yearbook* (New York: H. W. Wilson, 1964), pp. 312–14. "Givlio Natta: Biography," *Rubber Chem. Technology* 57 (May/June 1984): 658–61.

ZIEGLER, KARL

Prize: Chemistry, 1963. *Born:* November 26, 1898; Helsa, Oberhausen, Germany. *Died:* August 11, 1973; Mulheim, Germany. *Nationality:* German. *Education:* University of Marburg, Germany, Ph.D., 1920. *Career:* Marburg University, Germany, Professor, 1923–27; Heidelberg University, Germany, Professor, 1927–36; University of Halle, Germany, Professor and Administrator, 1936–43; Kaiser Wilhelm Institute, Germany, Director, 1943–69. *Other Awards:* Leibig Medal, 1935; Lavosier Medal, 1955; Swinburne Medal, 1964.

Citation: "For their discoveries in the field of the chemistry and technology of high polymers" (with Giulio Natta).

Life Work: Ziegler's field of investigation was polymerization, free radicals, large-ring compounds, and the synthesis of organometallic compounds. His research team found that certain organometallic substances, such as aluminum triethyl, catalyzed the self-condensation of ethylene to form not polyethylene but, rather, organometallic and unsaturated molecules of intermediate sizes. He found that a certain zirconium compound acted in conjunction with aluminum trimethyl to catalyze ethylene polymerization reaction. The production of polyethylene led to the polymerization of several other compounds. Working with the Italian scientist Giulio Natta, Ziegler developed the Ziegler-Natta catalysts to control the structure and orientation of the new polymers. They produce a much stronger plastic that can be soaked in hot water without softening.

Publications: "Catalysis of the Polymerization of Unsaturated Hydrocarbons by Alkali Organic Compounds," with L. Jakob, *Annalen* 511 (1934): 46–63. "The Importance of Alkali Metallo-organic Compounds for Synthesis," *Angewandte Chemie* 49 (1936): 455–60. "The Polymerization of Butadiene and the Production of Artificial Rubber," *Rubber Chem. Tech* 11 (1938): 601–607. "Organoalkali Compounds. XV. Controlled 1,2-and 1,4-Polymerization of Butadiene," with H. Grimm and R. Willer, *Annalen* 542 (1940): 90–122. *Praparative Organische Chemie* (Wiesbaden, Germany: Dieterichsche Verlags, 1948). "The Polymerization of Ethylene," *Bull. Soc. Chim. France* (1956): 1–6.

Bibliography: *Biographical Memoirs of the Fellows of the Royal Society* (London: Royal Society, 1975), vol. 21, p. 569. *Chemical and Engineering News* 41 (November 11, 1963): 22. "Karl Ziegler: Biography," *Rubber Chemistry and Technology* 57 (May/June 1984): G49–G57.

HODGKIN, DOROTHY CROWFOOT

Prize: Chemistry, 1964. *Born:* May 12, 1910; Cairo, Egypt. *Died:* July 29, 1994; Shipston-on-Stour, England. *Nationality:* British. *Education:* Oxford University, England, baccalaureate, 1932; Cambridge University, England, Ph.D., 1937. *Career:* Oxford University, England, Professor, 1934–77. *Other Awards:* Royal Medal, Royal Society, 1957; Copley Medal, Royal Society, 1976; Mikhail Lomonosov Gold Medal, 1982; Dimitrov Prize, 1984; Lenin Prize, 1987.

Citation: "For her determinations by X-ray techniques of the structures of important biochemical substances."

Life Work: Hodgkin's field of investigation was the crystallography of penicillin, vitamin B12, and other important biochemical substances. She found that penicillin contains an unusual component, known as a beta-lactam ring which is responsible for the drug's antibiotic activity. She was the first to use the computer successfully in such work to determine the structure of penicillin (1949) and later also studied the structure of insulin. Hodgkin was also an inveterate traveler, an avocation inherited from her archeologist father, and a worker for peace and communication between nations.

Publications: "X-rays Analysis and Protein Structure," *Cold Spring Harbor Symposia on Quantitative Biology* 14 (1949): 79–84. "X-ray Analysis of the Structure of Penicillin," *Advancement Sci* 6 (1949): 85–89. "X-ray Crystallogrphic Study of the Structure of Vitamin B–12," *Bull. Soc. Franc. Mineral et Cryst* 78 (1955): 106–15. *Wandering Scientists* (New Delhi: Indian Council for Cultural Relations, 1974). *Structural Studies on Molecules of Biological Interest* (New York: Oxford University Press, 1981).

Bibliography: *Asimov's Biographical Encyclopedia of Science and Technology* (Garden City, N.Y.: Doubleday, 1982), p. 834. *Biographical Encyclopedia of Scientists* (New York: Facts on File, 1981), pp. 386–87. *New York Times* Biographical Service, August 1, 1994, p. 1150.

WOODWARD, ROBERT BURNS

Prize: Chemistry, 1965. *Born:* April 10, 1917; Boston, Massachusetts. *Died:* July 8, 1979; Cambridge, Massachusetts. *Nationality:* American. *Education:* Massachusetts Institute of Technology, B.S., 1936; Massachusetts Institute of Technology, Ph.D., 1937; Wesleyan University, Connecticut, D.Sc., 1945. *Career:* Harvard University, Massachusetts, Professor, 1937–79. *Other Awards:* Ledlie Prize, Harvard University, 1955; Davy Medal, Royal Society, 1959; Pius XI Gold Medal, Pontifical Academy of Sciences, 1961; Priestley Medallion, Dickinson College, New Jersey, 1962; National Medal of Science, United States, 1964; Lavoisier Medal, Société Chimique de France, 1968; Decorated Order of the Rising Sun, Japan, 1970; Science Achievement Award, American Medical Association, 1971; Arthur C. Cope Award, American Chemical Society, 1973; Copley Medal, Royal Society, 1978.

Citation: "For his outstanding achievements in the art of organic synthesis."

Life Work: Woodward is considered to be the greatest synthetic organic chemist of modern times. His first achievement was the synthesis of quinine. Later he created a protein analogue by joining units of amino acids into a long chain. He followed it with the synthesis of a number of compounds, including strychnine, cortisone, chlorophyll, lanosterol, lysergic acid, reserpine, prostaglandin F2a, colchicine, and vitamin B12. As head of the Woodward Research Institute in Basel, Switzerland, a unit of Ciba-Geigy, he synthesized cephalosporin C, an antibiotic. Although Woodward is best known for his syntheses, he made broader contributions to organic chemistry by applying the techniques of physical chemistry to the field. He made use of the electronic theory of molecules and popularized the use of spectroscopy. The Woodward Rule relate ultraviolet spectra to the number and type of linkages between carbon atoms and side groups. In collaboration with Roald Hoffmann, he devised the principle of conservation of orbital symmetry when bonding of atoms occurs in chemical reactions.

Publications: "Total Synthesis of Quinine," with W. E. Doering, *Journal of the American Chemical Society* 66 (1944): 849. "Total Synthesis of a Steroid," with others, *Journal of the American Chemical Society* 73 (1951): 2403–2404. "The Total Synthesis of Cholesterol," with F. Sondheimer and D. Taub, *Journal of the American Chemical Society* 73 (1951): 3548. "The Total Synthesis of Cortisone," with F. Sondheimer and D. Taub, *Journal of the American Chemical Society* 73 (1951): 4057. "The Total Synthesis of Reserpine," with others, *Journal of the American Chemical Society* 78 (1956): 2023–25. "Total Synthesis of Vitamin B-12," *Pure and Applied Chemistry* 33 (1973): 145–77.

Bibliography: *Biographical Memoirs of the Fellows of the Royal Society* (London: Royal Society, 1981), pp. 629–95. M. Bowden, *Robert Burns Woodward and the Art of Organic Synthesis* (Philadelphia: Beckman Center, 1992). *Current Biography Yearbook* (New York: H. W. Wilson, 1952), pp. 647–49.

MULLIKEN, ROBERT SANDERSON

Prize: Chemistry, 1966. *Born:* June 7, 1896; Newburyport, Massachusetts. *Died:* October 31, 1986; Arlington, Virginia. *Nationality:* American. *Education:* Massachusetts Institute of Technology, B.S., 1917; University of Chicago, Illinois, Ph.D., 1921. *Career:* Bureau of Mines, United States, Engineer, 1917; United States Army, 1918–19; University of Chicago, Illinois, Professor, 1919–26; New York University, Professor, 1926–28; University of Chicago, Illinois, Professor, 1928–61. *Other Awards:* Lewis Gold Medal, American Chemical Society, 1960; Richards Gold Medal, 1960; Debye Award, 1963; Kirwood Medal, 1964; Willard Gibbs Gold Medal, 1965.

Citation: "For his fundamental work concerning chemical bonds and the electronic structure of molecules by the molecular orbital method."

Life Work: Mulliken's field of investigation was the interpretation of molecular spectra and with the application of quantum theory to the electronic states of molecules. With Frederick Hund, he developed the molecular-orbital theory of chemical bonding, which is based on the idea that electrons in a molecule move in the field produced by all the nuclei. The atomic orbitals of isolated atoms become molecular orbitals, extending over two mor more atoms in the molecule. He showed how the relative energies of these orbitals could be obtained from the spectra of the molecules. Another of Mulliken's contributions is the application of electronegativity, the ability of a particular atom in a molecule to draw electrons to itself. Using the computer, Mulliken delineated the behavior of charge-transfer complexes (relatively weak associations of different molecules that share electrons and interact strongly with light). He also made major contributions to the theory and interpretation of molecular spectra.

Publications: "The Assignment of Quantum Numbers for Electrons in Molecules," *Physics Review* 32 (1928): 186–22. "The Assignment of Quantum Numbers for Electrons in Molecules. II. Correlation of Molecular and Atomic Electron States," *Physics Review* 32 (1928): 761–72. "Electronic States of Diatomic Carbon, and the C-C

Bond," *Physics Review* 56 (1939): 778–81. "Quantum-Mechanical Methods and the Electronic Spectra and Structure of Molecules," *Chemical Reviews* 41 (1947): 201–206

Bibliography: *Biographical Encyclopedia of Scientists* (New York: Facts on File, 1981), pp. 752–52. *Biographical Memoirs of the Fellows of the Royal Society* (London: Royal Society, 1990), vol. 35, p. 327. *Current Biography Yearbook* (New York: H.W. Wilson, 1967), pp. 307–309.

EIGEN, MANFRED

Prize: Chemistry, 1967. *Born:* May 9, 1927; Bochum, Germany. *Nationality:* German. *Education:* University of Göttingen, Germany, Doctor Rerum Naturalium, 1951. *Career:* University of Göttingen, Germany, Researcher, 1951–53; Max Planck Institut, Germany, Professor and Administrator, 1953–. *Other Awards:* Otto Hahn Prize, German Chemical Society, 1962; Kirkwood Medal, 1963. Linus Pauling Medal, 1967; Faraday Medal, 1977.

Citation: "For their studies of extremely fast chemical reactions, effected by disturbing the equilibrium by means of very short pulses of energy" (with Ronald Norrish and George Porter).

Life Work: Eigen's first field of investigation was sonar waves and sound waves. In 1954 he introduced the so-called relaxation techniques for the study of extremely fast chemical reactions (those taking less than a millisecond). He created disturbance in a solution by means such as pulses of electric current, sudden changes in temperature or pressure, or changes in electric field and studied them through absorption spectroscopy. The first reaction he investigated was the formation of water molecule from the hydrogen ion H+ and the hydroxyl radical OH–. He later studied the dissociation and recombination of ions in pure water, diffusion-controlled proton transfer in liquids sound absorption by electrolyte solutions, and the kinetics of keto-enol tautomerism, in which compounds with different arrangements of atoms exist in equilibrium. Relaxation techniques are used to study enzyme-catalyzed reactions, the formation of polypeptides into helical coils, and the coding of biological information.

Publications: "Methods for Investigation of Ionic Reactions in Aqueous Solutions with Half Times as Short as 10^{-9} Sec.: Application to Neutralization and Hydrolysis Reactions," *Discussions of the Faraday Society* 17 (1954): 194–205. "Kinetics of Neutralization," with Leo De Maeyer, *Zeitschrift fur Elektrochemie* 59 (1955): 986–93. "Potential-Impulse Method for the Investigation of Very Rapid Ionic Reactions in Aqueous Solution," with J. Schoen, *Zeitschrift fur Elektrochemie* 59 (1955): 483–94. "A Temperature-Jump Method for the Examination of Chemical Relaxation," with G. Czerlinski, *Zeitschrift fur Elektrochemie* 63 (1959): 652–61. "Eine Kinetische Methode zur Untersuchung Schneller Prototroper Tautomerisierungsreaktionen," with G. Ilgenfritz and W. Kruse, *Chemische Berichte* 98 (May 1965): 1623–38.

Bibliography: *Contemporary Authors* (Detroit, Mich.: Gale Research Company, 1983), vol. 108, p. 140. *Science* 158 (November 10, 1967): 748–68.

NORRISH, RONALD GEORGE WREYFORD

Prize: Chemistry, 1967. *Born:* November 9, 1897; Cambridge, England. *Died:* June 7, 1978; Cambridge, England. *Nationality:* British. *Education:* Cambridge University, England, baccalaureate, 1921; Cambridge University, England, Ph.D., 1924. *Career:* British Army, 1916–19; Cambridge University, England, Profesor, 1925–65. *Other Awards:* Liversidge Medal, Chemical Society, 1958; Davy Medal, Royal Society, 1958; Bernard Lewis Gold Medal, Combustion Institute, 1964; Faraday Medal, Chemical Society, 1965; Longstaff Medal, Chemical Society, 1969.

Citation: "For their studies of extremely fast chemical reactions, effected by disturbing the equilibrium by means of very short pulses of energy" (with Manfred Eigen and George Porter).

Life Work: Norrish's field of investigation was photochemistry, especially the interaction of light with molecules and light emitted by chemical reactions. He established the role of formaldehyde as an intermediate compound that reacts with ultraviolet light to cause an explosion. He found that many photochemical processes involve chain reactions, including polymerization, in which many small molecules join together to form large molecules. After the war Norrish and George Porter investigated the chemistry of very fast chemical reactions to determine the presence of intermediate compounds. They devised a measurement technique called flash photolysis to detect fast transitional reactions that had been theoretically predicted but never observed.

Publications: Chemical Reactions Produced by Very High Light Intensities," with G. Porter, *Nature* 164 (1949): 658. "The Application of Flash Techniques to the Study of Fast Reactions," with G. Porter, *Discussions of the Faraday Society* 17 (1954): 40–46. "The Gas Phase Oxidation of n-Butenes," with K. Porter, *Proceedings of the Royal Society (London)* Series A272 (1963): 164–91. "The Kinetics and Anaylsis of Very Fast Reactions," *Chemistry in Britain* 1 (1965): 289–311.

Bibliography: *Biographical Memoirs of the Fellows of the Royal Society* (London: Royal Society, 1981), vol. 27, pp. 379–424. *The Excitement and Fascination of Science* (Palo Alto, Calif.: Annual Reviews, 1978), vol. 2, pp. 483–506. "Obiturary R. G. W. Norrish, 1897–1978." *Nature* 275 (September 7, 1978): 78–79.

PORTER, SIR GEORGE

Prize: Chemistry, 1967. *Born:* December 6, 1920; Stainforth, England. *Nationality:* British. *Education:* University of Leeds, England, B.Sc., 1941; Cambridge University, England, M.A., 1947; Cambridge University, England, Ph.D., 1949. *Career:* British Navy, 1941–45; Cambridge University, England, Professor, 1949–55; University of Sheffield, England, Professor, 1955–63; Royal Institution, England, Professor and Administrator, 1963–88. *Other Awards:* Corday-Morgan Medal, Chemical Society,

1955; Silvanus Thompson Medal, 1969; Davy Medal, Royal Society, 1971; Knighthood, 1972; Kalinga Prize, 1977; Robertson Prize, National Academy of Sciences, 1978; Rumford Medal, Royal Society, 1978; Communications Award, European Physical Society, 1978; Faraday Medal, Chemical Society, 1979; Longstaff Medal, 1981; Faraday Award, 1991.

Citation: "For their studies of extremely fast chemical reactions, effected by disturbing the equilibrium by means of very short pulses of energy" (with Manfred Eigen and Ronald Norrish).

Life Work: Porter and Ronald Norrish developed the technique of flash photolysis, in which a powerful flash of short-wavelength light breaks a photosensitive chemical into reactive intermediate components. A second, weaker light flash triggered at a known interval after the first flash illuminates the reaction zone, enabling a measurement of the resulting absorption spectra of the short-lived free radicals. By varying the time between the two flashes they were able to observe the course of chemical reactions that occur in a millionth of a second. By replacing the second flash with a continuous light source and using a very fast light detector they measured the concentration of the chemical continuously over time. Later, Porter used the same techniques to study more complex chemical reactions, such as the interaction of oxygen with hemoglobin.

Publications: "Chemical Reactions Produced by Very High Light Intensities," with R. Norrish, *Nature* 164 (1949): 658. "The Application of Flash Techniques to the Study of Fast Reactions," with R. Norrish, *Discussions of the Faraday Society* 17 (1954): 40–46. *Chemistry for the Modern World* (New York: Barnes and Nobel, 1962). *Progress in Reaction Kinetics* (New York: Pergamon Press, 1965).

Bibliography: *Biographical Encyclopedia of Scientists* (New York: Facts on File, 1981), pp. 647–48. *Science* 158 (November 10, 1967): 746–48.

ONSAGER, LARS

Prize: Chemistry, 1968. *Born:* November 27, 1903; Oslo, Norway. *Died:* October 5, 1976; Coral Gables, Florida. *Nationality:* Norwegian; later American citizen. *Education:* Norges Tekniske Hogskale, Norway, Chem. E., 1925; Yale University, Connecticut, Ph.D., 1935. *Career:* Brown University, Rhode Island, Professor, 1928–33; Yale University, Connecticut, Professor, 1933–72. *Other Awards:* Rumford Medal, American Academy of Sciences, 1953; Lorenz Medal, 1958; G. N. Lewis Medal, 1962; J. J. Kirkwood Medal, 1962; Willard Gibbs Medal, 1962; T. W. Richards Medal, 1964; Debye Award, 1965; Belfer Award, 1966.

Citation: "For the discovery of the reciprocal relations bearing his name, which are fundamental for the thermodynamics of irreversible processes."

Life Work: Onsager's field of investigation was the physics and chemistry of electrolytes. Using statistical mechanics based on the law of motion, he developed nonequilibrium thermodynamics to describe how simultaneous reactions influence each other in relationships, now called Onsager's reciprocal relations. Onsager also demonstrated that reciprocal relations were mathematically equivalent to a general principle of least dissipation, which states that the rate of increase of entropy in coupled irreversible processes is a minimum. Onsager made important contributions to statistical mechanics, the theory of phase transitions, turbulence, the quantum effects of superfluid helium, the behavior of liquid crystals, the properties of virus suspensions in water, and the behavior of polar liquids in applied electrical fields.

Publications: "Reciprocal Relations in Irreversible Processes," *Physical Review* 37 (1931): 405–26. "Reciprocal Relations in Irreversible Processes," *Physical Review* 38 (1931): 2265–79. "Initial Recombination of Ions," *Physical Review* 54 (1938): 554–57. "De Haas-van Alphen Effect in Zinc," with J. E. Robinson, *Physical Review* 74 (1948): 1235. "Fluctuations and Irreversible Processes," with S. Machlup, *Physical Review* 91 (1953): 1505–12.

Bibliography: *Biographical Memoirs of the Fellows of the Royal Society* (London: Royal Society, 1978), vol. 24, p. 445. *Current Biography Yearbook* (New York: H. W. Wilson, 1958), pp. 321–23.

BARTON, SIR DEREK HAROLD RICHARD

Prize: Chemistry, 1969. *Born:* September 8, 1918; Gravesend, Kent, England. *Died:* March 16, 1998; College Station, Texas. *Nationality:* British. *Education:* Imperial College, England, B.Sc., 1940; Imperial College, England, Ph.D., 1942; University of London, England, D.Sc., 1949. *Career:* British Government Service, Researcher, 1942–45; Imperial College, England, Professor, 1945–49; Harvard University, Massachusetts, Professor, 1949–50; University of London, England, Professor, 1950–55; University of Glasgow, Scotland, Professor, 1955–57; Imperial College, England, Professor, 1957–78; Institute of Chemistry and Natural Substances, France, Director, 1978–86; Texas A & M University, Professor, 1986–1998. *Other Awards:* Hoffman Prize, Imperial College, England, 1940; Harrison Memorial Prize, Chemical Society, 1948; Corday-Morgan Medal, Chemical Society, 1951; Fritzsche Award, American Chemical Society, 1959; Roger Adams Award, American Chemical Society, 1959; Davy Medal, Royal Society, 1961; Knighthood, 1972.

Citation: "For their contributions to the development of the concept of conformation and its application in chemistry" (with Odd Hassel).

Life Work: Barton's field of investigation was the structure of highly complex organic molecules. His method, known as conformational analysis, made it possible to understand and predict how steroids and carbohydrates behave under various conditions. He showed that the orientations in space of functional groups affects the rate of reaction in isomers. In demonstrating the distinctive stability of the chair conformation of cyclohexane, Barton drew a distinction between equatorial conformations, in which the hydrogen atoms lie in the same plane as the carbon ring, and the axial conformation where they are perpendicular to the ring. At Glasgow, Barton investigated many types of organic chemicals, including alkaloids. In 1960 he devised a method of producing chemical reactions by the use of light, known as the Barton Process.

Publications: "The Conformation of the Steroid Nucleus," *Experienta* 6 (1950): 316–20. "The Stereo-chemistry of Cyclohexane Derivatives," *Journal of the Chemical Society* (1953): 1027–40. "The Inaugural Simonsen Lecture. Some Aspects of Sesquiterpenoid Chemistry," *Proceedings of the Chemical Society* (1958): 61–66. "Recent Progress in Conformational Analysis," *Theoret Org. Chem., Papers Kekule Symposium, London* (1958): 127–43. "Recent Progress in Conformational Analysis," *Suomen Kemistilehte* 32A (1959): 27–33.

Bibliography: *The Biographical Dictionary of Scientists: Chemists* (New York: Bedrick, 1984), pp. 14–15. *Chemical and Engineering News* 47 (November 10, 1969): 11. *Science* 166 (November 7, 1969): 715–22. *Some Recollections of Gap Jumping* (Washington, D.C.: American Chemical Society, 1991).

HASSEL, ODD

Prize: Chemistry, 1969. *Born:* May 17, 1897; Oslo, Norway. *Died:* May 15, 1981; Oslo, Norway. *Nationality:* Norwegian. *Education:* University of Oslo, Norway, Candidate Real Degree, 1920; University of Berlin, Germany, D. Phil., 1924. *Career:* University of Oslo, Norway, Professor, 1925–64. *Other Awards:* Knight Order of St. Olav, 1971; Guineras Medal, 1964; Guldberg Waage Medal, 1964.

Citation: "For their contributions to the development of the concept of conformation and its application in chemistry" (with Derek Barton).

Life Work: Hassel's field of investigation was organic molecules, especially the structure of cyclohexane. This substance is composed of an unbroken chain, or ring, of six carbon atoms to which twelve atoms of hydrogen are attached. Through X-ray crystallography and electron diffraction, Hassel demonstrated that its structure resembled one of two forms: boat or chair and the molecules oscillated between the two forms a million times a second, but assumed the chair form most often. Hassel proposed that this was so because the chair form was more energy efficient. By showing that the form of a cyclohexane molecule affected the arrangement of its atoms, he made it possible to predict the chemical properties of the substance. After World War II, Hassel investigated the physical structure of charge-transfer compounds.

Publications: *Crystal Chemistry* (London: Heinemann, 1935). *U.S. Dept. Com., Office Tech. Serv.*, AD267293 (1961): 1–37. "Weak Intermolecular Bonds in Solids," *Dansk. Tidsskr. Farm* 36 (1962): 41–54. "Investigation of Molecular Structures," in *Selected Topics in Structure Chemistry* (Oslo: Universitétsforlaget, 1967).

Bibliography: *Chemical and Engineering News* 47 (November 10, 1969): 11. *Science* 166 (November 7, 1969): 715–22.

LELOIR, LUIS FEDERICO

Prize: Chemistry, 1970. *Born:* September 6, 1906; Paris, France. *Died:* December 2, 1987; Buenos Aires, Argentina. *Nationality:* Argentinian. *Education:* University of Buenos Aires, Argentina, M.D., 1932. *Career:* University of Buenos Aires, Argentina, Researcher, 1932–35; Cambridge University, England, Researcher, 1935–37; Institute of Physiology, Argentina, Researcher, 1937–44; United States, Exile, 1944–47; Biochemical Research Institute, Argentina, Researcher, 1947–87.

Citation: "For his discovery of sugar nucleotides and their role in the biosynthesis of carbohydrates."

Life Work: Leloir's field of investigation was lactose, or milk sugar. In a search for an enzyme to catalyze the reversible synthesis of lactose, Leloir identified two heat-stable cofactors, glucose-1, 6 disphosphate, and a nucleoside, uridine diphosphoglucose (UDPG). UDPG was found to serve as a glucose donor in the formation of disaccharides trehalose phosphate and sucrose phosphate. In 1959, after finding that glycogen (the storage form of glucose in animals) is formed from UDPG, Leloir analyzed the synthesis of starch in plants involving the sugar nucleotide, adenosine disphosphate (ADP) glucose. Leloir's discoveries—that the sugar nucleotides are principal actors in interconversion of sugars and polysaccharide formation—led to additional research in carbohydrate metabolism and on the medical implications of the discoveries.

Publications: "The Enzymic Transformation of Uridine Diphosphate into a Galactose Drivative," *Arch. Biochem. Biophys* 33 (1951): 186–90. "Carbohydrate Metabolism," with C. E. Cardini, *Ann. Rev. Biochem* 22 (1953): 179–210. "Uridine Coenzymes," *Proc. 3rd Intern. Congr. Biochem.,* Brussels (1955): 154–62. "Nucleotide and Saccharide Synthesis," *Conf. on Polysaccharides in Biol., Trans* (1958): 155–234.

Bibliography: *Biographical Memoirs of the Fellows of the Royal Society* (London: Royal Society, 1990), vol. 35, p. 201. *Chemical and Engineering News* 48 (November 2, 1970): 13. *The Excitement and Fascination of Science* (Palo Alto, Calif.: Annual Reviews, 1990), vol. 3, part 1, pp. 367–81. *Science* 170 (November 6, 1970): 604–609.

HERZBERG, GERHARD

Prize: Chemistry, 1971. *Born:* December 25, 1904; Hamburg, Germany. *Died:* March 4, 1999; Ottawa, Ontario, Canada. *Nationality:* German; later Canadian citizen. *Education:* Darmstadt Institute of Technology, Germany, Doctor of Engineering, 1928. *Career:* Darmstadt Institute of Technology, Germany, Professor, 1930–35; University of Saskatchewan, Canada, Professor, 1935–45; University of Chicago, Illinois, Professor, 1945–48; National Research Council, Canada, Researcher and Administrator, 1949–69. *Other Awards:* University of Liege Medal, 1950; Henry Marshall Tory

Medal, Canadian Royal Society, 1953; Jay Kissen Mookerjee Gold Medal, Indian Association for the Cultivation of Science, 1957; Frederic Ives Medal, Optical Society of America, 1965; Willard Gibbs Medal, American chemical Society, 1969; Faraday Medal, Chemical Society of London, 1970; Royal Medal, Royal Society, 1971; Linus Pauling Medal, American Chemical Society, 1971; Plyler Prize, 1985.

Citation: "For his contributions to the knowledge of electronic stucture and geometry of molecules, particularly free radicals."

Life Work: Herzberg's field of investigation was electromagnetic radiation. In 1929, by analyzing the spectra of molecular nitrogen, Herzberg demonstrated that the nitrogen nucleus was composed not merely of protons and electrons. Herzberg also discovered line spectra of diatomic oxygen, now designated Herzberg bands, important in the study of upper atmospheres. In the 1950s he turned to the spectroscopic analysis of free radicals (atoms or molecules with at least one unpaired electron). They have such fleeting lifetimes that they had not been observed until then. Using flash photolysis techniques, he made the first successful spectroscopic studies of free methyl and methylene. His work includes the first measurements of the Lamb shifts in deuterium, helium, and positive lithium ion.

Publications: *Atomic Spectra and Atomic Structure* (New York: Prentice-Hall, 1937). *Molekulspektren und Molekulstructur. Zweiatomige Molekule* (Dresden, Germany: T. Steinkopff, 1939). *Infrared and Roman Spectra of Polyatomic Molecules* (New York: D. Van Nostrand, 1945). "The Electronic Structure of the Nitrogen Molecule," *Physical Review* 69 (1946): 362–65. "Lamb Shift of the 1(2)S Ground State of Deuterium," *Proceedings of the Royal Society of London* 234A (1956): 516–28.

Bibliography: *Chemical and Engineering News* 49 (November 1, 1971): 5. *Current Biography Yearbook* (New York: H. W. Wilson, 1973), pp. 185–87.

ANFINSEN, CHRISTIAN BOEHMER

Prize: Chemistry, 1972. *Born:* March 26, 1916; Monessen, Pennsylvania. *Died:* May 14, 1995, Randallstown, Maryland. *Nationality:* American. *Education:* Swarthmore College, Pennsylvania, B.A., 1937; University of Pennsylvania, M.S., 1939; Harvard University, Massachusetts, Ph.D., 1943. *Career:* University of Pennsylvania, Professor, 1938–39; Carlsberg University, Denmark, Researcher, 1939–40; Harvard University, Massachusetts, Professor, 1941–50; National Heart Institute, Researcher, 1950–62; Harvard University, Massachusetts, Professor, 1962–63; National Institute of Arthritis, Metabolism, and Digestive Diseases, Researcher, 1963–81; John Hopkins University, Maryland, Professor, 1982–95. *Other Awards:* Public Service Award, Rockefeller Foundation, 1954; Myrtle Wreath, Hadassah, 1977.

Citation: "For his work on ribonuclease, especially concerning the connection between the amino acid sequence and the biologically active conformation."

Life Work: Anfinsen's field of investigation was enzymes. To understand how they functioned, he examined how radioactively labeled amino acids are incorporated into proteins. Using Frederick Sanger's methods, he sought to determine how many properties of an enzyme are governed solely by its amino acid sequence. For his investigations he selected bovine ribonuclease, an enzyme of 124 amino acids produced in the pancreas. The molecule of ribonuclease consists of one chain twisted into a ball and held together by four disulfide bridges. By chemical means the chemical bridges can be separated so that the enzyme becomes denatured, or a simple polypeptide chain with no power to hydrolyze. Once the bridges are broken, they can be reunited in any one of 105 ways. The minimum of chemical intervention was sufficient to induce the ribonuclease to adopt the one configuration that restores enzymatic activity. He proved that the amino acid sequence alone is sufficient to determine not only the enzyme's structure but also its function.

Publications: "Method for the Specific Proteolytic Cleavage of Protein Chains," with Michael Sela and Harold Tritsch, *Archives of Biochemistry and Biophysics* 65 (1956): 156–63. "Reductive Cleavage of Disulfide Bridges in Ribonuclease," with Michael Sela and Frederick H. White, *Science* 125 (1957): 691–92. *The Molecular Basis of Evolution* (New York: Wiley, 1959). "The Ribonucleases-Occurrence, Structure and Properties," in *Enzymes* (New York: Academic Press, 1961), vol. 5, pp. 95–122.

Bibliography: "The 1972 Nobel Prize for Chemistry," *Science* (November 3, 1972): 492–93. "Nobel Winners in Physics, Chemistry," *New York Times*, October 21, 1972, p. L14.

MOORE, STANFORD

Prize: Chemistry, 1972. *Born:* September 4, 1913; Chicago, Illinois. *Died:* August 23, 1982; New York, New York. *Nationality:* American. *Education:* Vanderbilt University, Tennessee, A.B., 1935; University of Wisconsin, Ph.D., 1938. *Career:* Rockefeller Institute for Medal Research, New York, Professor, 1939–42; Office of Scientific Research and Development, Washington, D.C., Researcher, 1942–45; Rockefeller Institute for Medal Research, New York, Professor, 1945–82. *Other Awards:* Founder's Medal, Vanderbilt University, 1935; Chromatography Award, American Chemical Society, 1963; Richard's Medal, American Chemical Society, 1972; Linderstrom-Lang Medal, Copenhagen, Denmark, 1972.

Citation: "For their contribution to the understanding of the connection between chemical structure and catalytic activity of the active centre of the ribonuclease molecule" (with William H. Stein).

Life Work: Moore's field of investigation was amino acid analysis. He and William H. Stein sought to advance methods of protein separation and purification through column chromotography and ion exchange chromotography. They purified bovine ribonuclease through the ion exchange method. From this highly purified enzyme they broke the polypeptide chain into pieces, separated the pieces by chromotography, and identified the amino acids present in each one. By 1960 the team had mapped out the complete amino acid sequence of ribonuclease. It was the second protein sequence and the first enzyme ever to be mapped. From these results they were able to locate and determine the components of the active center of ribonuclease. Later they applied the same techniques to analyze deoxyribonuclease.

Publications: "Structure and Activity of Pancreatic Ribonuclease," *Soc. Chim. Biol., Celebration Cinquantenaire, Conf. Rappt., Paris* (1964): 189–94. "Amino Acid Analysis: Aqueous Dimethyl Sulfoxide as Solvent for the Ninhydrin Reaction," *Journal of Biological Chemistry* 243 (1968): 6281–83. "Chemical Structures of Pancreatic Ribonuclease and Deoxyribonuclease," with William H. Stein, *Science* 180 (1973): 458–64. "The Precision and Sensitivity of Amino Acid Analysis," *Kagaku No Ryoiki Zokan* 106 (1976): 136–75.

Bibliography: *Biographical Memoirs. National Academy of Sciences* (Washington, D.C.: National Academy Press, 1987), vol. 56, 355. *Science* 178 (November 3, 1972): 492–93. *Science News* 102 (October 28, 1972): 276.

STEIN, WILLIAM HOWARD

Prize: Chemistry, 1972. *Born:* June 25, 1911; New York, New York. *Died:* February 2, 1980; New York, New York. *Nationality:* American. *Education:* Harvard University, Massachusetts, B.S., 1933; Columbia University, New York, Ph.D., 1938. *Career:* Rockefeller Institute, New York, Researcher, 1938–80. *Other Awards:* Award in Chromatography and Electrophoresis, 1964.

Citation: "For their contribution to the understanding of the connection between chemical structure and catalytic activity of the active centre of the ribonuclease molecule" (with Stanford Moore).

Life Work: Stein's field of investigation was the analysis of amino acids in proteins. Working with Stanford Moore, he developed paper chromotography and, later, column chromotography and ion exchange chromotography as standard tools in protein biochemistry. They focused on the enzyme ribonuclease, one of the many thousands of organic catalysts that regulate chemical reactions within living organisms.

Publications: "Amino-Acid Composition of Human Hemoglobin," with others, *Biochemica et Biophysica Acta* 24 (19757): 640–42. "Chemical Modifications of Ribonuclease," *Brookhaven Symposia in Biology* 13 (1960): 104–14. "Relations Between Structure and Activity of Ribonuclease," with Stanford Moore, *Proc. Intern. Congr. Biochem., 5th, Moscow* 4 (1961): 33–38. "Structure-Activity Relations in Ribonuclease," *Federation Proceedings* 23 (1964): 599–608. "Structure and the Activity of Ribonuclease," *Israel Journal of Medical Science* 1 (1965): 1229–43.

Bibliography: *Chemical and Engineering News* 50 (October 30, 1972): 2–3. *Dictionary of Scientific Biography* (New York: Scribner's), suppl. 2, pp. 851–55. *Science* 178

(November 3, 1972): 492 93. *Biographical Memoirs. National Academy of Sciences* (Washington, D.C.: National Academy Press, 1987), vol. 56, p. 415.

FISCHER, ERNST OTTO

Prize: Chemistry, 1973. *Born:* November 10, 1918; Muchen-Sölln, Germany. *Nationality:* German. *Education:* University of Munich, Germany, Dipl. Chem., 1949; University of Munich, Germany, Doctor Rerum Naturalium, 1952. *Career:* University of Munich, Germany, Professor, 1954–. *Other Awards:* Göttingen Academy Prize, 1957; Alfred Stock-Gedachtnis Prize, 1959.

Citation: "For their pioneering work, performed independently, on the chemistry of the organometallic, so called sandwich compounds" (with Geoffrey Wilkinson).

Life Work: Fischer's field of investigation was metal carbonyls, especially the structure of dicyclopentadienyl iron, or ferrocene, a compound remarkable for its chemical and thermal stability. He described ferrocene as an entirely new type of covalent complex. Using X-ray crystallography, Fischer determined that the two rings are parallel, forming a layered, or sandwich, structure with the iron atom positioned centrally between them. As a result, the central atom is bonded with each of the five carbon atoms in the upper and lower rings. Fischer's work was the foundation for the development of new cata-. lysts used in a variety of industrial processes. Fischer continued his study of transition metals whose properties are intermediate between metals and nonmetals, such as dibenzenechromium and analyzed metal complexes of arenes.

Publications: "The Nomenclature of Metal Compounds Containing Two Cyclopentadienyl Rings," *Z. Naturforsch* 9b (1954): 619–20. "New Results on Aromatic Metal Carbonyls," *Journal of Inorganic and Nuclear Chemistry* 8 (1958): 268–72. *Metal (pi)-Complexes*, with H. Werner (New York: Elsevier, 1966). "Transition Metal Carbonyl Carbene Complexes," *Pure and Applied Chemistry* 30 (1972): 353–72.

Bibliography: *Biographical Encyclopedia of Scientists* (New York: Facts on File, 1981), pp. 264–65. *Science* 182 (November 16, 1973): 699–700.

WILKINSON, GEOFFREY

Prize: Chemistry, 1973. *Born:* July 14, 1921; Todmorden, England. *Died:* September 26, 1996; London, England. *Nationality:* British. *Education:* University of London, England, B.Sc., 1941; University of London, England, Ph.D., 1946. *Career:* National Research Council of Canada, Scientific Officer, 1943–46; University of California, Researcher, 1946–50; Massachusetts Institute of Technology, Professor, 1950–51; Harvard University, Massachusetts, Professor, 1951–55; University of London, England, Professor,

1956–88. *Other Awards:* Inorganic Chemistry Award, American Chemical Society, 1966; Lavoisier Medal, French Chemical Society, 1968; Transition Metal Chemistry Award, Royal Society, 1972; Hiroshima University Medal, Japan, 1978; Royal Medal, Royal Society, 1981; Galileo Medal, University of Pisa, Italy, 1983; Longstaff Medal, 1987.

Citation: "For their pioneering work, performed independently, on the chemistry of the organometallic, so called sandwich compounds" (with Ernest Fischer).

Life Work: Wilkinson's field of investigation was inorganic complexes, especially complexes containing a metal hydrogen bond. Complexes of rhodium with triphenyl phosphine react with molecular hydrogen. The compound known as Wilkinson's Catalyst was the first such to be used as a homogeneous catalyst for adding hydrogen to the double bonds of alkenes. This type of compound can also be used as a catalyst for the reaction of hydrogen and carbon monoxide with alkenes. It is the basis for industrial low pressure processes for making aldehydes from ethene and propene. At Harvard, he went on to synthesize additional sandwich molecules, including compounds with carbonyls and nitrosyls. His further studies on the bonding abilities of transition metals helped to advance organometallic chemistry.

Publications: "The Structure of Iron Biscyclopentadienyl," with M. Rosenblum, M. C. Whiting, and R. B. Woodward, *Journal of the American Chemical Society* 74 (1952): 2125–26. *Advanced Inorganic Chemistry*, with F. A. Cotton (New York: Interscience, 1962). "Catalytically Active Rhodium (I) Complexes," German Patent 2, 136, 470 (February 10, 1972). "Hexamethyltungsten," U.S. Patent 3, 816, 491 (June 11, 1974). *Basic Inorganic Chemistry*, with F. A. Cotton (New York: Wiley, 1976).

Bibliography: "The 1973 Nobel Prize for Chemistry," *Science* (November 16, 1973): 699–701. "Three Win Nobel Physics Prize and Two the Chemistry Award." *New York Times*, October 24, 1973, pp. L1, L26.

FLORY, PAUL JOHN

Prize: Chemistry, 1974. *Born:* June 19, 1910; Sterling, Illinois. *Died:* September 9, 1985; Big Sur, California. *Nationality:* American. *Education:* Manchester College, Indiana, B.Sc., 1931; Ohio State University, M.S., 1931; Ohio State University, Ph.D., 1934. *Career:* DuPont Experimental Station, Delaware, Researcher, 1936–38; University of Cincinnati, Ohio, Professor, 1938–40; Standard Oil Development, Ohio, Researcher, 1940–43; Goodyear Tire and Rubber, Ohio, Administrator, 1943–48; Cornell University, New York, Professor, 1948–56; Mellon Institute, Pennsylvania, Administrator, 1956–61; Stanford University, California, Professor, 1961–75. *Other Awards:* Sullivant Medal, 1945; Baekeland Award, 1947; Cowyn Medal, 1954; Nichols Medal, 1962; High-Polymer Physics Prize, 1962; International Award, 1969; Chandler Medal, 1970; First Award for Excellence, 1971; Cresson Medal, 1971; Kirkwood Medal, 1971; National Medal of Science, 1975.

Citation: "For his fundamental achievements, both theoretical and experimental, in the physical chemistry of the macromolecules."

Life Work: Flory's field of investigation was the properties of polymers, such as polyvinyl chloride. Polymers are produced by smaller units, known as monomers, joined together in a process called polymerization. Flory became especially interested in the speed of polymer reactions. He formulated a theory to explain the rate at which some polymers developed a branched configuration forming meshlike networks characteristic of elastic polymers, such as rubber and silicone. He made several important discoveries, among them that the tensile strength of rubber is related predictably to flaws in the network structure, and that the configuration of small molecules in a solution can be accurately described only at the ideal theta point, now known as the Flory Temperature. He showed that viscosity is a reliable indicator of polymer length since the increase in viscosity is proportional to the cube of the structural radius of the molecule. He also described the configuration of proteins and polypeptides and published a paper on liquid crystals long before they were made.

Publications: *Principles of Polymer Chemistry* (Ithaca, N.Y.: Cornell University Press, 1953). *Statistical Mechanics of Chain Molecules* (New York: Interscience Publishers, 1969). *Selected Works of Paul J. Flory* (Stanford, Calif.: Stanford University Press, 1985).

Bibliography: *Biographical Encyclopedia of Scientists* (New York: Facts on File, 1981), pp. 271–72. *Current Biography Yearbook* (New York: H. W. Wilson, 1975), pp. 127–30.

CORNFORTH, SIR JOHN WARCUP

Prize: Chemistry, 1975. *Born:* September 7, 1917; Sydney, Australia. *Nationality:* British. *Education:* University of Sydney, Australia, B.S., 1937; Oxford University, England, M.Sc., 1938; Oxford University, England, D.Phil., 1941. *Career:* Medical Research Council, London, England, Researcher, 1946–62; Shell Research Laboratory, England, Director, 1962–75; University of Sussex, England, Professor, 1975–82. *Other Awards:* Corday-Morgan Medal, Chemistry Society, 1953; Flintoff Medal, Chemistry Society, 1966; CIBA Medal, 1966; Stouffer Prize, 1967; Davy Medal, Royal Society, 1968; Ernest Gunther Award, American Chemical Society, 1969; Prix Roussel, 1972; Royal Medal, Royal Society, 1976; Knighthood, 1977; Copley Medal, Royal Society, 1982.

Citation: "For his work on the stereochemistry of enzyme-catalyzed reactions."

Life Work: Cornforth's field of investigation was analysis of the steroid cholesterol. Using radioactive carbon labeling techniques Cornforth demonstrated the structural position of each acetic acid precursor in cholesterol and also identified the fourteen intermediate steps between mevalonic acid and squalene. Cornforth focused on stereochemistry, or three-dimensional geometry, of the molecular interactions between enzymes and their substrates in the synthesis of squalene from mevalonic acid. He labeled each of the six methylene hydrogens in mevalonic acid with deuterium or tritium, both isotopes of hydrogen. He showed that all enzyme substrate interactions between mevalonic acid and squalene as well as between terpenoid compounds are stereospecific or produced by a specific stereoisomer. He also identified the hydrogen atom of the coenzyme NADH that is transferred to molecular oxygen in biological oxidation reductions. Another focus of Cornforth's work was chirality, a stereochemical property describing the optical activity of organic compounds in solution. Beginning 1967 he worked on the problem of the chiral methyl group synthesizing and enzymatically assaying them. Cornforth then used acetic acid to study further the stereochemistry of enzyme-substrate reactions.

Publications: *The Chemistry of Penicillin*, with others (Princeton, N.J.: Princeton University Press, 1949). "Absolute Configuration of Cholesterol," with I. Youhotsky and G. Popjack, *Nature* 173 (1954): 536. "Total Synthesis of Steroids," *Progress in Organic Chemistry* 3 (1955): 1–43. "Stereoselective Synthesis of Squalene," with R. H. Cornforth and K. K. Mathew, *Journal of the Chemical Society* (1959): 2539–47. "Absolute Stereochemistry of Some Enzymic Processes," *Biochemical Journal* 86 (1963): 7.

Bibliography: *Biographical Encyclopedia of Scientists* (New York: Facts on File, 1981), p. 163. *Science* 190 (November 21, 1975): 722–73.

PRELOG, VLADIMIR

Prize: Chemistry, 1975. *Born:* July 23, 1906; Sarajevo, Bosnia. *Died:* January 7, 1998; Zürich, Switzerland. *Nationality:* Yugoslavian; later Swiss citizen. *Education:* Institute of Technology and School of Chemistry, Czechoslovakia, doctorate, 1929. *Career:* G. Z. Driza Laboratories, Prague, Czechoslovakia, Researcher, 1929–35; University of Zagreb, Yugoslavia, Researcher, 1929–35; University of Zagreb, Yugoslavia, Professor, 1935–42; Eidgenossische Technische Hochschule, Switzerland, Professor, 1942–76. *Other Awards:* Warner Medal, 1945; Stas Medal, 1962; Medal of Honor, Rice University, 1962; Marcel Benoist Award, 1965; Roger Adams Award; A. W. Hofman Medal; Davy Medal, Royal Society.

Citation: "For his research into the stereochemistry of organic molecules and reactions."

Life Work: Prelog's early field of investigation was stereochemistry. After studying the stereochemistry of the malarial drug quinine and its isomers, Prelog turned his attention to compounds containing medium-sized ring structures and to the mechanisms of transannular reactions, or stereochemical reactions between segments of medium ring structures. Using X-ray crystallography Prelog discovered an entirely new type of stereoisomerism, called cyclostereoisomerism. He developed a system of classification and nomenclature of stereoisomers called the Cahn-Ingold-Prelog system, describing the stereochemical structure of molecules with more than one asymmetrical center. Prlog and his colleagues synthesized vesperines, molecules with a rare type of symmetry, and studied the stereochemistry of nonactin and the enzyme fatty acid synthetase, actually a composite enzyme containing all the individual enzymes required for the biosynthesis of fatty acids. He discovered many new natural substances, including the first natural compound containing boron, boromycin.

Publications: "Conformation and Reactivity of Medium-sized Ring Compounds," *Pure Applied Chemistry* 6 (1963): 545–60. "Constitution of Rifamycins," *Pure Applied Chemistry* 7 (1963): 551–64. "Role of Certain Microbial Metabolites as Specific Complexing Agents," *Pure Applied Chemistry* 25 (1971): 197–210. "Chiral Ionophores," *Pure Applied Chemistry* 50 (1978): 893–904. "Structure and Properties of Boromycin and Products of Its Degradation," *Front. Bioorg. Chem. Mol. Biol* (1979): 87–96.

Bibliography: *Biographical Encyclopedia of Scientists* (New York: Facts on File, 1981), pp. 651–52. *Chemical and Engineering News* 53 (October 27, 1975): 4–5.

LIPSCOMB, WILLIAM NUNN

Prize: Chemistry, 1976. *Born:* December 9, 1919; Cleveland, Ohio. *Nationality:* American. *Education:* University of Kentucky, B.S., 1941; California Institute of Technology, Ph.D., 1946. *Career:* United States Office of Scientific Research and Development, Chemist, 1942–46; University of Minnesota, Professor, 1946–59; Harvard University, Massachusetts, Professor, 1959–90. *Other Awards:* Harrison Howe Award, American Chemical Society, 1958; Distinguished Service Award, American Chemical Society, 1968; George Ledlie Prize, Harvard University, Massachusetts, 1971; Peter Debye Award, American Chemical Society, 1973; Evans Award, Ohio State University; Remsen Award, American Chemical Society, Maryland Section, 1976; Alexander von Humboldt-Stiftung, 1979.

Citation: "For his studies on the structure of boranes illuminating problems of chemical bonding."

Life Work: Lipscomb is best known for his work on boranes. He proposed that boranes had three-center bonds in which an electron pair unites either three boron atoms or two boron atoms and one hydrogen atom. It proved to be the key to a new topological theory of bonding on boranes. He applied this theory to an understanding of reactivity in mixed carbon-boron hydrides, known as carbones. Boranes are also used in radiation cancer therapy. His work on boron hydrides involved new techniques that proved to have wider application in chemistry. In particular, Lipscomb produced a theory of chemical effects in nuclear magnetic resonance studies of complex molecules. He also worked on the quantum mechanics of complex molecules. Later, at Harvard, Lipscomb's focus shifted toward biochemistry, especially the elucidation of structures of complex proteins, using X-ray diffraction techniques. His main success has been his structural analysis of the digestive enzyme carboxypeptidase A and the regulatory enzyme ATcase.

Publications: "Valence in the Boron Hydrides," *Journal of Physical Chemistry* 61 (1957): 23–27. "Boron Hydrides," *Advances in Inorganic Chemistry and Radiochem-*

istry 1 (1959): 117–56. *Boron Hydrides* (New York: W. A. Benjamin, 1963). "Geometrical Theory of Boron Hydrides," *Inorganic Chemistry* 3 (1964): 1683–85. *Nuclear Magnetic Resonance Studies of Boron Hydrides and Related Compounds* (New York: W. A. Benjamin, 1969).

Bibliography: *Chemistry* 49 (December 1976): 2. *Science* 194 (November 1976): 709–10.

PRIGOGINE, ILYA

Prize: Chemistry, 1977. *Born:* January 25, 1917; Moscow, Russia. *Nationality:* Russian; later Belgian citizen and American resident. *Education:* Université Libre de Bruxelles, Belgium, baccalaureate, 1939; doctorate, 1942. *Career:* Université Libre de Bruxelles, Belgium, Professor and Administrator, 1947–; University of Texas, Austin, Professor and Administrator, 1967–. *Other Awards:* Prix Francqui, 1955; Prix Solvay, 1965; Bourke Medal, Chemical Society, England, 1972; Rumford Medal, Royal Society, 1976; Karcher Medal, American Crystallographic Association, 1978; Descartes Medal, University of Paris, France, 1979; Honda Prize, 1983; Artificial Intelligence Award, 1990.

Citation: "For his studies on the structure of boranes illuminating problems of chemical bonding."

Life Work: Prigogine's field of investigation was the thermodynamics of states far from equilibrium, known as dissipative structures, that play an extensive role in biological processes. Believing that nonequilibrium could be a source of organization and order, Prigogine conceived of dissipative structures in terms of a mathematical model with time-dependent nonlinear functions the describes the ability of systems to exchange matter or energy with their environment and to restabilize themselves spontaneously. Prigogine extended his theory of dissipative structures to the formation and development of biological systems, such as embryos, as well as social systems, vehicular traffic patterns, natural resource management, population growth, meteorology, and astronomy.

Publications: *Thermodynamique Chimique Conformement aux Methodes de Gibbs et De Donder* (Liege, Belgium: Desoer, 1944–51). *Treatise on Thermodynamics Based on the Methods of Gibbs and De Donder*, with R. Defay (London: Longmans, Green, 1954). *Introduction to Thermodynamics of Irreversible Processes*, with A. Bellemans and V. Mathot (New York: Interscience, 1962). *Order Out of Chaos* (New York: Bantam Books, 1984).

Bibliography: *Chemical and Engineering News* 55 (October 17, 1977): 4. *Current Biography Yearbook* (New York: H. W. Wilson, 1987), pp. 447–50. *Physics Today* 30 (December 1977): 79–80.

MITCHELL, PETER DENIS

Prize: Chemistry, 1978. *Born:* September 20, 1920; Mitcham, Surrey, England. *Died:* April 10, 1992; Bodmin, England. *Nationality:* British. *Education:* Cambridge University, England, B.A., 1943; Cambridge University, England, Ph.D., 1950. *Career:* Cambridge University, England, Professor, 1943–55; University of Edinburgh, Scotland, Professor, 1964–86. *Other Awards:* CIBA Medal and Prize, Biochemical Society, England, 1973; Warren Triennial Prize, Massachusetts General Hospital, 1974; Louis and Bert Freedman Foundation Award, New York Academy of Sciences, 1974; Wilhelm Feldberg Foundation Prize, Anglo/American Science Exchange, 1976; Lewis S. Rosenstiel Award, Brandeis University, 1977; Medal Federal European Biochemistry Society, 1978; Copley Medal, Royal Society, 1981.

Citation: "For his contribution to the understanding of biological energy transfer through the formulation of the chemiosmotic theory."

Life Work: Mitchell's field of investigation was oxidative phosporylation, the process by which ATP is made by coupling adenosine diphosphate (ADP) to an inorganic phosphate. Mitchell suggested a physical mechanism by which an electrochemical gradient is created across the cellular membrane. Enzymic reactions are essentially vectorial; that is, they transport something. When the enzymes were taken into membranes, the direction of these reactions became apparent. When an enzyme complex is so firmly set in a membrane the reaction route traverses the barrier catalyzing the dislocation of a chemical group. This process was named vectorial metabolism. Between 1961 and 1966, Mitchell formulated chemiosmotic hypothesis, an extreme but elegant solution to the problem of energy coupling in the mechanisms of oxidative and photosynthetic phosophrylation. He proposed that the respiratory chain is an alternating sequence of carriers for hydrogen and electrons so arranged in the inner mitochondrial membrane that they transport protons across the membrane. Since the mitochondrial membrane does not permit a passive flow of protons, respiration creates an electrochemical ramp or slope for hydrogen ions with the inner matrix being electrically negative and alkaline relative to the exterior. Protons on the outer surface gravitate back into the matrix, traveling down the ramp with the help of the proton current.

Publications: *Chemiosmotic Coupling in Oxidative and Photosynthetic Phosphorylation* (Bodmin, Cornwall, England: Glynn Research, 1966). *Chemiosmotic Coupling and Energy Transduction* (Bodmin, Cornwall, England: Glynn Research, 1968). *Chemiosmotic Proton Circuits in Biological Membranes*, with P. C. Hinkle and V. P. Skulachev (Reading, Mass.: Addison-Wesley, 1981).

Bibliography: *Biographical Encyclopedia of Scientists* (New York: Facts on File, 1981), p. 564. *Biographical Memoirs of the Fellows of the Royal Society* (London: Royal Society, 1994), vol. 40, p. 281. *Science* 202 (December 8, 1978): 1174–76.

BROWN, HERBERT CHARLES
(BROVARNIK, HERBERT CHARLES)

Prize: Chemistry, 1979. *Born:* May 22, 1912; London, England. *Nationality:* British; later American citizen. *Education:* Wright Junior College, Illinois, A.S., 1935; University of Chicago, Illinois, B.S., 1936; University of Chicago, Illinois., Ph.D., 1938. *Career:* University of Chicago, Illinois, Professor, 1936–43; Wayne State University, Michigan, Professor, 1943–47; Purdue University, Indiana, Professor, 1947–78. *Other Awards:* Purdue Sigma Xi Research Award, 1951; Nichols Medal, American Chemical Society, 1959; American Chemical Society Award for Creative Research in Synthetic Organic Chemistry, 1960; H. N. McCoy Award, 1965; Linus Pauling Medal, 1968; National Medal of Science, 1969; Roger Adams Medal, 1971; Charles Frederick Chandler Medal, 1973; Madison Marshall Award, 1975; Chemical Pioneer Award, 1975; CCNY Scientific Achievement Award Medal, 1976; Elliot Cresson Medal, 1978; C. K. Ingold Medal, 1978; Priestly Medal, 1981; Perkin Medal, 1982; Kosolapoff Medal, 1987; Oesper Award, 1990.

Citation: "For their development of the use of boron- and phosphorus-containing compounds, respectively, into important reagents in organic synthesis" (with Georg Wittig).

Life Work: Brown's field of investigation was compounds of boron. In 1936 he found a simple way of making diborane and sodium borohydride, a reagent used extensively in organic chemistry for reduction. By reacting diborane with alkenes he produced a new class of compounds called organoboranes. Diborane was used to synthesize uranium borohydride. Reduction carried out with diborane or sodium borohydride provides synthetic routes to new compounds. The work also opened up lines of fundamental research in physical organic chemistry, such as the quantitative relationship between molecular structure and reactivity. In 1955 Brown discovered a process called hydroboration by adding diborane to carbon-carbon double bonds to produce organoboranes. This process is used to convert olefins to alcohols or to saturated compounds. Brown's work transformed organoboranes to one of the most versatile chemical intermediates with a number of important technical applications.

Publications: *Hydroboration* (New York: W. A. Benjamin, 1962). *Boranes in Organic Chemistry* (Ithaca, N.Y.: Cornell University Press, 1972). *Organic Syntheses via Boranes,* with others (New York: Wiley-Interscience, 1975). *The Nonclassical Ion Problem* (New York: Plenum Press, 1977).

Bibliography: *Asimov's Biographical Encyclopedia of Science and Technology* (Garden City, N.Y.: Doubleday, 1982), p. 843. *Biographical Encyclopedia of Scientists* (New York: Facts on File, 1981), p. 114.

WITTIG, GEORG FRIEDRICH KARL

Prize: Chemistry, 1979. *Born:* June 16, 1897; Berlin, Germany. *Died:* August 26, 1987; Heidelberg, Germany. *Nationality:* German. *Education:* University of Marburg, Germany, Ph.D., 1923. *Career:* University of Marburg, Germany, Professor, 1926–32; Technische Hochschule, Braunschweig Institute of Technology, Germany, Professor, 1932–37; University of Freiburg, Germany, Professor, 1944–56; University of Heidelberg, Germany, Professor, 1956–67. *Other Awards:* Adolf von Baeyer Medal, Society of German Chemists, 1953; Silver Medal, University of Helsinki, 1957; Dannie Heineman Award, Gottinger Academy of Sciences, 1965; Otto Hahn Prize, Germany, 1967; Silver Medal, City of Paris, 1969; Paul Karrer Medal, University of Zürich, 1972; Medal of the Bruylants Chair, University of Leuwen, 1972; Roger Adams Award, American Chemical Society, 1973; Karl Ziegler Prize, Society of German Chemists, 1975; Ordens Grosses Verdienstkreuz, 1980.

Citation: "For their development of the use of boron- and phosphorus-containing compounds, respectively, into important reagents in organic synthesis" (with Herbert C. Brown).

Life Work: Wittig's field of investigation was the mechanism of chemical reactions and molecular rearrangements in five organic groups that became covalently bonded to Group V elements in the periodic table, such as nitrogen, phosphorus, and arsenic. In the course of his research he came across a family of products called ylides, a Group V quarternary salt. He found that ylides react smoothly with carbonyl compounds. This process yields an olefin with a new carbon-carbon double bond in place of the carbonyl group. Now known as the Wittig reaction, it is an enormously useful tool for organic synthesis. With Wittig reactions chemists can now join two carbon structures easily and reliably by using an appropriate alkyl halide and a carbonyl compound. It is used in the preparation of vitamins A and D and steroids as well as natural pest control agents.

Publications: "Course of Reactions of Pentaphenylphosphorus and Certain Derivatives," *Annalender Chemie, Justus Liebigs* 580 (1953): 44–57. "Triphenylphosphine-methylene as an Olefin-forming Reagent," *Chemisches Berichte* 87 (1954): 1318–30. "Triphenylphosphinemethylenes as Olefin-forming Reagents," *Chemisches Berichte* 87 (1954): 1318–30. "Triphenylphosphinemethylenes as Olefin-forming Reagents," *Chemisches Berichte* 88 (1955): 654–66. "Metallizability of Quaternary Ammonium and Phosphonium Salts," *Annalender Chemie, Justus Liebigs* 562 (1956): 177–78.

Bibliography: *Biographical Dictionary of Scientists, Chemists* (New York: Peter Bedrick Books, 1983), pp. 148–49. *Modern Scientists and Engineers* (New York: McGraw-Hill, 1980), vol. 3, pp. 341–42.

BERG, PAUL

Prize: Chemistry, 1980. *Born:* June 30, 1926; New York, New York. *Nationality:* American. *Education:* Pennsylvania State University, B.S., 1948; Case Western Reserve University, Ohio, Ph.D., 1952. *Career.* Washington University, St. Louis, Missouri, Professor, 1955–74; Stanford University, California, Professor, 1974–. *Other Awards:* Eli Lilly Award, 1959; California Scientist of the Year, 1964; V. D. Mattia Prize, Roche Institute for Molecular Biochemistry, 1972; Albert Lasker Medical Research Award, 1980; Gairdner Foundation Award, 1980; National Medal of Science, 1983.

Citation: "For his fundamental studies of the biochemistry of nucleic acids, with particular regard to recombinant DNA."

Life Work: Berg's field of investigation was DNA and RNA, especially the role of adaptors, later known as transfer RNA. Working on the genes of simian virus 40, a monkey tumor virus, Berg tried to create a recombinant DNA that serves as a vector from more than one type of organism. Although he later abandoned his efforts to recombine DNA, his techniques enabled researchers to manipulate genes to create new pharmaceuticals, such as interferon and growth hormones.

Publications: "Contributions of Nucleic Acids to the Specificity of Protein Synthesis," *Probl. Neoplastic Disease; Symp., New York* (1962): 15–34. "Viral Genome in Transformed Cells," *Proceedings of the Royal Society, Series B* (1971): 65–76. "Potential Biohazards of Recombinant DNA Molecules," with others, *Proceedings of the National Academy of Sciences U.S.A.* (1974): 2593–94.

Bibliography: *New York Times* Biographical Service, October 1980, p. 1359. *Science* 210 (November 21, 1980): 887–89.

GILBERT, WALTER

Prize: Chemistry, 1980. *Born:* March 21, 1932; Boston, Massachusetts. *Nationality:* American. *Education:* Harvard University, Massachusetts, B.A., 1953; Harvard University, Massachusetts, A.M., 1954; Cambridge University, England, D. Phil., 1957. *Career:* Harvard University, Massachusetts, Professor, 1957–82; Biogen, Inc., Massachusetts, Researcher, 1982–84; Harvard University, Massachusetts Professor, 1984–. *Other Awards:* U.S. Steel Foundation Award, National Academy of Sciences, 1968; Ledlie Prize, Harvard University, Massachusetts, 1969; Warren Triennial Prize, Massachusetts General Hospital, 1977; Louis and Bert Freedman Foundation Award, New York Academy of Sciences, 1977; Prix Charles-Leopold Mayer, Académie des Sciences, France, 1977; Louisa Gross Horwitz Prize, Columbia University, New York, 1979; Gairdner Prize, 1979; Albert Lasker Basic Science Award, 1979.

Citation: "For their contributions concerning the determination of base sequences in nucleic acids" (with Frederick Sanger).

Life Work: Gilbert's field of investigation was the repressor molecule that inactivates the transcription process by binding to the DNA and preventing RNA polymerase from moving along it. By 1966 Gilbert had isolated the repressor using an ingenious experimental procedure known as equilibrium dialysis, and by 1970 he had located the structure and location of the operator, the position on the DNA strand to which the repressor becomes attached. In 1973 he elucidated the sequence of the lac operator. Trying to determine the specific nucleotides in the lac operator that are most important in the binding process, Gilbert separated the DNA fragments according to length using gel electrophresis. By 1977 Gilbert had determined the entire sequence of bases for the protein and his method became one of the fundamental tools in the expanding field of recombinant DNA, or gene splicing.

Publications: "Protein Synthesis in *Escherichia coli*," *Cold Spring Harbor Symposium on Quantitative Biology* 28 (1963): 287–97. "Isolation of the Lac Repressor," with Benno Mueller-Hill, *Proceedings of the National Academy of Sciences U.S.* 56 (1966): 1891–98. "DNA Replication. The Rolling Circle Model," with David Dressler, *Cold Spring Harbor Symposium on Quantitative Biology* 33 (1968): 473–84. "The Lac Operator in DNA," with Benno Mueller-Hill, *Proceedings of the National Academy of Sciences U.S.* 58 (1968): 2415–21. "Repressors and Genetic Control," *Neurosci: Second Study Program* (1970): 946–54.

Bibliography: *Physics Today* 34 (January 1981): 17–18. *Science* 210 (November 21, 1980): 887–89.

SANGER, FREDERICK. *See* **1958**, p. 63.

FUKUI, KENICHI

Prize: Chemistry, 1981. *Born:* October 4, 1918; Nara, Japan. *Died:* January 9, 1998; Kyoto, Japan. *Nationality:* Japanese. *Education:* Kyoto Imperial University, Japan, bachelor's in engineering, 1941; Kyoto Imperial University, Japan, Ph.D., 1948. *Career:* Japanese Army Fuel Laboratory, Researcher, 1941–44; Kyoto Imperial University, Japan, Professor, 1944–82; Kyoto University of Industrial Arts, Japan, President, 1982–88. *Other Awards:* Japan Academy Medal, 1962; Order of Culture, Japan, 1981; Person of Cultural Merit, Japan, 1981.

Citation: "For their theories, developed independently, concerning the course of chemical reactions" (with Roald Hoffman).

Life Work: Fukui's field of investigation was the role of frontier orbitals in chemical reactions. Each molecule has many electrons, each with its orbital encompassing the entire molecule. A few of these molecular orbitals, called frontier orbitals, are significant in a reaction. He found that a chemical reaction was an interaction between the highest occupied molecular orbital of one compound with the lowest occupied molecular orbital of the other compound. One orbital shares its most loosely bound electrons with another, which accepts them at a site able to bind them tightly, creating a new orbital with an intermediate energy level. Fukui's discovery set the laws for many groups of organic-chemical reactions.

Publications: "Developments in Quantum-Mechanical Interpretation of the Reactivity of Unsaturated Hydrocarbons," *Journal of Japanese Chemistry* 6 (1952): 379–85. "Further Studies on the Frontier Electrons," *Journal of Japanese Chemistry* 8 (1954): 73–74. "Molecular Orbital Theory of Orientation in Aromatic, Heteroaromatic, and Other Conjugated Molecules," with others, *Journal of Chemical Physics* 22 (1954): 1433–42. "Theoretical Reactivity Index of Addition in the Frontier Electron Theory," with others, *Bulletin of the Chemical Society of Japan* 34 (1961): 230–32.

Bibliography: *Chemical and Engineering News* 59 (October 26, 1981): 6–7. *Science* 214 (November 6, 1981): 627–29.

HOFFMANN, ROALD (HOFFMAN, RONALD)

Prize: Chemistry, 1981. *Born:* July 18, 1937; Zloczow, Poland. *Nationality:* Polish; later American citizen. *Education:* Columbia University, New York, B.S., 1958; Harvard University, Massachusetts, M.A., 1960; Harvard University, Massachusetts, Ph.D., 1962. *Career:* Harvard University, Massachusetts, Researcher, 1962–65; Cornell University, New York, Professor, 1965–. *Other Awards:* American Chemical Society Award, 1969; Fresenius Award, 1969; Harrison Howe Award, 1969; Annual Award of International Academy of Quantum Molecular Sciences, 1970; Arthur C. Cope Award, American Chemical Society, 1973; Linus Pauling Award, 1974; Nichols Medal, 1980; Inorganic Chemistry Award, American Chemical Society, 1982; National Medal of Science, 1983; Priestley Medal, 1990.

Citation: "For their theories, developed independently, concerning the course of chemical reactions" (with Kenichi Fukui).

Life Work: Hoffmann is best known for the Woodward-Hoffmann rules, which predict whether a particular combination of chemicals will result in a reaction. Systems tend toward a configuration having the least energy. If a set of reactants will have less energy as a new compound than as discrete chemicals, the reaction will take place; no reaction will take place if the reverse is the case. Bonding between atoms occurs when their orbiting electrons overlap, that is, when the orbitals are symmetrical. The Woodward-Hoffmann rules predict mathematically whether a particular reaction will maintain that symmetry in concerted reactions in which several bonds are or broken simultaneously, rather than sequentially. The rules are considered to be the most important theoretical advance in organic chemistry in the latter part of the twentieth century.

Publications: "Orbital Symmetries and Endoexo Relationships in Concerted Cycloaddition Reactions," with R. B. Woodward, *Journal of the American Chemical Society* 87 (1965): 4388–89. "Orbital Symmetries and Orientational Effects in a Sigmatropic Reaction," with R. B. Woodward, *Journal of the American Chemical Society* 87 (1965): 4389–90. "Selection Rules for Concerted Cycloaddition Reactions," with R. B. Woodward, *Journal of the American Chemical Society* 87 (1965): 2046–48. "Stereochemistry of Electrocyclic Reactions," with R. B. Woodward, *Journal of the American Chemical Society* 87 (1965): 395–97. *Conservation of Orbital Symmetry*, with R. B. Woodward (Weinheim, Germany: Verlag Chemie, 1970). "Theoretical Aspects of the Coordination of Molecules to Transition Metal Centers," with T. A. Albright and D. L. Thorn, *Pure Applied Chemistry* 50 (1978): 1–9.

Bibliography: *Biographical Encyclopedia of Scientists* (New York: Facts on File, 1981), pp. 387–88. *Science* 214 (November 6, 1981): 627–29.

KLUG, AARON

Prize: Chemistry, 1982. *Born:* August 11, 1926; Dunbar, South Africa. *Nationality:* South African; later British resident. *Education:* University of Witwatersrand, South Africa, B.Sc., 1946; University of Cape Town, South Africa, M.Sc., 1947; Cambridge University, England, Ph.D., 1949. *Career:* Cambridge University, England, Professor, 1949–53; Birkbeck College, London, England, Professor and Administrator, 1954–61; Cambridge University, England, Professor and Administrator, 1962–. *Other Awards:* Heineken Prize, Royal Netherlands Academy of Science, 1979; Louisa Gross Horowitz Prize, Columbia University, 1981; Copley Medal, 1985; Harden Medal, 1985; Baly Medal, 1987.

Citation: "For his development of crystallographic electron microscopy and his structural elucidation of biologically important nuclei acid-protein complexes."

Life Work: Klug's field of investigation was the biochemical processes by which oxygen and carbon dioxide are exchanged in hemoglobin. He first studied tobacco mosaic virus and the virus that causes polio. He devised a technique called crystallographic electron microscopy, in which images obtained with an electron microscope are subjected to diffraction by laser light. The resulting pattern is then interpreted to reveal the structure of the object. He applied this procedure to the study of chromatin, the compound of histones and DNA that makes up the chromosomes of higher organisms. He showed that each histone is a stubby, cylindrical molecule around which a section of continuous DNA is coiled. The histones themselves are gathered into coils so that a single strand of human DNA, which is about six feet in length, fits within the nucleus of a cell, which is less than a hundredth of a millimeter in diameter.

Publications: "Reaggregation of the A-protein of Tobacco Mosaic Virus," with R. E. Franklin, *Biochim. et Biophys. Acta* 23 (1957): 199–201. "Joint Probability Distributions of Structure Factors and the Phase Problem," *Acta Cryst* 11 (1958): 515–43. "Architecture of Plant Viruses," *Biochemical Journal* 88 (1963): 24. "An Optical Method for the Analysis of Periodicities in Electron Micrographs, and Some Observations on the Mechanism of Negative Staining," with J. Berger, *Journal of Molecular Biology* 10 (1964): 565–69.

Bibliography: *Chemical and Engineering News* 60 (October 25, 1982): 4–5. *Science* 218 (November 12, 1982): 653–55.

TAUBE, HENRY

Prize: Chemistry, 1983. *Born:* November 30, 1915; Neudorf, Saskatchewan, Canada. *Nationality:* Canadian; later U.S. citizen. *Education:* University of Saskatchewan, Canada, B.S., 1935; University of California, M.S., 1937; University of California, Ph.D., 1940. *Career:* University of California, Professor, 1940–41; Cornell University, New York, Professor, 1941–46; University of Chicago, Illinois, Professor, 1946–62; Stanford University, California, Professor, 1961–. *Other Awards:* Harrison Howe Award, 1961; Chandler Medal, Columbia University, 1964; Kirkwood Award, Yale University and American Chemical Society, 1966; Distinguished Service in Advancement of Inorganic Chemistry Award, 1967; National Medal of Science, 1977; Monsanto Co. Award, 1981; Welch Award, 1983; Priestley Medal, 1984; Oesper Award, 1986; Kosolapoff Award, 1990.

Citation: "For his work on the mechanisms of electron transfer reactions, especially in metal complexes."

Life Work: Taube's field of investigation was radioisotopes. He developed experimental methods using radioisotopes to describe the oxidation-reduction and substitution reactions. Substitution reactions involve the transfer of an atom from one molecule to another. In oxidation-reduction, or redox, reactions, electrons are transferred. Loss of electrons in terms of oxidation and electron gain is termed reduction. Taube went on to study coordination chemistry, the bonding and reactions of materials. In coordination compounds a central atom or ion is surrounded by a group of ions called ligands. Taube demonstrated that metal ions in solutions form chemical bonds with water molecules He also described the relationships that exist between rates of redox reactions, rates of ligand-substitution reactions, the electron structure of certain transition metals, and the electron configuration of metals and metal complexes. In 1969 he described and prepared a new species of positively charged ion, called a mixed-valence cation, now known as the Creutz-Taube ion. His research on the relation between rates of substitution of oxygen atoms and electron structure in transition metals contributed to an understanding in quantum mechanical terms of cellular hydroxylation and cytochrome enzyme systems.

Publications: "Rates and Mechanisms of Substitution in Inorganic Complexes in Solution," *Chemical Reviews* 50 (1952): 69–126. "Evidence for a Bridged Activated Complex for Electron Transfer Reactions," with Howard Myers, *Journal of the American Chemical Society* 76 (1954): 2103–11. "Electron-Transfer Reactions of Ruthenium Ammines," with T. J. Meyer, *Inorganic Chemistry* 7 (1968): 2369–79. "A Direct Approach to Measuring the Franck-Codon Barrier to Electron Transfer Between Metal Ions," with C. Creutz, *Journal of the American Chemical Society* 91 (1969): 3988–89. *Electron Transfer Reactions of Complex Ions in Solution* (New York: Academic Press, 1970). "Redetermination of the Hexaaminecobalt (III/II) Electron-Self-Exchange Rate," with Anders Hammershoi and Daniel Geselowitz, *Inorganic Chemistry* 23 (1984): 979–82.

Bibliography: "Electron-Transfer Work Earns Taube a Nobel," *Chemical Week* (October 26, 1983): 15–16. "The 1983 Nobel Prize in Chemistry," *Science* (December 1983): 986–87. "Nobel Prize Winner Henry Taube Discusses His Research," *Science* (January 9, 1984): 43–44.

MERRIFIELD, ROBERT BRUCE

Prize: Chemistry, 1984. *Born:* July 15, 1921; Fort Worth, Texas. *Nationality:* American. *Education:* University of California, Los Angeles, B.A., 1943, University of California, Los Angeles, Ph.D., 1949. *Career:* Philip R. Park Research Foundation, Researcher, 1943–44; University of California, Los Angeles, Medical School, Researcher, 1948–49; Rockefeller Institute for Medical Research, New York, Researcher, 1949–57; Rockefeller University, New York, Professor, 1957–92. *Other Awards:* Lasker Award, 1969; Gairdner Award, 1970; Intra-Sci Award, 1970; Award for Creative Work in Synthetic Organic Chemistry, American Chemical Society, 1972; Nichols Medal, 1973; Alan E. Pierce Award, American Peptide Symposium, 1979; Rudinger Award, 1990.

Citation: "For his development of methodology for chemical synthesis on a solid matrix."

Life Work: Merrifield's field of investigation was protein chemistry. He devoted his efforts to the development of improved methods of peptide synthesis, such as the solid-state peptide synthesis. Using this technique, he synthesized the nonapeptide hormone bradykinin, a powerful vasodilator. He completed the first working model of an automated solid-phase peptide synthesizer in 1965. Using this device, Merrifield synthesized several peptide hormones, including bradykinin, oxytocin, and angiotensin. In 1969 Merrifield synthesized ribonuclease.

Publications: "Solid-Phase Peptide Synthesis: The Synthesis of a Tetrapeptide," *Journal of the American Chemical Society* 85 (1963): 2149–54. "Solid-Phase Synthesis of the Cyclododecadepsipeptide Valinomycin," with B. F. Gisin and D. C. Tosteson, *Journal of the American Chemical Society* 91 (1969): 2691–95. "An Assessment of Solid Phase Peptide Synthesis," *Peptides: Structural Function, Proceedings of the Amer-*

ican Peptide Symposium, 8th (1983): 33–44. "SN2 Deprotection of Synthetic Peptides with a Low Concentration of Hydrogen Fluroide in Dimethyl Sulfide: Evidence and Application in Peptide Synthesis," with James P. Tam and William F. Heath, *Journal of the American Chemical Society* 105 (1983): 6442–55. "Solid-Phase Synthesis of Cecropin A and Related Peptides," with D. Andreu and H. G. Boman, *Proceedings of the National Academy of Sciences USA* 80 (1983): 6475–79.

Bibliography: *Current Biography Yearbook* (New York: H. W. Wilson, 1985), pp. 20–22. "R. Bruce Merrifield: Designer of Protein-Making Machine," *Chemical and Engineering News* (August 2, 1971): 22–26.

HAUPTMAN, HERBERT AARON

Prize: Chemistry, 1985. *Born:* February 14, 1917; Bronx, New York. *Nationality:* American. *Education:* City College of New York, B.S., 1937; Columbia University, New York, M.A., 1939; University of Maryland, Ph.D., 1955. *Career:* United States Census Bureau, Statistician, 1940–42; United States Air Force, 1942–43, 1946–47; United States Naval Research Laboratory, Researcher, 1947–70; Medical Foundation of Buffalo, New York, Administrator, 1970–. *Other Awards:* Belden Prize, 1934; Pure Science Award, Sigma Xi, 1959; A. L. Paterson Award, American Crystallographic Association, 1984.

Citation: "For their outstanding achievements in the development of direct methods for the determination of crystal structures" (with Jerome Karle).

Life Work: Hauptman's field of investigation was X-ray crystallography. Along with Jerome Kalre, he developed a mathematical method for determining three-dimensional crystal structures of important molecules, such as hormones, vitamins, and antibiotics. By analyzing the intensity of dots shown on film, they calculated the angles at which the X rays were deflected to construct an accurate picture of the molecular structures being observed. By relating the dots to the positions of the atoms in the molecules, they reduced the time needed to construct a three-dimensional structure from years to a few days.

Publications: "The Phases and Magnitudes of the Structure Factors," with J. Karle, *Acta Cryst* 3 (1950): 181–87. "Solution of Structure-Factor Equations," with J. Karle, *Acta Cryst* 4 (1951): 188–89. *Solution of the Phase Problem I. The Centrosymmetric Crystal,* with J. Karle (Ann Arbor, Mich.: American Crystallographic Association, 1953). "A Theory of Phase Determination for the Four Types of Non-centrosymmetric Space Groups," with J. Karle, *Acta Cryst* 9 (1956): 635–51. *Table of All Primitive Roots for Primes Less than 5000* (Washington, D.C.: Naval Research Laboratory, 1970). *Crystal Structure Determination: The Role of the Cosine Seminvariants* (New York: Plenum Press, 1972).

Bibliography: *New York Times,* October 27, 1985, p. 1. *Science* 231 (January 24, 1986): 362–64.

KARLE, JEROME

Prize: Chemistry, 1985. *Born:* June 18, 1918; Brooklyn, New York. *Nationality:* American. *Education:* City College of New York, B.S., 1937; Harvard University, Massachusetts, M.A., 1938; University of Michigan, Ph.D., 1943. *Career:* Manhattan Project, Illinois, Researcher, 1943–44; United States Navy Project, Michigan, Researcher, 1944–46; Naval Research Laboratory, Maryland, Researcher and Administrator, 1946–. *Other Awards:* Pure Science Award, Sigma Xi, 1959; Navy Distinguished Civilian Service Award, 1968; Hillebrand Award, American Chemical Society, 1969; Robert Dexter Conrad Award, 1976; A. L. Paterson Award, American Crystallographic Association, 1984.

Citation: "For their outstanding achievements in the development of direct methods for the determination of crystal structures" (with Herbert A. Hauptman).

Life Work: Karle's field of investigation was X-ray crystallography. Working with Herbert Hauptman, he developed a method of constructing an electron density map of a substance showing the exact position of the atoms and, therefore, its molecular structure. When a beam of X rays is directed at a crystal, some of the rays pass through the crystal while others are deflected by the electrons surrounding rhe nuclei of the atoms. The deflected rays are recorded on film as thousands of dots forming a characteristic pattern. Through precise mathematical formulas they calculated the phase of the X-ray beam, that is, how much each of these rays had been displaced when traveling through the crystal.

Publications: "The Phases and Magnitudes of the Structure Factors," with H. Hauptman, *Acta Cryst* 3 (1950): 181–87. "Solution of Structure-Factor Equations," with H. Hauptman, *Acta Cryst* 4 (1951): 188–89. *Solution of the Phase Problem. I. The Centrosymmetric Crystal*, with H. Hauptman (Ann Arbor, Mich.: American Crystallographic Association, 1953). "A Theory of Phase Determination for the Four Types of Non-centrosymmetric Space Groups," with H. Hauptman, *Acta Cryst* 9 (1956): 635–51.

Bibliography: *New York Times*, October 27, 1985, p. 1. *Science* 231 (January 24, 1986): 362–64.

HERSCHBACH, DUDLEY ROBERT

Prize: Chemistry, 1986. *Born:* June 18, 1932; San Jose, California. *Nationality:* American. *Education:* Stanford University, California, B.S., 1954; Stanford University, California, M.S., 1955; Harvard University, Massachusetts, M.A., 1956; Harvard University, Massachusetts, Ph.D., 1958. *Career:* University of California, Berkeley, Professor, 1959–63; Harvard University, Massachusetts, Professor, 1963–. *Other Awards:*

Pure Chemistry Award, American Chemical Society, 1965; Spiers Medal, 1976; Centenary Medal, British Chemical Society, 1977; Linus Pauling Medal, 1978; Polanyi Medal, 1982; Langmuir Prize, 1983; National Medal of Science, 1991; Heyrovsky Medal, 1992.

Citation: "For their contributions concerning the dynamics of chemical elementary processes" (with Yuan T. Lee and John C. Polyani).

Life Work: Herschbach's field of investigation was molecular beam dynamics. Herschbach built an apparatus in which two molecular beams—one consisting of potassium atoms and the other of molecules of carbon, hydrogen, and iodine—crossed each other. Details of the reaction taking place at the intersection of the beams were studied with a device called a surface ionization detector. Based on the directions and recoil energies at which the reaction products emerged he found that much of the released chemical energy appeared as vibrations in the reaction products. Further reactions were studied disclosing a wide variety including mechanisms called rebound and stripping, some that were intermediate, and others that proceeded by way of formation and decomposition. The released energy appeared more in the form of internal excitation of the product molecules than in the velocities at which they traveled. To study more complex molecules with far greater precision, he and Yuan T. Lee constructed a new supermachine, a movable mass spectrometer that used nozzles to create beams. It had improved differential pumping to provide better vacuums, time-of-flight product velocity analysis and computers for data acquisition.

Publications: "Molecular Beam Kinetics: Evidence for Preferred Geometry in Interhalogen Exchange Reactions," *Journal of Chemical Physics* 51 (1969): 455–56. "Supersonic Molecular Beams of Alkali Dimers," *Journal of Chemical Physics* 54 (1971): 2393–2409. "Molecular Beam Kinetics: Reactions of Hydrogen and Deuterium Atoms with Diatomic Alkali Molecules," *Journal of Chemical Physics* 54 (1971): 2410–23. *Chemical Kinetics* (London: Butterworths, 1976).

Bibliography: *New York Times*, October 16, 1986, p. B19. *Physics Today* 40 (1987): 17–19. *Research and Development* 28 (1986): 37–38.

LEE, YUAN TSEH

Prize: Chemistry, 1986. **Born:** November 29, 1936; Hsinchu, Taiwan. **Nationality:** Chinese; later U.S. citizen. **Education:** National Taiwan University, B.S., 1959; National Tsing Hua University, Taiwan, M.S., 1961; University of California, Ph.D., 1965. **Career:** University of Chicago, Illinois, Professor, 1968–74; University of California, Berkeley, Professor, 1974–. **Other Awards:** Ernest Orlando Lawrence Award, 1981; Harrison E. Howe Award, 1983; Peter Debye Award, 1986; National Medal of Science, 1986.

Citation: "For their contributions concerning the dynamics of chemical elementary processes" (with Dudley R. Herschbach and John C. Polyani).

Life Work: Lee's field of investigation was ion molecule reactions and the dynamics of molecular scattering. Working with Dudley R. Herschbach, Lee helped to create the first new universal crossed molecular beam apparatus with a rotatable ultra-high vacuum mass spectrometer as a detector that applied magnetic and electrical fields to deflect different ions along different paths, thus separating and identifying them. The technique enabled the researchers to analyze the velocities, directions, and energies of reaction products from which they could deduce the mechanisms of reaction, the dynamics of collision between individual molecules, angular momentum in the reactions, and the distribution of chemically released energy between the velocity of flight and internal vibrations.

Publications: "Molecular Beam Kinetics: Evidence for Preferred Geometry in Interhalogen Exchange Reactions," *Journal of Chemical Physics* 51 (1969): 455–56. "Molecular Beam Kinetics: Reaction of Hydrogen and Deuterium Atoms with Diatomic Alkali Molecules," *Journal of Chemical Physics* 54 (1971): 2410–23. "Studies with Crossed Laser and Molecular Beams," *Physics Today* 33 (1980): 52–59. "Molecular Beam Studies of Elementary Chemical Processes," *Science* 236 (1986): 673–74.

Bibliography: *New York Times*, October 16, 1986, p. B19. *Science* 234 (1986): 673–74.

POLANYI, JOHN CHARLES

Prize: Chemistry, 1986. *Born:* January 23, 1929; Berlin, Germany. *Nationality:* German; later English and now Canadian citizen. *Education:* Manchester University, England, B.S., 1949; Manchester University, England, Ph.D., 1952. *Career:* National Research Council, Researcher, 1952–54; Princeton University, New Jersey, Researcher, 1954–56; University of Toronto, Canada, Professor, 1956–. *Other Awards:* Marlow Medal, 1962; Steacie Prize, 1965; Henry Marshall Tory Medal, 1977; Remsen Award, 1978; Wolf Prize, 1982; Killam Memorial Prize, 1988; Royal Medal, 1989.

Citation: "For their contributions concerning the dynamics of chemical elementary processes" (with Dudley R. Herschbach and Yuan T. Lee).

Life Work: Polanyi's life work was the molecular basis of chemical reactions. In 1958 he studied enhanced reaction rates in vibrationally excited hydrogen chloride in the hear-releasing reaction of atomic hydrogen and molecular chlorine. The excitation was chemical in origin and constituted infrared chemiluminescence. To overcome vibrational and rotational relaxation sprays of reagent gases crossed in the center of an evacuated chamber, recoding the infrared emission from newborn reaction products and then removing the products by condensation at the liquid-nitrogen-cooled vessel walls before they had time to relax. By arresting the relaxation, the researchers determined the detailed rate constants, that is, the rates at which the reaction created products with specific states of vibrational, rotational, and translational excitation. A major technological outgrowth of Polanyi's work was chemical lasers.

Publications: "Quenching and Vibrational-energy Transfer of Excited Iodine Molecules," *Canadian Journal of Chemistry* 36 (1958): 121–30. "Energy Distribution Among Reagents and Products of Atomic Reactions," *Journal of Chemical Physics* 31 (1959): 1338–51. "An Infrared Maser Dependent on Vibrational Excitation," *Journal of Chemical Physics* 34 (1961): 347–48. "Some Concepts in Reaction Dynamics," *Science* 236 (1987): 680–90.

Bibliography: *Chemical Week* 139 (1986): 8–10. *Maclean's* 99 (1986): 60. *Science* 234 (1986): 673–74.

CRAM, DONALD JAMES

Prize: Chemistry, 1987. *Born:* April 22, 1919; Chester, Vermont. *Died:* June 17, 2001; Palm Desert, California. *Nationality:* American. *Education:* Rollins College, Florida, B.S., 1941; University of Nebraska, M.S., 1942; Harvard University, Massachusetts, Ph.D., 1947. *Career:* Merck and Company, New Jersey, Researcher, 1942–45; University of California, Los Angeles, Professor, 1947–90. *Other Awards:* American Chemical Society Award, 1953, 1965; Herbert Newby McCoy Award, 1965, 1975; Society of Chemical Manufacturing Association Award, 1965; Arthur C. Cope Award, 1974; Roger Adams Award, 1985; Willard Gibbs Award, 1985; Tolman Medal, 1985; Seaborg Award, 1989; National Medal of Science, 1993.

Citation: "For their development and use of molecules with structure-specific interactions of high selectivity" (with Jean-Marie Lehn and Charles J. Pedersen).

Life Work: Cram's field of investigation was enzymes, especially their ability to recognize other molecules and bind with them. He built on the work of Charles Pedersen, who had synthesized a new type of molecule called crown ether, in which atoms of oxygen and carbon combined in an essentially ringlike shape. Its ringlike shape allowed it to bind easily with a metal ion. Pedersen's synthetic compound had a flat shape and was three-dimensional and thus provided an ideal method for Cram to develop a host-guest chemistry in which each host molecule would accept a specific guest molecule. His research has been of enormous importance in the growth of coordination chemistry, organic synthesis, analytic chemistry, and bioinorganic and bio-organic chemistry. Cram's host-guest chemistry also makes it possible to separate materials with great efficiency. Continuing to develop new forms of synthetic molecules Cram has created structures called cancerands—hemispheric molecules that bond together at their rims, thus creating prison cells that trap molecules inside.

Publications: "Chiral, Hinged, and Functionalized Multiheteromacrocycles," *Journal of the American Chemical Society* 95 (1973): 2691–92. "Chiral Recognition in Molecular Complexing," *Journal of the American Chemical Society* 95 (1973): 2692–93. "Host-Guest Chemistry," *Science* 183 (1974): 803–809. "The Design of Molecular Hosts, Guests, and Their Complexes," *Science* 240 (1988): 760–67.

Bibliography: *From Design to Discovery* (Washington, D.C.: American Chemical Society, 1990). *New York Times*, October 15, 1987, p. A14. *Science* 238 (1987): 611–12.

LEHN, JEAN-MARIE PIERRE

Prize: Chemistry, 1987. *Born:* September 30, 1939; Rosheim, Bas Rhin, France. *Nationality:* French. *Education:* University of Strasbourg, France, B.S., 1960; University of Strasbourg, France, Ph.D., 1963. *Career:* National Center for Scientific Research, France, Researcher, 1960–66; University of Strasbourg, France, Professor, 1966–69; Université Louis Pasteur, France, Professor, 1970–79; College of France, Paris, Professor, 1979–. *Other Awards:* Gold Medal, Italy, 1981; Paracelsus Prize, 1982; von Humboldt Prize, 1983; Ziegler Prize, 1989.

Citation: "For their development and use of molecules with structure-specific interactions of high selectivity" (with Donald J. Cram and Charles J. Pedersen).

Life Work: Lehn's field of investigation was supramolecular chemistry, the chemistry of the intermolecular bond, the process by which molecules recognize and react to each other. He found that the three-dimensional, flat and ringlike crown ether, synthesized by Charles Pedersen, react with other molecules at only a few contact points and thus were more selective. In 1969 Lehn succeeded in producing elaborate three-dimensional molecules, called cryptands, in the laboratory. More rigid and more complex than crown ethers, they resembled biological locks to be opened by specific molecular keys. Later, Lehn produced a synthetic molecule that acts as a host for acetyl choline, a substance in the chemical process that sends messages through the nervous system to the human brain.

Publications: "Kinetic and Conformational Studies by Nuclear Magnetic Resonance. XI. Ring Inversion in Tetrahydro–1, 3-Oxazines," *Bulletin Soc. Chim. France* 3 (1968): 1172–77. "Cryptates, Cation Exchange Rates," *Journal of the American Chemical Society* 92 (1970): 2916–18. "Cation and Cavity Selectivities of Alkali-and Alkaline-Earth Cryptates," *Journal of the Chemical Society D.* (1971): 440–41. "Cryptates," *Recherche* 2 (1971): 276–77.

Bibliography: *New York Times*, October 15, 1987, p. A14. *Science* 238 (1987): 611–12.

PEDERSEN, CHARLES JOHN

Prize: Chemistry, 1987. *Born:* October 3, 1904; Fusan, Korea. *Died:* October 26, 1989; Salem, New Jersey. *Nationality:* American. *Education:* University of Dayton,

Ohio, B.S., 1926; Massachusetts Institute of Technology, M.S., 1927. *Career:* DuPont Company, Delaware, Researcher, 1927–69. *Other Awards:* American Chemical Society Award, 1968.

Citation: "For their development and use of molecules with structure-specific interactions of high selectivity" (with Donald J. Cram and Jean-Marie Lehn).

Life Work: Pedersen's field of investigation was oxidative degradation and stabilization. At the beginning of his career he he began to search for deactivators—chemical compounds that suppress the catalytic activity of metals. This search led him to coordination chemistry, the study of how metallic ions bond with nonmetallic ions or ligands. In 1960 Pedersen discovered a new molecule in which the atoms formed an unusually large ring consisting of eighteen atoms, twelve of which were carbon rings and six were oxygen atoms with two carbons between each oxygen. The structure resembled a royal crown and Pedersen named this new molecule crown ether, or 18-crown-6. Until this time no one had ever made a synthetic compound that could form stable bonds with sodium ions. The crown ethers could also bond with other alkali metal ions, such as potassium, lithium, rubidium, and cesium. The discovery elucidated how cells transport sodium and potassium across cell membranes. Crown ethers can also be used to separate metal mixtures. Pedersen's work laid the foundation for the field of supermolecular chemistry.

Publications: "Macrocyclic Polyethers with Aromatic Groups and Their Cationic Complexes," French Patent 1,440,716 (June 3, 1966). "Cyclic Polyethers and Their Complexes with Metal Salts," *Journal of American Chemical Society* 89 (1967): 7017–36. "Macrocyclic Polyethers," British Patent 1,149,229 (April 16, 1969). "Macrocyclic Polyether Compounds and Their Ionic Complexes," German Patent 1,963,528 (July 2, 1970).

Bibliography: *New York Times*, October 15, 1987, p. A14. *Science* 238 (1987): 611–12.

DEISENHOFER, JOHANN

Prize: Chemistry, 1988. *Born:* September 30, 1943; Zusamaltheim, Germany. *Nationality:* German. *Education:* Technical University, Munich, Germany, M.S., 1971; Max Planck Institute for Biochemistry, Germany, Ph.D., 1974. *Career:* Max Planck Institute for Biochemistry, Germany, Researcher, 1974–88; University of Texas Southwestern Medical Center, Professor, 1988–. *Other Awards:* Biological Physics Prize, American Physical Society, 1986; Bayer Prize, 1988.

Citation: "For the determination of the three-dimensional structure of a photosynthetic reaction centre" (with Robert Huber and Hartmut Michel).

Life Work: Deisenhofer's fields of investigation were photosynthesis and X-ray crystallography. After colaureate Hartmut Michel crystallized the membrane-bound protein photosynthetic reaction center of the *Rhodopseudomonas viridis* bacterium, Deisenhofer and his other colaureate, Robert Huber, used X-ray crystallography to elucidate the positions of the approximately ten thousand atoms in the protein complex. In addition to its importance in the understanding of photosynthesis, the work had other applications, since membrane-bound proteins are also important in many disease states.

Publications: "X-ray Structure of a Membrane Protein Complex," with R. Huber and H. Michel, *Journal of Molecular Biology* 180 (1984): 385–98. "Structure of the Protein Subunits in the Photosynthetic Reaction Center of *Rhodopseudomonas viridis* at 3 Angstrom Resolution," with R. Huber and H. Michel, *Nature* 318 (1985): 19–26. "Experience with Various Techniques for the Refinement of Protein Structures," *Methods Enzymol* (1985): 115.

Bibliography: *Chemical Week* 143 (1988): 11–12. *New York Times*, October 20, 1988, p. B12.

HUBER, ROBERT

Prize: Chemistry, 1988. *Born:* February 20, 1937; Munich, Germany. *Nationality:* German. *Education:* Technical University, Munich, Germany, Ph.D., 1963. *Career:* Technical University, Munich, Germany, Professor, 1976; Max Planck Institute for Biochemistry, Germany, Director, 1972–. *Other Awards:* E. K. Frey Prize, 1972; Otto Warburg Medal, 1977; Emil von Behring Prize, 1982; Keilin Medal, 1987; Richard Kuhn Medal, 1987; Frey-Werle Medal, 1989; Kone Award, 1990; Krebs Medal, 1992.

Citation: "For the determination of the three-dimensional structure of a photosynthetic reaction centre" (with Johann Deisenhofer and Hartmut Michel).

Life Work: Huber's field of investigation was X-ray crystallography. He developed crystallographic techniques that are now standard in laboratories around the world. In collaboration with Hartmut Michel and Johann Deisenhofer, Huber analyzed the ten thousand atoms that make up the photosynthetic reaction center and provided a complete three-dimensional analysis of a membrane protein. This work has given theoretical chemists an indispensable tool to understand biologic electron transfer that takes place in photosynthesis.

Publications: "X-ray Structure of a Membrane Protein Complex," with J. Deisenhofer and H. Michel, *Journal of Molecular Biology* 180 (1984): 385–98. "Structure of the Protein Subunits in the Photosynthetic Reaction Center of *Rhodopseudomonas viridis* at 3 Angstrom Resolution," with J. Deisenhofer and H. Michel, *Nature* 318 (1985): 19–26. "Structural Basis for Antigen-Antibody Recognition," *Science* 233 (1986): 702–703.

Bibliography: *New York Times*, October 20, 1988, p. A1. *Physics Today* 42 (1989): 17–18.

MICHEL, HARTMUT

Prize: Chemistry, 1988. *Born:* July 18, 1948; Ludwigsburg, Germany. *Nationality:* German. *Education:* University of Wurzburg, Germany, Ph.D., 1977. *Career:* University of Wurzburg, Germany, Researcher 1977–79; Max Planck Institute for Biochemistry, Germany, Researcher, 1979–87; Max Planck Institute for Biophysics, Germany, Director, 1987–. *Other Awards:* Biophysics Prize, American Physical Society, 1986; Otto Klung Prize, 1986; Otto Bayer Prize, 1988.

Citation: "For the determination of the three-dimensional structure of a photosynthetic reaction centre" (with Johann Deisenhofer and Robert Huber).

Life Work: Michel's field of investigation was photosynthesis, the process by which plants trap energy from the sun and convert it to nutrients. Working with a membrane protein called bacteriorhodopsin, he found that it is possible to crystallize membrane proteins, even though they were not water soluble. In 1979 he produced the first three-dimensional crystals of a membrane protein. Michel turned his attention to the photosynthetic reaction center of the purple bacterium *Rhodopseudomonas viridis*, made up of four different proteins and fourteen other components bound to the bacterium's membrane. In 1981 Michel X rayed the first reaction crystal. Later, with Johann Deisenhofer and Robert Huber, he provided a complete three-dimensional analysis of a membrane protein.

Publications: "Crystallization of Membrane Proteins," *Trends in Biochemical Science* 8 (1983): 56–59. "X-ray Structure of a Membrane Protein Complex," with J. Deisenhofer and R. Huber, *Journal of Molecular Biology* 180 (1984): 385–98. "Structure of the Protein Subunits in the Photosynthetic Reaction Center of *Rhodopseudomonas viridis* at 3 Angstrom Resolution," with J. Deisenhofer and R. Huber, *Nature* 318 (1985): 19–26.

Bibliography: *New York Times*, October 20, 1988, p. B12. *Science* 242 (1988): 672–73.

ALTMAN, SIDNEY

Prize: Chemistry, 1989. *Born:* May 7, 1939; Montreal, Quebec, Canada. *Nationality:* Canadian; later U.S. citizen. *Education:* Massachusetts Institute of Technology, B.S., 1960; University of Colorado, Ph.D., 1967. *Career:* Harvard University, Massachusetts, Researcher, 1967–69; Yale University, Connecticut, Professor, 1969–.

Citation: "For their discovery of catalytic properties of RNA" (with Thomas R. Cech).

Life Work: Altman's life work was RNA, especially the structure of precursor RNA into which DNA is transcribed. Precursor RNA is made up of a transfer RNA strand with additional sequences on each end of the strand. By producing mutations in transfer RNA genes, Altman developed the first method for isolating precursor RNA from bacterial cells. Altman found that additional sequences found on each end of the precursor RNA were edited away in the enzyme, which they called ribonuclease P, which cut RNA at a very precise point. Similar work by Thomas R. Cech confirmed the discovery that RNA acts a genetic code and as an enzyme and catalyst.

Publications: *Transfer RNA* (Cambridge, Mass.: Massachusetts Institute of Technology Press, 1978). "Transfer-RNA Processing Enzymes," *Cell* 23 (1981): 3–4. "Gene Coding for a Protamine-like Protein," *Cell* 26 (1981): 299–304. "Aspects of Biochemical Catalysis," *Cell* 36 (1984): 237–39.

Bibliography: *New York Times*, October 13, 1989, p. A10. *Science* 246 (October 20, 1989): 325–26.

CECH, THOMAS ROBERT

Prize: Chemistry, 1989. *Born:* December 8, 1947; Chicago, Illinois. *Nationality:* American. *Education:* Grinnell College, Iowa, B.A., 1970; University of California, Ph.D., 1975. *Career:* Massachusetts Institute of Technology, Resident, 1975–77; University of Colorado, Professor, 1977–. *Other Awards:* Passano Foundation Award, 1984; Harrison Howe Award, 1984; Pfizer Award, 1985; U.S. Steel Award, 1987; V. D. Mattia Award, 1987; Newcombe-Cleveland Award, 1988; Heineken Prize, 1988; Horwitz Prize, 1988; Gairdner Foundation Award, 1988; Lasker Research Award, 1988; Rosentiel Award, 1989; Warren Prize, 1989; Hopkins Medal, 1992.

Citation: "For their discovery of catalytic properties of RNA" (with Sidney Altman).

Life Work: Cech's field of investigation was ribosomal RNA (rRNA), one of the three types of RNA manufactured by DNA transcription. Cech chose to study Tetrahymena rRNA genes, which are located on small, extrachromosomal DNA molecules. These molecules may be copied ten thousand times over in active cells. Cech found that much of the length of the rDNA matched the rRNA, but that there also existed addtional pieces of rDNA not found in the rRNA. These intervening pieces were called introns. In order to locate and isolate the enzyme responsible for splicing (removing the introns), Cech transcribed Tetrahymena rRNA in pre-RNA in a test tube in the absence of all cell material except cell nuclei. It was only the second time that RNA splicing had been done in the test tube. The experiments proved that RNA itself was acting as a biological catalyst or an enzyme. The pre-rRNA prepared from bacteria genetically engineered bacteria that carried a Tetrahymena rDNA gene was named ribosome, an RNA enzyme.

Publications: "RNA as an Enzyme," *Scientific American* 255 (November 1986): 64–74. "The Chemistry of Self-splicing RNA and RNA Enzymes," *Science* 236 (June 19, 1987): 1532–40. "Ribozymes and Their Medical Implications," *Journal of the*

American Medical Association (November 25, 1988): 3030–35. "Defining the Inside and Outside of a Catalytic RNA Molecule," *Science* 245 (July 21, 1989): 276–83.

Bibliography: *New York Times*, October 13, 1989, p. A10. *Science* 246 (October 20, 1989): 325–26.

COREY, ELIAS JAMES

Prize: Chemistry, 1990. *Born:* July 12, 1928; Methuen, Massachusetts. *Nationality:* American. *Education:* Massachusetts Institute of Technology, B.S., 1948; Massachusetts Institute of Technology, Ph.D., 1951. *Career:* University of Illinois, Professor, 1951–59; Harvard University, Massachusetts, Professor, 1959–. *Other Awards:* Intrascience Foudation Award, 1968; Ernest Guenther Award, 1968; Harrison Howe Award, 1971; Ciba Foundation Medal, 1972; Evans Award, Ohio State University, 1972; Linus Pauling Award, 1973; Dickson Prize, 1973; George Ledlie Prize, 1973; Nichols Medal, 1977; Buchman Award, 1978; Franklin Medal, 1978; J. G. Kirkwood Award, 1980; Wolf Prize, 1986; National Medal of Science, 1988; Japan Prize, 1989; Gold Medal Award, 1990.

Citation: "For his development of the theory and methodology of organic synthesis."

Life Work: Corey discovered the retrosynthetic analysis, which begins with the structure of the finished synthesized molecule and works backward. The molecule is conceptually dissected into progressively simpler structures, resulting in an analytic tree that branches from the target molecule back to several possible compounds. By analyzing the pathways represented by the branches, the chemist can select the appropriate process and materials for the synthesis. At Harvard from 1959, Corey performed the first successful synthesis of one of the three prostaglandin families and developed a single intermediate, known as the Corey lactone aldehyde, from which prostagladins could be synthesized. As part of his research Corey developed fifty new and improved synthetic reactions.

Publications: "General Methods for the Construction of Complex Molecules," *Pure and Applied Chemistry* 14 (1967): 19–37. "Total Synthesis of Humulene," *Journal of the American Chemical Society* 89 (1967): 2758–59. "Total Syntheses of Prostaglandins," *Proceedings of the Robert A. Welch Foundation Conference on Chemical Research* 12 (1968): 51–79. *The Logic of Chemical Synthesis* (New York: Wiley, 1989).

Bibliography: *New York Times*, October 18, 1990, p. A12. *Science* 250 (October 26, 1990): 510–11.

ERNST, RICHARD ROBERT

Prize: Chemistry, 1991. *Born:* August 14, 1933; Winterhur, Zürich, Switzerland. *Nationality:* Swiss. *Education:* ETH-Zürich, Diploma, Chemistry, 1956; D.Sc., 1962. *Career:* Varian Associates, California, Researcher, 1963–68; Federal Institute of Technology, Switzerland, Researcher, 1968–. *Other Awards:* Benoist Prize, 1986; Kirkwood Medal, 1989; Ampere Prize, 1990; Wolf Prize, 1991; Horwitz Prize, 1991.

Citation: "For his contributions to the development of the methodology of high resolution nuclear magnetic resonance (NMR) spectroscopy."

Life Work: Ernst's field of investigation was nuclear magnetic resonance (NMR), which determined the atomic composition and structure of molecules. Ernst devised a technique for improving the speed of NMR studies by submitting the samples to all the relevant radio frequencies in one quick broadband burst, making all the atoms resonate at once. The output represented the sum of all the resonances of the all the different atoms present. The individual resonances were separated out by a mathematical technique called Fourier transform. In 1971 he improved the Fourier transform NMR with a two-dimensional NMR. It involved hitting a sample with two separate bursts of radio waves. Resonances caused by the first burst are modified by the second burst.

Publications: "Recent Developments in Fourier Spectroscopy," *Pulsed Nucl. Magn. Resonance Spin Dyn. Solids, Proc. Spec. Colloq. Ampere 1st* (1973): 40–52. "Two-Dimensional Spectroscopy," *Chimia* 29 (1975): 179–83. "Recent Advances in Two-Dimensional Spectroscopy," *Proc. Colloq. Spectrosc. Int., Invited Lect., 20th* 2 (1977): 175–81.

Bibliography: *Chemical and Engineering News* 69 (October 21, 1991): 4. *Science* 254 (October 25, 1991): 518.

MARCUS, RUDOLPH ARTHUR

Prize: Chemistry, 1992. *Born:* July 21, 1923; Montreal, Quebec, Canada. *Nationality:* Canadian; later U.S. citizen. *Education:* McGill University, Canada, B.Sc., 1943; Ph.D., 1946. *Career:* National Research Council, Canada, Researcher, 1946–51; Polytechnic Institute of Brooklyn, New York, Professor, 1951–64; University of Illinois, Professor, 1964–78; California Institute of Technology, Professor, 1978–. *Other Awards:* Langmuir Award, 1978; Robinson Medal, 1982; Chandler Medal, 1983; Wolf Prize, 1985; Faraday Medal, 1988; Debye Award, 1988; Gibbs Medal, 1988; National Medal of Science, 1989; Evans Award, 1990; Hirschfelder Prize, 1993.

Citation: "For his contributions to the theory of electron transfer reactions in chemical systems."

Life Work: Marcus is credited with the Marcus Theory, which uses simple yet extremely useful equations to predict how electron energy transfer rates vary within specified parameters. In addition, these equations show rates for self-exchange transfers in molecules and those for corresponding cross-reactions. According to the theory electron transfer between reacting molecules occur only when the system is at the intersection of the reactant and product free energy curves. By increasing molecular force, the chemical reactions are actually slowed down. The Marcus Theory shed light on many complex chemical reactions, including corrosion and photosynthesis in plants.

Publications: "Theory of Oxidation-Reduction Reactions Involving Electron Transfer," *J. Chem. Phys.* 24 (1956): 966–78. "Theory of Electrochemical and Chemical Electron-Transfer Processes," *Can. J. Chem.* 37 (1959): 155–63. "Theory of Electron-transfer Reactions and of Related Phenomena," *Exchange Reactions, Proc. Symp. Upton, N.Y.* (1965): 1–6.

Bibliography: *Physics Today* 46 (January 1993): 16–20. *Science* 258 (October 23, 1992): 544.

MULLIS, KARY BANKS

Prize: Chemistry, 1993. ***Born:*** December 28, 1944; Lenoir, North Carolina. ***Nationality:*** American. ***Education:*** Georgia Institute of Technology, B.S., 1966; University of California, Ph.D., 1973. ***Career:*** Cetus Corp., California, Researcher, 1979–86; Xytronyx, Inc., California, Researcher, 1986–88; Consultant, 1988–. ***Other Awards:*** Preis Award, 1990; Allan Award, 1990; Gairdner Foundation Award, 1991; Koch Award, 1992; Chiron Corp. Award, 1992; Japan Prize, 1992.

Citation: "For contributions to the developments of methods within DNA-based chemistry" (with Michael Smith); "for his invention of the polymerase chain reaction (PCR) method."

Life Work: Mullis's field of investigation was oligopolymerides. He discovered a technique for doubling the amount of the target DNA fragment or gene in a sample. He combined DNA with the oligonucleotide primers, the DNA polymerase, and all four types of nucleotides. In a reaction that mimics the process of DNA synthesis as it occurs in nature, the nucleotide building blocks are added one by one to the primer until a new strand of DNA, complementary to the original, is synthesized. By repeating the reaction, called polymerase chain reaction (PCR), as many as a billion copies of an entire strand of DNA could be synthesized in relatively short period of time. The process was patented in 1987 followed by the invention of the Termal Cycler using PCR.

Publications: "Transcription Termination at and Tryptophan Operon Attenuator is Decreased In Vitro by an Oligomer Complementary to a Segment of the Leader Transcript," *Proc. Natl. Acad. Sci. USA* 79 (1982): 2181–85. "Isolation of a cDNA Clone for the Human HLA-DR Antigen Alpha Chain by Using a Synthetic Oligonucleotide as a Hybridization Probe," *Proc. Natl. Acad. Sci. USA* 79 (1982): 5966–70. "Enzymic

Amplification of Beta-globin Genomic Sequences and Restriction Site Analysis for Diagnosis of Sickle Cell Anemia," *Science* 230 (1985): 1350–54.

Bibliography: *Chemical and Engineering News 71* (October 18, 1993): 6. *New Scientist* 140 (October 23, 1993): 4.

SMITH, MICHAEL

Prize: Chemistry, 1993. *Born:* April 26, 1932; Blackpool, England. *Died:* October 4, 2000; Vancouver, British Columbia, Canada. *Nationality:* English; later Canadian citizen. *Education:* University of Manchester, England, B.Sc., 1953; Ph.D., 1956. *Career:* Vancouver Laboratory Fisheries Board, Canada, Researcher, 1961–66; University of British Columbia, Canada, Researcher, 1966–. *Other Awards:* Gairdner Foundation Award, 1986.

Citation: "For contributions to the developments of methods within DNA-based chemistry" (with Kary B. Mullis); "for his fundamental contributions to the establishment of oligonucleiotide-based, site-directed mutagenesis and its development for protein studies."

Life Work: Smith's work created specific mutations in the DNA allowing for customized proteins. The method he developed is site-directed mutagenesis, a process by which DNA molecule strands are manipulated and reprogrammed for changed proteins whose actions differ from those of the original proteins and can be controlled. Smith's genetic engineering techniques are used for a host of purposes, including correcting hereditary diseases, developing strains of plant life and cancer therapies. Later, Smith developed a strain of yeast that could be implanted in the human gene for insulin.

Publications: "Cellular Adaptation to the Environment," *Environ. Physiol. Anim.* (1976): 231–58. "The First Complete Nucleotide Sequencing of an Organism's DNA," *Am. Sci.* 67 (1979): 57–67. "Applications of Synthetic Oligodeoxyribonucleotides to Problems in Molecular Biology," *Nucleic Acids Symp. Ser.* 7 (1980): 387–95.

Bibliography: *Chemical and Engineering News* 71 (October 18, 1993): 6. *New Scientist* 140 (October 23, 1993): 4.

OLAH, GEORGE ANDREW

Prize: Chemistry, 1994. *Born:* May 22, 1927; Budapest, Hungary. *Nationality:* Hungarian; later U.S. citizen. *Education:* Technical University of Budapest, Hungary, Ph.D., 1949. *Career:* Technical University of Budapest, Hungary, Professor, 1949–54; Central Chemical Research Institute, Hungary, Researcher, 1954–56; Dow Chemical

Co., Canada and U.S., Researcher, 1957–65; Case Western Reserve University, Ohio, Professor, 1965–77; University of Southern California, Professor, 1977–. *Other Awards:* Baekeland Award, 1966; Morley Medal, 1977; Humboldt Award, 1979; Mendeleev Medal, 1992.

Citation: "For his contribution to carbocation chemistry."

Life Work: Olah's field of investigation was saturated hydrocarbons, especially the stabilization and recombination of carbocations—short-lived, positively charged fragments of hydrocarbon molecules that had eluded detailed study because of their instability. By using superacids (strong acids whose acidity is billions of times stronger than 100 percent sulfuric acid) to split the hydrocarbon molecules, Olah isolated and stabilized their carbocations and studied them with conventional techniques such as magnetic resonance spectroscopy. The chemistry in superacids showed that carbons in some concations bind simultaneously to five or even six other atoms. This represented the foundation for the chemistry of saturated hydrocarbon at high acidities, where such transformations as alkylization and isomerization to produce high-octane gasoline and even conversion of natural gas to higher hydrocarbons can be readily carried out.

Publications: *Carbonium Ions* (New York: Interscience Publishers, 1969–76). *Carbocations and Electrophilic Reactions* (New York: Wiley, 1973). *Superacids* (New York: Wiley, 1984). *Hydrocarbon Chemistry* (New York: John Wiley, 1995).

Bibliography: *Chemical and Engineering News* 72 (October 17, 1994): 4. *New York Times* Biographical Service, 1994, p. 1570.

CRUTZEN, PAUL J.

Prize: Chemistry, 1995. *Born:* December 3, 1933; Amsterdam, Netherlands. *Nationality:* Dutch; later German resident. *Education:* University of Stockholm, Sweden, Ph.D. *Career:* University of Stockholm, Sweden, Researcher and Professor, 1959–74; National Council on Atmospheric Research (NCAR), Colorado, Researcher, 1974–80; Max Planck Institute for Chemistry, Germany, 1980–. *Other Awards:* Szilard Prize, 1985; Tyler Prize, 1989; Volvo Prize, 1991.

Citation: "For their work in atmospheric chemistry, particularly concerning the formation and decomposition of ozone" (with Mario J. Molina and F. Sherwood Rowland).

Life Work: Crutzen's field of investigation was stratospheric ozone. After analysis of the solar spectrum Crutzen was able to derive the approximate levels of stratospheric ozone, including their vertical distribution. In his paper on the catalytic ozone destruction, Crutzen showed how the balance of the ozone layer was being destroyed by nitrogen compounds that react chemically with ozone. In addition, he showed the link between the thickness of the ozone layer and chemicals released by bacteria in the soil, indicating that the earth operates as a system linking ocean, air, and land.

Publications: "SST's Threat to the Earth's Ozone Shield," *Ambio* 1 (1972): 41–51. "Estimates of Possible Variations in Total Ozone Due to Natural Causes and Human Activities," *Ambio* 3 (1974): 201–10. "Upper Limits on Atmospheric Ozone Reductions Following Increased Application of Fixed Nitrogen to the Soil," *Geophys. Res. Lett.* 3 (1976): 169–72. *Atmospheric Change* (New York: W. H. Freeman, 1995).

Bibliography: *New York Times*, October 12, 1995, p. A1

MOLINA, MARIO J.

Prize: Chemistry, 1995. *Born:* March 19, 1943; Mexico City, Mexico. *Nationality:* Mexican; later U.S. citizen. *Education:* Academy Hispano Mexicana, B.A., 1969; University of California, Ph.D., 1972. *Career:* University Nacional Autonoma de Mexico, Professor, 1967–68; University of California, Professor, 1972–82; Jet Propulsion Laboratory, Maryland, Researcher, 1983–89; Massachusetts Institute of Technology, Professor, 1989–. *Other Awards:* Tyler Award, 1983; Esselen Award, 1987.

Citation: "For their work in atmospheric chemistry, particularly concerning the formation and decomposition of ozone" (with Paul J. Crutzen and F. Sherwood Rowland).

Life Work: Molina's field of investigation was chlorofluorocarbons (CFCs). With F. Sherwood Rowland he developed the OFC ozone depletion theory. He investigated the seasonal depletion of ozone over Antarctica as a result of the chemistry of polar atmospheric clouds, some of which consist of ice crystals. He showed that chlorine activation reactions take place very efficiently in the presence of ice under polar conditions. He was also able to link chlorine peroxide with the rapid loss of ozone in the polar atmosphere.

Publications: "Stratospheric Sink for Chlorofluoromethanes, Chlorine Atom-Catalyzed Destruction of Ozone," with F. Rowland, *Int. Conf. Environ. Impact Aerosp. Oper. High Atmos., 2nd* (1974): 99–104; *Nature (London)* 249 (1974): 810–12. "Unmeasured Chlorine Atom Reaction Rates Important for Stratospheric Modeling of Atom-Catalyzed Removal of Ozone," with F. Rowland, *J. Phys. Chem.* 79 (1975): 667–69.

Bibliography: *New York Times*, October 12, 1995, p. A1.

ROWLAND, FRANK SHERWOOD

Prize: Chemistry, 1995. *Born:* June 28, 1927; Delaware, Ohio. *Nationality:* American. *Education:* Ohio Wesleyan, A.B., 1948; University of Chicago, Illinois, M.S.,

1951; Ph.D., 1952. *Career:* Princeton University, New Jersey, Professor, 1952–56; University of Kansas, Professor, 1956–64; University of California, Professor, 1964–. *Other Awards:* Wiley Jones Award, 1975; Billard Award, 1977; Tyler Prize, 1983; Dana Award, 1987; Wadsworth Award, 1989; Japan, 1989; Dickson Prize, 1991.

Citation: "For their work in atmospheric chemistry, particularly concerning the formation and decomposition of ozone" (with Paul J. Crutzen and Mario J. Molina).

Life Work: Rowland's field of investigation was chlorofluorocarbons (CFCs). Together with Mario J. Molina, he linked the depletion of ozone to CFCs, which were brought up into the stratosphere before any ultraviolet rays could break up their molecules. They also estimated the mean atmospheric lifetime of CFCs to be 40 to 80 years for some and 7 to 150 years for others.

Publications: "Stratospheric Sink for Chlorofluoromethanes, Chlorine Atom-catalyzed Destruction of Ozone," with M. Molina, *Int. Conf. Environ. Impact Aerosp. Oper. High Atmos., 2nd,* (1974): 99–104; *Nature (London)* 249 (1974): 810–12. "Unmeasured Chlorine Atom Reaction Rates Important for Stratospheric Modeling of Atom-catalyzed Removal of Ozone," with M. Molina, *J. Phys. Chem* 79 (1975): 667–69.

Bibliography: *New York Times,* October 12, 1995, p. A1.

CURL, ROBERT FLOYD, JR.

Prize: Chemistry, 1996. *Born:* August 23, 1933; Alice, Texas. *Nationality:* American. *Education:* Rice University, Houston, Ph.D., 1951. *Career:* Rice University, Research Professor, 1958–. *Other Awards:* Clayton Prize, Institute of Mechanical Engineers, 1958; Humboldt Prize, 1984; American Physical Society International Prize for New Materials, 1992.

Citation "For their discovery of fullerenes" (with Harold W. Kroto and Richard E. Smalley).

Life Work: Curl's theory of fine and hyperfine structure provided a solid foundation for an interpretation of the spectra of stable free radicals. In 1971 Curl began working in the field of laser spectroscopy, using continuous-wave dye lasers to explore high resolution electronic spectra of small molecules. From 1979 he explored the electronic spectrum of a molecule in the process of chemical reaction by direct excitation of the reaction complex followed by fluorescence emission from an atom produced by this excitation. In 1984 he began an intensive study of semiconductor clusters.

Publications: "Probing C60," with R. E. Smalley, *Science* 49 (November 18, 1988): 247–56. "Rate and Measurement of the Recombinant Reaction *C3+H3+C3H3,*" *Journal of Physical Chemistry* 18 (1994): 192–97. "The Reaction of NH2 with O," *Journal of Physical Chemistry* 58 (1994): 79–83.

Bibliography: William H. Aldersey, *The Most Beautiful Molecule* (New York: Wiley, 1995). *American Men and Women of Science* (New Providence, N.J.: R. R. Bowker, 1996). J. Baggott, *Perfect Symmetry* (New York: Oxford University Press, 1994). *New York Times*, October 10, 1996, p. D21. *Science News* 150 (October 19, 1996): 247.

KROTO, HAROLD W.

Prize: Chemistry, 1996. *Born:* October 7, 1939; Wesbech, England. *Nationality:* British. *Education:* University of Sheffield, Ph.D., 1964. *Career:* Bell Telephone Laboratories, 1966–67; University of Sheffield, Professor, 1967–. *Other Awards:* International Prize for New Materials of the American Physical Society; Italgas, Prize for Innovation in Chemistry; Royal Society of Chemistry Longstaff Medal, Hewlett Packard Europhysics Prize, 1994.

Citation: "For their discovery of fullerenes" (with Robert F. Curl Jr. and Richard E. Smalley).

Life Work: At Rice University, Kroto, along with Robert F. Curl Jr. and Richard E. Smalley, discovered Fullerenes, hollow, spherical clusters of carbon atoms bonded together into highly symmetrical cagelike structures. Bonds in the prototype molecule $C60$ resemble the seams on a soccer ball. Geometrically it is a polygon with sixty vertices and thirty-two faces, twelve of which are pentagons and twenty of which are octagons.

Publications: "Space, Stars, C60 and Soot," *Science* 242 (November 25, 1988): 1139–45. *The Fullerenes: New Horizons for the Chemistry, Physics, and Astrophysics of Carbon*, with D. R. Walter (New York: Cambridge University Press, 1993). The Fullerenes, with J. E. Flischer and D. E. Cox (New York: Pergamon, 1993). *Molecular Rotation Spectra* (New York: Dover, 1995).

Bibliography: *Financial Times*, October 10, 1996, p. 4. *Larousse Dictionary of Scientists* (New York: Larousse, 1994). *New York Times*, October 10, 1996, p. D21. *Technology Review* 17 (January 1994): 59–63.

SMALLEY, RICHARD E.

Prize: Chemistry, 1996. *Born:* June 6, 1943, Akron, Ohio. *Nationality:* American. *Education:* Hope College, University of Michigan, Ann Arbor, B.S., 1965; Princeton University, M.S., 1971. *Career:* Rice University, Gene and Norman Hackerman Professor, 1976–. *Other Awards:* American Physical Society, 1991; United States Department of Energy, 1992; American Chemical Society, 1992; European Physical Society, 1994.

Citation: "For their discovery of fullerenes" (with Robert F. Curl Jr. and Harold W. Kroto).

Life Work: Smalley is an authority on cluster chemistry, the study of aggregates of atoms or molecules that range in size between the microscopic and the visible, especially clusters of metal atoms of potential use in electronic semiconductor materials. His laboratory instrument, the laser supersonic cluster beam apparatus, could vaporize almost any material into plasma of atoms and be used to study the remaining clusters.

Publications: "Probing 60," with Robert F. Curl, *Science* 49 (November 18, 1988): 247–56. "Great Balls of Carbon: The Story of Buckminster Fullerene," *Sciences* 18 (March/April 1991): 42–44. "Self-Assembly of the Fullerenes," *Accounts of Chemical Research* 24 (1992): 91–93.

Bibliography: "The All-Star Buckyball," *Scientific American,* 269 (September 1993): 46. *New York Times,* October 10, 1996, p. D21. *Technology Review* 17 (January 1994): 59–63.

BOYER, PAUL D.

Prize: Chemistry, 1997. ***Born:*** 1918, Provo, Utah. ***Nationality:*** American. ***Education:*** Brigham Young University; University of Wisconsin, Madison, Ph.D. ***Career:*** University of Minnesota, Professor, 1945–56; University of California, Los Angeles, Hill Professor, 1956–63; University of California, Los Angeles, Director, Molecular Biology Institute, 1965–83; University of California, Los Angeles, Professor Emeritus, Chemistry and Biochemistry, 1990–; ***Other Awards:*** American Chemical Society McCoy Award for Chemical Research, 1976; Tolman Medal, 1984; Rose Award, American Society for Biochemical and Molecular Biology, 1989.

Citation: "For their elucidation of the enzymatic mechanism underlying the synthesis of adenosine triphosphate (ATP)" (with John E. Walker).

Life Work: Boyer's fields of investigation were the chemistry and mechanism of action of enzymes, oxidative phosphorylation and photophosphorylation, especially ATP, the energy carrier in living cells. ATP consists of a molecule of adenosine linked to a chain of three phosphate groups by high-energy bonds. Removal of a phosphate group releases the stored energy for use by cells. In the process, ATP becomes adenosine diphosphate. With help from chemical energy in food, a phosphate can be added to ADP, producing more ATP.

Publications: *Enzymes* (New York: Academic Press, 1975). "Oxygen 18—Probe of Enzymic Reactions of Phosphate Compounds," with D. D. Hackney and K. E. Stempel, *Methods in Enzymology* 64 (1980): 60–83. "The Binding Change Mechanism for ATP Synthase—Some Probabilities and Possibilities," *Biochemica et Biophysica Acta* 1140 (1993): 215–50. "From Human Serum Albumin to Rotational Catalysis by ATP Synthase," *FASEB Journal* 9 (April 1995): 559–61. "The ATP Synthase—A Splendid Molecular Machine," *Annual Review in Biochemistry* 66 (1997): 717–49.

Bibliography: *New York Times,* October 16, 1997, p. A16.

SKOU, JENS C.

Prize: Chemistry, 1997. *Birth:* October 8, 1918; Copenhagen, Denmark. *Nationality:* Danish. *Education:* University of Copenhagen, Aarhus University, Denmark, Ph D *Career:* Aarhus University, Professor of Physiology, 1963–76; Aarhus University, Professor of Biophysics, 1977–.

Citation: "For the first discovery of an ion-transporting enzyme, Na+, K+-ATPase."

Life Work: Skou's field of investigation was ATP synthase, an enzyme responsible for making adenosine triphosphate (ATP), the universal energy carrier in living cells. Transport of ATPase through cell membranes helps to maintain normal concentrations of sodium, potassium, and other chemicals in cells. Sodium concentration inside cells is lower than outside, and potassium concentration is higher inside the cells than outside. When a nerve cell transmits an impulse sodium ions pour into the cell, increasing their internal concentration. They must be transported out of the cell for it to fire again. That transport requires energy, which sodium potassium ATPase acquires by detaching phosphate groups from ATP molecules. Later, more ion pumps were discovered with similar structures and functions. A calcium pump helps to control muscle contraction and a hydrogen pump produces hydrochloric acid in the stomach. Stomach ulcers and gastritis are treated by inhibiting the action of the pump enzyme.

Publications: "The Influence of Some Cations on an Adenosine Triphosphatase from Peripheral Nerves," *Biochemica et Biophysica Acta* 23 (1957): 394–401. "The Na. K-ATPase," with M. Esmann, *Journal of Bioenergetics and Biomembranes* 24 (1992): 249–61.

Bibliography: *New York Times*, October 16, 1997, p. A16.

WALKER, JOHN E.

Prize: Chemistry 1997. *Born:* 1941; Halifax, England. *Nationality:* British. *Education:* University of Oxford, Ph.D., 1970. *Career:* MRC Laboratory of Molecular Biology, Senior Scientist, Oxford, England, 1982–.

Citation: "For their elucidation of the enzymatic mechanism underlying the synthesis of adenosine triphosphate (ATP)" (with Paul D. Boyer).

Life Work: Walker's field of investigation was ATP synthase, an enzyme responsible for making adenosine triphosphate (ATP), the universal energy carrier in living cells. By means of energy-rich chemical bonds, the molecule ATP captures the chemical energy released from food and makes it available to cells for muscle contraction, transmission of nerve impulses, construction of cell components, and other processes. It serves this critical function, often described as the energy currency of cells.

Publications: "The Mitochondrial Transport Family," *Current Opinion in Structural Biology* 2 (1992): 519–26. "The Mechanism of ATP Synthesis," *Biochemist* 15 (1994): 31–35. "The Regulation of Catalysis in ATP Synthase," *Current Opinion in Structural Biology* 4 (1994): 912–18. "Structure at 2.8 Resolution of F1-ATPase from Bovine Heart Mitochonrida," *Nature* 370 (1994): 621–28.

Bibliography: *New York Times*, October 16, 1997, p. A16.

KOHN, WALTER B.

Prize: Chemistry, 1998. *Birth:* March 9, 1923, Vienna, Austria. *Nationality:* British. *Education:* University of Toronto, Canada, Ph.D., 1945; Harvard University, Ph.D., 1951. *Career:* University of California, San Diego, Professor, 1960–79; University of California, San Diego, Founding Director, Institute for Theoretical Physics, 1960–79; University of California, San Diego, Professor, Department of Physics, 1979–84, Institute for Theoretical Physics, Professor, 1984–91; University of California, San Diego, Professor of Physics Emeritus, 1991–. *Other Awards:* Buckley Prize, 1960; Davission-Germer Prize, 1977; National Medal of Science, 1988; Feenberg Medal, 1991; Niels Bohr/UNESCO Gold Medal, 1998.

Citation: "For his development of the density-functional theory."

Life Work: Kohn's field of investigation was electron density. The development of quantum mechanics in physics in the early 1900s offered chemists the potential for a deep new mathematical understanding of their science. Nevertheless, describing the quantum mechanics of large molecules, which are very complex systems, involved what appeared to be impossibly difficult computations. Chemists were stymied until the 1960s, when computers for solving these complex equations became available. Quantum chemistry, the application of quantum mechanics to chemical problems, emerged as a new branch of chemistry and is now used to study the inner structure of matter. Kohn's work was crucial in opening and guiding the development of this new field. Before Kohn, chemists thought that a description of the quantum mechanics of molecules required precise knowledge of the motion of every electron in every atom in a molecule. Kohn showed that it is sufficient only to know the average number of electrons at any one point in space, i.e., the electron density. For determining that information Kohn introduced a computational method known as the density-functional theory which is widely used as the basis for solving many problems in chemistry, such as calculating the geometrical structure of large molecules, such as enzymes.

Publications: "Theory of the Insulating State," *Physical Review* 133 (1964): A171. "Quantum Density Oscillations in an Inhomogeneous Electron Gas," with L. J. Sham, *Physical Review* 137 (1965): A1697. "Wannier Functions and Self-Consistent Metal Calculations," *Physical Review* 382 (1974): B10. "Local Density-Functional Theory of Frequency-Dependent Linear Response," with E. K. U. Gross, *Physical Review Letters* 55 (1985): 2850.

Bibliography: *New York Times*, October 14, 1998, p. A16.

POPLE, JOHN ANTHONY

Prize: Chemistry, 1988. *Birth:* October 31, 1925; Burnham-on-Sea, England. *Nationality:* British. *Education:* University of Cambridge, Ph.D., 1951. *Career:* Carnegie-Mellon University, Professor, 1964–93; Northeastern University, Professor, 1993–. *Other Awards:* Irving Langmuir Award, American Chemical Society, 1970; Harrison Howe Award, 1971; Marlow Medal, Faraday Society, 1958; Gilbert Newton Lewis Award, 1972; Morley Award, 1976; Pittsburgh Award, 1975; Pauling Award, 1977; Scientist Award, Alexander von Humboldt Fund, 1981; G. Willard Whelan Award, University of Chicago, 1981; Evans Award, Ohio State University, 1982; Wolf Prize, Jerusalem, 1992.

Citation: "For his development of computational methods in quantum chemistry."

Life Work: Pople's field of investigation was the application of quantum mechanics to the structure of molecules and theories of physical properties. Pople's research led to the discovery of a new approach for analyzing the electronic structure of molecules, based on the fundamental laws of quantum mechanics. He put the approach, called theoretical model chemistry, into a computer program that allowed scientists to create computer models of chemical reactions that were difficult or impossible to run in a laboratory. One use of such information was, in the development of new drugs, to determine how a molecule would react inside the body. In the early 1990s, Pople incorporated Kohn's density-functional theory into the program, making possible the analysis of more complex molecules. The original Gaussian 70 program was updated and marketed commercially.

Publications: *High-Resolution Nuclear Magnetic Resonance* (New York: McGraw-Hill, 1959). *Approximate Molecular Orbital Theory*, with D. L. Beveridge (New York: McGraw-Hill, 1970. *Ab Initio Molecular Orbital Theory* (New York: Wiley, 1986).

Bibliography: *Journal of Physical Chemistry* 1994 (July 12 1990): 5431–34. *New York Times*, October 14, 1998, p. A16.

ZEWAIL, AHMED H.

Prize: Chemistry, 1999. *Birth:* February 26, 1946, Damanhur, Egypt. *Nationality:* Egyptian; later U.S. citizen. *Education:* University of Alexandria, M.S., 1967; University of Pennsylvania, Ph.D., 1974; *Career:* California Institute of Technology, Linus Pauling Professor of Chemical Physics, 1976–; University of Texas at Austin, Distinguished Visiting Professor, 1977; Wayne State University, Professor, 1985–. *Other Awards:* Buck-Whitney Medal, American Chemical Society, 1985; Harrison Howe Award, 1989; King Faisal International Prize in Science 1989; Hoechst Prize, 1990; Carl Zeiss International Award, 1992; Earl K. Pyler Prize, American Physical Society,

1993; Wolf Prize in Chemistry, 1993; Medal Royal, Netherlands Academy of Arts and Sciences, 1993.

Citation: "For his studies of the transition states of chemical reactions using femtosecond spectroscopy."

Life Work: Zewail's fields of investigation were nonlinear laser spectroscopy, radiationless processes in molecules, energy transfer in solids, picosecond spectroscopy, solar photovoltaic conversion, and laser-induced chemistry. Zewail laid the foundations of new field called femtochemistry, which uses ultrafast laser flashes to probe the innermost secrets of chemical reactions. The flashes take place on the same scale in which chemical reactions occur –fs, (femtoseconds.). One femtosecond is 0.000000000000001 second, or a millionth of a billionth of a second. Femtochemistry allows scientists to study chemical reactions in slow motion, visualizing in real time what actually happens when chemical bonds break and new bonds form. During reactions, molecules are pushed over an invisible energy barrier. At the top of the barrier, called the *transition state*, they assume different forms, and substances called intermediates are formed in the split second during which a reaction proceeds from the original reactants to the final products. Zewail's femtosecond spectroscopy supplied the method to study such chemical reactions, using laser technology capable of producing light flashes lasting no more than ten femtoseconds, the same time scale as the events in chemical reactions. In femtosecond spectroscopy, molecules are mixed together in a vacuum chamber. An ultrafast laser then beams in two pulses. The first, called the pump pulse, supplies energy needed to drive the molecules up the energy barrier to the transition state. A second, weaker beam called the probe pulse is tuned to the wavelength necessary for detecting the original molecules or an altered form of the molecules. The pump pulse starts the reaction and the probe pulse examines the ongoing reaction by analyzing characteristic spectra or light patterns. Femtochemistry is increasingly important in elucidating structures of short-lived intermediates in a reaction chain.

Publications: "The Validity of the Diradical Hypothesis: Direct Femtosecond Studies of the Transition State Structures," with S. Pederson and J. L. Hurek, *Science* 266 (1944): 1359–64. *Photochemistry and Photobiology* (Newark, N.J.: Gordon & Breach, 1983). "The Birth of Molecules," *Scientific American* (December 1990): 40–46. *The Chemical Bond: Structure and Dynamics* (New York: Academic Press, 1992). *Femtochemistry: Ultrafast Dynamics of the Chemical Bond* (River Edge, N.J.: World Scientific Publishing, 1994).

Bibliography: *New York Times*, October 13, 1999, p. A18.

HEEGER, ALAN J.

Prize: Chemistry, 2000. *Birth:* January 22, 1936, Sioux City, Iowa. *Nationality:* American. *Education:* University of Nebraska, B.S., 1953; University of California, Ph.D., 1961. *Career:* University of Pennsylvania, Department of Physics, Professor,

1962–67; Laboratory for Research into Structure of Matter, Director, 1974–81; University of California, Santa Barbara, Department of Physics, Professor, 1967–82; Institute for Polymers and Organic Solids, Director, 1982–99; UNIAX Corporation, Chief Scientist, 1999–. *Other Awards:* Oliver Buckley Prize in Solid State Physics, 1983; John Scott Award and Medal, 1989.

Citation: "For the discovery and development of conductive polymers" (with Alan J. MacDiarmid and Hideki Shirakawa).

Life Work: Heeger's fields of investigation are semiconducting polymers and light emission from semiconducting polymers (both photoluminescence and electroluminescence). His main research covers spectroscopic studies (including ultrafast femtosecond time-resolved spectroscopy), quantitative measurement of photoluminescene and electroluminescence quantum efficiencies, optical gain/loss of conjugated polymer/oligomer laser materials, and photoconductivity. His work has elucidated the fundamental electronic structure of polymers as well as light-emitting diodes, light-emitting electrochemical cells and lasers, all fabricated from semiconducting polymers.

Publications: "Synthesis of Electrically Conducting Organic Polymers: Halogen Derivatives of Polyacetylene (Ch)n," with A. A. MacDiarmid and H. Shirakawa, *Journal of Chemical Society, Chemical Communications* (summer 1977). "Synthesis of Highly Conducting Films of Derivatives of Polyacetylene (CHx)," with A. A. MacDiarmid and H. Shirakawa, *Journal of the American Chemical Society* 100 (1978): 1013. *Nonlinear Optical Properties of Polymers* (Pittsburgh: Materials Research, 1988).

Bibliography: *New York Times*, October 11, 2000, p. A16.

MacDIARMID, ALAN G.

Prize: Chemistry, 2000. *Born:* 1929. *Nationality:* New Zealander. *Education:* University of New Zealand, B.S., 1953; University of Wisconsin, Ph.D., 1958; Cambridge University, Ph.D., 1961. *Career:* University of Pennsylvania, Blanchard Professor of Chemistry, 1965–.

Citation: "For the discovery and development of conductive polymers" (with Alan J. Heeger and Hideki Hirakawa).

Life Work: MacDiarmid is the codiscoverer of conducting polymers, more commonly known as synthetic metals. By chemical and electrochemical doping of polyacetylene, the prototype conducting polymer and the rediscovery of polyaniline, he established that polymer plastics can be made to conduct electricity if alternating single and double bonds link their carbon atoms, and electrons are removed either through oxidation or introduced through reduction. The extra electrons or corresponding holes can then move along the doped molecule, making the conjugated polymer conduct electricity almost as well as a metal. In 1973 he began research on polymeric materials with metallic conductivity. He has also investigated light-emitting organic polymers. Some twenty-five years after the initial discovery, conducting organic polymers are now being developed for applications ranging from light-emitting diodes in electronic displays to cheap replacements for the electronic chip. MacDiarmid's experimented with a metallic looking film of the inorganic polymer sulphur nitride. He joined with Hidecki Shirakawa and Alan J. Heeger to discover that iodine doping boosted the electrical conductivity of trans-polyacetylene 10 million times and published their results in a seminal 1977 paper. Technological opportunities for the application of these materials in such diverse areas as rechargeable batteries, electromagnetic interference shielding, antistatic dissipation, stealth applications, corrosion inhibition, flexible plastic transistors, and electrodes, electroluminiscent polymer displays, and artificial nerves and sensors have resulted from the discovery.

Publications: "Synthesis of Electrically Conducting Organic Polymers: Halogen Derivatives of Polyacetylene (CHn)," with A. Heeger and H. Shirakawa, *Journal of Chemical Society, Chemical Communications* (summer 1977). "Synthesis of Highly Conducting Films of Derivatives of Polyacetylene (CHx)," with A. Heeger and H. Shirakawa, *Journal of the American Chemical Society* 100 (1978): 1013. "Plastics That Conduct Electricity," with R. B. Kaner, *Scientific American* 106 (February 1988).

Bibliography: *New York Times*, October 11, 2000, p. A16.

SHIRAKAWA, HIDEKI

Prize: Chemistry, 2000. *Born:* 1936. *Nationality:* Japanese. *Education:* Tokyo Institute of Technology, Ph.D., 1966. *Career:* University of Tsukuba, Japan, Professor of Materials Science, 1970–.

Citation: "For the discovery and development of conductive polymers" (with Alan J. Heeger and Alan J. MacDiarmid).

Life Work: Shirakawa explored an unprecedented new area of polymer science by converting insulating polyacetylene into an electrically conducting one. This was triggered by an accident in which one of his researchers added a thousand times too much catalyst during the synthesis of a polymer, resulting in a silvery film possessing many properties of a metal. Later, he was invited to the University of Pennsylvania to work with Alan J. Heeger and Alan G. MacDiarmid on doping polyacetylene with different substances. They found that one doping regimen yielded a film whose electrical conductivity was enhanced by a factor of 10 million. Further research revelaed thatorgànic plastic could be made to glow by a process called electrolumiscence. That, in turn, led to LEDs.

Publications: "Synthesis of Electrically Conducting Organic Polymers: Halogen Derivatives of Polyacetylene (CHn)," with A. Heeger and A. A. MacDiarmid, *Journal of Chemical Society, Chemical Communications* (summer 1977). "Synthesis of Highly Conducting Films of Derivatives of Polyacetylene (CHx)," with A. Heeger and A. A. MacDiarmid, *Journal of the American Chemical Society* 100 (1978): 1013.

Bibliography: *New York Times*, October 11, 2000, p. A16.

PHYSICS

RÖNTGEN, WILHELM CONRAD

Prize: Physics, 1901. *Born:* March 27, 1845; Lennep, Germany. *Died:* February 10, 1923; Munich, Germany. *Nationality:* German. *Education:* Polytechnic, Switzerland, engineering diploma, 1868; Polytechnic, Switzerland, Ph.D., 1869. *Career:* University of Zürich, Switzerland, Researcher, 1869; University of Wurzburg, Germany, Researcher, 1870–72; University of Strasbourg, Germany, Professor, 1872–75; Agricultural Academy, Hohenheim, Germany, Professor, 1875–76; University of Strasbourg, Germany, Professor, 1876–79; University of Giessen, Germany, Professor, 1879–88; University of Wurzburg, Germany, Professor, 1888–1900; University of Munich, Germany, Professor, 1900–23. *Other Awards:* Rumford Medal, Royal Society, 1896; Royal Order of Merit, Bavaria, 1896; Baumgaertner Prize, Vienna Academy, 1896; Elliot-Cresson Medal, Franklin Institute, Philadelphia, Pennsylvania, 1897; Prix Lacaze, Paris, 1897; Mattencei Medal, Rome, 1897; Otto-Wahlbuch-Stiftung Prize, Hamburg, 1898; Order of Merit of St. Michael, I Class, 1900; Silver Medal of Prince Regent Luitpold, 1900; Barnard Medal, Columbia University, New York, 1900; Komitur of the Order of the Italian Crown, 1900; Order Pour le Merite for Science and Art, France, 1911; Helmholtz Medal, Germany, 1919.

Citation: "In recognition of the extraordinary services he has rendered by the discovery of the remarkable rays subsequently named after him."

Life Work: Röntgen's experiments led to the discovery that X rays had the ability to pass through almost all objects to different extent, depending on the thickness and density. While holding a small lead disk between the screen and a cathode tube, he made the dramatic discovery that the bones in his hand produced a dark shadow of the soft tissues of his hand. X rays not only caused fluorescence but also affected a photographic plate, which darkened after development where it had been struck by the rays.

Publications: "On a New Kind of Rays, a Preliminary Communication," *Sitzungsberichte Phys.-Med. Ges. Wurzburg* (1895): cxxxvii. "On a New Kind of Rays, Continued," *Sitzungsberichte Phys.-Med. Ges. Wurzburg* (1896): XI. "Further Observations on the Properties of X-rays," *Math. U. Naturw. Mitt. a.d. Sitzungsberichte Preuss. Akad. Wiss., Physik.-Math. Kl.* (1897): 392.

Bibliography: *Dictionary of Scientific Biography* (New York: Scribner's, 1975), vol. 11, pp. 529–31. Otto Glasser, *Dr. W. C. Roentgen* (Springfield, Ill.: Thomas, 1945). W. Robert Nitske, *The Life of Wilhelm Conrad Roentgen, Discoverer of the X-Ray* (Tucson: University of Arizona Press, 1971).

LORENTZ, HENDRIK ANTOON

Prize: Physics, 1902. *Born:* July 18, 1853; Arnhem, Netherlands. *Died:* February 4, 1928; Haarlem, Netherlands. *Nationality:* Dutch. *Education:* University of Leiden, Netherlands, B.Sc., 1871; University of Leiden, Netherlands, Ph.D., 1875. *Career:* University of Leiden, Netherlands, Professor, 1878–1912; Teyler Laboratory, Haarlem, Netherlands, Director, 1912–23. *Other Awards:* Rumford Medal, Royal Society, 1908; Copley Medal, Royal Society, 1918.

Citation: "In recognition of the extraordinary service they rendered by their researches into the influence of magnetism upon radiation phenomena" (with Pieter Zeeman).

Life Work: Lorentz's field of investigation was electrons. He developed Maxwell's electromagnetic theory of light with the hypothesis that in matter extremely small particles, called electrons, are the carriers of certain specific charges. He determined that frequencies of oscillations of electrons determined the frequencies in the emitted light. Furthermore, he suggested that a magnetic field should alter the motion of the electrons and slightly vary the oscillation frequencies, splitting the spectral lines into multiples. By the turn of the century, Lorentz was recognized as the world's leading theoretical physicist whose work embraced electricity, magnetism, optics, kinetics, thermodynamics, mechanics, statistical analysis, and hydrodynamics. In 1904 he published his best-known equations, known as Lorentz Transformations, which described a shortening of the dimensions of a moving body along the direction of motion and a change in the perception of time. The Lorentz Transformations had far-reaching consequences for physical theory and strongly influenced the development of Einstein's Theory of Relativity and quantum mechanics.

Publications: *Lectures on Theoretical Physics*, 8 vols. (London: Macmillan and Co., 1927–31). *H. A. Lorentz, Collected Papers*, 9 vols. (The Hague: M. Nijhoff, 1934–39).

Bibliography: *Dictionary of Scientific Biography* (New York: Scribner's, 1973), vol. 8, pp. 487–500. G. L. de Haas-Lorentz, *H. A. Lorentz. Impressions of His Life and Work*, trans. Joh. C. Fagginger Auer (Amsterdam: North-Holland, 1957).

ZEEMAN, PIETER

Prize: Physics, 1902. *Born:* May 25, 1865; Zonnemaire Zeeland, Netherlands. *Died:* October 9, 1943; Amsterdam, Netherlands. *Nationality:* Dutch. *Education:* University of Leiden, Netherlands, Ph.D., 1893. *Career:* University of Leiden, Netherlands, Professor, 1893–97; University of Amsterdam, Netherlands, Professor, 1897–1935. *Other Awards:* Gold Medal, Netherlands Scientific Society of Haarlem, 1892; Rumford Medal, Royal Society, 1922.

Citation: "In recognition of the extraordinary service they rendered by their researches into the influence of magnetism upon radiation phenomena" (with Hendrik Lorentz).

Life Work: Zeeman was an assistant to Hendrik Lorentz and was closely involved in the latter's experiments on light and magnetism. Zeeman proved Lorentz's hypothesis that a magnetic field would cause the electrically charged particles in matter to oscillate in different modes, with slightly different frequencies from that of the undisturbed particles and that the single spectral line would not merely broaden but split into three distinct lines. The splitting of the lines (now known as the Zeeman Effect) permitted an estimation of the ratio of the electric charge to the mass of the vibrating particle, a ratio that was surprisingly large, and a determination that the charge was negative. The name cathode rays was given to the particles flowing from the negative electrode (cathode) to the positive electrode (anode) in the discharge tube. The Zeeman Effect became an essential tool in the exploration of the atom and the determination of the magnetic field of stars.

Publications: *Researches in Magneto-Optics* (London: Macmillan, 1913). *Verhandelingen van Dr. P. Zeeman over Magneto-Optische Verschijnselen* (Leiden, Netherlands: E. Ijdo, 1921). P. Velthuys-Bechthold, *Inventory of the Papers of Pieter Zeeman* (Haarlem, Netherlands: Rijksarchief in Noord-Holland, 1993).

Bibliography: *Dictionary of Scientific Biography* (New York: Scribner's, 1973), vol. 10, pp. 524–26. *Obituary Notices of Fellows of the Royal Society of London* 4 (1944): 591–95.

BECQUEREL, ANTOINE HENRI

Prize: Physics, 1903. *Born:* December 15, 1852; Paris, France. *Died:* August 25, 1908; Le Croisic, France. *Nationality:* French. *Education:* École des Pontes-et-Chaussees, France, ingenieur, 1877; École des Pontes-et-Chaussees, France, docteur-es-sciences, 1888. *Career:* École Polytechnique, Paris, France, Professor, 1876–1908; concurrently employed at Museum of Natural History, National Administration of Bridges and Highways, and National Conservatory of Arts and Trades. *Other Awards:* Legion of Honour, France, 1900; Rumford Medal, 1908; Barnard Medal, 1908; Helmholtz Medal, 1908.

Citation: "In recognition of the extraordinary services he has rendered by his discovery of spontaneous radioactivity."

Life Work: Becquerel's field of investigation was X rays, which had been discovered earlier by Wilhelm Röntgen. His experiments led him to the discovery that uranium compounds emitted spontaneous radiation, whether they were luminescent or not. The mysterious radiation that was an intrinsic property of uranium came to be known as Becquerel rays.

Publications: "Emission de Radiations Nouvelles par l'Uranium Metallique," *Comptes Rendus de l'Académie des Sciences, Paris* 122 (1896): 1086–88. "Sur Diverses Proprietes des Rayons Uraniques," *Comptes Rendus de l'Académie des Sciences, Paris* 123

(1896): 855–58. "Sur le Rayonnement des Corps Radio-Actifs," *Comptes Rendus de l'Académie des Sciences, Paris* 129 (1899): 1205–1207. "Sur la Radioactivite de l'Uranium," *Comptes Rendus de l'Académie des Sciences, Paris* 133 (1901): 977–80. "Recherches sur Une Propriete Nouvelle de la Matiere. Activite Radiante Spontanee ou Radioactivite de la Matiere," *Memories de l'Académie des Sciences, Paris* 46 (1903).

Bibliography: *Dictionary of Scientific Biography* (New York: Scribner's, 1970), vol. 1, pp. 558–61. Albert Ranc, *Henri Becquerel et la Decouverte de la Radioactivitie* (Paris: Éditiones de la Liberte, 1946).

CURIE, MARIE (SKLODOWSKA, MARIA). *See* Chemistry, 1911, pp. 21–22.

CURIE, PIERRE

Prize: Physics, 1903. *Born:* May 15, 1859; Paris, France. *Died:* April 19, 1906; Paris, France. *Nationality:* French. *Education:* University of Paris-Sorbonne, France, license es sciences, 1875; University of Paris-Sorbonne, France, license in physical sciences, 1877; University of Paris-Sorbonne, France, doctor of science, 1895. *Career:* University of Sorbonne, France, Researcher, 1878–82; University of Sorbonne, France, Professor, 1882–1906. *Other Awards:* La Caze Prize, Académie des Sciences, 1901; Davy Medal, Royal Society, 1903; Matteuci Gold Medal, Italian Society of Sciences, 1904.

Citation: "In recognition of the extraordinary services they have rendered by their joint researches on the radiation phenomena discovered by Professor Henri Becquerel" (with Marie Curie).

Life Work: Studying Becquerel radiation (which he named radioactivity) Curie sought to find out whether any substances other than uranium compounds emit Becquerel rays. He found that pitchblende, a mineral ore, emitted more Becquerel rays than the uranium and thorium compounds in it could possibly produce. In 1898 the Curies isolated and identified two new elements responsible for the hyperradioactivity—polonium and radium. In 1902 they isolated one-tenth of a gram of radium chloride from several tons of pitchblende. The radium salt glowed with a bluish light and emitted heat.

Publications: *Oeuvres de Pierre Curie* (Paris: Gauthier-Villars, 1908).

Bibliography: M. Curie, *Pierre Curie*, trans. Charlotte and Vernon Kellogg (New York: Macmillan, 1923). *Dictionary of Scientific Biography* (New York: Scribner's, 1971), vol. 3, pp. 503–508.

STRUTT, JOHN WILLIAM (LORD RAYLEIGH)

Prize: Physics, 1904. *Born:* November 12, 1842; Lanford Grove, Essex, England. *Died:* June 30, 1919; Witham, Essex, England. *Nationality:* British. *Education:* Cambridge University, England, B.A., 1865. *Career:* Cambridge University, England, Laboratory Director, 1879–84; Royal Institute, England, Professor, 1887–1905; Cambridge University, England, Chancellor, 1908–19. *Other Awards:* Royal Medal, 1882; Bressa Prize, Italy, 1891; Hodgkins Prize, Smithsonian, 1895; Matteuci Medal, Italy, 1895; Barnard Medal, Columbia University, New York, 1895; Faraday Medal, Chemical Society, 1895; Copley Medal, 1899; Albert Medal, Royal Society of the Arts, 1905; Rumford Medal, 1914; Cresson Medal, Franklin Institute, 1914.

Citation: "For his investigations of the densities of the most important gases and for his discovery of argon in connection with these studies."

Life Work: Lord Rayleigh's field of investigation was gas densities as related to atomic weights. Studying nitrogen, he discovered that nitrogen obtained from the decomposition of ammonia was less dense than nitrogen obtained from air. He concluded that the latter was more impure than the former because it contained a small quantity of other gases. In 1895 he and William Ramsay identified the elusive gas and named it *argon*, Greek for "inert." They later found that argon contained many other inert gases, such as neon, krypton, xenon, and helium. They are collectively known as the "noble gases" because of their resistance to chemical reactions. In 1900 he published the Rayleigh-Jeans radiation law on the relationship between temperature and wavelength for blackbody radiation.

Publications: *The Theory of Sound*, 2 vols. (London: Macmillan, 1877–78). *Scientific Papers*, 6 vols. (Cambridge: Cambridge University Press, 1899–1920).

Bibliography: *Dictionary of Scientific Biography* (New York: Scribner's, 1976), vol. 13, pp. 100–107. Robert Lindsay, *Lord Rayleigh* (Elmsford, N.Y.: Pergamon, 1970). Robert John Strutt, *Life of John William Strutt* (Madison: University of Wisconsin Press, 1965).

LENARD, PHILIPP EDUARD ANTON VON

Prize: Physics, 1905. *Born:* June 7, 1862; Pressburg, Hungary. *Died:* May 20, 1947; Messelhausen, Germany. *Nationality:* Hungarian; later German citizen. *Education:* University of Heidelberg, Germany, Ph.D., 1886. *Career:* University of Heidelberg, Germany, Research, 1887–90; University of Bonn, Germany, Research, 1891–94; University of Breslau, Germany, Professor, 1894–95; Technische Hochschule, Aachen, Germany, Professor, 1895–96; University of Heidelberg, Germany, Professor, 1896–98; University of Kiel, Germany, Professor, 1898–1907; University of Heidelberg, Germany, Professor, 1907–31. *Other Awards:* Rumford Medal, Royal Society, 1904; Franklin Medal, Franklin Institute, 1905.

Citation: "For his work on cathode rays."

Life Work: Lenard's field of investigation was cathode rays. His major scientific contribution was his discovery in 1902 that a free electron (which he called a cathode ray) must have at least a certain energy to ionize a gas (or cause it to be electrically charged), by knocking a bound electron out of an atom. His estimate of the ionization potential (required energy) for hydrogen was remarkably accurate. He also proved that the photoelectric effect produces the same electrons found in cathode rays, that the photoelectrons are not merely discharged from the metal surface, but ejected with a certain velocity and that the number of emitted electrons rises with the intensity of radiation but that their velocities never exceed a certain limit.

Publications: *Uber Kathodenstrahlen* (Leipzig, Germany: J. A. Barth, 1906). *Uber Aether und Materie* (Heidelberg, Germany: C. Winter, 1911). *Uber Relativitatsprinzip, Aether, Gravitation* (Leipzig, Germany: S. Hirzel, 1920).

Bibliography: *Dictionary of Scientific Biography* (New York: Scribner's, 1973), vol. 8, pp. 180–83. *Nobel Prize Winners: Physics* (Pasadena, Calif.: Salem Press, 1988), vol. 1, pp. 87–95.

THOMSON, SIR JOSEPH JOHN

Prize: Physics, 1906. *Born:* December 18, 1856; Manchester, England. *Died:* August 30, 1940; Cambridge, England. *Nationality:* British. *Education:* Owens College, England, engineering degree, 1876; Cambridge University, England, B.A., 1880. *Career:* Cambridge University, England, Professor, 1883–1918. *Other Awards:* Royal Medal, Royal Society, 1894; Hughes Medal, 1902; Hodgkins Medal, Smithsonian Institution, 1902; Knighthood, 1908; Order of Merit, 1912; Copley Medal, Royal Society, 1914; Franklin Medal, 1923; Scott Medal, 1923; Mescart Medal, Paris, 1927; Guthrie Medal and Prize, 1928; Dalton Medal, 1931; Faraday Medal, Institution of Civil Engineers, 1938.

Citation: "In recognition of the great merits of his theoretical and experimental investigations on the conduction of electricity by gases."

Life Work: Thomson's field of investigation was conduction in gases and cathode rays. Repeating Hertz's experiments, he demonstrated that cathode rays were in fact deflected by electric fields. The deflection of the cathode rays by electric forces indicated that the particles forming the cathode rays were negatively electrified. The result removed the discrepancy between the effects of magnetic and electric forces on the cathode particles. It also provided a method of measuring the velocity of these particles. The resulting mass of the particle-electric charge ratio for the cathode ray corpuscles proved to be one thousand times larger than the corresponding value for a hydrogen ion. He had discovered a new entity, one thousand times lighter than the simplest atom. He concluded that the atom is not the ultimate limit to the subdivision of matter and went on to devise a model of the atom as a diffuse sphere of positive electrical charge in which negatively charged electrons are distributed. Between 1906 and 1914 Thomson embarked on a second great period of experimental activity. He studied canal rays or positive rays that stream toward a cathode in a discharge tube. He defined their characteristics and separated the different kind of atoms and atomic groupings present in them. He demonstrated an entirely new way of separating atoms, showing that certain atomic groups could exist even though they have no stable existence under ordinary conditions. He found that samples of the inert gas neon contained atoms with two different atomic weights. The discovery of these isotopes contributed to the understanding of the heavy radioactive elements, such as uranium and radium.

Publications: *A Treatise on the Motion of Vortex Rings* (London: Macmillan, 1883). *Elements of the Mathematical Theory of Electricity and Magnetism* (Cambridge: Cambridge University Press, 1895). *The Conduction of Electricity Through Gases* (Cambridge: Cambridge University Press, 1903). *Electricity and Matter* (Westminster, England: Constable, 1904). *The Corpuscular Theory of Matter* (New York: Scribner's, 1907). *Atomic Theory.* Oxford: Clarendon Press, 1914).

Bibliography: *Biographical Memoirs of the Fellows of the Royal Society* (London: Royal Society, 1939–41), vol. 3, pp. 587–609. *Dictionary of Scientific Biography* (New York: Scribner's, 1976), vol. 13, pp. 362–72. *Obituary Notices of Fellows of the Royal Society* (London: Royal Society, 1941), vol. 3, p. 587. Robert J. S. Rayleigh, *The Life of J. J. Thomson* (Cambridge: Cambridge University Press, 1943). J. J. Thomson, *Recollections and Reflections* (London: G. Bell, 1936).

MICHELSON, ALBERT ABRAHAM

Prize: Physics, 1907. *Born:* December 19, 1852; Strelno, Germany. *Died:* May 9, 1931; Pasadena, California. *Nationality:* German; later U.S. citizen. *Education:* United States Naval Academy, Maryland, baccalaureate, 1873. *Career:* United States Naval Academy, Maryland, Professor, 1875–79; Germany and France, Student, 1879–82; Case School of Applied Science, Ohio, Professor, 1883–89; Clark University, Massachusetts, Professor, 1889–93; University of Chicago, Illinois, Professor, 1893–1929. *Other Awards:* Rumford Medal, Royal Society, 1889; Grand Prix, Paris Exposition, 1900; Matteuci Medal, Rome, Italy, 1904; Copley Medal, Royal Society, 1907; Elliott Cresson Medal, 1912; Draper Medal, National Academy of Sciences, 1916.

Citation: "For his optical precision instruments and the spectroscopic and metrological investigations carried out with their aid."

Life Work: Michelson invented the interferometer, an apparatus that uses the interference of light to measure various phenomena involving light. In 1881, working in Berlin, he succeeded in using the interferometer to detect the earth's motion through ether. He proved that the hypothesis of a stationary ether is incorrect. He repeated the experiment in collaboration with Edward W. Morley in 1887. The resulting Michelson-Morley experiment confirmed that the speed of light was unaffected by the motion of the earth. Later, at Clark University, he used the interferometer to define the length of a meter in terms of the wavelength of one of the spectral lines of cadmium. Between 1887 and 1897 he conducted research on light emitted by excited atoms. He discovered that almost all spectral lines were composed of a number of closely spaced sublines, a phenomenon that was later explained by quantum theory.

Publications: *Velocity of Light* (Chicago: University of Chicago Press, 1902). *Light Waves and Their Uses* (Chicago: University of Chicago Press, 1903). *Studies in Optics* (Chicago: University of Chicago Press, 1927).

Bibliography: *Biographical Memoirs. National Academy of Sciences* (Washington, D.C.: National Academy of Sciences, 1938), vol. 19, pp. 120–47. *Dictionary of Scientific Biography* (New York: Scribner's, 1974), vol. 9, pp. 371–74. Dorothy M. Livingston, *The Master of Light: A Biography of Albert A. Michelson* (New York: Scribner's, 1973).

LIPPMANN, GABRIEL JONAS

Prize: Physics, 1908. *Born:* August 16, 1845; Hollerich, Luxembourg. *Died:* July 13, 1921; at sea. *Nationality:* French. *Education:* Heidelberg University, Germany, Ph.D.; University of Paris-Sorbonne, France, D.Sc., 1875. *Career:* Sorbonne University, Paris, France, Professor, 1878–1921.

Citation: "For his method of reproducing colours photographically based on the phenomenon of interference."

Life Work: Lippmann's field of investigation was electrocapillarity. His investigations into the production of electricity by mechanically deforming the mercury surface led him to a general theory, published in 1881, that knowledge of a particular physical phenomenon enables the prediction of the existence and magnitude of its converse. He applied this insight to piezoelectricity, the generation of electricity by the compression or expansion of certain crystals, such as quartz. Mechanical forces change the crystal dimensions as they produce electric charge. In 1891 Lippmann demonstrated a method for producing permanent color photographs using the principle of interference. Lippmann's plates were clear glass coated on one side with a relatively thick photosensitive emulsion. The plateholder, during an exposure, backed the uncoated glass face with mercury, forming a shiny, reflective surface. Color-linked interference patterns between incoming light from the object and reflected light from the mercury became fixed in the distribution of silver grains produced chemically during development.

Publications: "Extension du Principe de Carnot a la Theorie des Phenomenes Electriques," *Comptes Rendus de l'Académie des Sciences* 82 (1876): 1425. "Photographies Colorees du Spectre, sur Albumine et sur Gelatine Bichromatees," *Comptes Rendus de* *l'Académie des Sciences* 115 (1892): 575. "Sur un Coelostat," *Comptes Rendus de l'Académie des Sciences* 120 (1895): 1015.

Bibliography: *Annales de Physique* 16 (1921): 156. *Dictionary of Scientific Biography* (New York: Scribner's, 1981), vol. 7, pp. 387–88. Ernest Lebon, *Gabriel Lippmann* (Paris: Gauthier-Villars, 1911).

BRAUN, CARL FERDINAND

Prize: Physics, 1909. *Born:* June 6, 1850; Fulda, Germany. *Died:* April 20, 1918; Brooklyn, New York. *Nationality:* German. *Education:* University of Berlin, Germany, Ph.D., 1872. *Career:* University of Wurzburg, Germany, Researcher, 1872–74; St. Thomas Gymnasium, Leipzig, Germany, Professor, 1874–76; University of Marburg, Germany, Professor, 1876–80; University of Strasbourg, France, Professor, 1880–83; Technical High School, Karlsruhe, Germany, Professor, 1883–85; University of Tübingen, Germany, Professor, 1885–95; University of Strasbourg, France, Professor, 1895–1915.

Citation: "In recognition of their contributions to the development of wireless telegraphy" (with Guglielmo Marconi).

Life Work: Braun's field of investigation was wireless telegraphy. Guglielmo Marconi had devised a transmitter that sent wireless messages through the air, but it had a range of only nine miles. Braun developed a transmitter, employing a sparkless antenna circuit with a superior range. Power from the Braun transmitter, generated in an oscillatory circuit, was coupled magnetically to the antenna circuit by a transformer effect instead of including the antenna directly in the power circuit. An essential feature of the Braun system was the inclusion of a condenser in the circuit containing the spark gap. At the receiver Braun used direct coupling between the condenser circuit and the aerial; through resonance the oscillations from the transmitting station produced the maximum effect at the receiving station. In 1899 he founded Professor Braun's Telegraph Company, which developed other innovations including the crystal detector, a forerunner of the transistor.

Publications: *Uber den Einfluss von Steifigkeit, Befestigung und Amplitude auf die Schwingungen von Saiten* (Berlin: Druck von G. Schade, 1872). *Uber Elektrische Kraftubertragung Inbesondere uber Drehstrom* (Tübingen, Germany: H. Laupp'sche Buchhandlung, 1892). *Drahtlose Telegraphie durch Wasser und Luft* (Leipzig, Germany: Veit and Co., 1901). *Anleitung fur das Photographieren von Tieren* (Berlin: Deutsche Landwirtschafts-Gesellschaft, 1927).

Bibliography: *Dictionary of Scientific Biography* (New York: Scribner's, 1970), vol. 2, pp. 427–28. *Nobel Prize Winners: Physics* (Pasadena, Calif.: Salem Press, 1988), vol. 1, pp. 137–45.

MARCONI, GUGLIELMO

Prize: Physics, 1909. *Born:* April 25, 1874; Bologna, Italy. *Died:* July 20, 1937; Rome, Italy. *Nationality:* Italian. *Education:* No college degrees. *Career:* Inventor and Entrepreneur, Italy. *Other Awards:* Order of Saint Anne, Russia, 1900; Commander of the Order of Saint Maurice and Saint Lazarus, 1902; Grand Cross of the Order of the Crown of Italy, 1902; Freedom of the City of Rome, 1903; Grand Cross Order of Alphonso XII, 1907; Grand Cordon Order of the Rising Sun, 1907; Albert Medal, Royal Society of Arts, 1910.

Citation: "In recognition of their contributions to the development of wireless telegraphy" (with Carl Braun).

Life Work: Marconi's field of investigation was wireless telegraphy. He sent his initial messages across the English Channel using a battery of antennas, each 150 feet high. To give the signal more energy, he added a condenser and tuning coils to the transmitter. The condenser magnified the effect of the oscillations produced by the sparking apparatus and the coils induced the antenna to oscillate precisely to the period of the enhanced oscillations. Tuned to one another, these two circuits prevented destructive interference and minimized signal diminution. At the same time he improved signal reception by adding tuning coils to the receiver. In 1902 Marconi sent the first wireless message across the Atlantic, and in 1907 he opened the first transatlantic commercial wireless service. In 1905 he patented a directional aerial and, in 1912, an improved timed spark system for generating transmission waves.

Publications: "Wireless Telegraphy," *Proceedings of the Institution of Electrical Engineers* 28 (1899): 273. "Wireless Telegraphy," *Proceedings of the Royal Institution of Great Britain* 16 (1899–1901): 247–56. "Syntonic Wireless Telegraphy," *Royal Society of Arts Journal* 49 (1901): 505. "The Progress of Electric Space Telegraphy," *Proceedings of the Royal Institution of Great Britain* 17 (1902–1904): 195–210. "Recent Advances in Wireless Telegraphy," *Proceedings of the Royal Institution of Great Britain* 18 (1905–1907): 31–45.

Bibliography: B. Birch, *Gugliemo Marconi* (New York: Exley, 1990). B. L. Jacot de Boinod and D. M. B. Collier, *Marconi: Master of Space* (London: Hutchinson, 1935). *Dictionary of Scientific Biography* (New York: Scribner's, 1974), vol. 9, pp. 98–99. Orrin E. Dunlap Jr., *Marconi: The Man and His Wireless* (New York: Macmillan, 1937). Degna Marconi, *My Father, Marconi* (New York: McGraw-Hill, 1962).

WAALS, JOHANNES DIDERIK VAN DER

Prize: Physics, 1910. *Born:* November 23, 1837; Leiden, Netherlands. *Died:* March 8, 1923; Amsterdam, Netherlands. *Nationality:* Dutch. *Education:* Leiden University,

Netherlands, Teaching Certificate, 1865; Leiden University, Netherlands, Doctorate, 1873. *Career:* High School Teacher, Deventer, Netherlands, 1864–66; Teacher and Principal, The Hague, Netherlands, 1866–77; University of Amsterdam, Netherlands, Professor, 1877–1907.

Citation: "For his work on the equation of state for gases and liquids."

Life Work: Van der Waals is best noted for the equation that bears his name. It related to the kinetic theory of gases and held that the attraction between molecules gives rise to an internal pressure that tends to hold the population of molecules together. As the volume increases due to an increase in externally applied pressure, the internal pressure increases much faster. If it equals or exceeds the external pressure, the molecules cling together without an external pressure. At that point the gas liquefies. There are no essential differences between a gas and a liquid because both are governed by the same forces. His equation applied to all gases, depending in each case only on the critical temperature, pressure, and volume, and not on the nature of the gas. This was the basis for his Law of Corresponding States, which makes it possible to calculate the state of any gas or liquid for any temperature and pressure if its critical temperature is known.

Publications: *Over de Continuiteit van den Gasen-Vloeistoftoestand* (Leiden, Netherlands: A. W. Sijthoff, 1873). *Le Continuitat des Gasformigen und Flussigen Zustandes* (Leipzig, Germany:J. A. Barth, 1881). *Lehrbuch der Thermodynamik in Ihrer Anwendung auf das Gleichgewicht von System mit Gasformig-flussigen Phasen* (Leipzig, Germany: Maas und Van Suchtelen, 1908). *De Relativiteitstheorie* (Haarlem, Netherlands: F. Bohn, 1923). *Lehrbuch der Thermostatik, das Heisst, des Thermischen Gleich Gewichtes Materieller System* (Leipzig, Germany: J. A. Barth, 1927).

Bibliography: *Dictionary of Scientific Biography* (New York: Scribner's, 1976), vol. 4, pp. 109–11. R. E. Oesper, "Johannes Diderik van der Waals," *Journal of Chemical Education* 31 (1954): 599.

WIEN, WILHELM CARL WERNER OTTO FRITZ FRANZ

Prize: Physics, 1911. *Born:* January 13, 1864; Gaffken, Germany. *Died:* August 30, 1928; Munich, Germany. *Nationality:* German. *Education:* University of Berlin, Germany, Ph.D., 1886. *Career:* Germany, Landowner, 1886–90; State Physico-Technical Institute, Germany, Researcher, 1890–96; Technische Hochschule, Aachen, Germany, Professor, 1896–99; University of Giessen, Germany, Professor, Professor, 1896–99; University of Giessen, Germany, Professor, 1899–1900; University of Wurzburg, Germany, Professor, 1900–20; University of Munich, Germany, Professor, 1920–28.

Citation: "For his discoveries regarding the laws governing the radiation of heat."

Life Work: Wien's field of investigation was hydrodynamics, especially the behavior of sea waves and cyclones, and thermal radiation, the emissions of bodies due to their temperature. In 1893 Wien investigated blackbody radiation based on the laws of thermodynamics. He calculated changes in temperature affecting the energy radiated at each different wavelength or color. A heated body emits radiation over a range, or spectrum, of wavelengths, but not uniformly. The curve of radiated energy versus wavelength shifts to shorter or longer wavelengths as the temperature rises or falls, in accordance with what is now known as Wien's Displacement Law. The wavelength at the peak of radiation multiplied by the absolute temperature remains a constant. Since the curve retains its basic shape as the temperature changes, knowledge of the curve at any one temperature permits a construction of the curve at any other temperature on the basis of Wien's law. In 1896 Wien extended his calculations to a theoretical explanation of the shape of the energy distribution curve to formulate Wien's Distribution Law. Investigating the discharge of electricity through gases at very low pressure through vacuum tubes, Wien established that cathode rays were particles carrying negative electric charge and canal rays were positively charged atoms or ions of residual gases in the discharge tubes.

Publications: *Lehrbuch der Hydrodynamik* (Leipzig, Germany: S. Hirzel, 1900). *Kanalstrahlen* (Leipzig Germany: Akademische Verlagsgesellschaft, 1917). *Aus Dem Leben und Wirken eines Physikers* (Leipzig, Germany J. A. Barth, 1930).

Bibliography: *Ausdem Leben und Wirken Eines Physikers* (Berlin: Deutsches Verlags, 1930). *Deutsches Biographisches Jahrbuch* (Berlin: Deutsches Verlags, 1931), vol. 10, pp. 302–10. *Dictionary of Scientific Biography* (New York: Scribner's, 1976), vol. 14, pp. 337–42. Max Steenbeck, *Wilhelm Wien und Sein Einfluss auf die Physik Seiner Zeit* (Berlin: Akademie-Verlag, 1964).

DALÉN, NILS GUSTAF

Prize: Physics, 1912. *Born:* November 30, 1869; Stenstorp, Sweden. *Died:* December 9, 1937; Lidingo, Sweden. *Nationality:* Swedish. *Education:* Chalmers Tekniska Hogskola, Sweden Civil Engineering Degree, 1896. *Career:* Laval Steam Turbine Co., Sweden, Researcher, 1897–1900; Swedish Carbide and Acetylene Co., Sweden, Administrator and Researcher, 1901–1903; Gas Accumulator Co., Engineer and Researcher, 1906–12; Inventor, 1912–37. *Other Awards:* Morehead Medal, International Acetylene Association, 1933.

Citation: "For his invention of automatic regulators for use in conjunction with gas accumulators for illuminating lighthouses and buoys."

Life Work: Dalén's principal legacy is the gas accumulator, which is a unit comprising acetylene, acetone, porous mass, and container. His device contained a substance called aga, which could be transported without danger of detonation from shock. He made another improvement when he invented a regulator to control the pressure of the gas inside the container. Later, he devised the sun valve that assured the accumulator provided gas only at night or in overcast weather.

Publications: *Chemische Technologie de Papiers* (Leipzig, Germany: J. A. Barth, 1911).

Bibliography: *Biographical Encyclopedia of Scientists* (New York: Facts on File, 1981), p. 179. *Svensk Biografiskt Lexikon* (Stockholm: Albert Bonners Forlag 1931), vol. 3, pp. 36–50. Erik Wastberg, *Gustaf Dalén* (Stockholm: Hokerberg, 1938).

KAMERLINGH ONNES, HEIKE

Prize: Physics, 1913. *Born:* September 21, 1853; Groningen, Netherlands. *Died:* February 21, 1926; Leiden, Netherlands. *Nationality:* Dutch. *Education:* University of Groningen, Netherlands, Candidates Degree, 1871; University of Heidelberg, Germany, Ph.D., 1879. *Career:* University of Leiden, Netherlands, Professor, 1882–1923. *Other Awards:* Rumford Medal, Royal Society, 1912.

Citation: "For his investigations on the properties of matter at low temperatures which led, inter alia, to the production of liquid helium."

Life Work: Kamerlingh Onnes's field of investigation was cryogenics, the study of the effects of low temperatures. Between 1906 and 1908 he was able to produce liquid hydrogen and liquid helium. Using liquid helium, he achieved temperatures as low as $1.04°K$. He investigated the properties of substances at these low temperatures, especially the absorption spectra of elements, the phosphorescence of various compounds, the viscosity of liquefied gases, and their magnetic properties. His most important discovery came in 1911, when he observed that the electrical resistance of some metals completely vanishes at low temperatures. This phenomenon is called superconductivity.

Publications: "Algemeene Theorie der Vloeistoffen" ["General Theory of Fluids"], *Verhandelingen der Kon. Akademie van Wetenschappen (Amsterdam)* 21 (1881): 9. "On the Cryogenic Laboratory at Leiden and on the Production of Very Low Temperatures," *Communications from the Laboratory of Physics at the University of Leiden* 14 (1894). "The Liquefaction of Helium," *Communications from the Physical Laboratory at the University of Leiden* 108 (August 1908); translated from *Bijvoegsel aan het Verslag van de Gewone Vergadering der Wis-en Naturkundige Afdeeling der Kon. Akademie van Wetenschappen te Amsterdan* (June 1908): 163–79. "Further Experiments with Liquid Helium. G. On the Electrical Resistance of Pure Metals, etc. VI. On the Sudden Change in the Rate at Which the Resistance of Mercury Disappears," *Communications from the Physical Laboratory of the University of Leiden* 124c (December 1911); translated from *Verslagen van de Afdeeling Naturrkunde der Kon. Akademie van Wetenschappen te Amsterdam* (December 30, 1911): 799–802. "Further Experiments with Liquid Helium. P. On the Lowest Temperature Yet Obtained," *Transactions of the Faraday Society* 18, (December 1922); part 2, reprinted in *Communications from the Physical Laboratory of the University of Leiden* 159 (1922): 3–32. *Through Measurement to Knowledge* (London: Kluwer Academic Publishers, 1991).

Bibliography: *Dictionary of Scientific Biography* (New York: Scribner's, 1973), vol. 7, pp. 220–22. "Heike Kamerlingh Onnes—1853–1926," *Proceedings of the Royal Society* A113 (January 1927): i–vi.

LAUE, MAX THEODOR FELIX VON

Prize: Physics, 1914. *Born:* October 9, 1879; Pfaffendorf, Germany. *Died:* April 24, 1960; Berlin Germany. *Nationality:* German. *Education:* University of Berlin, Germany, Dr. Phil., 1903. *Career:* University of Berlin, Germany, Professor, 1906–1909; University of Munich, Germany, Professor, 1909–12; University of Zürich, Switzerland, Professor, 1912–14; University of Frankfurt am Main, Germany, Professor, 1914–18; University of Berlin, Germany, Professor and Administrator, 1919–43; University of Göttingen, Germany, Professor and Administrator, 1946–51; Fritz Haber Institute of Physical Chemistry, Berlin, Germany, Director, 1951–58. *Other Awards:* Max Planck Medal, German Physical Society, 1932; Bimala-Churn-Law Gold Medal, Indian Association for the Cultivation of Science, India, 1950; Knight, Ordre Pour le Merité, 1952; Grand Cross with Star for Federal Service, 1953; Officer of the Legion of Honour, France, 1957.

Citation: "For his discovery of the diffraction of X rays by crystals."

Life Work: Laue's field of investigation was to determine whether X rays were a form of electromagnetic radiation with a very short wavelength. Laue proved that X rays were indeed electromagnetic waves, like light, in which, scattered by individual atoms, they would emerge from a crystal in many directions and create a diffraction pattern consisting of points of reinforcement, where the rays converged in phase and areas of destructive interference, where rays converged more or less out of phase. The Laue Diagram showed true electromagnetic wave interference in which waves passing through the dark points all had the same wavelength, even when the incident X rays contained a mixture of different wavelengths.

Publications: "Interferenzerscheinungen bei Rontgenstrahlen," with W. Friedrich and P. Knipping, *Bayerische Akademie der Wissenschaften zu Munchen. Sitzungsberichte Mathematisch-Physikalischen Klasse* (June 1912): 303–22. "Eine Quantitative Prufung der Theorier fu die Interferenzerscheinungen bei Rontgenstrahenlen," *Bayerische Akademie der Wissenschaften zu Munchen. Sitzungsberichte Mathematisch-Physikalischen Klasse* (July 1212): 363–73. *Bayerische Akademie der Wissenschaften zu Munchen. Sitzungsberichte Mathematisch-Physikalischen Klasse* (1913): 971–88. *Uber die Auffindung der Rontgenstrahlinterferenzen* (Karlsruhe, Germany: C. F. Mullersche Hofbuchhandlung, 1920). *Die Relativitatstheorie* [*The Theory of Relativity*], 2 vols. (Braunschweig, Germany: F. Vieweg & Sohn, 1921). *Rontgenstrahlinterferenzen* [*X-ray Interference*] (Leipzig, Germany: Akademische Verlagsgesellschaft, 1941). *Gerschichte der Physik* (Bonn: Universitäts Verlag, 1946); *History of Physics*, trans. Ralph Oesper (New York: Academic Press, 1950). *Theorie der Supraleitung* (Berlin: Springer,

1947); *Theory of Superconductivity*, trans. Lothar Meyer and William Band (New York: Academic Press, 1952).

Bibliography: *Biographical Memoirs of the Fellows of the Royal Society* (London: Royal Society, 1960), vol. 6, pp. 135–56. *Dictionary of Scientific Biography* (New York: Scribner's, 1973), vol. 8, pp. 50–53. "My Development as a Physicist: An Autobiography," in *Fifty Years of X-ray Diffraction*, by Peter Paul Ewald (Utrecht, Netherlands: N. V. A. Obsthoek's Uitgeversmaatschappy, 1962), pp. 278–307.

BRAGG, SIR WILLIAM HENRY

Prize: Physics, 1915. *Born:* July 2, 1862; Westward, Cumberland, England. *Died:* March 12, 1942; London, England. *Nationality:* British. *Education:* Cambridge University, England, M.A., 1884. *Career:* University of Adelaide, Australia, Professor, 1885–1909; Leeds University, England, Professor, 1909–15; University of London, England, Professor, 1915–25; Royal Institution, England, Professor and Administrator, 1923–42. *Other Awards:* Barnard Gold Medal, Columbia University, New York, 1915; Rumford Medal, Royal Society, 1915; Gold Medal, Societa Italiana de Scienze, 1917; Knighthood, 1920; Copley Medal, Royal Society, 1930; Franklin Medal, Franklin Institute, 1930; Faraday Medal, Institution of Electrical Engineers, 1936; John J. Carty Medal, National Academy of Sciences, 1938; Institute of Metals Medal, 1939.

Citation: "For their services in the analysis of crystal structure by means of X rays" (with W. L. Bragg).

Life Work: Bragg's field of investigation was X-ray diffraction. Bragg investigated the penetrative power of alpha particles, which are emitted from all radioactive atoms as they decay, that is, as their nuclei disintegrate into nuclei of other atoms. He found that the alpha particles emitted by a given radioactive substance form well-defined groups, with all the particles in one group traveling the same distance before being absorbed. Alpha particles are emitted with only certain initial velocities. The radioactive parent nucleus disintegrates in stages, each intermediate daughter nucleus emitting an alpha particle with a different initial velocity. The distance an alpha particle traveled could identify the type of nucleus from which the particle came. Bragg invented an instrument called an X-ray spectrometer for detecting and measuring wavelengths of diffracted X rays. Working with his son, W. L. Bragg, he determined the structure of various crystals. They discovered that compounds such as sodium chloride are composed not of molecules but of arrays of sodium ions. Together, father and son laid the foundations of X-ray crystallography.

Publications: *Studies in Radioactivity* (London: Macmillan, 1912). "X-rays and Crystal Structure," *Science* (December 14, 1914): 795–802. *An Introduction to Crystal Analysis* (London: Bell and Sons, Ltd., 1928). *The Crystalline State*, with W. L. Bragg, 4 vols. (London: G. Gell, 1933–53). *Atomic Structure of Minerals*, with W. L. Bragg (London: Oxford University Press, 1937).

Bibliography: Gwendolyn M. Caroe, *William Henry Bragg. 1862–1942* (Cambridge: Cambridge University Press, 1978). *Dictionary of Scientific Biography* (New York: Scribner's, 1970), vol. 2, pp. 397–400. *Obituary Notices of the Fellows of the Royal Society* (London: Royal Society, 1943), vol. 4, pp. 277–300.

BRAGG, SIR WILLIAM LAWRENCE

Prize: Physics, 1915. *Born:* March 31, 1890; Adelaide, Australia. *Died:* July 1, 1971; Ipswich, England. *Nationality:* British. *Education:* University of Adelaide, Australia, M.A., 1908; Cambridge University, England, M.A., 1912. *Career:* Cambridge University, England, Professor, 1914–15; British Army, 1915–19; Manchester University, England, Professor, 1919–37; National Physical Laboratory, England, Director, 1937–38; Cambridge University, England, Professor, 1938–53; Royal Institution, England, Professor and Administrator, 1954–65. *Other Awards:* Barnard Gold Medal, Columbia University, New York, 1915; Gold Medal, Societa Italiana di Scienze, 1917; Military Cross, 1918; Hughes Medal, Royal Society, 1931; Knighthood, 1941; Royal Medal, Royal Society, 1946; Roebling Medal, Mineral Society of America, 1948; Commander, Order of Leopold of Belgium, 1961.

Citation: "For their services in the analysis of crystal structure by means of X rays" (with W. H. Bragg).

Life Work: Bragg's field of investigation was X-ray diffraction. He proposed that specific diffraction patterns of atoms in crystals are due to the specific arrangement of the atoms in different kinds of crystals. In 1913 he published an equation, later called Bragg's Law, that described the angles at which an X-ray beam should be aimed to determine the structure of a crystal from the diffraction of X rays reflected off the crystal's planes. Bragg used the equation to analyze various crystals using the X-ray spectrometer invented by his father, W. H. Bragg. Their investigations established the distinction between molecular compounds and ionic compounds. By creating a standard procedure for X-ray analysis, the Braggs laid the foundation of X-ray crystallography.

Publications: *X-rays and Crystal Structure*, with W. H. Bragg (London: G. Bell and Sons, 1915). *The Crystalline State*, with W. H. Bragg, 4 vols. (London: G. Bell, 1933–53). *Atomic Structure of Minerals*, with W. H. Bragg (London: Oxford University Press, 1937). *The Development of X-Ray Analysis* (London: G. Bell, 1975).

Bibliography: *Biographical Memoirs of the Fellows of the Royal Society* (London: Royal Society, 1975), pp. 75–143. *Dictionary of Scientific Biography* (New York: Scribner's, 1978), vol. 15, pp. 61–64. *The Legacy of Sir Lawrence Bragg* (Northwood, England: Science Reviews, Ltd., 1990). "Reminiscences of Fifty Years of Research," *Proceedings of the Royal Institution of Great Britain* 41 (1966): 92–100.

BARKLA, CHARLES GLOVER

Prize: Physics, 1917. *Born:* June 27, 1877; Widness, Lancashire, England. *Died:* October 23, 1944; Edinburgh, Scotland. *Nationality:* British. *Education:* University of Liverpool, England, B.Sc., 1898; University of Liverpool, England, M.Sc., 1899; Cambridge University, England, B.A., 1901; University of Liverpool, England, D.Sc., 1904. *Career:* University of Liverpool, England, Researcher, 1905–1909; University of London, England, Professor, 1909–13; University of Edinburgh, Scotland, Professor, 1913–44. *Other Awards:* Hughes Medal, 1917.

Citation: "For his discovery of the characteristic Röntgen radiation of the elements."

Life Work: Barkla's field of investigation was X rays. His experiments proved that X rays are pulses of electromagnetic waves resulting from the deceleration of electrons striking the anode of a cathode-ray tube. In 1903 Barkla published a work on secondary radiation, that is, radiation emitted whenever X rays fall upon a substance due entirely to the scattering of the primary beam. He found that the scattering increased proportionally to the presumed atomic weight of the scattering substance. He showed that the secondary radiation has two components: unchanged X rays scattered from the primary beam (called K radiation) and less penetrating or softer radiation (called L radiation) produced by and characteristic of the scattering substance. The softer (or characteristic radiation) increases in penetrating power according to the position of the X-radiated element in the periodic table.

Publications: "Secondary Roentgen Radiation," *Philosophical Magazine*, 6th series, 11 (June 1906): 812–28. "The Spectra of the Fluorescent Roentgen Radiations," *Philosophical Magazine* 22 (September 1911): 396–412. *Radiation and Matter* (Greenock, England: Telegraph Printing Works, 1920).

Bibliography: *Dictionary of Scientific Biography* (New York: Scribner's, 1970), vol. 1, pp. 456–59. *Obituary Notices of Fellows of the Royal Society of London* (London: Royal Society, 1947), pp. 341–66. Reginald Stephenson, "The Scientific Career of Charles Glover Barkla," *American Journal of Physics* 35 (February 1967): 141–52.

PLANCK, MAX KARL ERNST LUDWIG

Prize: Physics, 1918. *Born:* April 23, 1858; Kiel, Germany. *Died:* October 4, 1947; Göttingen, Germany. *Nationality:* German. *Education:* University of Munich, Germany, Ph.D., 1879. *Career:* University of Munich, Germany, Professor, 1880–85; University of Kiel, Germany, Professor, 1885–89; University of Berlin, Germany, Professor, 1889–1928. *Other Awards:* Copley Medal, Royal Society, 1929.

Citation: "In recognition of the services he rendered to the advancement of Physics by his discovery of energy quanta."

Life Work: Planck's field of investigation was thermodynamics and its application to physical chemistry and electrochemistry. From 1896 he devoted his attention to the problem of radiation from hot bodies, especially the blackbody problem, which is concerned with the quantitative accounting for the observed energy distribution of radiation. In 1900 he succeeded in deriving a formula that explained this problem with remarkable accuracy. Planck introduced a radical concept in his formula, according to which the energy of the oscillators did not vary continuously, as in conventional physics, but had discrete values that increased in finite steps. Each step of energy equaled a constant number (called Planck's Constant) multiplied by the frequency. The discrete bits of energy were later called quanta. His concept revolutionized modern physics and led to the birth of quantum theory. Later, Planck derived the Fokker-Planck equation, which describes the behavior of a system of particles subjected to small random impulses.

Publications: *Vorlesungen uber Thermodynamik* (Leipzig, Germany: Veit, 1897). "Zur Theorie des Gesetzes der Energieverteilung im Normalspektrum," *Verhandlungen der Deutschen Physikalischen Gesellschaft* 2 (1900): 237–45. "Uber die Elementarquanta der Materie und der Elektrizitat," *Annalen der Physik* 4 (1901): 564–66. *Vorlesungen uber die Theorie der Warmestrahlung* (Leipzig, Germany: Barth, 1906).

Bibliography: *Dictionary of Scientific Biography* (New York: Scribner's, 1975), vol. 11, pp. 7–17. A. Hermann, *Max Planck in Selbstzeugnissen und Bilddokumenten* (Hamburg: Rowohlt, 1973). *Max Planck* (Halle/Salle, Germany: Deutsche Akademie der Naturforscher Leopoldina, 1990). *Obituary Notices of Fellows of the Royal Society* (London: Royal Society, 1948), pp. 160–88.

STARK, JOHANNES

Prize: Physics, 1919. **Born:** April 15, 1874; Schickenhof, Bavaria, Germany. **Died:** June 21, 1957; Traunstein, Bavaria, Germany. **Nationality:** German. **Education:** University of Munich, Germany, Ph.D., 1897. **Career:** University of Munich, Germany, Professor, 1897–1900; University of Göttingen, Germany, Professor, 1900–1906; Technische Hochschule, Hannover, Germany, Professor, 1906–1909; Technische Hochschule, Aachen, Germany, Professor, 1909–17; University of Greifswald, Germany, Professor, 1917–20; University of Wurzburg, Germany, Professor, 1920–22. **Other Awards:** Baumgartner Prize, Vienna Academy of Sciences, 1910; Vahlbruch Prize, Göttingen Academy of Sciences, 1914; Matteuci Medal, Rome, 1921.

Citation: "For his discovery of the Doppler effect in canal rays and the splitting of spectral lines in electric fields."

Life Work: Stark's field of investigation was the behavior of ions in electric fields. In 1904 Stark founded the *Jahrbuch der Radioaktivitat und Elektronik* to publish research papers in the area of particle physics. Stark is also known for his modification of the photo-equivalence law proposed by Albert Einstein in 1906. Now known as the Stark-Einstein law, it states that each molecule involved in a photochemical reaction absorbs only one quantum of the radiation that causes the reaction. In 1905 he observed the Doppler shift in canal rays, which are positive ions accelerated in a vacuum toward an electrode and which pass through spaces or canals in the electrode. In 1913 Stark produced a splitting of the spectral lines of hydrogen by means of an electric field, a phenomenon known as the Stark effect.

Publications: *Die Elektrizitat in Gasen* (Leipzig, Germany: J. A. Barth, 1902). "Der Doppler-Effekt bei den Kanalstrahlen und die Spektra der Positiven Atomionen," *Physikalische Zeitschrift* 6 (1905): 892–97. "Elementarquantum der Energie, Modell der Negativen und Positiven Elektrizitat," *Physikalische Zeitschrift* 8 (1907); 881–84. *Prinzipien der Atomdynamik*, 3 vols. (Leipzig, Germany: S. Hirzel, 1910–15).

Bibliography: *Dictionary of Scientific Biography* (New York: Scribner's, 1975), vol. 12, pp. 613–66. *Nobel Prize Winners: Physics* (Pasadena, Calif.: Salem Press, 1988), vol. 1, pp. 233–41.

GUILLAUME, CHARLES EDOUARD

Prize: Physics, 1920. *Born:* February 15, 1861; Fleurier, Switzerland. *Died:* June 13, 1938; Sevres, France. *Nationality:* Swiss; later French resident. *Education:* Zürich Polytechnic, Switzerland, Ph.D., 1883. *Career:* International Bureau of Weights and Measures, France, Administrator and Researcher, 1883–1936. *Other Awards:* Grand Officer, Legion of Honour, 1937.

Citation: "In recognition of the service he has rendered to precision measurements in Physics by his discovery of anomalies in nickel steel alloys."

Life Work: Guillaume's first work was to determine the accuracy of the mercury thermometer. He summarized his careful evaluation in his *Traite de Thermometrie* in 1889. Turning next to the measurement of length, he searched for an alloy that could be used in local metrology laboratories as a reliable and affordable substitute for the expensive platinum-iridium standard meter bar owned by each of the nations that had participated in the first Conference on Weights and Measures in 1889. He found it in invar, a nickel steel alloy containing 36 percent nickel, 0.4 percent manganese, 0.1 percent carbon, and 63.5 percent iron that had a coefficient of expansion less than one-tenth that of iron. He developed a number of methods for tempering, drawing, and rolling invar in ways that controlled its thermal expansivity. Through further research, he developed another alloy called elinar, containing 36 percent nickel, 12 percent chrtomium, and 52 percent iron. Steel tuning forks and steel balance wheels for watches are made of elinar. An early champion of the metric system, Guillaume helped in the adoption of the system throughout Europe.

Publications: *Traite Pratique de Thermometrie de Precision* (Paris: Gauthier-Villars, 1889). "Recherches sur les Aciers au Nickel. Proprietes Metrologiques," *Comptes Rendus Hebdomadaires des Seances de l'Académie des Sciences* 124 (1897): 752.

"Recherches sur les Aciers au Nickel. Proprietes Magnetiques et Deformations Perma-
nentes," *Comptes Rendus Hebdomadaires des Seances de l'Académie des Sciences* 124
(1897): 1515. "Recherches sur les Aciers au Nickel. Dilatations aux Temperatures
Elevees: Resistance Electrique," *Comptes Rendus Hebdomadires des Seances de
l'Académie des Sciences* 125 (1897): 235. "Recherches sur les Aciers au Nickel. Variations de Volumes des Alliages Irreversibles," *Comptes Rendus Hebdomadaires des
Seances de l'Académie des Sciences* 126 (1898): 738. *Les Etats de la Matiere* (Paris:
Société Astronomique de France, 1908).

Bibliography: *Dictionary of Scientific Biography* (New York: Scribner's, 1972), vol. 5,
pp. 582–83. *Nobel Prize Winners: Physics* (Pasadena, Calif.: Salem Press, 1988), vol. 1,
pp. 243–51.

EINSTEIN, ALBERT

Prize: Physics, 1921. *Born:* March 14, 1879; Ulm, Germany. *Died:* April 18, 1955;
Princeton, New Jersey. *Nationality:* German; later Swiss and U.S. citizen. *Education:*
University of Zürich, Switzerland, Ph.D., 1905. *Career:* Swiss Patent Office, Berne,
Switzerland, Patent Examiner, 1902–1908; University of Zürich, Switzerland, Pro-
fessor, 1909–11; Karl-Ferdinand University, Prague, Austria, Professor, 1911–12;
Technische Hochschule, Bern, Switzerland, Professor, 1912–14; Kaiser Wilhelm Insti-
tute, Germany, Director, 1914–33; Princeton University, New Jersey, Professor,
133–55. *Other Awards:* Barnard Medal, Columbia University, 1920; Copley Medal,
Royal Society, 1925; Gold Medal, Royal Astronomical Society, 1926; Max Planck
Medal, 1929; Franklin Medal, Franklin Institute, 1935.

Citation: "For his services to Theoretical Physics, and especially for his discovery of the
law of the photoelectric effect."

Life Work: Einstein's contributions to science were manifold. His early work explained
Brownian motion, the chaotic zigzagging of particles suspended in a liquid. Another
paper explained the photoelectric effect, the emission of electrons from a metal surface
irradiated by ultraviolet rays or other electromagnetic radiation. Building on Planck's
work on quanta, Einstein related the photon to the energy of the ejected electron. Each
photon ejected one electron. The electron's kinetic energy equaled the energy from the
photon left over after expenditure of the energy required to dislodge the electron from
its attachment to the metal. Faster electrons were produced by radiation of a higher frequency because its photons contained more energy. Einstein demonstrated that light
had a dual nature, as a wave and also as a particle. In 1905 Einstein followed with one
of his most dramatic achievements, the Special Theory of Relativity, based on two universal assumptions: (1) that all laws of physics have equal validity for any two observers,
regardless of their relative motion, and (2) that light always travels through free space
at the same velocity, regardless of the motion of its source. These assumptions were
expressed by the formula $E = mc^2$ where m is mass, a kind of frozen energy, and c is the

velocity of light. The formula changed ideas of space and time and established the equivalence of mass and energy. The emission of photons of light is compensated by a reduction in the mass of the source. In 1915 Einstein developed his General Theory of Relativity, which encompassed all kinds of motion and accelerations. Einstein also replaced many of Newton's concepts, especially the theory of gravitational attraction between bodies by a space-time geometry in which bodies influence the characteristics of space in their vicinity. Under his Equivalence Principle, gravitational and inertial effects are indistinguishable. In 1916 Einstein introduced into quantum theory the idea of stimulated emission of radiation, a process that underlies the action of modern lasers.

Publications: *Relativity, The Special and the General Theory: A Popular Exposition*, trans. Robert W. Lawson (London: Methuen, 1920). *The Meaning of Relativity: Four Lectures Delivered at Princeton University, May 1921*, trans. Edwin Plimpton Adams (London: Methuen, 1921). *Investigations on the Theory of the Brownian Movement*. trans. A. D. Cowper (London: Methuen, 1926). *The Evolution of Physics: The Growth of Ideas from Early Concepts to Relativity and Quanta*, with Leopold Infeld (New York: Simon & Schuster, 1938).

Bibliography: *Autobiographical Notes* (New York: Simon & Schuster, 1993). Ronald W. Clark, *Einstein: The Life and Times* (New York: World Publishing, 1971). *Dictionary of Scientific Biography* (New York: Scribner's, 1971), vol. 4, pp. 312–33. Philipp Frank, *Einstein, His Life and Times*, trans G. Rosen (New York: A. A. Knopf, 1947). Banesh Hoffmann and Helen Dukas, *Albert Einstein—Creator and Rebel* (New York: Viking, 1972). Abraham Pais, "*Subtle Is the Lord . . .*" *The Science and Life of Albert Einstein* (New York: Oxford University Press, 1982). Anton Reiser, *Albert Einstein, a Biographical Portrait* (New York: Boni, 1930).

BOHR, NIELS HENRIK DAVID

Prize: Physics, 1922. *Born:* October 7, 1885; Copenhagen, Denmark. *Died:* November 18, 1962; Copenhagen, Denmark. *Nationality:* Danish. *Education:* University of Copenhagen, Denmark, baccalaureate, 1907; University of Copenhagen, Denmark, M.S., 1909; University of Copenhagen, Denmark, Ph.D., 1911. *Career:* Cambridge University, England, Professor, 1911–12; University of Manchester, England, Professor, 1913–14; Victoria University, England, Professor, 1914–16; University of Copenhagen, Denmark, Professor and Administrator, 1916–62. *Other Awards:* Gold Medal, Royal Danish Academy of Sciences, 1907; Hughes Medal, Royal Society, 1921; H. C. Oerstad Medal, Society for the Propagation of Natural Science, 1924; Norwegian Gold Medal, University of Oslo, 1924; Barnard Medal, Columbia University, New York, 1925; Mateucci Medal, Societa Italiana della Scienze, Rome, Italy, 1925; Franklin Medal, Franklin Institute, 1926; Faraday Medal, Chemical Society of London, England, 1930; Planck Medal, Deutsche Physikalische Gesellschaft, 1930; Copley Medal, Royal Society, 1938.

Citation: "For his services in the investigation of the structure of atoms and of the radiation emanating from them."

Life Work: Bohr is noted for his quantum theory which overturned the classical nuclear model of the atom. He suggested that electrons have a certain stable orbits in which they do not radiate energy. It is only when an electron jumps from one orbit to another that it gains or loses energy and then the gain or loss is always equal to the energy difference between the two orbits. Published in 1913, Bohr's theory established his reputation and his atomic model came to be known as the Bohr atom. It provided the bridge to the quantum theory. During the 1920s he made pivotal contributions to the Copenhagen Interpretation of quantum mechanics. It holds that rigid laws of cause and effect do not apply to subatomic phenomena, which can be understood only in terms of probability. Bohr also formulated two of the fundamental principles that guided the development of quantum mechanics: the correspondence principle and the complementarity principle. The former states that quantum-mechanical descriptions of the macroscopic world must correspond to the descriptions of classical mechanics. The latter states that the wavelike and particlelike character of matter and radiation are mutually exclusive properties, although both are necessary components of nature. During the 1930s Bohr turned to nuclear physics and proposed a liquid-drop model of the nucleus that accounted for many of the observed reactions. Escaping to the United States during wartime in 1943, Bohr made technical contributions to the development of the atomic bomb.

Publications: *The Theory of Spectra and Atomic Constitution: Three Essays* (Cambridge: Cambridge University Press, 1922). *Atomic Theory and the Description of Nature* (New York: Macmillan, 1934). *Atomic Physics and Human Knowledge* (New York: Wiley, 1958). *Essays, 1958–1962, on Atomic Physics and Human Knowledge* (New York: Interscience, 1963). *On the Constitution of Atoms and Molecules, Papers of 1913 Reprinted from the Philosophical Magazine* (New York: Benjamin, 1963).

Bibliography: *Dictionary of Scientific Biography* (New York: Scribner's, 1970), vol. 2, pp. 230–54. Henry Folse, *The Philosophy of Niels Bohr* (New York: North Holland, 1985). Ruth E. Moore, *Niels Bohr: The Man, His Science, and the World They Changed* (New York: Knopf, 1966). *Niels Bohr, His Life and Work as Seen by His Friends and Colleagues*, ed. S. Rozenthal (New York: Wiley, 1967). R. Spangenburg, *Niels Bohr* (New York: Facts on File, 1995).

MILLIKAN, ROBERT ANDREWS

Prize: Physics, 1923. *Born:* March 22, 1868; Morrison, Illinois. *Died:* December 19, 1963; San Marino, California. *Nationality:* American. *Education:* Oberlin College, Ohio, A.B., 1891; Oberlin College, Ohio, A.M., 1893; Columbia University, New York, Ph.D., 1895. *Career:* University of Chicago, Illinois, Professor, 1896–1921; California Institute of Technology, Professor and Administrator, 1921–46. *Other Awards:* Comstock Prize, National Academy of Sciences, 1913; Edison Medal, American Institute of Electrical Engineers, 1922; Hughes Medal, Royal Society, 1923; Faraday Medal, Chemical Society of London, 1924; Matteuci Medal, Societa Italiana della Scienze, 1925; Gold Medal, American Society of Mechanical Engineers, 1926; Messel Medal, Society of Chemical Industry, 1928; Gold Medal, Holland Society, 1928; Gold Medal, Radiological Society of North America, 1930; Gold Medal, Roosevelt Memorial Association, 1932; Newman Medal, 1934; Legion of Honor, France, 1936; Gold Medal, Franklin Institute, 1937; Gold Medal, Ulster-Irish Association of New York, 1938; Joy Kissen Mookerjee Gold Medal, Indian Association for the Cultivation of Science, 1939; Oersted Medal, American Association of Physics Teachers, 1940; Order of the Jade, China, 1940; Order Al Merito, Chile, 1944.

Citation: "For his work on the elementary charge of electricity and on the photoelectric effect."

Life Work: Milliken's early investigations provided evidence that electrons were fundamental particles of identical charge and mass. In 1913 he calculated the value of the electron charge. Studying photoelectric effect (in which light striking the surface of a metal causes electrons to be ejected) he helped convince physicists of the validity of Einstein's quantum theory. His research into portions of the electromagnetic spectrum by means of hot-spark spectrography and his work on the Brownian movement in gases helped to confirm the molecular theory. Later in life he studied cosmic rays and cosmic radiation.

Publications: "Quantum Theory and Its Relation to Photoelectric Phenomena," *Physik. Z.* 17 (1916): 217–21. *Electron: Its Isolation and Measurement and the Determination of Some of Its Properties* (Chicago: University of Chicago Press, 1917). "Radiation and the Electron," *Nature* 101 (1918): 234–37, 254–57. "High-Frequency Rays of Cosmic Origin," *Science* 62 (1925): 445–48. *Electrons, Protons, Photons, Neutrons and Cosmic Rays* (Chicago: University of Chicago Press, 1935).

Bibliography: *The Autobiography of Robert A. Millikan* (New York: Prentice-Hill, 1950). *Dictionary of Scientific Biography* (New York: Scribner's, 1974), vol. 9, pp. 395–400. Robert Kargon, *The Rise of Robert Millikan* (Ithaca, N.Y.: Cornell University Press, 1982).

SIEGBAHN, KARL MANNE GEORG

Prize: Physics, 1924. *Born:* December 3, 1886; Orebro, Sweden. *Died:* September 26, 1978; Stockholm, Sweden. *Nationality:* Swedish. *Education:* University of Lund, Sweden, B.S., 1908; University of Lund, Sweden, Dr.Sc., 1911. *Career:* University of Lund, Sweden, Professor, 1911–23; University of Uppsala, Sweden, Professor, 1923–37; Swedish Royal Academy of Sciences, Professor and Administrator, 1937–64. *Other Awards:* Hughes Medal, Royal Society, 1934; Rumford Medal, Royal Society, 1940; Duddel Medal, Physical Society of London, 1948.

Citation: "For his discoveries and research in the field of X-ray spectroscopy."

Life Work: Siegbahn's field of investigation was X rays, and he devised a number of instruments, such as spectrometers to measure wavelengths. With the help of these instruments he discovered many new lines in the K and L series and two new series M and N. Electrons circle in certain allowed orbits about the nucleus. The energy of a photon equals the energy difference between a higher and a lower orbit. The frequency of the radiation is proportional to the photon energy. In X rays the wavelengths are shorter and the frequencies higher. Accurate knowledge of radio wavelengths allowed scientists to probe the atomic structure.

Publications: *The Spectroscopy of X-rays* (London: Oxford University Press, 1925).

Bibliography: *Biographical Encyclopedia of Scientists* (New York: Facts on File, 1981), pp. 733–34. *Biographical Memoirs of the Fellows of the Royal Society* (London: Royal Society, 1991), vol. 37, p. 527. *Nobel Prize Winners: Physics* (Pasadena, Calif.: Salem Press, 1988), vol. 1, pp. 283–93.

FRANCK, JAMES

Prize: Physics, 1925. **Born:** August 26, 1882; Hamburg, Germany. **Died:** May 21, 1964; Göttingen, Germany. **Nationality:** German; later U.S. citizen. **Education:** University of Berlin, Germany, Ph.D., 1906. **Career:** University of Berlin, Germany, Professor, 1906–18; Kaiser Wilhelm Institute, Germany, Professor, 1918–20; University of Göttingen, Germany, Professor, 1920–33; University of Copenhagen, Denmark, Professor, 1934; Johns Hopkins University, MD, Professor, 1935–38; University of Chicago, Illinois, Professor, 1938–49. **Other Awards:** Max Planck Medal, German Physical Society, 1953; Rumford Medal, American Academy of Arts and Sciences, 1955.

Citation: "For their discovery of the laws governing the impact of an electron upon an atom" (with Gustav Hertz).

Life Work: Franck began his collaboration with Gusave Hertz in 1913, working on electron interaction with atoms in low-density noble gases. Their work on inelstic collisions led to the discovery of quantized transfer of energy between atoms and electrons. Their work showed that electrons impart energy to a mercury atom only in units that are integral multiples of of 4.9 electron volts. The atoms emit energy equal to the amount they absorb producing a spectral line of predictable wavelength. These experiments demonstrated the existence of the energy quanta. After World War I, Franck and his colleagues discovered metastable atoms that lose their excitation energy by colliding with particles. Metastable states play an important role in photosynthesis, where they are critical to the plant's ability to store energy. Working with Edward Condon, he developed the Franck-Condon principle, which allowed determination of basic chemical properties from spectroscopic measurements.

Publications: *Anregungen von quanten-sprungen durch Stosse*, with P. Jordan (Berlin: J. Springer, 1926). *Photosynthesis in Plants*, with W. E. Loomis (Ames: Iowa State College Press, 1949).

Bibliography: *Biographical Memoirs of the Fellows of the Royal Society* (London: Royal Society, 1965), vol. 11, pp. 53–74. *Current Biography Yearbook* (New York: H. W. Wilson, 1957), pp. 192–94. *Dictionary of Scientific Biography* (New York: Scribner's, 1972), vol. 5, pp. 117–18.

HERTZ, GUSTAV LUDWIG

Prize: Physics, 1925. *Born:* July 22, 1887; Hamburg, Germany. *Died:* October 30, 1975; Berlin, Germany. *Nationality:* German. *Education:* University of Berlin, Germany, Ph.D., 1911. *Career:* University of Berlin, Germany, Researcher, 1913–14; Germany Army, 1914–17; University of Berlin, Germany, Researcher, 1917–20; Philips Incandescent Lamp Factory, Netherlands, Researcher, 1920–25; University of Halle, Germany, Professor and Administrator, 1925–28; Charlottenburg Technological University, Berlin, Germany, Professor and Administrator, 1928–35; Siemens Company, Germany, Researcher and Administrator, 1935–45; Research Laboratory, USSR, Researcher and Administrator, 1945–54; Karl Marx University, Leipzig, Germany, Professor and Administrator, 1955–61. *Other Awards:* Max Planck Medal, 1961; German Physical Society, 1968.

Citation: "For their discovery of the laws governing the impact of an electron upon an atom" (with James Franck).

Life Work: Hertz and Franck were the first to measure directly the energy in a quantum. Their work confirmed that energy was absorbed by an atom only in specific amounts, which they calculated at 4.9 volts. The 4.9 volts was an excitation potential, that is, the energy or quantum required to boost or excite an electron from one energy state to another without severing its attachment to the atom. After World War I he developed a gas diffusion process for separating the isotopes of neon.

Publications: "Impacts Between Gas Molecules and Slowly Moving Electrons," with J. Franck, *Ber. Physike. Geog* (1913): 373–91. "A Connection Between Impact Ionization and Electron Affinity," with J. Franck, *Verh. Deut. Physik. Geo* 15 (1920): 929–34. "Collisions Between Electrons and Molecules of Mercury Vapor and the Ionizing Voltage for the Same," *Verh. Deut. Physik. Geo* 16 (1922): 457–67. *Lehrbuch der Kernphysik*, 3 vols. (Leipzig: B. G. Teubner, 1958–62).

Bibliography: *Nobel Prize Winners: Physics* (Pasadena, Calif.: Salem Press, 1988), vol. 1, pp. 305–13. *Physics Today* 29 (January 1976): 83–85.

PERRIN, JEAN BAPTISTE

Prize: Physics, 1926. *Born:* September 30, 1870; Lille, France. *Died:* April 17, 1942; New York, New York. *Nationality:* French. *Education:* École Normale Supérieure, France, D.Sc., 1897. *Career:* École Normale Supérieure, France, Researcher, 1894–97; University of Paris, France, Professor, 1897–1940. *Other Awards:* Joule Prize, Royal Society, 1896; La Caze Prize, French Academy of Sciences, 1914.

Citation: "For his work on the discontinuous structure of matter, and especially for his discovery of sedimentation equilibrium."

Life Work: Perrin's field of investigation was the structure of the atom. His study of colloids (suspensions of fine particles) led him to Brownian motion. To prove the existence of molecules, he segregated—after months of centrifuging—a few tenths of a gram of uniform particles of gamboge, a yellowish material made from vegetable sap. Perrin also studied sedimentation, or sinking, of small suspended particles. In such a state, the upward momentum gained from molecular collisions will oppose the downward pull of gravity. So long as the suspension is undisturbed, an equilibrium will eventually be reached, after which the concentrations of particles at various depths will remain unchanged. His goal was to establish the discontinuous nature of matter and to prove the reality of atoms and molecules.

Publications: "Rayons Cathodiques et Rayons de Roentgen," *Annales de Chimie et de Physique* 11 (1897): 496–554. *Traite de Chimie Physicque. Les Principes* (Paris: Gauthier-Villars, 1903). "Mouvement Brownien et Realite Moleculaire," *Annales de Chimie et de Physique* 18 (1909): 1–114. *Les Atomes* (Paris: Alcan, 1913). *Oeuvres Scientifiques de Jean Perrin* (Paris: Centre National de la Recherche Scientifique, 1950).

Bibliography: *Dictionary of Scientific Biography* (New York: Scribner's, 1973), vol. 10, pp. 524–26. Mary Jo Nye, *Molecular Reality* (London: MacDonald, 1972).

COMPTON, ARTHUR HOLLY

Prize: Physics, 1927. *Born:* September 10, 1892; Wooster, Ohio. *Died:* March 15, 1962; Berkeley, California. *Nationality:* American. *Education:* College of Wooster, Ohio, B.S., 1913; Princeton University, New Jersey, M.A., 1914; Princeton University, New Jersey, Ph.D., 1916. *Career:* University of Minnesota, Professor, 1916–17; Westinghouse Lamp Co., Pennsylvania, Researcher, 1917–19; Cambridge University, England, Researcher, 1919–20; Washington University, Missouri, Professor, 1920–23; University of Chicago, Illinois, Professor, 1923–45; Washington University, Missouri, Professor and Administrator, 1945–61. *Other Awards:* Rumford Medal, American Academy of Arts and Sciences, 1927; Gold Medal, Radiological Society of North America, 1928; Matteuci Medal, Italian Academy of Sciences, 1933; Franklin Medal,

Franklin Institute, 1940; Hughes Medal, Royal Society, 1940; Washington Award, Western Society of Engineers, 1945; Franklin Medal, American Philosophical Society, 1945; Congressional Medal of Merit, 1946.

Citation: "For his discovery of the effect named after him."

Life Work: Compton's field of investigation was the interaction of matter and energy. He made precise measurements of the wavelengths of X rays scattered from a target. He found that the scattered radiation was of two types, one with a wavelength the same as that of the primary rays and the other longer. The increase in wavelength, which became known as the Compton Effect, was proportional to the angle of the scattering. An X-ray energy particle or quantum colliding with an electron in the target gives up some of its energy to the electron; consequently, the particle has a lower energy after the collision, corresponding to a lower frequency or longer wavelength of radiation. His finding explained why scattered gamma rays were more absorbable than primary gamma rays. The Compton Effect provided strong support for Einstein's thesis that light behaves like a particle as well as a wave. During the 1920s Compton conducted other significant X-ray research showing that light and X rays behave similarly. This work established the study of X rays as a branch of optics. Compton's work contributed to an understanding of the magnetism of ferromagnetic materials, such as iron. In the 1930s he became interested in cosmic rays and the interaction of gamma rays and electrons in cosmic rays.

Publications: "A Quantum Theory of the Scattering of X-Rays by Light Elements," *Physical Review* 21 (1923): 483–502. "Polarization of Secondary X-Rays," with C. F. Hagenow, *Journal of the Optical Society of America* 8 (1924): 487–91. "X-Ray Spectra from a Ruled Reflection Grating," with R. L. Doan, *Proceedings of the National Academy of Sciences, USA* 11 (1925): 598–601. *X-Rays and Electrons* (Princeton, N.J.: D. Van Nostrand Company, 1926). *X-Rays in Theory and Experiment*, with S. K. Allison (Princeton, N.J.: D. Van Nostrand Company, 1935).

Bibliography: *Biographical Memoirs of National Academy of Sciences* (Washington, D.C.: National Academy of Sciences, 1965), pp. 81–110. *The Cosmos of Arthur Holly Compton* (New York: Knopf, 1967). *Dictionary of Scientific Biography* (New York: Scribner's, 1971), vol. 3, pp. 366–72.

WILSON, CHARLES THOMSON REES

Prize: Physics, 1927. *Born:* February 14, 1869; Glencorse, Midlothian, Scotland. *Died:* November 15, 1959; Carlops, Peeblesshire, Scotland. *Nationality:* Scottish. *Education:* Owens College, England, B.Sc., 1887; Cambridge University, England, B.A., 1892. *Career:* Cavendish Laboratory, England, Researcher, 1892–96; Bradford Grammar School, Yorkshire, England, Teacher, 1894; Cambridge University, England, Professor, 1896–1934. *Other Awards:* Hughes Medal, Royal Society, 1911; Hopkins Prize, Cambridge Philosophical Society, England, 1920; Gunning Prize, Royal Society of Edinburgh, Scotland, 1921; Royal Medal, Royal Society, 1922; Howard Potts Medal, Franklin Institute, 1925; Copley Medal, Royal Society, 1935.

Citation: "For his method of making the paths of electrically charged particles visible by condensation of vapour."

Life Work: Wilson's field of investigation was the condensation of water. Using a primitive X-ray tube he demonstrated that water droplets in clouds form by condensing around ions. He improved the design of the expansion chamber, which came to be known as the cloud chamber. Conducting further cloud-chamber experiments, he invented a new form of electroscope that was one hundred times more sensitive than any in use at the time and produced important information on the behavior of ions in gases and their effects on the atmosphere. He detected the passage of charged subatomic alpha and beta particles that ionize gas particles in their paths. He recorded on photographic emulsion trails formed by water vapor condensing around ionized molecules.

Publications: "A Method of Making Visible the Paths of Ionizing Particles Through a Gas," *Proceedings of the Royal Society of London* Series A. 85 (1911): 285–88. "An Expansion Apparatus for Making Visible the Track of Ionizing Particles in Gases and Some Results Obtained by Its Use," *Proceedings of the Royal Society of London* Series A 87 (1913): 277–92. "The Acceleration of Beta-Particles in Strong Electrical Fields Such as Those of Thunderclouds," *Proceedings of the Cambridge Philosophical Society* 22 (1925): 534–38.

Bibliography: *Biographical Memoirs of the Fellows of the Royal Society* (London: Royal Society, 1960), vol. 6, pp. 269–95. *Dictionary of Scientific Biography* (New York: Scribner's, 1981), vol. 14, pp. 420–23.

RICHARDSON, SIR OWEN WILLANS

Prize: Physics, 1928. *Born:* April 26, 1879; Dewsbury, England. *Died:* February 15, 1959; Alton, England. *Nationality:* British. *Education:* University of London, England, B.Sc., 1900; Cambridge University, England, M.A., 1904; University of London, England, D.Sc., 1904. *Career:* Cavendish Laboratory, England, Researcher, 1900–1906; Princeton University, New Jersey, Professor, 1906–14; University of London, England, Professor, 1914–44. *Other Awards:* Hughes Medal, Royal Society, 1920; Royal Medal, Royal Society, 1930; Knighthood, 1939.

Citation: "For his work on the thermionic phenomenon and especially for the discovery of the law named after him."

Life Work: Richardson described both theoretically and experimentally how heated metal elements emit streams of changed particles. On the basis of this work he proved that an electron gas can evaporate from a hot surface. He formulated an empirical law that relates the rate of electron emission to the composition of the filament and to the temperature of its surface. Richardson's law states that the rate of electron emission increases very rapidly as the temperature of the surface is increased, obeying the same statistical relationships as atomic and molecular gases. His other research concerned the emission of electrons from illuminated matter (the photoelectric effect) the interaction of X rays with matter, the emission of light by matter, the gyromagnetic effect and thermodynamics, or the behavior of systems made up of enormous number of particles. In 1909 he coined the term thermionics to describe the emission of electric charges from hot bodies.

Publications: *The Electron Theory of Matter* (Cambridge: Cambridge University Press, 1914). *The Emission of Electricity from Hot Bodies* (London: Longmans, Green and Co., 1916). *Molecular Hydrogen and Its Spectrum* (New Haven, Conn.: Yale University Press, 1934).

Bibliography: *Biographical Memoirs of the Fellows of the Royal Society* (London: Royal Society, 1959), vol. 5, pp. 207–15. *Dictionary of Scientific Biography* (New York: Scribner's, 1981), vol. 11, pp. 419–23.

BROGLIE, LOUIS-VICTOR PIERRE RAYMOND DE

Prize: Physics, 1929. *Born:* August 15, 1892; Dieppe, France. *Died:* March 19, 1987; Lovveciennes, Yvelines, France. *Nationality:* French. *Education:* University of Paris, France, licence in history, 1910; University of Paris, France, licence in science, 1913; University of Paris, France, D.Sc., 1924. *Career:* University of Paris, France, Professor, 1924–62. *Other Awards:* Henri Poincare Medal, Académie des Sciences, 1929; Max Planck Medal, Germany Physical Society, 1938; Kalinga Prize, UNESCO.

Citation: "For his discovery of the wave nature of electrons."

Life Work: De Broglie's field of investigation was the behavior of electrons, atoms, and X rays. De Broglie asserted that if waves could act as particles, particles could act as waves. He extended to matter the Einstein-Bohr theory of wave-particle duality. However, waves and matter are different. Matter has a rest mass and can either be motionless or move at various velocities. Light has no rest mass and moves only at one velocity. In parallel with the link between the wavelength of light and the energy in a photon, de Broglie proposed that a matter wavelength is related to momentum, which is directly related to kinetic energy. The faster the electron the higher the frequency. Thus, whether matter and radiation appear as particles or waves depends on the observer's circumstances. Applied to the atom this meant that a negative electron is attracted to a positive nucleus. The electron must travel at a particular speed to circle the nucleus at a certain distance. The speed and the orbit must remain compatible in order for the centripetal force to balance the centrifugal. A particular electron speed corresponds to a particular momentum and to a particular electron wavelength. In order for the electron waves to be in phase (at the same point in a frequency cycle) and not interfere destructively with themselves, the circumference of the orbits must equal an integral number of electron wavelengths. Waves associated with material particles are now called de Broglie Waves. De Broglie's ideas constitute the foundation of wave mechanics and led to the development of electron microscopes.

Publications: "Recherches sur la Theorie des Quanta," *Annales de Physique* 3 (January–February 1925): 22–128. *La Mecanique Ondulatoire* (Paris: Gauthier-Villars, 1928); *Selected Papers on Wave Mechanics*, with L. Brillouin, trans. W. M. Deans (London: Blackie & Son Limited, 1928). *An Introduction to the Study of Wave Mechanics*, trans H. T. Flint. (London: Methuen & Co., Ltd., 1930). *Matter and Light: The New Physics*, trans W. H. Johnston (New York: W. W. Norton, 1939). *Nonlinear Wave Mechanics: A Causal Interpretation*, trans Arthur J. Knodel and Jack C. Miller (New York: Elsevier, 1960). *The Current Interpretation of Wave Mechanics, a Critical Study*, trans Express Translation Service (New York: Elsevier, 1964).

Bibliography: *Current Biography Yearbook* (New York: H. W. Wilson, 1955), pp. 67–69. G. Lochak, *Louis de Broglie* (Paris: Flammarion, 1992). *Modern Scientists and Engineers* (New York: McGraw-Hill, 1980), vol. 1, pp. 143–44. *Nobel Prize Winners: Physics* (Pasadena, Calif.: Salem Press, 1988), vol. 1, pp. 361–70.

RAMAN, SIR CHANDRASEKHARA VENKATA

Prize: Physics, 1930. *Born:* November 7, 1888; Trichinopoly, India. *Died:* November 21, 1970; Bangalore, India. *Nationality:* Indian. *Education:* Presidency College, India, B.A., 1902; Presidency College, India, M.A., 1907. *Career:* Indian Finance Department, Researcher, 1907–17; Calcutta University, India, Professor, 1917–33; Indian Institute of Science, Professor, 1933–48; Raman Institute of Research, Bangalore, Director, 1948–70. *Other Awards:* Knighthood, 1929; Mateucci Medal, Italy, 1929; Hughes Medal, Royal Society, 1930; Franklin Medal, Franklin Institute, 1941.

Citation: "For his work on the scattering of light and for the discovery of the effect named after him."

Life Work: Raman's life work was the scattering of light. He observed that scattered light is accompanied by a feebler type of secondary radiation, whose wavelength differs from that of the primary radiation. In 1928 he demonstrated that secondary radiation consists of light at a number of different wavelengths, mostly longer and of lower energy than the original beam of light. Wavelengths thus produced depend on the nature of the molecules doing the scattering and are characteristic of the transmitting substance. When the wavelength of the illuminating light source is changed, the induced light emissions also change their wavelengths, although the energy shifts between the primary and secondary radiation remain constant. These energy shifts, named the Raman Effect, are used in the investigation of molecular structures.

Publications: "Dynamical Theory of the Motion of Bowed Strings," *Bulletin Indian Association for the Cultivation of Science* 11 (1914). "On the Molecular Scattering of Light in Water and the Color of the Sea," *Proceedings of the Royal Society* 64 (1922).

"A New Radiation," *Indian Journal of Physics* 2 (1928): 387. "Crystals and Photons," *Proceedings of the Indian Academy of Science* 13A (1941): 1. *The Physiology of Vision* (Bangalore: Indian Academy of Sciences, 1968).

Bibliography: *Dictionary of Scientific Biography* (New York: Scribner's, 1975), vol. 11, pp. 264–67. *Nobel Prize Winners: Physics.* (Pasadena, Calif.: Salem Press, 1988), vol. 1, pp. 371–80.

HEISENBERG, WERNER KARL

Prize: Physics, 1932. *Born:* December 5, 1901; Wurzburg, Germany. *Died:* February 1, 1976; Munich, Germany. *Nationality:* German. *Education:* University of Munich, Germany, Ph.D., 1923; University of Göttingen, Germany, Dr. Phil. Habil., 1924. *Career:* University of Copenhagen, Denmark, Professor, 1924–27; University of Leipzig, Germany, Professor, 1927–41; University of Berlin, Germany, Professor, 1942–45; University of Göttingen, Germany, Professor, 1946–58; University of Munich, Germany, Professor, 1958–70. *Other Awards:* Barnard Medal, Columbia University, New York, 1930; Max Planck Medal, German Physical Society, 1933; Grotius Medal, Hugo Grotius Stiftung, 1956; Sigmund Freud Prize, Deutsche Akademie für Sprache und Dichtung, 1970; Niels Bohr Gold Medal, Dansk Ingeniorforening, 1970.

Citation: "For the creation of quantum mechanics, the application of which has, inter alia, led to the discovery of the allotropic forms of hydrogen."

Life Work: Heisenberg's field of investigation was quantum mechanics. He regarded quantum events as a different level of phenomena not accurately pictured by easily visualized models, such as orbiting electrons. In 1927 he published a paper stating his famous Uncertainty Principle (also known as the Copenhagen Interpretation), a consequence of matrix multiplications. Order is irrelevant in ordinary mathematics but not in matrices. In dealing with certain pairs of quantities, such as particle momentum and position, the answer is determined by the order and sequence, because the specification of one particle affects the value of the other so that it is impossible to know both with precision at the same time. This imprecision is stated mathematically that the product of two errors cannot be less than Planck's Constant. In the everyday world, the Uncertainty Principle has little effect, but at the atomic level it is significant, because an electron cannot be assigned a definite velocity and position at the same time. Observation disturbs and alters what is being observed. Thus, quantum-mechanical descriptions are only statements of relative probabilities of possible experimental outcomes rather than exact predictions. The principle helped to predict two forms of hydrogen molecules.

Publications: "Uber Quantentheoretische Umdeutung Kinematischer und Mechanischer Beziehungen," *Zeitschrift fur Physik* 33 (1925): 879–983. "Mehrkorper-problem und Resonanz in der Quantenmechanik," *Zeitschrift fur Physik* 38 (1926): 411–26; 41 (1927): 239–67. "Uber den Anschaulichen Inhalt der Quantentheoretischen Kinematik und Mechanik," *Zeitschrift fur Physik* 43 (1927); 172–98. *The Physical Principles* *of the Quantum Theory*, trans. Carl Eckart and Frank C. Hoyt (Chicago: University of Chicago Press, 1930). *Philosophic Problems of Nuclear Science*, trans. F. C. Hayes (New York: Pantheon, 1952). *Physics and Philosophy: The Revolution in Modern Science* (New York: Harper, 1958). *Werner Heisenberg: A Bibliography of His Writings* (Berkeley: University of California Press, 1984).

Bibliography: *Biographical Memoirs of the Fellows of the Royal Society* (London: Royal Society, 1977), vol. 22, pp. 213–51. D. Cassidy, *Uncertainty* (New York: W. H. Freeman, 1992). Elisabeth Heisenberg, *Inner Exile: Recollections of a Life with Werner Heisenberg*, trans. Steve Capalari (Boston: Birkhauser, 1984). Armin Hermann, *Werner Heisenberg, 1901–1976*, trans. Timothy Nevill (Bonn-Bad Godesberg, Germany: Inter Nationes, 1976).

DIRAC, PAUL ADRIEN MAURICE

Prize: Physics, 1933. *Born:* August 8, 1902; Bristol, England. *Died:* October 20, 1984; Tallahassee, Florida. *Nationality:* British; later U.S. resident. *Education:* Bristol University, England, B.Sc., 1921; Cambridge University, England, Ph.D., 1926. *Career:* Cambridge University, England, Professor, 1927–69; Florida State University, Professor, 1971–84. *Other Awards:* Royal Medal, Royal Society, 1939; Copley Medal, Royal Society, 1952; Max Planck Medal, German Institute, 1952.

Citation: "For the discovery of new productive forms of atomic theory" (with Erwin Schrödinger).

Life Work: Dirac's major contribution to the study of electrons was the Dirac Equation, published in 1928, which incorporated relativity in the wave equation by introducing the relativistic expression for particle motion. It predicted the electron's magnetic properties and posited the electron spin. His theory indicated a possible negative energy, which is an antielectron or a reversed twin. He also showed than an electron could fall into a vacant hole, equivalent to the meeting of an electron and an antielectron in which they annihilate each other, their energy reappearing as a photon of radiation. He also predicted that a photon of sufficient energy could produce an electron-antielectron pair. The Dirac Equation helped to clarify the scattering of X rays by matter. Dirac also discovered the statistical distribution of energy in electron systems, now known as Fermi-Dirac Statistics.

Publications: *The Principles of Quantum Mechanics* (London: Clarendon Press, 1930). *The Development of Quantum Theory* (New York: Gordon and Breach Science Publishers, 1971). *Spinors in Hibert Space* (New York: Plenum Press, 1974). *General Theory of Relativity* (New York: Wiley, 1975). *The Selected Works of P. A. M. Dirac* (Cambridge: Cambridge University Press, 1995).

Bibliography: H. Krage, *Dirac* (Cambridge: Cambridge University Press, 1990). Behram N. Kursunoglu and Eugene P. Wigner. *Paul Adrien Maurice Dirac* (New York:

Cambridge University Press, 1987). *Modern Scientists and Engineers* (New York: McGraw-Hill, 1980), vol. 1, pp. 292–93.

SCHRÖDINGER, ERWIN

Prize: Physics, 1933. **Born:** August 12, 1887; Vienna, Austria. **Died:** January 4, 1961; Vienna, Austria. **Nationality:** Austrian. **Education:** University of Vienna, Austria, Ph.D., 1910. **Career:** University of Vienna, Austria, Researcher, 1910–14; Austrian Army, 1914–20; University of Stuttgart, Germany, Professor, 1920; University of Jena, Germany, Professor, 1920–21; University of Breslau, Germany, Professor, 1921; University of Zürich, Switzerland, Professor, 1921–27; University of Berlin, Germany, Professor, 1927–33; Oxford University, England, Researcher, 1933–36; University of Graz, Austria, Professor, 1936–38; Fondation Francqui, Belgium, Professor, 1939–40; Royal Irish Academy, Professor, 1940; Dublin Institute for Advanced Studies, Ireland, Professor, 1940–56; University of Vienna, Austria, Professor, 1956–58. *Other Awards:* Matteuci Medal, 1955; Planck Medal, 1958.

Citation: "For the discovery of new productive forms of atomic theory" (with P. A. M. Dirac).

Life Work: Much of Schrödinger's work revolved around his efforts to apply the wave descriptions of electrons to a consistent quantum theory. In 1926 he formulated the Schrödinger Wave Equation, which described matter mathematically in terms of a wave function. His theory, called wave mechanics, proved more popular with physicists than the earlier matrix mechanics. Together, the two theories provided the general framework for describing quantum phenomena. Wave mechanics was a simple and elegant solution to a number of problems in atomic physics.

Publications: "Quantisierung als Eigenwert-problem. Erste Mitteilung," *Ann. Phys.* 79 (1926): 361. "Quantisierung Zweite Mitteilung," *Ann. Phys.* 79 (1926): 489. "Quantisierung Dritte Mitteilung," *Anns. Phys.* 80 (1926): 437. "Quantisierung Vierte Mitteilung," *Ann. Phys.* 81 (1926): 109. *What is Life?* (Cambridge: Cambridge University Press, 1945). *Space-Time Structure* (Cambridge: Cambridge University Press, 1950). *Statistical Thermodynamics* (Cambridge: Cambridge University Press, 1952).

Bibliography: *Dictionary of Scientific Biography* (New York: Scribner's, 1975), vol. 12, pp. 217–22. C. W. Kilmister, *Schrödinger: A Centenary Celebration of a Polymath* (Cambridge, Cambridge University Press, 1987). *What Is Life?* (Cambridge: Cambridge University Press, 1992).

CHADWICK, SIR JAMES

Prize: Physics, 1935. *Born:* October 20, 1891; Bollington, England. *Died:* July 24, 1974; Cambridge, England. *Nationality:* British. *Education:* University of Manchester, England, baccalaureate, 1911; University of Manchester, England, M.Sc., 1913. *Career:* Cambridge University, England, Researcher, 1919–35; University of Liverpool, England, Professor, 1935–48; Manhattan Project, British Mission, England, Administrator, 1943–48; Cambridge University, England, Professor, 1948–59. *Other Awards:* Hughes Medal, Royal Society, 1932; MacKenzie Davidson Medal, 1932; Knighthood, 1945; United States Medal for Merit, 1946; Transenter Medal, 1946; Melchett Medal, 1946; Faraday Medal, Institution of Electrical Engineers, 1950; Copley Medal, Royal Society, 1950; Franklin Medal, Franklin Institute, 1951; Guthrie Medal, 1967.

Citation: "For the discovery of the neutron."

Life Work: Chadwick's field of investigation was the neutron. Lord Rutherford had proposed in 1920 that nuclei might also contain electrically neutral particles he later named neutrons. He showed that the capture of an alpha particle by a beryllium nucleus could result in the formation of a nucleus of the element carbon and the release of a neutron. The high penetrating power of the neutron follows from its lack of charge, which enables it to pass through matter unaffected by the electric fields in atoms, interacting with nuclei only by direct hit. Chadwick also confirmed Rutherford's hypothesis that the neutron's mass would be similar to that of the proton by analyzing the exchange of energy between neutrons and ejected protons. The demonstration of the neutron's existence paved the way for further advances in physics. The neutron also had a practical use as an atom smasher.

Publications: *Radioactivity and Radioactive Substances* (London: Sir Isaac Pitman and Sons, 1921). "The Existence of a Neutron," *Proceedings of the Royal Society of London* A136 (1929); 692–708. *Radiations from Radioactive Substances,* with E. Rutherford and C. D. Ellis (Cambridge: Cambridge University Press, 1930). "The Neutron" (Bakerian Lecture), *Proceedings of the Royal Society of London* A142 (1933): 1–25. "The Neutron and its Properties," *British Journal of Radiology* 6 (1933): 24–32. "Evidence for a New Type of Disintegration Produced by Neutrons," with N. Feather and W. T. Davies, *Proceedings of the Cambridge Philosophical Society* 30 (1934): 357–64.

Bibliography: *Biographical Memoirs of the Fellows of the Royal Society* (London: Royal Society, 1976), vol. 22, pp. 11–70. "Chadwick's Neutron," *Contemporary Physics* 6 (1974): 565–712.

ANDERSON, CARL DAVID

Prize: Physics, 1936. *Born:* September 3, 1905; New York, New York. *Died:* January 11, 1991; San Marino, California. *Nationality:* American. *Education:* California Institute of Technology, B.S., 1927; California Institute of Technology, Ph.D., 1930. *Career:* California Institute of Technology, Professor and Administrator, 1930–77. *Other Awards:* Gold Medal, American Institute of the City of New York, 1935; Elliott Cresson Medal, Franklin Institute, 1937; Presidential Certificate of Merit, 1945; John Ericsson Gold Medal, American Society of Swedish Engineers, 1960.

Citation: "For his discovery of the positron."

Life Work: In 1932 Anderson announced his discovery of the positron, a positively charged particle with about the mass of an electron. The discovery confirmed the existence of antimatter. When an electron meets a positron, the two are annihilated, producing a burst of gamma rays. Conversely, if gamma rays of high energy are stopped, they vanish, leaving in their place a newly created electron-positron pair. These transformations confirmed the equivalence of mass and energy.

Publications: "Energies and Cosmic-Ray Particles," *Physical Review* (August 15, 1932): 405–21. "Positive Electron," *Physical Review* 43 (March 15, 1933): 491–94. "Cosmic-Ray Positive and Negative Electrons," *Physical Review* 44 (September 1, 1933): 406–16. "Mechanism of Cosmic-Ray Counter Action," with others, *Physical Review* 45 (March 15, 1934): 352–63. "The Positron," *Nature* 133 (March 1934): 313–16.

Bibliography: *Current Biography Yearbook* (New York: H. W. Wilson, 1951), pp. 15–17. *Nobel Prize Winners: Physics* (Pasadena, Calif.: Salem Press, 1988), vol. 1, 437–47. *New York Times* Biographical Service, January 12, 1991, p. 26.

HESS, VICTOR FRANZ

Prize: Physics, 1936. *Born:* June 24, 1883; Schloss Waldstein, Austria. *Died:* December 17, 1964; Mount Vernon, New York. *Nationality:* Austrian; later U.S. citizen. *Education:* University of Graz, Austria, Ph.D., 1906. *Career:* University of Graz, Austria, Researcher, 1906–1908; Vienna Veterinary College, Austria, Professor, 1908–10; University of Vienna, Austria, Professor, 1910–20; University of Graz, Austria, Professor, 1920–21; U.S. Radium Corp., New York, Researcher, 1921–23; University of Graz, Austria, Professor, 1923–31; University of Innsbruck, Austria, Professor, 1931–37; University of Graz, Austria, Professor, 1937–38; Fordham University, New York, Professor, 1938–58. *Other Awards:* Lieben Prize, Austrian Academy of Sciences, 1919; Abbe Prize, Carl Zeiss Foundation, 1932.

Citation: "For his discovery of cosmic radiation."

Life Work: Hess's field of investigation the source of ionizing radiation in the atmosphere. Using balloons he demonstrated that ionization was reduced with increasing height from the earth but that it increased from one thousand meters upward. He concluded that ionization was attributable to the penetration of the earth's atmosphere from outer space by hitherto unknown radiation.

Publications: *Die Elektrische Leitfahigkeit der Atmosphare und Ihre Ursachen* (Brunswick, Germany: F. Viewig and Sohn, 1926). *Die Weltraumstrahlung und Ihre Biologischen Wirkungen* (Zürich: Drell Fussli, 1940). "The Discovery of Cosmic Radiation," *Thought* (1940): 1–12. "Work in the USA," *Oesterreichische Hochschulzeitung* (January 15, 1955): 4.

Bibliography: *Dictionary of Scientific Biography* (New York: Scribner's, 1972), vol. 6, pp. 354–56. *Nobel Prize Winners: Physics* (Pasadena, Calif.: Salem Press, 1988), vol. 1, pp. 427–35. J. G. Wilson, "Obituary Notice," *Nature* 207 (1965): 352.

DAVISSON, CLINTON JOSEPH

Prize: Physics, 1937. *Born:* October 22, 1881; Bloomington, Illinois. *Died:* February 1, 1958; Charlottesville, Virginia. *Nationality:* American. *Education:* University of Chicago, Illinois, B.S., 1908; Princeton University, New Jersey, Ph.D., 1911. *Career:* Carnegie Institute of Technology, Pennsylvania, Professor, 1911–17; Bell Telephone Laboratories, New Jersey, Researcher, 1917–46; University of Virginia, Professor, 1947–49. *Other Awards:* Comstock Prize, National Academy of Sciences (U.S.), 1928; Elliot Cresson Medal, Franklin Institute, 1931; Hughes Medal, Royal Society, 1935.

Citation: "For their experimental discovery of the diffraction of electrons by crystals" (with G. P. Thomson).

Life Work: Working at Western Electric, Davisson investigated thermionics and the emission of electrons from metals under electron bombardment. In 1919 Davisson set out to study the interaction of electrons with metal surfaces, as their energies and angles, by directing an electron beam against such a surface as well. He measured the scattering of electrons by polycrystalline metals and noticed scatter patterns caused by the wavelike nature of the electron. This confirmed de Broglie's electron wave theory. Davisson's later application of electron beams to crystal physics was applied to the design of microwave sources for radar applications as well as to the physics and design of quarts oscillators.

Publications: "Dispersion of Hydrogen and Helium on Bohr's Theory," *Physical Review, 2nd Series* 8 (1916): 20–27. "Scattering of Electrons by Nickel," with C. H. Kunsman, *Science, New Series* 54 (1921: 522–24. "Thermionic Work Function of Tungsten," with L. H. Germer, *Physical Review, 2nd Series* 20 (1922): 300–30. "Reflection and Refraction of Electrons by a Crystal of Nickel," with L. H. Germer, *Proceedings of the National Academy of Sciences, USA* 14 (1928): 619–27.

Bibliography: *Biographical Memoirs. National Academy of Sciences* (Washington, D.C.: National Academy of Sciences, 1962), vol. 36, pp. 51–84. *Dictionary of Scientific Biography* (New York: Scribner's, 1971), vol. 3, pp. 597–98.

THOMSON, SIR GEORGE PAGET

Prize: Physics, 1937. *Born:* May 3, 1892; Cambridge, England. *Died:* September 10, 1975; Cambridge, England. *Nationality:* British. *Education:* Cambridge University, England, baccalaureate, 1914. *Career:* Cambridge University, England, Professor, 1919–22; University of Aberdeen, Scotland, Professor, 1922–30; Imperial College of Science, England, Professor, 1930–52; Cambridge University, England, Professor and Administrator, 1952–62. *Other Awards:* Hughes Medal, Royal Society, 1939; Knighthood, 1943; Royal Medal, Royal Society, 1949; Faraday Medal, Institution of Electrical Engineers, 1960.

Citation: "For their experimental discovery of the diffraction of electrons by crystals" (with Clinton J. Davisson).

Life Work: Thomson investigated the interaction of electrons with thin, solid films in a vacuum. Using a thin celluloid film as a target, he found that many of the energetic electrons that passed through the film were deflected to form diffuse rings on a photographic plate behind the target. As electron energies were increased, the deflection angles decreased, confirming a wavelike behavior of electrons. He also contributed to the efforts to achieve nuclear fission.

Publications: *The Atom*, with J. J. Thomson (London: Oxford University Press, 1930). *Wave Mechanics of Free Electrons* (New York: McGraw-Hill, 1930). *Theory and Practice of Electron Diffraction*, with W. Cochrane (New York: Macmillan, 1939). *The Foreseeable Future* (London: Cambridge University Press, 1955). *The Inspiration of Science* (London: Oxford University Press, 1961).

Bibliography: *Biographical Memoirs of the Fellows of the Royal Society* (London: Royal Society, 1977), vol. 23, pp. 529–56. *Current Biography Yearbook* (New York: H. W. Wilson, 1947), pp. 635–37.

FERMI, ENRICO

Prize: Physics, 1938. *Born:* September 29, 1901; Rome, Italy. *Died:* November 28, 1954; Chicago, Illinois. *Nationality:* Italian; later U.S. citizen. *Education:* University of Pisa, Italy, Ph.D., 1922. *Career:* University of Florence, Italy, Professor, 1924–26; University of Rome, Italy, Professor, 1926–38; Columbia University, New York, Professor, 1939–45; University of Chicago, Illinois, Professor, 1945–54. *Other Awards:*

Hughes Medal, 1942; Franklin Medal, Franklin Institute, 1947; Barnard Gold Medal, Columbia University, 1950; Rumford Medal, 1953; Fermit Prize, 1954.

Citation: "For his demonstrations of the existence of new radioactive elements produced by neutron irradiation, and for his related discovery of nuclear reactions brought about by slow neutrons."

Life Work: Fermi's field of investigation was the nucleus of the atom. In 1933 he proposed a theory of beta decay, which explained how the nucleus spontaneously emits electrons. Fermi's theory included a new type of force called the weak interaction, which acts between neutrons and protons of the nucleus and is responsible for beta decay. Fermi realized the significance of the neutron as a powerful tool for inciting nuclear reactions, and they further eliminated the need for costly accelerators. Building on the discovery of artificial radioactivity by Frederic Joliot and Irene Joliot-Curie, Fermi and his colleagues bombarded each element in the periodic table with neutrons, hoping to produce new radioactive substances by the attachment of neutrons to nuclei. In the process, they created hundreds of new radioactive substances. When he bombarded uranium element 92, the heaviest naturally occurring element, he caused a nuclear fission, although he did not realize it. In 1935 he discovered that neutrons were actually more effective in causing reactions if their speed was slowed down by passing them through water or paraffin. After emigrating to the United States, Fermi continued to work on a self-sustaining, controlled nuclear fission. In 1939 he suggested to the U.S. Department of the Navy the possibility of an atomic weapon using a powerful chain reaction. In 1942, when the United States created the Manhattan Project to build an atomic bomb, Fermi was given the responsibility for chain reaction and plutonium research and in that capacity directed the construction of the world's first nuclear reactor.

Publications: *Collected Papers,* 2 vols. (Chicago: University of Chicago Press, 1962–65).

Bibliography: *Dictionary of Scientific Biography* (New York: Scribner's, 1971), vol. 4, pp. 576–83. Laura Fermi, *Atoms in the Family* (Chicago: University of Chicago Press, 1954). B. Pontkorvo, *Enrico Fermi* (Pordenone, Italy: Edizioni Studio Tesi, 1993). Emilio Segrè, *Enrico Fermi, Physicist* (Chicago: University of Chicago Press, 1970).

LAWRENCE, ERNEST ORLANDO

Prize: Physics, 1939. *Born:* August 8, 1901; Canton, South Dakota. *Died:* August 27, 1958; Palo Alto, California. *Nationality:* American. *Education:* University of South Dakota, B.A., 1922; University of Minnesota, M.A., 1923; Yale University, Connecticut, Ph.D., 1925. *Career:* Yale University, Connecticut, Professor, 1925–28; University of California, Berkeley, Professor and Administrator, 1928–58. *Other Awards:* Elliott Cresson Medal, Franklin Institute, 1937; Hughes Medal, Royal Society, 1937; Duddell Medal, Royal Physical Society, 1940; Faraday Medal, 1952; American Cancer Society Medal, 1954; Enrico Fermi Award, 1957; Sylvanus Thayer Award, 1958.

Citation: "For the invention and development of the cyclotron and for results obtained with it, especially with regard to artificial radioactive elements."

Life Work: Lawrence is best known for the development of the cyclotron, a circular accelerator in which particles were accelerated in a series of steps rather than in one large, high-voltage surge. Its design depended on the fact that the charged particles in a uniform magnetic field travel in circles because the direction of the particle is constantly deflected. The first crude cyclotron was built in 1930, and each successive model was larger and could accelerate particles to energies of many million electron volts. Cyclotrons were ideal experimental instruments. The particle beam was unidirectional, had adjustable energy, and was far more intense than from any radioactive source. Cyclotrons also opened a vast new field of research and led to the discovery of many new elements not found naturally on earth. Radioactive isotopes obtained through bombardment of the atoms of many different elements became new tools in the cure of many diseases, such as cancer. Almost all the uranium in the atomic bomb dropped on Hiroshima in 1945 was produced by Lawrence and his associates. After the war Lawrence supervised the development of Bevatron accelerators capable of propelling particles to energies reaching billions of electron volts. The Lawrence Livermore Laboratories are named after him.

Publications: "On the Production of High Speed Protons," with N. E. Edlefsen, *Science* 72 (1930): 376–77. "Disintegration of Lithium by Swiftly Moving Protons," with M. S. Livingston and M. G. White, *Physical Review* 42 (1932): 150–51. "An Improved Cyclotron," with Donald Cooksey, *Science* 86 (1937): 411. "High Energy Physics," *American Scientist* 36 (1948): 41–49. "High-Current Accelerators," *Science* 122 (1955): 1127–32.

Bibliography: *Biographical Memoirs. National Academy of Sciences* (Washington, D.C.: National Academy of Sciences, 1970), vol. 41, pp. 251–94. Herbert Childs, *An American Genius: The Life of Ernest Lawrence* (New York: Dutton, 1968). *Dictionary of Scientific Biography* (New York: Scribner's, 1973), vol. 8, pp. 93–96.

STERN, OTTO

Prize: Physics, 1943. *Born:* February 17, 1888; Sohrau, Germany. *Died:* August 17, 1969; Berkeley, California. *Nationality:* Germany; later U.S. citizen. *Education:* University of Breslau, Germany, Ph.D., 1912. *Career:* Technische Hochschule, Zürich, Switzerland, Professor, 1913–14; University of Frankfurt, Germany, Professor, 1914–21; University of Rostock, Germany, Professor, 1921–22; University of Hamburg, Germany, Professor, 1923–33; Carnegie Institute of Technology, Pennsylvania, Professor, 1933–45.

Citation: "For his contribution to the development of the molecular ray method and his discovery of the magnetic moment of the proton."

Life Work: Using the method of molecular beams, Stern verified Maxwell's equation expressing the distribution of velocities of gas molecules. This led him to an investigation of the magnetic moment of atoms. Because atoms contain electrically charged particles in motion, which constitute an electric current, they behave like small magnets. The magnetic moment describes the strength and direction of magnetism. In the Stern-Gerlach experiment, a molecular beam was passed between the poles of a nonuniform magnet, which caused a deflection of the beam. It confirmed quantum theory predictions that atoms would only deflect one way or the other, splitting the beam into two. Later Stern confirmed the Broglie formula regarding the wave properties of large particles by directing a beam of helium gas through toothed wheels onto the surface of a lithium fluoride crystal. He also measured the magnetic moment of the proton, the nucleus of the hydrogen atom.

Publications: "Zur Kinetischen Theorie des Campfdrucks Einatomiger Fester Stoffe und uber die Entropiekonstante Einatomiger Gase," *Physikalische Zeitschrift* 14 (1913): 629–32. "Die Entropie Fester Losungen," *Annalen der Physik, 4th Series* 49 (1916): 823–41. "Ein Weg zur Experimentellen Prufung der Richtungsquantelung im Magnetfield," *Zeitschrift fur Physik* 7 (1921): 249–53. "Das Magnetische Moment des Silberatoms," with W. Gerlach, *Zeitschrift fur Physik* 9 (1922): 353–55. "Uber die Richtungsquantelung im Magnetfeld," with W. Gerlach, *Annalen der Physik, 4th Series* 74 (1924): 673.

Bibliography: *Biographical Memoirs of the National Academy of Sciences* (Washington, D.C.: National Academy of Sciences, 1973), pp. 215–36. *Dictionary of Scientific Biography* (New York: Scibner's, 1976), vol. 13, pp. 40–43. I. Estermann, *Recent Research in Molecular Beams* (New York: Academic Press, 1959), pp. 1–7.

RABI, ISIDOR ISAAC

Prize: Physics, 1944. *Born:* July 29, 1898; Rymanov, Austria. *Died:* January 11, 1988; New York, New York. *Nationality:* Austrian; later U.S. citizen. *Education:* Cornell University, New York, B.Chem., 1919; Columbia University, New York, Ph.D., 1927. *Career:* Columbia University, New York, Professor, 1929–67. *Other Awards:* Sigma Xi Semicentennial Prize, 1936; Elliott Cresson Medal, Franklin Institute, 1942; United States Medal for Merit, 1948; King's Medal, England, 1948; Commander, Order of the Southern Cross, Brazil, 1952; Henrietta Szold Award, 1956; Barnard Medal, 1960; Priestly Memorial Award, Dickinson College, 1964; Niels Bohr International Gold Medal, 1967; Atoms for Peace Award, 1967; Tribute of Appreciation, United States Department, 1978; Pupin Gold Medal, Columbia University, 1981; Franklin D. Roosevelt Four Freedoms Medal, 1985; Public Welfare Medal, National Academy of Sciences, 1985; Vannevar Bush Award, 1986; Weizmann Medallion, 1987.

Citation: "For his resonance method for recording the magnetic properties of atomic nuclei."

Life Work: Rabi's field of investigation was nuclear spin, a property of electrons in a magnetic field. The spin axis can be oriented in either of two ways, the energies of which depend on the magnetic moment associated with the spin as well as on the magnetic field strength. The nucleus of an atom also interacts with magnetic fields by means of the nuclear spin and its associated magnetic moment. Rabi predicted that a molecular beam could be split into more than two parts. The number of subbeams would depend upon the interactions of the nuclear and electron spins with each other and with the applied magnetic field, and each subbeam would be composed of atoms that shared the same nuclear and electron spins. By applying a weak radiofrequency signal to a molecular beam in a magnetic field, Rabi made atoms change their spin orientation. Adjusting the frequency of the radio signal allowed him to make precise measurements of nuclear spin and of the strength of the nucleus's own magnetic field. His discovery helped in an understanding of the behavior of the nucleus.

Publications: "The Principal Magnetic Susceptibilities of Crystals," *Physical Review* 29 (1927): 174–85. "Nuclear Spin in Isotopic Mixtures," *Physical Review* 45 (1934): 334. "A New Method of Measuring Nuclear Magnetic Moment," with others, *Physical Review* 53 (1938): 318. "Molecular Beam Resonance Method for Measuring Nuclear Magnetic Moments. The Magnetic Moments of 3-LI–6, 3-Li–7, and 9-F–19," with others, *Physical Review* 55 (1939): 526–35. "The Radiofrequency Spectra of Atoms," with P. Kusch and S. Millman, *Physical Review* 57 (1940): 765–80. *Science: The Center of Culture* (New York: World Publishing, 1970).

Bibliography: *My Life and Times as a Physicist* (Clarement, Calif.: Claremont College, 1960). John Rigden, *Rabi: Scientist and Citizen* (New York: Basic Books, 1987).

PAULI, WOLFGANG ERNST

Prize: Physics, 1945. *Born:* April 25, 1900; Vienna, Austria. *Died:* December 15, 1958; Zürich, Switzerland. *Nationality:* Austrian; later Swiss citizen. *Education:* University of Munich, Germany, Ph.D., 1921. *Career:* University of Göttingen, Germany, Researcher, 1921–22; University of Copenhagen, Denmark, Researcher, 1922–23; University of Hamburg, Germany, Professor, 1923–28; Eidgenossische Technishe Hochschule, Zürich, Switzerland, Professor, 1928–58. *Other Awards:* Lorentz Medaille, 1930; Franklin Medal, 1952; Max Planck Medal, 1958.

Citation: "For the discovery of the Exclusion Principle, also called the Pauli Principle."

Life Work: Pauli's field of investigation was atomic structure and the behavior of atoms in magnetic fields. In 1925 Pauli suggested that electrons have a property later identified as spin, or intrinsic angular momentum. Pauli introduced a two-valuedness property to the electron. In a magnetic field, an electron with spin has two possible orientations, that is, with the spin axis parallel or antiparallel to the direction of the field. The orbital motion of the electron in the atom defines another axis that can be oriented in various ways with respect to an externally imposed magnetic field. Various possible combinations of spin and orbital orientation differ slightly in energy, causing a proliferation in the number of atomic energy states. Transitions between each of the sublevels and some other orbits correspond to different wavelengths of light, thus accounting for the fine splitting of the spectral lines. Pauli extended his analysis to explain why electrons in an atom do not all occupy the lowest energy level. In Pauli's model the allowed energy states or orbits of electrons are described by the four quantum numbers of each electron. These numbers define the electron's basic energy level, its orbital angular momentum, its magnetic moment, and its spin orientation. Each of the quantum numbers can assume only certain values, and only certain combinations of values are possible. On this basis, Pauli formulated the exclusion principle, which states that no two electrons in a system can have an identical set of quantum numbers. Thus, each shell of an atom can have only a limited number of electron orbits, determined by the possible values of the quantum numbers. Pauli's exclusion principle was critical to an understanding of the structure and behavior of atoms, the atomic nucleus and the properties of metals. It explains the chemical interaction of the elements, and their organization in the periodic table. Pauli's contributions helped to expand quantum mechanics so that it could describe high-energy particles and the interaction of particles with light and other forms of electromagnetic fields. This field came to be known as relativistic quantum electrodynamics. In the 1930s Paul also predicted the existence of an undetected particle, later named neutrino, observed during the beta decay of atomic nuclei.

Publications: "Relativitatstheorie," *Encyklopaide der Mathematischen Wissenschaften* (Leipzig, 1921), vol. 2, pp. 539–775; *Theory of Relativity*, trans G. Field (New York: Pergamon Press, 1958). "Uber den Zusammenhang des Abschlusses der Elektronengruppen im Atom mit der Komplexstruktur der Spektren," *Zeitschrift fur Physik* 31 (1925): 765. *Naturerklarung und Psyche*, with C. G. Jung (Zürich: Rascher, 1952). *Collected Scientific Papers*, ed. R. Kronig and V. F. Weisskopf (New York: Interscience Publishers, 1964).

Bibliography: *Current Biography Yearbook* (New York: H. W. Wilson, 1946), pp. 468–70. *Dictionary of Scientific Biography* (New York: Scribner's, 1974), vol. 10, pp. 422–25. Markus Fierz and V. F. Weisskopf, eds., *Theoretical Physics in the Twentieth Century: A Memorial Volume to Wolfgang Pauli* (New York: Interscience Publishers, 1960). *Writings on Physics and Philosophy* (Berlin: Springer-Verlag, 1994).

BRIDGMAN, PERCY WILLIAMS

Prize: Physics, 1946. *Born:* April 21, 1882; Cambridge, Massachusetts. *Died:* August 20, 1961; Randolph, New Hampshire. *Nationality:* American. *Education:* Harvard University, Massachusetts, B.A., 1904; Harvard University, Massachusetts, M.A., 1905; Harvard University, Massachusetts, Ph.D., 1908. *Career:* Harvard University, Massachusetts, Professor, 1908–54. *Other Awards:* Rumford Medal, American Academy of Arts and Sciences, 1929; Cresson Medal, Franklin Institute, 1932; Comstock Prize,

National Academy of Sciences, 1933; Bakhius-Roozeboom Medal, Royal Academy of Sciences, Netherlands, 1933; Bingham Medal, Society of Rheology, 1935; Research Corporation of America Award, 1937.

Citation: "For the invention of an apparatus to produce extremely high pressures, and for the discoveries he made therewith in the field of high pressure physics."

Life Work: In 1905 Bridgman invented a leakproof method, known as the Bridgman Seal, for sealing pressure vessels. It ensures that the sealing gasket, made of rubber or soft metal, is always compressed to a higher pressure than the pressure to be contained. This device enabled Bridgman to measure the compressibility, density, and melting point of hundreds of materials as a function of applied pressure and temperature. His work proved that many materials are polymorphic under high pressure and that their crystal structure changed to allow tighter packing of the atoms in the crystal. His studies revealed two new forms of phosphorus and hot ice, or ice that is stable under pressure of 290,000 pounds per square inch. Using special equipment Bridgman was able to study materials at 1.5 million pounds per square inch. During World War I, Bridgman developed sound development systems for antisubmarine warfare.

Publications: *The Logic of Modern Physics* (New York: Macmillan, 1927). *The Physics of High Pressure* (New York: Macmillan, 1931). *The Nature of Thermodynamics* (Cambridge: Harvard University Press, 1941). *The Thermodynamics of Electrical Phenomena in Metals and a Condensed Collection of Thermodynamic Formulas* (New York: Dover Publications, 1961). *Collected Experimental Papers* (Cambridge: Harvard University Press, 1964).

Bibliography: *Biographical Memoirs of the Fellows of the Royal Society* (London: Royal Society, 1962), vol. 8, pp. 26–40. *Dictionary of Scientific Biography* (New York: Scribner's, 1971), vol. 2, pp. 457–61. *Reflections of a Physicist* (New York: Philosophical Library, 1950).

APPLETON, SIR EDWARD VICTOR

Prize: Physics, 1947. *Born:* September 6, 1892; Bradford, England. *Died:* April 21, 1965; Edinburgh, Scotland. *Nationality:* British. *Education:* Cambridge University, England, B.A., 1913. *Career:* Cambridge University, England, Researcher, 1917–24; London University, England, Professor, 1924–36; Cambridge University, England, Professor, 1936–49; University of Edinburgh, Scotland, Administrator, 1949–65. *Other Awards:* Knighthood, 1941; Medal of Merit (U.S.), 1947; French Legion of Honor, 1947; Albert Medal, Royal Society of Arts, 19590; Gunning Victoria Jubilee Prize, Royal Society, Scotland, 1960; Medal of Honor, Institute of Radio Engineers of America, 1962.

Citation: "For his investigations of the physics of the upper atmosphere especially for the discovery of the so-called Appleton layer."

Life Work: Appleton's field of investigation was the propagation of radio waves in atmosphere. Using frequency modulation radar, he provided the first experimental proof of the existence of the ionosphere. This paved the way for the invention of the radar. Two years later Appleton discovered a second nonconducting layer some 150 miles above the surface of the earth, called the Appleton Layer. His second discovery is the basis of direct worldwide radio broadcasts. Continuing to investigate the ionosphere, Appleton established that it was controlled by sunlight, and that it is affected by particles emitted by the sun as well as by solar ultraviolet emissions and lunar tides.

Publications: "Equivalent Heights of the Atmospheric Ionized Regions in England and America," *Nature* 123 (1929): 445. *The Thermionic Value* (London: Methuen, 1931). *Thermionic Vacuum Tubes* (New York: E. P. Dutton, 1933). "Some Problems of Atmospheric Physics. Atmospheric Ozone," *Journal of the Royal Society of Arts* 85 (1937): 299–307. "New Material for Old," *J. Inst. Civil Engrs. (London)* 8 (1939–40): 448–68.

Bibliography: *Biographical Memoirs of the Fellows of the Royal Society* (London: Royal Society, 1966), vol. 12, pp. 1–21. *Dictionary of Scientific Biography* (New York: Scribner's, 1970), vol. 1, pp. 195–96.

BLACKETT, PATRICK MAYNARD STUART

Prize: Physics, 1948. *Born:* November 18, 1897; London, England. *Died:* July 13, 1974; London, England. *Nationality:* British. *Education:* Cambridge University, England, B.A., 1921: Cambridge University, England, M.A., 1923. *Career:* British Navy, 1914– 19; Cambridge University, England, Professor, 1923–33; University of London, England, Professor, 1933–37; University of Manchester, England, Professor, 1937–53; Imperial College of Science and Technology, England, Professor, 1953–65. *Other Awards:* Royal Medal, Royal Society of London, 1940; American Medal for Merit, 1946; Dalton Medal, 1949; Copley Medal, Royal Society, 1956; Order of Merit, 1967.

Citation: "For his development of the Wilson cloud chamber method, and his discoveries therewith in the fields of nuclear physics and cosmic radiation."

Life Work: Blackett's field of investigation was cosmic rays. Using a Wilson counter-controlled cloud chamber to photograph the track of charged particles passing through the chamber, he confirmed the existence of the positron discovered earlier. He also confirmed Einstein's theorem that energy is transformed into matter by proving that showers of positron-electron pairs rose from gamma rays.

Publications: "Some Photographs of the Tracks of Penetrating Radiation," with G. P. S. Ochialini, *Proceedings of the Royal Society of London* A139 (1934): 699. "Some Experiments on the Production of Positive Electrons," with J. Chadwick and G. P. S. Occhialini, *Proceedings of the Royal Society of London* A144 (1934): 235. *Cosmic Rays. The Halley Lecture* (Oxford: Clarendon Press, 1936). *Military and Political Conse-*

quences of Atomic Energy (London: Turnstile Press, 1948). "The Elementary Particles of Nature." *British Journal of Radiology* 31 (1958): 1.

Bibliography: *Biographical Memoirs of the Fellows of the Royal Society* (London: Royal Society, 1975), vol. 21, pp. 1–115. Bernard Lovell, *PMS Blackett: A Biographical Memoir* (London: Royal Society, 1976).

YUKAWA, HIDEKI

Prize: Physics, 1949. *Born:* January 23, 1907; Tokyo, Japan. *Died:* September 8, 1981; Kyoto, Japan. *Nationality:* Japanese. *Education:* Kyoto Imperial University, Japan, M.S., 1929; Osaka University, Japan, Doctor of Science, 1938. *Career:* Kyoto Imperial University, Japan, Professor, 1932–70. *Other Awards:* Imperial Prize, Japan Academy, 1940; Decoration of Cultural Merit, 1943; Lomonosov Gold Medal, 1964; Order of Merit, Germany, 1964; Order of Rising Sun Japan, 1977.

Citation: "For his prediction of the existence of mesons on the basis of theoretical work on nuclear forces."

Life Work: Yukawa's field of investigation was a problem that had puzzled physicists: Why does the nucleus of an atom not split apart? The mystery was the cohesion of the protons (which repel each other) and the cohesion of the neutrons to each other and to the protons. In 1935 Yukawa proposed a strong nuclear binding force associated with a hypothetical exchange particle with a large mass, calculated at two hundred times that of the electron. This particle could not be detected in ordinary nuclear reactions because of its high energy, but could be detected in violent collisions between cosmic rays and atomic nuclei. Later called the meson, the new particle was found to be a pair, one light (discovered by Carl D. Anderson) and the other heavy. Yukawa's heavy meson was found in the earth's upper atmosphere where primary cosmic rays collided with nuclei for the first time.

Publications: "On the Interaction of Elementary particles. I," *Proceedings of the Physical-Mathematical Society of Japan* 17 (1935): 48. *Introduction to Quantum Mechanics* (Tokyo: Kobundo, 1947). *Introduction to the Theory of Elementary Particles*, 2 vols. (Tokyo: Iwanami shoten, 1948). *Yukawa Hideki Jishenshu* (*Selected Works of Hideki Yukawa*), 5 vols. (Tokyo: Asahi Shimbunsha, 1971). *Creativity and Intuition: A Physicist Looks at East and West*, trans J. Bester (Tokyo: Kodansha International, 1973). *Hideki Yukawa Scientific Works* (Tokyo: Iwanami Shoten, 1979).

Bibliography: *Biographical Memoirs of the Royal Society* (London: Royal Society, 1983), pp. 661–76. *Tabbito, the Traveler*, trans. L. Brown and R. Yoshida (Singapore: World Scientific, 1982).

POWELL, CECIL FRANK

Prize: Physics, 1950. *Born:* December 5, 1903; Tonbridge, England. *Died:* August 9, 1969; Bellano, Lake Como, Italy. *Nationality:* British. *Education:* Cambridge University, England, baccalaureate, 1925; Cambridge University, England, Ph.D., 1927. *Career:* Bristol University, England, Professor, 1928–69. *Other Awards:* Charles Vernon Boys Prize, 1947; Hughes Medal, Royal Society, 1949; Rutherford Medal and Prize, 1960; Royal Medal, Royal Society, 1951; Lomonosov Gold Medal, Soviet Academy of Sciences, 1967; Guthrie Medal and Prize, Institute of Physics and Physical Society, 1969.

Citation: "For his development of the photographic method of studying nuclear processes and his discoveries regarding mesons made with this method."

Life Work: Powell's field of investigation was tracking of electrically charged particles by using photographic plates. Using special emulsion and film developing techniques, Powell discovered a new charged particle in cosmic radiation: the pion or pi-meson. Its mass is 273 times that of the electron and about one-seventh that of a proton. It is short-lived, decaying into muon and a neutrino. The pion is largely responsible for the forces between protons and neutrons that bind the atomic nucleus together. This discovery led to the subsequent detection of many other new subatomic particles. Powell also discovered the K-mesons which are heavier and shorter lived than the pi-meson.

Publications: *The Study of Elementary Particles by the Photographic Method* (London: Pergamon Press, 1959). "Cosmic Radiation," *Proceedings of the Institute of Electrical Engineers* 107B (1960): 389–94. "The Role of Pure Science in European Civilization," *Physics Today* 18 (1965): 56–64. "Promise and Problems of Modern Science," *Nature* 216 (1967): 543–46. *Selected Papers of Cecil Frank Powell*, ed. E. H. S. Burhop, W. O. Lock, and M. G. K. Menon (Amsterdam: North Holland, 1972).

Bibliography: *Biographical Memoirs of the Fellows of the Royal Society* (London: Royal Society, 1971), pp. 541–63. *Dictionary of Scientific Biography* (New York: Scribner's, 1975), vol. 11, pp. 117–18.

COCKCROFT, SIR JOHN DOUGLAS

Prize: Physics, 1951. *Born:* May 27, 1897; Todmorden, Yorkshire, England. *Died:* September 18, 1967; Cambridge, England. *Nationality:* British. *Education:* University of Manchester, England, M.Sc.Tech., 1922; Cambridge University, England, B.A., 1924; Cambridge University, England, B.A., 1924; Cambridge University, England, Ph.D., 1928. *Career:* Cambridge University, England, Professor, 1928–39; British Government Service, 1939–44; British Atomic Energy Projects, 1944–59; Cambridge University, England, Professor, 1959–67. *Other Awards:* Hughes Medal, 1938; American Freedom Medal, 1947; Knighthood, 1948; Chevalier de la Legion d'Honneur, 1950; Royal Medal, Royal Society, 1954; Faraday Medal, 1955; Kelvin Gold Medal, 1956; Niels Bohr International Gold Medal, 1958; Grand Cross, Order of Alfonso X, Spain, 1958; Atoms for Peace Award, 1961.

Citation: "For their pioneer work on the transmutation of atomic nuclei by artificially accelerated atomic particles." (with Ernest Walton).

Life Work: As director of the famed Cavendish Laboratory in Cambridge, England, Cockcroft worked on improving particle acceleration using the direct method. Inspired by the theories of George Gamow, Cockcroft transmuted lithium and hydrogen into helium, thus becoming the first scientist to split the atom by artificial means. Using a device capable of applying 600,000 volts of electricity to a tube containing hydrogen, Cockcroft bombarded lithium with hydrogen nuclei or protons.

Publications: "The Design of Coils for the Production of Strong Magnetic Fields," *Philosophical Transactions of the Royal Society* A227 (1928): 317–43. "Experiments with High Velocity Positive Ions," with E. T. S. Walton, *Proceedings of the Royal Society* A129 (1930): 477–89. "Experiments with High Velocity Positive Ions. I. Further Developments in the Method of Obtaining High Velocity Positive Ions," with E. T. S. Walton, *Proceedings of the Royal Society* A136 (1932): 619–30. "Experiments with High Velocity Positive Ions. II. The Disintegration of Elements by High Velocity Protons," *Proceedings of the Royal Society* A137 (1932): 229–42.

Bibliography: *Biographical Memoirs of the Fellows of the Royal Society* (London: Royal Society, 1968), vol. 14, 139–88. *Dictionary of Scientific Biography* (New York: Scribner's, 1971), vol. 3, pp. 328–31. Guy Hartcup and T. E. Allibone, *Cockcroft and the Atom* (Bristol, England: Adam Hilger, 1984).

WALTON, ERNEST THOMAS SINTON

Prize: Physics, 1951. *Born:* October 6, 1903; Dungarvan, Ireland. *Died:* June 25, 1995; Belfast, Ireland. *Nationality:* Irish. *Education:* Methodist College, Ireland, B.A., 1922; Trinity College, Ireland, M.A., 1926 Trinity College, Ireland, M.Sc., 1927 Cambridge University, England, Ph.D., 1930. *Career:* Lord Rutherford's Research Assistant, 1927–34; Trinity College, Dublin, Ireland, Professor, 1934–74. *Other Awards:* Hughes Medal, Royal Society, 1938.

Citation: "For their pioneer work on the transmutation of atomic nuclei by artificially accelerated atomic particles." (with John Cockcroft).

Life Work: While working for Rutherford at Cambridge, Walton built a linear accelerator which became a prototype for subsequent atom-smashers. Using voltages of about 400 kilowatts, with a proton current of a few microamperes, Walton and John Cockcroft were able to bombard lithium atoms with sufficient force to transform each lithium nucleus into two helium nuclei—the first successful transmutation of elements by human means. Their experiments demonstrated the enormous energies available in atomic nuclei and provided the first experimental confirmation of Einstein's equations showing the equivalence of mass and energy.

Publications: "Production of High Speed Electrons by Indirect Means," *Cambridge Philosophical Society Proceedings* (October 1929): 469–81. "Experiments with High Velocity Positive Ions," with P. I. Dee, *Royal Society Proceedings* A (September 1, 1933): 733–42. "High Velocity Positive Ions, Part 3: Disintegration of Li, B, and C by Diplons," with J. Cockcroft, *Royal Society Proceedings* A (May 1, 1934): 704–20. "Part 4: Production of Induced Radioactivity by Protons and Diplons," with J. Cockcroft and C. W. Gilbert, *Royal Society Proceedings* A (January 1, 1935): 225–40.

Bibliography: *Current Biography Yearbook* (New York: H. W. Wilson, 1952), pp. 618–20. *Modern Men of Science* (New York: McGraw-Hill, 1966), pp. 509–10. *Nobel Prize Winners: Physics* (Pasadena, Calif.: Salem Press, 1988), vol. 2, pp. 591–600. *New York Times* Biographical Service, June 28, 1995, p. 938.

BLOCH, FELIX

Prize: Physics, 1952. *Born:* October 23, 1905; Zürich, Switzerland. *Died:* September 10, 1983; Zürich, Switzerland. *Nationality:* Swiss, later U.S. citizen. *Education:* University of Leipzig, Germany, Ph.D., 1928. *Career:* University of Zürich, Switzerland, Researcher, 1928–29; University of Utrecht, Netherlands, Researcher, 1929–30; University of Leipzig, Germany, Researcher, 1931–32; University of Leipzig, Germany, Professor, 1932–33; Stanford University, California, Professor, 1934–71.

Citation: "For their development of new methods for nuclear magnetic precision measurements and discoveries in connection therewith" (with Edward M. Purcell).

Life Work: Because of Bloch's contributions to the theory of superconductivity and to the theoretical understanding of magnetic systems, a number of theorems and effects are named after him: the Bloch theory on superconductivity, the Bloch law concerning the temperature dependence of magnetization in a ferromagnetic material, Bloch walls, the transition region between areas of a ferromagnetic material with different magnetic orientations, and the Bloch-Gruneisen relationship concerning the temperature dependence of the electrical conductivity of metals. After leaving Germany for the United States in 1933, Bloch investigated the properties of neutron, measured its magnetic moment, and investigated the properties of uranium isotopes. After World War II, Bloch described a method of measuring nuclear magnetic moments that was both precise and nondestructive. Called nuclear magnetic resonance (NMR), it is one of the great analytic tools of chemistry and is used also in medicine, as in computer-assisted tomography (CAT) scanners. NMR techniques also led to the development of radio astronomy.

Publications: "The Magnetic Moment of the Neutron," *Ann. Inst. Henri Poincare* 8 (1938): 63–78. "Nuclear Induction," *Physical Review* 70 (1946): 460–74. "Chemical

Analysis by Nuclear Inductions," with William W. Hansen, U.S. Patent 2, 561, 481. July 24, 1951. "Dynamical Theory of Nuclear Induction. II," *Physical Review* 102 (1956): 104–35.

Bibliography: Marvin Chodorow, *Felix Bloch and the Twentieth Century Physics* (Houston: Rice University Press, 1980). *Nobel Prize Winners: Physics* (Pasadena, Calif.: Salem Press, 1988), vol. 2, pp. 601–10.

PURCELL, EDWARD MILLS

Prize: Physics, 1952. *Born:* August 30, 1912; Taylorville, Illinois. *Died:* March 7, 1997; Cambridge, Massachusetts. *Nationality:* American. *Education:* Purdue University, Indiana, B.S.E.E., 1933; Harvard University, Massachusetts, A.M., 1935; Harvard University, Massachusetts, Ph.D., 1938. *Career:* Harvard University, Massachusetts, Professor, 1938–40; Massachusetts Institute of Technology, Researcher, 1941–45; Harvard University, Massachusetts, Professor, 1946–80. *Other Awards:* Oersted Medal, American Association of Physics Teachers, 1968; National Medal of Science, 1980; Harvard Medal, 1986.

Citation: "For their development of new methods for nuclear magnetic precision measurements and discoveries in connection therewith" (with Felix Bloch).

Life Work: Purcell's field of investigation was the nuclear magnetic moment. Working independently but at the same time as Felix Bloch, he developed a technique for this purpose that was nondestructive and precise. It involved placing the sample to be studied between the poles of a small magnet activated by radio signals. The field of the magnet fluctuated with a frequency corresponding to that of the controlling radio waves. The small magnet, in turn, was placed in the much stronger field of a large nonfluctuating magnet. The strong fixed field caused the nuclei in the sample to precess at a fixed frequency. When the fluctuation frequency of the weak field exactly matched the precessional frequency of the nuclei, the spin orientation of the nuclei would suddenly reverse, an effect called nuclear magnetic resonance (NMR). This effect allowed the precision frequency as well as the nuclear magnetic moment to be determined with precision. NMR soon came to be a great tool in chemical analysis as well as medical diagnosis. In 1951 Purcell found that interstellar hydrogen atoms emit electromagnetic radiation at a radio frequency corresponding to a wavelength of 21 centimeters. To detect this wavelength, Purcell built the first radio telescope using NMR. Radio telescopes have allowed the mapping of the overall structure of the galaxy despite galactic dust clouds.

Publications: "Relaxation Effects in Nuclear Magnetic Resonance Absorption," with N. Bloembergen and R. V. Pound, *Physical Review* 73 (1948): 679–712. "I. Rigid Crystal Lattices," with others, *Journal of Chemical Physics* 17 (1949): 972–81. "A Precise Determination of the Proton Magnetic Moment in Bohr Magnetons," with J. H. Gardner *Physical Review* 76 (1949): 1262–63. "Interactions between Nuclear Spins in Molecules," with N. F. Ramsey, *Physical Review* 85 (1952): 143–44.

Bibliography: *Current Biography Yearbook* (New York: H. W. Wilson, 1954), pp. 519–21. *Nobel Prize Winners: Physics.* (Pasadena, Calif.: Salem Press, 1988), vol. 2, 611–20.

ZERNIKE, FRITS

Prize: Physics, 1953. *Born:* July 16, 1888; Amsterdam, Netherlands. *Died:* March 10, 1966; Naarden, Netherlands. *Nationality:* Dutch. *Education:* University of Amsterdam, Netherlands, Ph.D., 1915. *Career:* University of Groningen, Netherlands, Professor, 1913–58. *Other Awards:* Gold Medal, Dutch Society for Sciences, 1912; Rumford Medal, Royal Society, 1952.

Citation: "For his demonstration of the phase contrast method, especially for his invention of the phase contrast microscope."

Life Work: Zernike is credited with the discovery of the phase-contrast microscope. His field of investigation was optics, especially the effect of flaws in diffraction gratings. A diffraction grating is a clear glass or mirror whose surface is scored by a large number of fine, closely spaced, equidistant grooves, which divide the transmitted or reflected light into many slitlike sources. Repetitive errors in the groove spacing produce extra lines, called ghosts, on either side of a prominent bright line. Zernike found that ghosts represented phase shifts in the light cycle. Phases differ because light travels at different speeds in different substances. In his experiments Zernike converted the phase change into an amplitude change by superimposing the light passing through a transparent object on a uniform background illumination representing a small portion of the direct light deliberately advanced in phase by a quarter of a wavelength. The background illumination was introduced by a phase plate (a glass plate with an etched plate in it) into the light path in the focal plane of the microscope objective lens. Zernike's phase-contrast microscope proved useful in viewing colorless organisms.

Publications: "Die Beugung von Rontgenstrahlen in Flussigkeiten als Effect der Molekulanordnung," with J. A. Prins, *Z. Phys.* 41 (1927): 184. "Diffraction Theory of the Knife-Edge Test and Its Improved Form, the Phase-Contrast Method," *Mon. Nat. Roy. Astron. Soc.* 94 (1934): 377. "Das Phasenkontrastverfahren bei der Mikroskopschen Beobachtung," *Z. Techn. Phys.* 16 (1935): 454. "The Propagation of Order in Cooperative Phenomena," *Physica* 7 (1940): 565. "A Precision Method for Measuring Small Phase Differences," *Journal of the Optical Society of America* 40 (1950): 326.

Bibliography: *Biographical Memoirs of the Fellows of the Royal Society* (Cambrdige: Royal Society, 1967), vol. 13, pp. 393–402. *Dictionary of Scientific Biography* (New York: Scribner's, 1976), vol. 14, pp. 616–17.

BORN, MAX

Prize: Physics, 1954. *Born:* December 11, 1882; Breslau, Germany. *Died:* January 5, 1970; Göttingen, Germany. *Nationality:* German; later British citizen. *Education:* University of Göttingen, Germany, Ph.D., 1907. *Career:* Cambridge University, England, Researcher, 1907–1908; University of Breslau, Germany, Researcher, 1908–1909; University of Göttingen, Germany, Professor, 1909–12; University of Chicago, Illinois, Researcher, 1912–15; University of Berlin, Professor, 1915–19; German Army, 1915–19; University of Frankfurt, Germany, Professor, 1919–21; University of Göttingen, Germany, Professor, 1921–33; Cambridge University, England, Professor, 1933–36; University of Edinburgh, Scotland, Professor, 1936–53. *Other Awards:* Stokes Medal, England, 1934; Macdougall-Brisbane and Gunning-Victoria Jubilee Prize, Royal Society of Edinburgh, Scotland, 1945, 1950; Max Planck Medaille, Germany, 1948; Hughes Medal, Royal Society, 1950; Grotius Medal, Munich, Germany, 1956.

Citation: "For his fundamental research in quantum mechanics, especially for his statistical interpretation of the wave function."

Life Work: Born's field of investigation was quantum theory, applying the theory of wave mechanics and matrix mechanics to the theory of atomic scattering. Born devised the principle known as Born approximation. Born created a new picture of atomic structure that transformed physics and chemistry. Born worked with Heisenberg and Bohr on the statistical interpretation of quantum mechanics, now known as the Copenhagen Interpretation. He maintained that quantum mechanics gives only a statistical description of a particle's location.

Publications: *Zur Begrundung der Matrizenmechanik* (Stuttgart: E. Battenberg, 1962). *Zur Statistischen Deutung der Quantentheorie*, 2 vols. (Stuttgart: E. Battenberg, 1962). *Ausgewoehlte Abhandlungen*, 2 vols. (Göttingen: Vandenhoek and Ruprecht, 1963).

Bibliography: *Dictionary of Scientific Biography* (New York: Scribner's, 1978), vol. 15, pp. 39–44. *Mein Leben. Die Errinerungen des Nobelpreistragers* (Munich: Nymphenburger Verlagshandlung, 1975). *Physics in My Generation* (New York: Pergamon Press, 1956).

BOTHE, WALTHER WILHELM GEORG

Prize: Physics, 1954. *Born:* January 8, 1891; Oranienburg, Germany. *Died:* February 8, 1957; Heidelberg, Germany. *Nationality:* German. *Education:* University of Berlin, Germany, Ph.D., 1914. *Career:* Germany Army, 1915–20; University of Berlin, Germany, Professor, 1920–30; Giessen University, Germany, Professor, 1930–32; Max Planck Institute, Germany, Researcher and Administrator, 1932–57. *Other Awards:* Ordre Pour le Merité, peace class, 1952; Max Planck Prize, 1953; Grossen Verdeinstkreuz Bundesrepublik, 1954.

Citation: "For the coincidence method and his discoveries made therewith."

Life Work: Bothe's field of investigation was the deflection of alpha and beta particles by matter. Working with Geiger, he devised a way of using Geiger counters in what came to be known as the coincidence method, which used two counters each with a hydrogen-filled cylinder to record the scatter quantum and the recoil electron produced by each collision. He found that the scatter quantum and the recoil electron occurred often, resulting almost always from a single collision. It disproved Bohr's theory that at the atomic level the interactions of individual particles do not have to conserve either energy or momentum.

Publications: "Ein Weg zur Experimentellen Nachprufund der Theorie von Bohr, Kraners and Slater," *Zeitschrift fur Physik* 26 (1924): 44. "Uber des Wesen des Comptoneffekts," *Zeitschrift fur Physik* 32 (1925): 639. *Atlas Typischer Nebelkammerbilder,* with Wolfgang Gentner (Berlin: J. Springer, 1940). "Das Wesen der Hohenstrahlung," *Zeitschrift fur Physik* 56 (1959): 75.

Bibliography: *Current Biography Yearbook* (New York: H. W. Wilson, 1955), pp. 55–56. *Dictionary of Scientific Biography* (New York: Scribner's, 1973), vol. 2, pp. 337–39. *Nobel Prize Winners: Physics* (Pasadena, Calif.: Salem Press, 1988), vol. 2, pp. 643–52.

KUSCH, POLYKARP

Prize: Physics, 1955. *Born:* January 26, 1911; Blankenburg, Germany. *Died:* March 20, 1993; Dallas, Texas. *Nationality:* American. *Education:* Case Institute of Technology, Ohio, B.S., 1931; University of Illinois, M.S., 1933; University of Illinois, Ph.D., 1936. *Career:* University of Minnesota, Researcher, 1936–37; Columbia University, New York, Professor, 1937–41; Westinghouse Electric and Manufacturing Company, Researcher, 1941–42; Columbia University, New York, Researcher, 1942–44; Bell Telephone Laboratories, New Jersey, Researcher, 1944–46; Columbia University, New York, Professor and Administrator, 1946–72; University of Texas at Dallas, Professor, 1972–82. *Other Awards:* Illinois Achievement Award, University of Illinois, 1975.

Citation: "For his precision determination of the magnetic moment of the electron."

Life Work: Using magnetic resonance, Kusch studied the magnetic moment of the electron and measured the ratio of the total intrinsic and orbital magnetic moments of beams of atoms in different energy states. The result was always the same: The intrinsic magnetic moment of the electron is larger than its orbital magnetic moment by a little more than one-tenth of a percent. His work was an integral part of the field of quantum electrodynamics.

Publications: "The Radiofrequency Spectra of Atoms," with S. Millman and I. I. Rabi, *Physical Review* 57 (1940): 765–80. "The Magnetic Moment of the Electron," with

H. M. Foley, *Physical Review* 74 (1948): 250–63. "The Magnetic Moment of the Proton," with H. Taub, *Physical Review* 75 (1949): 1481–92. "The World of Science and the Scientist's World," *Bulletin of the Atomic Scientists* 24 (October 1968): 38–43. "A Personal View of Science and the Future," in *The Future of Science; 1975 Nobel Conference Organized by Gustavus Adolphus College* (New York: John Wiley & Sons, 1977), pp. 39–55.

Bibliography: *Current Biography Yearbook* (New York: H. W. Wilson, 1956), pp. 348–50. *National Cyclopedia of American Biography* (New York: James T. White, 1960), vol. I, pp. 35. *Nobel Prize Winners: Physics* (Pasadena, Calif.: Salem Press, 1988), vol. 2, pp. 663–72. *New York Times* Biographical Service , March 23, 1993, p. 401.

LAMB, WILLIS EUGENE, JR.

Prize: Physics, 1955. *Born:* July 12, 1913; Los Angeles, California. *Nationality:* American. *Education:* University of California, B.S., 1934; University of California, Ph.D., 1938. *Career:* Columbia University, New York, Professor, 1938–51; Stanford University, California, Professor, 1951–56; Oxford University, England, Professor, 1956–62; Yale University, Connecticut, Professor, 1962–74; University of Arizona, Professor, 1974–. *Other Awards:* Rumford Award, American Academy of Arts, 1953; Research Corporation Award, 1955; Yeshiva Award, 1962.

Citation: "For his discoveries concerning the fine structure of the hydrogen spectrum."

Life Work: Lamb's field of investigation was the meta-stable states of atoms. Unlike the excited or high-energy state of an atom, which decays quickly by decaying to a lower-energy state, meta-stable states last much longer. Pursuing this interest, Lamb studied the absorption and emission of microwave radiation by atoms. In a hydrogen atom, a single electron moves around the nucleus in a series of orbits, in each of which the electron has a definite energy. For the electron to rise from a lower to a higher orbit, the atom must absorb a photon whose energy corresponds to the energy difference between the orbits. In the reverse process, an atom emits a photon of the appropriate energy. Such transitions give atomic hydrogen a spectrum of distinct, sharply defined lines. The so-called Lamb Shift describes atoms making the transition to a short-lived state by absorbing the radiation. The two energy levels are not identical but are separated by a small amount of energy. In later life Lamb made contributions to beta decay, cosmic-ray showers, interactions of neutrons and matter, magnetic oscillators, and lasers.

Publications: "Fine Structure of the Hydrogen Atom by a Microwave Method," with Robert C. Retherford, *Physical Review* 72 (1947): 241–43. "Formation of Metastable Hydrogen Atoms by Electron Bombardment of H–2," with Robert C. Retherford, *Physical Review* 75 (1949): 1332. "The Fine Structure of Singly Ionized Helium," with Miriam Skinner, *Physical Review* 78 (1950): 539–50. "Fine Structure of n–3 Hydrogen by a Radio-Frequency Method," with T. M. Sanders, *Physical Review* 103 (1956):

313–14. *Laser Physics*, with M. Sargent and M. O. Scully (Reading, Mass.: Addison-Wesley Publishing Co., 1974).

Bibliography: *Current Biography Yearbook* (New York: H. W. Wilson, 1956), pp. 357–58. *National Cyclopedia of American Biography* (New York: James T. White, 1963), vol. J, p. 238. *Nobel Prize Winners: Physics* (Pasadena, Calif.: Salem Press, 1988), vol. 2, pp. 653–62.

BARDEEN, JOHN

Prize: Physics, 1956; Physics, 1972. *Born:* May 23, 1908; Madison, Wisconsin. *Died:* January 30, 1991; Boston, Massachusetts. *Nationality:* American. *Education:* University of Wisconsin, B.S., 1928; University of Wisconsin, M.A., 1929; Princeton University, New Jersey, Ph.D., 1936. *Career:* Gulf Research and Development, Geophysicist, 1930–33; Harvard University, Massachusetts, Fellow, 1935–38; University of Minnesota, Professor, 1938–41; U.S. Naval Ordinance Laboratory, Physicist, 1941–45; Bell Telephone Laboratories, New Jersey, Physicist, 1945–51; University of Illinois, Professor, 1951–75. *Other Awards:* Ballantine Medal, Franklin Institute, 1952; Buckley Prize, American Physical Society, 1954; John Scott Medal, City of Philadelphia, 1955; Fritz London Award, 1962; Vincent Bendix Award, American Society of Engineering Education, 1966; Michelson-Morley Award, Case Western Reserve University, Ohio, 1968; Medal of Honor, Institute of Electrical and Electronic Engineering, 1971; James Madison Medal, Princeton University, New Jersey, 1973; Franklin Institute Medal, 1975; Presidential Medal of Freedom, 1977; Lomonosov Medal, 1987.

Citation: 1956: "For their researches on semiconductors and their discovery of the transistor effect" (with Walter H. Brattain and William Shockley). 1972: "For their jointly developed theory of superconductivity, usually called the BCS-theory" (with Leon N. Cooper and John R. Schrieffer).

Life Work: Bardeen was a codiscoverer of the semiconductor and the transistor which, because of their small size, rugged structure, low cost, and low energy consumption, rapidly replaced vacuum tubes. Superconductivity had been discovered in 1911 by the Dutch physicist Heike Kamerlingh Onnes, who found that some metals lose all resistance to the flow of electric current at temperatures a few degrees above absolute zero. In 1933 the German physicist Walther Meissner discovered that superconductors are diamagnetic, that is, they reject a magnetic field. In 1950 several American physicists discovered that different isotopes of a given metal became superconducting at different temperatures and that the critical temperature was inversely proportional to the atomic mass. Bardeen suggested that the superconductivity of a metal involved an interaction between conduction electrons and the vibrations of atoms in the metal body and that their link to atomic vibrations also coupled the electrons to each other. Working with Bardeen were two of his students, Leon N. Cooper and J. Robert Schrieffer. Cooper discovered the Cooper pairs, which are electrons (one positive and the other negative) that become paired through the concentration of positive charge that binds them together. Bardeen and his colleagues showed that Cooper pairs interact to compel many of the free electrons in a semiconductor to flow in unison. They form a single quantum state that encompasses the entire metal body. The critical temperature at which superconductivity appears represents the degree of reduction of thermal vibrations required to allow the influence of Cooper pairs to predominate in coordinating the movement of free electrons. The BCS Theory is considered one of the most important in theoretical physics in the twentieth century. It has been used to predict superfluidity (the absence of viscosity and surface tension) in helium 3. It has also made possible the construction of powerful electromagnets used in the study of nuclear fusion, in magnetohydrodynamics, in high-energy particle accelerators, in magnetically levitating trains, and in the construction of electric generators.

Publications: "Interaction between Electrons and Lattice Vibrations," *Canadian Journal of Physics* 34 (1956): 1171–89. "Research Leading to the Point-Contact Transistor," *Science* 126 (1957): 105–13. "Theory of Superconductivity," *Physical Review* 108 (1957): 1175–204. "Critical Fields and Currents in Superconductors," *Reviews of Modern Physics* 34 (1962): 667–75. "Review of the Present Status of the Theory of Superconductivity," *IBM Journal of Research* 6 (1962): 3–11. "Electron-phonon Interactions and Superconductivity," *Science* 181 (1973): 1209–14. *A Collection of Professor John Bardeen's Publications on Semiconductors and Superconductivity* (Urbana: University of Illinois Press, 1988).

Bibliography: *Biographical Memoirs of the Royal Society* (London: Royal Society, 1994), vol. 39, p. 19. *Modern Men of Science* (New York: McGraw-Hill, 1966–68), vol. 1, p. 1920. Bernard Weinraub, "Six Americans Win Nobel Prizes in Physics and Chemistry Fields," *New York Times*, October 21, 1972, pp. 1, 14.

BRATTAIN, WALTER HOUSER

Prize: Physics, 1956. *Born:* February 10, 1902; Hsiamen, China. *Died:* October 13, 1987; Seattle, Washington. *Nationality:* American. *Education:* Whitman College, Washington, B.S., 1924; University of Oregon, M.A., 1926; University of Minnesota, Ph.D., 1929. *Career:* Bureau of Standards, Washington, D.C., Researcher, 1928–29; Bell Telephone Laboratories, New Jersey, 1929–67; Whitman College, Washington, Professor, 1967–72. *Other Awards:* Stuart Ballantine Medal, Franklin Institute, 1952; John Scott Medal, Philadelphia, Pennsylvania, 1955; National Inventors Hall of Fame, 1974.

Citation: "For their researches on semiconductors and their discovery of the transistor effect" (with John Bardeen and William Shockley).

Life Work: Brattain worked with William Shockley and John Bardeen to construct a device that displayed for the first time the transistor effect. The device, called a point contact transistor, consisted of two closely spaced gold film contacts on one face of a block of germanium crystal containing a small concentration of impurities, and a third terminal on the opposite face. A positive bias voltage was placed between one gold contact (the emitter) and the third terminal (base) and a negative bias (collector) between the second gold contact and the base. A signal applied to the emitter influenced the current flowing in the collector-base circuit. This model has been constantly improved, with the junction transistor and the field-effect transistor. Most later transistors were made of silicon instead of germanium.

Publications: "Nature of the Forward Current in Germanium Point Contacts," with J. Bardeen, *Physical Review* 74 (1948): 231–32. "The Transistor, a Semi-Conductor Triode," with J. Bardeen, *Physical Review* 74 (1948): 230–31. "Physical Principles Involved in Transistor Action," with J. Bardeen, *Physical Review* 75 (1949): 1208–25. "Surface Properties of Semiconductors," *Science* 126 (1957): 151–53. "The Distribution of Potential Across the Low-Index Crystal Planes of Germanium Contacting on Aqueous Solution," with P. J. Boddy, *Proceedings of the National Academy of Sciences* 48 (1962): 2005–12.

Bibliography: *Biographical Memoirs. National Academy of Sciences* (Washington, D.C.: National Academy Press, 1994), vol. 63, p. 69. *Current Biography Yearbook* (New York: H. W. Wilson, 1957), pp. 68 70. *National Cyclopedia of American Biography* (New York: James T. White, 1960), vol. 1, pp. 404–405. *New York Times* Biographical Service, October 14, 1987, p. 1040. *Nobel Prize Winners: Physics* (Pasadena, Calif.: 1988), vol. 2, pp. 695–704.

SHOCKLEY, WILLIAM BRADFORD

Prize: Physics, 1956. *Born:* February 13, 1910; London, England. *Died:* August 12, 1989; Palo Alto, California. *Nationality:* American. *Education:* California Institute of Technology, B.S., 1932; Massachusetts Institute of Technology, Ph.D., 1936. *Career:* Bell Telephone Laboratories, New Jersey, Researcher, 1936–42; United States Navy, Research Director, 1942–44; Bell Telephone Laboratories, New Jersey, Researcher, 1945–55; Shockley Semiconductor Laboratories, Director, 1955–58; Shockley Transistor Corporation, President, 1958–60; Shockley Transistor Unit, Director, 1960–63; Consultant, 1963–65; Stanford University, California, Professor, 1963–75. *Other Awards:* Medal of Merit (U.S.), 1946; Morris Liebmann Prize, Institute of Radio Engineers, 1951; O. E. Buckley Prize, American Physical Society, 1953; Comstock Prize, National Academy of Sciences, 1954; Wilhelm Exner Medal, Oesterreichischer Gewerberein, 1963; Holley Medal, American Society of Mechanical Engineers, 1963; Public Service Achievement Award, National Aeronautics and Space Administration, 1969; Gold Medal, Institute of Electrical and Electronics Engineers, 1972; National Inventors Hall of Fame, 1974; Medal of Honor, Institute of Electrical and Electronics Engineers, 1980; California Inventor's Hall of Fame, 1983.

Citation: "For their researches on semiconductors and their discovery of the transistor effect" (with John Bardeen and Walter H. Brattain).

Life Work: As director of the solid-state physics research program at Bell Labs, Shockley and and his associates, John Bardeen and Walter H. Brattain, studied semiconductors. It had been known that semiconductors involved two kinds of charge carriers, electrons and holes. The electrons available for conduction were those in excess of the number binding the atoms together into a solid crystal. Holes represented missing electrons. Since an electron carries a negative charge, an unfilled electron state behaves like a positive charge of the same magnitude. Holes move in the opposite direction. When a nearby electron moves forward to fill a hole, it leaves a new hole behind, so that the hole appears to move backward. Impurities introduced into the pure crystal in the form of atoms that do not exactly fit into the regular crystal structure produce regions of excess electrons or excess holes. In 1947 the team made the first successful amplifying semiconductor device or transistor ("transfer" + "resistor"). Its basic action was the introduction of holes into the germanium by the emitter contact and the flow of holes directly to the collector contact where they increased the collector current. The transistor was developed further with, first, a junction transistor and, later, the field-effect transistor.

Publications: "Density of Surface States on Silicon Deduced from Contact Potential Measurements," with W. Brattain, *Physical Review* 72 (1947): 345. "Modulation of Conductance of Thin Films of Semiconductors by Surface Charges," with G. L. Pearson, *Physical Review* 74 (1948): 232–33. "Investigation of Hole Injection in Transistor Action," with J. R. Haynes, *Physical Review* 75 (1949): 691. *Electrons and Holes in Semiconductors* (New York: D. Van Nostrand Co., 1950). "The Mobility and Life of Injected Holes and Electrons in Germanium," with J. R. Haynes, *Physical Review* 81 (1951): 835–43. "Statistics of the Recombinations of Holes and Electrons," with W. T. Read, *Physical Review* 87 (1952): 835–42.

Bibliography: *Current Biography Yearbook* (New York: H. W. Wilson, 1953), pp. 569–71. *Modern Men of Science* (New York: McGraw-Hill, 1966), p. 430. *New York Times* Biographical Service, August 14, 1989, p. 776. *Nobel Prize Winners: Physics* (Pasadena, Calif.: Salem Press, 1988), vol. 2, pp. 673–82.

LEE, TSUNG-DAO

Prize: Physics, 1957. *Born:* November 25, 1926; Shanghai, China. *Nationality:* Chinese; later U.S. citizen. *Education:* National Chekiang University, China, baccalaureate, 1944; University of Chicago, Illinois, Ph.D., 1950. *Career:* University of California, Berkeley, Researcher, 1950–51; Institute for Advanced Study, Princeton, New Jersey, Researcher, 1951–53; Columbia University, New York, Professor, 1953–60; Institute for Advanced Study, New Jersey, Researcher, 1960–63; Columbia University, New York, Professor, 1963–. *Other Awards:* Albert Einstein Commemorative Award in Science, Yeshiva University, 1957; Science Award, Newspaper Guild of New York, 1957.

Citation: "For their penetrating investigation of the so-called parity laws which has led to important discoveries regarding the elementary particles" (with Chen Ning Yang).

Life Work: Lee and his associate Chen Ning Yang worked to prove the right-left symmetry in weak interactions. The law of conservation of parity stated that particle interactions and the mirror image of such interactions obey the same physical laws and are indistinguishable from each other. Known physical interactions involved four forces: strong force (which holds the nucleus together), electromagnetic force (which acts on charged particles), weak force (which acts in the emission of particles during radioactive decay), and gravitation. One problem in this construct was the two apparently different kinds of K-mesons, unstable particles found in the debris created by the high-energy bombardment of atomic nuclei. In their decay, K-meson (*theta*) decayed into two pi-mesons while the other, named *tau*, decayed into three, although both had the same mass and lifetime. In their experiments, Lee and Wang they found that parity law was not conserved in the decay of cobalt. They found that the *mu*-mesons and electrons failed to exhibit the forward-backward symmetry expected under the law of conservation of parity.

Publications: "Interaction of Mesons with Nucleons and Light Particles," with C. N. Yang and M. Rosenbluth, *Physical Review* 75 (1949): 905. "Mass Degeneracy of the Heavy Mesons," with C. N. Yang, *Physical Review* 102 (1956): 290–91. "Question of Parity Conservation in Weak Interactions," with C. N. Yang, *Physical Review* 104 (1956): 254–58. "Parity Nonconservation and a Two-Component Theory of the Neutrino," with C. N. Yang, *Physical Review* 105 (1957): 1671–75. "Remarks on Possible Noninvariance under Time Reversal and Charge Conjugation," with C. N. Yang, *Physical Review* 106 (1957): 340–45. *Particle Physics and Introduction to Field Theory* (New York: Harwood Academic Press, 1981). *T. D. Lee: Selected Papers* (Boston: Birkhauser, 1987).

Bibliography: *Current Biography Yearbook* (New York: H. W. Wilson, 1958), pp. 240–41. *Nobel Prize Winners: Physics* (Pasadena, Calif.: Salem Press, 1988), vol. 2, pp. 715–25. *Physics Teacher* 20 (May 1982): 281–88.

YANG, CHEN NING

Prize: Physics, 1957. *Born:* September 22, 1922; Hofei, Anwhei, China. *Nationality:* Chinese; later U.S. citizen. *Education:* National Southwest Associated University, China, B.Sc., 1942; Tsinghua University, China, M.Sc., 1944; University of Chicago, Illinois, Ph.D., 1948. *Career:* University of Chicago, Illinois, Professor, 1948–49; Institute for Advanced Study, New Jersey, Professor, 1949–65; State of University of New York, Stony Brook, Professor and Administrator, 1965–. *Other Awards:* Albert Einstein Commemorative Award, 1957; Rumford Prize, 1980; National Medal of Science, 1986; Liberty Award, 1986; Franklin Medal, 1993.

Citation: "For their penetrating investigation of the so-called parity laws which has led to important discoveries regarding the elementary particles" (with Tsung-Dao Lee).

Life Work: Working with Tsung-Dao Lee, Yang investigated the validity of the law of conservation of parity, one of the symmetries of nature. It states that the total parity is the same before and after an interaction. It means that nature is neither left-handed nor right-handed, so the mirror image of a particular interaction obeys the same laws as the interaction itself. This law was apparently contradicted by the fact that two different kinds of K-mesons, one called *theta* and the other *tau*, decayed into two *pi*-mesons and three mesons respectively. The experiments of Lee and Wang established that parity conservation was totally absent in weak interactions. Yang and Lee proposed that *theta* and *tau* were indeed the same particle, capable of two different types of decay. The failure of the law of conservation of parity opened the door to a host of theoretical and experimental projects.

Publications: "Interaction of Mesons with Nucleons and Light Particles," with T. D. Lee and M. Rosenbluth, *Physical Review* 75 (1949): 905. "Reflection Properties of Spin Fields and a Universal Fermi-Type Interaction," with J. Tiomno, *Physical Review* 79 (1950): 495–98. "Mass Degeneracy of the Heavy Mesons," with T. D. Lee, *Physical Review* 102 (1956): 290–91. "Question of Parity Conservation in Weak Interactions," with T. D. Lee, *Physical Review* 104 (1956): 254–58. "Parity Nonconservation and a Two-Component Theory of the Neutrino," with T. D. Lee, *Physical Review* 105 (1957): 1671–75. "Remarks on Possible Noninvariance under Time Reversal and Charge Conjugation," with T. D. Lee, *Physical Review* 106 (1957): 340–45. *Selected Papers, 1945–80, with Commentary* (San Francisco, Calif.: W. H. Freeman, 1983).

Bibliography: *Biographical Encyclopedia of Scientists* (New York: Facts on File, 1981), p. 866. *Nobel Prize Winners: Physics* (Pasadena, Calif.: Salem Press, 1988), vol. 2, pp. 705–13.

CHERENKOV, PAVEL ALEKSEYEVICH

Prize: Physics, 1958. *Born:* July 28, 1904; Novaya Chigla, Russia. *Died:* January 6, 1990; USSR. *Nationality:* Russian. *Education:* Voronezh University, USSR, graduate, 1928; Physics Institute, USSR Academy of Science, Doctorate of Physico-Mathematical Sciences, 1940. *Career:* Lebedev Physic Institute, USSR, Researcher and Administrator, 1930–1990. *Other Awards:* Stalin Prize, 1946; Order of Lenin, 1964.

Citation: "For the discovery and the interpretation of the Cherenkov effect" (with Il'ja Frank and Igor Tamm).

Life Work: Cherenkov's field of investigation was light produced when high-energy radiation is absorbed by liquid solutions. Through his investigations of gamma rays, he established the effect known as Cherenkov radiation. Gamma rays which have higher energy and different frequencies compared to X rays, emitted by radium produced a faint blue glow in a liquid. Cherenkov established that the blue glow was not due to fluoresesence. He found that the polarization of blue light was parallel, not perpendicular, to the path of the incoming gamma rays. The blue light was not emitted in all directions, but traveled forward from the incoming gamma rays and formed a cone of illumination whose axis was the gamma-ray path. When a gamma ray strikes an electron in a liquid and ejects it from the parent atom, Cherenkov radiation arises when the electron travels faster than light. After many years the practical application of Cherenkov radiation was recognized when Cherenkov counters were developed for counting and measuring the velocity of high-speed single particles such as those found in particle accelerators and cosmic rays. It was used in the discovery of the antiproton in 1955.

Publications: "Visible Glow and Pure Liquids under the Influence of Gamma-Rays," *Compt. Rend. Acad. Sci. U.R.S.S.* 2 (1934): 451–54. "Visible Radiation Produced by Electrons Moving in a Medium with Velocities Exceeding that of Light," *Physical Review* 52 (1937): 378–79. "Visible Radiation of Pure Liquids under the Action of Fast Electrons," *Bull. Acad. Sci. U.R.S.S., Classe sci. Mat. Nat., Ser. Phys* (1937): 455–91. "Absolute Output of Radiation Caused by Electrons Moving within a Medium with Super-Light Speed," *Trudy, Fiz. Inst. Im. P.N. Lebedeva, Akad. Nauk. S.S.S.R.* 2 (1944): 3–62.

Bibliography: *Asimov's Biographical Encyclopedia of Science and Technology* (Garden City, N.Y.: Doubleday, 1982), p. 801. *Nobel Prize Winners: Physics* (Pasadena, Calif.: Salem Press, 1988), vol. 2, pp. 727–34.

FRANK, IL'JA MIKHAILOVICH

Prize: Physics, 1958. *Born:* October 23, 1908; Leningrad, Russia. *Died:* June 22, 1990; Moscow, USSR. *Nationality:* Russian. *Education:* Moscow State University, USSR, baccalaureate, 1930; Moscow State University, USSR, Doctor of Physio-mathematical Sciences, 1935. *Career:* State Optical Institute, USSR, Professor, 1931–34; Lebedev Institute of Physics, USSR, Professor, 1934–90. *Other Awards:* Stalin Prize, 1946, 1954, 1971; Order of Lenin, 1974; Vavilov Gold Medal, 1979; Lenin Prize, 1979.

Citation: "For the discovery and the interpretation of the Cherenkov effect" (with Pavel Cherenkov and Igor Tamm).

Life Work: Frank and Igor Tamm worked to confirm Cherenkov radiation, which explained the blue glow from refractive media subjected to gamma rays. They showed that the effect was due to the properties of an electron moving uniformly through a medium faster than the speed of light in that medium. Their theory explained why the polarization of Cherenkov radiation was parallel to the incident radiation rather than perpendicular to it. Continuing his studies in the field, Frank formulated the theory of transition radiation, or the form of radiation that arises from the altered electric field of a uniformly moving particle as it crosses the interface between two media having different optical properties.

Publications: "The Excitation Function and the Absorption Curve in the Optical Dissociation of Thallium Iodide," *Physik Z. Sowjetunion* 2 (1932): 319–36. "Coherent Visible Radiation of Fast Electrons Passing through Matter," with I. Tamm, *Compt. Rend. Acad. Sci. U.R.S.S.* 14 (1937): 109–14. "Visible Radiation of Pure Liquids under the Action of Rapid Electrons," with I. Tamm and P. A. Cherenkov, *Bull. Acad. Sci. U.R.R.S., Classe Sci. Math, Nat., Ser. Phys* (1938): 29–30. "A New Type of Nuclear Reactions (The Splitting of Uranium and Thorium Nuclei under the Influence of Neutrons)," *Priroda* 9 (1939): 20–27.

Bibliography: *Biographical Encyclopedia of Scientists* (New York: Facts on File, 1981), pp. 280–81. *Modern Men of Science* (New York: McGraw-Hill, 1966), p. 182. *New York Times* Biographical Service, June 25, 1990, p. 597. *Nobel Prize Winners: Physics* (Pasadena, Calif.: Salem Press, 1988), vol. 2, pp. 735–43.

TAMM, IGOR YERGENEVICH

Prize: Physics, 1958. *Born:* July 8, 1895; Vladivostok, Russia. *Died:* April 12, 1971; Moscow, USSR. *Nationality:* Russian. *Education:* Moscow State University, USSR, degree in physics, 1918; Moscow State University, USSR, doctorate, 1933. *Career:* Crimean University, USSR, Professor and Administrator, 1918–20; Odessa Polytechnical Institut, USSR, Professor, 1920–22; Sverdlov Communist University, USSR, Professor, 1922–24; Moscow University, USSR, Professor and Administrator, 1924–71. *Other Awards:* Order of Lenin 1946, 1953; Stalin Prize, 1946; Order of Red Banner of Labor, 1949.

Citation: "For the discovery and the interpretation of the Cherenkov effect" (with Pavel Cherenkov and Il'ja Frank).

Life Work: Tamm made two significant discoveries in the quantum theory of metals. He explained the photoelectric emission of electrons from metals, and he discovered Tamm surface levels, special bound-energy states occupied by electrons at the surface of a crystal. Studying the atomic nucleus he predicted that the neutron, despite its lack of charge, possesses a negative magnetic moment. He did so on the basis of his beta theory on the forces that hold the nucleus together. Hideki Yukawa's discovery of mesons confirmed Tamm's work on nuclear bonding. In 1936–37 he and Ilya Frank provided the experimental basis for Cherenkov radiation by describing electrons moving faster than the speed of light in a medium. This research led to the development of superlight optics, which has practical applications in plasma physics. Later, he took part in the development of the Tamm-Dankov method widely used in theoretical studies of nucleon-nucleon and nucleon-meson interactions. The method describes the interaction of elementary particles at speeds approaching that of light. Tamm also developed a cascade theory of cosmic ray showers.

Publications: "Exchange Forces Between Neutrons and Protons, and Fermi's Theory," *Nature* 133 (1934): 981. "Nuclear Magnetic Moments and the Properties of the Neutron," *Nature* 134 (1934): 380. "Izluchenie Elektrona pri Ravnomernom Ovizhenii v Prelomliaiushchei Srede" ["Theory of the Electron in Uniform Motion in a Refracting Medium"], *Trudy Fizicheskago Instituta* 2 (1944): 63. "K Reliativistskoi Teorii Vzaimodeistvia Nuklonov" ["Toward a Relativistic Theory of the Mutual Interaction of Nucleons"], *Zhurnal Eksperimentalnogo I Teoricheskogo Fizika* 24 (1954): 3. "Teorii Magnitnykh Termoiadernykh Reaktsy" ["Theory of Magnetic Thermodynamic Reactors"], *Fizika Plazmy I Problemy Upravliaemykh Termoiadernykh Reaktsy* (1958): 3–19, 31–41. *Osnovy Teorii Elektrichestva* [Principles of the Theory of Electricity] (Moscow: n.p., 1966).

Bibliography: *Current Biography Yearbook* (New York: H. W. Wilson, 1963), pp. 412–14. *Dictionary of Scientific Biography* (New York: Scribner's, 1973), vol. 13, pp. 239–42. "In Memory of Igor Evgenevich Tamm," *Soviet Physics-Uspekhi* 14 (1972): 669–70.

CHAMBERLAIN, OWEN

Prize: Physics, 1959. *Born:* July 10, 1920; San Francisco, California. *Nationality:* American. *Education:* Dartmouth College, New Hampshire, B.S., 1941; University of Chicago, Illinois, Ph.D., 1949. *Career:* Manhattan Project, United States, Researcher, 1942–46; Argonne National Laboratory, Illinois, Senior Researcher, 1946–48; University of California, Berkeley, Professor, 1948–1989. *Other Awards:* Guggenheim Fellow, 1957.

Citation: "For their discovery of the antiproton" (with Emilio Segrè).

Life Work: Chamberlain's field of investigation was the investigation of the scattering of fast-moving protons and neutrons. He and Emilio Segrè used the Bevatron to discover the antiproton by devising an elaborate system of magnets and magnetic focusing devices to identify antiprotons, electronic counters and timers to measure velocity, and photographic emulsions to record final annihilations.

Publications: "Observation of Antiprotons," with others, *Physical Review* 100 (1955): 947–50. "Antiproton Star Observed in Emulsion," with others, *Physical Review* 101 (1956): 909–10. "Example of an Antiproton Nucleon Annihilation," with others, *Physical Review* 102 (1956): 921–23.

Bibliography: *Current Biography Yearbook* (New York: H. W. Wilson, 1960), pp. 83–85. *Modern Scientists and Engineers* (New York: McGraw-Hill, 1980), vol. 1, p. 191. *Nobel Prize Winners: Physics* (Pasadena, Calif.: Salem Press, 1988), vol. 2, pp. 767–75.

SEGRÈ, EMILIO GINO

Prize: Physics, 1959. *Born:* February 1, 1905; Rome, Italy. *Died:* April 22, 1989; Lafayette, California. *Nationality:* Italian; later U.S. citizen. *Education:* University of Rome, Italy, Ph.D., 1928. *Career:* University of Rome, Italy, Professor, 1932–36; University of Palermo, Italy, Researcher, 1936–38; University of California, Berkeley, Researcher, 1938–43; Los Alamos Laboratory of the Manhattan Project, NM, Researcher, 1943–46; University of California, Berkeley, Professor, 1946–72; University of Rome, Italy, Professor, 1974–75. *Other Awards:* Hofmann Medal, German Chemical Society, 1954; Cannizzaro Medal, Académie Nazionale dei Lincei, 1956; Commander of Merit, Republic of Italy, 1959.

Citation: "For their discovery of the antiproton" (with Owen Chamberlain).

Life Work: Segrè was a pioneer in the field of nuclear physics. In 1935 he, Enrico Fermi, and others discovered slow neutrons, which are important in the production of nuclear power. In the late 1930s he identified trace amounts of element 43, which he named Technetium; synthesized an artificial element with atomic number 85, named astatine; and codiscovered, with Glenn T. Seaborg, the element with the atomic number 94, plutonium-239. In the 1950s he collaborated with Owen Chamberlain to identify the antiproton, a negatively charged twin of the positive proton, with the help of the Bevatron, an accelerator capable of propelling particles to energies reaching billions of electron volts.

Publications: "Observation of Antiprotons," with others, *Physical Review* 100 (1955): 947–50. "Antiproton Star Observed in Emulsion," with others, *Physical Review* 101 (1956): 909–10. "Antiprotons," with others, *Nature* 177 (1956): 11–12. "Proton-Antiproton Elastic and Charge Exchange Scattering at About 120 Mev," with others, *Physical Review* 110 (1958): 994–95. *Nuclei and Particles* (New York: W. A. Benjamin, 1964). *Enrico Fermi, Physicist* (Chicago: University of Chicago Press, 1970).

Bibliography: *Current Biography Yearbook* (New York: H. W. Wilson, 1960), pp. 369–71. *A Mind Always in Motion.* (Berkeley: University of California Press, 1993). *Nobel Prize Winners: Physics* (Pasadena, Calif.: Salem Press, 1988), vol. 2, pp. 755–65.

GLASER, DONALD ARTHUR

Prize: Physics, 1960. *Born:* September 21, 1926; Cleveland, Ohio. *Nationality:* American. *Education:* Case Institute of Technology, Ohio, B.S., 1946; California Institute of Technology, Ph.D., 1950. *Career:* University of Michigan, Professor, 1949–59; University of California, Berkeley, Professor, 1959–. *Other Awards:* Henry Russel Award, University of Michigan, 1955; Charles Vernon Bays Prize, Institute of Physics, 1958; American Physics Society Prize, 1959; Gold Medal, Case Institute of Technology, 1967; Alumni Distinguished Service Award, California Institute of Technology, 1967.

Citation: "For the invention of the bubble chamber."

Life Work: Glaser's field of investigation was elementary particles found in cosmic radiation, which bombard the earth at high velocities. When they interact with matter, they often give rise to new particles. To track such particles, Glasser built large cloud chambers using pressurized, superheated liquid as a medium. To boil the liquid, he used radiation. Using a series of small glass chambers of different shapes, each containing superheated ether, Glasser record the paths of ionizing radiation. Glasser's technique was the mirror image of C. T. R. Wilson's cloud chamber. Whereas the latter produced a track of liquid droplets in a gas, the former produced a track of gaseous bubbles in a liquid. Later, he constructed a bubble chamber using liquid hydrogen in 1953 and liquefied xenon gas in 1956.

Publications: "Some Effects of Ionizing Radiation on the Formation of Bubbles in Liquids," *Physical Review* 87 (August 15, 1952): 665. "Progress Report on the Development of Bubble Chambers," *Nuovo Cimento Supplement* 11 (1953): 361–68. "Characteristics of Bubble Chambers," with D. C. Rahm, *Physical Review* 97 (January 15, 1955: 474–79. "Bubble Counting for the Determination of the Velocities of Charged Particles in Bubble Chambers," with D. C. Rahm and C. Dodd, *Physical Review* 102 (July 15, 1956): 1653–58.

Bibliography: *Current Biography Yearbook* (New York: H. W. Wilson, 1961), pp. 1976–78. *Nobel Prize Winners: Physics* (Pasadena, Calif.: Salem Press, 1988), vol. 2, pp. 777–85.

HOFSTADTER, ROBERT

Prize: Physics, 1961. *Born:* February 5, 1915; New York, New York. *Died:* November 17, 1990; Stanford, California. *Nationality:* American. *Education:* City College of New York, B.S., 1935; Princeton University, New Jersey, M.A., 1938; Princeton University, New Jersey, Ph.D., 1938. *Career:* University of Pennsylvania, Researcher, 1939–40; Princeton University, New Jersey, Professor, 1940–41; City College of New York, Professor, 1941–42; National Bureau of Standards, Washington, D.C., Researcher, 1942–43; Norden Laboratories Corporation, New York, Researcher, 1943–46; Princeton University, New Jersey, Professor, 1946–50; Stanford University, California, Professor and Administrator, 1950–85. *Other Awards:* Kenyon Prize in Mathematics and Physics, 1935; California Scientist of the Year, 1958; Townsend Harris Medal, City College of New York, 1962; Rontgen Medal, 1985; National Science Medal, 1986; Cultural Foundation Prize, Fiuggi, Italy, 1986.

Citation: "For his pioneering studies of electron scattering in atomic nuclei and for his thereby achieved discoveries concerning the structure of the nucleons."

Life Work: Hofstadter's early research on crystals as detectors of high-energy particles and radiation led to the development of a scintillation detector using a crystal of the sodium salt iodine doped with a small quantity of the element thallium. When the crystal is struck by an energetic atomic particle or by a photon, it emits a burst of light whose intensity is proportional to the energy of the particle or photon. This became one of the basic measuring tools for nuclear radiation studies. In 1950 Hofstadter turned to the study of nuclear structure using an electron accelerator that could sort out electrons according to their energy and angle of deflection. He measured the deflection of electrons that had not generated additional particles in their encounter with a nucleus. By this means, he measured the size, shape, density, and skin thickness of many atomic nuclei. With the more powerful Stanford accelerator, Hoftsadter probed the internal structure of protons and neutrons, the constituent elements of a nucleus. He discovered that protons and neutrons are different aspects of a single entity called the nucleon.

Publications: "High-Energy Electron Scattering and the Charge Distributions of Selected Nuclei," with B. Hahn and D. G. Ravenhall, *Physical Review* 101 (1956): 1131–42. *High Energy Electron Scattering Tables*, with Robert C. Herman (Stanford, Calif.: Stanford University Press, 1960). *Nuclear and Nucleon Structure* (Stanford, Calif.: Stanford University Press, 1963). *Nucleon Structure: Proceedings* (Stanford, Calif.: Stanford University Press, 1964).

Bibliography: *Current Biography Yearbook* (New York: H. W. Wilson, 1962), pp. 212–14. *New York Times* Biographical Service, November 19, 1990, p. 1098. *Nobel Prize Winners: Physics* (Pasadena, Calif.: Salem Press, 1988), vol. 2, pp. 787–95.

MÖSSBAUER, RUDOLF LUDWIG

Prize: Physics, 1961. *Born:* January 31, 1929; Munich, Germany. *Nationality:* German. *Education:* Technische Hoschschule, Germany, B.S., 1952; Technische Hochschule, Germany, M.S., 1955; Technische Hochshule, Germany, Ph.D., 1958. *Career:* Max Planck Institute, Germany, Researcher, 1955–57; Institute of Technology, Germany, Researcher, 1958–60; California Institute of Technology, Researcher and Professor, 1960–64; Technische Universität, Munich, Professor and Administrator, 1964–72; Institute Max von Laue, France, Director, 1972–77; Institute of Technology, Germany, Professor, 1977–. *Other Awards:* Research Corporation Award, New York, 1960; Röntgen Award, University of Gieson, Germany, 1961; Elliot Cresson Medal, Franklin Institute, 1961; Bavarian Order of Merit, 1962; Guthrie Medal Institute of Physics, London, 1974; Lomonosov Gold Medal, 1984; Einstein Medal, 1986.

Citation: "For his researches concerning the resonance absorption of gamma radiation and his discovery in this connection of the effect which bears his name."

Life Work: Mössbauer is best known as the discoverer of the effect named after him. His field of investigation was gamma rays, especially their emission and absorption by atomic nuclei. Mössbauer found a way to demonstrate the gamma-ray resonance fluorescence in which absorbed and emitted photons have equal energy. Studying gamma-ray atoms of the radioactive isotope of the metal iridium, he found that individual nuclei emitting or absorbing gamma rays transferred the interaction momentum directly to the surrounding crystal. The emitted and absorbed gamma-ray photons showed no frequency shift. This phenomenon is now called the Mössbauer shift. With their remarkably constant wavelengths and frequencies, fluorescence gamma rays are used as measuring tools for gauging the effect oif such natural forces as gravity, electricity, and magnetism. The Mössbauer effect has applications in archeology, chemical analysis, solid state science, and atomic physics.

Publications: "Nuclear Resonance Absorption of Gamma Rays in Iridium-191," *Naturwissenschaften* 45 (1958): 538–39. "Nuclear Resonance Fluorescence of Gamma Radiation in Iridium-191," *Z. Physik* 151 (1958): 124–43. "Nuclear Resonance Absorption of Gamma Rays in Iridium-191," *Z. Naturforsch* 14a (1959): 211–16. "Nuclear Resonance Absorption of Gamma Radiation in Re-87 Not Broadened by Doppler Effect," with Herbert W. Weidemann, *Z. Physik* 159 (1960): 33–48. "Hyperfine Structure Splitting of Recoil-free Gamma Lines," with F. W. Stanek and H. W. Wiedemann, *Z. Physik* 151 (1961): 388–91.

Bibliography: *Current Biography Yearbook* (New York: H. W. Wilson, 1962), pp. 306–308. *Nobel Prize Winners: Physics* (Pasadena, Calif.: Salem Press, 1988), vol. 2, pp. 797–807. *Physics Today* 15 (December 1962): 56.

LANDAU, LEV DAVIDOVICH

Prize: Physics, 1962. *Born:* January 22, 1908; Baku, Russia. *Died:* April 1, 1968; Moscow, USSR. *Nationality:* Russian. *Education:* Leningrad State University, USSR, baccalaureate, 1924; Kharkov Institute of Mechanical Engineering, USSR, Ph.D., 1934. *Career:* University of Leningrad, USSR, Researcher and Professor, 1931–35; Kharkov University, USSR, Researcher and Administrator, 1935–37; Institute of Physical Problems of the USSR Academy of Sciences, USSR, Researcher, 1937–68. *Other Awards:* Fritz London Award, 1960; Lenin Prize, 1962; Stalin Prize, 1965.

Citation: "For his pioneering theories for condensed matter, especially liquid helium."

Life Work: Landau was an extremely versatile genius whose work extended over such fields as the origin of stars, sound dispersion, light scattering, magnetic properties of materials, superconductivity, and the motion of electrically charged particles. He made important contributions to quantum field theory, low-temperature physics, and studies of the nature and interactions of elementary particles. Landau explained superfluids, such as helium-1 and helium-2, by proposing the existence of two components of motion, or excitation: phonons, representing the relatively normal straight line propagation of sound waves at low values of momentum or energy, and rotons, representing rotational motion with higher values of momentum and energy. When phonons and rotons collided, the former predominated at temperatures above 1°K and phonons below 0.6°K. Investigating a rare isotope of helium with an atomic weight of 3, he predicted a new type of wave propagation called zero sound. He also contributed to the development of the Soviet atomic bomb.

Publications: *Teoriia Polia* [Field Theory], with E. Lifshits (Moscow: n.p., 1941). "Teoriia Sverkhtekuchesti Gelia–2" ["Theory of the Superfluidity of Helium II"], *Zhurnal Eksperimentalnoe I Theoreticheskoi Fiziki* 11 (1941): 592. *Kvantovaia Mekhanika* [Quantum Mechanics], with E. Lifshits (Moscow: n.p., 1948). "O Zakonakh Sokhranenia pri Slabykh Vzaimodeistviakh" ["On the Laws of Conservation in Weak Interactions"], *Zhurnal Eksperimentalnoe I Theoreticheskoi Fiziki* 32 (1957): 2. *Collected Papers of L. D. Landau* (New York: Pergamon, 1965).

Bibliography: M. Besserab, *Landau* (Moscow: Moskowskii Rabochii, 1990). *Current Biography Yearbook* (New York: H. W. Wilson, 1963), pp. 231–33. *Dictionary of Scientific Biography* (New York: Scribner's, 1973), vol. 7, pp. 616–19.

GOEPPERT-MAYER, MARIA

Prize: Physics, 1963. *Born:* June 28, 1906; Kattowitz, Poland. *Died:* February 20, 1972; San Diego, California. *Nationality:* German; later U.S. citizen. *Education:* University of Göttingen, Germany, Ph.D., 1930. *Career:* Johns Hopkins University, Baltimore, MD, Volunteer Researcher, 1930–39; Columbia University, New York, Volunteer Lecturer, 1939–45; Sarah Lawrence College, New York, Professor, 1942–45; University of Chicago, Fermi Institute, Illinois, Professor, 1946–60; University of California, San Diego, Professor, 1960–72.

Citation: "For their discoveries concerning nuclear shell structure" (with J. Hans D. Jensen).

Life Work: Mayer's field of investigation was magic numbers. Atomic nuclei contain protons and neutrons but certain nuclei were unaccountably abundant and therefore presumed to be stable. Abundance and stability coincide because an unstable nucleus is likely to change by radioactive decay into another one. Thus, stable nuclei persist and accumulate. In the abundant nuclei, either the number of protons or the number of neutrons equals one of the magic numbers, 2, 8, 20, 28, 50, 82, or 126. Atomic stability is chemical since chemical reactions are governed by the loss, gain, or sharing of electrons. Chemical properties recur in cycles, or periods, as the atomic number increases. The recurring stability of certain atomic numbers was explained on the basis of atomic energy levels related to the angular momentum of electrons moving around the nucleus. As the atomic number rises and electrons are added one by one, each additional electron occupies the next available level and the total energy rises step by step. The energy levels are not equal but occur in clusters of smaller steps separated by unusually large steps. These clusters are called shells. A shell is closed by the chemical element in whose atom the outermost electron occupies the last level before a large step. An electron of the next highest atomic number starts the next shell. Mayer showed that the atomic nucleus has shells with the protons and neutrons revolving around each other and spinning in orbit. Nuclei are stable when the shells of protons or neutrons were full.

Publications: *Statistical Mechanics*, with J. E. Mayer (New York: Wiley, 1940). "Nuclear Configurations in the Spin-Orbit Coupling Model," *Physical Review*, Series 2, 78 (April 1, 1950): 16–23. "The Structure of the Nucleus," *Scientific American* 184 (March 1951): 22–26. "Electromagnetic Effects Due to Spin-Orbit Coupling," with J. H. D. Jensen, *Physical Review* 85 (1952): 1040–41. *Elementary Theory of Nuclear Shell Structure*, with J. H. D. Jensen (New York: Wiley, 1955).

Bibliography: *Biographical Memoirs. National Academy of Sciences* (Washington, D.C.: National Academy of Sciences, 1979), vol. 50, pp. 310–28. Joan Dash, *A Life of One's Own* (New York: Harper & Row, 1973), pp. 226–369. *Physics Today* 25 (May 1972): 77, 79.

JENSEN, JOHANNES HANS DANIEL

Prize: Physics, 1963: *Born:* June 25, 1907; Hamburg, Germany. *Died:* February 11, 1973; Heidelberg, Germany. *Nationality:* German. *Education:* University of Hamburg, Germany, Dr. rerum naturalium, 1932. *Career:* University of Hamburg, Germany, Professor, 1932–41; Hanover Institute of Technology, Germany, Professor, 1941–48; University of Heidelberg, Germany, Professor, 1949–69.

Citation: "For their discoveries concerning nuclear shell structure" (with Maria Goeppert-Mayer).

Life Work: Jensen's field of investigation was the shell in nuclear structure. Shells are groups of orbital energy. Atomic energy levels cluster naturally in shells separated by relatively large steps of energy between the electrons that fill one shell and the electron that fills the next higher shell. The shell model explains the periodic table, which arranges elements according to atomic number and groups them according to similarity of chemical behavior. Properties recur in cycles, or periods, as the atomic number rises. Jensen's model showed a nucleus of orbiting protons and neutrons with strong spin-orbit coupling. His theory of nuclear energy levels related to orbital angular moments and the effect of nucleon spin explained the existence of all seven known magic numbers: 2, 8, 20, 28, 50, 82, and 126.

Publications: "Systematics of the Binding Energies of Atomic Nuclei," with H. Steinwedel, *Naturwissenschaften* 33 (1946): 249–50. "Interpretation of Prefverred Nucleon Numbers in the Structure of Atom Nuclei," with H. E. Suess and O. Haxel, *Naturwissenschaften* 36 (1949): 153–55. "Electromagnetic Effects Due to Spin-Orbit Coupling," with M. Goeppert-Mayer, *Physical Review* 85 (1952): 1040–41. "Nuclear Structure and Nuclear Transformation," *Zeitschrift fur Elektrochemie* 58 (1954): 546–53. *Elementary Theory of Nuclear Shell Structure*, with M. Goeppert-Mayer (New York: Wiley, 1955).

Bibliography: *Modern Men of Science* (New York: McGraw-Hill, 1966), p. 257. *Nobel Prize Winners: Physics* (Pasadena, Calif.: Salem Press, 1988), vol. 2, pp. 841–49. *Physics Today* 16 (December 1963): 21.

WIGNER, EUGENE PAUL

Prize: Physics, 1963. *Born:* November 17, 1902; Budapest, Hungary. *Died:* January 1, 1995; Princeton, New Jersey. *Nationality:* Hungarian; later U.S. citizen. *Education:* Tecnische Hochschule, Germany, Chemical Engineering Degree, 1924; Technische Hochschule, Germany, Doctorate in Engineering, 1925. *Career:* Technische Hochschule, Berlin, Germany, Professor, 1926–27; University of Göttingen, Germany, Professor, 1927–28; Technische Hochschule, Berlin, Germany, Professor, 1928–30; Princeton University, New Jersey, Professor, 1930–36; University of Wisconsin, Professor, 1936–38; Princeton University, New Jersey, Professor, 1938–71. *Other Awards:* Medal of Merit, 1946; Franklin Medal, Franklin Institute, 1950; Enrico Fermi Award; Atoms for Peace Award; Max Planck Medal, German Physical Society, 1961; George Washington Award; Semmeweiss Medal; National Science Medal, 1969; Pfizer Award, 1971; Albert Einstein Award, 1972; Golden Plate Medal; Wigner Medal, 1978; Founders Medal, International Cultural Foundation, 1982; Medal, Hungarian Central Research Institute, 1985; American Preparedness Award, 1985; Lord Foundation Award, 1989.

Citation: "For his contributions to the theory of the atomic nucleus and the elementary particles, particularly through the discovery and application of fundamental symmetry principles."

Life Work: Wigner's field of research was the group theory. He formulated symmetry principles and, with group theory, applied them in atomic, nuclear, and elementary particle physics. Wigner worked out the theory of neutron absorption and showed that nuclear forces did not depend on electric charge. His work also included research in theories of chemical reaction rates and the solid state and part of the design of the first large-scale nuclear reactor in 1943. In the late 1930s and early 1940s, along with other physicists, he convinced the U.S. government of the need for an atomic bomb project. His book *Gruppentheorie und Ihre Anwendung auf die Quantenmechanik der Atomspektren* was widely used as an advanced text in quantum mechanics.

Publications: *Gruppentheorie und Ihre Anwendung auf die Quantenmechanik der Atomspektren* (Braunschweig, Germany: Vieweg, 1931); *Group Theory and Its Application to the Quantum Mechanics of Atomic Spectra*, trans. J. J. Griffin (New York: Academic Press, 1959). *Nuclear Structure*, with Leonard Eisenbud (Princeton, N.J.: Princeton University Press, 1958). *The Physical Theory of Neutron Chemical Reactors*, with Alvin Martin Weinberg (Chicago: University of Chicago Press, 1958). *Symmetries and Reflections: Scientific Essays of Eugene P. Wigner* (Bloomington: Indiana University Press, 1967). *The Collected Works of Eugene Paul Wigner* (Berlin: Springer-Verlag, 1993).

Bibliography: *Current Biography Yearbook* (New York: H. W. Wilson, 1954), pp. 657–59. *McGraw-Hill Encyclopedia of World Biography* (New York: McGraw-Hill, 1973), vol. 11, pp. 357–58. *Nobel Prize Winners: Physics* (Pasadena, Calif.: Salem Press, 1988), vol. 2, pp. 819–28. *The Recollections of Eugene P. Wigner* (New York: Plenum Press, 1992).

BASOV, NICOLAY GENNADIYEVICH

Prize: Physics, 1964. *Born:* December 14, 1922; Usman, USSR. *Died:* July 1, 2001; Moscow, Russia. *Nationality:* Russian. *Education:* Moscow Institute of Engineering Physics, USSR, Candidaat, 1950; Lebedev Institute of Physics, Soviet Academy of Sciences, USSR, Ph.D., 1956. *Career:* P. N. Lebedev Physical Institute, Researcher and Administrator, Moscow, USSR, 1950–2001. *Other Awards:* Lenin Prize, 1959, 1964; Order of Lenin, 1967, 1969, 1972, 1975, 1982; Gold Medal, Czechoslovakian Academy of Sciences, 1975; A. Volta Gold Medal, Italian Physical Society, 1977; Hen Kel Gold Medal, 1986; Kalinga Prize, 1986; Gold Medal, Slovak Academy of Sciences, 1988; Lomonosov Gold Medal, 1990; Teller Medal, 1991.

Citation: "For fundamental work in the field of quantum electronics, which has led to the construction of oscillators and amplifiers based on the maser-laser principle" (with Aleksandr Prokhorov and Charles H. Townes).

Life Work: Basov's field of investigation was the molecular oscillator, now known as maser (for "microwave amplification by stimulated emission of radiation"). Stimulated radiation was part of Einstein's equation. Basov used it to amplify incoming radiation and to create a molecular oscillator. To do so, he inverted the equilibrium condition by increasing the numbers of excited molecules (relative to the number in the ground state) through the segregation of the former by means of electric or magnetic fields.

Publications: "Application of Molecular Beams to the Radio Spectroscopic Study of the Rotation Spectra of Molecules," with A. M. Prokhorov, *Zh. Eksp. Teor. Fiz.* 27 (1954): 431–38. "Possible Methods of Obtaining Active Molecules for a Molecular Oscillator," with O. N. Krokhin and Y. M. Popov, *Soviet Physics-JETP* 1 (1956): 184–85. "Theory of the Molecular Generator and the Molecular Power Amplifier," with A. M. Prokhorov, *Zh. Eksp. Teor. Fiz.* 30 (1956): 560–63. "Generation, Amplification, and Detection of Infrared and Optical Radiation by Quantum Mechanical Systems," with O. N. Krokhin and Y. M. Popov, *Soviet Physics-Uspekhi* (March-April 1961): 702–28.

Bibliography: *New York Times,* October 30, 1964, p. 23. *Nobel Prize Winners: Physics* (Pasadena, Calif.: Salem Press, 1988), vol. 2, pp. 869–68. J. M. Perlado, "N. G. Basov and Laser Technology in the USSR," *Arbor* 121 (1985): 87–97.

PROKHOROV, ALEKSANDR MIKHAILOVICH

Prize: Physics, 1964. *Born:* July 11, 1916; Atherton, Australia. *Nationality:* Australian; later Russian citizen. *Education:* Leningrad State University, USSR, baccalaureate, 1939; Institute of Physics, Academy of Sciences, USSR, doctorate, 1948. *Career:* Institute of Physics, Academy of Sciences, USSR, Researcher and Administrator, 1939–. *Other Awards:* Lenin Prize, 1959; Order of Lenin; Lomosonov Gold Medal, 1988.

Citation: "For fundamental work in the field of quantum electronics, which has led to the construction of oscillators and amplifiers based on the maser-laser principle" (with Nicolay Basov and Charles H. Townes).

Life Work: Prokhorov's field of interest was radio spectroscopy. His research focused on a class of molecules called asymmetric tops, and microwave absorption spectra. Together with Basov, he worked on the development of molecular oscillators, now known as masers, utilizing Einstein's principle of stimulated emission. They did so by segregating excited molecules from those in the ground state with electric or magnetic fields, they created a population of molecules at an upper energy level. Incoming radiation whose frequency matched the difference between the excited and ground levels would then trigger stimulated emission of radiation of the same frequency, resulting in amplification. His later work proved useful in the development of lasers.

Publications: "Application of Molecular Beams to the Radio Spectroscopic Study of the Rotation Spectra of Molecules," with N. G. Basov, *Zh. Eksp. Teor. Fiz.* 27 (1954): 431–38. "Theory of the Molecular Generator and the Molecular Power Amplifier," with N.G. Basov, *Zh. Eksp. Teor. Fiz.* 30 (1956): 560–63. "Quantum Electronics," *Fiz Mat. Spisanie, Bulgar, Akad. Nauk.* 8 (1965): 165–71. "Quantum Electronics," *Usp Fiz. Nauk* 85 (1965): 599–604.

Bibliography: *The Great Soviet Encyclopedia* (New York: Macmillan, 1978), vol. 21, p. 257. *New York Times*, October 30, 1964, p. 23. *Nobel Prize Winners: Physics* (Pasadena, Calif.: Salem Press, 1988), vol. 2, pp. 869–79.

TOWNES, CHARLES HARD

Prize: Physics, 1964. *Born:* July 28, 1915; Greenville, South Carolina. *Nationality:* American. *Education:* Furman University, South Carolina, B.A., 1933; Furman University, South Carolina, B.S., 1935; Duke University, North Carolina, M.A., 1936; California Institute of Technology, Ph.D., 1939. *Career:* Bell Telephone Laboratories, New Jersey, Researcher, 1939–48; Columbia University, New York, Professor, 1948–61; Massachusetts Institute of Technology, Professor and Administrator, 1961–67; University of California, Berkeley, Professor, 1967–86. *Other Awards:* Comstock Award, 1959;

Stuart Ballantine Medal, 1959, 1962; Thomas Young Medal, 1963; Medal of Honor, IEEE, 1967; Mees Medal, 1968; Wilhelm Exner Award, Austria, 1970; National Inventors Hall of Fame, 1976; Earle K. Plyler Prize, 1977; Niels Bohr International Gold Medal, 1979; National Science Medal, 1983; Commonwealth Award, 1993.

Citation: "For fundamental work in the field of quantum electronics, which has led to the construction of oscillators and amplifiers based on the maser-laser principle" (with Nicolay Basov and Aleksandr Prokhorov).

Life Work: Independent of Nicolay Basov and Aleksandr Prokhorov, Townes developed the maser by using stimulated emission to release excess energy of excited molecules thus amplifying the radiation that triggered the release. He was able to create a large population of excited molecules, compared with those in the ground state, through positive feedback in a resonant circuit arrangement, similar to an oscillator. Maser was developed as a sensitive low-noise amplifier for microwave reception. In radio astronomy it permitted detection of radio sources at great distances from earth. Townes's work also inspired the discovery of laser.

Publications: "Molecular Microwave Oscillator and New Hyperfine Structure in the Microwave Spectrum of NH_3," with J. P. Gordon and H. J. Zeiger, *Physical Review* Series 2, 95 (July 1, 1954): 282–84. *Microwave Spectroscopy*, with A. L. Schawlow (New York: McGraw-Hill, 1955). *Quantum Electronics: A Symposium* (New York: Columbia University Press, 1960). *Venus: Strategy for Exploration. Report of a study by the Space Science Board. C. H. Townes, chair* (Washington, D.C.: National Academy of Sciences, 1970).

Bibliography: *Asimov's Biographical Encyclopedia of Science and Technology* (Garden City, N.Y.: Doubleday, 1984), pp. 855–57. *Current Biography Yearbook* (New York: H. W. Wilson, 1963), pp. 423–25. *A Life in Physics* (Berkeley: University of California Press, 1994).

FEYNMAN, RICHARD PHILLIPS

Prize: Physics, 1965. *Born:* May 11, 1918; New York, New York. *Died:* February 15, 1988; Los Angeles, California. *Nationality:* American. *Education:* Massachusetts Institute of Technology, B.S., 1939; Princeton University, New Jersey, Ph.D., 1942. *Career:* Princeton University Atomic Bomb Project, New Jersey, Researcher, 1941–43; Los Alamos Atomic Bomb Project, New Mexico, Researcher, 1943–45; Cornell University, New York, Professor, 1945–50; California Institute of Technology, Professor, 1950–88. *Other Awards:* Einstein Award, 1954; Oersted Medal, 1972; Niels Bohr International Gold Medal, 1973.

Citation: "For their fundamental work in quantum electrodynamics, with deep-ploughing consequences for the physics of elementary particles" (with Julian S. Schwinger and Sin-Itiro Tomonaga).

Life Work: Feynman formulated a modified theory of quantum electrodynamic interactions as flowing from a space-time path. A particle is said to propagate from the initial to the final point of a path and the possible interactions along the way may be expressed in terms of their relative probabilities. Feynman devised computational rules and a pictorial representation, known as the Feynman diagram, presenting the probabilities as a complex series. Feynman's work successfully accounted for the Lamb shift and the electron's magnetic moment. His work, combined with the work of Julian S. Schwinger and Shinchiro Tomonaga, in the field of quantum electrodynamics, resulted in Feynman-Schwinger-Tomonaga theory, one of the most accurate physical theories known today. Later, Feynman provided an atomic explanation for the theory of liquid helium developed by Lev Landau. With his colleague Murray Gell-Mann, he was also responsible for an important theory of weak interactions such as beta particle emission by radioactive nuclei. He also worked on the strong forces holding the atomic nucleus together and on the subnuclear particles or partons, of which protons and neutrons are composed.

Publications: *Quantum Electrodynamics* (Reading, Mass.: Benjamin/Cummings, Advanced Book Program, 1961). *Theory of Fundamental Processes* (New York: W. A. Benjamin, 1961). *Feynman Lectures on Physics*, 3 vols. (Reading, Mass.: Addison-Wesley, 1963–69). *Quantum Mechanics and Path Integrals* (New York: McGraw-Hill, 1965). *The Character of Physical Law* (Cambridge: Massachusetts Institute of Technology Press, 1967). *Photon Hadron Interactions* (Reading, Mass.: W. A. Benjamin, 1972).

Bibliography: *Current Biography Yearbook* (New York: H. W. Wilson, 1955), pp. 205–207. J. Gleick, *Genius* (London: Little, Brown, 1992). *Nobel Prize Winners: Physics* (Pasadena, Calif.: Salem Press, 1988), vol. 2, pp. 901–10. *Science* 150 (October 29, 1965): 588–89. *Surely You're Joking, Mr. Feynman* (New York: Bantam, 1985).

SCHWINGER, JULIAN SEYMOUR

Prize: Physics, 1965. **Born:** February 12, 1918; New York, New York. **Died:** July 16, 1994; Los Angeles, California. **Nationality:** American. **Education:** Columbia University, New York, BA, 1936; Columbia University, New York, Ph.D., 1939. **Career:** University of California, Berkeley, Researcher, 1939–41; Purdue University, Indiana, Professor, 1941–43; University of Chicago, Illinois, Researcher, 1943; Massachusetts Institute of Technology, Researcher, 1943; Massachusetts Institute of Technology, Researcher, 1943–45; Harvard University, Massachusetts, Professor, 1945–72; University of California, Los Angeles, Professor, 1975–88. **Other Awards:** C. L. Mayer Nature of Light Award, 1949; University Medal, Columbia University, New York, 1951; Einstein Prize, 1951; National Medal of Science for Physics, 1964; Humbolt Award, 1981; Monie A. Fest Award, 1986; Castiglione di Sicilia Award, 1986; American Academy of Achievement Award, 1987.

Citation: "For their fundamental work in quantum electrodynamics, with deepploughing consequences for the physics of elementary particles" (with Richard P. Feynman and Sin-Itiro Tomonaga).

Life Work: Schwinger's field of investigation was the fundamental nature of matter. His work combined quantum mechanics and the special theory of relativity. Working independently, he and Shinchiro Tomonaga sought to revise Dirac's quantum electrodynamics, which predicted that every electron had both an infinite mass and an infinite electric charge. This was false because the electron's mass and charge were known to be finite. Schwinger and Tomonaga adopted a procedure, a mathematical technique called renormalization, according to which the measured mass of the electron consists of two components: the actual electron mass and the mass associated with the cloud of virtual photons that the electron continually emits and reabsorbs. The infinite mass of the photon cloud and the infinite but negative charge of the electron nearly cancel each other, leaving a small, finite residue of the negative bare charge corresponding to the commonly observed value. Schwinger and Tomonaga introduced some new concepts, such as infinite negative masses. Because an electron cannot be separated from its cloud of virtual particles, the infinite bare mass cannot be observed and only finite positive masses can be observed. Schwinger has also made important contributions to nuclear physics and electromagnetic theory. In 1957 he predicted two forms of neutrino, one associated with the electron and the other with a heavier particle called *muon*.

Publications: "Quantum Electrodynamics," *Physical Review* 74 (November 15, 1948): 39–61. "On Gauge Invariance and Vacuum Polarization," *Physical Review* 82 (1951): 664–79. "A Theory of the Fundamental Interactions," *Annals of Physics* 2 (1957): 407–34. *Quantum Electrodynamics* (New York: Dover, 1958). "Gauge Invariance and Mass II," *Physical Review* 128 (1962): 2425–29. *Particles Sources and Fields* (Reading, Mass.: Addison-Wesley, 1970).

Bibliography: *Current Biography Yearbook* (New York: H. W. Wilson, 1967), pp. 379–81. *New York Times* Biographical Service, July 20, 1994, p. 1077. *Nobel Prize Winners: Physics* (Pasadena, Calif.: Salem Press, 1988), vol. 2, pp. 891–900. *Science* 150 (October 29, 1965): 588–89. S. Schweber, *QED and the Men Who Made It* (Princeton, N.J.: Princeton University Press, 1994).

TOMONAGA, SIN-ITIRO

Prize: Physics, 1965. *Born:* March 31, 1906; Tokyo, Japan. *Died:* July 8, 1979; Tokyo, Japan. *Nationality:* Japanese. *Education:* Kyoto Imperial University, Japan, B.A., 1929; Tokyo Imperial University, Japan, D.Sc., 1939. *Career:* Tokyo University, Japan, Professor, 1939–70. *Other Awards:* Japan Academy Prize, 1948; Lomonosov Medal, Russia, 1964.

Citation: "For their fundamental work in quantum electrodynamics, with deep-ploughing consequences for the physics of elementary particles" (with Richard P. Feynman and Julian S. Schwinger).

Life Work: Tomonaga's field of investigation was quantum electrodynamics. Like Schwinger, Tomanaga devised a mathematical procedure called renormalization, according to which the measured mass of the electron consists of two components: the real or bare mass that an electron would have if it could be observed in isolation, and the mass associated with the cloud of virtual photons and other virtual particles that the electron continually emits and reabsorbs. The bare mass is not only infinite but also negative. When the two contributions to the total mass are added, the infinities cancel each other, leaving only a small finite residue that corresponds to the measured mass. A similar approach explained the infinite charge of the electron. Only finite and positive masses are measurable. An electron can never be separated from its cloud of virtual particles, with the result that the infinite bare mass and charge are forever unobservable. Renormalization helped to overcome the obvious errors in Dirac's theory of quantum mechanics.

Publications: *Quantum Mechanics* (Tokyo: Misuzu Publishing Company, 1949); English publication in two volumes (Amsterdam: North-Holland Publishing Company, 1962–66). *Scientific Papers of Tomonaga*, 2 vols. (Tokyo: Misuzu Shobo Publishing Company, 1971–76).

Bibliography: *Modern Men of Science* (New York: McGraw-Hill, 1966), pp. 483–84. *Nobel Prize Winners: Physics* (Pasadena, Calif.: Salem Press, 1988), vol. 2, pp. 881–89. S. Schweber, *QED and the Men Who Made It* (Princeton, N.J.: Princeton University Press, 1994). Robert L. Weber, *Pioneers of Science, Nobel Prize Winners in Physics* (London: Institute of Physics, 1980), pp. 205–206.

KASTLER, ALFRED

Prize: Physics, 1966. *Born:* May 3, 1902; Guebwiller, France. *Died:* January 7, 1984; Bandol, France. *Nationality:* French. *Education:* École Normale Supérieure, France, Teaching degree, 1926; University of Bordeaux, France, Docteur des Sciences Physiques, 1936. *Career:* Clermont-Ferrant University, France, Professor, 1936–38; University of Bordeaux, France, Professor, 1938–41; École Normale Supérieure, France, Professor, 1941–68; CNRS, France, Director, 1968–72. *Other Awards:* Holweck Prize, London Physical Society, 1954; C. E. K. Mees International Medal, Optical Society of America, 1962; Award in Scientific Research, Academy of Sciences, 1963; Science Prize, City of Paris, 1963.

Citation: "For the discovery and development of optical methods for studying Hertzian resonances in atoms."

Life Work: Kastler's field of investigation was the interaction between light and electrons in atoms. The atoms of a particular element have a unique level of allowed energy levels corresponding to orbits. Information about an atom's characteristic energy levels or atomic structure is conveyed by a spectrum that shows that atomic energy levels are in fact clusters of sublevels or substates, representing different contributions from electron properties, such as spin. The most advanced technique used in Kastler's time was radio-frequency spectroscopy, particularly atomic beam-magnetic resonance, but it had several limitations. To overcome these limitations, Kastler developed double resonance, a powerful method using light. He followed it with another method, called optical pumping, which enabled him to shift electrons in atoms from one magnetic sublevel of the ground state to another. The techniques enabled physicists to orient the nuclei of mercury and cadmium vapor atoms in desired directions, to precisely measure certain magnetic properties of the nuclei, and for studying Hertzian resonances in atoms. Optical pumping played an important part in the development of the laser and in the construction of atomic clocks and magnetometers.

Publications: *La Diffusion de la Lumière par les Milieux Troubles* (Paris: Hermann, 1952). *Polarisation, Matière et Rayonnement, Volume Jubilaire en l'Honneur d'Alfred Kastler* (Paris: Presses Universitaires de France, 1969). *Cette Etrange Matière* (Paris: Stock, 1976).

Bibliography: *Association Amicale des Anciens eleves de l'École Normale Supérieure (Annuaire)*, 1985, pp. 60–65. *Current Biography Yearbook* (New York: H. W. Wilson, 1967), pp. 216–18. *New York Times*, November 4, 1966, pp. 1, 28. "Notices sur les membres decedes: Kastler (Alfred)."

BETHE, HANS ALBRECHT

Prize: Physics, 1967. *Born:* July 2, 1906; Strassburg, Germany. *Nationality:* German; later U.S. citizen. *Education:* Goethe Gymnasium, Germany, baccalaureate, 1924; University of Munich, Germany, Ph.D., 1928. *Career:* University of Frankfurt, Germany, Professor, 1928–29; University of Stuttgart, Germany, Professor, 1929–30; University of Munich and University of Tübingen, Germany, Professor, 1930–33; University of Manchester, England, Professor, 1933–34; University of Bristol, England, Professor, 1934–35; Cornell University, New York, Professor, 1937–75. *Other Awards:* Morrison Prize, New York Academy of Science, 1938; U.S. Medal of Merit, 1946; Draper Medal, National Academy of Sciences, 1948; Max Planck Medal, 1955; Enrico Fermi Prize, 1961; Eddington Medal, Royal Astronomical Society, 1963; National Medal of Science, 1975; Vannevar Bush Award, 1985; Einstein Peace Prize, 1993.

Citation: "For his contributions to the theory of nuclear reactions, especially his discoveries concerning the energy production in stars."

Life Work: Bethe's field of investigation was the mechanism that supplies the thermonuclear energy of the sun and other stars. Bethe's calculations suggested the fusion of two protons (hydrogen nuclei) to form deuterium or heavy hydrogen, causing the release of energy in the form of a positron and a neutrino. In the fusion of two protons, the emission of a positive charge converts one of the protons into a neutron. For more massive starts Bethe proposed a six-step carbon-nitrogen cycle. Continuing his studies of atomic nuclei, he demonstrated that the newly discovered meson might be linked to the force that holds nuclei together. He also investigated the highly complex shock waves generated by explosives.

Publications: "Energy Production in Stars," *Physical Review* 55 (1939): 434. *Elementary Nuclear Theory* (New York: John Wiley and Sons, Inc., 1947). *Quantum Mechanics of One-and Two-Electron Atoms*, with E. E. Salpeter (New York: Plenum, 1958). *Splitting of Atoms in Crystals* (New York: Plenum, 1962). *Intermediate Quantum Mechanics*, with Roman W. Jackiw (San Francisco: Benjamin-Cummings, 1968).

Bibliography: Jeremy Bernstein, *Hans Bethe: Prophet of Energy* (New York: Basic Books, 1980). *Modern Men of Science* (New York: McGraw Hill, 1966), pp. 37–39. *National Cyclopedia of American Biography* (New York: James T. White, 1960), vol. I, pp. 320–21. *Nobel Prize Winners: Physics* (Pasadena, Calif.: Salem Press), vol. 2, pp. 923–34.

ALVAREZ, LUIS WALTER

Prize: Physics, 1968. *Born:* June 13, 1911; San Francisco, California. *Died:* September 1, 1988; Berkeley, California. *Nationality:* American. *Education:* University of Chicago, Illinois, B.S., 1932; University of Chicago, Illinois, M.Sc., 1934; University of Chicago, Illinois, Ph.D., 1936. *Career:* University of California, Berkeley, Professor, 1936–78. *Other Awards:* Collier Trophy, 1946; Medal for Merit, 1948; John Scott Medal, 1953; California Scientist of the Year, 1960; Einstein Medal, 1961; National Medal of Science, 1964; Michaelson Award, 1965; National Inventors Hall of Fame, 1978; Wright Prize, 1981; Rockwell Medal, 1986; Enrico Fermi Award, 1987.

Citation: "For his decisive contributions to elementary particle physics, in particular the discovery of a large number of resonance states, made possible through his development of the technique of using hydrogen bubble chamber and data analysis."

Life Work: Working at the University of California, Berkeley, Alvarez worked on a number of inventions: the artificial isotope mercury 198; a method for producing beams of very slow neutrons, which led the way to the measurement of the neutron's magnetic moment; tritium; the radioactive isotope of hydrogen; and helium 3. Working at MIT, he developed three important radar systems: a microwave radar system that could locate planes lost in foul weather; the Eagle, a high-altitude radar device to facilitate pinpoint bombing; and the microwave early warning set, which transmitted images of aerial combat. Using high-speed computers and bubble chambers, Alvarez studied many subatomic particles produced by the new accelerators. As a result of these studies, the number of known particles rose to over 100. Many of them were short-lived resonance states, which could not be observed directly but whose existence could be deduced by an increase in the sudden increase in the number of other particles at certain energy states.

Publications: "The Lifetime of the t-Meson," with S. Goldhaber, *Nuovo Cimento* 2 (1955): 344. "Catalysis of Nuclear Reactions by u Mesons," with others, *Physical Review* 105 (1957): 1127. "K-Interactions in Hydrogen," with others, *Nuovo Dimento*

5 (1957): 1026. "Elastic Scattering of 1.6-Mev Gamma Ray from H, Li, C, and Al Nuclei," with F. S. Crawford and M. L. Stevenson *Physical Review* 112 (1958): 1267. *Strong Interactions* (New York: Academic Press, 1966). "Recent Developments in Particle Physics," *Science* 165 (September 12, 1969): 1071.

Bibliography: *Alvarez: Adventures of a Physicist* (New York: Basic Books, 1987). *Science* 162 (November 8, 1968): 645.

GELL-MANN, MURRAY

Prize: Physics, 1969. *Born:* September 15, 1929; New York, New York. *Nationality:* American. *Education:* Yale University, Connecticut, B.S., 1948; Massachusetts Institute of Technology, Ph.D., 1951. *Career:* Princeton University, New Jersey, Professor, 1951–52; University of Chicago, Illinois, Professor, 1952–55; California Institute of Technology, Pasadena, Professor, 1955–. *Other Awards:* Dannie Heineman Prize, American Physical Society and American Institute of Physics, 1959; Franklin Medal, Franklin Institute, Pennsylvania, 1967; Research Corporation Award, 1969.

Citation: "For his contributions and discoveries concerning the classification of elementary particles and their interactions."

Life Work: Gell-Mann's field of investigation was subatomic physics. The fundamental experimental tools of this field were particle accelerators, which helped to create numerous subatomic particles. Some of these particles exhibited what was known as strange behavior, which made it difficult to determine whether they were governed by the strong force or the weak force, two of the fundamental forces governing all nature (the other two being gravity and electromagnetism). Gell-Mann tried to reformulate the concept called independence, a method of grouping particles in a way that emphasized their similarities. Gell-Mann devised a scheme for grouping strange particles and proposed as their characteristic property a concept called strangeness. Conservation of strangeness explained why the decay of strange particles is not governed by the strong force. Strange particles, once created, survive until they decay by means of weak interaction. In 1961 Gell-Mann expanded this concept by introducing another concept, called families. He called this scheme the Eightfold Way because some families are grouped into families of eight members. The scheme is also known as the SU3 symmetry. His Eightfold Way was similar to Mendeleev's periodic table, where certain spaces are left empty pending the discovery of elements with the correct ensemble of properties. Two years later he discovered fractionally charged particles, called quarks, with George Zweig.

Publications: "Isotopic Spin and New Unstable Particles," *Physical Review* 92 (1953): 833. *Lectures on Weak Interactions of Strongly Interacting Particles, Delivered at the Summer School in Theoretical Physics, Bangalore, 1961* (Bombay: Tata Institute of Fundamental Research, 1961). *Lecture Notes on Special Topics in Relativistic Quantum Theory* (Cambridge: Massachusetts Institute of Technology Press, 1963). "A Schematic Model of Baryons and Mesons," *Physics Letters* 8 (February 1, 1964): 214. *The Eight-*

fold Way: A Review with a Collection of Reprints, with Y. Ne'eman (New York: W. A. Benjamin, 1964).

Bibliography: *Current Biography Yearbook* (New York: H. W. Wilson, 1966), pp. 124–66. *Science* (November 8, 1969): 715–22.

ALFVÉN, HANNES OLOF GÖSTA

Prize: Physics, 1970. *Born:* May 30, 1908; Norrkoeping, Sweden. *Died:* April 2, 1995; Djursholm, Sweden. *Nationality:* Swedish. *Education:* University of Uppsala, Sweden, Ph.D., 1934. *Career:* University of Uppsala, Sweden, Professor, 1934–37; Nobel Institute of Physics, Sweden, Researcher, 1937–40; Royal Institute of Technology, Professor, 1940–67; University of California, San Diego, Professor, 1967–88. *Other Awards:* Gold Medal, Royal Astronomical Society, 1967; Lomonosov Gold Medal, Soviet Academy of Sciences, 1971; Franklin Medal, Franklin Institute, Pennsylvania, 1971; Bowie Gold Medal, 1987; Dirac Medal, 1994.

Citation: "For fundamental work and discoveries in magneto-hydrodynamics with fruitful applications in different parts of plasma physics."

Life Work: Alfvén's field of investigation was magnetohydrodynamics and plasma physics. Plasma, found on the sun and others stars, is a gaslike mixture of electrons, stripped from atoms and molecules by high-energy collisions and the charged ions the collisions produce. When these particles enter the earth's magnetic field they are diverted toward the poles, where they produce the auroral displays. Alfvén showed that plasma is associated with a magnetic field and that under certain conditions the magnetic field could become frozen in the plasma. Alfvén developed the concept that a charged particle rotated about a guiding center which was itself drifting along magnetic field lines. He applied this principle to magnetic storms and auroras. The concept of a magnetic mirror is important in controlled thermonuclear fusion requiring the confinement of hot plasmas whose contact would destroy the walls of any container. His ideas also explained such phenomena as the Van Allen radiation belt. In 1942 Alfvén predicted that magnetic field lines in a plasma acted like stretched rubber bands to transmit a disturbance called a hydromagnetic wave, named the Alfvén wave. Alfvén waves explain small variations in the earth's magnetic field. Studying the solar sunspots, he concluded that they were regions of intense magnetic fields embedded in the body of the sun. Alfvén established a new field of physics called magnetohydrodynamics which is important not only to thermonuclear fusion, but also hypersonic flight, rocket propulsion, and reentry of space vehicles.

Publications: *Cosmical Electrodynamics* (Oxford: Clarendon Press, 1950). *On the Origin of the Solar System* (Oxford: Clarendon Press, 1954). *Cosmical Electrodynamics: Fundamental Principles*, with Carl-Gunne Falthammar (Oxford: Clarendon Press, 1963). *Worlds-Antiworlds: Antimatter in Cosmology* (San Francisco: W. H. Freeman, 1966). *Structure and Evolutionary History of the Solar System*, with Gustaf Arrhenius (Dordrecht: D. Reidel, 1975).

Bibliography: *New York Times* Biographical Service, October 28, 1970, pp. 2707–2708. *Physics Today* 23 (December 1970): 61–63.

NÉEL, LOUIS EUGÈNE FÉLIX

Prize: Physics, 1970. *Born:* November 22, 1904; Lyons, Rhone, France. *Died:* November 17, 2000; Brive-Corrèze, France. *Nationality:* French. *Education:* École Normale Supérieure, France, Agrege de l'Université, 1928; University of Strasbourg, France, Docteur es Sciences, 1932. *Career:* University of Strasbourg, France, Professor, 1937–45; University of Grenoble, France, Professor, 1945–76. *Other Awards:* Prix Holweck, 1952; Gold Medal (C.N.R.S.), 1965; Croix de Guerre, 1940; Grand Croix, Legion d'Honeur, 1953.

Citation: "For fundamental work and discoveries concerning antiferromagnetism and ferrimagnetism which have led to important applications in solid state physics."

Life Work: Néel's field of investigation was magnetic properties of solids, especially antiferromagnetism and ferromagnetism, both of which have important applications in solid-state physics. Néel proposed that in certain substances the interactions of neighboring atoms caused their magnetic fields to be oriented in opposite directions. The crystal lattices of such substances consist of two identical interpenetrating sublattices, each composed of atoms with magnetic fields oriented in a single direction. This orientation occurs when temperatures go below a certain point, called the Néel point. In 1948 Néel proposed another form of magnetization called ferrimagnetism, found in ferrites, a class of minerals that includes megnetite. Néel's research also include studies of magnetic creep and palaeomagnetism.

Publications: *Exposés sur l'Energie* (Paris: Institute de France, 1978). *Ouevres Scientifique de Louis Néel* (Paris: Centre National de la Recherche Scientifique, 1978). *Selected Works of Louis Néel* (New York: Gordon and Breach, 1988).

Bibliography: *New York Times* Biographical Service, October 28, 1970, pp. 2707–2708. *Science* (November 6, 1970): 604–609.

GABOR, DENNIS

Prize: Physics, 1971. *Born:* June 5, 1900; Budapest, Hungary. *Died:* February 8, 1979; London, England. *Nationality:* Hungarian; later British citizen. *Education:* Technische Hochschule, Germany, diploma, 1924; Technische Hochschule, Germany, Dr. Elect. Eng., 1927. *Career:* Siemens and Halske, Berlin, Germany, Researcher, 1927–33; British Thomson-Houston Co., Rugby, England, Researcher, 1933–48; Imperial College, London, England, Professor, 1949–67. *Other Awards:* Thomas

Young Medal and Prize, 1967; Cristoforo Columbo Prize, Genoa, Italy, 1967; Rumford Medal, Royal Society, 1968; Michelson Medal, Franklin Institute, Pennsylvania, 1968; Medal of Honor, Institute of Electrical and Electronics Engineers, 1970; Semmelweis Medal, American Hungarian Medical Association, 1970; Holweck Prize, French Physical Society, 1971; George Washington Award, American Hungarian Studies Foundation, 1973.

Citation: "For his invention and development of the holographic method."

Life Work: Gabor's field of investigation was holography. His work to improve the electron lens found in electron microscopes led to the concept of holography, a term he coined. A hologram captures information absent from a normal photograph by taking advantage of a property of light waves known as a relative phase. To produce a three-dimensional hologram, a single beam of light is split into two beams. The daughter beam, called the reference beam, passes straight to the film, while the other is reflected off the object before it strikes the film. Because the two beams travel different distances to reach the same point, they produce an interference pattern of dark and light fringes, representing points on the film where the intersecting waves are in or out of phase, respectively. To achieve a holographic effect, all light waves in an original unsplit beam must be completely in phase with one another. Such light, called coherent light, is produced only by lasers.

Publications: "A New Microscopic Principle," *Nature* (May 15, 1948): 777–78. "Microscopy by Reconstructed Wave-Fronts," *Proceedings of the Royal Society* A197 (1949): 454. "Microscopy by Reconstructed Wave Fronts: II," *Proceedings of the Royal Society* B64 (1951): 244. *Inventing the Future* (New York: Knopf, 1964). *Innovations: Scientific, Technological, and Social* (London: Oxford University Press, 1970).

Bibliography: *Biographical Memoirs of the Fellows of the Royal Society* (London: Royal Society, 1980), vol. 26, pp. 107–47. *New York Times*, November 3, 1971, pp. 1, 28.

BARDEEN, JOHN. *See* 1956, pp. 177–78.

COOPER, LEON NEIL

Prize: Physics, 1972. *Born:* February 28, 1930; New York, New York. *Nationality:* American. *Education:* Columbia University, New York, A.B., 1951; Columbia University, New York, A.M., 1953; Columbia University, New York, Ph.D., 1954. *Career:* Princeton University, New Jersey, Researcher, 1954–55; University of Illinois, Researcher, 1955–57; Ohio State University, Professor, 1957–58; Brown University, Rhode Island, Professor, 1958–. *Other Awards:* Comstock Prize, National Academy of Science, 1968; Descartes Medal, Académie de Paris, 1977; John Jay Award, Columbia University, New York, 1985.

Citation: "For their jointly developed theory of superconductivity, usually called the BCS-theory" (with John Bardeen and John R. Schrieffer).

Life Work: Cooper is best known for his discovery of Cooper pairs, bound pairs of electrons created by interaction between electrons and a crystal lattice. This was the basis of the general theory of superconductivity (BCS) developed by Bardeen, Cooper, and Schreiffer. It states that interaction between Cooper pairs allows a large fraction of the free electrons in the superconducting material to cooperate. In the resulting state the electrons move in lockstep. The pairing force that holds the electrons in their coordinated motion is stronger than the thermal vibrations of the metal atoms.

Publications: "Microscopic Theory of Superconductivity," with J. Bardeen and J. R. Schrieffer, *Physical Review* 106 (1957): 162–64. "Theory of Superconductivity," with J. Bardeen and J. R. Schrieffer, *Physical Review* 108 (1957): 1175–1204. "Specific Heat Measurements and the Energy Gap in Superconductors," *Physical Review Letters* 3 (1959): 17. "Superconductivity in the Neighborhood of Metallic Contacts," *Physical Review Letters* 6 (1961): 689–90. *An Introduction to the Meaning and Structure of Physics* (New York: Harper & Row, 1968). "Origin of the Theory of Superconductivity," *IEEE Transactions on Magnetics MAG–23* (March 1987): 376.

Bibliography: *Physics Today* 25 (December 1972): 73–75. *Science* 178 (November 3, 1972): 489–91.

SCHRIEFFER, JOHN ROBERT

Prize: Physics, 1972. *Born:* May 31, 1931; Oak Park, Illinois. *Nationality:* American. *Education:* Massachusetts Institute of Technology, B.S., 1953; University of Illinois, M.S., 1954; University of Illinois, Ph.D., 1957. *Career:* University of Chicago, Illinois, Professor, 1957–59; University of Illinois, Professor, 1959–62; University of Pennsylvania, Professor, 1962–79; University of California, Santa Barbara, Professor, 1979–91; Florida State University, Professor, 1992–. *Other Awards:* Buckley Prize, 1968; Comstock Prize, National Academy of Sciences, 1968; John Ericsson Medal, American Society of Swedish Engineers, 1976; National Medal of Science, 1984.

Citation: "For their jointly developed theory of superconductivity, usually called the BCS-theory" (with John Bardeen and Leon N. Cooper).

Life Work: Schreiffer worked with Bardeen and Cooper in the formulation of BCS theory of superconductivity. Building on the discovery of Cooper pairs by Cooper, Schreiffer discovered a method of analyzing the motions of large numbers of pairs of interacting electrons in a superconducting solid. Cooper and Schreiffer demonstrated that the interaction between Cooper pairs compels many of the free electrons in a superconducting substance to move in lockstep. Below a critical temperature, the pairing force that holds the electrons in their coordinated motion is stronger than the thermal vibrations of the metal atoms, as a result of which the superconducting elec-

trons drift coherently without loss of energy. The practical applications of superconductivity have been impressive in magnetohydrodynamics, the construction of electromagnets, magnetic levitation, and the working of the Josephson effect.

Publications: "Microscopic Theory of Superconductivity," with L. N. Cooper and J.
Bardeen, *Physical Review* 106 (1957): 162–64. "Theory of Superconductivity," with J.
Bardeen and L. N. Cooper, *Physical Review* 108 (1957): 1175–1204. "Recent
Advances in the Theory of Superconductivity," *Physica* 26 (1960): S1–S16. *Theory of
Superconductivity* (Reading, Mass.: W. A. Benjamin, 1964, rev. ed., 1983).

Bibliography: *Physics Today* 25 (December 1972): 73–75. *Science* 178 (November 3,
1972): 489–91.

ESAKI, LEO

Prize: Physics, 1973. *Born:* March 12, 1925; Osaka, Japan. *Nationality:* Japanese.
Education: University of Tokyo, Japan, B.S., 1947; University of Tokyo, Japan, Ph.D.,
1959. *Career:* Kobe Kogyo Corporation, Japan, Researcher, 1947–56; Sony Corpora-
tion, Japan, Researcher, 1956–60; International Business Machines, New York,
Researcher, 1960–92; University of Tsukuba, Japan, President, 1992–. *Other Awards:*
Nishina Memorial Award, 1959; Asahi Press Award, 1960; Toyo Rayon Foundation
Award, 1961; Morris N. Liebmann Memorial Prize, 1961; Stuart Ballantine Medal,
Franklin Institute, Pennsylvania, 1961; Japan Academy Award, 1965; Order of Cul-
ture, Japan, 1974; Science Achievement Award, U.S.-Asia Institute, 1983; Interna-
tional Prize for New Materials, American Physical Society, 1985; IEEE Medal of
Honor, 1991.

Citation: "For their experimental discoveries regarding tunneling phenomena in semiconductors and superconductors, respectively" (with Ivar Giaever).

Life Work: Esaki's field of investigation was tunneling by electrons in semiconductors.
He worked with junction diodes, in which adjacent regions in a semiconductor are
doped with electrically active impurities of opposite polarity. The diode conducts current freely in one direction but the junction presents a barrier to the flow of current in
the opposite direction. The relation of current to voltage appeared to be "fuzzy." When
the diodes had large tunneling currents, they developed a negative resistance. A circuit
incorporating such negative resistance generates high-frequency oscillations. These
tunnel diodes are called Esaki diodes and have junctions only ten-billionths of a meter.
Later, at IBM, Esaki pioneered in the investigation of semiconductor superlattices,
which are complex structures made by depositing fine layers of different semiconductors in such a way that the entire structure is one crystal. Superlattice materials are used
in high-speed computers.

Publications: "Properties of Heavily-Doped Ge and Narrow p-n Junctions," *Solid
State Phys. Electronics Telecommun., Proc. Intern. Conf., Brussels* 1 (1958): 514–23.

"New Horizons in Semimetal Alloys," *IEEE Spectrum* 3 (1966): 74–80, 85–86. "Tunneling Studies on the Group 5 Semimetals and the 4–6 Semiconductors," *Journal of the Physical Society of Japan*, supp. 21 (1966): 589–97. "Tunneling in Solids," *Electron. Struct. Solids, Lect. Chania Conf.*, 2nd (1968): 1–40.

Bibliography: *Modern Men of Science* (New York: McGraw-Hill, 1966), 156–57. *New York Times* Biographical Service, October 24, 1973, p. 1640. *Science* 182 (November 16, 1973): 701–704.

GIAEVER, IVAR

Prize: Physics, 1973. *Born:* April 5, 1929; Bergen, Norway. *Nationality:* Norwegian; later U.S. citizen. *Education:* Norwegian Institute of Technology, Norway, Bachelor of Engineering, 1952; Rensselaer Polytechnical Institute, New York, Ph.D., 1964. *Career:* Norwegian Army, 1952–53; Norwegian Patent Office, Oslo, Patent Examiner, 1953–54; General Electric Company, Canada, Engineer, 1954–56; General Electric Company, United States, Researcher, 1956–88; Rensselaer Polytechnic, New York, Professor, 1988–. *Other Awards:* Oliver E. Buckley Prize, American Physical Society, 1965; Guggenheim Fellow, 1970; V. K. Zworykin Award, National Academy of Engineering, 1974.

Citation: "For their experimental discoveries regarding tunneling phenomena in semiconductors and superconductors, respectively" (with Leo Esaki).

Life Work: Giaever's field of investigation was the electrical behavior of junctions formed by metal contacts separated by thin insulating layers. Gaiever devised a technique for observing and measuring forbidden energies in superconductors that affect the electrical behavior of an insulated junction. Forbidden energies are created through the interaction of electrons with the atomic vibrations in the material. His discovery is useful in detecting gravitational waves, for ore prospecting, for communication through water and through mountains, and for the study of electromagnetic fields through the heart and brain.

Publications: "Energy Gap in Superconductors Measured by Electron Tunneling," *Physical Review Letters* 5 (1960): 147. "Electron Tunneling between Two Superconductors," *Physical Review Letters* 5 (1960): 464. "Detection of the A. C. Josephson Effect," *Physical Review Letters* 14 (1965): 904. "Magnetic Coupling Between Two Adjacent Superconductors," *Physical Review Letters* 15 (1965): 825.

Bibliography: *Nobel Prize Winners: Physics* (Pasadena, Calif.: Salem Press, 1988), vol. 3, pp.1027–36. *Physics Today* 14 (December 1961): 38–41. *Science* 182 (November 16, 1973): 701–704.

JOSEPHSON, BRIAN DAVID

Prize: Physics, 1973. *Born:* January 4, 1940; Cardiff, Wales. *Nationality:* British. *Education:* Cambridge University, England, B.A., 1960; Cambridge University, England, M.A., 1964; Cambridge University, England, Ph.D., 1964. *Career:* Cambridge University, England, Professor, 1965–. *Other Awards:* New Scientist Award, 1969; Research Corporation Award, 1969; Fritz London Medal, 1970; Guthrie Medal, 1972; Van der Pol Medal, 1972; Elliott Cresson Medal, 1972; Hughes Medal, 1972; Holweck Medal, 1973; Faraday Medal, 1982; Sir George Thompson Medal, 1984.

Citation: "For his theoretical predictions of the properties of a supercurrent through a tunnel barrier, in particular those phenomena which are generally known as the Josephson effects."

Life Work: Josephson's field of investigation was the tunneling effect in semiconductors. He extended Gaiever's analysis to include the case of an insulated junction between two superconductors. He predicted that currents could flow between two superconductors even with no voltage difference between them and that a high-frequency alternating current would flow when a voltage was applied across the junction—the Josephson effects. The Josephson effects allowed increased precision in the ratio of the electronic charge to Max Planck's constant. It also led to the creation of a new primary quantum standard for voltage. By putting two Josephson junctions in a loop it became possible to develop sensors for magnetic fields that are extraordinarily sensitive. Such a device is called superconducting quantum interference device (SQUID). Josephson devices are also used in computer circuitry.

Publications: "Potential Differences in the Mixed State of Type II Superconductors," *Physics Letters* 16 (1965): 242–43. "Macroscopic Field Equations for Metals in Equilibrium," *Physical Review* 152 (1966): 211–17. "Inequality for the Specific Heat. I. Derivation," *Proceedings of the Physical Society* 92 (1967): 269–75. "Inequality for the Specific Heat. II. Application of Critical Phenomena," *Proceedings of the Physical Society* 92 (1967): 276–84. "Equation of State Near the Critical Point," *Proceedings of the Physical Society, London (Solid State Physics)* 2 (1969): 1113–15. *Consciousness and the Physical World* (New York: Pergamon Press, 1980).

Bibliography: *New York Times*, October 24, 1973, pp. 1, 26. *Nobel Prize Winners: Physics* (Pasadena, Calif.: Salem Press, 1988), vol. 3, pp.1037–44.

HEWISH, ANTONY

Prize: Physics, 1974. *Born:* May 11, 1924; Fowey, England. *Nationality:* British. *Education:* Cambridge University, England, B.A., 1948; Cambridge University, England, M.A., 1950; Cambridge University, England, Ph.D., 1952. *Career:* Cambridge University, England, Professor, 1952–89. *Other Awards:* Hamilton Prize, Cambridge

University, England, 1951; Eddington Medal, Royal Astronomical Society, 1968; Charles Vernon Boys Prize, Institute of Physics and Physical Sciences, 1970; Dellinger Gold Medal, International Union of Radio Sciences, 1972; Michelson Medal, Franklin Institute, Pennsylvania, 1973; Hopkins Prize, Cambridge Philosophical Society, 1973; Holweck Medal and Prize, Institute of Physics and French Physical Society, 1974; Hughes Medal, Royal Society, 1977.

Citation: "For their pioneering research in radio astrophysics: Ryle for his observations and inventions, in particular of the aperture synthesis technique, and Hewish for his decisive role in the discovery of pulsars" (with Martin Ryle).

Life Work: Hewish's field of investigation was radio astrophysics and his research led to the discovery of pulsars. In 1954, while observing radio emission from solar corona, Hewish predicted that radio sources with small angular diameters would scintillate (whereas those with large enough angular diameters do not) because the waves emanating from them bend slightly as they travel through interplanetary space occupied by variably dense gas. The result, called interplanetary scintillation (IPS), would be variations in strength of received signal, similar to the twinkling of the stars. Later he measured the velocity of the solar wind. A Hewish-designed radio telescope, completed in 1967, provided evidence of IPS in pulses of radio waves of very stable frequency from pulsars (pulsing stars). In 1968 it was proved that pulsars are spinning neutron stars accompanied by an enormously powerful magnetic field and surrounded by an electrically conducting gas cloud of low-density emitting rotating beam.

Publications: *Seeing Beyond the Visible* (London: English Universities Press, 1970). "Small Stars Raise Large Problems," *Physics Bulletin* 25 (1974): 459–61.

Bibliography: *Nobel Prize Winners: Physics* (Pasadena, Calif.: Salem Press, 1988), vol. 3, pp. 1053–59. *Science* 186 (November 15, 1974): 620–21.

RYLE, SIR MARTIN

Prize: Physics, 1974. **Born:** September 27, 1918; Brighton, England. **Died:** October 14, 1984; Cambridge, England. **Nationality:** British. **Education:** Oxford University, England, baccalaureate, 1945. **Career:** Telecommunications Research Establishment, England, Researcher, 1939–45; Cambridge University, England, Professor and Administrator, 1945–82. **Other Awards:** Hughes Medal, Royal Society, 1954; Gold Medal, Royal Astronomical Society, 1964; Henry Draper Medal, National Academy of Sciences, U.S.A., 1965; Knighthood, 1966; Royal Medal, Royal Society, 1973.

Citation: "For their pioneering research in radio astrophysics: Ryle for his observations and inventions, in particular of the aperture synthesis technique, and Hewish for his decisive role in the discovery of pulsars" (with Antony Hewish).

Life Work: Ryle's field of investigation was radio astrophysics. He built powerful radio telescopes by spacing his antennas many wavelengths apart and connecting them to a single receiver. With these he was able to reach 6 billion light years into space and to locate radio stars. He also demonstrated the method of aperture synthesis, which allows high resolving power in two dimensions. Later, with a large-aperture synthesis telescope with eight forty-two-foot-diameter dishes, he studied the fine structure of distant radio sources and galaxies. With them, he was able to study quasars (quasi-stellar objects), remote starlike objects that emit many times more energy than entire galaxies.

Publications: "The New Cambridge Radio Telescope," *Nature* 194 (May 12, 1962): 517–18. "High-Resolution Observations of the Radio Sources in Cygnus and Cassiopeia," with B. Elsmore and Ann C. Neville, *Nature* 205 (March 27, 1965): 1259–62. "Observations of Radio Galaxies with the One-Mile Telescope at Cambridge," with B. Elsmore and Ann C. Neville, *Nature* 207 (September 4, 1965): 1024–27. "The 5-km Radio Telescope at Cambridge," *Nature* 239 (October 20, 1972): 435–38.

Bibliography: *Biographical Memoirs of the Fellows of the Royal Society* (London: Royal Society, 1986), vol. 32, p. 495. *New York Times* Biographical Service, October 16, 1974, p. 1491. *Nobel Prize Winners: Physics* (Pasadena, Calif.: Salem Press, 1988), vol. 3, pp. 1045–52.

BOHR, AAGE NIELS

Prize: Physics, 1975. *Born:* June 19, 1922; Copenhagen, Denmark. *Nationality:* Danish. *Education:* University of Copenhagen, Denmark, M.S., 1946; University of Copenhagen, Denmark, Ph.D., 1954. *Career:* Department of Scientific and Industrial Research, London, England, Researcher, 1943–45; Institute for Theoretical Physics, Copenhagen, Researcher, 1946–49; Columbia University, New York, Researcher, 1949–50; University of Copenhagen, Denmark, Researcher and Professor, 1950–. *Other Awards:* Dannie Heineman Prize, American Physical Society and American Institute for Physics, 1960; Pope Pius XI Medal, 1963; Atoms for Peace Award, Ford Motor Company Fund, 1969; H. C. Orsted Medal, 1970; Rutherford Medal and Prize, Institute of Physics, London, 1972; John Price Wetherill Medal, Franklin Institute, Pennsylvania, 1974; Ole Romer Medal, 1976.

Citation: "For the discovery of the connection between collective motion and particle motion in atomic nuclei and the development of the theory of the structure of the atomic nucleus based on this connection" (with Ben R. Mottelson and James Rainwater).

Life Work: Bohr's field of investigation was the atom and his theories provided the bridge between Rutherford's atom and the world of quantum theory. Applying the latter to the problem of atomic structure, Bohr suggested that electrons have certain allowed stable orbits in which they do not radiate energy. It is only when an electron jumps from one orbit to another that it gains or loses energy, and then the gain or loss is always precisely equal to the energy difference between the two orbits. Bohr's revolutionary model offered a clue to the baffling spectra of the elements. When light from a glowing element is passed through a prism, it does not produce a continuous spectrum including all colors, but rather a sequence of discrete bright lines, separated by wider dark regions. In the Bohr atom, each distinct wavelength represents light emitted by electrons as they jump from a specific allowed orbit to another orbit of lower energy. During the 1920s Bohr made significant contributions to the Copenhagen Interpretation of quantum mechanics. Bohr also formulated two of the fundamental principles that guided the development of quantum mechanics: the correspondence principle and the complementarity principle. Turning to nuclear physics in 1930, Bohr proposed a liquid drop model of the nucleus that provided the theoretical basis for nuclear fission.

Publications: "On the Quantization of Angular Momenta in Heavy Nuclei," *Physical Review* 81 (January 1, 1951): 134–38. "Nuclear Magnetic Moments and Atomic Hyperfine Structure," *Physical Review* 81 (February 1, 1951): 331–35. *Rotational States of Atomic Nuclei* (Copenhagen: Munksgaard, 1954). *Collective and Individual-Particle Aspects of Nuclear Structure*, with B. Mottelson (Copenhagen: Munksgaard, 1957). *Nuclear Structure*, 2 vols., with B. Mottelson (New York: W. A. Benjamin, 1969–75).

Bibliography: *Physics Today* 28 (December 1975): 69–71. *Science* 190 (November 28, 1975): 868–70.

MOTTELSON, BEN ROY

Prize: Physics, 1975. *Born:* July 9, 1926; Chicago, Illinois. *Nationality:* American; later Danish citizen. *Education:* Purdue University, Indiana, B.S., 1947; Harvard University, Massachusetts, M.A., 1948; Harvard University, Massachusetts, M.A., Ph.D., 1950. *Career:* Institute for Theoretical Physics, Denmark, Researcher, 1950–51; U.S. Atomic Energy Commission, Researcher, 1951–53; CERN, Theoretical Study Group, Researcher, 1953–56; Nordic Institute for Theoretical Atomic Physics, Denmark, Professor and Administrator, 1957–.

Citation: "For the discovery of the connection between collective motion and particle motion in atomic nuclei and the development of the theory of the structure of the atomic nucleus based on this connection" (with Aage Bohr and James Rainwater).

Life Work: Mottelson's field of investigation was the behavior of protons and neutrons in a large nucleus. Working with Aage Bohr, he was able to integrate two theoretical models: Bohr's own liquid drop model and the shell model offered by Mayer and Jensen. Another colleague, James Rainwater, had developed the football model, which was the basis of the new model proposed by Bohr and Mottelson. It established the connection between the collective motion and particle motion in the atomic nuclei. While retaining the liquid drop surface, the Bohr-Mottelson model proposed that the shell structure of the nucleus can be deformed. When the outermost shell of a nucleon has a full complement of nucleons, it is spherical, but when the outer shell is incomplete, it becomes distorted into the shape of a football. The distorted nuclei have various new modes of vibration and rotation, including surface waves and breathing modes.

Publications: *Collective and Individual-Particle Aspects of Nuclear Structure,* with A. Bohr (Copenhagen: Munksgaard, 1957). *Lectures on Selected Topics in Nuclear Structure* (Bombay: Tata Institute of Fundamental Research, 1964). *Nuclear Structure,* with A. Bohr, 2 vols. (New York: W. A. Benjamin, 1969–75). "Elementary Modes of Excitation in the Nucleus," *Reviews of Modern Physics* 48 (July 1976): 375–83.

Bibliography: *Asimov's Biographical Encyclopedia of Science and Technology* (Garden City, N.Y.: Doubleday, 1982), p. 833. *Kraks Blaa Bog 1984* (Copenhagen: Krak, 1985), p. 754. *Physics Today* 28 (December 1975): 69, 71–72.

RAINWATER, LEO JAMES

Prize: Physics, 1975. *Born:* December 9, 1917; Council, Idaho. *Died:* May 31, 1986; Yonkers, New York. *Nationality:* American. *Education:* California Institute of Technology, B.S., 1939; Columbia University, New York, M.A., 1941; Columbia University, New York, Ph.D., 1946. *Career:* Columbia University, New York, Professor, 1946–82. *Other Awards:* Ernest Orlando Lawrence Memorial Award, Atomic Energy Commission, 1963.

Citation: "For the discovery of the connection between collective motion and particle motion in atomic nuclei and the development of the theory of the structure of the atomic nucleus based on this connection" (with Aage Bohr and Ben R. Mottelson).

Life Work: Rainwater's field of investigation was the fundamental structure of the nucleus. His work mediated the liquid drop theory of Aage Bohr and the shell model of Mayer and Jensen by proposing that the orbital shells in the nucleus are distorted by centrifugal forces into a shape more like a football than a sphere. Using Rainwater's insight, Bohr and Mottelson developed a complete theory of nuclear behavior establishing a connection between the collective motion and particle motion in atomic nuclei. The collective action of the nucleons causes the surface of the nuclei to behave like a liquid drop when the outermost shell has a full complement of nucleons. However, the nucleus has a shell structure capable of being deformed into a football shape when the outermost shell is only partly filled.

Publications: "Nuclear Energy Level Argument for a Spheroidal Nuclear Model," *Physical Review* 79 (August 10, 1950): 432–34. "Mu-Meson Physics," *Annual Review of Nuclear Science* 7 (1957): 1–30. "Increasing Synchrocyclotron Currents and the Space Charge Limit," *AD 636708* (1965): 1–8.

Bibliography: *New York Times* Biographical Service, June 3, 1986, p. 733. *Nobel Prize Winners: Physics* (Pasadena, Calif.: Salem Press, 1988), vol. 3, pp. 1079–87. *Science* 190 (November 28, 1975): 868–70.

RICHTER, BURTON

Prize: Physics, 1976. *Born:* March 22, 1931; Brooklyn, New York. *Nationality:* American. *Education:* Massachusetts Institute of Technology, B.S., 1952; Massachusetts Institute of Technology, Ph.D., 1956. *Career:* Stanford University, California, Professor, 1956–. *Other Awards:* Ernesto Orlando Lawrence Medal, 1975.

Citation: "For their pioneering work in the discovery of a heavy elementary particle of a new kind" (with Samuel C. C. Ting).

Life Work: Richter's field of investigation was quantum electrodynamics. Working on two major accelerators, the Stanford Linear Accelerator Center (SLAC) and the Stanford Positron-Electron Accelerating Ring (SPEAR) Richter and his colleagues discovered a new hadron, which he named psi. Working independently, Samuel C. C. Ting's team at MIT also discovered the same particle at the same time. Ting chose the name J, and later the two names were combined as J/psi. J/psi was remarkable in that it had a lifetime ten thousand times longer than any similar particle. This discovery provided the experimental evidence of the existence of a fundamental particle called *charm*. Charm turned out to be a quark that complemented the three other known quarks—up, down, and strange—discovered by Gell-Mann and Zweig.

Publications: "Low Mass Anomaly in Photoproduction of Pion Pairs," *Physical Review Letters* 9 (1962): 217–20. *Instabilities in Stored Particle Beams*, with M. Sands and A. M. Sessler (Springfield, Va.: CFSTI, 1965). "High-energy Photoproduction," *U.S. Atomic Energy Commission CONF–670923* (1967): 309–36. "Two-body Photoproduction," *U.S. Atomic Energy Commission SLAC-PUB–501* (1968): 1–57. "Plenary Report on e(+)e(-) Hadrons," *Proceedings of the International Conference on High Energy Physics 17th* (1974): 20–35.

Bibliography: *Nobel Prize Winners: Physics* (Pasadena, Calif.: Salem Press, 1988), vol. 3, pp. 1089–97. *Science* (November 19, 1976): 825–26.

TING, SAMUEL CHAO CHUNG

Prize: Physics, 1976. *Born:* January 27, 1936; Ann Arbor, Michigan. *Nationality:* American. *Education:* University of Michigan, B.S.E., 1959; University of Michigan, M.S., 1960; University of Michigan, Ph.D., 1962. *Career:* Columbia University, New York, Professor, 1964–67; Massachusetts Institute of Technology, Professor, 1967–. *Other Awards:* Ernest Orlando Lawrence Award, 1976; A. E. Eringen Medal, 1977.

Citation: "For their pioneering work in the discovery of a heavy elementary particle of a new kind" (with Burton Richter).

Life Work: Ting's field of investigation was pair production, the simultaneous generation of an electron and its antiparticle, the positron by a collision between a particle of radiation and a nuclear target. He worked with several electron accelerators at Harvard, Hamburg (Deutsches Elektronen-Synchrotron), MIT, and Brookhaven. Working with a highly sophisticated spectrometer he discovered a new particle he named J. It turned out to be the same particle that Richter had discovered a few days earlier, named psi. J/psi was the combined name that was finally adopted for the new particle. Physicists explained J/psi in terms of a fourth quark named charm.

Publications: "Timelike Momenta in Quantum Electrodynamics," with Stanley J. Brodsky, *Physical Review* 145 (1966): 1018–22. "Leptonic Decays of Vector Mesons," *U.S. Atomic Energy Commission CONF–670923* (1967): 452–83. "Electrodynamics at Small Distances, Leptonic Decays of Vector Mesons, and Photoproduction of Vector Mesons," *Int. Conf. High-Energy Phys., Proc. 14th* (1968): 43–71. "Summary of Photoproduction and Leptonic Decays of Vector Mesons," *U.S. Atomic Energy Commission DESY–68/29* (1968): 1–18. *The Search for Charm, Beauty, and Truth at High Energies,* with G. Bellini (New York: Plenum Press, 1984).

Bibliography: *Physics Today* 29 (December 1976): 17. *Science* 194 (November 19, 1976): 825–26.

ANDERSON, PHILIP WARREN

Prize: Physics, 1977. *Born:* December 13, 1923; Indianapolis, Indiana. *Nationality:* American. *Education:* Harvard University, Massachusetts, B.S., 1943; Harvard University, Massachusetts, M.A., 1947; Harvard University, Massachusetts, Ph.D., 1949. *Career:* Bell Telephone Laboratories, New Jersey, Researcher, 1949–84; Cambridge University, England, Professor, 1967–75; Princeton University, New Jersey, Professor, 1975–84. *Other Awards:* Oliver E. Buckley Prize, 1964; Dannie Heineman Prize, 1975; Guthrie Medal, 1978; National Medal of Science, 1982.

Citation: "For their fundamental theoretical investigations of the electronic structure of magnetic and disordered systems" (with Nevill Mott and John H. van Vleck).

Life Work: Anderson's field of investigation was superconductivity, the complete absence of electrical resistance in certain substances at very low temperatures. He worked on the theory of dirty superconductors. Predicting an anisoptropic phase in superconducting liquid helium, Anderson moved to a study of the behavior of electrons in amorphous (noncrystalline) solids. He showed that under certain conditions, the so-called free electrons of an amorphous solid are tied to specific positions, a phenomenon known as Anderson localization. Amorphous semiconductors are used in photocopiers and solar cells.

Publications: "The Limits of Validity of the van Vleck–Weisskopf Line Shape Formula," *Physical Review* 76 (1949): 471. "An Approximate Quantum Theory of the Antiferromagnetic Ground State," *Physical Review* 86 (1952): 694–701. "New Method in the Theory of Superconductivity," *Physical Review* 110 (1958): 985–86.

"New Approach to the Theory of Superexchange Interactions," *Physical Review* 115 (1959): 2–13. "Generalized B.C.S. States and Aligned Orbital Angular Momentum in the Proposed Low-Temperature Phase of Liquid Helium–3," *Physica* 26 (1960). 5137–42. *Concepts in Solids* (New York: W. A. Benjamin, 1963). *Basic Notions of Condensed Matter Physics* (Menlo Park, Calif.: Benjamin/Cummings, 1984).

Bibliography: *Biographical Encyclopedia of Scientists* (New York: Facts on File, 1981), pp. 18–19. *Physics Today* 30 (December 1977): 77–78.

MOTT, SIR NEVILL FRANCIS

Prize: Physics, 1977. *Born:* September 30, 1905; Leeds, England. *Died:* August 8, 1996; Milton Keynes, England. *Nationality:* British. *Education:* Cambridge University, England, BA, 1927; Cambridge University, England, Massachusetts, 1930. *Career:* Cambridge University, England, Professor, 1930–33; University of Bristol, England, Professor, 1933–54; Cambridge University, England, Professor, 1954–71. *Other Awards:* Hughes Medal, 1941; Royal Medal, 1953; Knighthood, 1962; Copley Medal, 1972; Ordre Nationale Merite, 1977.

Citation: "For their fundamental theoretical investigations of the electronic structure of magnetic and disordered systems" (with Philip E. Anderson and John H. van Vleck).

Life Work: Mott's field of investigation was the structural properties of metals. He proposed a theory of transition metals in which he identified two groups of electrons, one primarily responsible for electrical conductivity and the other for magnetic and scattering properties. In 1937 Mott refined the band theory to account for the interaction between electrons, Mott explained why certain substances change from insulators to conductors when their electron density is altered. These changes are now called Mott transitions. In the 1960s Mott began to investigate the electronic structure of magnetic and disordered systems. This led to collaboration with Anderson on electrical conduction in semiconductors. Mott extended Anderson's theory of localization to explain a number of electronic properties of disordered materials. Mott's concept of mobility edge describes the critical energy level that separates mobile electrons from trapped electrons.

Publications: *The Theory of Atomic Collisions*, with H. S. W. Massey (Oxford: Clarendon Press, 1933). *The Theory of Properties of Metals and Alloys*, with H. Jones (New York: Dover, 1936). *Electronic Processes in Ionic Crystals*, with R. W. Gurney (Oxford: Clarendon Press, 1948).

Bibliography: *A Life in Science* (Philadelphia: Taylor and Francis, 1986). *Physics Today* 30 (December 8, 1977): 77–78. *Science* 198 (November 18, 1977): 713–15.

VAN VLECK, JOHN HASBROUCH

Prize: Physics, 1977. *Born:* March 13, 1899; Middletown, Connecticut. *Died:* October 27, 1980; Cambridge, Massachusetts. *Nationality:* American. *Education:* University of Wisconsin, B.S., 1920; Harvard University, Massachusetts, M.A., 1921; Harvard University, Massachusetts, Ph.D., 1922. *Career:* Harvard University, Massachusetts, Professor, 1922–23; University of Minnesota, Professor, 1923–28; University of Wisconsin, Professor, 1928–34; Harvard University, Massachusetts, Professor, 1934–69. *Other Awards:* Chevalier Legion of Honor, France, 1959; Albert A. Michelson Award, Case Institute of Technology, 1963; Irving Langmuir Award, General Electric Foundation, 1965; National Medal of Science, 1966; Distinguished Service Award, University of Wisconsin Alumni Association, 1967; Cresson Medal, Franklin Institute, Pennsylvania, 1971; Lorentz Medal, Netherlands Academy, 1974.

Citation: "For their fundamental theoretical investigations of the electronic structure of magnetic and disordered systems" (with Philip E. Anderson and Nevill Mott).

Life Work: Van Vleck is known as the father of modern magnetism for his work *The Theory of Electric and Magnetic Susceptibilities* (1932), which helped to establish the new science of solid-state physics. The term Van Vleck paramagnetism explains paramagnetism in certain gases and solids. He helped to develop the crystal field theory by which the quantum mechanical energy levels of an atom or an ion in a crystal can be calculated. After World War II, Van Vleck's studies of magnetic resonance, a response of electrons, nuclei or atoms to electromagnetic radiation led to the development of nuclear magnetic resonance spectrometry and magnetic resonance imaging.

Publications: "Quantum Theory of the Specific Heat of Hydrogen. I. Relation to the New Mechanics, Band Spectra and Chemical Constants," *Physical Review* 28 (1926): 980–1021. "Dielectric Constants and Magnetic Susceptibilities in the New Quantum Mechanics. Part I. A General Proof of the Langevin-Debye Formula," *Physical Review* 29 (1927): 727–44. "The New Quantum Mechanics," *Chemical Reviews* 5 (1928): 467–507. *The Theory of Electric and Magnetic Susceptibilities* (New York: Oxford University Press, 1932). "The Theory of Antiferromagnetism," *Journal of Chemical Physics* 9 (1941): 85–90.

Bibliography: *Biographical Memoirs of the National Academy of Sciences* (New York: Columbia University Press, 1987), vol. 56, pp. 501–40. *Biographical Memoirs of the Royal Society* (London: Royal Society, 1982), vol. 28, pp. 627–65.

KAPITSA, PYOTR LEONIDOVICH

Prize: Physics, 1978. *Born:* July 8, 1894; Kronstadt, Russia. *Died:* April 8, 1984; Moscow, USSR. *Nationality:* Russian. *Education:* Petrograd Polytechnical Institute,

USSR, baccalaureate, 1918; Cambridge University, England, Ph.D., 1923. *Career:* Petrograd Polytechnical Institute, USSR, Professor, 1918–21; Cambridge University, England, Researcher and Professor, 1921–35; USSR Academy of Sciences, Institute for Physical Problems, Director, 1935–46, 1955–84; Physiotechnical Institute, Moscow, USSR, Professor, 1947–84. *Other Awards:* Stalin Prize, 1941, 1943; Faraday Medal Council of Electrical Engineers of England, 1942; Five Orders of Lenin, 1943; Order of the Red Banner of Labor, 1943; Franklin Medal, 1944.

Citation: "For his basic inventions and discoveries in the area of low-temperature physics."

Life Work: Kapitsa's fields of investigation was electromagnetism and low-temperature physics. At Cambridge, England, he built a novel machine for liquefying helium. Back in Moscow from 1934, he discovered superfluids, which have low viscosity and increased heat conductivity and defy gravity. After World War II Kapitsa focused his research on plasmas and microwave generators. Plasmas are gases heated to such high temperatures that they are stripped of their electrons and become electrified ions. They are used in fusion reactors.

Publications: *Collected Papers* (Oxford: Oxford University Press, 1946–47). *Elektronika Bol'shikh Moshchnostei* (Moscow: n.p., 1962). *Teoriia, Eksperiment, Praktika* [Theory, Experiment, Practice] (Moscow: n.p., 1966).

Bibliography: *Kapitza in Cambridge and Moscow* (Amsterdam: North-Holland, 1990). Lawrence Badash, *Kapitza, Rutherford, and the Kremlin* (New Haven, Conn.: Yale University Press, 1985). *Peter Kapitza on Life and Science* (New York: Macmillan, 1968). *Science* 202 (December 1, 1978): 960–62.

PENZIAS, ARNO ALLAN

Prize: Physics, 1978. *Born:* April 26, 1933; Munich, Germany. *Nationality:* German; later U.S. citizen. *Education:* City College of New York, B.S., 1954; Columbia University, New York, M.A., 1958; Columbia University, New York, Ph.D., 1962. *Career:* Bell Laboratories, New Jersey, Researcher and Administrator, 1961–. *Other Awards:* Henry Draper Medal, 1977; Herschel Medal, 1977; Townsend Harris Medal, 1979; Newman Award, City College of New York, 1983; Joseph Handleman Prize, 1983; Priestley Award, 1989; Pender Award, 1992.

Citation: "For their discovery of cosmic microwave background radiation" (with Robert W. Wilson).

Life Work: Penzias's field of investigation was radio astronomy. Using the horn antenna, he and Wilson measured the intensities of several extraterrestrial radio sources. Their technique enabled them to distinguish and subtract radio noise from their measurements. In 1964, while measuring radio signals from Cassiopeia A, they found more noise than could be accounted for. This radio noise had long wavelengths well below the visible range. They corresponded to the dominant wavelength emitted by a black-body, as predicted by the big-bang cosmology. In the 1960s Penzias investigated the origin of chemical elements and detected seven interstellar molecules.

Publications: "Interstellar Carbon Monoxide, Carbon-13 Monoxide, and Carbon Monoxide-Oxygen–18," with Keith B. Jefferts and Robert W. Wilson, *Astrophysics Journal* 165, part 1 (1971): L63. "Interstellar Carbon Monosulfide," with others, *Astrophysics Journal* 168, part 2 (1971): L53-L58. "Interstellar C N Excitation at 2.65 mm," with Keith B. Jefferts and Robert W. Wilson, *Physics Review Letters* 28 (1972): 772–75. "Millimeter-Wavelength Radio-Astronomy Techniques," with C. A. Burrus, *Annu. Rev. Astron. Astrophys* 11 (1973): 51–72.

Bibliography: *Current Biography Yearbook* (New York: H. W. Wilson, 1985), pp. 328–31. *New York Times*, October 18, 1978, p. 5.

WILSON, ROBERT WOODROW

Prize: Physics, 1978. *Born:* January 10, 1936; Houston, Texas. *Nationality:* American. *Education:* Rice University, Texas, B.A., 1957; California Institute of Technology, Ph.D., 1962. *Career:* Owens Laboratories, United States, 1962–63; Bell Laboratories, New Jersey, 1963–. *Other Awards:* Henry Draper Medal, Royal Astronomy Society, 1977; Herschel Medal, National Academy of Sciences, 1977.

Citation: "For their discovery of cosmic microwave background radiation" (with Arno A. Penzias).

Life Work: In 1960 Wilson and Penzias converted a horn-reflector antenna at Holmdel, New Jersey, into a telescope for radio astronomy for measuring the intensities of extraterrestrial radio sources. It enabled them to distinguish and subtract radio noise from their measurements. Measuring signals from Cassiopeia A, a supernova remnant, they picked up more radio noise than could be accounted for. This unexplained radiation corresponded to the emission by a blackbody. Blackbodies emit a spectrum of radiation rather than a wavelength, but each temperature is characterized by a dominant wavelength at which the emission is most intense.

Publications: "Isotropy of Cosmic Background Radiation at 4080 Megahert," with A. A. Penzias, *Science* 156 (1967): 1100–1101. "Measurement of the Flux Density of CAS A at 4080 Ma/s," with A. A. Penzias, *Astrophysical Journal* 142 (1965): 1149–56. "Interstellar CN Excitation at 2.64 mm," with A. A. Penzias and K. B. Jefferts, *Physics Review Letters* 28 (1972): 772–75.

Bibliography: "The 1978 Nobel Prize in Physics." *Science* 205 (December 1, 1978): 962–65. *Nobel Prize Winners: Physics* (Pasadena, Calif.: Salem Press, 1988,), vol. 3, pp. 1163–70.

GLASHOW, SHELDON LEE

Prize: Physics, 1979. *Born:* December 5, 1932; New York, New York. *Nationality:* American. *Education:* Cornell University, New York, A.B., 1954; Harvard University, Massachusetts, M.A., 1955; Harvard University, Massachusetts, Ph.D., 1958. *Career:* Institute of Theoretical Physics, Copenhagen, Denmark, Researcher, 1958–60; California Institute of Technology, Researcher, 1960–61; Stanford University, California, Professor, 1961–62; University of California, Berkeley, Professor, 1962–66; Harvard University, Massachusetts, Professor, 1966–1982; Texas A & M, Professor, 1983–. *Other Awards:* J. R. Oppenheimer Memorial Prize, 1977; George Ledlie Prize, 1978; Castiglione di Silica Prize, 1983.

Citation: "For their contributions to the theory of the unified weak and electromagnetic interaction between elementary particles, including, inter alia, the prediction of the weak neutral current" (with Abdus Salam and Steven Weinberg).

Life Work: Glashow's field of investigation was a theory unifying all the forces observed in nature. In classical physics, there were four independent forces at work in the universe: gravitation, electromagnetism, strong force, and weak force. The work of Glashow, Salam, and Weinberg led to the unification of electromagnetism and the weak force as the electroweak force. In 1960 Glashow proposed to link electromagnetism and the weak force based on a concept called gauge symmetry. Glashow predicted the existence of four particles that would serve as carriers of the four forces: photon (electromagnetic force), W+, W–, and Zo (weak force). All four particles are massless. When two particles interact by means of the electromagnetic force, their electric charges are not altered, but in weak interactions a unit of electric charge is transferred. The major failing of Glashow's theory was the apparently unlimited range of the weak force. This problem was later solved by Weinberg and Salam, working independently, based on the gauge symmetry. Their mechanism, called spontaneous symmetry, left the photon massless while giving mass to the three weak force particles.

Publications: "Symmetries of Strong Interactions," *Proceedings of the International School of Physics "Enrico Fermi" Course XXXIII, Varenna, 6th–18th July 1964* (New York: Academic Press, 1966), pp. 189–225. "Divergencies of Massive Yang-Mills Theories: Higher Groups," with J. Iiopoulos, *Physical Review D: Particles and Fields* 4 (September 15, 1971): 1918–19. "Toward a Unified Theory: Threads in a Tapestry," *Science* 210 (1980): 1319–23.

Bibliography: *Physics Today* 32 (December 1979): 17–19. *Science* 206 (December 14, 1979): 1290–92.

SALAM, ABDUS

Prize: Physics, 1979. *Born:* January 29, 1926; Jhang Maghiana, Pakistan. *Died:* November 21, 1996; Oxford, England. *Nationality:* Pakistani; later British resident. *Education:* University of Punjab, Pakistan, M.A., 1946; Cambridge University, England, B.A., 1948; Cambridge University, England, Ph.D., 1952; Cambridge University England, D.Sc., 1957. *Career:* Institute for Advanced Study, Princeton, New Jersey, Researcher, 1951; University of Punjab, Lahore, Pakistan, Professor, 1951–54; Cambridge University, England, Professor, 1954–56; Imperial College London, England, Professor, 1957–. *Other Awards:* Hopkins Prize, Cambridge University, England, 1957; Adams Prize, 1958; Pride of Performance Award, Pakistan, 1959; Maxwell Medal, Physical Society, London, England, 1961; Hughes Medal, 1964; Atoms for Peace Award, 1968; Guthrie Medal and Prize, 1976; Royal Medal, Royal Society, 1978; Matteuci Medal, Academia Nazionale di Lincei, Rome, Italy, 1978; John Tate Medal, American Institute of Physics, 1978; Einstein Medal, 1979; Josef Stefan Medal, 1980; Peace Medal, 1981; Lomonosov Gold Medal, 1983; Copley Medal, 1990.

Citation: "For their contributions to the theory of the unified weak and electromagnetic interaction between elementary particles, including, inter alia, the prediction of the weak neutral current" (with Sheldon L. Glashow and Steven Weinberg).

Life Work: Salam and his colleagues, Glashow and Weinberg, sought a unified theory by unifying electromagnetism with weak force into a single electroweak force based on a concept called gauge symmetry. Glashow's theory of electroweak force predicted the existence of four carrier particles, the photon (electromagnetism) and three called W+, W–, and Zo (weak force). However, none of the particles had a mass, a premise under which all of them had infinite range. Working independently, Salam proposed a theory, called spontaneous symmetry, that obviated the problem by giving mass to the three weak force particles but left the photon massless. This theory was validated by Gerardus 't Hooft in 1971, and later by the discovery of the W and Z particles by CERN.

Publications: "Gauge Unification of Fundamental Forces," *Proc.-Eur. Conf. Part. Phys* (9th) 2 (1977): 1187–1207. "Gauge Unification of Fundamental Forces," *Proc. Int. Conf. Winter Sch. Front. Theor. Phys.* (1977): 29–35. "Gauge Unification of the Four Fundamental Forces," *Phys. Contemp. Needs* 2 (1978): 419–56. "The Electroweak Force, Grand Unification and Superunification," *Phys. Scr.* 20 (1979): 227–34. *Selected Papers of Abdus Salam* (River Edge, N.Y.: Word Scientific, 1994).

Bibliography: Abdul Ghani, *Abdus Salam Khanachi* (Pakistan: Ma'Aref, 1982). *Physics Today* 32 (December 1979): 17–19. *Science* 206 (December 14, 1979): 1290–92. J. Singh, *Abdus Salam, A Biography* (New York: Penguin Books, 1992).

WEINBERG, STEVEN

Prize: Physics, 1979. *Born:* May 3, 1933; New York, New York. *Nationality:* American. *Education:* Cornell University, New York, A.B., 1954; Princeton University, New Jersey, Ph.D., 1957. *Career:* Columbia University, New York, Professor, 1957–59; University of California, Berkeley, Professor, 1959–69; Massachusetts Institute of Technology, Professor, 1969–73; Harvard University, Massachusetts, Professor, 1973–83; University of Texas, Austin, Professor, 1983–. *Other Awards:* J. R. Oppenheimer Prize, 1973; Dannie Heineman Mathematical Physics Prize, 1977; American Institute of Physics—U.S. Steel Foundation Science Writing Award, 1977; Elliott Cresson Medal, Franklin Institute, Pennsylvania, 1979; Madison Medal, 1991; National Medal of Science, 1991.

Citation: "For their contributions to the theory of the unified weak and electromagnetic interaction between elementary particles, including, inter alia, the prediction of the weak neutral current" (with Sheldon L. Glashow and Abdus Salam).

Life Work: Weinberg's research was focused on a unified theory of natural forces. There are four forces at work in the universe: gravitation, electromagnetism, strong force, and weak force. Weinberg and his colleagues, Salam and Glashow, used a concept called gauge symmetry to unify electromagnetism and weak force into a single electroweak force. In 1960 Glashow proposed the existence of four particles as carriers of electromagnetism and the weak force: photon (electromagnetism), W+, W–, and Zo (weak force). The theory suffered from the fact that the particles were massless, giving them an unlimited range that did not accord with experimental evidence. Weinberg rectified this problem with a solution called spontaneous symmetry breaking in which the photon was left massless while the other three particles had mass. According to Weinberg, the electromagnetic and weak forces are identical at extremely high energy, but at lower energies W and Z particles are seldom created and the differences between the two forces are more conspicuous than their similarities.

Publications: *Gravitation and Cosmology: Principles and Applications of the General Theory of Relativity* (New York: Wiley, 1972). "Recent Progress in Gauge Theories of the Weak, Electromagnetic and Strong Interactions," *Reviews of Modern Physics* 46 (1974): 255–77. *The First Three Minutes: A Modern View of the Origin of the Universe* (New York: Basic Books, 1977). "Limits of Massless Particles," *Physics Letters* B 96 (1980): 59–62. "Charges from Extra Dimensions," *Physics Letters* B 125 (1983): 265–69. *The Discovery of Subatomic Particles* (New York: Scientific American Library, 1983).

Bibliography: *Physics Today* 32 (December 1979): 17–19. *Science* 206 (December 14, 1979): 1290–92.

CRONIN, JAMES WATSON

Prize: Physics, 1980. *Born:* September 29, 1931; Chicago, Illinois. *Nationality:* American. *Education:* Southern Methodist University, Texas, B.S., 1951; University of Chicago, Illinois, Ph.D., 1955. *Career:* Brookhaven National Laboratory, Researcher, 1955–58; Princeton University, New Jersey, Professor, 1958–71; University of Chicago, Illinois, Professor, 1971–. *Other Awards:* Research Corporation Award, 1968; Ernest Orlando Lawrence Award, 1977; John Price Wetherill Medal, Franklin Institute, Pennsylvania, 1975.

Citation: "For the discovery of violations of fundamental symmetry principles in the decay of neutral K-mesons" (with Val L. Fitch).

Life Work: Cronin's research concerned the three fundamental rules of research: the symmetry of charge conjugation (C), parity (P), and time reversal symmetry (T). Scientists had noted imperfections in all three. Cronin and Fitch, working with beams of neutral K-mesons, now called kaons, found evidence of clear violation of the symmetry. When K-mesons decay, about 1 in 500 events fail the symmetry test. The violation led physicists to rethink their explanation of physical phenomena. It also explained one theory of how the universe evolved. If, in the early moments of the Big Bang, matter and antimatter were formed in equal amounts, they would have annihilated each other. Lack of symmetry would allow antiparticles to decay faster than particles and consequently disappear sooner, leaving an excess of particles as the substance of the universe.

Publications: "Experimental Status of CP Violation," *AEC Accession Number 19428, Report Number ANL–7130* (1965): 17–28. "Coupling Constant Relations for 1 (±) and Induced 0 (±) Mesons," with Y. Nambu, *Nuovo Cimento* 41A (1966): 380–85. "Experimental Developments in Weak Interactions," *Proc. Int. Conf. Particles Fields* (1967): 3–20. "Weak Interactions and CP Violation-Experimental," *Int. Conf. High-Energy Phys., Proc.,* 14th (1968): 281–303.

Bibliography: *New York Times* Biographical Service, October 1980, p. 1374. *Science* 210 (November 7, 1980): 619–21.

FITCH, VAL LOGSDON

Prize: Physics, 1980. *Born:* March 10, 1923; Merriman, Nebraska. *Nationality:* American. *Education:* McGill University, Canada, B.Eng., 1948; Columbia University, New York, Ph.D., 1954. *Career:* Columbia University, New York, Professor, 1953–54; Princeton University, New Jersey, Professor, 1954–. *Other Awards:* Research Corporation Award, 1968; Ernest Orlando Lawrence Award, 1968; John Wetherill Medal, Franklin Institute, Pennsylvania, 1976; National Medal of Science, 1993.

Citation: "For the discovery of violations of fundamental symmetry principles in the decay of neutral K-mesons" (with James W. Cronin).

Life Work: Fitch's field of investigation was the principle of symmetry. Together with Cronin, he studied neutral K-mesons, or kaons, unstable particles with about half the mass of the proton, produced in high-energy collisions to determine whether they violated the three basic symmetry relationships or conservation rules of physics, designated C, P, and T. These symmetries governed particles and antiparticles, left and right parity, and time-reversal. Fitch and Cronin found that the decay of K-mesons violated CPT symmetries. Symmetry violations led scientists to speculate on the reasons matter and antimatter, created according to the Big Bang Theory of the birth of the universe, had not totally annihilated each other.

Publications: "Mass Difference of Neutral K Meson," with P. A. Piroue and R. B. Perkins, *Nuovo Cimento* 22 (1961): 1160–70. "The K(+) Decay Probability," with C. A. Quarles, *Physical Review* 140B (1965): 1088–91. "Experiments on Time-Reversal Invariance," *Nucl. Particle Phys. Annu* 1 (1967): 117–20. "Charge Assymetries," *Comments Nucl. Particle Phys* 2 (1968): 6–9.

Bibliography: *Physics Today* 33 (December 1980): 17–19. *Science* 210 (November 7, 1980): 619–21.

BLOEMBERGEN, NICOLAAS

Prize: Physics, 1981. *Born:* March 11, 1920; Dordrecht, Netherlands. *Nationality:* Dutch; later U.S. citizen. *Education:* University of Utrecht, Netherlands, B.A., 1941; University of Utrecht, Netherlands, M.A., 1943; Leiden University, Netherlands, Ph.D., 1948. *Career:* Harvard University, Massachusetts, Professor, 1949–. *Other Awards:* Guggenheim Fellow, 1957; Buckley Prize, American Physical Society, 1958; Morris Liebman Award, IEEE, 1959; Ballantine Medal, Franklin Institute, Pennsylvania, 1961; Half Moon Trophy, Netherlands Club, New York, 1972; National Medal of Science, 1975; Lorentz Medal, Royal Dutch Academy, 1978; Frederic Ives Medal, Optical Society of America, 1979; von Humboldt Senior Scientist Award, Munich, Germany, 1980; Medal of Honor, IEEE, 1983; Dirac Medal, University of New South Wales, Australia, 1983.

Citation: "For their contribution to the development of laser spectroscopy" (with Arthur L. Schawlow).

Life Work: Bloembergen's early work dealt with masers. In 1956 he proposed a three-level design principle in which a solid material, such as a crystal, would be stimulated by radiation of an appropriate frequency to the highest of three particular levels. When natural relaxation caused a drop to the next level, there would be stimulated emission. Radiation of a frequency corresponding to the difference between the two lowest levels would stimulate the emission of the desired radiation. Bloembergen is one of the founders of nonlinear optics, a field theory of the interaction of electromagnetic radiation and matter. He made a significant contribution to laser design by showing that nonlinear optical behavior could produce high-frequency beams. By suggesting how three laser beams could interact to produce a fourth whose frequency can be controlled, he provided a theoretical basis for the tunable laser.

Publications: *Nuclear Magnetic Relaxation* (The Hague: M. Nijhoff, 1948). "Nuclear Magnetic Relaxation in Semiconductors," *Physica* 20 (1954): 1130–33. "Proposal for a New-Type Solid-State Maser," *Physical Review* 104 (1956): 324–27. "The Zero-Field Solid-State Maser as a Possible Time Standard," *Quantum Electronics Symposium, High View, New York* (1959): 160–66. *Nonlinear Optics* (Reading, Mass.: W. A. Benjamin, 1965).

Bibliography: *Nobel Prize Winners: Physics* (Pasadena, Calif.: Salem Press, 1988), vol. 3, pp. 1219–28. *Science* 214 (November 4, 1981): 629–33.

SCHAWLOW, ARTHUR LEONARD

Prize: Physics, 1981. *Born:* May 5, 1921; Mt. Vernon, New York. *Died:* April 28, 1999; Palo Alto, California. *Nationality:* American. *Education:* University of Toronto, Canada, B.A., 1941; University of Toronto, Canada, M.A., 1942; University of Toronto, Canada, Ph.D., 1949. *Career:* Columbia University, New York, Researcher, 1949–51; Bell Telephone Laboratories, New Jersey, Researcher, 1951–61; Stanford University, California, Professor, 1961–91. *Other Awards:* Ballantine Medal, Franklin Institute, Pennsylvania, 1962; Thomas Young Medal and Prize, Institution of Physics and the Physics Society of London, England, 1963; Liebmann Prize, IEEE, 1964; California Scientist of the Year, 1973; Frederick Ives Medal, Optical Society of America, 1976; Schawlow Medal, 1982; National Medal of Science, 1991.

Citation: "For their contribution to the development of laser spectroscopy" (with Nicolaas Bloembergen).

Life Work: Schawlow's field of investigation was lasers. His main contributions to laser were adjustable frequency (tunable) lasers. From 1960 he has been in the forefront of laser spectroscopy. The tunable laser was a significant contribution because the laser's light is highly monochromatic, highly intense, and adjustable to the desired frequencies. Working with Theodore W. Hansch, Schawlow managed to overcome the problem of Doppler broadening in spectroscopy by isolating the absorption spectra due only to atoms with no component of motion parallel to the laser beam. In 1972 he used the first Doppler-free optical spectra of atomic hydrogen to measure the Rydberg constant. He has also devised laser labeling to simplify the spectra of molecules.

Publications: "Significance of the Results of Microwave Spectroscopy for Nuclear Theory," *Annals of the New York Academy of Sciences* 55 (1952): 955–65. "Infrared and Optical Masers," with Charles H. Townes, *Physical Review* 112 (1958): 1940–49.

"Simultaneous Optical Maser Action in Two Ruby Satellite Lines," with G. E. Devlin, *Physical Review Letters* 6 (1961): 605–607. *Microwave Spectroscopy*, with Charles H. Townes (New York: McGraw Hill, 1955).

Bibliography: *Physics Today* 34 (December 1981): 17–20. *Science* 214 (November 6, 1981): 629–33.

SIEGBAHN, KAI MANNE BOERJE

Prize: Physics, 1981. *Born:* April 20, 1918; Lund, Sweden. *Nationality:* Swedish. *Education:* University of Uppsala, Sweden, B.Sc., 1939; University of Uppsala, Sweden, Licentiate of Philosophy, 1942; University of Stockholm, Sweden, Ph.D., 1944. *Career:* Nobel Institute of Physics, Sweden, Researcher, 1942–51; University of Stockholm, Sweden, Professor, 1951–54; Uppsala University, Sweden, Professor, 1954–84. *Other Awards:* Knight of the Order of the North Star, 1955; Bjoerken Prize, 1977; Celsius Medal, 1962; Sixten Heyman Award, 1971; Harrison Howe Award, 1973; Maurice F. Hasler Award, 1975; Charles Frederick Chandler Medal, 1976; Torbern Bergman Medal, 1979; Pittsburgh Award of Spectroscopy, 1982; Rontgen Medal, 1985; Fiuggi Award, 1986; Humboldt Award, 1986.

Citation: "For his contribution to the development of high-resolution electron spectroscopy."

Life Work: Siegbahn's field of investigation was high-resolution spectroscopy, the determination of the different energies of electrons emitted by atoms during some forms of radioactive decay. He devised a method known as *magnetic double-focusing* to achieve greater resolution in spectroscopy. He also applied electron spectroscopy to atomic physics and recorded the first photoelectron spectrum. Among other discoveries, he detected evidence of chemical shifts and chemical bonding when atoms combine in various ways. His high-resolution analysis, now known as *electron spectroscopy for chemical analysis* (ESCA) has become a standard laboratory procedure.

Publications: "X-Ray Spectroscopy in the Precision Range of $1:10^5$," with K. Edvarson, *Nuclear Physics* 1 (1956): 137–59. *ESCA—Atomic, Molecular and Solid State Structure Studied by Means of Electron Spectroscopy*, with others, Nova Acta Regiae Societatis Scientarium Upsaliensis, Series IV, Volume 20 (Uppsala, Sweden: Almquist and Wiksells Boktryckeri Ab, 1967). *ESCA—Applied to Free Molecules*, with others (Amsterdam/London: North-Netherlands, 1969). "ESCA Applied to Liquids," with Hans Siegbahn, *Journal of Electron Spectroscopy and Related Phenomena* 2 (1973): 319–25. "Electron Spectroscopy for Atoms, Molecules, and Condensed Matter," *Review of Modern Physics* 54 (July 1982): 709–28.

Bibliography: J. Hecht and R. Brookfield, "Physicists Keep Nobel Prizes in the Family," *New Scientist* 92 (October 22, 1981): 224–25. Jack M. Hollander and David Shirley, "The 1981 Nobel Prize in Physics," *Science* 214 (November 6, 1981): 629–31.

Walter Sullivan, "Physics: To the Heart of the Matter." *New York Times*, October 20, 1981, sec. 3, p. 2.

WILSON, KENNETH GEDDES

Prize: Physics, 1982. *Born:* June 8, 1936; Waltham, Massachusetts. *Nationality:* American. *Education:* Harvard University, Massachusetts, B.A., 1956; California Institute of Technology, Ph.D., 1961. *Career:* Harvard University, Massachusetts, Fellow, 1959–62; Ford Foundation Fellow, 1962–63; Cornell University, New York, Professor, 1963–. *Other Awards:* Heineman Prize, 1973; Boltzmann Medal, 1975; Wolf Prize, 1980; Franklin Medal, 1983; A. C. Eringer Medal, 1984; Rahman Prize, 1993.

Citation: "For his theory for critical phenomena in connection with phase transitions."

Life Work: Wilson's field of investigation was the critical phenomenon, the special behavior of materials near certain environmental conditions, such as temperature and pressure, at which materials undergo striking changes. These special conditions are called the critical point. Wilson applied renormalization group analysis to achieve a successful method for characterizing behavior near the critical point and making quantitative estimates of system properties with the aid of computers.

Publications: "Renormalization Group and Critical Phenomena. I. Renormalization Group and the Kadanoff Scaling Picture," *Physics Reviews* B4 (November 1, 1971): 3174–83. "Renormalization Group and Critical Phenomena. II. Phase-Space Cell Analysis of Critical Behavior." *Physics Reviews* B4 (November 1, 1971): 3184–3205.

Bibliography: *Nobel Prize Winners: Physics* (Pasadena, Calif.: Salem Press, 1988), vol. 3, pp. 1253–60. *Physics Today* 35 (December 1982): 17–19.

CHANDRASEKHAR, SUBRAMANYAN

Prize: Physics, 1983. *Born:* October 19, 1910; Lahore, India. *Died:* August 21, 1995; Chicago, Illinois. *Nationality:* Indian; later U.S. citizen. *Education:* Madras University, India, M.A., 1930; Cambridge University, England, Ph.D., 1933. *Career:* Cambridge University, England, Professor, 1933–37; University of Chicago, Professor, 1937–86. *Other Awards:* Bruce Medal, Astronomical Society of the Pacific, 1952; Gold Medal, Royal Astronomical Society, 1953; Rumford Medal, American Academy of Arts and Sciences, 1957; Royal Medal, Royal Society, 1962; National Science Medal, 1966; Henry Draper Medal, 1971; Dannie Heineman Prize, 1974; Copley Medal, 1984.

Citation: "For his theoretical studies of the physical processes of importance to the structure and evolution of the stars."

Life Work: Chandrasekhar's field of investigation was the internal constitution of stars. Using quantum mechanics and the theory of relativity he analyzed the behavior of stellar matter, with special attention to electrons, as a star becomes smaller and denser. If a star is small enough, the gravitational pressures promoting collapse will be balanced by outward pressures as the star reaches equilibrium at the size of a white dwarf. However, if the stellar mass is above a certain magnitude, the so-called Chandrasekhar limit, the electrons will become so compressed that their velocities will approach that of light, a condition called *relativistic degeneracy*. His calculations predicted what are now known as black holes. In 1934 he predicted that a shrinking dead star of a mass two or three times that of the sun would develop so much energy in its outer layers that it will explode as a supernova. Its thick shell would be blown out into space and the remnant would shrink to a stable neutron star. At Chicago, Chandrasekhar investigated stellar dynamics, especially dynamic friction, and developed his theory of radiative transfer important for an understanding of stellar atmospheres and luminosity and spectral line formation. The Chandrasekhar limit is one of the foundations of modern astrophysics.

Publications: *An Introduction to the Study of Stellar Structure* (Chicago: University of Chicago Press, 1939). *Principles of Stellar Dynamics* (Chicago: University of Chicago Press, 1942). *Hydrodynamic and Hydromagnetic Stability* (London: Clarendon, 1961). *Ellipsoidal Figures of Equilibrium* (New Haven, Conn.: Yale University Press, 1969). *The Mathematical Theory of Black Holes* (London: Clarendon, 1983).

Bibliography: *Current Biography Yearbook* (New York: H. W. Wilson, 1986), pp. 6–9. *New York Times* Biographical Service, October 1973, pp. 1176–77. *Science* 222 (November 25, 1983): 883+. K. Wali, *Chandra* (New Delhi, India: Viking, 1991).

FOWLER, WILLIAM ALFRED

Prize: Physics, 1983. *Born:* August 9, 1911; Pittsburgh, Pennsylvania. *Died:* March 14, 1995; Pasadena, California. *Nationality:* American. *Education:* Ohio State University, B.Eng., 1933; California Institute of Technology, Ph.D., 1936. *Career:* California Institute of Technology, Professor and Administrator, 1936–82. *Other Awards:* Naval Ordinance Development Award, United States Navy, 1945; Medal of Merit, 1948; Lamme Medal, Ohio State University, 1952; Medal, University Liege, 1955; Scientist of the Year Award, California, 1958; Barnard Medal, Columbia University, New York, 1965; Apollo Achievement Award, National Aeronautics and Space Administration, 1969; Bonner Prize, American Physical Society, 1970; Vetlesen Prize, 1973; National Medal of Science, 1974; Benjamin Franklin Fellow, Royal Society of the Arts, 1975; Edington Medal, Royal Astronomical Society, 1978; Bruce Gold Medal, Astronomical Society of the Pacific, 1979; Sullivant Medal, Ohio State University, 1985; Fowler Award, 1986.

Citation: "For his theoretical and experimental studies of the nuclear reactions of importance in the formation of the chemical elements in the universe."

Life Work: In 1955 Fowler formulated a comprehensive theory that summarized the nuclear reactions leading to the synthesis of all the naturally occurring elements. By combining the data of nuclear astrophysics and the theory of stellar structure, Fowler created a basic model of star development. The model consists of six steps: (1) A cloud of gas—mostly hydrogen and helium—contracts under its own gravitational attraction. (2) When the cloud becomes sufficiently dense and hot, hydrogen fuses into helium and the cloud becomes a star. (3) As a massive star contracts following the exhaustion of hydrogen, helium fuses into carbon and the star expands greatly to become a red giant. (4) The core will undergo repeated cycles of nuclear fuel exhaustion, core contraction, and reignition until the reside consists mainly of iron. (5) When the iron core becomes too massive it blows up into a supernova and then collapses. (6) These processes scatter some of the synthesized heavy elements into space, where they become part of future stellar systems.

Publications: "Synthesis of the Elements in Stars," with E. M. Burbridge, G. R. Burbridge, and F. Hoyle, *Review of Modern Physics* 29 (1957): 547. *Nucleosynthesis in Massive Stars and Supernovae,* with F. Hoyle (Chicago: University of Chicago Press, 1964). *Nuclear Astrophysics* (Philadelphia: American Philosophical Society, 1967).

Bibliography: *New Scientist* 100 (October 27, 1983): 254–55. *Science* 22 (November 25, 1983): 881–83.

MEER, SIMON VAN DER

Prize: Physics, 1984. *Born:* November 24, 1925; The Hague, Netherlands. *Nationality:* Dutch. *Education:* Technical University, Netherlands, physical engineering degree, 1955. *Career:* Dutch Philips Company, Researcher, 1952–56; European Organization for Nuclear Research, Researcher, 1956–90. *Other Awards:* Duddell Medal and Prize, England, 1982.

Citation: "For their decisive contributions to the large project, which led to the discovery of the field particles W and Z, communicators of weak interaction" (with Carlo Rubbia).

Life Work: Van der Meer's initial work was the design of the particle accelerator, the proton synchrotron, at CERN. He developed a pulsed focusing device called a neutrino horn, designed to increase the intensity of beams of neutrinos and a small storage ring to measure the magnetic properties of the muon. In 1976 he joined Carlo Rubbia's team for the discovery of the hypothetical W and Z particles. Rubbia and over one hundred scientists built an intricate 1,200-ton detection chamber for this purpose. Van der Meer solved the problem of supplying the antiprotons with the use of a special accumulator storage ring. Protons and antiprotons were given an acceleration to energies of the order of 300 billion electron volts in the four-mile-diameter storage ring, in which particles and antiparticles circled in opposing directions and collided head-on at six well-defined points. The collisions of protons and antiprotons racing 50,000 laps per second around a circle 1,250 miles in circumference were the most violent produced on earth up to that time. The accumulator storage ring was based on van der Meer's concept of stochastic cooling. All the W and Z particles were discovered in 1983.

Publications: "Stochastic Cooling Theory and Devices," *Lawrence Berkeley Laboratory Report LBL-7574* (1978): 93–97. "Stochastic Cooling in the CERN Antiproton Accumulator," *IEEE Trans. Nucl. Sci.* NS28–3 Part I (1981): 1994–98. "Recent Experience with Antiproton Cooling," with others, *IEEE Trans. Nucl. Sci.* 30–4 Part I (1983): 2587–89. "Antiproton Production and Collection for the CERN Antiproton Accumulator," with others, *IEEE Trans. Nucl. Sci.* 30–4 Part I (1983): 2778–80.

Bibliography: *New York Times*, October 18, 1984, p. B13. *Nobel Prize Winners: Physics* (Pasadena, Calif.: Salem Press, 1988), vol. 3, pp. 1291–99. *Science* 227 (January 11, 1985): 131–34.

RUBBIA, CARLO

Prize: Physics, 1984. *Born:* March 31, 1934; Gorizia, Italy. *Nationality:* Italian. *Education:* University of Pisa, Italy, Ph.D., 1958. *Career:* European Organization of Nuclear Research, Geneva, Switzerland, Researcher, 1961–; concurrently associated with Harvard University, Massachusetts, Professor, 1970–. *Other Awards:* Ledlie Prize, 1985; Jesolo d'Oro, 1986.

Citation: "For their decisive contributions to the large project, which led to the discovery of the field particles W and Z, communicators of weak interaction" (with Simon van der Meer).

Life Work: Rubbia's field of investigation was the three previously unobserved bosons W+, W–, and Zo, predicted by the electroweak force proposed by Glashow. Early in his investigation, he discovered the existence of neutral currents, the flow of uncharged particles resulting from the exchange of Zo particles. Working with a team of over one hundred scientists, Rubbia and his colleagues built a 1,200-ton detection chamber in which a stream of protons and a stream of antiprotons circled in the same ring-shaped tunnel in opposite directions and then were brought together in a head-on collision. Particles and antiparticles received a final acceleration of 300 billion electron volts and, since they have opposite charges, they traveled the ring in opposite directions, colliding at six well-defined points. The team discovered all the four particles of the electroweak force.

Publications: "The Physics of the Proton Antiproton Collider," *Proc. HEP83, Int. Europhys. Conf. High Energy Phys.* (1983): 860–79. "The HPW Proton-Decay Experiment," with others, *AIP Conf. Proc.* (1984): 77–88.

Bibliography: *Current Biography Yearbook* (New York: H. W. Wilson, 1985), pp. 26–29. *New York Times*, October 18, 1984, p. B13. *Science* (January 11, 1985): 131–34.

KLITZING, KLAUS VON

Prize: Physics, 1985. *Born:* June 28, 1948; Schroda, Germany. *Nationality:* German. *Education:* Technical University, Berlin, Germany, baccalaureate, 1969; University of Wurzburg, Germany, Ph.D., 1972. *Career:* University of Wurzburg, Germany, 1970–78; Technical University, Munich, Germany, Professor, 1978–80; Max Planck Institute, Stuttgart, West Germany, Researcher, 1980–. *Other Awards:* Walter-Schottky Prize, 1981; Hewlett Packard Europhysics Prize, 1982.

Citation: "For the discovery of the quantized Hall effect."

Life Work: Klitzing's field of investigation was the physics of semiconductors, especially X-ray spectroscopy and luminescence. He focused on the Hall effect, which measured the concentration of electrons in a semiconductor. In his experiments, he used a silicon that was part of a transistor in which the mobile electrons were confined to a thin surface layer. The Hall voltage then dropped from its normal smooth variation. The electrical resistance was measured at 25,813 ohms: the ratio of two fundamental constants of nature—Planck's constant and the square of the electrical charge of the electron. The phenomenon, named quantum Hall effect, is the new absolute standard of electrical resistance.

Publications: "Resonance Structure in the High Field Magnetoresistance of Tellurium," with G. Landwehr, *Solid State Communications* 9 (1971): 1251–54. "An Observation by Photoconductivity of Strain Splitting of Shallow Bulk Donors Located Near to the Surface in Silicon MOS Devices," with R. J. Nicholas and R. A. Stradling, *Solid State Communications* 20 (1976): 77–80. "New Method for High-Accuracy Determination of the Fine-Structure Constant Based on Quantized Hall Resistance," with G. Dorda and M. Pepper, *Physical Review Letters* 45 (1980): 494. "Electron Spin Resonance on GaAs-Al(x)Ga(1-x) As Heterostructures," with D. Stein, *Physical Review Letters* 51 (1983): 130–33.

Bibliography: *New York Times*, October 17, 1985, p. 1. *Nobel Prize Winners: Physics* (Pasadena, Calif.: Salem Press, 1988), vol. 3, pp. 1301–11. *Science* 231 (February 21, 1986): 820–22.

BINNIG, GERD KARL

Prize: Physics, 1986. *Born:* July 20, 1947; Frankfurt, Germany. *Nationality:* German. *Education:* Goethe University, Germany, Diploma, 1973; University of Frankfurt, Germany, Ph.D., 1978. *Career:* IBM, Switzerland, Researcher, 1978–. *Other Awards:* Physics Prize, German Physical Society, 1982; Otto Klung Prize, 1983; Hewlett-Packard Europhysics Prize, 1984; King Faisal International Prize, Saudi Arabia, 1984; Eliot Cresson Medal, 1987; Minnie Rosen Award, Ross University, New York, 1988.

Citation: "For their design of the scanning tunneling microscope" (with Heinrich Rohrer).

Life Work: Binnig's field of investigation was the surfaces of materials. To probe the surfaces of materials, Binnig and his colleague Heinrich Rohrer tried a variant of an effect of quantum mechanics known as tunneling. Their work led to the development of the scanning tunneling microscope, in which electrons tunnel through a vacuum by means of tunneling current. The scanning tunneling microscope has become a standard tool in many research laboratories for use in semiconductor physics, microelectronics, chemical catalysis, and the study of DNA molecules.

Publications: "Scanning Tunneling Microscopy," *IBM Journal of Research and Development* 30 (1986): 355–69. "Atomic Resolution with Atomic Force Microscope," *Europhysics Letters* 3 (1987): 1281–86. "Scanning Tunneling Microscopy: From Birth to Adolescence," *Review of Modern Physics* 59 (1987): 615–25. "Smectic Liquid Crystal Monolayers on Graphite Observed by STM," *Science* 245 (1989): 43–46.

Bibliography: *Research and Development* 23 (1986): 37–38. *Science* 234 (1986): 821–22.

ROHRER, HEINRICH

Prize: Physics, 1986. *Born:* June 6, 1933; Buchs, Switzerland. *Nationality:* Swiss. *Education:* Federal Institute of Technology, Switzerland, Diploma, 1955; Federal Institute of Technology, Switzerland, Ph.D., 1960. *Career:* Swiss Institute of Technology, Switzerland, Researcher, 1960–61; Rutgers University, New Jersey, Researcher, 1961–63; IBM, Switzerland, Researcher, 1963–. *Other Awards:* Hewlett-Packard Europhysics Prize, 1984; King Faisal International Prize, Saudi Arabia, 1984; Eliot Cresson Medal, 1987.

Citation: "For their design of the scanning tunneling microscope" (with Gerd Binnig).

Life Work: Rohrer's field of investigation was superconductivity. Working with Binnig, he tried to get electrons to tunnel through a vacuum. This approach led to the invention of a new instrument called the scanning tunneling microscope, which can measure the flow of electrons as a tunneling current.

Publications: "Scanning Tunneling Microscopy," *IBM Journal of Research and Development* 30 (1986): 355–69. "A Study of Graphite Surface Using the Scanning Tunneling Microscope and Electronic Structure Calculations," *Surface Sciences* 81 (1987): 26–38. "Topography of Defects at Atomic Resolution Using the STM," *Surface Sciences* 181 (1987): 139–44. "Scanning Tunneling Microscopy: From Birth to Adolescence," *Review of Modern Physics* 59 (1987): 615–25.

Bibliography: *Science* 234 (1986): 821–22. *Science News* 130 (1986): 262–63.

RUSKA, ERNST

Prize: Physics, 1986. *Born:* December 25, 1906; Heidelberg, Germany. *Died:* May 27, 1988; Berlin, Germany. *Nationality:* German. *Education:* Technical University, Berlin, Germany, Certified engineer, 1931; Technical University, Berlin, Germany, Ph.D., 1933. *Career:* Fernseh Corporation, Germany, Engineer, 1933–37; Siemens Company, Germany, Engineer, 1937–56; Institute of Electron Microscopy, Max Planck Society, Germany, 1956–72. *Other Awards:* Senckenberg Prize, 1939; Leibniz Silver Medal, 1941; Lasker Award, 1960; Duddell Medal and Prize, 1975; Cothenius Medal, 1975.

Citation: "For his fundamental work in electron optics, and for the design of the first electron microscope."

Life Work: Ruska is best known as the inventor of the electron microscope. In the late 1920s Ruska discovered that magnetic coils act as a lens for electrons. He also succeeded in building a magnetic lens with a short enough focal length to be used to obtain an image of an object irradiated with electrons. He first built an electron microscope in 1931 and developed it over the next several years until it was developed commercially in 1937. The electron microscope developed by Ruska is known as a transmission microscope. It led to the development of other types of microscopes, such as the scanning electron microscope.

Publications: "The Electron Microscope," *Zeitschrift fur Physik* 78 (1932): 318–39. "Images of Metal Forces in the Electron Microscope," *Zeitschrift fur Physik* 83 (1933): 187–93. "Images of Surfaces Which Reflect Electrons in the Electron Microscope," *Zeitschrift fur Physik* 83 (1933): 492–97. "Magnetic Objective for the Electron Microscope," *Zeitschrift fur Physik* 89 (1934): 90–128. *The Early Development of Electron Lenses and Electron Microscopy* (Stuttgart, Germany: S. Hirzel Verlag, 1980).

Bibliography: *Nobel Prize Winners: Physics* (Pasadena, Calif.: Salem Press, 1988), vol. 3, pp. 1315–21. *Physics Today* 40 (1987): 17–20. *Science* 234 (1986): 821–22.

BEDNORZ, JOHANNES GEORG

Prize: Physics, 1987. *Born:* May 16, 1950; Nevenkirchen, West Germany. *Nationality:* West German; later Swiss resident. *Education:* University of Munster, Germany, B.S., 1976; Federal Institute of Technology, Switzerland, Ph.D., 1982. *Career:* IBM, Switzerland, Researcher, 1982–. *Other Awards:* Marcel-Benoist Prize, 1986; Victor Moritz Goldschmidt Prize, 1987; Robert Wichard Pohl Prize, 1987; Fritz London Memorial Award, 1987; Dannie Heineman Prize, 1987; Otto Klung Prize, 1987; Hewlett-Packard Europhysics Prize, 1988.

Citation: "For their important break-through in the discovery of superconductivity in ceramic materials" (with K. Alexander Müller).

Life Work: Bednorz's field of investigation was high-temperature superconductivity. Superconductivity, discovered by Heike Kamerlingh Onnes in 1911, had remained impracticable for many years because it required cooling mercury to 4°K. By 1980s, the limit had been raised to 23°K, still outside most practical applications. After years of trial and error, Bednorz and K. Alexander Müller tried a newly synthesized oxide of copper mixed with barium and lanthanum. They raised the record to 35°K, thus making the dream of practical superconductivity a reality.

Publications: "Possible High T. Superconductivity in the Ba-La-Cu-O Systems," *Zeitschrift fur Physik B* 64 (1986): 189–93. "The Discovery of a Class of High Temperature Superconductors," *Science* 237 (1987): 1133–39. "The Discovery of Superconductivity at High Temperature," *Recherche* (France) 19 (January 1988): 52–60.

Bibliography: *Nobel Prize Winners: Physics* (Pasadena, Calif.: Salem Press, 1988), vol. 3, pp. 1336–48. *Science* 238 (1987): 481–82.

MÜLLER, KARL ALEXANDER

Prize: Physics, 1987. *Born:* April 20, 1927; Basel, Switzerland. *Nationality:* Swiss. *Education:* Federal Institute of Technology, Switzerland, M.S., 1952; Federal Institute of Technology, Switzerland, Ph.D., 1958. *Career:* Batelle Institute Switzerland, Researcher, 1959–63; IBM, Switzerland, Researcher, 1963–. *Other Awards:* Marcel-Benoist Foundation Prize, 1986; Fritz London Memorial Award, 1987; Dannie Heineman Prize, 1987; Robert Wichard Pohl Prize, 1987; Hewlett-Packard Europhysics Prize, 1988.

Citation: "For their important break-through in the discovery of superconductivity in ceramic materials" (with J. Georg Bednorz).

Life Work: Müller and Bednorz collaborated in making superconductivity achievable at practical temperatures. First observed in 1911, superconductivity research had stalled for over half a century because of the difficulty and the cost of cooling mercury to 4°K. In 1986, Müller and Bednorz successfully tested a newly synthesized oxide of copper, barium, and lanthanum to achieve superconductivity at 23°K.

Publications: "Inhomogeneous Superconductivity Transitions in Granular Al," *Physical Review Letters* 45 (1980): 832–36. "Possible T. Superconductivity in the Ba-La-Cu-O System," *Zeitschrift fur Physik B* 64 (1986): 189–93. "The Discovery of a Class of High-Temperature Superconductors," *Science* 237 (1987): 1133–39. "The Discovery of Superconductivity at High Temperature," *Recherche* (France) 19 (January 1988): 52–60.

Bibliography: *New York Times*, October 15, 1987, p. A14. *Nobel Prize Winners: Physics* (Pasadena, Calif.: Salem Press, 1988), vol. 3, pp. 1336–48.

LEDERMAN, LEON MAX

Prize: Physics, 1988. *Born:* July 15, 1922; New York, New York. *Nationality:* American. *Education:* City College of New York, B.S., 1943; Columbia University, New York, A.M., 1948; Columbia University, New York, Ph.D., 1951. *Career:* Columbia University, New York, Professor, 1951–79; Fermi National Accelerator Lab, Illinois, Administrator, 1979–89; University of Chicago, Illinois, Professor, 1989–92; Illinois Institute of Technology, Professor, 1992–. *Other Awards:* National Medal of Science, 1965; Townsend Harris Medal, 1973; Elliot Cresson Medal, 1976; Wolf Prize, 1983; Fermi Prize, 1992.

Citation: "For the neutrino beam method and the demonstration of the doublet structure of the leptons through the discovery of the muon neutrino" (with Melvin Schwartz and Jack Steinberger).

Life Work: Lederman's field of investigation was the neutrino. Together with Melvin Schwartz and Jack Steinberger, he decided to test the weak force by using the technique of colliding particle beams. The particle studied for this purpose was the neutrino, a particle with no electrical charge and virtually no mass. It rarely interacts with other particles except for rare interactions with the weak force. The goal was to create a concentrated beam of neutrinos and to isolate uncontaminated weak force interactions. The first part of the experiment consisted of creating a flood of subatomic particles in a synchrotron and then eliminating all particles except neutrinos. The result was a neutron beam. The team used the neutron beam to test the two-neutron theory, according to which there were two types of neutrons, the muon type, produced by muons, and the pion type, produced by beta decay. The experiment confirmed the two-neutrino theory.

Publications: "The Two-Neutrino Experiment," *Scientific American* 208 (1963): 60–70. *From Quarks to the Cosmos* (New York: Scientific American Library, 1989).

Bibliography: *Nobel Prize Winners: Physics* (Pasadena, Calif.: Salem Press, 1989), vol. 3, pp. 1353–64. *Physics Today* 42 (1989): 17–19. *Science* 242 (1988): 669–70.

SCHWARTZ, MELVIN

Prize: Physics, 1988. *Born:* November 2, 1932; New York, New York. *Nationality:* American. *Education:* Columbia University, New York, B.A., 1953; Columbia University, New York, Ph.D., 1958. *Career:* Brookhaven National Laboratories, New York, Researcher, 1956–58; Columbia University, New York, Professor, 1958–66; Stanford University, California, Professor, 1966–79; Digital Pathways, California, President, 1979–91; Columbia University, New York, Professor, 1991. *Other Awards:* Hughes Prize, 1964; Guggenheim Fellow Award, 1968.

Citation: "For the neutrino beam method and the demonstration of the doublet structure of the leptons through the discovery of the muon neutrino" (with Leon M. Lederman and Jack Steinberger).

Life Work: Schwartz's field of investigation was particle physics. He collaborated with Lederman and Steinberger in the discovery of the neutron beam and the confirmation of the two-neutrino theory. Challenged to devise a way to observe and measure the weak force, Schwarz came up with the idea of using neutrinos for the purpose. Neutrinos are particles with no electrical charge and virtually no mass, and they interact only with the weak force. With the goal of collecting neutrons in one place where their interactions with the weak force could be studied they created a flood of subatomic particles in a synchrotron from which all particles except neutrinos were eliminated. The result was a neutrino beam. Using the neutrino beam, they confirmed the two neutrino theory according to which there were two types of neutrinos: muon types, formed from the decay of a pion, and the electron type, produced by beta decay.

Publications: "Observation of High-Energy Neutrino Reactions and the Existence of Two Kinds of Neutrinos," *Physical Reviews Letters* 9 (1962): 36. "Neutrino Physics," *Reports on Progress in Physics* 28 (1965): 61–75. "Search for Intermediate Bosons," *Physical Reviews Letters* 15 (1965): 42. *Principles of Electrodynamics* (New York: McGraw-Hill, 1972).

Bibliography: *Nobel Prize Winners, Physics* (Pasadena, Calif.: Salem Press, 1989), vol. 3, pp. 1353–64. *Physics Today* 42 (1989): 17–19. *Science* 242 (1988): 669–70.

STEINBERGER, JACK

Prize: Physics, 1988. *Born:* May 25, 1921; Bad Kissingen, Germany. *Nationality:* German; later U.S. citizen. *Education:* University of Chicago, Illinois, B.S., 1942; University of Chicago, Illinois, Ph.D., 1948. *Career:* University of California, Berkeley, Professor, 1949–50; Columbia University, New York, Professor 1950–68; European Center for Nuclear Research, Director, Researcher and Administrator, 1968–86; Scuola Normale, Italy, Professor 1986–. *Other Awards:* Medal of Science, 1988.

Citation: "For the neutrino beam method and the demonstration of the doublet structure of the leptons through the discovery of the muon neutrino" (with Leon M. Lederman and Melvin Schwartz).

Life Work: Steinberg's field of investigation was particle physics. He collaborated with Lederman and Schwartz in the discovery of the neutron beam and the confirmation of the two-neutron theory. Challenged to devise an experiment to observe and measure weak interactions, the team decided to focus on neutrinos. Neutrinos are particles with no electrical charge and virtually no mass. They react only with the weak force. The goal was to create a concentrated beam of neutrinos and to study their uncontaminated weak force interactions. They used the Brookhaven National Laboratory's alternating gradient synchrotron to create a flood of subatomic particles and then to eliminate all particles except the neutrinos. The result was a neutrino beam. The beam was used to confirm the two-neutrino theory. Physicists had suggested that there were two types of neutrinos: the muon type, derived from the decay of a pion, and the electron type, derived from beta decay.

Publications: "Observation of High-Energy Neutrino Reactions and the Existence of Two Kinds of Neutrinos," *Physical Reviews Letters* 9 (1962): 36. "Resonances in Strange-Particle Production," *Physical Reviews* 128 (1962): 1930. "Lifetime of the 4-Meson," *Physical Reviews Letters* 11 (1963): 436.

Bibliography: *Nobel Prize Winners: Physics* (Pasadena, Calif.: Salem Press, 1989), vol. 3, pp. 1353–64. *Physics Today* 42 (1989): 17–19. *Science* 242 (1988): 669–70.

DEHMELT, HANS GEORG

Prize: Physics, 1989. *Born:* September 9, 1922; Gorlitz, Germany. *Nationality:* German; later U.S. citizen. *Education:* University of Göttingen, Germany, Ph.D., 1950. *Career:* University of Göttingen, Researcher, 1950–52; Duke University, North Carolina, Researcher, 1952–55; University of Washington, Professor, 1955–. *Other Awards:* Davisson-Germer Prize, 1970; Humbolt Prize, 1974; Basic Research Award, International Society of Magnetic Resonance, 1980; Rumford Prize, 1985.

Citation: "For the development of the ion trap technique" (with Wolfgang Paul).

Life Work: During the 1950s Dehmelt experimented with polarized atoms and measuring the light they emitted or absorbed as they changed magnetic orientation. Such changes are called quantum transitions. When an atom changes orientation, it absorbs or emits light of very specific frequencies, called resonance frequencies, which can be measured with high resolution spectroscopy. Producing polarized atoms required Dehmelt to temporarily trap and hold a beam of polarized electrons, a technique designed to assure more precise measurements of resonance frequencies. In 1959 he developed his first version of a Penning trap for electrons. He next turned to measuring the electron's gyromagnetic ratio (the ratio between its magnetic moment and its spin) with the aid of a laser side-band cooling that measured frequencies with the continuous Stern-Gerlach technique. Refining the technique, Dehmelt and his colleagues succeeded in measuring the gyromagnetic ratio of the electron to an accuracy of 4 parts per trillion. Another outgrowth of Dehmelt's work is the shelved optical electron amplifier to make very accurate frequency measurements, working on ions instead of electrons and using visible light rather than radio waves.

Publications: "Spin Resonance of Free Electrons Polarized by Exchange Collisions," *Physical Review* 109 (1958): 381–85. "Spin Resonance of Free Electrons," *Journal of Physical Radium* 19 (1958): 866–71. "Radiofrequency Spectroscopy of Stored Ions. I. Storage," *Advances in Atomic Molecular Physics* 3 (1967): 53–72. "Radiofrequency

Spectroscopy of Stored Ions. II. Spectroscopy," *Advances in Atomic Molecular Physics* 5 (1969): 109–54.

Bibliography: *New York Times*, October 13, 1989, pp. 1, 10. *Science* 246 (October 20, 1989): 327–28.

PAUL, WOLFGANG

Prize: Physics, 1989. **Born:** August 10, 1913; Lorenzkirch, Germany. **Died:** December 6, 1993; Bonn, Germany. **Nationality:** German. **Education:** Technical University, Berlin, Germany, Ph.D., 1939. **Career:** University of Göttingen, Germany, Professor, 1944–52; University of Bonn, Germany, Professor, 1952–83. **Other Awards:** Humboldt Prize, 1979; Robert W. Pohl Prize, 1989.

Citation: "For the development of the ion trap technique" (with Hans G. Dehmelt).

Life Work: In the 1950s Paul and his associates devised the first ion traps, now called Paul traps. These electrical "bottles" have advanced high-precision measurement of atoms and can be used to test the theory of quantum mechanics.

Publications: "A New Mass Spectrometer without Magnetic Field," *Z. Naturforsch* 89 (1953): 448–50. "Production of Elementary Particles in the Laboratory," *Naturwissenschaften* 46 (1959): 277–83. "Survey of Methods of Producing Sources of Polarized Protons," *Helvetica Physica Acta Supplement* 6 (1961): 17–25.

Bibliography: *New York Times*, October 13, 1989, pp. 1, 10. *Science* 246 (October 20, 1989): 327–28. *New York Times* Biographical Service, December 8, 1993, p. 1681.

RAMSEY, NORMAN FOSTER, JR.

Prize: Physics, 1989. **Born:** August 27, 1915; Washington, D.C. **Nationality:** American. **Education:** Columbia University, New York, A.B., 1937; Cambridge University, England, B.A., 1937; Cambridge University, England, M.A., 1941; Columbia University, New York, Ph.D., 1940; Cambridge University, England, D.Sc., 1954. **Career:** University of Illinois, Researcher, 1940–42; Columbia University, New York, Professor, 1942–47; Harvard University, Massachusetts, Professor, 1947–. **Other Awards:** E. O. Lawrence Award, 1960; Medal of Honor, IEEE, 1983; Rabi Prize, 1985; Monie Ferst Award, 1985; Compton Medal, 1985; Oersted Medal, 1988; National Medal of Science, 1988; Pupin Medal, 1992; Einstein Medal, 1993.

Citation: "For the invention of the separated oscillatory fields method and its use in the hydrogen maser and other atomic clocks."

Life Work: Ramsey studied and measured a wide variety of atomic and molecular properties and laid the foundations for the theories behind the development of nuclear magnetic resonance and magnetic resonance imaging. His first task was to measure magnetic moments more accurately. To do so he invented a new method, the separated oscillatory field method, which passes a molecular beam through two rotating magnetic fields separated by a long region containing only a static magnetic field. This invention has led to the development of atomic clocks, which use the magnetic resonance frequencies of atoms as a standard for timekeeping. Ramsey also shared with Daniel Kleppner the invention of the atomic hydrogen maser (microwave amplification by stimulated emission of radiation).

Publications: "A New Molecular-Beam Resonance Method," *Physical Review* 76 (1949): 996. "A Molecular-Beam Resonance Method with Separated Oscillating Fields," *Physical Review* 78 (1950): 695–99. "Radiofrequency Spectra of Hydrogen and Deuterium by a New Molecular-Beam Resonance Method," *Physica* 17 (1951): 328–32. *Molecular Beams* (Oxford: Claredon Press, 1956).

Bibliography: *New York Times*, October 13, 1989, pp. 1, 10. *Science* 246 (October 20, 1989): 327–28.

FRIEDMAN, JEROME ISAAC

Prize: Physics, 1990. *Born:* March 28, 1930; Chicago, Illinois. *Nationality:* American. *Education:* University of Chicago, Illinois, A.B., 1950; University of Chicago, Illinois, M.S., 1953; University of Chicago, Illinois, Ph.D., 1956. *Career:* University of Chicago, Illinois, Researcher, 1956–67; Stanford University, California, Researcher, 1957–60; Massachusetts Institute of Technology, Professor, 1960–. *Other Awards:* Panofsky Prize, 1989.

Citation: "For their pioneering investigations concerning deep inelastic scattering of electrons on protons and bound neutrons, which have been of essential importance for the development of the quark model in particle physics" (with Henry W. Kendall and Richard E. Taylor).

Life Work: Friedman, Henry Kendall, and Richard Taylor were part of a team that observed the first traces of quarks that had eluded physicists for many years. Quarks are clusters of subatomic particles first predicted by Gell-Mann in 1964. The team worked at the Stanford Linear Accelerator Center (SLAC), a two-mile-long particle accelerator. In a series of experiments called Deep Inelastic Scattering, they sent beams of electrons traveling at nearly the speed of light toward targets of hydrogen or liquid deuterium. Along with quarks, the team identified particles called gluons, electrically neutral particles that bind quarks together.

Publications: "Electron-Proton Elastic Scattering at High Momentum Transfer," with H. W. Randall and R. E. Taylor, *Physical Review Letters* 20 (1968): 292. "High Energy

Inelastic Electron-Proton Scattering at Six Degrees and Ten Degrees," with H. W. Randall and R. E. Taylor, *Physical Review Letters* 23 (1969): 930. "Observed Behavior of Highly Inelastic Electron-Proton Scattering," with H. W. Randall and R. E. Taylor, *Physical Review Letters* 23 (1969): 935.

Bibliography: *New York Times*, October 18, 1990, p. A12. *Science* 250 (October 26, 1990): 508–509.

KENDALL, HENRY WAY

Prize: Physics, 1990. ***Born:*** December 9, 1926; Boston, Massachusetts. ***Died:*** February 15, 1999; Tallahassee, Florida. ***Nationality:*** American. ***Education:*** Amherst College, Massachusetts, B.A., 1950; Massachusetts Institute of Technology, Ph.D., 1955. ***Career:*** Massachusetts Institute of Technology, Researcher, 1954–56; Stanford University, California, Professor, 1956–61; Massachusetts Institute of Technology, Professor, 1961–. ***Other Awards:*** Panofsky Prize, 1989.

Citation: "For their pioneering investigations concerning deep inelastic scattering of electrons on protons and bound neutrons, which have been of essential importance for the development of the quark model in particle physics" (with Jerome I. Friedman and Richard E. Taylor).

Life Work: Kendall's field of investigation was subatomic particles. Working with the Stanford Linear Accellerator, Kendall and his colleagues, Jerome Friedman and Richard Taylor, were able to observe the first traces of quarks. Quarks were predicted by Gell-Mann as clusters of small subatomic particles. In a series of experiments called Deep Inelastic Scattering, they sent beams of electrons traveling at nearly the speed of light toward targets of liquid hydrogen or deuterium. Along with quarks, the team also identified particles called gluons, electrically neutral particles that bind quarks together.

Publications: "Electron-Proton Elastic Scattering at High Momentum Transfer," with J. I. Friedman and R. E. Taylor, *Physical Review Letters* 20 (1968): 292. "High-Energy Inelastic Electon-Proton Scattering at Six Degrees and Ten Degrees," with J. I. Friedman and R. E. Taylor, *Physical Review Letters* 23 (1969): 930. "Observed Behavior of Highly Inelastic Electron-Proton Scattering," with J. I. Friedman and R. E. Taylor, *Physical Review Letters* 23 (1969): 935. *Energy Strategies* (Cambridge, Mass.: Union of Concerned Scientists, 1980).

Bibliography: *New York Times*, October 18, 1990, p. A12. *Science* 250 (October 26, 1990): 508–509.

TAYLOR, RICHARD E.

Prize: Physics, 1990. *Born:* November 2, 1929; Medicine Hat, Alberta, Canada. *Nationality:* Canadian; later American resident. *Education:* University of Alberta, Canada, B.S., 1950; University of Alberta, Canada, M.S., 1952; Stanford University, California, Ph.D., 1962. *Career:* Boursier Laboratory, France, Researcher, 1958–61; Lawrence Laboratory, California, Researcher, 1961–62; Stanford University, California, Professor, 1962–. *Other Awards:* Panofsky Prize, 1989.

Citation: "For their pioneering investigations concerning deep inelastic scattering of electrons on protons and bound neutrons, which have been of essential importance for the development of the quark model in particle physics" (with Jerome I. Friedman and Henry W. Kendall).

Life Work: Together with Friedman and Kendall, Taylor used the Stanford Linear Accelerator to prove the existence of the quark by bombarding hydrogen and deuterium with high-energy electrons. Their experiments, called Deep Inelastic Scattering, sent beams of electrons traveling at nearly the speed of light to shatter the components of the nucleus and release the quarks, clusters of the smallest particles and building blocks of the universe. Along the way, they also identified particles called gluons, electrically neutral particles that bind quarks together. All matter on earth, including human bodies, consist of more than 99 percent quarks with associated gluons.

Publications: "Electron-Proton Elastic Scattering at High Momentum Transfer," with J. I. Friedman and H. W. Kendall, *Physical Review Letters* 20 (1968): 292. "High-Energy Inelastic Electron-Proton Scattering at Six Degrees and Ten Degrees," with J. I. Friedman and H. W. Kendall, *Physical Review Letters* 23 (1969): 930. "Observed Behavior of Highly Inelastic Electron-Proton Scattering," with J. I. Friedman and H. W. Kendall, *Physical Review Letters* 23 (1969): 935.

Bibliography: *New York Times,* October 18, 1900, p. A12. *Science* 250 (October 26, 1990): 508–509.

GENNES, PIERRE-GILLES DE

Prize: Physics, 1991. *Born:* October 24, 1932; Paris, France. *Nationality:* French. *Education:* Lycée Claude-Bernard à Paris, France, B.A.; École Normale Supérieure, France, Ph.D., 1957. *Career:* Center for Atomic Studies, France, Researcher, 1955–61; University of Paris, France, Professor, 1961–71; Collège de France, Professor, 1971–. *Other Awards:* Ampere Prize, 1977; Harvey Prize, 1989; Wolf Prize, 1990.

Citation: "For discovering that methods developed for studying order phenomena in simple systems can be generalized to more complex forms of matter, in particular to liquid crystals and polymers."

Life Work: Gennes's fields of investigation were superconductors, liquid crystals, and polymers. He discovered that the same principles govern the phase transitions of both magnets and superconductors. He showed that a phase change in liquid crystals transforms them from transparent to opaque, permitting the scattering of light. He also mathematically developed the links between liquid crystals and superconductors. He explained polymer dynamics and developed mathematical principles that determined the geometrical arrangement of monomer groups within a polymer chain. His work has had many practical applications in the development of synthetic polymers and the improvement of natural polymers. Yet another field wherein his contributions are significant is the study of gels and adhesives. The Royal Swedish Academy of Sciences has called him "the Isaac Newton of our time."

Publications: *The Physics of Liquid Crystals* (Oxford: Oxford University Press, 1974). *Sealing Concepts in Polymer Physics* (Ithaca, N.Y.: Cornell University Press, 1979). *Simple Views on Condensed Matter* (New York: World Scientific Publishing Co., 1992).

Bibliography: *Chemical and Engineering News* 69 (October 21, 1991): 4. *Science* 254 (October 25, 1991): 518.

CHARPAK, GEORGES

Prize: Physics, 1992. *Born:* August 1, 1924; Dubrovica, Poland. *Nationality:* Polish; later French citizen. *Education:* École des Mines de Paris, France, B. Engineering, 1948; Collège de France, Ph.D., 1953. *Career:* National Center for Scientific Research, France, Researcher, 1948–59; European Center for Nuclear Research, Switzerland, Researcher, 1959–.

Citation: "For his invention and development of particle detectors, in particular the multiwire proportional chamber."

Life Work: In 1968 Charpak created a wire proportional chamber for particle detectors. It tracked both the paths and the energies of charged particles that spray out from a collision, allowing researchers to pinpoint individual particle trajectories while handling hundreds of thousands of such events per event. It records up to 1 million tracks per second and sends the data directly to a computer for analysis. In 1974 he used another type of detection chamber, known as a *drift chamber*, to measure the spherical drift in the study of protein structure by X-ray diffraction. From 1978 he developed avalanche multistep chambers for the study of particles. After 1992 he created a new detector for biological uses. By using the Charpak system, patients will be subjected to fewer X-rays than before.

Publications: "Recent Progress in Particle Detection," *IEEE Transactions in Nuclear Science* 19 (1972): 152–57. "Multiwire Proportional Chambers," *Report* JINR-D-5805 (1970): 271–50. "Multiwire and Multipurpose Development of Multiwire Proportional Chambers," *CERN Cour* 12 (1972): 362–64.

Bibliography: *Physics Today* 46 (January 1993): 17. *Science* 258 (October 23, 1992): 543. *La Vie a Fil Tendú* (Paris: O. Jacob, 1993).

HULSE, RUSSELL ALAN

Prize: Physics, 1993. *Born:* November 28, 1950; New York, New York. *Nationality:* American. *Education:* Cooper Union, New York, B.S., 1970; University of Massachusetts, M.S., 1972; Ph.D., 1975. *Career:* National Radio Astronomy Observatory, New Jersey, Researcher, 1975–77; Princeton University, New Jersey, Researcher, 1977–.

Citation: "For the discovery of a new type of pulsar, a discovery that has opened up new possibilities for the study of gravitation" (with Joseph H. Taylor Jr.).

Life Work: Hulse's field of investigation was pulsars. With Joseph Taylor, he embarked on a systematic search for pulsars. They discovered a binary pulsar, one subject to the gravitational pull of another object, presumably another pulsar. The work provided strong experimental support for the existence of gravitational waves and for Einstein's theories.

Publications: "Discovery of a Pulsar in a Binary System," with J. H. Taylor, *Astrophysical Journal* 195 (1975): L51. "Charge Exchange as a Recombination Mechanism in High-Temperature Plasmas," *Report PPPL–1633* (1980). "Charge Exchange as a Recombination Mechanism in High-Temperature Plasmas," *J. Phys. B.* 13 (1980): 3895–907.

Bibliography: *Physics Today* 46 (December 1993): 17. *Science* 262 (October 22, 1993): 507.

TAYLOR, JOSEPH HOOTON, JR.

Prize: Physics, 1993. *Born:* March 29, 1941; Philadelphia, Pennsylvania. *Nationality:* American. *Education:* Haverford College, Pennsylvania, B.A., 1963; Harvard University, Massachusetts, Ph.D., 1968. *Career:* University of Massachusetts, Professor, 1969–80; Princeton University, New Jersey, Professor, 1980–. *Other Awards:* Heineman Prize, 1980; Tomella Foundation Prize, 1985; Draper Medal, 1985; Magellanic Premium Award, 1990; Carty Medal, 1991; Wolf Prize, 1992.

Citation: "For the discovery of a new type of pulsar, a discovery that has opened up new possibilities for the study of gravitation" (with Russell A. Hulse).

Life Work: Taylor was a codiscoverer with Hulse of the first binary pulsar sighted by a terrestrial telescope. The system manifested several of the effects predicted by Einstein including the bending of the path of the radio waves and a precession in the system's axis of rotation.

Publications: "Discovery of a Pulsar in a Binary System," with R. Hulse, *Astrophysical Journal* 195 (1975): L51; "Further Observations of the Binary Pulsar PSR1913+16." *Astrophysical Journal* 206 (1976): L53. *Pulsars* (San Francisco: W. H. Freeman, 1977). "Further Tests of Relativistic Gravity Using the Binary Pulsar PSR 1913+16," *Astrophysical Journal* 345 (1989): 434.

Bibliography: *Physics Today* 46 (December 1993): 17. *Science* 262 (October 22, 1993): 507.

BROCKHOUSE, BERTRAM NEVILLE

Prize: Physics, 1994. *Born:* Lethbridge, Alberta, Canada; July 15, 1918. *Nationality:* Canadian. *Education:* University of British Columbia, Canada, B.A., 1947; University of Toronto, Canada, M.A., 1948, Ph.D., 1950. *Career:* University of Toronto, Ontario, Canada, Professor, 1949–50; Atomic Energy of Canada, Researcher, 1950–62; McMaster University, Ontario, Canada, Professor, 1962–84. *Other Awards:* Buckley Prize, 1962; Dudell Medal, 1963; Canadian Association of Physicists Medal, 1967; Tory Medal, 1973.

Citation: "For pioneering contributions to the development of neutron scattering techniques for studies of condensed matter" (with Clifford G. Shull); "for the development of neutron spectroscopy."

Life Work: Brockhouse's field of investigation was neutron spectroscopy. His first actual experiments studied the scattering of neutrons by highly absorbing elements. In 1956 he completed the first true triple-axis crystal spectrometer. He developed a number of instruments to facilitate neutron scattering, including the filter-chopper apparatus and the beryllium detector.

Publications: "Resonant Scattering of Slow Neutrons," *Canadian Journal of Physics* 31 (1953): 432–52. "Energy Distribution of Neutrons Scattered by Paramagnetic Substances," *Physics Reviews* 99 (1955): 601–603. "Slow-neutron Spectrometry—A New Tool for the Study of Energy Levels in Condensed Systems," *Physics Reviews* 98 (1955): 1171.

Bibliography: *New York Times* Biographical Service, October 13, 1994, p. 1570. *Physics Today* 47 (December 1994): 17.

SHULL, CLIFFORD GLENWOOD

Prize: Physics, 1994. *Born:* September 23, 1915; Pittsburgh, Pennsylvania. *Nationality:* American. *Education:* Carnegie Institute of Technology, Pennsylvania, B.S.,

1937; New York University, Ph.D., 1941. *Career:* Texas Co., Researcher, 1941–46; Oak Ridge National Laboratories, Tennessee, Researcher, 1946–55; Massachusetts Institute of Technology, Professor, 1955–86. *Other Awards:* Carnegie Mellon University Alumni Award, 1968; Humboldt Award, 1979; Tennessee Governor Award, 1986; Aminoff Prize, 1993; Frank Prize, 1993.

Citation: "For pioneering contributions to the development of neutron scattering techniques for studies of condensed matter" (with Bertram N. Brockhouse); "for the development of the neutron diffraction technique."

Life Work: Shull's field of investigation was neutron scattering. Neutrons, like X rays, produce waves that scatter when they interact with crystals. Neutron waves of specific lengths produce specific patterns of scattered waves. Neutrons are not electrically charged and hence do not interact with electrons. Working at Oak Ridge, Shull tried to create a monochromatic beam of neutrons with equal velocities. He created this beam to probe solid objects and to produce neutron diffraction patterns that revealed the atomic structure of the object. The neutron scattering technique has influenced every area of condensed matter physics. Later, Shull discovered the first evidence of antiferromagnetism.

Publications: "Determination of X-ray Diffraction Line Widths," *Phys. Rev.* 70 (1946): 679–84. "X-ray Scattering at Small Angles by Finely Divided Solids," *J. Applied Phys.* 18 (1947): 295–313. "Highly Polarized Neutron Beams by Bragg Reflection from Ferromagnetic Crystals," *Phys. Rev.* 81 (1951): 626.

Bibliography: *New York Times* Biographical Service, October 13, 1994, p. 1570. *Physics Today* 47 (December 1994): 17.

PERL, MARTIN L.

Prize: Physics, 1995. *Born:* June 24, 1927; New York, New York. *Nationality:* American. *Education:* Polytechnic Institute of New York, B.A., 1948; Columbia University, New York, Ph.D., 1955. *Career:* General Electric, New York, Researcher, 1948–50; University of Michigan, Professor, 1955–63; Stanford University, California, Professor, 1963–. *Other Awards:* Wolf Prize, 1982.

Citation: "For pioneering experimental contributions to lepton physics" (with Frederick Reines); "for the discovery of the tau lepton."

Life Work: Perl's field of investigation was particle physics. He concentrated on the physics of strong interactions, using spark chambers to measure the elastic scattering of pions on protons. He also tried to solve two classic puzzles relating to the connection between muons and electrons, particularly why the muon is 207 times heavier than the electron even though their properties are the same, and why the decay of the muon to an electron produces a neutrino and an antineutrino. This led him to search for a hypothetical particle called the lepton, using an electron-positron collider. By 1975 he and his colleagues had identified the lepton as well as family of elementary particles (tau, tau neutrino, top quark, and bottom quark).

Publications: *High Energy Hadron Physics* (New York: Wiley, 1974). "Evidence for, and Properties of the Tau Lepton," *Report 1977, SLAC-PUB-2055, CONF-7710107–1.* "Comments on the Tau Heavy Lepton," *Exp. Meson Spectrosc. Int. Conf., 5th* (1977): 118–31.

Bibliography: *New York Times*, October 12, 1995, p. A12.

REINES, FREDERICK

Prize: Physics, 1995. *Born:* March 16, 1918; Patterson, New Jersey. *Died:* August 26, 1998; Orange, California. *Nationality:* American. *Education:* Stevens Institute of Technology, New Jersey, B.S., 1939; New York University, M.S., 1941, Ph.D., 1944. *Career:* Los Alamos Scientific Laboratory, New Mexico, Researcher, 1944–59; Case Institute of Technology, Ohio, Professor, 1959–66; University of California, Professor, 1966–88. *Other Awards:* Oppenheimer Prize, 1981; National Medal of Science, 1983; Michelson Morley Award, 1990; Rossi Prize, 1990; Franklin Medal, 1992; Panofsky Prize, 1992.

Citation: "For pioneering experimental contributions to lepton physics" (with Martin L. Perl); "for the detection of the neutrino."

Life Work: Reines and his associate Clyde L.Cohen proved successfully the existence of the neutrino, which had been predicted by Wolfgang Pauli in 1930 to explain the process of beta decay.

Publications: "Neutron Spectra from Proton Recoils in Photographic Emulsions," *Phys. Rev.* 74 (1948): 1565. "A Proposed Experiment to Detect the Free Neutrino," *Phys. Rev.* 90 (1953): 492–93. "Detection of the Free Neutrino," *Phys Rev.* 92 (1953): 830–31.

Bibliography: *New York Times*, October 12, 1995, p. A12.

LEE, DAVID M.

Prize: Physics, 1996. *Born:* January 20, 1931; Rye, New York. *Nationality:* American. *Education:* Harvard University, B.S., 1952; University of Connecticut, M.S., 1955; Yale University, Ph.D., 1959. *Career:* Cornell University, 1959–; Visiting Professor, University of Florida, 1974–75; Professor, University of California, San Diego, 1976–1988; Professor, University of Grenoble, France, 1988. *Other Awards:* Sir Francis Simon Memorial Prize, 1976; Oliver E. Buckley Solid State Physics Prize of the American Physical Society, 1979.

Citation: "For their discovery of superfluidity in helium-3" (with Douglas D. Osheroff and Robert C. Richardson).

Life Work: The structure of helium helped scientists to understand how the first structures began to form in space microseconds after the big bang. Experts believe that in the early universe cosmological phase transitions had formed strange, linelike defects called cosmic strings. The team discovered superfluidity by accident, but in their initial measurements a problem occurred when the temperature dropped below absolute zero. They observed that such a superfluid condition was also magnetic. A new kind of sound known as zero sound was also uncovered.

Publications: "Evidence for a New Phase of Solid He3," with D. D. Osheroff and R. C. Richardson, *Physical Review Letters* 28 (April 1972): 885. "Superfluid Helium 3," with N. David Mermin, *Scientific American* (December 1976): 57–71. "The Extraordinary Phases of Liquide He3," *Reviews of Modern Physics* 69 (July 1997): 645–65.

Bibliography: *New York Times*, October 10, 1996, p. D21. *Science News* 150 (October 19, 1996): 247.

OSHEROFF, DOUGLAS D.

Prize: Physics, 1996. *Born:* August 1, 1945; Aberdeen, Washington. *Nationality:* American. *Education:* California Institute of Technology, B.S., 1967; Cornell University, M.S., 1969, Ph.D., 1973. *Career:* AT&T Bell Laboratories, 1973–1987; Stanford University, 1987–. *Other Awards:* Simon Memorial Prize of the British Institute of Physics, 1989; John D. and Catherine T. MacArthur Prize, 1981; Oliver E. Buckley Solid State Physics Prize, 1981.

Citation: "For their discovery of superfluidity in helium-3" (with David M. Lee and Robert C. Richardson).

Life Work: The team discovered superfluidity in helium-3 by accident while attempting to discover an antiferromagnetic phase in helium-3. Superfluid helium can be used as a quantum microscope to study quantum mechanics. Superfluidity is also magnetic. A new kind of sound, known as zero sound, was also discovered. The structure of helium has helped scientists to understand how the first structures began to form in space microseconds after the Big Bang. Helium-3 is anisotropic, that is, it displays different properties in different directions along which the property is measured.

Publications: "Evidence for a New Phase of Solid He3," with D. M. Lee and R. C. Richardson, *Physical Review Letters* 28 (April 1972): 885. "Novel Magnetic Properties of Solid Helium–3," with M. C. Cross, *Physics Today* 28 (February 1987): 142–47.

Bibliography: *New York Times*, October 10, 1996, p. D21. *Science News* 150 (October 19, 1996): 247.

RICHARDSON, ROBERT C.

Prize: Physics, 1996. Birth: June 26, 1937; Washington, D.C. *Nationality:* American. *Education:* Virginia Polytechnic Institute, B.S., 1956, M.S., 1960; Duke University, Ph.D., 1966. *Career:* Cornell University, 1966. *Other Awards:* Simon Memorial Prize of the British Physical Society, 1974; Buckley Prize of the American Physical Society, 1981.

Citation: "For their discovery of superfluidity in helium-3" (with David M. Lee and Douglas D. Osheroff).

Life Work: Superfluidity in helium-3 was discovered by accident when trying to discover an antiferromagnetic phase in helium-3. Using a specially built apparatus, the trio examined the behavior of helium-3 when it had been cooled to a temperature near absolute zero. A problem with the thermometer's readings led the scientists to monitor the internal pressure of the sample under external pressure that was increased over time. As they did so, they observed superfluidity in the sample for the first time. The discovery allows scientists to observe the world of quantum mechanics and also provide answers regarding the origin of the universe. Helium-3 may also help scientists to understand and develop high-temperature superconductors and to make materials that become superconducting closer to room temperature.

Publications: "Evidence for a New Phase of Solid He3," with D. M. Lee and D. D. Osheroff, *Physical Review Letters* 28 (April 1972): 885. "Low Temperature Science— What Remains for the Physicist?" *Physics Today* (August 1981): 144–46. "Experimental Techniques in Condensed Matter Physics at Low Temperatures," *Physics Today* (1988): 129–31.

Bibliography: *New York Times*, October 10, 1996, p. D21. *Science News* 150 (October 19, 1996): 247.

CHU, STEVEN

Prize: Physics, 1997. *Birth:* February 28, 1948; St. Louis, Missouri. *Nationality:* American. *Education:* University of Rochester, B.S., 1970; University of California, Berkeley, Ph.D., 1976. *Career:* Stanford University, Professor of Physics and Applied Physics, 1987–; Stanford University, Theodore and Frances Geballe Professor of Humanities and Sciences, 1990–. *Other Awards:* Broida Prize, American Physical Society, 1987; Arthur Schawlow Prize for Laser Sciences, 1994; Richtinger Memorial Prize, American Physical Society, 1990; King Faisal Prize for Science, 1993; William F. Meggers Award, Optical Society of America, 1994.

Citation: "For development of methods to cool and trap atoms with laser light" (with Claude Cohen-Tannoudji and William D. Phillips).

Life Work: In 1985 Chu, working at Bell Laboratories, developed the original method for cooling atoms. The techniques were needed because atoms and molecules in gases move fast, at about 2,500 miles per hour, so detailed observations are difficult. To slow atomic and molecular motion, temperatures needed to be chilled to absolute zero (0°K), where gases condense and freeze. Chu made an apparatus that allowed gases to be chilled to within a fraction of a degree of absolute zero without freezing. It consisted of six laser beams that bombard the gas's constituent particles from all directions, slowing their motion. The laser light acts like an extremely thick liquid, called optical molasses. Sodium atoms were cooled to 240 microkelvins, equal to the theoretical Doppler limit. In 1987 the system was augmented by a magnetooptical trap, which prevented atoms from falling from the optical molasses. According to the Nobel Academy, Chu constructed an atomic fountain, in which the laser cooled atoms are sprayed up from a trap like jets of water. The discovery was the basis of a new generation of atomic clocks that are accurate to one second in 3 billion years.

Publications: "Laser Manipulation of Atoms and Particles," *Science* 253 (August 23, 1991): 861–66. "Laser Trapping of Neutral Particles," *Scientific American* 71 (February 1992).

Bibliography: *American Scientist* 86 (January/February 1988): 22–25. *New York Times*, October 16, 1997, p. A16. *New York Times*, June 30, 1998, p. F1.

COHEN-TANNOUDJI, CLAUDE NESSIM

Prize: Physics, 1997. *Birth:* April 1, 1933, Constantine, Algeria. *Nationality:* French. *Education:* École Normale Supérieure, Ph.D., 1962. *Career:* Professor, Faculte des Sciences, Collège de France, 1964–73. *Other Awards:* Ampere Prize, 1980; Lilienfeld Prize, American Physical Society, 1990; Charles Townes Award, Optical Society of America, 1993; Harvey Prize, 1995; CNRS Gold Medal, 1996.

Citation: "For development of methods to cool and trap atoms with laser light" (with Steven Chu and William D. Phillips).

Life Work: Cohen-Tennoudji and his colleagues made important advances in chilling temperatures to within 1°K, which corresponds to a speed of only 0.8 inches per second. He explained the results in terms of the structure of the lowest energy levels of the sodium atom. He overcame the recoil limit associated with an atom's recoil velocity from emitting a single photon, by converting the slowest atoms to a dark state in which they do not absorb photons. This discovery has applications in the Bose-Einstein condensation in dilute gases and also atomic clocks, atomic interferometers for ultra-high precision measurements of the gravitational acceleration, atomic lithography of integrated circuits, and atom lasers.

Publications: *Photons and Atoms* (New York: Wiley, 1989). "New Mechanisms for Laser Cooling," with W. D. Phillips, *Physics Today* (October 1990): 33–44. *Quantum*

Mechanics, 2 vols. (New York: Wiley, 1993). *Atoms in Electromagnetic Fields* (River Edge, N.J.: World Scientific, 1994).

Bibliography: *New York Times,* October 16, 1997, p. A16. *Science* (May 26, 1995): 1212–14.

PHILLIPS, WILLIAM D.

Prize: Physics, 1997. *Birth:* November 5, 1948; Wilkes-Barre, Pennsylvania. *Nationality:* American. *Education:* Juniata College, Pennsylvania, B.S., 1970; Massachusetts Institute of Technology, Ph.D., 1976. *Career:* National Institute of Standards and Technology, Physicist, 1978–. *Other Awards:* Silver Medal, U.S. Department of Commerce, 1983; Gold Medal, 1993.

Citation: "For development of methods to cool and trap atoms with laser light" (with Steven Chu and Claude Cohen-Tannoudji).

Life Work: Phillips's field of investigation was the manipulation of atoms by laser cooling and trapping and atom optics and the application of these and other techniques to atomic clocks. Phillips and his associates developed several new methods for measuring temperature and achieved temperatures of $40°K$, a temperature much lower than the Doppler limit.

Publications: "Cooling and Trapping Atoms," with H. J. Metcalf, *Scientific American* (March 1987): 36–44. "New Mechanisms for Laser Cooling," with C. N. Cohen-Tannoudji, *Physics Today* (October 1990): 33–44. "Laser Manipulation of Atoms and Ions," *Proceedings of the International School of Physics,* 118 (1992).

Bibliography: *New York Times,* October 16, 1997, p. A16.

LAUGHLIN, ROBERT B.

Prize: Physics, 1998. *Birth:* November 1, 1950; Visalia, California. *Nationality:* American. *Education:* Massachusetts Institute of Technology, Ph.D. 1979. *Career:* Stanford University, Professor, 1993–. *Other Awards:* E. O. Lawrence Award for Physics, 1985; Oliver E. Buckley Prize, American Physical Society, 1986; Franklin Institute Medal, 1998.

Citation: "For their discovery of a new form of quantum fluid with fractionally charged excitations" (with Horst L. Störmer and Daniel C. Tsui).

Life Work: In 1982 Stormer and Tsui carried out experiments in which, using low temperatures and strong magnetic fields, they found more steps in the Hall resistance that suggested that the involved particles had fractional electrical charges. This mystified scientists who could not explain this phenomenon. A year later, Laughlin, at Bell Labs and then Lawrence Livermore National Laboratory, solved the mystery with a theoretical explanation. He proposed that the low temperature and the intense magnetic field made the electrons condense into a new kind of quantum fluid. Earlier, scientists had observed other quantum fluids at very low temperatures in liquid helium and in superconductor materials. Laughlin's quantum fluid exhibited many unusual properties, including one in which the participating electrons behaved as fractionally charged quasiparticles. Laughlin showed that such quasiparticles had exactly the right electric charges to explain Stormer and Tsui's findings. This was confirmed later by experiments using microelectronics.

Publications: "Quantized Hall Conductivity in Two Dimensions," *Physical Review B* 23 (May 15, 1981): 5632–33. "Excitons in the Fractional Quantum Hall Effect," *Physica B&C* 126 (November 1984): 254–59. "Fractional Statistics, Gas with Spin and Stability of the Superfluid State," *Physical Review B* 48 (October 1, 1993): 10382–90.

Bibliography: *New York Times*, October 14, 1998, p. A16.

STORMER, HORST L.

Prize: Physics, 1998. *Birth:* April 6, 1949; Frankfurt am Main, Germany. *Nationality:* German. *Education:* University of Frankfurt, B.S., 1970; University of Stuttgart, Ph.D., 1977. *Career:* Bell Labs, New Jersey, AT&T, Department Head, 1983–. *Other Awards:* Oliver E. Buckley Prize, 1991; Otto Klung Prize, 1994.

Citation: "For their discovery of a new form of quantum fluid with fractionally charged excitations" (with Robert B. Laughlin and Daniel C. Tsui).

Life Work: Stormer and Tsui discovered in 1982 a new aspect of the Hall effect, first demonstrated by the American physicist Edwin H. Hall in 1879. Hall found that when a conductor carrying an electric current is placed in a magnetic field that is perpendicular to the current flow, an electric field is created that is perpendicular to both the current and the magnetic field, because the magnetic field deflects the flow of electrons toward one side of the current-carrying material. This electric field gives rise to the Hall voltage, and the ratio of this voltage to the current is called the Hall resistance. In 1980 the German physicist Klaus von Klitzing discovered a variation of the Hall effect called the integer quantum Hall effect. For moderate applied magnetic fields, the Hall resistance changes smoothly with changes in the strength of the field. However, in high magnetic fields and temperatures near absolute zero using semiconductor devices, in which the electron motion was confined to two dimensions, the Hall resistance was quantized, that is, it changed not discretely but in discrete steps. When Stormer and Tsui used lower temperatures and stronger fields, they found more steps in the Hall resistance in which the involved particles had fractional electric charges, such as one-seventh of an electron. It was an indirect demonstration of the existence of quasiparticles.

Publications: "The Fractional Quantum Hall Effect," with J. P. Eisenstein, *Science* (June 22, 1990): 1510. "Composite Fermions," with D. Tsui, *Physics News* (1994).

Bibliography: *New York Times*, October 14, 1998, p. A16.

TSUI, DANIEL C.

Prize: Physics, 1998. *Birth:* February 28, 1939; Henan, China. *Nationality:* Chinese; later U.S. citizen. *Education:* Augustana College, B.A., 1961; University of Chicago, Ph.D., 1967. *Career:* Bell Labs, Director, 1968–82; Arthur Legrand Doty Professor of Electrical Engineering, Princeton University, 1982–. *Other Awards:* Oliver E. Buckley Condensed Matter Physics Prize, American Physical Society, 1984.

Citation: "For their discovery of a new form of quantum fluid with fractionally charged excitations" (with Robert B. Laughlin and Horst L. Störmer).

Life Work: Tsui and Stormer carried out experiments on the Hall effect and Hall resistance and its variation, called the integer quantum Hall effect, using samples of very high purity, lower temperatures, and higher magnetic fields. They discovered many new Hall resistance steps with values equal to the same constant divided by various fractions. The fractional quantum Hall effect was later explained by Laughlin.

Publications: "The Fractional Quantum Hall Effect," *IIEE Journal of Quantum Electronics* 22 (1986). "Composite Fermions," with H. Stormer, *Physics News* (1994).

Bibliography: *New York Times*, October 14, 1998, p. A16. *Notable Twentieth-Century Scientists* (Farmington Hills, Mich.: Gale, 1996).

'T HOOFT, GERARDUS

Prize: Physics, 1999. *Birth:* July 5, 1946; Den Helder, Netherlands. *Nationality:* Dutch. *Education:* University of Utrecht, Ph.D., 1972. *Career:* Researcher, European Center for Nuclear Research, Switzerland, 1972–74; Professor, Institute for Theoretical Physics, University of Utrecht, Netherlands, 1974–. *Other Awards:* Winkler Prins Prize, 1974; Azko Prize, 1977; Lorentz Medal, 1986; Dannie Heineman Prize, 1979; Wolf Prize, 1981; Pius XI Medal, 1983; Franklin Medal, Franklin Institute, 1995; Spinoza Premium, 1995; Gian Carlo Wick Medal, 1997; Oskar Klein Silver Medal, 1999; High Energy Physics Prize, 1999.

Citation: "For elucidating the quantum structure of electroweak interactions in physics" (with Martinus J. G. Veltman).

Life Work: 't Hooft's fields of investigation are the building blocks of the universe, especially gauge theories in elementary particle physics. Forces among elementary particles are either very weak, or they must be mediated by gauge fields. These fields are based on the same principles as the electro-magnetic fields, but are more complicated. He has also worked on quantum gravity and black holes, trying to devise laws of physics governing the behavior of tiny black holes.

Publications: "Gauge Theories of the Forces between Elementary Particles," *Scientific American* (June 1980): 90. *In Search of the Ultimate Buliding Blocks* (Cambridge: Cambridge University Press, 1997).

Bibliography: *New York Times*, October 13, 1999, p. A8. *New York Times*, October 17, 1999, pp. 4, 6.

VELTMAN, MARTINUS J. G.

Prize: Physics, 1999. *Birth:* June 27, 1931; Waalvijk, Netherlands. *Nationality:* Dutch. *Education:* University of Utrecht, Ph.D., 1963. *Career:* Researcher, CERN, Switzerland, 1963–66; Professor, University of Utrecht, Netherlands, 1966–81; John D. MacArthur Professor of Physics, University of Michigan, Professor Emeritus, 1981–. *Awards:* Von Humboldt Award, 1989; Fifth Physica, Leipzig, 1990; Dutch Order of the Lion of Queen Beatrix, 1992; High Energy and Particle Physics Prize, 1993; P. A. M. Dirac Medal and Prize, 1996.

Citation: "For elucidating the quantum structure of electroweak interactions in physics" (with Gerardus 't Hooft).

Life Work: Veltman is one of the developers of the gauge theories. His fields of investigation are the field theoretical aspects of gauge theories, and their applications to elementary particle physics, radiative corrections in the Standard Model, the Higgs sector of the Standard Model and its implications on the new physics beyond the Standard Model, and the vacuum structure of field theories. In the 1960s scientists formulated the electroweak theory, which unites electromagnetism and the weak interactions (which govern radioactive decay). However, this theory gave unreasonable results and therefore was suspect. In mathematical terms, there is a conflict because the force-mediating particles in electromagnetism are massless, noninteracting photons, but those in the electroweak interaction include the massive and interactive W and Z bosons. The electroweak theory is a nonabelian gauge theory, more complex than an abelian theory such as quantum electrodynamics. Veltman developed a computer program for simplifying the complicated expressions that arise in quantum field theories. His work had great impact on the development of particle physics and provided a method for performing precise calculations in the field.

Publications: *Diagrammatica: The Path to Feynman Diagrams* (New York: Cambridge University Press, 1995). "The Higgs Boson," *Scientific American* (November 1986): 88.

Bibliography: *Economist* (October 16, 1999). *New York Times*, October 13, 1999, p. A8. *New York Times*, October 17, 1999, pp. 4, 6.

ALFEROV, ZHORES I.

Prize: Physics, 2000. *Born:* March 15, 1930; Vitebsk, Belorussia, USSR. *Nationality:* Russian. *Education:* V. I. Ulyanov (Lenin) Electrotechnical Institute, Leningrad (St. Petersburg) Doctor of Science in Physics and Mathematics, Ioffe Institute, 1970. *Career:* Physicotechnical Institute, Staff Member and Researcher, 1953–67; Head of the Laboratory, 1967–87; Director, 1987–. *Other Awards:* Ballantine Medal of the Franklin Institute, 1971; Lenin Prize, 1972; Hewlett-Packard Europhysics Prize, 1978; GaAs Symposium Award and H. Welker Medal, 1987; Karpinski Prize, 1989; Ioffe Prize, 1996; Nicholas Holonyak Jr. Award, 2000.

Citation: "For basic work on information and communication technology" (with Jack S. Kilby and Herbert Kroemer); "for developing semiconductor heterostructures used in high-speed- and opto-electronics" (with Herbert Kroemer).

Life Work: Alferov and Herbert Kroemer received half the prize for their work on semiconductor heterostructures (sandwich structures made of numerous semiconductor layers, tailored to produce certain electronic effects, or to emit light), semiconductor layers, epitaxial growth techniques (ability to lay down very thin layers of atoms in a highly controlled manner and optoelectronics (combining the information processing abilities of both electrons and photons) usually based on gallium arsenide, stacked on top of each other. Alferov and Kroemer independently proposed ideas to build semiconductor lasers from heterostructure devices. He built the first semiconductor laser from gallium arsenide and aluminum arsenide in 1969. This breakthrough was the key to fiber optics, CD players, bar code readers, laser pointers, mobile phones and laser diodes, which drive the flow of information through the Internet, and the light-emitting diodes used in modern car brake lights.

Publication: "The History and Future of Semiconductor Heterostructures from the Point of View of a Russian Scientist," *Physica Scripta* T68 (1996): 32.

Bibliography: *New York Times*, October 11, 2000, p. A16. *New York Times*, October 12, 2000, p. A3.

KILBY, JACK S.

Prize: Physics, 2000. *Born:* November 8, 1923; Jefferson City, Missouri. *Nationality:* American. *Education:* University of Illinois, Urbana-Champaign, B.S. 1947; University of Wisconsin, Madison, M.S., 1950. *Career:* Texas Instruments, 1958–83; Texas A &

M University, professor, 1978–85. *Other Awards:* National Medal of Science, 1970; National Inventors Hall of Fame, 1982; Stuart Ballantine Medal, 1967; Vladimir Zworykin Award, 1975; Holley Medal, 1982; IIEE's Medal of Honor, 1986; Cledo Brunetti Award, 1978; David Sarnoff Award, 1966.

Citation: "For basic work on information and communication technology" (with Zhores I. Alferov and Herbert Kroemer); "for his part in the invention of the integrated circuit."

Life Work: Kilby's invention of the monolithic integrated circuit, the microchip, in 1958 at Texas Instruments laid the conceptual and technical foundation for the entire field of modern microelectronics. Kilby used geranium and gold connectors and embedded the entire set of components in a single block of semiconductor—an element that conducts electricity between insulators and metals. It has been described as the nerve cell of the information age. It was this breakthrough that made possible the sophisticated high-speed computers with large capacity semiconductor memories. He later coinvented the hand held calculator and the thermal printer used in portable data terminals.

Publication: "Invention of the Integrated Circuit," *IIEE Transactions on Electronic Devices* ED-27, no. 7 (July 1976): 648.

Bibliography: *New York Times*, October 11, 2000, p. A16. *Notable Twentieth-Century Scientists* (Farmington Hills, Mich.: Gale, 1996).

KROEMER, HERBERT

Prize: Physics, 2000. *Born:* August 25, 1928, Weimar, Germany. *Nationality:* German; later U.S. citizen. *Education:* Doctorate in Physics, University of Gottingen, 1952. *Career:* RCA Laboratories, Princeton and Varian Associates, Palo Atlo, Calif., 1957–76; University of California, Santa Barbara, Professor, 1976–. *Other Awards:* J. J. Ebers Award of the Electron Devices Group of IEEE, 1973; Heinrich Welker Medal of the International Symposium on GaAs and Related Compounds; Joack Morton Award, 1986; Alexander von Humboldt Research Award, 1994.

Citation: "For basic work on information and communication technology" (with Zhores I. Alferov and Jack S. Kilby); "for developing semiconductor heterostructures used in high-speed- and opto-electronics" (with Zhores I. Alferov).

Life Work: Kroemer pioneered a radical new kind of transistor called a heterotransistor which can handle much higher frequencies than its predecessors. Independent of Alferov, he came up with the idea of using techology to fire laser light. This breakthrough was the key to fiber optics, CD players, bar code readers, and light-emitting diodes used in modern car brake lights. Kroemer was one of the early pioneers in molecular beam epitaxy, concentrating on applying the technology to untried new materials systems, such as GaP and GaAs on silicon. Since 1985 his work has moved to 6.1Å group of materials,

InAs, GaSb, and AlSb. His current research continues to involve a combination of these materials in a number of projects at the forefront of the heterostructure field.

Publications: "Heterostructure Bipolar Transistors and Integrated Circuits," *Proceedings IIEE* 70 (1982): 13–25. *Quantum Mechanics* (Paramus, N.J.: Prentice-Hall, 1994). "Bond Offsets and Chemical Bonding: The Basis for Heterostructure Applications," *Physica Scripta* T68 (1996): 10.

Bibliography: *New York Times*, October 11, 2000, p. A6.

PHYSIOLOGY
OR
MEDICINE

BEHRING, EMIL ADOLPH VON

Prize: Physiology or Medicine, 1901. *Born:* March 15, 1854; Hansdorf, Germany. *Died:* March 31, 1917; Marburg, Germany. *Nationality:* German. *Education:* Friedrich-Wilhelms University, Germany, M.D., 1878; Friedrich-Wilhelms University, Germany, Ph.D., 1880. *Career:* Charite Hospital, Berlin, Germany, Intern, 1880–81; Prussian Army, Surgeon, 1881–87; Academy for Military Medicine, Berlin, Germany, Professor, 1888–89; Institute of Hygiene, Berlin, Germany, Researcher, 1889–93; University of Halle, Germany, Professor, 1894–95; University of Marburg, Germany, Professor and Administrator, 1895–1917. *Other Awards:* Officer, Legion of Honor, 1895; Prize, Paris Académie d' Médicine, 1895; Prize, Institute of France, 1895; Nobility, Prussia, 1901; Iron Cross, Germany, World War I.

Citation: "For his work on serum therapy, especially its application against diphtheria, by which he has opened a new road in the domain of medical science and thereby placed in the hands of the physician a victorious weapon against illness and deaths."

Life Work: Behring's field of investigation was tetanus and diphtheria. In 1890 he showed that rabbits and mice immunized against tetanus developed the ability to render harmless the toxic substance which the tetanus bacillus produces. Extending this finding to diphtheria, he showed that nonimmune animals could be protected against the toxin by an injection of antitoxin from immune animals. In 1913 he produced a vaccine that provided a lasting protection against the disease.

Publications: "Uber das Zustandekommen der Diptherie-Immunitat und der Tetanus-Immunitat bei Thieren," with S. Kitasato, *Deutsche Medizinische Wochenschrift* 16 (1890): 113–14 *Gesammelte Abhandlungen zur Atiologischen Therapie von Ansteckenden Krankeiten* (Leipzig, Germany: Thieme, 1893). *Gesammelte Abhandlungen. Nene Folge* (Bonn: A. Marcus and E. Webers, 1915).

Bibliography: *Dictionary of Scientific Biography* (New York: Scribner's, 1970), vol. 1, pp. 575–78. A. S. Macnalty, "Emil von Behring." *British Medical Journal* 1 (1954): 668–70. Hellmuth Unger, *Emil von Behring, Sein Lebenswerk Als Vovergangliches Erbe* (Hamburg: Hoffman und Campe, 1948). Heinz Zeiss and R. Bieling, *Behring, Gestalt und Werk* (Berlin: Grunewald, B. Schultz, 1940).

ROSS, SIR RONALD

Prize: Physiology or Medicine, 1902. *Born:* May 13, 1857; Almora, India. *Died:* September 16, 1932; London, England. *Nationality:* British. *Education:* St. Bartholomew's Medical School Hospital, England, MRCS diploma (medical degree), 1879. *Career:* Indian Medical Service, Doctor, 1881–99; School of Tropical Medicine, Liverpool, England, Professor, 1899–1917; London, England, Physician, 1917–23;

Hospital for Tropical Diseases, Ross Institute, London, England, Director, 1923–32. *Other Awards:* Parke Gold Medal, 1895; Cameron Prize, 1901; Royal Medal, Royal Society, 1909; Knighthood, 1911.

Citation: "For his work on malaria, by which he has shown how it enters the organism and thereby has laid the foundation for successful research on this disease and methods of combating it."

Life Work: Ross's field of investigation was malaria. Working in India, he worked on the mosquito as a carrier of malaria. He came across a genus of the species *Anopheles*, which transmits the disease to both humans and birds.

Publications: "On Some Peculiar Pigmented Cells Found in Two Mosquitoes Fed on Malarial Blood," *British Medical Journal* 2 (1897): 1786–88. *The Prevention of Malaria* (London: J. Murray, 1910). *Studies on Malaria* (London: J. Murray, 1928).

Bibliography: *Dictionary of Scientific Biography* (New York: Scribner's, 1975), vol. 11, pp. 555–57. R. L. Megroz, *Ronald Ross, Discoverer and Creator* (London: Allen and Unwin, 1931). Sir Ronald Ross, *Memoirs, with a Full Account of the Great Malaria Problem and Its Solution* (London: J. Murray, 1923).

FINSEN, NIELS RYBERG

Prize: Physiology or Medicine, 1903. *Born:* December 15, 1860; Thorshavn, Denmark. *Died:* September 24, 1904; Copenhagen, Denmark. *Nationality:* Danish. *Education:* University of Copenhagen, Denmark, M.D., 1890. *Career:* University of Copenhagen, Denmark, Professor, 1890–93; Finsen Ray Institute, Copenhagen, Denmark, Founder and Director, 1896–1904. *Other Awards:* Knight of the Order of Dannebrog, 1899; Danish Gold Medal for Merit; Cameron Prize, University of Edinburg, Scotland, 1904.

Citation: "In recognition of his contribution to the treatment of diseases, especially lupus vulgaris, with concentrated light radiation, whereby he has opened a new avenue for medical science."

Life Work: Finsen's field of investigation was phototherapy, or the therapeutic effect of light. From earlier investigations he knew that light inhibits the growth of certain bacterial colonies and also kills bacteria. In 1889 a Swedish scientist had discovered that ultraviolet light irritates biological tissues. Finsen also found that red light helped to cure smallpox lesions. Finsen extended his investigations to artificial light, especially light generated by electrical carbon arcs. He used this technique to successfully treat patients of lupus vulgaris, a disfiguring skin disease.

Publications: "Red Light Treatment of Smallpox," *British Medical Journal* 2 (1895): 1412–14. *Om Anvendelse i Medicinen af Koncentrede Kemiske Lysstraaler* [On the Use in Medicine of Concentrated Chemical Rays] (Copenhagen: F. Hegel and Son, 1896).

Phototherapy (London: E. Arnold, 1901). *Om Bekaempelse af Lupus Vulgaris Med Rede Gorelse for de i Danmark Opnaaede Resultater* (Copenhagen: Gyldendalske Boghandels Forlag, 1902). *Die Bekampfung des Lupus Vulgaris* (Jena, Germany: G. Fischer, 1903).

Bibliography: *Dictionary of Scientific Biography* (New York: Scribner's, 1970), vol. 4, pp. 620–21. Paul De Kruif, *Men Against Death* (New York: Harcourt, Brace, 1934), pp. 283–99.

PAVLOV, IVAN PETROVICH

Prize: Physiology or Medicine, 1904. *Born:* September 27, 1849; Ryazan, Russia. *Died:* February 27, 1936; Leningrad, USSR. *Nationality:* Russian. *Education:* Military Medical Academy, Russia, graduate, 1879; Military Medical Academy, Russia, M.D., 1883. *Career:* Military Medical Academy, St. Petersburg, Russia, Professor, 1888–1924; Institute of Experimental Medicine, St. Petersburg, Russia, Director, 1891–1936. *Other Awards:* Gold Medal, University of St. Petersburg, Russia, 1875; Copley Medal, Royal Society, 1915.

Citation: "In recognition of his work on the physiology of digestion, through which knowledge on vital aspects of the subject has been transformed and enlarged."

Life Work: Pavlov's field of investigation was surgery of the internal organs, such as the digestive system. Working with animals, he discovered how each part of the digestive system adds a different combination of chemicals to food, breaking it down to absorbable units of protein, fat, and carbohydrate. His experiments on the influence of the nervous system on the actions of the internal organs led to his observations of conditioned reflexes. These investigations occupied him for the rest of his life.

Publications: *The Work of the Digestive Glands,* (Philadelphia: J.B. Lippincott, 1910). *Conditioned Reflexes* (London: Oxford University Press, 1927). *Polnoe Sobranie Sochiney* [Completed Collected Works] (Moscow: Academy of Sciences, 1954).

Bibliography: Boris P. Babkins, *Pavlov: A Biography* (Chicago: University of Chicago Press, 1949). *Dictionary of Scientific Biography* (New York: Scribner's, 1974), vol. 10, pp. 431–36. J. A. Gray, *Ivan Pavlov* (New York: Penguin, 1981). Albert Parry, *The Russian Scientist* (New York: Macmillan, 1973), pp. 78–89.

KOCH, HEINRICH HERMANN ROBERT

Prize: Physiology or Medicine, 1905. *Born:* December 11, 1843; Clausthal, Germany. *Died:* May 27, 1910; Baden-Baden, Germany. *Nationality:* German. *Education:* University of Göttingen, Germany, M.D., 1866. *Career:* Hamburg, Germany, Doctor,

1866; Lagenhagen Lunatic Asylum, Germany, Doctor, 1866–68; Poznan, Germany, Doctor, 1868; Rakwitz, Germany, Doctor, 1869; German Army, Doctor, 1870–71; Wollstein, Germany, Doctor, 1872–80; Health Department, Berlin, Germany, Doctor, 1880–85; Berlin University, Germany, Professor and Administrator, 1885–90; Institute for Infectious Diseases, Berlin, Germany, Director, 1891–1904. *Other Awards:* Harben Medal, 1901; Prussian Order Pour le Mérite, 1906; Robert Koch Medal, 1908.

Citation: "For his investigations and discoveries in relation to tuberculosis."

Life Work: Koch's field of investigation was epidemic diseases. In a series of experiments he proved that anthrax bacillus was the sole cause of anthrax in cattle. It was the first clear demonstration of the bacterial origin of any disease. In 1882 he followed by isolating the bacterium that causes tuberculosis. His principles and methods for obtaining a proof of the cause of a disease laid the foundations of medical microbiology. Sent to India by the German government, Koch isolated the microbe responsible for cholera. Eventually, he helped to develop public health measures for controlling most of the infectious diseases of the time, especially typhoid fever, typhus, rinderpest, plague, and sleeping sickness.

Publications: *Investigations into the Etiology of Traumatic Infective Diseases* (London: New Sydenham Society, 1880). "Etiology of Tuberculosis," *American Review of Tuberculosis* 25 (1932): 285–323. "Etiology of Anthrax, Bases on the Ontogeny of the Anthrax Bacillus," *Medical Classics* 2 (1937–38): 787–820. "Methods for Studying, Preserving and Photographing Bacteria," in *Microbiology Contributions from 1776–1908.* (New Brunswick, N.J.: Rutgers University Press, 1960), pp. 67–73.

Bibliography: C. Barlowe, *Robert Koch* (Portland, Ore.: Heron Books, 1971). Thomas D. Brock, *Robert Koch* (New York: Springer-Verlag, 1988). *Dictionary of Scientific Biography* (New York: Scribner's 1973), vol. 7, pp. 420–35.

GOLGI, CAMILLO

Prize: Physiology or Medicine, 1906. *Born:* July 7, 1843; Corteno, Italy. *Died:* January 21, 1926; Pavia, Italy. *Nationality:* Italian. *Education:* University of Padua, Italy, M.D., 1865. *Career:* Pavia, Italy, Doctor and Researcher, 1865–72; University of Pavia, Italy, Professor, 1875–78; University of Siena, Italy, Professor, 1879–80; University of Pavia, Italy, Professor, 1880–1918.

Citation: "In recognition of their work on the structure of the nervous system" (with Santiago Ramón y Cajal).

Life Work: Golgi is best known for his method of microscopic study by staining individual nerve cells. Golgi found that by immersing the hardened slices of nerve tissues in a silver nitrate solution, the neurons were stained black, which made them stand out boldly against the background. This method was adopted by other neuroanatomists. Golgi himself classified different types of neurons and made many important discoveries about the structure of individual neurons and the central nervous system. His most famous discovery was that of the Golgi apparatus or the fine network of interlaced threads in a nerve cell. Later in life he concentrated his research on malaria.

Publications: *Opera Omnia* [*Collected Works*], 4 vols (Milan: U. Hoepli, 1903–29).

Bibliography: J. Chorobski, "Camillo Golgi, 1843–1926," *Archives of Neurology* (Chicago) 33 (1935): 163–70. *Dictionary of Scientific Biography* (New York: Scribner's, 1973), vol. 5, pp. 459–61.

RAMON Y CAJAL, SANTIAGO

Prize: Physiology or Medicine, 1906. *Born:* May 1, 1852; Petilla de Aragon, Spain. *Died:* October 18, 1934; Madrid, Spain. *Nationality:* Spanish. *Education:* University of Zaragoza, Spain, licentiate in medicine, 1873; University of Zaragoza, Spain, doctorate in medicine, 1877. *Career:* Army Medical Service, 1874–76; University of Zaragoza, Spain, Professor, 1876–83; University of Valencia, Spain, Professor, 1833–87; University of Barcelona, Spain, Professor, 1887–92; University of Madrid, Spain, Professor, 1892–1922; Institute Cajal, Madrid, Researcher, 1922–34. *Other Awards:* Fauvelle Prize, 1896; Rubio Prize, 1897; Moscow Prize, 1900; Martinez y Molina Prize, 1902; Helmholtz Gold Medal, 1905; Echegaray Medal, 1922.

Citation: "In recognition of their work on the structure of the nervous system" (with Camillo Golgi).

Life Work: Ramon y Cajal's field of investigation was the nervous system. Using Golgi's silver nitrate method for staining nerve tissues, he published detailed and accurate descriptions of the structures of the individual neurons. He was able to trace each fiber to a specific nerve cell. He developed the neuron doctrine according to which the nervous system consists of many independent cells rather than a single network. Motor and sensory neurons had discrete functions although they interacted at synapses where two adjacent neurons met. An individual nerve cell consists of up to several thousand protruding fibers, called dendrites. One of these fibers, the axon, is different because it is longer, thicker, and covered with an insulating layer of fat called myelin. The dendrites are all on one side of the cell, pointing toward the outside, whereas the axons all extend in the direction of the brain. This persuaded Ramon y Cajal to formulate his theory of dynamic polarization, according to which nerve impulses are received by the dendrites but are transmitted by the axon. His description of the cellular structure is the foundation for studies of cerebral localization, which deals with the distribution of functions among the various parts of the brain.

Publications: *Manual de Anatomia Pathologica General* (Madrid: Moya, 1896). *Textura del Systema Nervioso del Hombre y de los Vertebrados* (Madrid: Moya, 1899–1904). *Degeneration and Regeneration of the Nervous System* trans. Raoul M. Day (London: Oxford University University Press, 1928).

Bibliography: Dorothy F. Cannon, *Explorer of the Human Brain: The Life of Santiago Ramon y Cajal. 1852–1934* (New York: Schuman, 1949). *Dictionary of Scientific Biography* (New York: Scribner's, 1975), vol. 11, pp. 273–76. Santiago Ramon y Cajal, *Recollections of My Life* (Cambridge: Massachusetts Institute of Technology Press, 1966).

LAVERAN, CHARLES LOUIS ALPHONSE

Prize: Physiology or Medicine, 1907. *Born:* June 18, 1845; Paris, France. *Died:* May 18, 1922; Paris, France. *Nationality:* French. *Education:* University of Strasbourg, France, M.D., 1867. *Career:* French Army, Surgeon, 1870–96; Pasteur Institute, Paris, France, Researcher, 1897–1922. *Other Awards:* Breant Prize, 1884; Jenner Medal, 1902; Moscow Prize, 1906; Commander of Legion of Honor, 1912.

Citation: "In recognition of his work on the role played by protozoa in causing diseases."

Life Work: Laveran's field of investigation was malaria. Working with French soldiers in Algeria, he found the malarial parasite *Plasmodium* inside the red blood cells of malarial patients. Later he worked on *Trypanosomiasis*, or African sleeping sickness, and found the tyrpanosomes, protozoans that are transmitted to human beings through flies.

Publications: *Traite des Fieures Palustres avec la Description des icrobes du Paludisme* (Paris: O. Doin, 1884). *Du Paludisme et de Son Hematozoaire* (Paris: G. Masson, 1891) *Les Hematozoaires de L'Homme et des Animaux* (Paris: Rueff, 1895). *Trypanosome et Trypanosomiases* (Paris: Masson, 1912).

Bibliography: *Dictionary of Scientific Biography* (New York: Scribner's, 1973), vol. 8, pp. 65–66. "Le Professeur Laveran," *Bulletin de la Société de Pathologie Exotique* 15 (1922): 373–78.

EHRLICH, PAUL

Prize: Physiology or Medicine, 1908. *Born:* March 14, 1854; Strehlen, Germany. *Died:* August 20, 1915; Bad Homburg, Germany. *Nationality:* German. *Education:* University of Leipzig, Germany, M.D., 1878. *Career:* Charite Hospital and University of Berlin, Germany, Doctor and Researcher, 1878–87; Robert Koch Institute, Berlin, Germany, Researcher and Administrator, 1890–95; State Institute for the Investigation and Control of Serum, Stieglitz, Germany, Director, 1896–99; Royal Institute for Experimental Therapy, Frankfurt, Germany, Director, 1899–1915. *Other Awards:* Geheimer Obermedizinalrat, 1907; Privy Councilor, 1911; Liebig Medal, Society of German Chemists, 1911; Cameron Prize, Edinburg, 1914.

Citation: "In recognition of their work on immunity" (with Ilya Mechnikov)

Life Work: Ehrlich's field of investigation was immunology. Early in his career, Ehrlich developed new dyes with specific affinities for different cell types that enabled him to distinguish different types of white blood cells, a crucial discovery for hematology. He set up standards for toxins, antitoxins, and serum samples that was later widely adopted and remains in use today. In 1899 he published his groundbreaking side-chain theory as applied to immunology. It states that antibodies can be produced only by direct chemical interactions between toxins or other antigens and cells. In response to such interactions, the cell overproduces the receptors that bind to the toxins in the blood-stream. Antibodies are therefore receptors (or reactive side-chains) of cells affected by the antigens. In 1906 Ehrlich discovered Salvarsan, a cure for syphilis.

Publications: *The Collected Papers of Paul Ehrlich,* ed. F. Himmelweit (New York: Pergamon Press, 1956–58).

Bibliography: E. Baumler, *Paul Ehrlich* (New York: Holmes and Meier, 1984). *Dictionary of Scientific Biography* (New York: Scribner's, 1971), vol. 4, pp. 295–305. Martha Marquandt, *Paul Ehrlich* (New York: Henry Schuman, 1951).

MECHNIKOV, ILYA ILYICH

Prize: Physiology or Medicine, 1908. *Born:* May 15, 1845; Kharkov, Russia. *Died:* July 15, 1916; Paris, France. *Nationality:* Russian; later French resident. *Education:* University of Kharkov, Russia, graduate, 1864; University of St. Petersburg, Russia, M.S., 1867; University of St. Petersburg, Russia, doctorate, 1868. *Career:* University of Odessa, Russia, Professor, 1867–69; University of St. Petersburg, Russia, Professor, 1870; University of Novorossiia, Russia, Professor, 1870–72; Messina, Sicily, Researcher, 1882–86; Bacteriological Institute, Odessa, Russia, Director, 1886–87; Pasteur Institute, Paris, France, Administrator to Director, 1888–1916. *Other Awards:* Copley Medal, 1908.

Citation: "In recognition of their work on immunity" (with Paul Ehrlich).

Life Work: Mechnikov's field of investigation was pathology. Studying the transparent starfish larvae he found mobile cells surround and engulf foreign bodies. If the foreign body was small enough the phagocytes (wandering cells) completely absorbed the invader and also resorbed and erased other tissues that were no longer needed. He concluded that phagocytes functioned as policing or sanitizing agents. Mechnikov characterized disease as a struggle between the morbid outside agents and the mobile cells of the organism itself. Cure results from the victory of the cells and immunity is the sign that they have acquired the ability to ward off further onslaught. Mechnikov's theory was a fundamental contribution to the nature of the immune response.

Publications: *Lectures on the Comparative Pathology of Inflammation, Delivered at the Pasteur Institute in 1891* (London: K. Pau, Trench, Trubner and Co., 1893). *Immunity in Infectious Diseases* (Cambridge: Cambridge University Press, 1907). *The Pro-*

longation of Life: Optimistic Studies (New York: G. P. Putnam's Sons, 1912). *The Nature of Man: Studies in Optimistic Philosophy* (London: Watts and Company, 1938).

Bibliography: *Dictionary of Scientific Biography* (New York: Scribner's, 1973), vol. 9, pp. 33–35. Olga Mechnikov, *The Life of Elie Metchnikoff, 1845–1916* (New York: Houghton-Mifflin, 1921). A. Tauber, *Metchnikoff and the Origins of Immunology* (New York: Oxford University Press, 1991).

KOCHER, EMIL THEODOR

Prize: Physiology or Medicine, 1909. *Born:* August 25, 1841; Berne, Switzerland. *Died:* July 27, 1917; Berne, Switzerland. *Nationality:* Swiss. *Education:* University of Berne, Switzerland, M.D., 1869. *Career:* University of Berne, Switzerland, Professor, 1872–1911.

Citation: "For his work on the physiology, pathology and surgery of the thyroid gland."

Life Work: Kocher was one of the greatest surgical innovators of his time. Among his contributions was a method of treating wounds with chlorine solutions. For certain injuries and diseases of the brain he developed the technique of trephination, which involved the surgical removal of a small section of the skull to relieve intercranial pressure. He was also an authority on gunshot wounds. His most important contribution, however, was his description of the functioning of the thyroid gland and the development of surgical procedures to correct malfunctions of the gland, including goiters. The thyroid gland synthesizes and secretes thyroid hormones, thyroxine and tri-iodothyronine, into the bloodstream. These hormones are critical to normal cellular metabolism. Excessive hormone output results in hyperthyrodism and reduced output in hypothyroidism and cretinism. When the supply of iodine in the human diet is too low, the thyroid gland may enlarge, resulting in goiter. Kocher established the procedure for proper thyroid surgery by not removing the entire gland but leaving the four parathyroid glands or the surrounding tissue. Kocher performed more than five thousand thyroidectomies and became the most famous thyroid surgeon in Europe.

Publications: *Chirurgische Operationslehre* (Jena, Germany: G. Fischer, 1892). *Operative Surgery* (New York: W. Wood and Co., 1894). *Vorlesungen uber Chirurgische Infektionskrankheiten* 2 vols., with E. Tavel (Basel, Switzerland: C. Sallman, 1895–1909).

Bibliography: *A Biographical Dictionary of Scientists* (New York: Wiley, 1969), pp. 295–96. T. Boni, *Theodor Kocher, 1841–1917* (Berne: Huber, 1991). Edgar Bonjour, *Theodor Kocher* (Berne: P. Haupt, 1981).

KOSSEL, KARL MARTIN LEONHARD ALBRECHT

Prize: Physiology or Medicine, 1910 *Born:* September 16, 1853; Rostock, Germany. *Died:* July 5, 1927; Heidelberg, Germany. *Nationality:* German. *Education:* University of Strasbourg, France, M.D., 1878. *Career:* University of Strasbourg, France, Professor, 1877–83; Berlin Physiological Institute, Germany, Director, 1883–87; University of Berlin, Germany, Professor, 1887–95; University of Marburg, Germany, Professor, 1895–1901; University of Heidelberg, Germany, Professor and Administrator, 1901–27.

Citation: "In recognition of the contributions to our knowledge of cell chemistry made through his work on proteins, including the nucleic substances."

Life Work: Kossel's earliest studies explored the chemical constituents of nuclein, a phosphorus-rich material discovered in the nuclei of pus cells. He isolated nuclein from yeast and determined the constituents of nucleic acids to be pyramidines, which includes thymine, cytosine, and urasil. He linked nuclein to the growth of tissues. He isolated histone, a simple, basic protein, from the nuclei of goose red blood cells.

Publications: *Leitfaden fur Medicinisch-Chemische Kurse* (Berlin: Fischer Medecin, 1888). *Die Gewebe des Menschlichen Korpers und Ihre Mikroskopische Untersuchung*, with W. Behrens and P. Schiefferdecker (Brunswick, Germany: Herald Braha, 1889). *The Protamines and Histones* (New York: Longmans, Green and Co., 1928).

Bibliography: "Albrecht Kossel zum Gedachtnis," *Hoppe-Seyler's Zeitschrift fur Physiologische Chemie* 177 (1928): 1–14. *Dictionary of Scientific Biography* (New York: Scribner's, 1973), vol. 7, pp. 466–68.

GULLSTRAND, ALLVAR

Prize: Physiology or Medicine, 1911. *Born:* June 5, 1862; Landskrona, Sweden. *Died:* July 21, 1930; Uppsala, Sweden. *Nationality:* Swedish. *Education:* Royal Caroline Institute, Sweden, M.D., 1888; Royal Caroline Institute, Sweden, Ph.D., 1890. *Career:* Royal Caroline Institute, Stockholm, Sweden, Lecturer, 1892–94; University of Uppsala, Sweden, Professor, 1894–1930. *Other Awards:* Grafe Medal, Deutsche Opthalmologische Gesellschaft, 1927.

Citation: "For his work on the dioptrics of the eye."

Life Work: Gullstrand's field of investigation was the structure of the eye. His goal was to elucidate the refractive index of the eye and the mechanism known as accommodation (the ability of the eye to focus an image) and to combine them into a general mathematical model. He determined that the lens of the eye continually changes its refractive index in order to produce an accurate image on the retina. He also introduced two new instruments for use in clinical examination of the eye—the slit lamp and the Gullstrand ophthalmoscope.

Publications: *Allgemeine Theorie der Monochromatischen Aberrationen and Ihre Nachsten Ergebnisse fur die Opththalmologie* (Uppsala, Sweden: Berling, 1900). *Die Optische Abbildung in Heterogenen Medien und die Dioptrik der Kristallinge des Menschen* (Uppsala, Switzerland: Almquist & Wiksells, 1908). *Einfuhrung in die Methoden der Dioptrik des Auges des Menschen* (Leipzig, Germany: S. Hirzil, 1911).

Bibliography: "Allvar Gullstrand," *Zeitschift fur Opthalmologische Optik* 18 (1930): 129–34. *Dictionary of Scientific Biography* (New York: Scribner's, 1972), vol. 5, pp. 590–91.

CARREL, ALEXIS

Prize: Physiology or Medicine, 1912. *Born:* June 28, 1873; Sainte Foy-les-Lyon, France. *Died:* November 5, 1944; Paris, France. *Nationality:* French. *Education:* University of Lyons, France, Bachelor of Letters, 1889; University of Lyons, France, Bachelor of Science, 1890; University of Lyons, France, M.D., 1900. *Career:* Lyons Hospital, France, Intern, 1896–1900; University of Lyons, France, Professor, 1900-1902; University of Chicago, Illinois, Researcher, 1905-1906; Rockefeller Institute, New York, Researcher, 1906–44. *Other Awards:* Legion d'Honneur, France, 1930; Nordhoff-Jung Prize for Cancer Research, 1930; Newman Foundation Award, University of Illinois, 1937; Rotary Club of New York Service Award, 1939.

Citation: Carrel: "In recognition of his work on vascular suture and the transplantation of blood vessels and organs."

Life Work: Early in his career Carrel devised a way to rejoin severed blood vessels. He not only succeeded in suturing arteries and veins, but was able to restore the flow of blood through severed vessels. By coating his instruments and threads with paraffin jelly, he was able to prevent clotting. In 1906 he conducted his first experiment in organ transplantation.

Publications: *Treatment of Infected Wounds,* with George Dehelly (New York: Hoeber, 1917). *The Culture of Organs,* with Charles A. Lindbergh (New York: Hoeber, 1938). *Man, the Unknown* (New York: Harper and Brothers, 1939).

Bibliography: *Dictionary of Scientific Biography* (New York, Scribner's, 1971), vol. 3, pp. 90–91. T. I. Malanin, *Surgery and Life: The Extraordinary Career of Alexis Carrel* (New York: Harcourt, Brace, Jovanovich, 1979). A. May, *The Two Lions of Lyons* (Rockville, Md.: Kabel Publishers, 1992). Robert Soupalt, *Alexis Carrel, 1873–1944* (Paris: Plon, 1952).

RICHET, CHARLES ROBERT

Prize: Physiology or Medicine, 1913. *Born:* August 26, 1850; Paris, France. *Died:* December 4, 1935; Paris, France. *Nationality:* French. *Education:* University of Paris, France, M.D., 1877; University of Paris, France, D.Sc., 1878. *Career:* Collège de France, Paris, Professor, 1876–87; University of Paris, France, Professor, 1887–1927. *Other Awards:* French Biological Society Institute Award, 1879; Cross of the Legion of Honor, 1926.

Citation: "In recognition of his work on anaphylaxis."

Life Work: Richet's field of investigation was microbiology. He proposed the idea that microbial diseases in animals may be caused by a toxin that is counteracted by chemical substances in the blood, extending his studies of hemotherapy to humans. In 1901, while investigating the toxicity of muscle plasma when injected directly into a vein, he discovered the phenomenon known as *anaphylaxis*, which is the reverse of normal immunization. In such cases, reinjection of smaller doses of the same poison, causes death. Now known as *anaphylactic shock*, it appears as exaggerated allergic reaction to foreign proteins or antigens. Thus, certain overly sensitive individuals can react to serum injections with vomiting, itching, lower blood pressure, paralysis of higher brain function, labored breathing, and low temperature.

Publications: *Physiology and Histology of the Cerebral Convolutions* (New York: W. Wood and Co., 1879). *La Chaleur Animale* (Paris: F. Alcan, 1889). *Dictionaire de Physiologie*, 10 vols., with P. Langlois and L. Lapicque (Paris: F. Alcan, 1895–1928). *Traite de Metapsychique* (Paris: F. Alcan, 1923).

Bibliography: *Biographical Dictionary of Scientists* (New York: Wiley, 1969), p. 443. *Dictionary of Scientific Biography* (New York: Scribner's, 1975), vol. 11, pp. 425–32. S. Wolf, *Brain, Mind, and Medicine* (New Brunswick, N.J.: Transaction Publishers, 1993).

BARANY, ROBERT

Prize: Physiology or Medicine, 1914. *Born:* April 22, 1876; Vienna, Austria. *Died:* April 8, 1936; Uppsala, Sweden. *Nationality:* Austrian; later Swedish resident. *Education:* University of Vienna, Austria, M.D., 1900. *Career:* University of Vienna, Austria, Professor and Researcher, 1903–14; Austrian Army, 1914–17; University of Uppsala, Sweden, Professor and Administrator, 1917–36. *Other Awards:* Politzer Prize, 1912; Belgian Academy of Sciences Prize, 1913; ERB Medal, German Neurological Society, 1913; Guyot Prize, 1914; Swedish Medical Society Medal, 1925.

Citation: "For his work on the physiology and pathology of the vestibular apparatus."

Life Work: Barany's field of investigation was nystagmus, which occasions vertigo. Vertigo arises from the overstimulation of the vertibular apparatus in the human ear, which consists of three tiny perpendicular loops of fluid filled tissue in the inner ear and serves as the organ of balance. Endolymph, the fluid in these canals, does not move in synchronization with the body but sloshes slightly like water in a bucket. The sloshing action is sensed by the cells in the vestibular apparatus and this sensation is used by the eye to create a sense of balance. The vestibular apparatus is a pair, one on each side of the head. Vertigo occurs when the eye and the vestibular apparatus are not in agreement and have different inputs. Barany demonstrated that the vestibular apparatus was sensitive to heat. Known as the caloric (or heat-related) reaction, this discovery was valuable in diagnosing patients with inner-ear infections.

Publications: *Untersuchungen uber den Vestibular-Apparat des Ohres* (Berlin: O. Coblentz, 1906). *Physiologie und Pathologie des Bogengang-Apparatus beim Menschen* (Leipzig, Germany: F. Deuticke, 1907). *Funktionelle Prufung des Vestibular-Apparatus*, with K. Wittmaack (Jena, Germany: G. Fischer, 1911). *Die Radikaloperation des Ohres ohne Gehoergangsplastik* (Leipzig, Germany: F. Deuticke, 1923).

Bibliography: *Dictionary of Scientific Biography* (New York: Scribner's, 1971), vol. 1, pp. 446–47. Ernst Wodak, *Der Baranysche Zeigeversuch* (Berlin: Urban and Schwarzenberg, 1927).

BORDET, JULES JEAN BAPTISTE VINCENT

Prize: Physiology or Medicine, 1919. *Born:* June 13, 1870; Soignies, Belgium. *Died:* April 6, 1961; Brussels, Belgium. *Nationality:* Belgian. *Education:* University of Brussels, Belgium, M.D., 1892. *Career:* Middlekerke Hospital, Belgium, Physician, 1892–94; Institut Pasteur, Paris, France, Researcher, 1894–1901; Institut Pasteur de Brabant, University of Brussels, Belgium, Professor and Administrator, 1901–40. *Other Awards:* Prix de la Vaille, Paris, 1911; Hansen Prize, 1913; Pasteur Medal, Swedish Medical Society, 1913.

Citation: "For his discoveries relating to immunity."

Life Work: Bordet's field of investigation was bacteriology and immunology. He demonstrated that serum consists of two substances: alexine, now known as complement, which is a bactericidal substance; and sensibilizer, now known as the antibody, which is the preventative substance. Continuing his work at the Pasteur Institute, Bordet established that hemagglutination (clumping) and hemolysis (destruction) of red blood cells are caused by bacteriolysis. He explained this phenomenon with a concept known as antigenic specificity, which states that proteins or antigens can be distinguished by using specific antiserums, or blood serums containing specific antibodies. Because complement combines with an antigen only if the antigen is bound to an antibody Bordet formulated the complement-fixation reaction. He also developed the indirect hemagglutination test in which red blood cells are used as carriers for foreign antigens and are agglutinated by complement and the appropriate antibody. Bordet devised complement-fixation tests, such as the Wassermann reaction for the diagnosis of syphilis. Later Bordet worked on the bacteriology of whooping cough and influenza.

Publications: *Studies in Immunity*, with others (New York: Wiley, 1909). *Traite de l'Immunite dans les Maladies Infectieuses* (Paris: Masson et cie, 1920). *Infection et immunite* (Paris: Flammarion, 1947).

Bibliography: *Biographical Memoirs of the Fellows of the Royal Society* (London: Royal Society, 1962), vol. 8, pp. 18–25. *Dictionary of Scientific Biography* (New York: Scribner's, 1971), vol. 2, pp. 300–301.

KROGH, SCHACK AUGUST STEENBERG

Prize: Physiology or Medicine, 1920. *Born:* November 15, 1874; Grenaa, Jutland, Denmark. *Died:* September 13, 1949; Copenhagen, Denmark. *Nationality:* Danish. *Education:* University of Copenhagen, Denmark, M.Sc., 1899; University of Copenhagen, Denmark, Ph.D., 1903. *Career:* University of Copenhagen, Denmark, Professor, 1899–1949. *Other Awards:* Seegan Prize, Vienna Academy of Sciences, 1906; Baly Medal, Royal College of Physicians, London, 1945.

Citation: "For his discovery of the capillary motor regulating mechanism."

Life Work: Early in life Krogh was a zoologist who researched the larvae of an aquatic organism, corethra. To aid his research he invented a microtonometer for measuring the pressure or tension of a gas dissolved in a fluid. His doctoral dissertation was on pulmonary and cutaneous respiration. Using the microtonometer to measure the partial gas pressures of oxygen and carbon dioxide in the blood and lungs Krogh demonstrated that the exchange of gases takes place in the lung by diffusion alone. With Christian Bohr, father of Niels Bohr, he described the effects of varying carbon dioxide concentrations on the dissociation of oxygen from hemoglobin. From 1916, as professor of zoology at the University of Copenhagen, he investigated the physiological regulation of capillary blood flow and oxygen delivery to the blood and cells. Capillaries open and close asynchronously, that is, out of rhythm with arterial pressure changes. Krogh proved that the number of functioning capillaries was controlled by local mechanical, chemical, and temperature stimuli and that the capillary diffusion surface was directly related to oxygen consumption. Krogh's analysis of pulmonary gas exchange and the regulation of capillary blood flow have many medical applications, such as the use of hypothermia during open heart surgery.

Publications: *Meddelelser fra Akademiet for de Tekniske Videnskaber* 1 (1949): 39–50.

Bibliography: *Dictionary of Scientific Biography* (New York: Scribner's, 1973), vol. 7, pp. 501–504. B. Schmidt-Nielsen, *August and Marie Krogh* (New York: Oxford University Press, 1995). *Yale Journal of Biology and Medicine* 24 (1951): 83–102.

HILL, ARCHIBALD VIVIAN

Prize: Physiology or Medicine, 1922. *Born:* September 26, 1886; Bristol, Gloucestershire, England. *Died:* June 3, 1977; Cambridge, England. *Nationality:* British. *Education:* Cambridge University, England, M.A., 1906; Cambridge University, England, Sc.D., 1907. *Career:* British Army, 1914–19; University of Manchester, England, Professor, 1920–23; University of London, England, Professor, 1923–51.

Citation: "For his discovery relating to the production of heat in the muscle."

Life Work: Hill's field of investigation was the energy exchanges that occur in muscles, especially the mechanics of muscle contraction. He proposed that muscle produces heat in animals in two separate phases, during contraction and after contraction, and that oxygen is needed only during the second phase. He confirmed Otto Meyefoff's finding that some lactic acid, formed from glycogen, is burned during contraction and that the rest is restored to its precursor. During moderate exercise, most of the lactic acid is oxidized in the muscle shortly after the exertion stops. However, during strenuous exercise, large amounts of lactic acid accumulate in the muscles and are diffused into the blood and body tissues. To describe this process, Hill coined the term "oxygen debt." Oxygen debt explains the deep breathing that follows exercise.

Publications: *Muscular Activity* (Baltimore: Williams and Wilkins, 1926). *Living Machinery* (New York: Harcourt Brace, 1927). *Muscular Movement in Man* (New York: McGraw-Hill, 1927). *Trails and Trials in Physiology* (Baltimore: Williams and Wilkins, 1965).

Bibliography: *Biographical Memoirs of the Fellows of the Royal Society* (London: Royal Society, 1978), vol. 24, pp. 71–149. *Perspectives in Biology and Medicine* 14 (1977): 27–42.

MEYERHOF, OTTO FRITZ

Prize: Physiology or Medicine, 1922. *Born:* April 12, 1884; Hanover, Germany. *Died:* October 6, 1951; Philadelphia, Pennsylvania. *Nationality:* German; later U.S. citizen. *Education:* University of Heidelberg, Germany, M.D., 1909. *Career:* University of Heidelberg, Germany, Researcher, 1909–11; University of Kiel, Germany, Professor, 1912–24; Kaiser Wilhelm Institute of Biologie, Berlin-Dahlem, Germany, Researcher, 1924–29; Kaiser Wilhelm Institute of Physiology, Heidelberg, Germany, Director, 1929–38; Research Centre Nationale, Paris, France, Director, 1938–40; University of Pennsylvania, Professor, 1940–51.

Citation: "For his discovery of the fixed relationship between the consumption of oxygen and the metabolism of lactic acid in the muscle."

Life Work: Meyerhof's field of investigation was the thermodynamics of cell reactions and the bioenergetics of cell processes. Meyehoff's experiments compared correlations among cellular oxygen consumption (respiration), cellular heat production (thermodynamics), the biochemical events in cells, and the mechanical work performed by specialized muscle cells. He explained cellular function in physical terms by measuring oxygen consumption and lactic acid production in both the presence and absence of oxygen. Since, in the presence of oxygen, only one-fifth of the cellular lactic acid is fully oxidized to carbon dioxide and water, he concluded that cellular energy is generated by the oxidative process and is used by the cell in a cyclic reaction to resynthesize glucose molecules from the residual lactate in the cells.

Publications: *Chemical Dynamics of Life Phenomena* (London: J. B. Lippincott, 1924). *Die Chemischen Vorgange in Muskel* (Berlin: J. Springer, 1930). *Chie de la Contraction Musculaire* (Bordeaux: Delmas, 1932).

Bibliography: *Biographical Memoirs. National Academy of Sciences* (New York: Columbia University Press, 1960), vol. 34, pp. 152–82. *Dictionary of Scientific Biography* (New York: Scribner's, 1974), vol. 9, p. 359.

BANTING, SIR FREDERICK GRANT

Prize: Physiology or Medicine, 1923. *Born:* November 4, 1891; Alliston, Ontario, Canada. *Died:* February 21, 1941; Newfoundland, Canada. *Nationality:* Canadian. *Education:* Victoria College, Toronto, Ontario, Canada, M.B., 1916; University of Toronto, Ontario, Canada, M.D., 1922. *Career:* University of Western Ontario, London, Ontario, Canada, Researcher, 1920–21; University of Toronto, Ontario, Canada, Professor, 1921–41. *Other Awards:* Starr Gold Medal, University of Toronto, 1922; George Armstrong Peters Prize, University of Toronto 1922; John Scott Medal, American Philosophical Society, 1923; Charles Mickle Fellowship, University of Toronto, 1923; Reeve Prize, University of Toronto, 1923; Rosenberger Gold Medal, Chicago, Illinois, 1924; Cameron Prize, Edinburgh, Scotland, 1927; Flavelle Medal, Royal Society of Canada, 1931; Knighthood, 1934; Apothecaries' Medal, London, Ontario, Canada, 1934.

Citation: "For the discovery of insulin" (with John J. R. McLeod).

Life Work: Banting's field of investigation was the role of insulin in diabetes. Together with Best, an assistant, he extracted insulin from the islet (of Langerhans) cells of the pancreas of dogs. In 1922 the first patient was successfully treated with insulin. Later, he determined the appropriate dosage levels for humans.

Publications: "Internal Secretion of Pancreas," with C. H. Best, *Journal of Laboratory and Clinical Medicine* 7 (February 1922): 251–326. "Pancreatic Extracts in Diabetes," with others, *Journal of the Canadian Medical Association* 12 (March 1922): 141–46. "Effect of Pancreatic Extract (Insulin) on Normal Rabbits," *American Journal of Phys-*

iology 62 (September 1922): 162–76. "Insulin in Treatment of Diabetes Mellitus," with W. R. Campbell and A .A. Fletcher, *Journal of Metabolic Research* 2 (November-December 1922): 547–604.

Bibliography. M. Bliss, *Banting* (Toronto: University of Toronto Press, 1992). *Dictionary of National Biography* (London: Oxford University Press, 1959), pp. 54–55. *Dictionary of Scientific Biography* (New York: Scribner's, 1970), vol. 1, pp. 440–43. Seale Harris, *Banting's Miracle: The Story of the Discoverer of Insulin* (Philadelphia: Lippincott, 1946). Lloyd Stevenson, *Sir Frederick Banting* (Toronto: Ryerson Press, 1946).

MACLEOD, JOHN JAMES RICKARD

Prize: Physiology or Medicine, 1923. *Born:* September 6, 1986; Cluny, Scotland. *Died:* March 16, 1935; Aberdeen, Scotland. *Nationality:* Scottish. *Education:* Marischal College, Scotland, M.B., 1898; Marischal College, Scotland, Ch.B., 1898; Cambridge University, England, D.P.H., 1902. *Career:* Western Reserve University, Cleveland, Ohio, Professor, 1903–18; University of Toronto, Ontario, Canada, Professor and Administrator, 1918–28; University of Aberdeen, Scotland, Professor, 1928–35. *Other Awards:* Cameron Prize, University of Edinburgh, Scotland, 1923.

Citation: "For the discovery of insulin" (with Frederick G. Banting).

Life Work: Macleod's field of investigation was respiration and carbohydrate metabolism. Working at the Western Reserve University in Ohio, Macleod developed an experimental model of glycosuria, and performed experiments to determine the role of the central nervous system in the development of diabetes mellitus. When, in 1916, Edward Sharpey-Schafer suggested the name *insuline* for a hypothetical substance that reduced blood glucose, Macleod changed it to *insulin*. In 1918 he provided his research facilities to a young surgeon for an experimental project on diabetes. In the same year, Banting and Best succeeded in extracting insulin from the islets of Langerhans of the pancreas of dogs. In 1922 the first patient with diabetes was successfully treated with insulin.

Publications: *Practical Physiology*, with others (London: E. Arnold, 1902). *Recent Advances in Physiology*, with Leonard Hill (New York: Longmans, Green, 1906). *Diabetes: Its Pathological Physiology* (New York: Longmans, Green, 1913). *Fundamentals of Human Physiology*, with R. G. Pearce (St. Louis: C.V . Mosby, 1916). *Physiology and Biochemistry in Modern Medicine*, with R. G. Pearce (St. Louis: C. V. Mosby, 1918). *Carbohydrate Metabolism and Insulin* (New York: Longmans, Green, 1926).

Bibliography: C. H. Best, "The Late John James Rickard MacLeod, M.B., Ch.B., LL.D., F.R.C.P.," *Canadian Medical Association Journal* 32 (1935): 556. *Dictionary of Scientific Biography* (New York: Scribner's, 1973), vol. 8, pp. 614–15. M. Williams, *John James Rickard MacLeod* (Edinburgh, Scotland: Royal College of Physicians, 1993).

EINTHOVEN, WILLEM

Prize: Physiology or Medicine, 1924. *Born:* May 22, 1860; Semarang, Dutch East Indies. *Died:* September 29, 1927; Leiden, Netherlands. *Nationality:* Dutch. *Education:* University of Utrecht, Netherlands, Ph.D., 1885. *Career:* University of Leiden, Netherlands, Professor, 1885–1927.

Citation: "For his discovery of the mechanism of the electrocardiogram."

Life Work: Einthoven's field of investigation was electrophysiology, the study of electrical phenomena occurring in the normal functions of the body. To measure the cardiac currents associated with the heartbeat, Einthoven designed an apparatus that could record small, fluctuating differences called the string galvanometer, an instrument consisting of a fine quartz wire held under tension in a magnetic field. A normal electrocardiogram (ECG or EKG) shows three waves (P, QRS, and T). The first records electrical activity of the atria and the other two record ventricular currents. This invention revolutionized cardiology.

Publications: *Sterescopie door Kleurveschil* (Utrecht, Netherlands: Utrechtsche Drukkerij, 1885). *Over de Beteekenis der Electrophysiologie als een Ouderdeel Van de Leer der Levensverrichtingen* (Leiden, Netherlands: Brill, 1906). *Das Saitengalvenometer und die Messung der Aktionsstrome des Herzens* (Stockholm: Norstedt, 1926).

Bibliography: *Dictionary of Scientific Biography* (New York: Scribner's, 1971), vol. 4, pp. 333–35. S. Hogenwerf, *Leven en Werken van Willem Einthoven* (N.p.: Hoorn, 1925). H. Snellen, *Willem Einthoven* (Boston: Kluwer Academic Publishers, 1995).

FIBIGER, JOHANNES ANDREAS GRIB

Prize: Physiology or Medicine, 1926. *Born:* April 23, 1867; Silkeborg, Denmark. *Died:* January 30, 1928; Copenhagen, Denmark. *Nationality:* Danish. *Education:* University of Copenhagen, Denmark, baccalaureate, 1883; University of Copenhagen, Denmark, M.D., 1890; University of Copenhagen, Denmark, Ph.D., 1895. *Career:* University of Copenhagen, Denmark, Researcher, 1891–94; Blegdams Hospital for Contagious Diseases, Copenhagen, Denmark, Physician, 1894–97; University of Copenhagen, Denmark, Professor, 1897–1928. *Other Awards:* Nordhoff-Jung Cancer Prize, 1927.

Citation: "For his discovery of the Spiroptera carcinoma."

Life Work: Fibiger's field of investigation was cell biology of cancers. He established the connection between nematodes and stomach cancers. In 1913 he published his first studies of rodent cancers caused by the larvae of the parasite *S. neoplastica*. Later, he made numerous studies of coal tar cancers.

Publications: *Bakteriologiske Studier over Diphtheri* (Copenhagen: det Schulothecke Forlag, 1895). *Investigations on the Spiropetera Cancer* (Copenhagen: Andr. Fred. Host and Son, Bianco Lunos Bogtrykkeri, 1918–19). *Experimental Production of Tar Cancer in White Mice*, with Fridtjof Bang (Copenhagen: Andr. Fred. Host and Son, Bianco Lunos Bogtrykkeri, 1921). *Investigations Upon Immunisation against Metastasis Formation in Experimental Cancer*, with Paul Moller (Copenhagen: Andr. Fred. Host and Son, Bianco Lunos Bogtrykkeri, 1927).

Bibliography: V. Meisen, *Prominent Danish Scientists* (Copenhagen: Levin and Munkegaard, 1932). K. Secher, *Johannes Fibiger* (Copenhagen: Nordisk Vorlag, 1947).

WAGNER VON JAUREGG, JULIUS

Prize: Physiology or Medicine, 1927. *Born:* March 7, 1857; Wels, Austria. *Died:* September 27, 1940; Vienna, Austria. *Nationality:* Austrian. *Education:* University of Vienna, Austria, Ph.D., 1880. *Career:* University of Vienna, Austria, Professor, 1881–1928. *Other Awards:* Cameron Prize, 1935; Gold Medal, American Committee for Research on Syphilis, 1937.

Citation: "For his discovery of the therapeutic value of malaria inoculation in the treatment of dementia paralytica."

Life Work: Wagner von Jauregg's field of investigation was neurology and psychiatry. He investigated the physiological causes of mental diseases, especially cretinism, a form of thyroid deficiency that results from an absence of iodine in the diet. He proposed that these diseases could be prevented by the use of iodized salt. He also studied paresis, which occurs during the tertiary phase of syphilis, when the syphilis spirochete enters the central nervous system causing progressive insanity, paralysis, and eventually death. In 1887 he proposed that psychoses might be cured by deliberately inducing high fevers. He was successful in curing general paresis by inducing noninfectious malaria and then curing it with quinine. The success of the procedure has not been fully explained.

Publications: "Uber die Einwirkung Fieberhafter Erkankungen auf Psychosen," *Jahrbuch fur Psychiatrie und Neurologie* 7 (1887): 94–131. "Zur Reform des Irrenwesens," *Viennaer Klinische Wochenscrift* 14 (1901): 293–96. *Myxoden und Kretinismus*, (Leipzig, Germany: F. Deuticke, 1915). "Uber die Einwirkung der Malaria auf die Progressive Paralyse," *Psychiatrischneurologische Wochenschrift* 20 (1918–19): 132–34. *Fieber und Infektionstherapie* (Vienna: Verlag fur Medizin, Weidmann, 1936).

Bibliography: *Dictionary of Scientific Biography* (New York: Scribner's, 1976), vol. 14, pp. 114–16. *Grosse Nervenarzte* (Stuttgart, Germany: G. Thieme, 1956), pp. 254–66.

NICOLLE, CHARLES JULES HENRI

Prize: Physiology or Medicine, 1928. *Born:* September 21, 1866; Rouen, France. *Died:* February 28, 1936; Tunis, Tunisia. *Nationality:* French; later Tunisian resident. *Education:* Rouen School of Medicine, France, M.D., 1893. *Career:* Rouen School of Medicine, France, Professor, 1895–1903; Pasteur Institute, Tunis, Tunisia, Director, 1903–36. *Other Awards:* Prix Montyon, 1909, 1912, 1914; Prix Osiris, 1927; Gold Medal, Tunis, 1928.

Citation: "For his work on typhus."

Life Work: Nicolle's field of investigation was typhus, a tropical disease caused by *Rickettsia* microorganisms. He discovered that typhus is spread by lice. He also explained the phenomenon known as inapparent infection, in which uninfected carriers transmitted the disease to others.

Publications: "Recherches Experimentales sur le Typhus Exanthematique," *Annales de l'Institut Pasteur* 24 (1910): 243–75; 25 (1911): 97–144; 26 (1912): 250–80, 332–35. *Naissance, Vie et Mort des Maladies Infectieuses* (Paris: F. Alcan, 1930). *Biologie de l'Invention* (Paris: F. Alcan, 1932). *Destindes Maladies Infectieuses* (Paris: Presses Universitaires de France, 1939).

Bibliography: *Dictionary of Scientific Biography* (New York: Scribner's, 1978), supp., pp. 453–55. G. Lot, *Charles Nicolle et la Biologie Conquerante* (Paris: Seghers, 1961).

EIJKMAN, CHRISTIAAN

Prize: Physiology or Medicine, 1929. *Born:* August 11, 1858; Nijkerk, Netherlands. *Died:* November 5, 1930; Utrecht, Netherlands. *Nationality:* Dutch. *Education:* University of Amsterdam, Netherlands, M.D., 1883. *Career:* Dutch Army, 1886–87; Medical School, Java, Indonesia, Director, 1888–96; University of Utrecht, Netherlands, Professor, 1896–1928. *Other Awards:* John Scott Medal, Philadelphia, 1923.

Citation: "For his discovery of the antineuritic vitamin."

Life Work: Eijkman's field of investigation was bacteriology. He set out to the Dutch East Indies to study beri-beri, a fatal disease common among rice-eating peoples. Eijkman's researches proved that beri-beri was caused by a nutritional deficiency or the lack of a specific natural substance found in certain foods. In 1911 the Polish scientist Casimir Funk extracted this substance from the outer husks of rice grains. Funk coined the term *vitamine,* later shortened to *vitamin.* The substance that he identified was vitamin B, or thiamine.

Publications: *Specifieke Antistoffen* (Haarlem, Netherlands: de Erven F. Bohn, 1901). *Onzichtbare Smetstoffen* (Haarlem, Netherlands: de Erven F. Bohn, 1904). *Een en*

Ander over Voeding (Haarlem, Netherlands: de Erven F. Bohn, 1906). *Hygienische Strijdvragen* (Rotterdam: W. L. and J. Brusse, 1907).

Bibliography: *Dictionary of Scientific Biography* (New York: Scribner's, 1971), vol. 4, pp. 310–12. Barend Coeraad Jansen, *Het Levenswerk van Christiaan Eijkman, 1858–1930* (Haarlem, Netherlands: de Erven F. Bohn, 1959). *Polyneuritis in Chickens or the Origins of Vitamin Research* (New Brunswick, N.J.: Hoffman-LaRoche, 1990).

HOPKINS, SIR FREDERICK GOWLAND

Prize: Physiology or Medicine, 1929. *Born:* June 30, 1861; Eastbourne, Sussex, England. *Died:* May 16, 1947; Cambridge, England. *Nationality:* British. *Education:* University of London, England, B.Sc., 1890; University of London, England, M.B., 1894. *Career:* Guy's Hospital, London, England, Researcher, 1894–97; Cambridge University, England, Professor, 1898–1943. *Other Awards:* Baly Medal, Royal College of Physicians, 1915; Royal Medal, Royal Society, 1918; Cameron Prize, University of Edinburgh, Scotland, 1922; Knighthood, 1925; Copley Medal, 1926; Albert Medal, 1934; Order of Merit, 1935; Harben Medal, 1937.

Citation: "For his discovery of the growth-stimulating vitamins."

Life Work: Hopkins's field of investigation was biochemistry. He isolated and identified tryptophan, an amino acid needed for growth. He concluded that protein quality depended on the types of amino acids present and that a good diet needed more than quality proteins, but what he termed accessory food factors, named vitamines by the Polish scientist Casimir Funk. He conducted important studies on intermediary metabolism, the complex series of oxidation and reduction reactions by which cells obtain energy. He explained intermediary metabolism as a series of chemical steps in which lactic acid accumulated in muscles when oxygen is depleted. Later Hopkins isolated and named glutathione, a tripeptide, and xanthine oxidase, an enzyme that catalyzes the oxidation of the purines xanthine and hypoxanthine to uric acid.

Publication: *Hopkins and Biochemistry, 1861–1947* (Cambridge: W. Heffer, 1949).

Bibliography: Ernest Baldwin, *Gowland Hopkins* (London: VandenBerghs, 1961). *Dictionary of Scientific Biography* (New York: Scribner's, 1972), vol. 6, pp. 493–502.

LANDSTEINER, KARL

Prize: Physiology or Medicine, 1930. *Born:* June 14, 1868; Vienna, Austria. *Died:* June 26, 1943; New York, New York. *Nationality:* Austrian; later U.S. citizen. *Education:* University of Vienna, Austria, M.D., 1891. *Career:* University of Vienna, Austria, Professor, 1896–98; Pathological-Anatomical Institute, Vienna, Austria, Researcher, 1898–1907; Wilhelmina Hospital, Vienna, Austria, Physician, 1908–19; R. K. Zickenhuis Hospital, The Hague, Netherlands, Physician, 1919–22; Rockefeller Institute, New York, Researcher, 1922–43. *Other Awards:* Chevalier Legion of Honor, France, 1926; Hans Aronson Foundation Prize, Berlin, 1926; Paul Ehrlich Gold Medal, 1930; Dutch Red Cross Medal, 1933; Cameron Prize, University of Edinburgh, Scotland, 1938.

Citation: "For his discovery of human blood groups."

Life Work: Landsteiner's fields of investigation were hematology, immunology, and physiology. Investigating interagglutination of blood, he divided human blood into three groups: A, B, and C (later changed to O). Later, a fourth group, AB, was added. The blood grouping was achieved by mixing suspensions of red blood cells with test serums known as anti-A and anti-B. Landsteiner conceived of serological identification in which individual characteristics of blood could be used as markers to distinguish one human being from another. He postulated that paroxysmal cold hemoglobinuria was caused by an antibody that, when exposed to cold, combines with the red cells, and eventually, under warmer conditions, causes their breakdown in the body. He also attributed poliomyelitis to a virus belonging to the class of protozoa.

Publication: *Die Spezifizitat der Serologischen Reaktionen* (Berlin: Julius Springer, 1933).

Bibliography: *Dictionary of Scientific Biography* (New York: Scribner's, 1973), vol. 7, pp. 622–25. *Obituary Notices of Fellows of the Royal Society of London* (London: Royal Society, 1947), vol. 5, pp. 295–324. Paul Speiser, *Karl Landsteiner* (Vienna: Hallenek Brothers, 1961).

WARBURG, OTTO HEINRICH

Prize: Physiology or Medicine, 1931. *Born:* October 8, 1883; Freiburg, Germany. *Died:* August 1, 1970; Berlin, Germany. *Nationality:* German. *Education:* University of Berlin, Germany, Dr. der Chemie, 1906; University of Heidelberg, Germany, Dr. der Medizin, 1911. *Career:* Kaiser-Wilhelm Institute, Germany, Professor, 1913–70. *Other Awards:* German Order of Merit, 1944; Freedom of the City of Berlin, 1955; Paul Ehrlich Prize, 1962; Nordhoff-Jung Prize, 1963; Schneider Prize, 1963; Gold Medal, University of Wurzburg, 1965.

Citation: "For his discovery of the nature and mode of action of the respiratory enzyme."

Life Work: Warburg's fields of investigation were photosynthesis, cancer, and enzymes of cellular oxidation reactions. The analytic methods he developed included manometry, which measures changes in gas pressure; spectrophotometry, or the use of monochromatic light to measure reaction rates and quantities of metabolites; and tissue-slice techniques for testing oxygen consumption without mechanical destruction of cells. In 1913, while studying oxygen uptake in liver cells, Warburg discovered the subcellular particles called grana. He determined the biochemical changes that occur when normal cells become cancer cells by measuring the rates of oxygen consumption, using tissue slices in a manometer. He concluded that tumor cells prefer to use the anaerobic pathway to metabolize glucose and that normal cells are transformed into malignant cells because they are deprived of oxygen. He demonstrated that environmental substances, such as cyanide, were secondary causes of cancer. In the 1920s Warburg discovered the respiratory enzyme cytochrome oxidase, which catalyzes oxidative reactions on the surface of the grana or mitochondria. Using a technique of radiation physics Warburg found that the active conenzyme of cytochrome oxidase is a porphyrin molecule with iron acting as the oxygen transferring component. In the 1930s Warburg isolated and crystallized nine enzymes of the anaerobic pathway of glucose metabolism and two coenzymes: flavin adenine dinucleotide (FAD) and nicotinamide adenine dinucleotide phosphate (NADP). The discovery of NADP, which contains the vitamin nicotinic acid, clarified the coenzyme function of vitamins. In the field of photosynthesis, he determined how efficiently plants convert carbon dioxide and water into sugar and oxygen. He correlated the amount of light intensity in the photochemical reaction with rates of photosynthesis. He also discovered the electron carrier ferredoxin in green plants.

Publications: *Uber den Stoffwechsel der Tumoren* (Berlin: Springer, 1926). *The Metabolism of Tumours,* trans. Frank Dickens (London: Constable, 1930). *Uber die Katalytischen Wirkungen der Lebendigen Substanz* (Berlin: Springer, 1928). *Schwermetalle als Wirkungsgruppen von Fermenten* (Berlin: W. Saenger, 1948). *The Prime Cause and Prevention of Cancer* (Wurzburg, Germany: K. Triltsch, 1969).

Bibliography: *Biographical Memoirs of the Fellows of the Royal Society* (London: Royal Society, 1972), vol. 18, pp. 629–99. *Dictionary of Scientific Biography* (New York: Scribner's, 1976), vol. 14, pp. 172–77. Hans A. Krebs, *The Excitement and Fascination of Science* (Palo Alto, Calif.: Annual Reviews, 1965), vol. 1, pp. 531–44. *Otto Warburg: Biochemist and Eccentric* (New York: Oxford University Press, 1981). P. Werner, *Ein Genie Irrt Seltener-Otto Heinrich Warburg* (Berlin: Akademie Verlag, 1991).

ADRIAN, BARON EDGAR DOUGLAS

Prize: Physiology or Medicine, 1932. *Born:* November 30, 1889; London, England. *Died:* August 4, 1977; London, England. *Nationality:* British. *Education:* Cambridge University, England, M.A., 1911; Cambridge University, England, M.D., 1915. *Career:* British Army, 1916–19; Cambridge University, England, Professor and Administrator, 1920–75. *Other Awards:* Baly Medal, 1929; Royal Medal, Royal Society, 1934; Order of Merit, England, 1942; Copley Medal, Royal Society, 1946; Hughlings Jackson Medal, Royal Society of Medicine, 1947; Gold Medal, Royal Society of Medicine, 1950; Albert Gold Medal, Royal Society of Arts, 1953; Harben Medal, 1955; Made Baron, 1955; Chevalier Legion of Honour, France, 1956; Sherington Memorial

Medal, 1957; Medal for Distinguished Merit, British Medical Association, 1958; Jephcott Medal, Royal Society of Medicine, 1963.

Citation: "For their discoveries regarding the functions of neurons" (with Charles S. Sherrington).

Life Work: Adrian formulated a general theory of sensation by measuring various impulses in sensory and motor nerves. Human sensory receptors react to changes in the environment; after the change has occurred they adapt to the new state. The intensity with which the receptors react determines the rate at which impulses in the sensory nerves are produced. All sensory impulses are alike, but the brain interprets them according to the origin of the stimulation. The impulses are integrated by a central process, and the rise and decline of the sensation is related closely to the excitatory process in the receptor and the intervals between the impulses.

Publications: *The Basis of Sensation* (New York: W. W. Norton, 1928). *Mechanism of Nervous Action* (Philadelphia: University of Pennsylvania Press, 1932). *Physical Background of Perception* (Oxford: Clarendon Press, 1947).

Bibliography: *Biographical Memoirs of the Fellows of the Royal Society* (London: Royal Society, 1979), vol. 25, pp. 1–73. *Current Biography Yearbook* (New York: H. W. Wilson, 1955), pp. 1–3.

SHERRINGTON, SIR CHARLES SCOTT

Prize: Physiology or Medicine, 1932. *Born:* November 27, 1857; London, England. *Died:* March 4, 1952; Eastbourne, Sussex, England. *Nationality:* British. *Education:* Cambridge University, England, M.B., 1885. *Career:* Koch Laboratory, Berlin, Germany, Researcher, 1886–87; St. Thomas Hospital, London, England, Physician, 1887–90; University of London, England, Professor and Administrator, 1891–94; University of Liverpool, England, Professor, 1895–1913; Oxford University, England, Professor, 1913–35; University of Edinburgh, Scotland, Professor, 1936–38. *Other Awards:* Royal Medal, Royal Society, 1905; Knighthood, 1922; Order of Merit, England, 1924; Baly Gold Medal, 1927; Retzius Gold Medal, Royal Swedish Academy, 1927; Copley Medal, 1927.

Citation: "For their discoveries regarding the functions of neurons" (with Edgar D. Adrian).

Life Work: Sherrington's field of investigation was neurophysiology. His early research dealt with reflex actions. He spent many years mapping the areas supplied by nerves by each spinal root. He discovered that only two-thirds of the nerves in muscles are motor nerves, which bring instructions from the muscles to the central nervous system, and that the rest (proprioceptors) are sensory nerves, which deliver information from the muscles to the central nervous system. Nerves from a given root usually lead to more than one group of muscles, while a given muscle receives nerves from more than one root. Muscles, thus, do not function as individual units; rather, the nervous system is an integrated and well-coordinated whole. Sherrington's study of the functional relationships of individual nerves revealed the general principles under which the nervous system operates. One such principle is that there is a mutual interaction between two central processes, excitation and inhibition. Building on the neuroanatomical theories of Ramon y Cajal, Sherrington explained impulses as impulses transmitted by contacts between nerves and he gave synapse to the junction where one neuron interacts with the next.

Publications: *The Integrative Action of the Nervous System* (New Haven, Conn.: Yale University Press, 1906). *Man on His Nature* (London: Cambridge University Press, 1940). *Selected Writings of Sir Charles Sherrington* (Oxford: Oxford University Press, 1979).

Bibliography: *Dictionary of Scientific Biography* (New York: Scribner's, 1975), vol. 12, pp. 395–402. John C. Eccles and William C. Gibson, *Sherrington. His Life and Thought* (New York: Springer International, 1979). *Obituary Notices of Fellows of the Royal Society* (Cambridge: Royal Society, 1952), vol. 21, pp. 241–70.

MORGAN, THOMAS HUNT

Prize: Physiology or Medicine, 1933. *Born:* September 25, 1866; Lexington, Kentucky. *Died:* December 4, 1945; Pasadena, California. *Nationality:* American. *Education:* State College of Kentucky, B.S., 1886; State College of Kentucky, M.S., 1888; John Hopkins University, Maryland, M.D., Ph.D., 1890. *Career:* Bryn Mawr College, Pennsylvania, Professor, 1891–1903; Columbia University, New York, Professor, 1904–28; California Institute of Technology, Professor, 1928–45. *Other Awards:* Darwin Medal, 1924; Copley Medal, 1939.

Citation: "For his discoveries concerning the role played by the chromosome in heredity."

Life Work: Morgan's field of investigation was genetics. Developing Mendel's theory of heredity, he demonstrated that heredity follows predictable rules and that chromosomes are in fact directly involved in heredity. He found that while each organism independently possesses genes that control a given trait, certain traits, such as sex and the color of the eye, were linked, a phenomenon that Morgan called sex linkage. He speculated that the genes for these traits might be located close together on the same chromosome. Chromosomes in a pair could break and recombine, thus allowing them to exchange genes. The degree of linkage of two genes on a chromosome provides a measure of the linear distance between them. Using this principle, Morgan made maps showing the relative positions of the genes on the fruit fly's chromosomes.

Publications: *Regeneration* (New York: Macmillan, 1901). *Heredity and Sex* (New York: Columbia University Press, 1913). *The Scientific Basis of Evolution* (London:

Faber and Faber, 1932). *The Theory of the Gene* (New Haven, Conn.: Yale University Press, 1932).

Bibliography: Garland E. Allan, *Thomas Hunt Morgan: The Man and His Science* (Princeton, N.J.: Princeton University Press, 1978). A. Barahona, *El Hombre de las Moscas; Thomas H. Morgan* (Mexico City: Pangea, 1992). *Biographical Memoirs. National Academy of Sciences* (New York: Columbia University Press, 1959), vol. 33, pp. 383–436. *Dictionary of Scientific Biography* (New York: Scribner's, 1974), vol. 9, pp. 515–26.

MINOT, GEORGE RICHARDS

Prize: Physiology or Medicine, 1934. *Born:* December 2, 1885; Boston, Massachusetts *Died:* February 25, 1950; Brookline, Massachusetts *Nationality:* American. *Education:* Harvard University, Massachusetts, B.A., 1908; Harvard University, Massachusetts, M.D., 1912. *Career:* Massachusetts General Hospital, Boston, Physician, 1912–13; Johns Hopkins University, Baltimore, Maryland, Researcher, 1913–15; Massachusetts General Hospital, Boston, Physician, 1915–23; Peter Bent Brigham Hospital, Massachusetts, Physician, 1923–28; Collis P. Huntington Memorial Hospital, Maryland, Physician and Administrator, 1923–28; Harvard University, Massachusetts, Professor and Administrator, 1928–50. *Other Awards:* Kober Gold Medal, Association of American Physicians, 1928; Cameron Prize, University of Edinburg, Scotland, 1930; Gold Medal and Award, Popular Science Monthly, 1930; Moxon Medal, Royal College of Physicians, 1933; John Scott Medal, Philadelphia, 1935; Scroll Award, Association of Grocery Manufacturers of America, 1936.

Citation: "For their discoveries concerning liver therapy in cases of anaemia" (with William P. Murphy and George H. Whipple).

Life Work: Minot's field of investigation was pernicious anemia. Working with William P. Murphy and George H. Whipple, he discovered that massive doses of liver or liver extract produced remarkable improvement in patients. In 1948 it was shown that pernicious anemia resulted from a deficiency of vitamin B-12, a compound in liver.

Publications: "Development of Liver Therapy in Pernicious Anemia," *Lancet* 1 (1935): 361–64. *Pathological Physiology and Clinical Description of the Anemias* (New York: Oxford University Press, 1936).

Bibliography: *Biographical Memoirs: National Academy of Sciences* (New York: Columbia University Press, 1974), vol. 45, pp. 336–83. *Dictionary of Scientific Biography* (New York: Scribner's, 1974), vol. 9, pp. 416–17. F. M. Rackermann, *The Inquisitive Physician: The Life and Times of George Richards Minot* (Cambridge: Harvard University Press, 1956).

MURPHY, WILLIAM PARRY

Prize: Physiology or Medicine, 1934. *Born:* February 6, 1892; Stoughton, Wisconsin. *Died:* October 9, 1987; Brookline, Massachusetts. *Nationality:* American. *Education:* University of Oregon, A.B., 1914; Harvard University, Massachusetts, M.D., 1920. *Career:* U.S. Army, 1917–18; Rhode Island Hospital, Physician, 1920–22; Peter Bent Brigham Hospital, Massachusetts, Physician and Researcher, 1922–58. *Other Awards:* Cameron Prize, University of Edinburgh, Scotland, 1930; Commander, Order of White Rose First Rank, Finland, 1934; Bronze Medal for Science Exhibit, American Medical Association, 1934; Gold Medal, Human Society of Massachusetts, 1935; National Order of Merit Carlos J. Finlay, Cuba, 1952; Distinguished Achievement Award, Boston, Massachusetts, 1965; International Bicentennial Symposium Award, 1972; Gold Badge, Massachusetts Medical Society, 1973; Paul Harris Fellow Award, 1980.

Citation: "For their discoveries concerning liver therapy in cases of anaemia" (with George R. Minot and George H. Whipple).

Life Work: Murphy worked with Minot and Whipple to discover the curative property of liver in patients suffering from pernicious anemia.

Publications: *Anemia in Practice: Pernicious Anemia* (Philadelphia, Pennsylvania: W. B. Saunders, 1939).

Bibliography: *Asimov's Biographical Encyclopedia of Science and Technology* (Garden City, N.Y.: Doubleday, 1964), p. 507. *National Cyclopedia of American Biography* (New York: James T. White, 1946), vol. G, pp. 358–59.

WHIPPLE, GEORGE HOYT

Prize: Physiology or Medicine, 1934. *Born:* August 28, 1878; Ashland, New Hampshire. *Died:* February 1, 1976; Rochester, New York. *Nationality:* American. *Education:* Yale University, Connecticut, A.B., 1900; John Hopkins University, Maryland, M.D., 1905. *Career:* Holbrook School, New York, Teacher, 1901; Johns Hopkins University, Maryland, Professor, 1902–14; University of California, San Francisco, Professor and Administrator, 1914–21; University of Rochester, New York, Professor and Administrator, 1921–55. *Other Awards:* Warren Triennial Prize, 1910; Popular Science Monthly Award, 1929; William Wood Gerhard Gold Medal, 1934; Charles Mickle Fellowship, University of Toronto, 1938; Kober Medal, Georgetown University, 1939; Rochester Civic Medal, New York, 1943; Certificate of Honor, European Society for Hematology, 1959; Gold-Headed Cane Award, American Association of Pathologists and Bacteriologists, 1961; Kovalenko Medal National Academy of Sciences, 1962; Distinguished Service Award, American Medical Association, 1973; President's Medal, University of Rochester, New York, 1975.

Citation: "For their discoveries concerning liver therapy in cases of anaemia" (with George R. Minot and William P. Murphy).

Life Work: Whipple's field of investigation was the interrelationship of liver, bile, and hemoglobin. During his research he tried to induce long-term anemia in dogs by lowering the hemoglobin. He also found that liver was the best stimulator of hemoglobin production. This discovery was used by Minot and Murphy in their treatment of patients suffering from pernicious anemia.

Publications: "Icterus. A Rapid Change of Hemoglobin to Bile Pigments in the Circulation Outside the Liver," with C. W. Hooper, *Journal of Experimental Medicine* 17 (1913): 612–35. "Blood Regeneration Following Simple Anemia. IV. Influence of Meat, Liver, and Various Extractives, Alone or Combined with Standard Diets," with C. W. Hooper and F. S. Robscheit, *American Journal of Physiology* 53 (1920): 236–62. "Pigment Metabolism and Regeneration of Hemoglobin in the Body," *Archives of Internal Medicine* 29 (1922): 711–31. "Blood Regeneration in Severe Anemia. 14. A Liver Fraction Potent in Pernicious Anemia Fed Alone and Combined with Whole Liver, Liver Ash and Fresh Bile," with F. S. Robscheit-Robbins, *Journal of Experimental Medicine* 49 (1929): 215–27. *The Dynamic Equilibrium of Body Proteins. Hemoglobin, Plasma Proteins, Organ and Tissue Proteins* (Springfield, Ill.: Thomas, 1956).

Bibliography: George W. Corner, *George Hoyt Whipple and His Friends* (Philadelphia: Lippincott, 1963). *Perspectives in Biology and Medicine* 2 (spring 1959): 253–89.

SPEMANN, HANS

Prize: Physiology or Medicine, 1935. **Born:** June 27, 1869; Stuttgart, Wurtenberg, Germany. **Died:** September 12, 1941; Freiburg-im-Breisgau, Baden, Germany. **Nationality:** German. **Education:** University of Wurzburg, Germany, doctorate, 1895. **Career:** University of Wurzburg, Germany, Researcher, 1894–1908; University of Rostock, Germany, Professor, 1908–13; Kaiser Wilhelm Institute of Biology, Berlin-Dahlem, Germany, Director, 1914–18; University of Freiburg-im-Breisgau, Germany, Professor, 1919–35.

Citation: "For his discovery of the organizer effect in embryonic development."

Life Work: Spemann's field of investigation was developmental embryology, especially the development of embryos and the time sequence of that development. He concentrated on the time sequence, that is, which parts of an embryo are developed first and what the relationships are among the various parts. His experiments showed that there is an area in the embryo whose parts, when transplanted into an indifferent part of another embryo, there organize the primordia (the earliest discernible indications during embryonic development) for a second embryo. He named these parts organizers. The inductive stimulus does not prescribe the specific character of the induced organ but releases that already inherent in the reaction system. The structure of the reaction system merely triggers and directs the growth patterns.

Publications: *Experimentelle Beitrage zu einer Theorie der Entwicklung* (Berlin: J. Springer, 1936); *Embryonic Development and Induction* (New Haven, Conn.: Yale University Press, 1938).

Bibliography: *Dictionary of Scientific Biography* (New York: Scribner's, 1975), vol. 12, pp. 567–69. Otto Mangold, *Hans Spemann, ein Meister der Entwicklung-sphysiologie, sein Leben und sein Werk* (Stuttgart, Germany: Wissenschaftlich Verlagsgesellschaft, 1953). Hans Spemann, *Forschung und Leben, Erinnerungen* (Stuttgart, Germany: J. Engelhorns Nacht, 1943).

DALE, SIR HENRY HALLETT

Prize: Physiology or Medicine, 1936. ***Born:*** June 9, 1875; London, England. ***Died:*** July 23, 1968; Cambridge, England. ***Nationality:*** British. ***Education:*** Cambridge University, England, B.S., 1898; Cambridge University, England, B. Chir., 1903; Cambridge University, England, M.D., 1909. ***Career:*** Wellcome Physiological Research Laboratories, England, Director, 1904–14; National Institute for Medical Research, Hampstead, England, Researcher and Administrator, 1914–42; Royal Institution of Great Britain, Director, 1942–46. ***Other Awards:*** Gedge Prize, Cambridge University, England, 1900; Walsingham Medal, Cambridge University, England, 1900; Raymond Horton Smith Prize, 1909; Baly Medal, Royal College of Physicians, 1921; Cameron Prize, University of Edinburgh, Scotland, 1926; Medal of the Society of Apothecaries, 1932; Harrison Memorial Medal, Pharmaceutical Society of Great Britain, 1932; Knighthood, 1932; Addingham Medal, William Hoffmann Wood Trust, Leeds, England, 1935; Royal Medal, Royal Society, 1936; Copley Medal, Royal Society, 1937; Fothergillian Medal, Medical Society of London, 1938; Harben Gold Medal, Royal Institute of Public Health and Hygiene, 1943; Danbury Memorial Medal, Pharmaceutical Society of Great Britain, 1943; Dr. Bimala Churn Law Gold Medal, Indian Association for the Cultivation of Science, 1943; Order of Merit, 1944; USA Medal of Freedom with Silver Palm, 1947; Grand Croix de l'Ordre de la Couronne of Belgium, 1949; Pour le Mérite, West Germany, 1955; Gold Medal of Honour, Canadian Pharmaceutical Manufacturer's Association, 1955; Gold Albert Medal, Royal Society of the Arts, 1956; Schmiedeberg-Plakette, German Pharmacological Society, 1962.

Citation: "For their discoveries relating to chemical transmission of nerve impulses" (with Otto Loewi).

Life Work: Dale's field of investigation was neurology. He was the first to propose that nerve impulses were transmitted by a chemical called adrenaline. As director of the Burroughs Wellcome laboratories, he made two important discoveries, both by chance: the reversal of adrenaline by ergot, a chemical product of a fungus that grows on rye and other grains; and the pituitary gland hormone oxytocin, which facilitates contractions of the uterus and stimulates lactation. In 1910 he identified histamine, a chemical found in many vegetable and animal tissues. Four years later he isolated aceetylcholine from ergot. Later it was established that aceetylcholine was the transmitter of impulses in the sympathetic and parasympathetic nervous systems.

Publications: *Adventures in Physiology* (London: Pergammon Press, 1953). *An Autumn Gleaning* (London: Pergammon Press, 1954).

Bibliography: *Biographical Memoirs of the Fellows of the Royal Society* (London: Royal Society, 1970), vol. 16, pp. 77–174. *Dictionary of Scientific Biography* (New York: Scribner's, 1978), supp. I, pp. 104–107.

LOEWI, OTTO

Prize: Physiology or Medicine, 1936. *Born:* June 3, 1873; Frankfurt-am-Main, Germany. *Died:* December 25, 1961; New York, New York. *Nationality:* German; later U.S. citizen. *Education:* University of Strasbourg, France, M.D., 1896. *Career:* City Hospital, Frankfurt, Germany, Researcher, 1897–98; University of Marburg, Germany, Professor, 1898–1904; University of Vienna, Austria, Professor, 1905-1909; University of Graz, Austria, Professor, 1909–38; University of Brussels, Belgium, Professor, 1938–39; New York University, Professor, 1940–61. *Other Awards:* Austrian Distinguished Order for Art and Science, 1936; Cameron Prize, University of Edinburgh, Scotland, 1944.

Citation: "For their discoveries relating to chemical transmission of nerve impulses" (with Henry H. Dale).

Life Work: Loewi's field of investigation was physiology. His experiments proved the chemical transmission of nerve impulses. He named the transmitters *Vagusstoff* (vagus substance) and *Acceleranstoff* (accelerator substance).

Publications: "The Humoral Transmission of Nervous Impulse," *Harvey Lectures* 28 (1934): 218–33. "The Ferrier Lecture on Problems Connected with the Principle of Humoral Transmission of Nervous Impulses," *Proceedings of the Royal Society* 118B (1935): 299–316. "Die Chemische Ubertragung der Nervwirkung," *Schweizerische Medizinische Wochenschrift* 67 (1937): 850–55. "The Edward Gamaliel Janeway Lectures: Aspects of the Transmission of Nervous Impulse," *Journal of the Mount Sinai Hospital* 12 (1945): 803–16, 851–65.

Bibliography: *Biographical Memoirs of the Fellows of the Royal Society* (London: Royal Society, 1962), vol. 8, pp. 67–89. *Dictionary of Scientific Biography* (New York: Scribner's, 1973), vol. 8, pp. 451–56. Fred Lembreck and Wolfgang Giere, *The Excitement and Fascination of Science* (Palo Alto, Calif.: Annual Reviews, 1965), vol. 1, pp. 269–78. *Otto Loewi: Ein Lebensbild in Dokumenten* (New York: Springer, 1968).

SZENT-GYORGYI, ALBERT VON NAGYRAPOLT

Prize: Physiology or Medicine, 1937. *Born:* September 16, 1893; Budapest, Hungary. *Died:* October 22, 1986; Woods Hole, Massachusetts. *Nationality:* Hungarian; later U.S. citizen. *Education:* University of Budapest, Hungary, M.D., 1917; Cambridge University, England, Ph.D., 1927. *Career:* Austro-Hungarian Army, 1914–18; Researcher at various universities (Prague, Czechoslovakia; Berlin, Germany; Hamburg, Germany; Leiden, Netherlands; Liege, Belgium; Groningen, Germany; Budapest, Hungary; Minnesota; Cambridge, England), 1919–30; University of Szeged, Hungary, Professor and Administrator, 1931–45; University of Budapest, Hungary, Professor, 1945–47; Marine Biology Laboratories, Woods Hole, Maryland, Director, 1947–75; National Foundation for Cancer Research, Woods Hole, Massachusetts, Director, 1975–86. *Other Awards:* Cameron Prize, University of Edinburgh, Scotland, 1946; Lasker Award, American Heart Association, 1954.

Citation: "For his discoveries in connection with the biological combustion processes, with special reference to vitamin C and the catalysis of fumaric acid."

Life Work: Szent-Gyorgi's field of investigation was the mechanism of biological oxidation. He demonstrated that activation of both oxygen and hydrogen is necessary in cellular oxidation reactions. He also discovered enzymes of the dicarboxylic acids—succinic and citric acids–that catalyze oxidative reactions intermediate between pyruvate and carbon dioxide and water. This catalytic system is bound to intracellular structures, later shown to be mitochondria, the power centers of the cell. When he analyzed biological oxidation in plant cells, he discovered a hydrogen donor, a strong reducing substance. Because the substance contained six carbon atoms and was acidic, it was called first hexuronic acid, and later ascorbic acid or vitamin C. It was determined that lack of ascorbic acid led to scurvy. Later he discovered that plant pigments called flavonoids reduced the fragility of capillaries.

Publications: *On Oxidation, Fermentation, Vitamins, Health and Disease* (Baltimore: Williams and Wilkins, 1939). *Chemistry of Muscular Contraction* (New York: Academic Press, 1947). *Bioelectronics* (New York: Academic Press, 1968). *The Living State and Cancer* (New York: M. Dekker, 1978). *Essays and Scientific Papers of Albert Szent-Gyorgyi* (Szeged, Hungary: Albert Szent-Gyorgyi Medical University, 1991).

Bibliography: *Current Biography Yearbook* (New York: H. W. Wilson, 1955), pp. 596–99. *Encyclopedia of World Biography* (New York: McGraw-Hill, 1973), vol. 10, pp. 314–16. *The Excitement and Fascination of Science* (Palo Alto, Calif.: Annual Reviews, 1965), vol. 1, pp. 461–74. "Lost in the Twentieth Century," *Annual Review of Biochemistry* 32 (1963): 1–14. T. Szabo, *Albert Szent-Gyorgy and Szeged* (Szeged, Hungary: Szote Nyomba, 1993).

HEYMANS, CORNEILLE JEAN FRANÇOIS

Prize: Physiology or Medicine, 1938. *Born:* March 28, 1892; Ghent, Belgium. *Died:* July 18, 1968; Knokke, Belgium. *Nationality:* Belgian. *Education:* University of Ghent, Belgium, M.D., 1920. *Career:* University of Ghent, Belgium, Professor, 1923–68. *Other Awards:* Alvarenga Prize, Académie Royale de Médecine, Belgium; Gluge Prize, Académie Royal des Sciences, Belgium; Prix Quinquennal de Médecine du Gouvernement, Belgium; Pius XI Prize, Pontifica Academia Scientiarum, Rome; Purkinje Prize, Academy of Medicine, Czechoslovakia; Bourceret Prize, Académie de Médecine de Paris, France; Monthyon Prize, Institut de France; Schmiedeberg Plakette, Deutsche Pharmakologische Gesellschaft, Germany; Cyon Prize; Academy of Sciences, Bologna, Italy; Burgi Prize, University of Bern, Switzerland.

Citation: "For the discovery of the role played by the sinus and aortic mechanisms in the regulation of respiration."

Life Work: Heymans's field of investigation was the pathophysiology of the cardiovascular and respiratory systems, especially the function of the nervous system reflexes on the rate and rhythm of the heart, the level of pressure on circulation, and the rate of respiration. He demonstrated that the respiratory rate is regulated by the nervous system reflexes carried in the vagus (the tenth nerve that emanates from the medulla) and aortic nerves (in the abdomen). He showed that nervous reflexes originating in the cardioaortic body intervene in the response of the respiratory system the changes in blood pressure, and that carotid sinuses contain pressure receptors or baroreceptors which are sensitive to changes in blood pressure. Carotid sinuses and the cardioaortic body contain chemical receptors that are similar in structure to baroreceptors and are sensitive to certain stimuli. The respiratory gases and the hydrogen ion concentration of blood are maintained in equilibrium by nervous system reflexes, interconnecting vascular chemoreceptors, the medullary respiratory center, and the lungs. When the partial pressure of oxygen falls, the partial pressure of carbon dioxide rises, or the hydrogen ion concentration falls, nerve impulses from the vascular chemoreceptors to the medulla stimulate the rate of breathing. The partial pressure of oxygen is the effective stimulus of vascular chemoreceptors.

Publications: *The Artoid Sinus and Other Reflexogenic Vasosensitive Zones* (Paris: Press of French Universities, 1929). *Introduction to the Regulation of Blood Pressure and Heart Rate* (Springfield, Ill.: Thomas, 1950). *Reflexogenic Areas of the Cardiovascular System*, with E. Neil (London: Churchill, 1958).

Bibliography: *Biographical History of Medicine* (New York: Grune and Stratton, 1970), pp. 984–86. *Corneel Heymanns: A Collective Biography* (Ghent, Belgium: Archives Internationales de Pharmacodynamie et de Thérapie, 1972). *The Excitement and Fascination of Science* (Palo Alto, Calif.: Annual Reviews, 1965), vol. 1, pp. 163–76.

DOMAGK, GERHARD

Prize: Physiology or Medicine, 1939 (refused). *Born:* October 30, 1895; Lagow, Brandenburg, Germany. *Died:* April 24, 1964; Beirberg, Wurttenburg, Baden, Germany. *Nationality:* German. *Education:* University of Kiel, Germany, M.D., 1921. *Career:* Germany Army, 1914–18; University of Greifswald, Germany, Professor, 1921–25; University of Muenster, Germany, Professor, 1925–64; I. G. Farberindustrie, Elberfeld, Germany, Director of Research, 1928–64. *Other Awards:* Emil Fischer Memorial Plaque, 1937; Gold Medal of the Paris Exposition, 1938; Paul Ehrlich Gold Medal, 1939; Cameron Prize, University of Edinburgh, Scotland, 1939; Von Klebelsberg Award, University of Szeged, Hungary, 1940.

Citation: "For the discovery of the antibacterial effects of prontosil."

Life Work: Domagk's field of investigation was bacteriology. He discovered prontosil, the first of the so-called sulfa drugs, produced by natural micro-organisms, with remarkably effective therapeutic powers against streptococcal infections, pneumonia, meningitis, and gonorrhea.

Publications: "Ein Beitrag zur Chemotherapie der Bakteriellen Infektionen," *Deutsche Medizinische Wochenscrift* 61 (1935): 250–53. *Chemotherapie Bakterieller Infektionen,* with F. Hegler (Leipzig, Germany: Hirzel, 1940). *Pathologische Anatomie und Chemotherapie der Infektionskrankheiten* (Stuttgart, Germany: Thieme, 1947). *Chemotherapie der Tuberkulose mit Thiosemikarbazonen* (Stuttgart, Germany: Thieme, 1950).

Bibliography: *Biographical Memoirs of the Fellows of the Royal Society* (London: Royal Society, 1964), vol. 10, pp. 39–50. *Dictionary of Scientific Biography* (New York: Scribner's, 1971), vol. 4, pp. 153–56.

DAM, CARL PETER HENRIK

Prize: Physiology or Medicine, 1943. *Born:* February 21, 1895; Copenhagen, Denmark. *Died:* April 18, 1976; Copenhagen, Denmark. *Nationality:* Danish. *Education:* Polytechnic Institute, Denmark, M.S., 1920; University of Copenhagen, Denmark, D.Sc., 1934. *Career:* Royal School of Agriculture and Veterinary Medicine, Copenhagen, Denmark, Professor, 1920–23; University of Copenhagen, Denmark, Professor, 1923–41; University of Rochester, New York, Researcher, 1942–45; Rockefeller Institute for Medical Research, New York, Researcher, 1945–48; Polytechnic Institute, Copenhagen, Denmark, Professor, 1948–65. *Other Awards:* Christian Bohr Award in Physiology, 1939; Norman Medal, German Fat Research Society, 1960.

Citation: "For his discovery of vitamin K."

Life Work: Dam's field of investigation was biochemistry. In collaboration with Paul Karrer he discovered the fat-soluble substance from the chlorophyll of green leaves, which he called vitamin K (from the first letter of the German word *koagulation*) because of its ability to coagulate blood and prevent hemorrhage.

Publications: *Some Studies on Vitamin E* (Copenhagen: E. Munksgaard, 1941). "Vitamin K, Its Chemistry and Physiology," *Advances in Enzymology* 2 (1942): 285. "Medical Aspects of Vitamin K," *Lancet* 63 (1943): 353.

Bibliography: *Current Biography Yearbook* (New York: H. W. Wilson, 1949), pp. 134–36. *Dictionary of Scientific Biography* (New York: Scribner's, 1990), supp. II, pp. 196–202. *Modern Scientists and Engineers* (New York: McGraw-Hill, 1980), vol. 1, pp. 258–59.

DOISY, EDWARD ADELBERT

Prize: Physiology or Medicine, 1943. *Born:* November 13, 1893; Hume, Illinois. *Died:* October 23, 1986; St. Louis, Missouri. *Nationality:* American. *Education:* University of Illinois, A.B., 1914; University of Illinois, M.S., 1916; Harvard University, Massachusetts, Ph.D., 1920. *Career:* Harvard University, Massachusetts, Researcher, 1915–17; U.S. Army, 1917–19; Washington University, Missouri, Professor, 1919–23; St. Louis University, Missouri, Professor, 1923–65. *Other Awards:* Gold Medal, St. Louis Medical Society, 1935; Philip A. Conne Medal, Chemist's Club of New York, 1935; St. Louis Civic Award, 1939; Willard Gibbs Award, American Chemical Society, 1941; American Pharmaceutical Manufacturing Association Award, 1942; Squibb Award, 1944; Fleur de Lis, St. Louis University, Missouri, 1951; Commercial Solvent Award, 1952; Illini Achievement Award, University of Illinois, 1958; Barren Foundation Medal, 1972.

Citation: "For his discovery of the chemical nature of vitamin K."

Life Work: Doisy's early research consisted of the preparation of female sex hormones. With Edgar Allen he developed the Allen-Doisy vaginal smear test of estrogen potency; they also succeeded in purifying the hormones estrone, estriol, and estradio, which are used to treat gynecological disorders. His study of the chemical structure of vitamin K led to the discovery of two distinct active forms: K–1 from alfalfa and K–2 from fish meal. He also synthesiezed vitamin K–3 , called menadione. Vitamin K is essential for the synthesis of prothrombin, a blood clotting factor.

Publications: "The Constitution and Synthesis of Vitamin K1," with others, *Journal of Biological Chemistry* 131 (1939): 357–69. "The Isolation of Vitamin K1," with others, *Journal of Biological Chemistry* 130 (1939): 219–34. "The Isolation of Vitamin K2," with others, *Journal of Biological Chemistry* 131 (1939): 327–44. *Female Sex Hormones*, with others (Philadelphia: University of Pennsylvania Press, 1941).

Bibliography: *Current Biography Yearbook* (New York: H. W. Wilson, 1949), pp. 161–62. *Modern Scientists and Engineers* (New York: McGraw-Hill, 1980), vol. 1, pp. 298–99.

ERLANGER, JOSEPH

Prize: Physiology or Medicine, 1944. *Born:* January 5, 1874; San Francisco, California. *Died:* December 5, 1965; St. Louis, Missouri. *Nationality:* American. *Education:* University of California, B.S., 1895; Johns Hopkins University, Maryland, M.D., 1899. *Career:* Johns Hopkins University, Maryland, Professor, 1899–1906; University of Wisconsin, Professor, 1906–10; Washington University, Missouri, Professor, 1910–65.

Citation: "For their discoveries relating to the highly differentiated functions of single nerve fibres" (with Herbert S. Gasser).

Life Work: Erlanger's field of investigation was the regulation of blood pressure and the transmission of excitation from the auricles to the ventricles of the heart. He concentrated on studies of the electrical impulses in nerves. To measure these impulses, he devised an improved form of oscilloscope, which revealed that visible nerves are made up of nerve fibers with differing properties and sizes.

Publications: "A Study of the Metabolism in Dogs with Shortened Small Intestines," with A. W. Hewlett, *American Journal of Physiology* 6 (1901): 1–30. "On the Physiology of Heart-Block in Mammals, with Especial Reference to the Causation of Stokes-Adams Disease," *Journal of Experimental Medicine* 7 (1905): 676–724. "Studies in Blood Pressure Estimation by Indirect Methods. I. The Mechanism of the Oscillatory Methods," *American Journal of Physiology* 39 (1916): 401–46. "The Compound Nature of the Action Current of Nerve as Disclosed by the Cathode Ray Oscillograph," with H. S. Gasser, *American Journal of Physiology* 70 (1924): 624–66.

Bibliography: *Biographical Memoirs. National Academy of Sciences* (New York: Columbia University Press, 1970), vol. 41, pp. 111–39. *Dictionary of Scientific Biography* (New York: Scribner's, 1971), vol. 4, pp. 397–99. *The Excitement and Fascination of Science* (Palo Alto, Calif.: Annual Reviews, 1965), vol. 1, pp. 93–106. "A Physiologist Reminisces," *Annual Review of Physiology* 26 (1964): 1–14.

GASSER, HERBERT SPENCER

Prize: Physiology or Medicine, 1944. *Born:* July 5, 1888; Platteville, Wisconsin. *Died:* May 11, 1963; New York, New York. *Nationality:* American. *Education:* University of Wisconsin, A.B., 1910; University of Wisconsin, A.M., 1911; Johns Hopkins University, Maryland, M.D., 1915. *Career:* University of Wisconsin, Professor, 1911–16; Washington University, Missouri, Professor, 1916–31; Cornell University, New York, Professor, 1931–35; Rockefeller Institute for Medical Research, New York, Professor and Administrator, 1935–63. *Other Awards:* Kober Medal, American Association of Physicians, 1954.

Citation: "For their discoveries relating to the highly differentiated functions of single nerve fibres" (with Joseph Erlanger).

Life Work: Gasser's field of investigation was the transmission of nerve impulses. Together with Erlanger, he devised an oscillograph that recorded and amplified individual nerve impulses. They showed that different sensations were transmitted by axons of different widths and at different rates. What was previously thought to be a single action potential was in fact a collection of impulses from different types of nerves bound together in a single fiber. Action potential moved faster in thicker axons than in thinner ones. These differences, however, were not entirely consistent, for a given sensation may be transmitted at a variety of speeds.

Publications: "A Study of the Mechanism by Which muscular Exercise Produces Acceleration of the Heart," with W. J. Meek, *American Journal of Physiology* 34 (1914): 48–71. "An Experimental Study of Surgical Shock," with J. Erlanger and B.L. Elliott, *Journal of the American Medical Association* 69 (1917): 2089–92. "The Compound Nature of the Action Current of Nerve as Disclosed by the Cathode Ray Oscillograph," with J. Erlanger, *American Journal of Physiology* 70 (1924): 624–66. "The Classification of Nerve Fibers," *Ohio Journal of Science* 41 (1941): 145–59.

Bibliography: *Dictionary of Scientific Biography* (New York: Scribner's, 1972), vol. 5, pp. 290–91. *Herbert Spencer Gasser, 1888–1963: An Autobiographical Memoir* (New York: Academic Press, 1964).

CHAIN, SIR ERNST BORIS

Prize: Physiology or Medicine, 1945. *Born:* June 19, 1906; Berlin, Germany. *Died:* August 12, 1979; Mulranny, County Mayo, Ireland. *Nationality:* German; later Italian resident and British citizen. *Education:* Friedrich-Wilhelms University, Germany, Ph.D., 1930. *Career:* Charite Hospital, Berlin, Germany, Researcher, 1930–33; Cambridge University, England, Researcher, 1933–35; Oxford University, England, Professor, 1935–48; Instituto Superiore di Sanita, Rome, Italy, Professor and Administrator, 1948–61; University of London, England, Professor, 1961–73. *Other Awards:* Silver Berzelius Medal, Swedish Medical Society, 1946; Pasteur Medal, Institut Pasteur and Sociéte de Chimie Biologique, 1946; Harmsworth Memorial Fund, 1946; Paul Ehrlich Centenary Prize, 1954; Gold Medal for Therapeutics, Worshipful Society of Apothecaries, England, 1957; Knighthood, 1969; Marotta Medal, Societa Chimica Italiana, 1972; Carl Neuberg Medal, 1972; Hamburg Memorial Medal, Germany, 1972; Heymans Memorial Medal, 1974.

Citation: "For the discovery of penicillin and its curative effect in various infectious diseases" (with Alexander Fleming and Howard W. Florey).

Life Work: Chain's field of investigation was antibacterial substances, including lysozyme, discovered by Alexander Fleming. Fleming discovered penicillin in 1928 and

Chain spent the next ten years trying to purify and isolate the substance. He discovered that penicillin was not an enzyme but a relatively small organic molecule. He proposed that it incorporates a rare beta-lactam structure. To produce penicillin economically, he invented a freeze-drying technique in which a solution of penicillin was frozen, after which the water vapor was pumped away and condensed at a very low temperature.

Publications: "Penicillin as a Chemotherapeutic Agent," with others, *Lancet* 239 (1940): 226–28. "Further Observations on Penicillin," with others, *Lancet* 241 (1941): 177–89. *Antibiotics: A Survey of Penicillin, Streptomycin and other Antimicrobial Substances from Fungi, Actinomycetes, Bacteria and Plants*, with others (London: Oxford University Press, 1949).

Bibliography: *Biographical Encyclopedia of Scientists* (New York: Facts on File, 1981), p. 140. *Biographical Memoirs of the Fellows of the Royal Society* (London: Royal Society, 1983), vol. 29, pp. 42–91. R. W. Clark, *The Life of Ernst Chain* (New York: St. Martin's Press, 1985).

FLEMING, SIR ALEXANDER

Prize: Physiology or Medicine, 1945. *Born:* August 5, 1881; Lochfield Farm, Ayrshire, Scotland. *Died:* March 11, 1955; London, England. *Nationality:* Scottish. *Education:* University of London, England, M.D., 1903. *Career:* Shipping Company, London, Clerk, 1897–1901; St. Mary's Hospital, London, England, Physician and Researcher, 1906–55. *Other Awards:* Gold Medal, University of London, England, 1908; Cheadle Medal, 1908; John Scott Medal, Philadelphia, Pennsylvania, 1944; Knighthood, 1944; Cameron Prize, University of Edinburgh, Scotland, 1945; Louis Pasteur Medal, 1947; Medal for Merit, United States, 1947.

Citation: "For the discovery of penicillin and its curative effect in various infectious diseases" (with Ernst B. Chain and Howard W. Florey).

Life Work: Fleming's field of investigation was antibacterial substances. In 1922 he discovered by accident lysozyme, an enzyme that kills some bacteria without harming normal tissues. Again by accident, in 1928 he discovered the bacteriocidal mold Penicillium. Although he never fully investigated the therapeutic value of penicillin, his accidental discovery of the most famous antibiotic of modern times became the stuff of medical history.

Publications: "On the Use of Salvarsan in the Treatment of Syphilis," *Lancet* 1 (1911): 1631–34. "On a Remarkable Bacteriolytic Substance Found in Secretions and Tissues," *Proceedings of the Royal Society* 93B (1922): 306–17. "On the Antibacterial Action of Cultures of a *Penicillium*, with Special Reference to Their Use in the Isolation of B. *Influenzae*," *British Journal of Experimental Pathology* 10 (1929): 226–36. "Penicillin: Its Discovery, Development, and Uses in the Field of Medicine and Surgery," *Journal of the Royal Institute of Public Health and Hygiene* 8 (1945): 36–49,

63–71, 93–105. *Chemotherapy: Yesterday, Today, and Tomorrow* (Cambridge: Cambridge University Press, 1946). Shipton, R. *Bibliography of Sir Alexander Fleming. 1881–1955* (London: St. Mary's Hospital Medical School, 1993).

Bibliography: P. Bennett, *Alexander Fleming* (Boston: Wayland, 1992). *Dictionary of Scientific Biography* (New York: Scribner's, 1972), vol. 5, pp. 28–31. Laurence J. Ludovici, *Fleming, Discoverer of Penicillin* (London: A. Dakers, 1952). Gwyn Macfarlane, *Alexander Fleming: The Man and the Myth* (Cambridge: Harvard University Press, 1984). Andre Maurois, *The Life of Sir Alexander Fleming, Discoverer of Penicillin* (New York: Dutton, 1959).

FLOREY, SIR HOWARD WALTER

Prize: Physiology or Medicine, 1945. *Born:* September 24, 1898; Adelaide, Australia. *Died:* February 21, 1968; Oxford, England. *Nationality:* Australian; later British resident. *Education:* Adelaide University, Australia, B.S., 1921; Adelaide University, Australia, M.B., 1921; Oxford University, England, B.Sc., 1924; Oxford University, England, M.A., 1924; Cambridge University, England, Ph.D., 1927. *Career:* Cambridge University, England, Professor, 1926–31; University of Sheffield, England, Professor, 1931–35; Oxford University, England, Professor and Administrator, 1935–65; Australian National University, Canberra, Chancellor, 1965–68. *Other Awards:* Knighthood, 1944; Lister Medal, Royal College of Surgeons, 1945; Cameron Prize, University of Edinburgh, Scotland, 1945; Berzelius Silver Medal, Swedish Medical Society, 1945; Commander of the Legion of Honor, 1946; Harmsworth Memorial Award, 1946; Albert Gold Medal, Royal Society of the Arts, 1946; Medal in Therapeutics, Society of Apothecaries, London, England, 1946; Gold Medal, Royal Society of Medicine, 1947; Medal for Merit, United States, 1948; Addingham Gold Medal, 1949; Copley Medal, Royal Society, 1951; Royal Medal, 1951; Gold Medal, British Medical Association, 1964; Lomonossov Medal, USSR Academy of Sciences, 1964.

Citation: "For the discovery of penicillin and its curative effect in various infectious diseases" (with Ernst B. Chain and Alexander Fleming).

Life Work: Florey is remembered as the scientist who helped to develop penicillin as a commercially viable and medically proven antibiotic. He worked with Chain and Norman Heatley to devise new methods for growing penicillin mold in quantity and for extracting and purifying the substance. Later he and Chain were the first to conduct tests on mice and humans.

Publications: "The Secretion of Mucus by the Colon," *British Journal of Experimental Pathology* 11 (1930): 348–61. "Some Properties of Mucus, with Special Reference to Its Antibacterial Functions," with N.E. Goldsworthy, *British Journal of Experimental Pathology* 11 (1930): 192–208. "Penicillin as a Chemotherapeutic Agent," with others, *Lancet* 239 (1940): 226–28. "Further Observations on Penicillin," with others, *Lancet* 241 (1941): 177–88. *Antibiotics: A Survey of Penicillin, Streptomycin, and Other*

Antimicrobial Substances from Fungi, Actinomycetes, Bacteria and Plants (London: Oxford University Press, 1949).

Bibliography: *Biographical Memoirs of the Fellows of the Royal Society* (London: Royal Society, 1971), vol. 17, pp. 255–302. D. Chase, *Howard Florey, The Man Who Developed Penicillin* (South Melbourne: Macmillan Australia, 1991). *Dictionary of Scientific Biography* (New York: Scribner's, 1972), vol. 5, pp. 41–44. R. G. McFarlane, *Howard Florey* (London: Oxford University Press, 1979).

MULLER, HERMANN JOSEPH

Prize: Physiology or Medicine, 1946. *Born:* December 21, 1890; New York, New York. *Died:* April 5, 1967; Indianapolis, Indiana. *Nationality:* American. *Education:* Columbia University, New York, B.A., 1910; Columbia University, New York, M.A., 1911; Columbia University, New York, Ph.D., 1916. *Career:* Cornell University, New York, Professor, 1911–12; Columbia University, New York, Professor, 1912–15; Rice Institute, Texas, Professor, 1915–18; Columbia University, New York, Professor, 1918–20; University of Texas, Professor, 1920–36; Soviet Academy of Sciences Institute of Genetics, USSR, Researcher, 1933–37; University of Edinburgh, Scotland, Professor, 1937–40; Amherst College, Massachusetts, Professor, 1940–45; Indiana University, Professor, 1945–67. *Other Awards:* Cleveland Research Prize, American Association for the Advancement of Science, 1927; Kimber Award in Genetics, U.S. National Academy of Sciences, 1955; Virchow Medal, Virchow Society of New York, 1956; Darwin Medal, Linnean Society of London, 1958; Darwin Medal, Deutsche Akademie Naturforscher Leopoldina, 1959; Alexander Hamilton Award, Columbia University, New York, 1960; Humanist of the Year, Humanist Association, 1963; City of Hope Medical Centre Research Citation, 1964.

Citation: "For the discovery of the production of mutations by means of X-ray irradiation."

Life Work: Muller's field of investigation was genetics. Working on Darwin's theory of mutations as constant and that evolution proceeds in gradual steps Muller tried to devise a mutation rate. His research confirmed that most mutations are deleterious or lethal. He further demonstrated that the mutation rate does not depend on the environment and that they are produced at a constant rate whether needed or not. He found that environmental factors, especially X rays, could adversely affect genetics and heredity and cause mutations.

Publications: "Artificial Transmutation of the Gene," *Science* 66 (1927): 84–87. *Out of the Night: A Biologist's View of the Future* (London: V. Gollancz, 1936). *Genetics, Medicine and Man*, with C. C. Little and W. H. Snyder (Ithaca, N.Y.: Cornell University Press, 1947). *Studies in Genetics: The Selected Papers of H. J. Muller* (Bloomington: Indiana University Press, 1962).

Bibliography: *Biographical Memoirs of the Fellows of the Royal Society* (London: Royal Society, 1968), vol. 14, pp. 349–89. E. A. Carlson, *Genes, Radiation and Society: The Life and Work of H. J. Muller* (Ithaca, N.Y.: Cornell University Press, 1981). *Dictionary of Scientific Biography* (New York: Scribner's, 1974), vol. 9, pp. 564–65.

CORI, CARL FERDINAND

Prize: Physiology or Medicine, 1947. *Born:* December 5, 1896; Prague, Bohemia (now Czech Republic). *Died:* October 20, 1984; Cambridge, Massachusetts. *Nationality:* Czech; later U.S. citizen. *Education:* German University of Prague, Czechoslovakia, M.D., 1920. *Career:* University of Graz, Austria, Researcher, 1920–21; State Institute for the Study of Malignant Disease, Buffalo, New York, Researcher, 1922–31; Washington University, St. Louis, Missouri, Professor, 1931–66; Harvard University, Massachusetts, Professor, 1966–84. *Other Awards:* Midwest Award, American Chemical Society, 1946; Lasker Award, 1946; Squibb Award, 1947; Sugar Research Foundation Award, 1947, 1950; Willard Gibbs Medal, American Chemical Society, 1948.

Citation: "For their discovery of the course of the catalytic conversion of glycogen" (with Gerty T. Cori).

Life Work: Cori's field of investigation was carbohydrate metabolism, especially the biochemistry of glucose and glycogen. Glucose, a simple sugar molecule, is the principal energy source for living cells. Glycogen is the biochemical form in which glucose is stored in the liver. Dietary starch is converted to glucose, absorbed into the portal bloodstream, and carried to the liver, where it is converted into glycogen and stored for future use. The complete cycle by which glucose is converted into glycogen is known as the Cori Cycle. He discovered Glucose–1-phosphate, later kown as Cori ester, and also the biochemical mechanism of insulin, a hormone that is synthesized and secreted by the islets of Langerhans. Further, in 1936 he described the conversion of glucose–1-phosphate to glucose–6-phosphate by the enzyme phosphoglucomutase. In 1943 he isolated and purified phosphorylase in crystalline form which exists in both an active and an inactive form. The following year, he synthesized glycogen, thus establishing that the chemical pathway from glucose to glyogen has three steps.

Publications: "Mammalian Carbohydrate Metabolism," *Physiological Reviews* 11 (April 1931). "The Formation of Hexosephosphate Esters in Frog Muscle," with G. T. Cori, *Journal of Biological Chemistry* 116 (1936): 119–28. "Crystalline Muscle Phosphorylase. III. Kinetics," with A. A. Green and G. T. Cori, *Journal of Biological Chemistry* 151 (1943): 39–55. "The Enzymatic Conversion of Phosphorylase a to b," with G. T. Cori, *Journal of Biological Chemistry* 158 (1945): 321–32. "Glucose 6-Phosphatase of the Liver in Glycogen Storage Disease," with G. T. Cori, *Journal of Biological Chemistry* 199 (1952): 661–67.

Bibliography: *Biographical Memoirs of the Fellows of the Royal Society* (London: Royal Society, 1986), vol. 32, p. 65. *Biographical Memoirs. National Academy of Sciences*

(Washington, D.C.: National Academy Press, 1992), vol. 61, p. 111. *Current Biography Yearbook* (New York: H. W. Wilson, 1947), pp. 135–37. B. A. Houssay, "Carl F. and Gerty T. Cori." *Biochimica et Biophysica Acta* 20 (1956): 11–16.

CORI, GERTY THERESA RADNITZ

Prize: Physiology or Medicine, 1947. *Born:* August 15, 1896; Prague, Bohemia (now Czech Republic). *Died:* October 26, 1957; St. Louis, Missouri. *Nationality:* Czech; later U.S. citizen. *Education:* German University of Prague, Czechoslovakia, M.D., 1920. *Career:* Children's Hospital, Vienna, Austria, Researcher, 1920–22; State Institute for the Study of Malignant Diseases, Buffalo, New York, Researcher, 1922–31; Washington University, St. Louis, Missouri, Professor, 1931–57. *Other Awards:* Midwest Award, American Chemical Society, 1946; Squibb Award, 1947; Garvan Medal, 1948; Sugar Research Prize, National Academy of Sciences, 1950; Borden Award, Association of Medical Colleges, 1952.

Citation: "For their discovery of the course of the catalytic conversion of glycogen" (with Carl F. Cori).

Life Work: Gerty Cori worked with her husband, Carl, on the conversion of glucose to glycogen. They codiscovered the Cori cycle, which described the chemical pathway between dietary starch and glucose and between glucose and glycogen in the liver. They also discovered glucose–1-phosphate, which came to be known as the Cori ester and the biochemical mechanism of insulin action. The Coris described the the the transformation of glucose–6-phosphate into glucose–1-phosphate by the enzyme phosphoglucomutase. They isolated and purified phosphorylase enzyme in crystalline form which exists in both an active and an inactive form. In 1944 the Coris synthesized glycogen in a test tube.

Publications: "The Formation of Hexosephosphate Esters in Frog Muscle," with C. F. Cori, *Journal of Biological Chemistry* 116 (1936): 119–28. "Crystalline Muscle Phosphorylase. II. Prosthetic Group," with A. A. Green, *Journal of Biological Chemistry* 151 (1943): 31–38. "Crystalline Muscle Phosphorylase. III. Kinetics," with A. A. Green and C. F. Cori, *Journal of Biological Chemistry* 151 (1943): 39–55. "The Enzymatic Conversion of Phosphorylase a to b," with C.F. Cori, *Journal of Biological Chemistry* 158 (1945): 321–32. "Action of Amylo–1,6-Glycosidase and Phosphorylase on Glycogen and Amylopectin," with J. Larner, *Journal of Biological Chemistry* 188 (1951): 17–29. "Glucose 6-Phosphatase of the Liver in Glycogen Storage Disease," with C. F. Cori, *Journal of Biological Chemistry* 199 (1952): 661–67. "Glycogen Structure and Enzyme Deficiencies in Glycogen Storage Disease," *Harvey Lectures* 48 (1952–53): 145–71.

Bibliography: C. F. Cori, "The Call of Science," *Annual Review of Biochemistry* 38 (1969): 1–20. *Biographical Memoirs. National Academy of Sciences* (Washington, D.C.: National Academy Press, 1990), vol. 61, p. 111. *Current Biography Yearbook* (New

York: H. W. Wilson, 1947), pp. 135–37. *Dictionary of Scientific Biography* (New York: Scribner's, 1971), vol. 3, pp. 415–16. B. A. Houssay, "Carl F. and Gerty T. Cori," *Biochimica et Biophysica Acta* 20 (1956): 11–16.

HOUSSAY, BERNARDO ALBERTO

Prize: Physiology or Medicine, 1947. *Born:* April 10, 1887; Buenos Aires, Argentina. *Died:* September 27, 1971; Buenos Aires, Argentina. *Nationality:* Argentinian. *Education:* University of Buenos Aires, Argentina, Pharmacy Degree, 1904; University of Buenos Aires, Argentina, Doctorate in Medicine, 1910. *Career:* University of Buenos Aires, Argentina, Professor, 1907–69. *Other Awards:* National Award of Sciences, Buenos Aires, Argentina, 1923; Charles Mickle Fellowship, Toronto, Ontario, Canada, 1945; Banting Medal, American Diabetes Association, 1946; Research Award, American Pharmaceutical Manufacturers' Association, 1947; Baly Medal, Royal College of Physicians, England, 1947; James Cook Medal, Sydney Medal, 1948; Dale Medal, Society for Endocrinology, England, 1960; Weizmann Prize, 1967.

Citation: "For his discovery of the part played by the hormone of the anterior pituitary lobe in the metabolism of sugar."

Life Work: Houssay's field of investigation was physiology, especially the endocrine system. He described the pituitary as a master gland and determined its hormonal and regulatory relationships to the other glands in the endocrine system. His research particularly concerned the effects of pituitary hormones on carbohydrate metabolism and their relation to diabetes mellitus. He established that insulin and the hormones of the pituitary glands had a regulatory function in maintaining the blood levels of glucose and its cellular utilization and that glycogen is related to the development of diabetes. He further proved that carbohydrate metabolism and other metabolic processes are regulated by the balance maintained between the secretion of several endocrine glands. Diabetes and other metabolic diseases are a disturbance in this endocrine metabolism.

Publications: "Carbohydrate Metabolism," *New England Journal of Medicine* 214 (1936): 971. "The Hypophysis and Metabolism," *New England Journal of Medicine* 214 (1936): 961. "Diabetes as a Disturbance of Endocrine Regulation," *American Journal of Medical Science* 193 (1937): 581. "Advancement of Knowledge of the Role of the Hypophysis in Carbohydrate Metabolism During the Last Twenty-Five Years," *Endocrinology* 30 (1942): 884.

Bibliography: *Biographical Memoirs of the Fellows of the Royal Society* (London: Royal Society, 1974), vol. 20, pp. 247–70. M. Cereijido, *La Nuca de Houssay* (Buenos Aires: Fondo de Cultura Economica, 1990). *Current Biography Yearbook* (New York: H. W. Wilson, 1948), pp. 295–97. *The Excitement and Fascination of Science* (Palo Alto, Calif.: Annual Reviews, 1965), vol. 1, pp. 205–16.

MÜLLER, PAUL HERMANN

Prize: Physiology or Medicine, 1948. *Born:* January 12, 1899; Olten, Switzerland. *Died:* October 13, 1965; Basel, Switzerland. *Nationality:* Swiss. *Education:* University of Basel, Switzerland, doctorate, 1925. *Career:* Lonza Power Plant, Switzerland, Researcher, 1916–17; J. R. Geigy Company, Basel, Switzerland, Researcher, 1925–65.

Citation: "For his discovery of the high efficiency of DDT as a contact poison against several arthropods."

Life Work: Müller discovered DDT (p-dichloro-diphenyl-trichloroethane) as a synthetic insecticide that would kill insects on contact, but would be nontoxic to humans and plants, inexpensive, and chemically stable.

Publications: "Uber Konstitution und Toxische Wirkung von Naturlichen und Neuen Synthetischen. Insektentotenden Stoffen," with P. Lauger and H. Martin, *Helvetica Chimica Acta* 27 (1944): 899–928. "Uber Zusammenhange Zwischen Konstitution und Insektizider Werkung. I," *Helvetica Chimica Acta* 29 (1946): 1560–80.

Bibliography: *Current Biography Yearbook* (New York: H. W. Wilson, 1945), pp. 340–42. *Dictionary of Scientific Biography* (New York: Scribner's, 1974), vol. 9, pp. 576–77.

HESS, WALTER RUDOLPH

Prize: Physiology or Medicine, 1949. *Born:* March 17, 1881; Frauenfeld, Switzerland. *Died:* August 12, 1973; Locarno, Switzerland. *Nationality:* Swiss. *Education:* University of Zürich, Switzerland, M.D., 1906. *Career:* Zürich, Switzerland, Physician, 1905–12; Bonn, Germany, Physician, 1913–17; University of Zürich, Switzerland, Professor and Administrator, 1917–51. *Other Awards:* Marcel Benorst Prize, Switzerland, 1933; Ludwig Medal, German Society for Circulation Research, 1938.

Citation: "For his discovery of the functional organization of the interbrain as a coordinator of the activities of the internal organs."

Life Work: Hess's field of investigation was radioactive radiation and atmospheric ionization. To explain why radiation is higher in the atmosphere than on the ground, he sent instruments into the atmosphere by balloons. With the assistance of the Austrian Air Club, he made ten balloon ascents. He demonstrated that ionization was reduced with increasing height from the earth but increased noticeably from 2,700 feet upward. He also speculated that the radiation came from outer space rather than from the sun because there was no decrease in ionization during nighttime ascents.

Publications: *Die Funktionelle Organisation des Vegetativen Nervensystems* (Basel, Switzerland: B. Schwabe, 1948). *The Functional Organization of the Diencephalon*

(New York: Grune and Stratton, 1957). *The Biology of Mind* (Chicago: University of Chicago Press, 1964). *Biological Order and Brain Organization: Selected Works of W. R. Hess* (New York: Springer-Verlag, 1981).

Bibliography: D. J. Ingle, *A Dozen Doctors* (Chicago: University of Chicago Press, 1963). *Modern Scientists and Engineers* (New York: McGraw-Hill, 1980), vol. 2, p. 52. "W. R. Hess: The Control of the Autonomic Nervous System by the Hypothalamus," *Lancet* 1 (March 17, 1951): 627–29.

MONIZ, ANTONIO CAETANO DE ABREU FREIRE EGAS

Prize: Physiology or Medicine, 1949. *Born:* November 29, 1874; Avanca, Portugal. *Died:* December 13, 1955; Lisbon, Portugal. *Nationality:* Portuguese. *Education:* University of Coimbra, Portugal, M.D., 1899. *Career:* University of Coimbra, Portugal, Professor, 1902–11; University of Lisbon, Portugal, Professor, 1911–55. *Other Awards:* Grand Cross of Isabel la Catolica, Spain, 1952; Instrucao Publica, Portugal, 1953; Santiago de Espada, 1953; Commander, Legion of Honour, 1953.

Citation: "For his discovery of the therapeutic value of leucotomy in certain psychoses."

Life Work: Egas Moniz's field of investigation was neurology. He developed cerebral angiography, a procedure that uses X rays and radioactive iodine to make the blood vessels of the brain contrast with the surrounding tissues. He was the first neurosurgeon to direct a lobotomy in which prefrontal lobes were severed from the rest of the brain from patients suffering from severe anxiety or aggression. Although lobotomized patients were not all cured, many were able to return to normal lives without institutional care.

Publications: *Diagnostic des Tumeurs Cerebrales et Epreuve de L'Encephalographie Arterielle* (Paris: Masson, 1931). *A Vida Sexual [Fisiologia e Patologia]* (Lisbon: Abrantes, 1931). *L'Angiographie Cerebrale, Ses Applications et Resultats en Anatomie, Physiologie et Clinique* (Paris: Masson, 1934). *Cerebrale Arteriographie und Phlebographie* (Berlin: J. Springer, 1940).

Bibliography: *Dictionary of Scientific Biography* (New York: Scribner's, 1971), vol. 4, pp. 286–87. "Egas Moniz, 1874–1955," *Journal of the International College of Surgeons* 36 (1961): 261–71.

HENCH, PHILIP SHOWALTER

Prize: Physiology or Medicine, 1950. *Born:* February 28, 1896; Pittsburgh, Pennsylvania. *Died:* March 30, 1965; Ocho Rios, Jamaica. *Nationality:* American. *Education:*

Lafayette College, Pennsylvania, A.B., 1916; University of Pittsburgh, Pennsylvania, M.D., 1920; University of Minnesota, M.Sc., 1931. *Career:* St. Francis Hospital, Pittsburgh, Pennsylvania, Physician, 1921; University of Minnesota, Professor, 1921–57. *Other Awards:* Heberden Medal, London, 1942; Lasker Award, American Public Health Association, 1949; Page One Award, Newspaper Guild of New York, 1950; Passano Foundation Award, 1950; Scientific Award, American Pharmaceutical Manufacturers Association, 1950; Special Citation, American Rheumatism Association, 1951; Pennsylvania Ambassador Award, 1951; Northwestern University Centennial Award, 1951; Award of Merit, Masonic Foundation, 1951; Criss Award, 1951; Honor Award, Mississippi Valley Medical Society, 1952; Order of Carlos Finlay, Cuba.

Citation: "For their discoveries relating to the hormones of the adrenal cortex, their structure and biological effects" (with Edward C. Kendall and Tadeus Reichstein).

Life Work: Hench's field of investigation was rheumatoid arthritis. Working with arthritic patients he found that their pain diminished when they had jaundice. He postulated that an unknown substance X in jaundice was responsible for a remission of the symptoms. Meanwhile Edward Kendall, another researcher at the Mayo Clinic, had isolated thyroid hormone in 1914. He further isolated and identified the hormones of the adrenal glands which consist of an outer cortex and a central medulla that secrete epinephrine (adrenaline) into the bloodstream. The cells of the adrenal cortex, which synthesize and secrete adrenal corticosteroids into the bloodstream, are controlled by adrenocorticotropic hormone (ACTH), a hormonal secretion of the adrenal gland. There are two categories of adrenal corticosteroids of which glucocorticoids (cortisone and cortisol) metabolize carbohydrate, fat, and protein. Within a decade, Hench discovered that the administration of cortisone and ACTH to arthritic patients resulted in marked improvement in their condition.

Publications: *Chronic Arthritis: Chronic Infectious Arthritis, Chronic Senescent Arthritis, Gout* (Baltimore, Md.: Williams and Wilkins Company, 1940). "Effects of Cortisone Acetate and Pituitary ACTH on Rheumatoid Arthritis, Rheumatic Fever, and Certain Other Conditions," with E. Kendall, *Archives of Internal Medicine* 85 (1950): 545–666. *Cortisone, Hydrocortisone, and Corticotropin (ACTH) in the Treatment of Rheumatoid Arthritis* (Basel, Switzerland: Geigy, 1954).

Bibliography: *Current Biography Yearbook* (New York: H. W. Wilson, 1950), pp. 230–32. *Modern Scientists and Engineers* (New York: McGraw-Hill, 1980), vol. 2, pp. 42–43. L. G. Rowntree, *Amid Masters of the Twentieth Century Medicine* (Springfield, Ill.: C. C. Thomas, 1958).

KENDALL, EDWARD CALVIN

Prize: Physiology or Medicine, 1950. *Born:* March 8, 1886; Norwalk, Connecticut. *Died:* May 4, 1972; Rahway, New Jersey. *Nationality:* American. *Education:* Columbia University, New York, B.S., 1908; Columbia University, New York, M.S.,

1909; Columbia University, New York, Ph.D., 1910. *Career:* Parke, Davis, and Co., Detroit, Michigan, Researcher, 1910–11; St. Luke's Hospital, New York, Researcher, 1911–14; University of Minnesota, Professor and Administrator, 1914–51. *Other Awards:* John Scott Prize and Premium, Philadelphia, 1921; Chandler Medal, Columbia University, New York, 1925; Squibb Award for Outstanding Research in Endocrinology, 1945; Lasker Award, American Public Health Association, 1949; Page One Award, Newspaper Guild of New York, 1950; John Phillips Memorial Ward, American College of Physicians, 1950; Research Corporation Award, Research Corporation of New York, 1950; Remsen Memorial Award, Maryland Section of American Chemical Society, 1950; Research Award, American Pharmaceutical Manufacturers Association, 1950; Edgar F. Smith Award, American Chemical Society, 1950; Passano Award, 1950; Medal of Honor, Canadian Pharmaceutical Manufacturers Association, 1950; Dr. C. C. Criss Award, 1951; Award of Merit, Masonic Foundation for Medical Research and Humane Welfare, 1951; Cameron Award, University of Edinburgh, Scotland, 1951; Heberden Society Award, London, 1951; Kober Award, Association of American Physicians, 1952; Alexander Hamilton Medal, Alumni of Columbia College, 1961; Scientific Achievement Award, American Medical Association, 1965.

Citation: "For their discoveries relating to the hormones of the adrenal cortex, their structure and biological effects" (with Philip S. Hench and Tadeus Reichstein).

Life Work: Kendall's earliest research was to extract hormones from the thyroid gland. He was able to increase the concentration of the thyroid hormone in the thyroid gland. He continued to isolate and purify biologically active hormones from the thyroid gland, such as glutathione. Next he turned to the isolation and identification of the hormones of the adrenal glands, which discharge epinephrine, or adrenaline, into the bloodstream. The cells of the adrenal cortex are controlled by the pituitary gland, specifically by a secretion called *adrenocorticotropic hormone* (ACTH). There are two categories of ACTH of which glucocorticoids (cortisone and cortisol) are involved in the metabolism of carbohydrate, fat, and protein. Cortisone and cortisol also block biochemical reactions that intervene in the inflammatory response of tissue to injury or injection. After 1934, Kendall isolated and identified twenty-eight biologically inactive steroids from the adrenal cortex and six biologically active forms, A, B, C, D, E, and F. Of these E (Cortisone) and F (Cortisol or hydrocortisone) are the most important. By 1945, Kendall had clarified thirty of the thirty-eight biochemical steps in the biosynthesis of cortisone.

Publications: "The Isolation in Crystalline Form of the Compound Containing Iodin Which Occurs in the Thyroid: Its Chemical Nature and Physiological Activity," *Transactions of the Association of American Physicians* 30 (1914): 420–49. *Oxidative Catalysis* (New York: Columbia University Press, 1925). "The Identification of a Substance Which Possesses the Qualitative Action of Cortin," *Journal of Biological Chemistry* 116 (1936): 267–76. "Effects of Cortisone Acetate and Pituitary ACTH on Rheumatoid Arthritis, Rheumatic Fever, and Certain Other Conditions," with P. Hench, *Archives of Internal Medicine* 85 (1950): 545–666.

Bibliography: *Biographical Memoirs. National Academy of Sciences* (Washington, D.C.: National Academy of Sciences, 1975), vol. 48, pp. 249–92. *Dictionary of Scientific Biography* (New York: Scribner's, 1978), supp. I, pp. 258–59.

REICHSTEIN, TADEUS

Prize: Physiology or Medicine, 1950. *Born:* July 20, 1897; Wloclawek, Poland. *Died:* August 1, 1996; Basel, Switzerland. *Nationality:* Polish; later Swiss citizen. *Education:* Eidenossische Technische Hochschule, Switzerland, B.S., 1920; Eidenossische Technische Hochschule, Switzerland, Ph.D., 1922. *Career:* Eidenossische Technische Hochschule, Switzerland, Professor, 1922–38; University of Basel, Switzerland, Professor and Administrator, 1938–. *Other Awards:* Cameron Award, University of Edinburgh, Scotland, 1951; Copley Medal, Royal Society, 1968.

Citation: "For their discoveries relating to the hormones of the adrenal cortex, their structure and biological effects" (with Edward C. Kendall and Tadeus Reichstein).

Life Work: Reichstein began research on the adrenal cortical hormones in the 1930s. He isolated and identified five of these compounds including aldosterone, cortiscosterone and deoxycorticosterone. By 1942, he had isolated twenty-seven different adrenal corticosteroids. In 1943, he was granted a patent on a method for synthesizing one of the six hormones.

Publications: *Uber das Offenkettige Tropin und Einige Seiner Homologen* (Weida i. Thur, Germany: Thomas & Hubert, 1924). "Die Hormone der Nebennierenrinde," in *Handbuch der Biologischen Arbeitsmethoden*, ed. Emil Abderhalden (Berlin, 1938), vol. 5, pp. 1367–1439. "The Hormones of the Adrenal Cortex," with C.W. Shoppee, in *Vitamins and Hormones* (New York: Academic Press, 1943), pp. 346–414.

Bibliography: *Current Biography Yearbook* (New York: H. W. Wilson, 1951), pp. 512–14. "Tadeus Reichstein," *Journal of Chemical Education* 26 (1949): 529–30.

THEILER, MAX

Prize: Physiology or Medicine, 1951. *Born:* January 30, 1899; Pretoria, South Africa. *Died:* August 11, 1972; New Haven, Connecticut. *Nationality:* South African; later U.S. resident. *Education:* University of London, England, M.D., 1922. *Career:* Harvard University, Massachusetts, Professor, 1922–30; Rockefeller Foundation, New York, Researcher and Administrator, 1930–64; Yale University, New Haven, Connecticut, Professor, 1964–67; Rockefeller Foundation, New York, Researcher, 1967–72. *Other Awards:* Chalmers Medal, Royal Society of Tropical Medicine and Hygiene, England, 1939; Flattery Medal, Harvard University, Massachusetts, 1945; Lasker Award, American Public Health Association, 1949.

Citation: "For his discoveries concerning yellow fever and how to combat it."

Life Work: Theiler's field of investigation was yellow fever. In 1926, he found conclusive evidence that yellow fever was caused not by a bacterium but by a filterable virus. Theiler perfected a serum against yellow virus, called 17D, produced from the Asibi strain grown chicken embryos from which most of the nervous tissue had been removed.

Publications: "Studies on the Action of Yellow Fever Virus in Mice," *Annals of Tropical Medicine and Parasitology* 24 (1930): 249–72. "The Effect of Prolonged Cultivation in Vitro upon the Pathogenicity of Yellow Fever Virus," *Journal of Experimental Medicine* 65 (1937): 767–86. *Yellow Fever* (New York: McGraw-Hill, 1951), chap. 2. *The Anthropod-Borne Viruses of Vertebrates: An Account of the Rockefeller Foundation Virus Program* (New Haven, Conn.: Yale University Press, 1973).

Bibliography: *Biographical Encyclopedia of Scientists* (New York: Facts on File, 1981), pp. 778–79. *Current Biography Yearbook* (New York: H. W. Wilson, 1952), pp. 586–87.

WAKSMAN, SELMAN ABRAHAM

Prize: Physiology or Medicine, 1952. *Born:* July 2, 1888; Priluki, Ukraine. *Died:* August 16, 1973; Hyannis, Massachusetts. *Nationality:* Ukrainian; later U.S. citizen. *Education:* Rutgers University, New Jersey, B.Sc., 1915; Rutgers University, New Jersey, M.Sc., 1916; University of California, Ph.D., 1918. *Career:* Rutgers University, New Jersey, Professor, 1918–58. *Other Awards:* Nitrate of Soda Research Award, 1930; Passano Foundation Award, 1947; Award of the Carlsberg Laboratories, Denmark, 1948; New Jersey Agricultural Society Medal, 1948; Lasker Award, American Public Health Association, 1948; Emil Christian Hanson Medal, 1948; Leeuwenhoek Medal, Netherlands Academy of Sciences, 1950; Henrietta Szold Award, 1950; Commander, French Legion of Honour, 1950; British Shalom Humanitarian Award, 1952; Order of Merit of the Rising Sun, Japan, 1952; Great Cross of Public Health, Spain, 1954; St. Vincent Award for Medical Sciences, Academy of Sciences of Torino, Italy, 1954; Instituto Curlo Forlanini Medal, 1959; American Trudeau Medal, 1961; Commendatore Order of Southern Cross of Brazil, 1963.

Citation: "For his discovery of streptomycin, the first antibiotic effective against tuberculosis."

Life Work: Waksman's field of investigation was tuberculosis. He examined ten thousand different soil microbes seeking antibiotic agents that would destroy bacteria without destroying humans. His research led to the isolation of a number of antibiotics, including actinomycin, streptothricin, and streptomycin. The last became a particularly effective against strains of bacteria that are resistant to sulfa drugs and penicillin.

Publications: *Enzymes: Properties, Distribution, Methods and Applications,* with W. C. Davison (Baltimore: Williams and Wilkins, 1926). *Humus: Origin, Chemical Composition, and Importance in Nature* (Baltimore: Williams and Wilkins, 1936). *Neomycin: Its Nature, Formation, Isolation and Practical Application* (New Brunswick, N.J.: Rutgers University Press, 1953). *The Actinomycetes,* 3 vols. (Baltimore: Williams and Wilkins, 1959–62). *Scientific Contributions of Selman A. Waksman; Selected Articles Published in Honor of His 80th Birthday* (New Brunswick, N.J.: Rutgers University Press, 1968).

Bibliography: *National Cyclopedia of American Biography* (New York: James T. White, 1960), vol. I, pp. 312–13. Selman Waksman, *My Life with the Microbes* (New York: Simon and Schuster, 1954).

KREBS, SIR HANS ADOLF

Prize: Physiology or Medicine, 1953. *Born:* August 25, 1900; Hildesheim, Germany. *Died:* November 22, 1981; Oxford, England. *Nationality:* German; later British citizen. *Education:* University of Hamburg, Germany, M.D., 1925; Cambridge University, England, M.S., 1934. *Career:* Kaiser Wilhelm Institute, Berlin, Germany, Researcher, 1926–30; Municipal Hospital, Altona, Germany, Physician, 1930–32; University of Freiberg, Germany, Professor, 1932–33; Cambridge University, England, Professor, 1933–35; University of Sheffield, England, Professor, 1935–54; Oxford University, England, Professor, 1954–67. *Other Awards:* Lasker Award, 1953; Royal Medal, Royal Society, 1954; Gold Medal, Netherlands Society for Physics, Medical Science and Surgery, 1958; Knighthood, 1958; Copley Medal, 1961.

Citation: "For his discovery of the citric acid cycle."

Life Work: Krebs's field of investigation was biochemistry. He discovered the urea cycle, the process by which nitrogen and ammonia are eliminated from the body. He thus introduced the concept of cyclical processes in biochemistry. While studying the intermediate stages of carbohydrate metabolism he discovered the Krebs Cycle, or the tricarboxylic acid cycle. It is the final pathway in the breakdown of carbohydrates, proteins, and fats into carbon dioxide and water. The Krebs Cycle explains how the body converts food into energy. To determine how sugar is converted into other compounds, he investigated lactic and pyruvic acids. When pyruvic acid is oxidized, it forms an intermediate chemical called acetyl coenzyme A, and carbon dioxide is released during oxidation. Other acids are formed during oxidation. The discovery of the cyclic nature of intermediary metabolic reactions, an important milestone in biochemistry, provided a clue to the understanding of metabolic pathways.

Publications: "Metabolism of Acetoacetic Acid in Animal Tissues," with L. V. Eggleston, *Nature* 154 (August 12, 1944): 209–10. "Urea Synthesis in Mammalian Liver," with others, *Nature* (June 14, 1947): 808–809. "Tricarboxylic Acid Cycle," *Harvey Lectures* 44 (1950): 165–99. "A Survey of the Energy Transformations in Living Matter," with H. Kornberg, *Ergebn. Physiol. Biol. Chem. Exp. Pharmak* 49 (1957): 212. *The Metabolic Roles of Citrate* (London: Academic Press, 1968). *Essays in Cell Metabolism* (New York: Wiley, 1970).

Bibliography: *Biographical Memoirs. Royal Society of London* (London: Royal Society, 1984), vol. 30, p. 349. *Current Biography Yearbook* (New York: H. W. Wilson, 1954), pp. 384–85. F. Homes, *Hans Krebs* (New York: Oxford University Press, 1991–93). *Reminiscences and Reflections* (New York: Oxford University Press, 1982).

LIPMANN, FRITZ ALBERT

Prize: Physiology or Medicine, 1953. *Born:* June 12, 1899; Konigsburg, Germany. *Died:* July 25, 1986; Poughkeepsie, New York. *Nationality:* German; later U.S. citizen. *Education:* University of Berlin, Germany, M.D., 1924; University of Berlin, Germany, Ph.D., 1927. *Career:* Kaiser Wilhelm Institute, Berlin and Heidelberg, Germany, Researcher, 1927–30; Fischer's Laboratory, Berlin, Germany, Researcher, 1930–31; Rockefeller Institute for Medical Research, New York, Researcher, 1931–32; Carlsburg Foundation, Copenhagen, Denmark, Researcher, 1932–39; Cornell University, Ithaca, New York, Researcher, 1939–41; Massachusetts General Hospital, Boston, Researcher and Administrator, 1941–57; Harvard University, Massachusetts, Professor, 1949–57; Rockefeller University, New York, Professor, 1957–86. *Other Awards:* Carl Neuberg Medal, 1948; Mead Johnson and Company Award, 1948; National Medal of Science, 1966.

Citation: "For his discovery of co-enzyme A and its importance for intermediary metabolism."

Life Work: Lippmann's field of investigation was cellular energetics. He proposed that the principal source of energy in metabolic reactions in living cells was adenosine triphosphate (ATP), a central compound of the phosphate group that makes up the nucleotide molecular structure. He isolated and synthesized coenzyme A, a catalytic agent that releases cellular energy in all plants, animals and microorganisms. His finding elucidated the Krebs Cycle.

Publications: "Fermentation of Phosphogluconic Acid," *Nature* (October 3, 1936): 588–89. "Colored Intermediate on Reduction of Vitamin B1," *Nature* (November 13, 1937): 849. "Coupling Between Pyruvic Acid Dehydrogenation and Adenylic Acid Phosphorylation," *Nature* (February 18, 1939): 281. "Biosynthetic Mechanisms," *Harvey Lectures* 44 (1950): 99–123.

Bibliography: *Current Biography Yearbook* (New York: H. W. Wilson, 1954), pp. 413–14. *The Excitement and Fascination of Science* (Palo Alto, Calif.: Annual Reviews, 1990), vol. 3, part 1, pp. 383–415. *Wanderings of a Biochemist* (New York: Wiley, 1971).

ENDERS, JOHN FRANKLIN

Prize: Physiology or Medicine, 1954. *Born:* February 10, 1897; West Hartford, Connecticut. *Died:* September 8, 1985; Waterford, Connecticut. *Nationality:* American. *Education:* Yale University, Connecticut, A.B., 1920; Harvard University, Massachusetts, M.A., 1922; Harvard University, MA, Ph.D., 1930. *Career:* U.S. Army, 1917–20; Harvard University, Massachusetts, Professor, 1929–77. *Other Awards:*

Commander, Order National de la Republic de Haute Volta, 1951; Passano Foundation Award, 1953; Lasker Award, 1954; Kimball Award, 1954; Kyer Award, U.S. Public Health Service, 1955; Chapin Award, 1955; Bruce Award, American College of Physicians, 1956; Cameron Prize, University of Edinburgh, Scotland, 1960; Howard Taylor Ricketts Memorial Award, University of Chicago, 1962; New England Israel Freedom Award, 1962; Robert Koch Medal, Germany, 1962; Science Achievement Award, American Medical Association, 1963; Presidential Medal of Freedom, 1963.

Citation: "For their discovery of the ability of poliomyelitis viruses to grow in cultures of various types of tissue" (with Frederick C. Robbins and Thomas H. Weller).

Life Work: Enders's field of investigation was virus tissue culture and vaccine development. Trying to grow mumps virus in cultured chicken cells, Enders initiated continuous culture in which the tissues were preserved while the nutritive medium was removed. Next, Enders and his colleagues cultivated chicken pox and polio viruses. He succeeded in growing poliovirus in cultures of human tissues that are not nerve cells and growing cells in a solid layer.

Publications: *Immunity: Principles and Application in Medicine and Public Health*, with Hans Zinsser and Leroy D. Fothergill (New York: Macmillan, 1939). "Cultivation of the Lansing Strain of Poliomyelitis Virus in Cultures of Various Human Embryonic Tissues," *Science* 109 (January 28, 1949): 85–87. "Mumps," in *Viruland Ricketsial Infections of Man* (Philadelphia: Lippincott, 1959), pp. 780–89.

Bibliography: *Biographical Memoirs of the Fellows of the Royal Society* (London: Royal Society, 1987), vol. 33, p. 211. *Biographical Encyclopedia of Scientists* (New York: Facts on File, 1981), p. 239. *Current Biography Yearbook* (New York: H. W. Wilson, 1955), pp. 182–84.

ROBBINS, FREDERICK CHAPMAN

Prize: Physiology or Medicine, 1954. *Born:* August 25, 1916; Auburn, Alabama. *Nationality:* American. *Education:* University of Missouri, B.A., 1936; University of Missouri, B.S., 1938; Harvard University, Massachusetts, M.D., 1940. *Career:* Children's Hospital, Boston, Massachusetts, Physician, 1946–52; Harvard University, Massachusetts, Professor, 1950–52; Case Western Reserve University, Ohio, Professor and Administrator, 1952–80; Institute of Medicine, Bethesda, Maryland, Researcher, 1980–85. *Other Awards:* Bronze Star, 1945; Mead Johnson Prize, 1953; Medical Mutual Honor Award, 1969; Ohio Governor's Award, 1971.

Citation: "For their discovery of the ability of poliomyelitis viruses to grow in cultures of various types of tissue" (with John F. Enders and Thomas H. Weller).

Life Work: Robbins and his colleagues John Enders and Thomas Weller worked to improve earlier methods for growing cells in tissue cultures. They confirmed that viruses could multiply and spread in cultured cells. They invented the culture method, which used antibiotics to prevent bacteria from contaminating the cultures. With antibiotics, poliovirus could be grown from samples heavily loaded with other micro-organisms. As a result scientists could now substitute tissue cultures and changes in the cultures could be used to measure the infectiousness of a given virus strain. They also discovered that tissues could be protected from virus infection with antiserum from patients with poliomyelitis. This discovery aided the development of a polio vaccine.

Publications: "Cultivation of the Lansing Strain of Poliomyelitis Virus in Cultures of Various Human Embryonic Tissues," with T. H. Weller and J. F. Enders, *Science* 109 (January 28, 1949): 85–87. "Studies of the Cultivation of Poliomyelitis Viruses in Tissue Culture. I. The Propagation of Poliomyelitis Viruses in Suspended Cell Cultures of Various Human Tissues," with others, *Journal of Immunology* 69 (1952): 645–71.

Bibliography: *Biographical Encyclopedia of Scientists* (New York: Facts on File, 1981), p. 682. *Current Biography Yearbook* (New York: H. W. Wilson, 1955), pp. 182–84.

WELLER, THOMAS HUCKLE

Prize: Physiology or Medicine, 1954. *Born:* June 15, 1915; Ann Arbor, Michigan. *Nationality:* American. *Education:* University of Michigan, B.S., 1936; University of Michigan, M.S., 1937; Harvard University, Massachusetts, M.D., 1940. *Career:* Harvard University, Massachusetts, Professor and Administrator, 1940–81. *Other Awards:* Mead Johnson Award, American Academy of Pediatrics, 1953; Kimble Methodology Award, 1954; George Ledlie Prize, 1963; Weinstein Cerebral Palsy Award, 1973; Bristol Award, Infectious Diseases Society of America, 1980.

Citation: "For their discovery of the ability of poliomyelitis viruses to grow in cultures of various types of tissue" (with John F. Enders and Frederick C. Robbins).

Life Work: Weller, with his colleagues John Enders and Frederick Robbins, developed innovative methods for growing animal cells in tissue culture. They kept cells in the same test tube for a long time by changing the medium instead of transferring the cells to different containers. They avoided contamination by using both penicillin and strep-tomycin to keep bacteria from overgrowing the animal cells. They cultivated poliovirus in the cell cultures and injected mice with the culture medium. Later, they cultivated cells in a solid layer in bottles that were constantly rolled to keep the cells uniformly nourished. This was a landmark development in virology, because tissue culture became a viable substitute for the use of laboratory animals. Cultures could also test whether the virus is present in a sample and could test blood for antibodies.

Publications: "Cultivation of the Lansing Strain of Poliomyelitis Virus in Cultures of Various Human Embryonic Tissues," with F. C. Robbins and J. F. Enders, *Science* 109 (January 28, 1949): 85–87. "Studies of the Cultivation of Poliomyelitis Viruses in Sus-pended Cell Cultures of Various Human Tissues," with others, *Journal of Immunology* 69 (1952): 645–71.

Bibliography: *Biographical Encyclopedia of Scientists* (New York: Facts on File, 1981), p. 834. *Current Biography Yearbook* (New York: H. W. Wilson, 1955), pp. 182–84.

THEORELL, AXEL HUGO TEODOR

Prize: Physiology or Medicine, 1955. *Born:* July 6, 1903; Linkoping, Sweden. *Died:* August 15, 1982; Stockholm, Sweden. *Nationality:* Swedish. *Education:* University of Stockholm, Sweden, Bachelor of Medicine, 1924; University of Stockholm, Sweden, M.D., 1930. *Career:* University of Uppsala, Sweden, Professor, 1930–36; Nobel Medical Institute, Stockholm, Sweden, Professor and Administrator, 1937–70. *Other Awards:* First Class Commander, Royal Order of North Star, 1959; Legion d'Honneur, France, 1960; Officer, Order Southern Cross, Brazil, 1961.

Citation: "For his discoveries concerning the nature and mode of action of oxidation enzymes."

Life Work: Theorell's field of investigation was biological oxidation and bioenergetics. He was interested in cytochrome c, an enzyme that catalyzes oxidative reactions on the surface of mitochondria, the power plants of the cell. He separated crystalline cytochrome c into its two components: a coenzyme or a catalyst and an apoenzyme or pure protein, which work together to produce oxidative reactions. He crystallized and purified myoglobin from urine and heart muscle. He also investigated peroxidases, oxidative enzymes, and alcohol dehydrogenases. The kinetics of oxidative reactions is called the Theorell-Chance mechanism.

Publications: "The Heme-Protein Linkage in Hemoglobin and in Horseradish Peroxidase," *Arkiv Kemi Mineral. Geol.* 16A (1943): 1–18. "Catalases and Peroxidases," in *The Enzymes* (New York: Academic Press, 1951), pp. 397–427. "Function and Structure of Liver Alcohol Dehydrogenase," *Harvey Lectures* 61 (1967). 17–41. "Introduction to Mechanisms of Enzyme Actions," in *Metabolic Regulation and Enzyme Action* (London: Academic Press, 1970), pp. 179–80. "My Life with Proteins and Prosthetic Groups," in *Proteolysis and Physiological Regulation* (New York: Academic Press, 1975), pp. 1–27.

Bibliography: *Biographical Memoirs of the Fellows of the Royal Society* (London: Royal Society, 1983), vol. 29, pp. 585–621. *Current Biography Yearbook* (New York: H. W. Wilson, 1956), pp. 622–24.

COURNAND, ANDRÉ FRÉDÉRICK

Prize: Physiology or Medicine, 1956. *Born:* September 24, 1895; Paris, France. *Died:* February 19, 1988; Great Barrington, Massachusetts. *Nationality:* French; later U.S.

citizen. *Education:* University of Paris-Sorbonne, France, B.A., 1913; University of Paris-Sorbonne, France, P.C.B., 1914; University of Paris, France, M.D., 1930. *Career:* French Army, 1915–19; Columbia University, New York, Professor and Researcher, 1930–64. *Other Awards:* Croix de Guerre, France, 1930; Silver Medal, University of Paris, France, 1930; Andrea Retzius Silver Medal, Swedish Society of Internal Medicine, 1946; Lasker Award, 1949; John Phillips Memorial Ward, American College of Physicians, 1952; Gold Medal, Royal Academy of Medicine, Belgium, 1956; Jiminiz Diaz Prize, 1970.

Citation: "For their discoveries concerning heart catheterization and pathological changes in the circulatory system" (with Werner Forssmann and Dickinson W. Richards).

Life Work: Cournand developed a catheter for measuring blood pressure in the heart and blood flow through the lungs. In 1941 he performed the first human catheterization. He advanced a catheter through the right atrium and ventricle and into the pulmonary artery. His measurements of pulmonary blood pressure established the relationship between the oxygen content of the blood and the blood pressure in the pulmonary artery.

Publications: "Catheterization of the Right Auricle in Man," *Proceedings of the Society for Experimental Biology and Medicine* 46 (1941): 462–66. *Cardiac Catheterization in Congenital Heart Disease: A Clinical and Physiological Study in Infants and Children,* with J. S. Baldwin and A. Himmelstein (New York: Commonwealth Fund, 1949). *Pulmonary Circulation: Historical Background and Present Day Status of Knowledge in Man* (Leiden, Netherlands: Universitaire Pers, 1959).

Bibliography: *Current Biography Yearbook* (New York: H. W. Wilson, 1957), pp. 117–19. *From Roots to Late Budding: The Intellectual Adventures of a Medical Student* (New York: Gardner Press, 1985).

FORSSMANN, WERNER THEODOR OTTO

Prize: Physiology or Medicine, 1956. *Born:* August 29, 1904; Berlin, Germany. *Died:* June 1, 1979; Schopfheim, Germany. *Nationality:* German. *Education:* University of Berlin, Germany, M.D., 1929. *Career:* Augusta Viktoria Hospital, Eberswalde, Germany, Physician, 1929–30; Ferdinand Sauerbruch Clinic, Berlin, Germany, Physician and Researcher, 1931–32; City Hospital, Dresden, Germany, Physician and Researcher, 1933–38; German Army, Physician, 1939–45; Bad Kreuznach, Germany, Physician, 1946–58; Dusseldorf Evangelical Hospital, Germany, Physician, 1958–79. *Other Awards:* Leibnitz Medal, German Academy of Sciences, 1954; Grosses Bundesverdienst Kreuz, 1958, 1964; Gold Medal, Societa Medico Chirurgica di Ferrara, 1968; Ordentliches Mitglied der Rheinisch-Westfallschoen Akademy der Wissenschaften des Landes Nordrhein Westfalen, 1968; Commander, Ordre des Palmes Academiques, 1971.

Citation: "For their discoveries concerning heart catheterization and pathological changes in the circulatory system" (with André Cournand and Dickinson W. Richards).

Life Work: Forsmann was the first human being to experiment with catheterization, when he inserted a catheter into a vein of his own arm.

Publications: "Die Sondierung des Rechten Herzens," *Klinische Wochenschrift* 8 (1929): 2085–87. "Technik und Praktische Bedentung der Herzkatheterung fur die Funktionelle Diagnostik und die Therapie von Herzund Lungenerkrankungen," with W. Bolt and H. Rink, *Med. Klin., Berl* 48 (October 30, 1953): 1614–20.

Bibliography: *Current Biography Yearbook* (New York: H. W. Wilson, 1957), pp. 190–92. *Selbstversuch: Erinnerungen Eines Chirurgen* (Dusseldorf, Germany: Droste, 1972); translated as *Experiments on Myself: Memoirs of a Surgeon in Germany*, by Hilary Davies (New York: St. Martin's Press, 1974).

RICHARDS, DICKINSON WOODRUFF

Prize: Physiology or Medicine, 1956. *Born:* October 30, 1895; Orange, New Jersey. *Died:* February 23, 1973; Lakeville, Connecticut. *Nationality:* American. *Education:* Yale University, Connecticut, A.B., 1917; Columbia University, New York, M.A., 1922; Columbia University, New York, M.D., 1923. *Career:* Presbyterian Hospital, New York, Physician, 1923–27; National Institute for Medical Research, London, England, Researcher, 1927–28; Columbia University, New York, Professor, 1928–73. *Other Awards:* Chevalier Legion of Honor, France, 1956.

Citation: "For their discoveries concerning heart catheterization and pathological changes in the circulatory system" (with André Cournand and Werner Forssmann).

Life Work: Richards and Cournand used Forssmann's technique of inserting a catheter into the veins in the arm to measure respiratory gases in blood. In 1941 they used this technique for the first time on a patient to measure blood gases, cardiac output, blood pressure, and blood volume. The technique is now standard in the diagnosis and treatment of cardiovascular and pulmonary diseases.

Publications: "The Circulation in Traumatic Shock in Man," *Harvey Lectures* 39 (1943–44): 217. "Cardiac Output by the Catheterization Technique in Various Clinical Conditions," *Federation Proceedings* 4 (1945): 215. "Contributions of Right Heart Catheterization to the Physiology of Congestive Heart Failure," *American Journal of Medicine* 3 (1947): 434.

Bibliography: *Current Biography Yearbook* (New York: H. W. Wilson, 1957), pp. 457–59. *National Cyclopedia of American Biography* (New York: James T. White, 1960), vol. I, pp. 336–37.

BOVET, DANIEL

Prize: Physiology or Medicine, 1957. *Born:* March 23, 1907; Neuchatel, Switzerland. *Died:* April 9, 1992; Rome, Italy. *Nationality:* Swiss; later Italian citizen. *Education:* University of Geneva, Switzerland, M.S., 1927; University of Geneva, Switzerland, D.Sc., 1929. *Career:* Institut Pasteur, Paris, France, Researcher, 1929–47; Instituto Superiore di Sanita, Rome, Italy, Researcher, 1947–64; University of Sassari, Italy, Professor, 1964–71; Rome University, Italy, Professor, 1971–77. *Other Awards:* Martin Damourette Prize, France, 1936; General Nuteau Prize, Italy, 1941; Chevalier de la Legion d'Honneur, 1946; Burgi Prize, Switzerland, 1949; Addingham Gold Medal, England, 1952.

Citation: "For his discoveries relating to synthetic compounds that inhibit the action of certain body substances, and especially their action on the vascular system and the skeletal muscles."

Life Work: Bovet's field of investigation was the muscle-relaxant properties of curare, a highly toxic alkaloid extract. Bovet successfully created more than four hundred synthetic forms of curare, including gallamine and succinylcholine.

Publications: *Structure Chimique et Activite Pharmacodynamique du Systeme Nerveux Vegetatif*, with F. Bovet-Nitti (Basel, Switzerland: Karger, 1948). *Curare and Curare-like Agents*, with F. Bovet-Nitti and G. B. Marini-Bettolo (Amsterdam: Elsevier Publishing Co., 1959). *Controlling Drugs*, with others (San Francisco: Jossey-Bass, 1974).

Bibliography: *Biographical Encyclopedia of Scientists* (New York: Facts on File, 1981), pp. 98–99. *Biographical Memoirs of the Fellows of the Royal Society* (London: Royal Society, 1994), vol. 39, p. 59. *Current Biography Yearbook* (New York: H. W. Wilson, 1958), pp. 55–56.

BEADLE, GEORGE WELLS

Prize: Physiology or Medicine, 1958. *Born:* October 22, 1903; Wahoo, Nebraska. *Died:* June 9, 1989; Pomona, California. *Nationality:* American. *Education:* University of Nebraska, B.S., 1926; University of Nebraska, M.S., 1927; Cornell University, New York, Ph.D., 1931. *Career:* Cornell University, Ithaca, New York, Researcher, 1926–31; California Institute of Technology, Professor, 1931–35; Institut de Biologie, Paris, France, Researcher, 1935; Harvard University, Massachusetts, Professor, 1936–37; Stanford University, California, Professor, 1937–46; California Institute of Technology, Professor, 1946–61; University of Chicago, Illinois, Professor and Administrator, 1961–75. *Other Awards:* Lasker Award, American Public Health Association, 1950; Dyer Award, 1951; Emil C. Hansen Prize, Denmark, 1953; Albert Einstein Commemorative Award in Science, 1958; National Award of American Cancer Society,

1959; Kimber Genetics Award, National Academy of Science, 1960; Priestly Memorial Award, 1967; Donald Forsha Jones Medal, 1972.

Citation: "For their discovery that genes act by regulating definite chemical events" (with Edward L. Tatum).

Life Work: Beadle's field of investigation was biochemical genetics. He and Tatum grew colonies of *Neurospora*, the pink mold that forms on bread, on a culture medium that contained only a few nutrients essential to growth of the organism, and then irradiated the colony with X rays. The experiments proved that specific genes controlled the synthesis of specific cellular substances.

Publications: *An Introduction to Genetics*, with A. H. Sturtevant (Philadelphia: W. B. Saunders, 1939). *The Language of the Gene* (London: University of London Press, 1960). *Genetics and Modern Biology* (Philadelphia: American Philosophical Society, 1963). *The Language of Life*, with M. M. Beadle (New York: Doubleday, 1966).

Bibliography: *Biographical Memoirs. National Academy of Sciences* (Washington, D.C.: National Academy Press, 1990), vol. 59, p. 27. *Current Biography Yearbook* (New York: H. W. Wilson, 1956), pp. 37–39. *National Cyclopedia of American Biography* (New York: James T. White, 1964), vol. J, pp. 372–73. *New York Times* Biographical Service, June 12, 1989, p. 531.

LEDERBERG, JOSHUA

Prize: Physiology or Medicine, 1958. *Born:* May 23, 1925; Montclair, New Jersey. *Nationality:* American. *Education:* Columbia University, New York, B.A., 1944; Yale University, Connecticut, Ph.D., 1947. *Career:* University of Wisconsin, Professor, 1947–58; Stanford University, California, Professor and Administrator, 1958–78; Rockefeller University, New York, President, 1978–. *Other Awards:* Eli Lilly Award, 1953; Pasteur Award, Society of Illinois Bacteriologists, 1956; Procter Prize, 1982; National Medal of Science, 1989.

Citation: "For his discoveries concerning genetic recombination and the organization of the genetic material of bacteria."

Life Work: Lederberg's field of investigation was biochemical genetics. Lederberg knew that fungal organisms reproduced sexually. He wanted to prove that bacteria also reproduced sexually. He and Edward Tatum discovered that the bacterium *Escherichia coli* reproduced sexually by the conjugation of two separate bacterial cells. The bacterial daughter cell that is produced in this way divides, and new generations of cells are produced by successive divisions of its offspring. When two different strains are mated, offspring cells inherited certain traits from each parent strain, a process called sexual or genetic recombination. It involves the transfer of a full complement of chromosomes and their genes from one cell to the other. Later, Lederberg developed the technique of replica plating, a laboratory method that isolates mutations of a bacteria species by using ultraviolet light or other mutant-inducing agents. He proved that genetic mutations occur spontaneously. He also discovered the phenomenon of transduction in bacteria, which describes the transfer of fragments of chromosomal materials from one cell to another, thus altering the genetic code of the recipient cell. The order of genes on chromosomes may depend on transduction. This discovery led to the development of recombinant genetics, the manipulation of the genetic code to produce certain biochemical substances.

Publications: *Papers in Microbial Genetics* (Madison: University of Wisconsin Press, 1952). "Viruses, Genes and Cells," *Bacteriological Reviews* 21 (1957): 133–39. "Bacterial Reproduction," *Harvey Lectures* 53 (1959): 69–82. *Tables and Algorithms for Calculating Functional Groups of Organic Molecules in High Mass Spectrometry* (Palo Alto, Calif.: Stanford University Press, 1964).

Bibliography: *Biographical Encyclopedia of Scientists* (New York: Facts on File, 1981), pp. 479–80. *Current Biography Yearbook* (New York: H. W. Wilson, 1959), pp. 251–52. *The Excitement and Fascination of Science* (Palo Alto, Calif.: Annual Reviews, 1990), vol. 3, part 1, pp. 893–915.

TATUM, EDWARD LAWRIE

Prize: Physiology or Medicine, 1958. **Born:** December 14, 1909; Boulder, Colorado. **Died:** November 5, 1975; New York, New York. **Nationality:** American. **Education:** University of Wisconsin, A.B., 1931; University of Wisconsin, M.A., 1932; University of Wisconsin, Ph.D., 1934. **Career:** University of Wisconsin, Researcher, 1935; University of Utrecht, Netherlands, Researcher, 1936–37; Stanford University, California, Professor, 1937–45; Yale University, New Haven, Connecticut, Professor, 1948–56; Stanford University, California, Professor, 1956–57; Rockefeller Institute, New York, Professor, 1957–75. **Other Awards:** Remsen Award, American Chemical Society, 1953.

Citation: "For their discovery that genes act by regulating definite chemical events" (with George W. Beadle).

Life Work: Tatum worked with George Beadle to discover how genes function by making some of them defective. They grew colonies of *Neospora* on a culture medium that contained only nutrients essential to its growth and then irradiated the colonies with X rays. Their experiments proved that specific genes control the synthesis of specific cellular substances. Working with Joshua Lederberg, he demonstrated that bacterial cells, like fungi, reproduce by sexual means, a process they called sexual or genetic recombination.

Publications: "Genetic Control of Biochemical Reactions in Neurospora," with G. Beadle, *Proceedings of the National Academy of Sciences* 27 (1941): 499–506. "Genetic Control of Biochemical Reactions in Neurospora: An Aminobenziocless Mutant," with G. Beadle, *Proceedings of the National Academy of Sciences* 28 (1942): 234–64. "Gene Recombination in the Bacterium Escherichia Coli," with J. Lederberg, *Journal of Bac-

teriology 53 (1947): 673–84. "Sex in Bacteria: Genetic Studies, 1945–1952," with J. Lederberg, *Science* 118 (1953): 169–74.

Bibliography: *Biographical Memoirs. National Academy of Sciences* (Washington, D.C.: National Academy Press, 1990), vol. 59, p. 357. *Current Biography Yearbook* (New York: H. W. Wilson, 1959), pp. 437–39. *The Excitement and Fascination of Science* (Palo Alto, Calif.: Annual Reviews, 1990), vol. 3, part 1, pp. 775–79. *National Cyclopedia of American Biography* (New York: James T. White, 1964), vol. J, p. 475.

KORNBERG, ARTHUR

Prize: Physiology or Medicine, 1959. *Born:* March 3, 1918; Brooklyn, New York. *Nationality:* American. *Education:* City College of New York, B.S., 1937; University of Rochester, New York, M.D., 1941. *Career:* National Institutes of Health, Maryland, Researcher, 1942–52; Washington University, Missouri, Professor, 1953–59; Stanford University, California, Professor, 1959–. *Other Awards:* Paul-Lewis Laboratory Award, American Chemical Society, 1951; Silver Medal, Federal Security Agency, 1952; Lucy Wortham James Award, James Ewing Society, 1968; Max Berg Award, 1968; Science Achievement Award, American Medical Association, 1968; Borden Award, American Association of Medical Colleges, 1968; Albert Gallatin Medal, New York University, 1970; National Medal of Science, United States, 1980.

Citation: "For their discovery of the mechanisms in the biological synthesis of ribonucleic acid and deoxyribonucleic acid" (with Severo Ochoa).

Life Work: Kornberg's field of investigation was the biochemistry of enzymes. In 1953 he isolated and purified an enzyme responsible for synthesis of DNA . He called it DNA polymerase. The isolation and purification of DNA polymerase and the replication of DNA shaped further research in the field. The key step in the synthesis of DNA was the catalytic agent, the enzyme polymerase, a protein compound that synthesized the DNA chain in response to directions from a DNA template. These directions were dictated by the hydrogen-bonding relationship of adenine to thymine and guanine to cytosine-nucleotides or bases of DNA. This discovery had implications for the treatment of cancer and hereditary diseases.

Publications: *Harvey Lectures* 53 (1957–58): 83. *Enzymatic Synthesis of DNA* (New York: Wiley, 1961). "Enzymatic Synthesis of DNA. XXIII. Synthesis of Circular Replicative Form of Phage Phi X174DNA," with M. Goulian, *Proceedings of the National Academy of Sciences* 58 (1967): 1723–30. "Enzymatic Synthesis of DNA. XXIV. Synthesis of Infectious Phage X174DNA," with M. Goulian and R. Sinsheimer, *Proceedings of the National Academy of Sciences* 58 (1967): 2321–28. *DNA Replication* (New York: W.H. Freeman, 1980).

Bibliography: *Current Biography Yearbook* (New York: H. W. Wilson, 1968), pp. 210–12. *For the Love of Enzymes* (Cambridge: Harvard University Press, 1991). *New York Times*, October 16, 1959, p. 1.

OCHOA, SEVERO

Prize: Physiology or Medicine, 1959. *Born:* September 24, 1905; Luarca, Spain. *Died:* November 1, 1993; Madrid, Spain. *Nationality:* Spanish; later U.S. citizen. *Education:* Malaga College, Spain, B.A., 1921; University of Madrid, Spain, M.D., 1929. *Career:* Kaiser-Wilhelm Institute, Berlin, Germany, Researcher, 1929–37; Marine Biological Laboratory, England, Researcher, 1937; University of Oxford, England, Researcher, 1938–40; Washington University, Missouri, Researcher, 1941–42; New York University, Professor, 1942–75; Roche Institute of Molecular Biology, N.J., Researcher, 1975–85. *Other Awards:* Neuberg Medal Award, Society of European Chemists, 1951; Charles Meyer Price Award, Société de Chimie Biologique, 1955; Borden Award, Association of American Medical Colleges, 1958; New York University Medal, 1960; Order of the Rising Sun, 2nd Class Gold Medal, Japan, 1967; Quevedo Gold Medal, Spain, 1969; Albert Gallatin Medal, 1970; National Medal of Science, 1979.

Citation: "For their discovery of the mechanisms in the biological synthesis of ribonucleic acid and deoxyribonucleic acid" (with Arthur Kornberg).

Life Work: Ochoa's field of investigation was the structure of DNA and RNA. Every chromosome in every cell nucleus has resident genes that govern the inheritance of physical traits by directing the synthesis of proteins or enzymes. Genes are composed of DNA, a long macromolecule of the nitrogenous bases arranged in a double helical structure with sugars and phosphate groups. Protein synthesis occurs when the genetic information is passed to ribonucleic acid (RNA) containing ribose and uracil. Three types of RNA are involved in the sequential incorporation of amino acids into protein molecules: messenger RNA, ribosomal RNA, and transfer or soluble RNA. The genetic instructions for protein biosynthesis are encoded in the base sequences of DNA and RNA. Groups of three bases, or triplets, encode the incorporation of each amino acid into a molecule or protein. Ochoa isolated the bacterial enzyme polynucleotide phosphorylase, which catalyzes the synthesis of polyribonucleotides from ribonucleoside diphosphates in a reversible reaction. This work enabled him to decipher the triplet code for eleven amino acids. His synthesis of RNA and protein molecules in a test tube made possible the deciphering of the genetic code.

Publications: "Enzymatic Synthesis and Breakdown of Polynucleotides; Polynucleotide Phosphorylase," with M. Grunberg-Manago, *Journal of the American Chemical Society* 77 (1955): 3165–66. "Enzymatic Synthesis of Nucleic Acidlike Polynucleotides," with M. Grunberg-Manago and P .J. Ortiz, *Science* 122 (1955): 907–10. "Small Polyribonucleotides with 5^1 Phosphomonoester End- Groups," with L. A. Heppel and P. J. Ortiz, *Science* 123 (1956): 415–17. *La Clare Genetica, Base Quimica de la Herencia* (Barcelona, Spain: Real Academia de Ciencias y Artes de Barcelona, 1964). *Macromolecules: Biosynthesis and Function* (New York: Academic Press, 1970). *Viruses, Oncogenes, and Cancer* (New York: Karger, 1985).

Bibliography: *Current Biography Yearbook* (New York: H. W. Wilson, 1962), pp. 327–29. *The Excitement and Fascination of Science* (Palo Alto, Calif.: Annual Reviews,

1990), vol. 3, part 1, pp. 291–320. M. Gomez-Santos, *Severo Ochoa* (Madrid: Piramida, 1993). *Science* (October 23, 1959): 1099–1100.

BURNET, SIR FRANK MACFARLANE

Prize: Physiology or Medicine, 1960. *Born:* September 3, 1899; Traralgon, Victoria, Australia. *Died:* August 31, 1985; Melbourne, Australia. *Nationality:* Australian. *Education:* Melbourne University, Australia, M.A., 1922; Melbourne University, Australia, M.D., 1923; University of London, England, Ph.D., 1928. *Career:* Melbourne Hospital, Australia, Physician, 1923–24; Lister Institute, London, England, Researcher, 1926–27; Walter and Eliza Hall Institute for Medical Research, Melbourne, Australia, Physician and Administrator, 1928–65. *Other Awards:* Royal Medal, Royal Society, 1947; Knighthood, 1951; Lasker Award, 1952; Von Behring Prize, Marburg University, Germany, 1952; Galen Medal, Society of Apothecaries, 1958; Copley Medal, Royal Society, 1959.

Citation: "For discovery of acquired immunological tolerance" (with P. B. Medawar).

Life Work: Burnet's field of investigation was animal viruses. In the course of his work he refined techniques for cultivating viruses in chicken eggs. Burnet successfully induced immunological tolerance in chickens by exposing them to synthetic antigens. According to Burnet, an embryo contains examples of all the hundreds of millions of antibodies an adult animal can produce. Each antibody-producing cell can make only one type of antibody. During fetal development and early life any cell that encounters an antigen corresponding to its specific antibody is killed or inactivated.

Publications: *Biological Aspects of Infectious Disease* (New York: Macmillan, 1940). *Virus As Organism* (Cambridge: Harvard University Press, 1945). *Principles of Animal Virology* (New York: Academic Press, 1955). *Clonal Selection: Theory of Acquired Immunity* (Nashville, Tenn.: Vanderbilt University Press, 1959). *Immunology, Aging and Cancer* (San Francisco: W. H. Freeman, 1976).

Bibliography: "Fifty Years On," *British Medical Journal* 2 (1964): 1091. R. Norry, *Virus Hunter in Australia* (Melbourne: Nelson, 1966). C. Sexton, *The Seeds of Time* (Oxford: Oxford University Press, 1991).

MEDAWAR, PETER BRIAN

Prize: Physiology or Medicine, 1960. *Born:* February 28, 1915; Rio de Janeiro, Brazil. *Died:* October 2, 1987; London, England. *Nationality:* British. *Education:* Oxford University, England, B.A., 1935; Oxford University, England, M.A., 1939; Oxford University, England, D.Sci., 1945. *Career:* Oxford University, England, Researcher,

1938–47; Birmingham University, England, Professor and Administrator, 1947–51; University of London, England, Professor and Administrator, 1951–62; National Institute for Medical Research, Mill Hill, England, Researcher, 1962–71; Clinical Research Centre, England, Researcher, 1971–87. *Other Awards:* Edward Chapman Research Prize, 1938; Royal Medal, Royal Society, 1959; Copley Medal, Royal Society, 1969; Hamilton Fairley Medal, Royal College of Physicians, 1971.

Citation: "For discovery of acquired immunological tolerance" (with Frank Macfarlane Burnet).

Life Work: Medawar's field of investigation was immunology. He began by studying problems with skin transplants on burn victims, especially the graft rejection reaction. He found that the body rejected foreign tissue because of immunological differences. The agents in tissue rejection were lymphocytes, or small, colorless cells formed in the lymphoid tissue. All mammalian cells with nuclei contain proteins that can act as antigens (called histocompatibility antigens) that provoke immunological reactions. Medawar developed a biological glue, a concentrated form of the blood component fibrinogen, that could be used to join nerve endings in skin grafts. Later he confirmed Burnet's theory that the ability of the immune system to distinguish its own from what is foreign was determined not intrinsically but by experience. Thus, it accepts any antigen to which the body is exposed at an early age. He predicted that immunological tolerance could be produced in the laboratory by exposing animals to foreign tissues early in life.

Publications: *The Future of Man* (New York: Basic Books, 1960). "Transplantation of Tissues and Organs," *British Medical Bulletin* 27 (1965). *The Life Science: Current Ideas of Biology*, with J. S. Medawar (New York: Harper & Row, 1977). *Advice to a Young Scientist: Scientific Papers on Growth, Aging, Wound Healing and Transplantation* (New York: Harper Colophon Books, 1981).

Bibliography: *Current Biography Yearbook* (New York: H. W. Wilson, 1961), pp. 3030–35. J. Medawar, *A Very Decided Preference* (New York: W. W. Norton Co., 1990). *Memoirs of a Thinking Radish: An Autobiography* (Oxford: Oxford University Press, 1986).

BÉKÉSY, GEORG VON

Prize: Physiology or Medicine, 1961. *Born:* June 3, 1899; Budapest, Hungary. *Died:* June 13, 1972; Honolulu, Hawaii. *Nationality:* Hungarian; later U.S. citizen. *Education:* University of Budapest, Hungary, Ph.D., 1923. *Career:* Hungarian Telephone System, Communications Engineer, 1923–46; Karolinska Institute, Stockholm, Sweden, Researcher, 1946–47; Harvard University, Massachusetts, Professor, 1947–66; University of Hawaii, Professor, 1966–72. *Other Awards:* Denker Prize, 1931; Leibniz Medal, Akademie der Wissenschaften, Berlin, Germany, 1937; Academy Award, Academy of Science, Budapest, Hungary, 1946; Shambaugh Prize, 1950;

Howard Crosby Warren Medal, Society of Experimental Psychologists, 1955; Gold Medal, American Otological Society, 1957; Achievement Award, Deafness Research Foundation, 1961; Gold Medal, Acoustical Society of America, 1961.

Citation: "For his discoveries of the physical mechanism of stimulation within the cochlea."

Life Work: Békésy's field of investigation was the mechanical properties of the ear. He devised new microsurgical tools for opening and examining the middle and the inner ear. To investigate the movement of the basilar membrane, he measured volume elasticity of the vibrations, which he established are traveling waves. The basilar membrane is not uniform in thickness. It is thin and tightly stretched at the base of the cochlea (near the middle ear) and wider and floppier at the apex. One section of the cochlea moves more than the rest in response to a traveling wave. The location of this peak depends on the frequency of the stimulating vibration; for high sounds it is closer to the middle ear and for low sounds closer to the apex. The nerve fibers of the cochlea transmit this information to the brain which thus differentiates between low-pitched and high-pitched sounds. After World War II, at Harvard, Békésy constructed an enlarged model of the cochlea. In the model, although the traveling waves ran along the whole length of the membrane, only a section vibrated. It proved nervous inhibition plays an important role in the way sound is perceived.

Publications: *Experiments in Hearing* (New York: McGraw-Hill, 1960). *Sensory Inhibition* (Princeton, N.J.: Princeton University Press, 1967).

Bibliography: *Biographical Encyclopedia of Scientists* (New York: Facts on File, 1981), p. 60. *Current Biography Yearbook* (New York: H. W. Wilson, 1962), pp. 36–38. J. Daniel, *Békésy Gyorgy* (Budapest, Hungary: Akademiai Kaido, 1990). *The Excitement and Fascination of Science* (Palo Alto, Calif.: Annual Reviews, 1978), vol. 2, pp. 657–72.

CRICK, FRANCIS HARRY COMPTON

Prize: Physiology or Medicine, 1962. *Born:* June 8, 1916; Northampton, England. *Nationality:* British. *Education:* University of London, England, B.Sc., 1937; Cambridge University, England, Ph.D., 1954. *Career:* British Admiralty, Researcher, 1939–47; Strangeways Research Laboratory, Cambridge, England, Researcher, 1947–49; Cambridge University, England, Professor, 1949–77; Salk Institute for Biological Studies, San Diego, California, Professor, 1977–. *Other Awards:* Warren Triennial Prize, 1959; Albert Lasker Award, 1960; Prix Charles Leopold Mayer, French Academy of Sciences, 1961; Research Corporation Award, 1961; Gairdner Foundation Medal, 1962; Royal Medal, Royal Society, 1972; Copley Medal, Royal Society, 1976; Michelson-Morley Award, Cleveland, Ohio, 1981.

Citation: "For their discoveries concerning the molecular structure of nucleic acids and its significance for information transfer in living material" (with James D. Watson and Maurice H. F. Wilkins).

Life Work: Crick and Watson set out in 1951 to determine the chemical structure of DNA, which Maurice Wilkins had demonstrated is shaped like a double helix. They proposed a three-dimensional structure for the DNA molecule, and constructed a model from beads, pieces of wire, and cardboard. In this model, DNA consists of three strands of sugar and phosphate (deoxyribose phosphate) joined by pairs of bases inside the helix, one adenine paired with every thymine, and one guanine paired with every cytosine. These bases are attached to one another by hydrogen bonds. DNA replicates when the two parts of the molecule separate at the point of hydrogen bonding. One new molecule is then synthesized opposite each half of the old one. By 1961, three types of RNA had been discovered: messenger RNA, ribosomal RNA and transfer (or soluble) RNA. The genetic is read when messenger RNA receives genetic information from DNA in the nucleus of the cell and conveys it to ribosomes (the sites of protein synthesis) in the cytoplasm or the nonnuclear portion of the cell. Transfer RNA carries amino acids to the ribosomes. Messenger and ribosomal RNA then cooperate to join amino acids in the correct sequence to form protein molecules. The genetic code consists of triplets DNA and RNA bases for each of the twenty amino acids. Genes consist of many base triplets called codons.

Publications: "Structure for Deoxyribose Nucleic Acid," *Nature* 171 (April 25, 1953): 737. "Genetical Implications of the Structure of Deoxyribonucleic Acid," *Nature* 171 (May 30, 1953): 964–67. *The Genetic Code. III* (San Francisco: W. H. Freeman, 1966). *Of Molecules and Men* (Seattle: University of Washington Press, 1966). *Life Itself: Its Origin and Nature* (New York: Simon and Schuster, 1981).

Bibliography: *Asimov's Biographical Encyclopedia of Science and Technology* (Garden City, N.Y.: Doubleday, 1982), pp. 859–61. *Biographical Encyclopedia of Scientists* (New York: Facts on File, 1992).

WATSON, JAMES DEWEY

Prize: Physiology or Medicine, 1962. *Born:* April 3, 1928; Chicago, Illinois. *Nationality:* American. *Education:* University of Chicago, Illinois, B.S., 1947; University of Chicago, Illinois, Ph.B., 1947; Indiana University, Ph.D., 1950. *Career:* University of Copenhagen, Denmark, Researcher, 1950–51; Cambridge University, England, Researcher, 1951–53; California Institute of Technology, Researcher, 1953–55; Harvard University, Massachusetts, Professor, 1955–76; Cold Spring Harbor Laboratory, New York, Director, 1968–. *Other Awards:* John Collins Warren Prize, Massachusetts General Hospital, 1959; Eli Lilly Award, American Chemical Society, 1959; Albert Lasker Prize, American Public Health Association, 1960; Research Corporation Prize, 1962; Carty Medal, National Academy of Sciences, 1971; Presidential Medal of Freedom, 1977, 1989; Kaul Foundation Award, 1993; Copley, Medal, 1993.

Citation: "For their discoveries concerning the molecular structure of nucleic acids and its significance for information transfer in living material" (with Francis Crick and Maurice H. F. Wilkins).

Life Work: Watson and his colleagues, Crick and Maurice Wilkins, determined the double helix structure of the DNA. *See* Crick, Francis Harry Compton, p. 317.

Publications: "Structure for Deoxyribase Nucleic Acid," *Nature* 171 (April 25, 1953): 737. "Genetical Implications of the Structure of Deoxyribonucleic Acid," *Nature* 171 (May 30, 1953): 964–67. *Molecular Biology of the Gene* (Menlo Park, Calif.: W. A. Benjamin, 1965). *The DNA Story*, with J. Tooze (San Francisco: W.H. Freeman, 1981). *The Molecular Biology of the Cell*, with others (New York: Garland, 1983).

Bibliography: J. Baldwin, *DNA Pioneer* (New York: Walker and Co., 1994). *Current Biography Yearbook* (New York: H. W. Wilson, 1963), pp. 458–60. *The Double Helix* (New York: Atheneum, 1968).

WILKINS, MAURICE HUGH FREDERICK

Prize: Physiology or Medicine, 1962. *Born:* December 15, 1916; Pongaroa, New Zealand. *Nationality:* British. *Education:* Cambridge University, England, B.A., 1938; Cambridge University, England, Ph.D., 1940. *Career:* University of California, Berkeley, Researcher, 1944; St. Andrews University, Scotland, Professor, 1945; University of London, England, Professor and Administrator, 1946–81. *Other Awards:* Albert Lasker Award, American Public Health Association, 1960.

Citation: "For their discoveries concerning the molecular structure of nucleic acids and its significance for information transfer in living material" (with Francis Crick and James D. Watson).

Life Work: Wilkins clarified the complex molecular structure of the DNA molecule. He subjected DNA samples to X-ray diffraction analyses. It showed that the DNA molecule was shaped like a double helix. The structure was elucidated by Francis Crick and James Watson, who proposed a three-dimensional structure. This model enabled scientists to explain the process by which DNA replicates itself and also how it transfers genetic information.

Publications: "Crystallinity in Sperm Heads: Molecular Structure of Nucleoprotein in Vivo," with J. T. Randall, *Biochim. Biophys. Act* 10 (1953): 192–93. "The Molecular Configuration of Deoxyribonucleic Acid. I. X-ray Diffraction Study of a Crystalline form of the Lithium Salts," with others, *Journal of Molecular Biology* 2 (1960): 19. "The Molecular Structure of Deoxyribonucleic Acid (DNA)," *J. Chim. Phys* 58 (1961): 891–98. "Determination of the Helical Configuration of Ribonucleic Acid Molecules by X-ray Diffraction Study of Crystalline Amino-acid Transfer Ribonucleic Acid," with others, *Nature* 194 (1962): 1014.

Bibliography: *Current Biography Yearbook* (New York: H. W. Wilson, 1963), pp. 465–66. S. Johnson and T. R. Mertens, "An Interview with Nobel Laureate Maurice Wilkins," *American Biology Teacher* 51 (March 1989): 151–53.

ECCLES, SIR JOHN CAREW

Prize: Physiology or Medicine, 1963. *Born:* January 27, 1903; Melbourne, Australia. *Died:* May 2, 1997; Contra, Switzerland. *Nationality:* Australian; later British and U.S. resident. *Education:* Melbourne University, Australia, B.S., 1925; Melbourne University, Australia, M.B., 1925; Oxford University, England, M.A., 1929; Oxford University, England, Ph.D., 1929. *Career:* Oxford University, England, Professor, 1934–37; Kanematsu Memorial Institute of Pathology, Sydney, Australia, Director, 1937–44; University of Otago, Dunedin, New Zealand, Professor, 1944–51; Australian National University, Canberra, Australia, Professor, 1951–66; Institute for Biomedical Research, Illinois, Researcher, 1966–68; State University of New York at Buffalo, Professor and Administrator, 1968–75. *Other Awards:* Gotch Memorial Prize, 1927; Rolleston Memorial Prize, 1932; Knighthood, 1958; Baly Medal, 1961; Cothenius Medal, Deutsche Akademie der Naturforscher Leopoldina, 1963.

Citation: "For their discoveries concerning the ionic mechanisms involved in excitation and inhibition in the peripheral and central portions of the nerve cell membrane" (with Alan Hodgkin and Andrew Huxley).

Life Work: Eccles's work concerned the ionic mechanisms involved in the excitation and inhibition in the peripheral and central portions of the nerve cell membrane. He devised a method of monitoring and stimulating neurons in the spinal cords of live cats by inserting fine electrodes into individual nerve cells. To measure electrical activity in several linked neurons in an individual reflex arc, he used an electrical stimulating and recording device. Eccles showed that the firing of the stimulating (presynaptic) neuron at a synapse produces an excitatory postsynaptic potential (EPSP) in the stimulated neuron. Action potentials are set off by combinations of EPSPs because a single EPSP is insufficient to raise the postsynaptic neuron above the threshold of –40 millivolts, at which an action potential begins. Some of the neural circuits are inhibitory rather than excitatory. A neuron depends on the arithmetical sum of the incoming inhibitory postsynaptic potentials (IPSPs) and EPSPs. A particular neuron produces only one kind of chemical neurotransmitter.

Publications: *Reflex Activity of the Spinal Cord* (London: Oxford University Press, 1938). *The Neurophysiological Basis of Mind* (Oxford: Clarendon Press, 1965). *The Cerebellum as a Neuronal Machine* (Berlin: Springer-Verlag, 1967). *The Physiology of Nerve Cells* (Baltimore: Johns Hopkins Press, 1968). *The Inhibitory Pathways of the Central Nervous System* (Liverpool: Liverpool University Press, 1969).

Bibliography: *Current Biography Yearbook* (New York: H. W. Wilson, 1972), pp. 119–22. John Robinson, *100 Most Important People in the World Today* (New York: Putnam, 1970), pp. 237–40.

HODGKIN, SIR ALAN LLOYD

Prize: Physiology or Medicine, 1963. *Born:* February 5, 1914; Banbury, Oxfordshire, England. *Died:* December 20, 1998; Cambridge, England. *Nationality:* British. *Education:* Trinity College, Cambridge University, England, Ph.D. *Career:* Air Ministry and Ministry of Aircraft Production, England, Scientific Officer, 1939–45; Cambridge University, England, Professor and Administrator, 1945–52; Royal Society, England, Foulerton Research Professor, 1952–69; Cambridge University, England, Professor and Administrator, 1970–81. *Other Awards:* Baly Medal, 1955; Royal Medal, Royal Society, 1958; Copley Medal, 1965; Knighthood, 1972; Order of Merit, 1973; Lord Crook Medal, 1983; Helmerich Prize, 1988.

Citation: "For their discoveries concerning the ionic mechanisms involved in excitation and inhibition in the peripheral and central portions of the nerve cell membrane" (with John C. Eccles and Andrew Huxley).

Life Work: Hodgkin's field of investigation was the electrical nature of nerve impulses. His preliminary research was on shore crabs and squid. He found that their membranes underwent a large increase in conductance. His studies confirmed that the inner surface of the axonal membranes of a crab becomes more positive than the outer surface. The resting surface potential arises because the axonal membrane is permeable only to certain ions with the result that ions have different concentrations on either side of the membrane. The concentration of positively charged sodium ions is lower inside the membrane than outside and the reverse is true for positively charged potassium ions. Many of the large organic molecules inside the cell are negatively charged, permitting potassium ions, but not the sodium and organic ions, to pass through the pores in the membrane. The net result is a resting potential. Hodgkin developed the sodium hypothesis according to which sodium passes through a channel or gate into the cell making the inside of the axonal chamber positive. The action potential fluctuates in tandem with the external sodium concentration. Hodgkin and Andrew Huxley presented their theory in 1952 to explain the action potential as the movement of sodium ions into the cell followed by the movement of potassium ions out of the cell to restore the resting potential.

Publications: "Ionic Currents Underlying the Activity in the Giant Axon of the Squid," with A. Huxley and B. Katz, *Arch. Sci. Physiol* 3 (1949): 129–50. "Properties of Nerve Axons. I. Movement of Sodium and Potassium Ions during Nervous Activity," with A. Huxley, *Cold Spring Harbor Symposia on Quantitative Biology* 17 (1952): 43–52. "Movement of Radioactive Potassium and Membrane Current in a Giant Axon," with A. Huxley, *Journal of Physiology (London)* 121 (1953): 403–14. *The Conduction of the Nervous Impulse* (Liverpool: Liverpool University Press, 1971). *The Pursuit of Nature: Informal Essays on the History of Physiology* (Cambridge: Cambridge University Press, 1977).

Bibliography: *Biographical Encyclopedia of Scientists* (New York: Facts on File, 1981), p. 386. *Science* 142 (October 25, 1963): 468–70.

HUXLEY, SIR ANDREW FIELDING

Prize: Physiology or Medicine, 1963. *Born:* November 22, 1917; London, England. *Nationality:* British. *Education:* Cambridge University, England, B.A., 1938; Cambridge University, England, M.A., 1941. *Career:* Plymouth Marine Biology Laboratory, Massachusetts, Researcher, 1939–40; Cambridge University, England, Professor and Administrator, 1941–60; University of London, England, Professor, 1960–83; Cambridge University, England, Professor and Administrator, 1983–. *Other Awards:* Copley Medal, Royal Society, 1973; Knighthood, 1974.

Citation: "For their discoveries concerning the ionic mechanisms involved in excitation and inhibition in the peripheral and central portions of the nerve cell membrane" (with John C. Eccles and Alan Hodgkin).

Life Work: Huxley and Alan Hodgkin investigated the nerve impulse called action potential. Measuring the relative sizes of the resting and action potentials of crabs, they found that the change in membrane voltage during the action potential was, in fact, much greater than the resting potential. They showed that action potential was not caused by the movement of potassium ions alone, but involved sodium ions. The cell membrane contains voltage-sensitive sodium channels or gates that remain closed at the resting-potential stage and open when the axon is depolarized. When the gates open, the sodium ions rush from an area of relatively high concentration outside the axon to one of relatively low concentration inside the axon, making the inside temporarily positive. Using a voltage-clamp apparatus, they showed that action potential could be changed or eliminated by manipulating the external sodium concentration.

Publications: "Ionic Currents Underlying the Activity in the Giant Axon of the Squid," with A. Hodgkin and B. Katz, *Arch. Sci. Physiol* 3 (1949): 129–50. "Properties of Nerve Axons. I. Movement of Sodium and Potassium Ions during Nervous Activity," with A. Hodgkin, *Cold Spring Harbor Symposia on Quantitative Biology* 17 (1952): 43–52. "Movement of Radioactive Potassium and Membrane Current in a Giant Axon," with A. Hodgkin, *Journal of Physiology (London)* 121 (1953): 403–14. *Reflections on Muscle* (Princeton, N.J.: Princeton University Press, 1980).

Bibliography: *Biographical Encyclopedia of Scientists* (New York: Facts on File, 1981), p. 404. *Science* 142 (October 25, 1963): 468–70.

BLOCH, KONRAD E.

Prize: Physiology or Medicine, 1964. *Born:* January 21, 1912; Neisse, Germany. *Died:* October 15, 2000; Burlington, Massachusetts. *Nationality:* German; later U.S. citizen. *Education:* Technische Hochschule, Germany, Chem. Eng., 1934; Columbia University, New York, Ph.D., 1938. *Career:* Columbia University, New York, Professor,

1939–46; University of Chicago, Illinois, Professor, 1946–54; Harvard University, Massachusetts, Professor, 1954–78. *Other Awards:* Medal, Sociéte de Chimie Biologique, 1958; Fritzsche Award, American Chemical Society, 1964; Distinguished Service Award, University of Chicago School of Medicine, Illinois, 1964; Centennial Science Award, University of Notre Dame, Indiana, 1965; Cardano Medal, Lombardy Academy of Sciences, 1965; William Lloyd Evans Award, Ohio State University, 1968; National Medal of Science, 1988.

Citation: "For their discoveries concerning the mechanism and regulation of the cholesterol and fatty acid metabolism" (with Feodor Lynen).

Life Work: Bloch and Feodor Lynen clarified the role of acetic acid as a building block for cholesterol and fatty acids. Bloch discovered that cholesterol is a necessary ingredient of all body cells and is one of the female sex hormones and that all substances of a steroid nature are formed from cholesterol. He established the origin of all carbon atoms of the cholesterol skeleton and mapped the thirty-six separate steps in which acetic acid is converted into cholesterol. Bloch also studied the biosynthesis of glutathione, a tripeptide important in protein metabolism. He determined that acetyl coenzyme A is converted in an irreversible process to mevalonic acid which is transformed into chemically active isoprene from which the unsaturated hydrocarbon squalene and, finally, cholesterol are formed.

Publications: "Biological Conversion of Cholesterol to Cholic Acid," with B. Berg and D. Rittenberg, *Journal of Biological Chemistry* 149 (1943): 511–17. "The Utilization of AcOH for Fatty Acid Synthesis," with D. Rittenberg, *Journal of Biological Chemistry* 154 (1944): 311–12. "Biosynthesis of Squaline," with R. G. Langdon, *Journal of Biological Chemistry* 200 (1953): 129–34. *Lipide Metabolism* (New York: Wiley, 1960).

Bibliography: *The Excitement and Fascination of Science* (Palo Alto, Calif.: Annual Reviews, 1990), vol. 3, part 1, pp. 495–513. *New York Times,* October 16, 1964, pp. 1, 3. *Science* 146 (October 23, 1964): 504–506.

LYNEN, FEODOR FELIX KONRAD

Prize: Physiology or Medicine, 1964. *Born:* April 6, 1911; Munich, Germany. *Died:* August 6, 1979; Munich, Germany. *Nationality:* German. *Education:* University of Munich, Germany, Dr. Phil., 1937. *Career:* University of Munich, Germany, Professor, 1942–79. *Other Awards:* Neuberg Medal, American Society of European Chemists and Pharmacists, 1954; Justus von Liebig Medal, Gesellschaft Deutscher Chemiker, 1955; Carus Medal, Deutsche Akademie der Naturforscher Leopoldina, 1961; Otto Warburg Medal, Gesellschaft fur Physiologische Chemie, 1963; Norman Medaille, Deutsche Gesellschaft fur Fettnissenschaft, 1967.

Citation: "For their discoveries concerning the mechanism and regulation of the cholesterol and fatty acid metabolism" (with Konrad Bloch).

Life Work: Lynen's fields of investigation were intermediary metabolism, fatty acid oxidation, fatty acid biosynthesis, cholesterol synthesis, and the synthesis of rubber. The biosynthesis of both fatty acids and cholesterol begins with a chemically active form of acetate, a two-carbon molecule. Later, he discovered that the active form of acetate is acetyl coenzyme. Lynen also elucidated the mechanism of fatty acid biosynthesis beginning with acetyl coenzyme A, which combines with carbon dioxide in an irreversible step to form malonyl coenzyme A. A multiple enzyme complex contains all the enzymes required for fatty acid synthesis. Investigating biosynthesis, Lynen demonstrated that cholesterol is formed through the condensation of two molecules of acetyl coenzyme A to form acetoacetyl coenzyme A, a four-carbon molecule. The two coenzymes then combine to form coenzyme A, which is converted to mevalonic acid in a catalytic reaction cause by HMG coenzyme A reductase. Mevalonic acid is converted into chemically active isoprene, a hydrocarbon that is the building block of cholesterol. Cholesterol biosynthesis is also regulated by negative feedback.

Publications: "Acetyl Coenzyme A and the Fatty Acid Cycle," *Harvey Lecture Series* 48 (1953): 210–44. "Der Fettsaurecyclus," *Angewandte Chemie* 67 (1955): 463–70. "Phosphatkreislauf und Pasteur-Effekt," *Proceedings of the International Symposium on Enzyme Chemistry, Tokyo and Kyoto* (1957): 25–34. "Biosynthesis of Fatty Acids," *Proceedings of the Symposium on Drugs Affecting Lipid Metabolism* (1961): 3–15. "Cholesterol und Arteriosklerose," *Naturwiss. Rundschau* 25 (1972): 382–87.

Bibliography: *Biographical Memoirs of the Fellows of the Royal Society* (London: Royal Society, 1982), vol. 28, p. 261. *Current Biography Yearbook* (New York: H. W. Wilson, 1967), pp. 263–65. *Die Aktivierte Essigsaure und Ihre Folgen: Autobiograph* (New York: de Gruyter, 1976).

JACOB, FRANÇOIS

Prize: Physiology or Medicine, 1965. *Born:* June 17, 1920; Nancy, France. *Nationality:* French. *Education:* Lycée Carnot, France, baccalaureat, 1938; University of Paris, France, M.D., 1947; University of Paris, France, B.S., 1951; University of Paris, France, D.Sc., 1954. *Career:* French Army, 1940–45; Institut Pasteur, Paris, France, Researcher and Administrator, 1950–. *Other Awards:* Bronze Medal, French National Scientific Research Center, 1955; Essee Prize, Anti-Cancer League, 1958; Prix Charles Leopold Mayer, Académie des Sciences, 1962; Croix de la Libération, 1966; Grand Croix, Legion d'Honneur, 1966.

Citation: "For their discoveries concerning genetic control of enzyme and virus synthesis" (with André Lwoff and Jacques Monod).

Life Work: Jacob's field of investigation was the cellular genetics of bacteria. He and Elie Wollman determined that the bacterial cell chromosome is a circular structure attached to the membrane of the cell and that smaller genetic fragments may be added to or subtracted from it. Working with Monod, he discovered one of the three types of

RNA, messenger RNA, which receives genetic information from DNA lodged in the nucleus of the cell and conveys it to ribosomes—the site of protein synthesis—in the cytoplasm, the protoplasm of the cell outside the nucleus. The blueprint carried by messenger RNA orders the amino acids in the correct sequence to form protein molecules. They also discovered that DNA contains two different types of genes, structural and regulatory. The former transmit genetic codes from one generation of cells to the next and direct protein synthesis. The latter communicate with the structural genes and regulate all biochemical processes of the cell, enabling it to adapt to environmental changes. In a stable environment, regulatory genes inhibit or suppress structural genes. Jacob and Monod called the sets of structural and regulatory genes operons and the gene responsible for suppression and activation the operator gene. They found that bacteriophage particles contain structural and regulatory genes. During the noninfectious prophage phase of the bacteriophage, the structural gene responsible for phage replication is inhibited or suppressed. Jacob's viral theory of carcinogenesis states that viral particles are dormant in human cells and are activated by a variety of factors. Once activated, the virus can insert itself into the biochemical machinery of the cell, causing cancerous growth.

Publications: "Genetic Regulatory Mechanisms in the Synthesis of Proteins," with Jacques Monod, *Journal of Molecular Biology* 3 (1961): 356. "On the Regulation of Gene Activity: Beta-Galactosidase Formation in E. Coli," with Jacques Monod, *Cold Spring Harbor Symposia on Quantitative Biology* 26 (1961): 207. *Sexuality and Genetics of Bacteria*, with E. Wollman (New York: Academic Press, 1961). "Telenomic Mechanism's Cellular Metabolism, Growth and Differentiation," with Jacques Monod, *Cold Spring Harbor Symposia on Quantitative Biology* 26 (1961): 394–95.

Bibliography: *Current Biography Yearbook* (New York: H. W. Wilson, 1966), pp. 191–93. *Science* 150 (October 22, 1965): 462–63. *The Statue Within* (Paris: Seuil, 1990).

LWOFF, ANDRÉ MICHAEL

Prize: Physiology or Medicine, 1965. *Born:* May 8, 1902; Allier, France. *Died:* September 30, 1994; Paris, France. *Nationality:* French. *Education:* University of Paris, France, Licencie es Sciences, 1921; University of Paris, France, M.D., 1927; University of Paris, France, D.Sc., 1932. *Career:* Institut Pasteur, Paris, France, Researcher and Administrator, 1921–68; Cancer Research Institute, Villejuif, France, Researcher and Administrator, 1968–72. *Other Awards:* Medaille de la Résistance, France; Commander Legion d'Honneur, France; Lallemont Award, Académie des Sciences; Noury Award, Académie des Sciences; Longchampt Award, Académie des Sciences; Chausser Award, Académie des Sciences; Petit d'Ormoy, France; Charles Leopold Mayer Foundation Prize; Leeuwenhoek Medal, Royal Netherlands Academy of Sciences and Arts, 1960; Keilin Medal, British Biochemical Society, 1964; Einstein Award, 1967.

Citation: "For their discoveries concerning genetic control of enzyme and virus synthesis" (with François Jacob and Jacques Monod).

Life Work: Lwoff's field of investigation was growth factors, or specific substances which the organism is unable to synthesize but which are necessary for its growth and multiplication. He studied the biochemistry of thiamine, hematin, and nicotinamide. In the 1940s he turned his research to the genetics of bacteria and viruses. With Jacob and Monod he began to study lysogenic bacteria, or bacteria infected with phage particles and the process of cell destruction or lysogeny. In 1950, he discovered that when lysogenic bacterium, placed in a culture medium, divides into generations of daughter cells, the daughter cells were also lysogenic, thus proving that lysogeny is also a genetic trait. He also found that lysogenic bacteriophage differ from noninfectious or temperate phage particles, called prophage. When subjected to ultraviolet light prophage can be made to multiply and cause cell destruction. Phage particles and most other virus particles consist of an inner core of DNA and an outer coat of protein. When a bacterial cell is infected the prophage particle attaches itself to the chromosome of the cell. This led Lwoff to propose that viruses cause cancer as they reside in human cells and become active under certain conditions.

Publications: *L'Evolution Physiologique* (Paris: Hermann, 1944). *The Kinetosomes in Development, Reproduction, and Evolution* (New York: Wiley, 1950). *Problems of Morphogenesis in Ciliates* (New York: Wiley, 1950). *Biochemistry and Physiology of Protozoa* (New York: Academic Press, 1951–64). *Biological Order* (Cambridge: Massachusetts Institute of Technology Press, 1962).

Bibliography: *Asimov's Biographical Encyclopedia of Science and Technology* (Garden City, N.Y.: Doubleday, 1982), p. 787. *The Excitement and Fascination of Science* (Palo Alto, Calif.: Annual Reviews, 1978), vol. 2, pp. 301–26. *New York Times*, October 15, 1965, pp. 1, 36. *New York Times* Biographical Service, October 5, 1994, p. 1520. *Science* 150 (October 22, 1965): 462–63.

MONOD, JACQUES LUCIEN

Prize: Physiology or Medicine, 1965. **Born:** February 9, 1910; Paris, France. **Died:** May 31, 1976; Cannes, France. **Nationality:** French. **Education:** University of Paris, France, B.S., 1931; University of Paris, France, D.Sc., 1941. **Career:** University of Paris, France, Professor, 1931–41; Pasteur Institute, Paris, France, Researcher and Administrator, 1945–76. **Other Awards:** Montyon Physiology Prize, Paris Académie des Sciences, 1955; Louis Rapkine Medal, London, England, 1958; Chevalier de l'Ordre des Palmes Académiques, 1961; Charles Leopold Mayer Prize, Académie des Sciences, 1962; Officer de la Legion d'Honneur, 1963.

Citation: "For their discoveries concerning genetic control of enzyme and virus synthesis" (with François Jacob and André Lwoff).

Life Work: Monod's field of investigation was enzymatic adaptation, which describes the cycle of enzyme activation and suppression. He discovered that cellular energy is primarily used for biosynthetic processes rather than for maintenance of cellular structures. Working with Jacob, he proved the existence of messenger RNA that carries genetic instructions from DNA in the nucleus of the cell to ribosomes in the cytoplasm. They described the sets of genes into which DNA is organized as operons. An operon consists of the structural gene that directs and controls the synthesis of a specific cellular enzyme and a regulatory or operator gene. Normally the regulatory gene suppresses or inhibits the structural gene. When enzymes are activated, the regulatory gene is repressed by a cellular protein called the repressor protein, permitting the structural gene to synthesize messenger RNA and the cell to adapt to a new environment.

Publications: "Genetic Regulatory Mechanisms in the Synthesis of Proteins," with François Jacob, *Journal of Molecular Biology* 3 (1961): 356. "On the Regulation of Gene Activity: Beta Galactosidase Formation in E. Coli," with François Jacob, *Cold Spring Harbor Symposia on Quantitative Biology* 26 (1961): 207. *Chance and Necessity* (New York: Random House, 1971).

Bibliography: *Current Biography Yearbook* (New York: H. W. Wilson, 1971), pp. 277–79. *Dictionary of Scientific Biography* (New York: Scribner's, 1990), supp. II, pp. 636–49. *Science* 150 (October 22, 1965): 462–63.

HUGGINS, CHARLES BRENTON

Prize: Physiology or Medicine, 1966. *Born:* September 22, 1901; Halifax, Nova Scotia, Canada. *Died:* January 12, 1997; Halifax, Nova Scotia, Canada. *Nationality:* Canadian; later U.S. citizen. *Education:* Acadia University, Canada, B.A., 1920; Harvard University, Massachusetts, M.D., 1924. *Career:* University of Michigan Medical School, Surgery Intern and Instructor, 1924–26; University of Chicago Medical School, Illinois, Professor and Administrator, 1927–72; Acadia University, Nova Scotia, Chancellor, 1972–79. *Other Awards:* Gold Medal, American Medical Association, 1936, 1940; Award for Research, American Urological Association, 1948; Francis Amory Award, 1948; Gold Medal, Société Internationale d'Urologie, 1948; American Cancer Society Award, 1953; Bertner Award, M. D. Anderson Hospital, Texas, 1953; American Pharmaceutical Manufacturers Award, 1958; Gold Medal, American Association of Genito-Urinary Surgeons, 1955; Borden Award, Association of American Medical Colleges, 1955; Comfort Cruikshank Award, Middlesex Hospital, London, 1957; Cameron Prize, Edinburgh University, 1958; Valentine Prize, New York Academy of Medicine, 1962; Hunter Award, American Therapeutic Society, 1962; Lasker Award for Medical Research, 1963; Gold Medal for Research, Rudolph Virchow Society, 1964; Gold Medal in Therapeutics, Worshipful Society of Apothecaries of London, 1966; Gairdner Award, Toronto, 1966; Chicago Medical Society Award, 1967; Centennial Medal, Acadia University, Nova Scotia, 1967; Hamilton Award, Illinois Medical Society, 1967; Laurea and Award, American Urological Society, 1969; Sheen Award, American Medical Association, 1970; Distinguished Service Award, American Society of Abdominal Surgeons, 1971.

Citation: "For his discoveries concerning hormonal treatment of prostatic cancer."

Life Work: Huggins's field of investigation was the male genito-urinary system, especially the prostate gland. In his initial experiments he found that testosterone, the male sex hormone and steroid, stimulates growth and secretory activity of the prostate while estrogen, the female sex hormone, inhibits it. On this basis he established that testosterone promotes cancer of the prostate and estrogen inhibits it. His clinical experience led him to formulate two hypotheses concerning the biological behavior of cancer: first, cancers are not always autonomous and self-perpetuating, and second, the growth of some forms of cancer depends upon a hormonal environment. Later, his researches concentrated on cancer of the breast.

Publications: "The Business of Discovery in the Medical Sciences," *Journal of the American Medical Association* 194 (December 13, 1965): 1211–15. "Endocrine-Induced Regression of Cancers," *Science* 156 (1967): 1050–54. *Experimental Leukemia and Mammary Cancer: Induction, Prevention and Cure* (Chicago: University of Chicago Press, 1979).

Bibliography: *Current Biography Yearbook* (New York: H. W. Wilson, 1965), pp. 205–208. Paul Talalay, "The Scientific Contributions of Charles Brenton Huggins," *Journal of the American Medical Association* 192 (June 28, 1965): 1137–40.

ROUS, FRANCIS PEYTON

Prize: Physiology or Medicine, 1966. *Born:* October 5, 1879; Baltimore, Maryland. *Died:* February 16, 1970; New York, New York. *Nationality:* American. *Education:* Johns Hopkins University, Maryland, B.A., 1900; Johns Hopkins University, Maryland, M.A., 1901; Johns Hopkins University, Maryland, M.D., 1905. *Career:* University of Michigan, Professor, 1906–1908; Rockefeller Institute, New York, Professor, 1909–45. *Other Awards:* John Scott Medal, Philadelphia, Pennsylvania, 1927; Kobler Medal, Association of American Physicians, 1953; Bertner Foundation Award, University of Texas, 1954; Jessie Stevenson Kovalenko Award, National Academy of Sciences, 1954; Distinguished Service Award, American Cancer Society, 1957; Lasker Foundation Award, 1958; Karl Landsteiner Award, American Association of Blood Banks, 1958; New York Academy of Medicine Medal, 1959; Judd Award, Memorial Center for Cancer, New York, 1959; United Nations Prize, 1962; Gold-Headed Cane, American Association of Pathologists and Bacteriologists, 1964; National Medal of Science, United States, 1965; Paul Ehrlich-Ludwig Darmstaedter Prize, West Germany, 1966; Gold Medal, British Royal Society of Medicine, 1966.

Citation: "For his discovery of tumour-inducing viruses."

Life Work: Rous's investigation of chicken tumor by cell-free extracts (extracts of tumor tissue filtered to eliminate tumor cells) revealed that the cause of chicken sarcoma was a living virus. The chicken sarcoma was named the Rous sarcoma and the hypothetical causative agent as the Rous sarcoma virus. In 1942, he presented three hypotheses about the biology of cancers. First, viruses may infect the body in utero giving no sign of their presence until provoked by carcinogen. Second, chemical, or provocative carcinogens may cause tumors that appear spontaneously. Third, latent viruses and provocative chemical carcinogens may interact and cause tumors. During World War I, Rous devised a method for preserving blood, known as the ACD solution, containing acid, citrate, and dextrose. He also developed a new experimental method for separating cells from tissues by using trypsin, an enzyme synthesized by the pancreas. In the 1920s, he investigated the physiological function of the liver and gall bladder. They found that bile is reabsorbed by the intestines and recirculated to the liver by means of a special vascular system. He also found that bilirubin, a red bile pigment which causes jaundice, is made by means of a hemoglobin breakdown.

Publications: "A Sarcoma of the Fowl Transmissible by an Agent Separable from the Tumor Cells," *Journal of Experimental Medicine* 13 (1911): 397–411. "Transmission of a Malignant New Growth by Means of a Cell-Free Filtrate," *Journal of the American Medical Association* 56 (1911): 198. *The Modern Dance of Death* (London: Cambridge University Press, 1929). "The Virus Tumors and the Tumor Problem," *American Journal of Cancer* 28 (1936): 233–71. "Surmise and Fact on the Nature of Cancer," *Nature* 183 (1959): 1357–61.

Bibliography: *Biographical Memoirs of the Fellows of the Royal Society* (London: Royal Society, 1971), vol. 17, pp. 643–62. *Biographical Memoirs of the National Academy of Sciences* (Washington, D.C.: National Academy of Sciences, 1976), vol. 48, pp. 275–306. *Current Biography Yearbook* (New York: H. W. Wilson, 1967), pp. 354–57. *A Notable Career in Finding Out: Peyton Rous* (New York: Rockefeller University Press, 1971).

GRANIT, RAGNAR ARTHUR

Prize: Physiology or Medicine, 1967. *Born:* October 30, 1900; Helsinki, Finland. *Died:* July 9, 1998; Stockholm, Sweden. *Nationality:* Finnish; later Swedish citizen. *Education:* Helsingfors University, Finland, M.S., 1923; Helsingfors University, Finland, M.D., 1927. *Career:* University of Pennsylvania, Philadelphia, Fellow, 1929–31; Helsinki University, Finland, Professor, 1932–40; Royal Caroline Institute, Stockholm, Sweden, Professor, 1940–67. *Other Awards:* Lunsgaard Gold Medal, 1938; Jubilee Medal, Swedish Society of Physicians, 1947; Bjorken Prize, Uppsala University, 1948; Retzin Gold Medal, 1957; Donders Medal, 1957; 3rd International St. Vincent Prize, 1961; Jahre Prize, Oslo University, Norway, 1961; Sherrington Memorial Gold Medal, 1967; Purinje Gold Medal, 1969.

Citation: "For their discoveries concerning the primary physiological and chemical visual processes in the eye" (with Haldan Keffer Hartline and George Wald).

Life Work: Granit's field of investigation was electroneurophysiology. He discovered that strong illumination of parts of the retina inhibits the response of adjacent regions and enhances the perception of contrasts by the eye. His research confirmed that the visual image is elaborated by the interplay of excitation and inhibition in the nervous center of the retina itself. He investigated color vision and proved that the eye contains receptors (cone cells) with pigments sensitive to different wavelengths of light. His work established the spectral sensitivities of three types of cone cells: blue, green, and red. Later, he studied muscle spindles, which are specialized sense organs that respond to muscular tension and provide the feedback the body uses to control muscle response.

Publications: *On the Correlation of Some Sensory and Physiological Phenomena of Vision* (London: George Putman, 1938). *Sensory Mechanisms of the Retina* (New York: Hafner, 1963). *Receptors and Sensory Perception* (Westport, Conn.: Greenwood Press, 1975). *The Purposive Brain* (Cambridge: Massachusetts Institute of Technology Press, 1980).

Bibliography: *Hur det Kom Sig* [*A Memoir*] (N.p., 1983). *Science* (October 27, 1967): 468–71.

HARTLINE, HALDAN KEFFER

Prize: Physiology or Medicine, 1967. *Born:* December 22, 1903; Bloomsburg, Pennsylvania. *Died:* March 17, 1983; Fallston, Maryland *Nationality:* American. *Education:* Lafayette College, Pennsylvania, B.S., 1923; Johns Hopkins University, Maryland, M.D., 1927. *Career:* Johns Hopkins University, Baltimore, Maryland, Researcher, 1927–29; University of Pennsylvania, Professor, 1929–49; Johns Hopkins University, Baltimore, Maryland, Professor, 1949–53; Rockefeller University, New York, Professor, 1953–74. *Other Awards:* William H. Howell Award, 1927; Howard Crosby Warren Medal, 1948; A. A. Michelson Award, Case Institute, 1964; Lighthouse Award, New York City, 1969.

Citation: "For their discoveries concerning the primary physiological and chemical visual processes in the eye" (with Ragnar Granit and George Wald).

Life Work: Hartline's field of investigation was electrical impulses in single visual elements. In 1932 he made the first recordings of the activity of single optic nerve fibers. He found that the information recorded by the visual receptors constituted a kind of code. Different optic nerve fibers responded to light in different ways. His research demonstrated that individual retina ganglion cells, located several layers above the visual receptors, send fibers to the optic nerves. They respond best to particular combinations of excitation and inhibition in the receptors from which they receive input. Much of the visual information or data is processed in the thin layer of nervous tissue that is the retina. The response of an individual receptor unit is heavily dependent on the degree to which the neighboring receptors are illuminated. Thus, diffuse light produces weak visual responses while edges and contours are accentuated. All of the neuronal interactions in the retina are inhibitory.

Publications: *Studies on Excitation and Inhibition in the Retina: A Collection of Papers from the Laboratories of H. Keffer Hartline* (New York: Rockefeller University Press, 1974).

Bibliography: *Biographical Encyclopedia of Scientists* (New York: Facts on File, 1981), p. 355. *Biographical Memoirs of the Royal Society* (London: Royal Society, 1985), vol. 31, p. 261. *Science* 158 (October 27, 1967): 471–73.

WALD, GEORGE

Prize: Physiology or Medicine, 1967. **Born:** November 18, 1906; New York, New York. **Died:** April 12, 1997; Cambridge, Massachusetts. **Nationality:** American. **Education:** New York University, B.S., 1927; Columbia University, New York, M.A., 1928; Columbia University, New York, Ph.D., 1932. **Career:** National Research Council Fellow, 1932–34; Harvard University, Massachusetts, Professor, 1934–77. **Other Awards:** Eli Lilly Prize, American Chemical Society, 1939; Lasker Award, American Public Health Association, 1953; Proctor Medal, Association for Research in Ophthalmology, 1955; Rumford Medal, American Academy of Arts and Sciences, 1959; Ives Medal, Optical Society of America, 1966; Paul Karrer Medal, University of Zürich, Switzerland, 1967; T. Duckett Jones Award, Helen Hay Whitney Foundation, 1967; Bradford Washburn Medal, Boston Museum Society, 1968; Max Berg Award, 1969; Priestley Medal, Dickinson College, 1970.

Citation: "For their discoveries concerning the primary physiological and chemical visual processes in the eye" (with Ragnar Granit and Haldan Keffer Hartline).

Life Work: Wald's field of investigation was the physiology of the eye. The process of vision consists of light separating rhodopsin (a pigment) into two products, one of which, a protein, is called opsin and the other is vitamin A, a pigment. In 1950 Wald synthesized rhodopsin. He found that retinal (vitamin A aldehyde) is a molecule with a long arm of carbon atoms arranged in a number of ways, each called an isomer. In the most stable form the carbons are arrayed in a flat plane, the all-*trans* isomer, while another form of unilluminated retinal (*11-cis*) fits tightly into the opsin protein molecule. The vitamin A in every pigment is bent and twisted. What light does in vision is to straighten out the vitamin A molecule into its natural form. Everything else is a consequence of the light reaction. He also provided the biochemical basis for Ragnar Granit's theory that the human eye contains three kinds of cones, each of which is sensitive to a different band of the light spectrum.

Publications: *General Education in a Free Society* (Cambridge: Harvard University Press, 1945). *Twenty-Six Afternoons of Biology* (Reading, Mass.: Addison-Wesley, 1966). *Visual Pigments and Photoreceptors: Review and Outlook* (New York: Academic Press, 1974).

Bibliography: *Current Biography Yearbook* (New York: H. W. Wilson, 1968), pp. 412–14. "George Wald: The Man, the Speech," *New York Times Magazine*, August 17, 1969, pp. 28–29.

HOLLEY, ROBERT WILLIAM

Prize: Physiology or Medicine, 1968. *Born:* January 28, 1922; Urbana, Illinois. *Died:* February 11, 1993; Los Gatos, California. *Nationality:* American. *Education:* University of Illinois, A.B., 1942; Cornell University, New York, Ph.D., 1947. *Career:* Washington State College, Researcher, 1947–48; Cornell University, Ithaca, New York, Professor, 1948–66; Salk Institute of Biological Studies, La Jolla, California, Researcher, 1966–93. *Other Awards:* Distinguished Service Award, U.S. Department of Agriculture, 1965; Lasker Award, 1965; U.S. Steel Foundation Award, National Academy of Sciences, 1967.

Citation: "For their interpretation of the genetic code and its function in protein synthesis" (with Har Gobind Khorana and Marshall W. Nirenberg).

Life Work: Holley synthesized molecules of tranfer RNA with a nucleotide sequence specific for phenylalanine. They then determined the nucleotide sequence of the phenylalanine RNA. This was the first nucleic whose structure was deciphered. Holley also found that transfer RNA has a biologically active secondary structure. The primary structure is the sequence of bases in the nucleotide strand. The secondary structure resembles a three-leaf clover where the twist of the strand brings it in contact with itself.

Publications: "A New Method for Sequence Determination of Large Olegonucleotides," with others, *Biochem. Biophys. Res. Commun.* 17 (1964): 389–94. "Structure of a Ribonucleic Acid," with others, *Science* 147 (1965): 1462–65. "Structure of an Alanine Transfer Ribonucleic Acid," *Journal of the American Medical Association* 194 (1965): 868–71. "Experimental Approaches to the Determination of the Nucleotide Sequences of Large Oligonucleotides and Small Nucleic Acids," *Progr. Nucl. Acid Res. Mol. Biol.* (1968): 37–47.

Bibliography: *Current Biography Yearbook* (New York: H. W. Wilson, 1967), pp. 172–74. *New York Times* Biographical Service, February 14, 1993, p. 230. *Science* 162 (October 25, 1968): 433–36.

KHORANA, HAR GOBIND

Prize: Physiology or Medicine, 1968. *Born:* January 9, 1922; Raipur, India. *Nationality:* Indian; later U.S. citizen. *Education:* Punjab University, India, B.Sc., 1943; Punjab University, India, M.Sc., 1945; Liverpool University, England, Ph.D., 1948. *Career:* Federal Institute of Technology, Zürich, Switzerland, Researcher, 1948–49; Cambridge University, England, Researcher, 1950–52; University of British Columbia, Canada, Administrator, 1952–60; University of Wisconsin, Professor and Administrator, 1960–70; Massachusetts Institute of Technology, Professor, 1970–. *Other Awards:* Merck Award, Chemical Institute of Canada, 1958; Gold Medal, Professional

Institute of Public Service of Canada, 1960; Dannie-Heinneman Preiz, Göttingen, Germany, 1967; Remsen Award, Johns Hopkins University, 1968; American Chemical Society Award, 1968; Louisa Gross Horowitz Prize, 1968; Lasker Award, 1968; Gibbs Medal, American Chemical Society, 1974. Gairdner Foundation Award, 1980; National Medal of Science, 1987; Kayser Award, 1987.

Citation: "For their interpretation of the genetic code and its function in protein synthesis" (with Robert W. Holley and Marshall W. Nirenberg).

Life Work: In the early 1960s, Khorana set out to decipher the genetic code. Because there are four nucleotide bases in the DNA that encode for the twenty different amino acids, there are sixty-four possible triplet combinations. Khorana determined the base sequence in the triplet codes for each of the twenty amino acids. He synthesized nucleotide strands of DNA and RNA with all sixty-four base triplets and identified the base triplet codes. He also studied the secondary chemical structure of transfer RNA that carries amino acids to the ribosomes. It resembles a three-leaf clover, the middle leaf of which is complementary to the base sequence of messenger RNA. Later he synthesized the DNA gene of yeast and the gene of the intestinal bacterium *Escherichia coli*.

Publications: *Some Recent Developments in the Chemistry of Phosphate Esters of Biological Interest* (New York: Wiley, 1961). "Studies on Polynucleotides. LXVII. Initiation of Protein Synthesis in Vitro as Studied by Using Ribopolynucleotides with Repeating Nucleotide Sequences as Messengers," with others, *Journal of Molecular Biology* 25 (1967): 275–98. "Synthesis of Transfer RNA Genes," *Advan. Biosci* (1971): 89–102.

Bibliography: *Current Biography Yearbook* (New York: H. W. Wilson, 1970), pp. 222–24. *Science* 162 (October 25, 1968): 433–36.

NIRENBERG, MARSHALL WARREN

Prize: Physiology or Medicine, 1968. *Born:* April 10, 1927; New York, New York. *Nationality:* American. *Education:* University of Florida, B.S., 1948; University of Florida, M.S., 1952; University of Michigan, Ph.D., 1957. *Career:* National Institutes of Health, Bethesda, Maryland, Researcher and Administrator, 1957–. *Other Awards:* Molecular Biology Award, National Academy of Sciences, 1962; Biological Sciences Award, Washington Academy of Sciences, 1962; Paul Lewis Award, American Chemical Society, 1963; Modern Medicine Award, 1963; Medal, Department of Health, Education and Welfare, 1964; Harrison Howe Award, American Chemical Society, 1964; National Medal of Sciences, 1965; Hildebrand Award, American Chemical Society, 1966; Research Corporation Award, 1966; Gairdner Foundation Award of Merit, Canada, 1967; Prix Charles Leopold Meyer, French Academy of Sciences, 1967; Franklin Medal, Franklin Institute, 1968; Lasker Award, 1968; Priestly Award, 1968; Louisa Gross Horowitz Prize, 1968.

Citation: "For their interpretation of the genetic code and its function in protein synthesis" (with Robert W. Holley and Har Gobind Khorana).

Life Work: In the 1960s, Nirnberg performed an important series of experiments that enabled him to decipher the genetic code. First, he synthesized polyuracil, which was then placed in a cell-free experimental system. Polyuracil RNA directed the synthesis of a protein molecule consisting of a chain of molecules of the amino acid phenylalanine, whose triplet code is UUU. He then synthesized RNA with all possible triplet sequences. Some of the amino acids are encoded by more than one base triplet and some by nonsense triplets, because they do not encode any amino acids.

Publications: "The Genetic Code," *Scientific American* 208 (March 1963): 80–94. "RNA Code and Protein Synthesis," with others, *Cold Spring Symposium on Quantitative Biology* (1966): 11–14. "Genetic Memory," *Journal of the American Medical Association* 206 (1968): 1973–77.

Bibliography: *Current Biography Yearbook* (New York: H. W. Wilson, 1965), pp. 305–307. Donald Robinson, *100 Most Important People in the World Today* (New York: Putnam, 1970), pp. 204–206.

DELBRÜCK, MAX

Prize: Physiology or Medicine, 1969. *Born:* September 4, 1906; Berlin, Germany. *Died:* March 9, 1981; Pasadena, California. *Nationality:* German; later U.S. citizen. *Education:* University of Göttingen, Germany, Ph.D., 1930. *Career:* Kaiser Wilhelm Institute, Berlin, Germany, Researcher, 1932–37; California Institute of Technology, Researcher, 1937–39; Vanderbilt University, Tennessee, Professor, 1940–47; California Institute of Technology, Professor, 1947–76. *Other Awards:* Kimber Medal, National Academy of Sciences, 1965; Louisa Gross Horowitz Prize, 1969.

Citation: "For their discoveries concerning the replication mechanism and the genetic structure of viruses" (with Alfred Hershey and Salvador Luria).

Life Work: Delbrück's field of investigation was the genetics of the bacteriophage, a type of virus that infects bacterial cells. His experiments launched a new chapter in virus research and bacterial genetics and molecular biology. They showed that bacterial cell DNA underwent spontaneous mutations, which conferred upon the cell an immunity to lysis by bacteriophages. It was the first evidence that heredity in bacteria is mediated by genes.

Publications: "Mutation of Bacteria from Virus-Sensitive to Virus-Resistant," with S. Luria, *Genetics* 28 (1943): 491–511. "Induced Mutations in Bacterial Viruses," *Cold Spring Harbor Symposia on Quantitative Biology* 11 (1946): 33–37. *Uber Verebungschemie* (Cologne: Westdeutscher Verlag, 1963).

Bibliography: *Biographical Memoirs of the Fellows of the Royal Society* (London: Royal Society, 1982), vol. 28, pp. 59–60. E. P. Fischer and C. Lipson, *Thinking about Science: Max Delbrück and the Origins of Molecular Biology* (New York: Norton, 1988).

HERSHEY, ALFRED DAY

Prize: Physiology or Medicine, 1969. *Born:* December 4, 1908; Owosso, Michigan. *Died:* May 22, 1997; New York, New York. *Nationality:* American. *Education:* Michigan State University, B.S., 1930; Michigan State University, Ph.D., 1934. *Career:* Washington University, Missouri, Professor, 1934–50; Carnegie Institute at Cold Spring Harbor, New York, Researcher and Administrator, 1950–74. *Other Awards:* Lasker Award, American Public Health Association, 1958; Kimber Genetics Award, National Academy of Sciences, 1965.

Citation: "For their discoveries concerning the replication mechanism and the genetic structure of viruses" (with Max Delbrück and Salvador Luria).

Life Work: Hershey was a member of the Phage group (along with Max Delbrück and Salvador Luria) dedicated to bacteriophage research. In 1946 he discovered that different strains of bacteriophage may exchange genetic material. His experiments provided evidence of genetic exchange, which he called recombination. In 1952 he showed how bacteriophages infect bacterial cells, thus confirming that DNA is the genetic material of the bacteriophage. His work established that bacteriophage DNA is single-stranded, unlike the DNA of higher organisms, and that some bacteriophagic DNA is circular.

Publications: "Reproduction of Bacteriophage," *International Review of Cytology* 1 (1952): 119–34. "Nucleic Acid Economy in Bacteria Infected with Bacteriophage T2. II. Phage Precursor Nucleic Acid," *Journal of General Physiology* 37 (1953): 1–23. "Upper Limit to the Protein Content of the Germinal Substance of Bacterio-phage T2," *Virology* 1 (1955): 108–27.

Bibliography: *Biographical Encyclopedia of Scientists* (New York: Facts on File, 1981), p. 370. *Current Biography Yearbook* (New York: H. W. Wilson, 1970), pp. 175–77. *Science* (October 24, 1969): 479–81.

LURIA, SALVADOR EDWARD

Prize: Physiology or Medicine, 1969. *Born:* August 13, 1912; Turin, Italy. *Died:* February 6, 1991; Lexington, Massachusetts. *Nationality:* Italian; later U.S. citizen. *Education:* University of Turin, Italy, M.D., 1935. *Career:* Italian Army, 1935–38; Institute of Radium, Paris, France, Researcher, 1938–40; Columbia University, New York, Researcher, 1940–42; Indiana University, Professor, 1943–50; University of Illinois, Professor, 1950–59; Massachusetts Institute of Technology, Professor and Administrator, 1959–78. *Other Awards:* Lepetit Prize, 1935; Lenghi Prize, Academia Nazionale Lincei, 1965; Louisa Gross Horowitz Prize, Columbia University, 1969.

Citation: "For their discoveries concerning the replication mechanism and the genetic structure of viruses" (with Max Delbrück and Alfred Hershey).

Life Work: Luria's field of investigation was bacteriophages, especially the phenomenon of resistance, the appearance of bacterial variants resistant to both viruses and bactericidal drugs. His problem was to decide whether the resistant bacteria were spontaneously arising mutants or cells that became resistant as a result of an action of the phage on otherwise normal bacteria. His fluctuation test, published in 1943 with Max Delbrück, provided evidence for bacterial mutation. In 1951 he established that bacteriophage genes undergo spontaneous mutations and that phage protein rather than DNA carried the genetic information.

Publications: "Mutation of Bacteria from Virus-Sensitive to Virus-Resistant," with M. Delbrück, *Genetics* 28 (1943): 491–511. *The Multiplication of Viruses* (Vienna: Springer, 1958). *The Recognition of DNA in Bacteria* (San Francisco: W. H. Freeman, 1969). *A View of Life*, with S. Gould and S. Singer (Menlo Park, Calif.: Benjamin Cummings, 1981).

Bibliography: *Current Biography Yearbook* (New York: H. W. Wilson, 1970), pp. 258–60. S. Luria, *A Slot Machine, A Broken Test Tube* (New York: Harper & Row, 1984). *New York Times* Biographical Service, February 7, 1991, p. 108.

AXELROD, JULIUS

Prize: Physiology or Medicine, 1970. *Born:* May 30, 1912; New York, New York. *Nationality:* American. *Education:* City College of New York, B.S., 1933; New York University, M.A., 1941; George Washington University, Washington, D.C., Ph.D., 1955. *Career:* New York University, Researcher, 1933–49; National Institutes of Health, Maryland, Researcher and Administrator, 1950–. *Other Awards:* Meritorious Research Award, Association for Research on Nervous and Mental Diseases, 1965; Gairdner Award, 1967; Alumni Distinguished Achievement Award, George Washington University, 1968; Claude Bernard Professorship and Award, University of Montreal, 1969; Distinguished Service Award, 1970; Distinguished Service Award, Modern Medicine Magazine, 1970; Albert Einstein Award, Yeshiva University, 1971; Rudolph Virchow Medal, 1971; Myrtle Wreath Award, Hadassah, 1972; Torald Sollmann Award, American Society of Pharmacology and Experimental Therapeutics, 1973; Leibniz Medal, 1984; Salmon Medal, 1989; Thudicum Medal, 1989; Gerard Medal, 1991.

Citation: "For their discoveries concerning the humoral transmittors in the nerve terminals and the mechanism for their storage, release and inactivation" (with Ulf von Euler and Bernard Katz).

Life Work: Axelrod's field of investigation was amphetamines, a class of neurotransmitters related to a group of natural compounds called catecholamines that included adrenaline and noradrenaline. Axelrod isolated catechol-O-methyltransferase (COMT) one of the two most important enzymes that break down catecholamines in the body. His research showed that catecholamine-based impulses end when the neurotransmitter is reabsorbed by the presynaptic nerve terminal. Noradrenaline is released in discrete packets, or quanta, into the small vesicles, or storage granules, found in presynaptic cells. Axelrod discovered that psychoactive drugs act by modifying the normal recycling of catecholamines. They alter the amount of the transmitter packed into a vesicle, the rate of vesicle release, or the uptake of neurotransmitters by the presynaptic cell. Later Axelrod concentrated his research on the relationship between hormones and neurotransmiters and the effects of neurotransmitters on hormone production and the effects of hormones on neurotransmitter release.

Publications: "Reduction in the Accumulation of Norepinephrine 3H in Experimental Hypertension," with others, *Life Science* 5 (1966): 2283–91. "Control of Catechol Amine Metabolism," *Progress in Endocrinology, International Congress of Endocrinology, 3rd* (1968): 286–93. *The Pineal,* with R. Wurthman and D. Kelly (New York: Academic Press, 1968). "Biochemical Pharmacology of Catechol Amines and Its Clinical Implications," *Transactions of the American Neurological Association* 96 (1972): 179–86.

Bibliography: *People* 11 (February 5, 1979): 24. *Science* (October 23, 1970): 422–23.

EULER, ULF SVANTE VON

Prize: Physiology or Medicine, 1970. *Born:* February 7, 1905; Stockholm, Sweden. *Died:* March 10, 1983; Stockholm, Sweden. *Nationality:* Swedish. *Education:* Karolinska Institute, Sweden, M.D., 1930. *Career:* Karolinska Institute, Sweden, Professor and Administrator, 1930–71. *Other Awards:* Commander, Order of the North Star, Sweden; Cruzeiro do Sul, Brazil, 1952; Palmes Academiques, France, 1957; Gairdner Award, 1961; Jahre Prize, 1965; Stouffer Prize, 1967; Grand Cross at Merito Civil, Spain, 1979.

Citation: "For their discoveries concerning the humoral transmittors in the nerve terminals and the mechanism for their storage, release and inactivation" (with Julius Axelrod and Bernard Katz).

Life Work: In the mid–1920s Euler isolated a chemical similar to acetylcholine named substance P, a polypeptide that functions as a modulator of muscle activity. In 1935 he isolated another substance from the seminal fluid that lowers blood pressure, named prostaglandin. Next, Euler turned his attention to the analysis of tissue and nerve extracts. By 1946 he completed the isolation and identification of noradrenaline (norepinephrine) as the neurotransmitter in the sympathetic nervous system that coordinates the body's response to stress or strenuous activity. He developed fluorescent catecholamines (which are easily observed in tissues or extracts). Later he became an authority on aviation medicine.

Publications: "Hypertension after Bilateral Nephrectomy in the Rat," with E. Braun-Menendez, *Nature* 160 (1947): 905. *Noradrenaline: Chemistry, Physiology, Pharmacology, and Clinical Aspects* (Springfield, Ill.: Thomas, 1956). *Prostaglandins* (New

York: Academic Press, 1968). *Release and Uptake Functions in Adrenergic Nerve Granules* (Liverpool: Liverpool University Press, 1982).

Bibliography: *Biographical Encyclopedia of Scientists* (New York: Facts On File, 1981), p. 815. *Biographical Memoirs of Fellows of the Royal Society* (London: Royal Society, 1981), vol. 31, pp. 143–70. *The Excitement and Fascination of Science* (Palo Alto, Calif., Annual Reviews, 1978), vol. 2, pp. 675–86.

KATZ, SIR BERNARD

Prize: Physiology or Medicine, 1970. *Born:* March 26, 1911; Leipzig, Germany. *Nationality:* German; later British citizen. *Education:* University of Leipzig, Germany, M.D., 1934; University of London, England, Ph.D., 1938. *Career:* Sydney Hospital, Australia, Physician, 1939–42; British Army, 1942–45; University of London, England, Professor and Administrator, 1946–78. *Other Awards:* Garten Prize, University of Leipzig, 1934; Feldberg Foundation Award, 1965; Baly Medal, Royal College of Physicians, 1967; Copley Medal, Royal Society, 1967; Knighthood, 1969.

Citation: "For their discoveries concerning the humoral transmittors in the nerve terminals and the mechanism for their storage, release and inactivation" (with Julius Axelrod and Ulf von Euler).

Life Work: Katz's field of investigation was the transmission of nerve impulses to muscles. He employed new techniques in recording electrical impulses within individual neurons. They examined electrical activity in the end plate of muscles, directly across the synapse from activating neurons. In the absence of any form of stimulation, the end-plate region of the muscle fiber is not completely at rest but displays electrical activity in the form of discrete, randomly occurring miniature end-plate potentials. Each miniature end-plate potential arises from the synchronous impact of large multimolecular quantum of acetylcholine spontaneously discharged by the adjacent nerve terminal. The presynaptic region contains many small vesicles, each containing acetylcholine. He showed that neurotransmitter release depends on the movement of calcium ions. Each miniature end-plate potential corresponds to the action of a few thousand such molecules.

Publications: *Electric Excitation of Nerve: A Review* (London: Oxford University Press, 1939). *How Cells Communicate* (San Francisco: W. H. Freeman, 1961). *Nerve, Muscle, and Synapse* (New York: McGraw-Hill, 1966). *The Release of Neural Transmitter Substance* (Springfield, Ill.: Thomas, 1969).

Bibliography: *New York Times* Biographical Service, October 1970, p. 2589. *Science* 170 (October 23, 1970): 422–24.

SUTHERLAND, EARL WILBUR, JR.

Prize: Physiology or Medicine, 1971. *Born:* November 19, 1915; Burlingame, Kansas. *Died:* March 9, 1974; Miami, Florida. *Nationality:* American. *Education:* Washburn College, Kansas, B.S., 1937; Washington University, Missouri, M.D., 1942. *Career:* Washington University, Missouri, Professor, 1940–42; United States Army, 1942–45; Washington University, Missouri, Professor, 1945–53; Case Western Reserve University, Ohio, Professor, 1953–63; Vanderbilt University, Tennessee, Professor, 1963–73; University of Miami, Florida, Professor, 1973–74. *Other Awards:* Lasker Award, 1970; Achievement Award, American Heart Association, 1971; National Medal of Science, United States, 1973.

Citation: "For his discoveries concerning the mechanisms of the action of hormones."

Life Work: Sutherland's field of investigation was phosphorylase, an enzyme responsible for initiating the breakdown of glycogen in liver and muscle and the hormones epinephrine (found in the medullary portion of the adrenal glands) and glucagon (a secretion of the pancreas). He found that the initial step in glycogen breakdown is stimulated by epinephrine or glucagon, and then catalyzed by phosphorylase. The cycle of phosphorylation-dephosphorylation reaction is one of the body's basic biochemical energy-releasing processes. His experiments established that hormonal action is a molecular process and that both glucagon and epinephrine promote the active form of phosphorylase. During his research Sutherland found an unknown molecule, cyclic adnosine3',5'-monophsophate (cyclic AMP) which promotes the conversion of inactive phosphorylase (and other enzyme systems) to the active form and releases glucose within the cell. This discovery became the basis of the second messenger hypothesis of hormone action, which describes how hormones instruct their target tissues. Hormones such as epinephrine and glucagon are first messengers, which leave their sites of synthesis and circulate to the target tissues where they bind to basic receptors on the outer membranes of cells and signal them to increase the activity of the enzyme adenyl cyclase. This activity, in turn, instructs the cell to produce cyclic AMP, which serves as a second messenger to stimulate various enzymes to perform their specialized functions. Cyclic AMP is also involved in the activity of nerve cells and regulates cellular processes.

Publications: "Hormonal Regulatory Mechanisms," in *Proceedings of the Third International Congress of Biochemistry* (New York: Academic Press, 1955), pp. 318–27. "The Properties of an Adenine Ribonucleotide Produced with Cellular Particles, ATP, Mg++, and Epinephrine or Glucagon," with T. W. Rall, *Journal of the American Chemical Society* 79 (1957): 3068. "Formation of a Cyclic Adenine Ribonucleotide by Tissue Particles," with T. W. Rall, *Journal of Biological Chemistry* 232 (1958): 1065–76. "The Biological Role of Adenosine 3',5'-Phosphate," in *Harvey Lecture Series* (New York: Academic Press, 1962) vol. 57, pp. 17–33. "The Role of Cyclic 3', 5'-AMP in Responses to Catecholamines and Other Hormones," with G. A. Robison, *Pharmacological Reviews* 18 (1966): 145–61. *Cyclic AMP*, with G. A. Robinson and R. W. Butcher (New York: Academic Press, 1971).

Bibliography: *Biographical Memoirs of the National Academy of Sciences* (Washington, D.C.: National Academy of Sciences, 1978), vol. 49, pp. 319–50. *Time* 98 (October 25, 1971): 63.

EDELMAN, GERALD MAURICE

Prize: Physiology or Medicine, 1972. *Born:* July 1, 1929; New York, New York. *Nationality:* American. *Education:* Ursinus College, Pennsylvania, B.S., 1950; University of Pennsylvania, M.D., 1954; Rockefeller University, New York, Ph.D., 1960. *Career:* Rockefeller University, New York, Professor and Administrator, 1957–92. Scripps Research Institute, California, Researcher, 1992–. *Other Awards:* Spencer Morris Award, University of Pennsylvania, 1954; Eli Lilly Award, Harvey Society, 1965; Annual Alumni Award, Ursinus College, 1969; Albert Einstein Commemorative Award, Yeshiva University, 1974; Buchman Memorial Award, California Institute of Technology, 1975; Rabbi Shai Schaknai Memorial Prize, Hebrew University, 1977; Neurath Prize, 1986; Vogt Award, 1988; Warren Prize, 1992.

Citation: "For their discoveries concerning the chemical structure of antibodies" (with Rodney R. Porter).

Life Work: Edelman's field of investigation was the structure of antibodies, or blood proteins known as immunoglobulins (Igs), which are a crucial part of the body's chemical defenses because they can bind to and inactivate bacteria, viruses, and poisons. Edelman examined various methods of splitting IgG molecules, the most important Ig variety in the blood. In 1961, he split IgG molecules into two components called light and heavy chains. This enabled Porter to determine the basic structure of IgG molecule. During the early 1960s, Edelman, Porter, and others studied the sequences of amino acids in subsections of different myeloma proteins and established the precise sequence of all thirteen hundred amino acids. They now attempted to solve the central question of antibody diversity. Edelman suggested that antibody diversity arises from small errors that occur during the process of recombination.

Publications: "The Structure and Function of Antibodies," *Scientific American* 223 (August 1970): 34–42. *Cellular Selection and Regulation in the Immune Response* (New York: Raven Press, 1974). *Molecular Machinery of the Membrane* (Cambridge: Massachusetts Institute of Technology Press, 1975). *Dynamic Aspects of Neocortical Function*, with E. Gall and W. Cowan (New York: Wiley, 1985). *Molecular Basis of Neural Development*, with E. Gall and W. Cowan (New York: Wiley, 1985).

Bibliography: *Current Biography Yearbook* (New York: H. W. Wilson, 1995), p. 9. *New York Times*, May 22, 1988, sec. 6, pp. 16–19. *Science* 178 (October 27, 1972): 384–86.

PORTER, RODNEY ROBERT

Prize: Physiology or Medicine, 1972. *Born:* October 8, 1917; Liverpool, England. *Died:* September 6, 1985; Winchester, England. *Nationality:* British. *Education:* Liverpool University, England, B.S., 1939; Cambridge University, Ph.D., 1948. *Career:* National Institute for Medical Research, London, England, Researcher, 1949–60; London University, England, Professor, 1960–67; Oxford University, England, Professor, 1967–85. *Other awards:* Award of Merit, Gairdner Foundation, 1966; Ciba Medal, Biochemistry Society, 1967; Karl Landsteiner Memorial Award, American Association of Blood Banks, 1968; Royal Medal, Royal Society, 1973.

Citation: "For their discoveries concerning the chemical structure of antibodies" (with Gerald M. Edelman).

Life Work: Porter's field of study was the structure and function of antibodies, especially a class of proteins called immunoglobulins (Igs) that are found in the blood serum. All Ig molecules are of the same size and general composition, yet have an infinite range of antibody-combining specificity. To determine how antibodies combine diversity of function with uniformity of structure, Porter broke up purified Ig molecules with various enzymes. Working with Papain, a papaya juice enzyme, he broke up IgG, the most important Ig variety in the blood, into fragments. Pure Papain breaks IgG molecules into three pieces of two different types: fragment-crystallizable or Fc and fragment antigen-binding or Fab, the former making up one-third and the latter two-thirds. Using Edelman's technique of splitting IgG, Porter proposed the first satisfactory model of IgG structure in 1962.

Publications: *Defence and Recognition.* (Baltimore: University Park Press, 1973). *Chemical Aspects of Immunology* (Burlington, N.C.: Carolina Biological Supply Company, 1976). *Contemporary Topics in Molecular Immunology*, with G. Ada (New York: Plenum Press, 1976), vol. 6. *Biochemistry and Genetics of Complement: A Discussion* (London: Royal Society, 1984).

Bibliography: *Biographical Memoirs of the Fellows of the Royal Society* (London: Royal Society, 1987), vol. 33, p. 433. *New Scientist* (October 19, 1972): 142–43. *New York Times* Biographical Service, 1972, p. 1779. *Science* 178 (October 27, 1972): 384–86.

FRISCH, KARL VON

Prize: Physiology or Medicine, 1973. *Born:* November 20, 1886; Vienna, Austria. *Died:* June 12, 1982; Munich, Germany. *Nationality:* Austrian. *Education:* University of Munich, Germany, Ph.D., 1910. *Career:* University of Munich, Germany, Professor, 1919–14; Dobling Hospital, Vienna, Austria, Physician, 1914–19; University of Munich, Germany, Professor, 1912–21; University of Rostock, Germany, Professor,

1921–23; University of Breslau, Poland, Professor, 1923–25; University of Munich, Germany, Administrator, 1925–46; University of Graz, Austria, Professor and Administrator, 1946–50; University of Munich, Germany, Professor, 1950–58. *Other Awards:* Order Pour le Mérite fur Wissenschaften und Kunste, 1952; Magellan Prize, American Philosophical Society, 1956; Kalinga Prize, UNESCO, 1959; Balzan Prize, 1963.

Citation: "For their discoveries concerning organization and elicitation of individual and social behaviour patterns" (with Konrad Lorenz and Nikolaas Tinbergen).

Life Work: Frisch's field of investigation was ethology. He studied the behavior of honeybees. His experiments proved that bees are able to distinguish odors. He investigated the dance of the honeybees. He discovered that bees inform each other of the approximate direction, distance, and quantity of a new food source using a series of elaborate dances whose components contain the relevant information. If the food is close at hand, the informant bee performs a round dance; for food more than eighty-five meters away, the bee uses a tail wagging dance in the form of figure eight, at an angle with respect to the vertical dimension of the honeycomb that is equal to the angle of the food source with respect to the sun.

Publications: *The Dancing Bees: An Account of the Life and Senses of the Honeybee* (New York: Harcourt, Brace, 1955). *Man and the Living World* (New York: Harcourt, 1963). *Bees: Their Vision, Chemical Senses and Language* (Ithaca, New York: Cornell University Press, 1972). *Animal Architecture* (New York: Van Nostrand Reinhold, 1983).

Bibliography: *A Biologist Remembers* (New York: Pergamon, 1967). *Current Biography Yearbook* (New York: H. W. Wilson, 1974), pp. 130–33. "Karl von Frisch," *Biographical Memoirs of the Fellows of the Royal Society* (London: Royal Society, 1983), vol. 29, pp. 197–200.

LORENZ, KONRAD ZACHARIAS

Prize: Physiology or Medicine, 1973. *Born:* November 7, 1903; Vienna, Austria. *Died:* February 27, 1989; Altenburg, Austria. *Nationality:* Austrian. *Education:* University of Vienna, Austria, M.D., 1928; University of Vienna, Austria, Ph.D., 1933. *Career:* University of Vienna, Austria, Professor, 1928–40; University of Königsberg, Germany, Professor, 1940–42; German Army, 1942–44; Soviet Armenia, Prisoner of War, 1944–48; Institute of Comparative Ethology, Altenberg, Austria, Administrator, 1949–51; Max Planck Foundation, Germany, Administrator, 1951–73. *Other Awards:* Gold Medal, Zoological Society of New York, 1955; City Prize, Vienna, 1959; Gold Bolsche Medal, 1962; Austrian Distinction for Science and Art, 1964; Prix Mondial, Cino de Deuca, 1969; Kalinga Prize, UNESCO, 1970; Order Pour le Merite, 1972; Grosses Verdienstkreuz, 1974; Bayerischer Verdienstorden, 1974.

Citation: "For their discoveries concerning organization and elicitation of individual and social behaviour patterns" (with Karl von Frisch and Nikolaas Tinbergen).

Life Work: Lorenz and Nikolaas Tinbergen laid the foundations of modern ethology with their work on animal behavior. He established that animal instincts are caused not by reflexes, but by internally generated drives. These drives motivate an animal to seek a particular set of social or environmental stimuli. This so-called orientation behavior is highly variable; once the animal encounters certain cues (the sign stimuli or releasers) it automatically performs a stereotypical set of movements called *fixed action pattern* (FAP). Every animal has a distinctive system of FAPs and associated releasers which evolve in response to natural selection. In his work *On Aggression*, Lorenz described aggression as helpful to the survival of the fittest, as it facilitates such functions as the selection of mates, the establishment of social hierarchies, and maintenance of territories.

Publications: *On Aggression* (New York: Harcourt, Brace and World, 1966). *Evolution and Modification of Behavior* (Chicago: University of Chicago Press, 1967). *Studies in Animal and Human Behavior* (Cambridge: Harvard University Press, 1970–71).

Bibliography: *Current Biography Yearbook* (New York: H. W. Wilson, 1977), pp. 274–77. Richard Evans, *Konrad Lorenz: The Man and His Ideas* (New York: Harcourt, Brace, Jovanovich, 1975). F. Wukelits, *Konrad Lorenz* (Munich: Piper, 1990).

TINBERGEN, NIKOLAAS

Prize: Physiology or Medicine, 1973. *Born:* April 15, 1907; The Hague, Netherlands. *Died:* December 21, 1988; Oxford, England. *Nationality:* Dutch. *Education:* University of Leiden, Netherlands, Ph.D., 1932. *Career:* University of Leiden, Netherlands, Professor, 1933–49; German Prisoner of War, 1945–47; Oxford University, England, Professor, 1949–73. *Other Awards:* Bolsche Medal, 1969; Italia Prize for TV Documentaries, 1969; Godman-Savin Medal, British Ornithology Union, 1969; Jan Swammerdam Medal, 1973.

Citation: "For their discoveries concerning organization and elicitation of individual and social behaviour patterns" (with Karl von Frisch and Konrad Lorenz).

Life Work: Tinbergen's field of investigation was ethology. He studied killer wasps, arctic birds, sticklebacks, insects, and birds. With Konrad Lorenz, he formulated the theory that instincts arise from internal drives or impulses. Instinctive behavior consists of a stereotyped set of movements, the so-called fixed action patten (FAP), which is as distinct as a species's anatomical features. An animal performs an FAP in response to specific environmental stimuli or releasers. It also results from conflicts between two drives.

Publications: *The Animal in Its World: Explorations of an Ethologist, 1932–72* (Cambridge: Harvard University Press, 1972–73). *Early Childhood Autism: An Ethological Approach*, with E. A. Tinbergen (Berlin: P. Parry, 1972).

Bibliography: *Biographical Memoirs of the Fellows of the Royal Society* (London: Royal Society, 1990), vol. 36, p. 549. *Current Biography Yearbook* (New York: H. W. Wilson, 1975), pp. 414–16. *Psychology Today* (March 1974): 68–71.

CLAUDE, ALBERT

Prize: Physiology or Medicine, 1974. *Born:* August 24, 1898; Luxembourg, Belgium. *Died:* May 22, 1983; Brussels, Belgium. *Nationality:* Belgian; later U.S. citizen. *Education:* University of Liege, Belgium, M.D., 1928. *Career:* Rockefeller University, New York, Professor, 1929–72; University of Belgium, Professor, 1950–70; Institute Jules Bordet, Brussels, Belgium, 1948–71. *Other Awards:* British War Medal, 1918; Interallied Medal, 1918; Grand Cordon de l'Ordre de Leopold II, Belgium, 1927; Prize Fonds National de la echerche Scientifique, 1965; Medal, Belgian Académie of Médicine, 1968; Louisa G. Horowitz Prize, Columbia University, 1970; Paul Ehrlich Award, 1971; Ludwig Darmstaedter Prize, 1971.

Citation: "For their discoveries concerning the structural and functional organization of the cell" (with Christian de Duve and George E. Palade).

Life Work: To prove that tumors were caused by viruses, Claude proposed to identify the tumor agent. To separate the tumor agent from the rest of the cell he developed the technique of cell fractionation with the aid of a high-powered centrifuge. He then identified the agent as ribonucleic acid (RNA). In the course of his experiments, he separated the cell's nucleus from the cytoplasm and then the specialized parts of the cell including organelles and mitochondria from the cytoplasm. He reported that normal cells also contain particles of ribonucleic acid or microsomes and that they are the sites within the cells where protein is formed as well as the sites of respiration and energy generation. Using the first electron micrographs of layers of cultured cells, he found a lacelike network, called the endoplasmic reticulum, that specialized in the formation and transport of fats and proteins. The microscopic cellular anatomy was the subject of his later studies.

Publications: "Fractionation of Chicken Tumor Extracts by High-speed Centrifugation," *American Journal of Cancer* 30 (1937): 742–45. "Distribution of Nucleic Acids in the Cell and the Morphological Constitution of Cytoplasm," *Biological Symposia* 10 (1943): 111–29. "Fractionation of Mammalian Liver Cells by Differential Centrifugation. I and II," *Journal of Experimental Medicine* 84 (1946): 51–89. "The Nature of the Golgi Apparatus. I and II," with G. Palade, *Journal of Morphology* 85 (1949): 35–11.

Bibliography: *Biographical Encyclopedia of Scientists* (New York: Facts on File, 1981), p. 151. *New Scientist* (October 24, 1974): 255–56. *Science* 186 (November 8, 1974): 516–20.

DUVE, CHRISTIAN RENE MARIE JOSEPH DE

Prize: Physiology or Medicine, 1974. *Born:* October 2, 1917; Thames, Ditton, England. *Nationality:* Belgian; later U.S. resident. *Education:* University of Louvain, Belgium, M.D., 1941; University of Louvain, Belgium, M.Sc., 1946. *Career:* University of Louvain, Belgium, Professor, 1947–62; Rockefeller University, New York, Professor, 1962–88. *Other Awards:* Prix des Alumni, 1949; Prix Pfizer, 1957; Prix Franqui, 1960; Prix Quinquennal, Belge des Sciences Medicales, Belgium, 1967; International Award of Merit, Gairdner Foundation, Canada, 1967; Dr. H. P. Heineken Prijs, Netherlands, 1973; Grand Cross, Order of Leopold II, 1975.

Citation: "For their discoveries concerning the structural and functional organization of the cell" (with Albert Claude and George E. Palade).

Life Work: De Duve's field of investigation was the mechanism of insulin. He conducted a series of experiments designed to analyze the properties of a live cell enzyme involved in the metabolism of glucose. Using the analytical cell fractionation technique devised by Albert Claude to break the cells into their components, they studied the enzyme activity of the organelles, structures within the cells that perform specific functions for the cell as a whole. His first major discovery was the identification of a new organelle, the *lysosome,* and another subcellular organelle that contained the enzyme urate oxidase, called *peroxisome.* Lysosomes are saclike membrane like particles that contain several enzymes invoved in the cell's digestion of nutrient molecules. Peroxisomes have two metabolic functions: the conversion of a variety of intracellular molecules to water and the conversion of intracellular protein t glucose.

Publications: "Cytochrome Oxidase and Acid Phosphatase of Isolated Mitochondria," with F. Appelmans and R. Wattiaux, *Congr. Intern. Biochim.,* Resumes Communs., 2e Congr., Paris (1952). 278. "Lysosomes, a New Group of Cytoplasmic Particles," *Subcellular Particles, Symposium, Woods Hole, MA* (1958): 128–58. "Lysosomes and Chemotherapy," *Biological Approaches to Cancer Chemotherapy* (1960): 101–12. *A Guided Tour of the Living Cell* (New York: Scientific American Books, 1984).

Bibliography: *New York Times* Biographical Service, October 1974, p. 1405. *Science* 186 (November 8, 1974): 516–20.

PALADE, GEORGE EMIL

Prize: Physiology or Medicine, 1974. *Born:* November 19, 1912; Jassi, Romania. *Nationality:* Romanian; later U.S. citizen. *Education:* University of Bucharest, Romania, M.D., 1940. *Career:* University of Bucharest, Romania, Professor, 1935–45; Rockefeller University, New York, Professor, 1946–72; Yale University, Connecticut, Professor, 1972–90; University of California, San Diego, Professor, 1990–. *Other Awards:* Passano Award, American Medical Association, 1964; Lasker Award, 1966; Gairdner Special Award, 1967; Horowitz Prize, 1970; Warren Prize, Massachusetts General Hospital, 1977; National Medal of Science, 1986.

Citation: "For their discoveries concerning the structural and functional organization of the cell" (with Albert Claude and Christian de Duve).

Life Work: Palade's field of investigation was cell biology. Using cell fractionation and cell microscopy, Palade described the ultrastructural appearance of the cell and the biochemical functions of the structures or organelles within it: the mitochondria, the endoplasmic reticulum, the ribosomes, and the Golgi complex. He next investigated how the living cell synthesizes proteins and elucidated the pathways of protein synthesis and enzyme secretion in the pancreatic exocrine cell. He turned his attention to another process central to biology: the synthesis of cellular and intracellular membranes, the capsules that surround the cell itself, and the organelles within it. His vasicular theory held that ions and larger molecules from outside the cell are engulfed by vesicles or sacs that temporarily fuse with the membrane of the cell.

Publications: "The Nature of the Golgi Apparatus. I and II," with A. Claude, *Journal of Morphology* 85 (1949): 35–111. "Liver Microsomes. An Integrated Morphological and Biochemical Study," with P. Siekovitz, *J. Biophys. Biochem. Cytol.* 2 (1956): 171–200. "Pancreatic Microsomes. An Integrated Morphological and Biochemical Study," with P. Siekovitz, *J. Biophys. Biochem. Cytol* 2 (1956): 671–90. "Functional Changes in the Structure of Cell Components," *Subcellular Particles, Symposium, Woods Hole, MA* (1958): 64–80.

Bibliography: *Current Biography Yearbook* (New York: H. W. Wilson, 1967), pp. 324–26. *Science* 186 (November 8, 1974): 516–20.

BALTIMORE, DAVID

Prize: Physiology or Medicine, 1975. *Born:* March 7, 1938; New York, New York. *Nationality:* American. *Education:* Swarthmore College, Pennsylvania, B.A., 1960; Rockefeller University, New York, Ph.D., 1964. *Career:* Albert Einstein College of Medicine, New York, Researcher, 1964–65; Salk Institute, California, Researcher, 1965–68; Massachusetts Institute of Technology, Professor and Administrator, 1968–90; Rockefeller University, New York, Professor, 1990–. *Other Awards:* Gustav Stern Award, 1970; Warren Triennial Prize, Massachusetts General Hospital, 1971; Eli Lilly Award, 1971; U.S. Steel Foundation Award, 1974; Gairdner Foundation Annual Award, 1974.

Citation: "For their discoveries concerning the interaction between tumour viruses and the genetic material of the cell" (with Renato Dulbecco and Howard M. Temin).

Life Work: Baltimore's field of investigation was viral genetics. Working separately, Baltimore and Temin isolated an enzyme that incorporated viral genes into cellular DNA, and called it RNA-directed DNA polymerase. This process is called reverse transcription. At MIT, Baltimore partially synthesized the gene responsible for the biosynthesis of mammalian hemoglobin, the molecule in red blood cells that carries oxygen to the tissues. While continuing his search for the reverse transcriptase enzyme in other tumor-causing viruses, he discovered eight viruses that possess this enzyme. Known as retroviruses, they are known to play a role in hepatitis, some forms of cancer, and AIDS.

Publications: "Viral RNA-Dependent DNA Polymerase," *Nature (London)* 226 (1970): 1211–13. "RNA-Directed DNA Synthesis and RNA Tumor Viruses," *Advances in Virus Research* 17 (1972): 51–94. *Animal Virology*, with others (New York: Academic Press, 1976). *Activation and Regulation of Immunoglobin Synthesis in Malignant B Cells*, with others (Copenhagen: Munksgaard, 1979).

Bibliography: *Current Biography Yearbook* (New York: H. W. Wilson, 1983), pp. 25–28. *Science* 190 (November 14, 1975): pp. 650, 712–13.

DULBECCO, RENATO

Prize: Physiology or Medicine, 1975. *Born:* February 22, 1914; Catanzaro, Italy. *Nationality:* Italian; later U.S. citizen. *Education:* University of Torino, Italy, M.D., 1936. *Career:* University of Torino, Italy, Researcher, 1936–47; Indiana University, Researcher, 1947–49; California Institute of Technology, Professor, 1949–63; Salk Institute, California, Researcher, 1963–71; Imperial Cancer Research Fund, London, England, Administrator, 1971–77; Salk Institute, California, Professor, 1977–81. *Other Awards:* John Scott Award, City of Philadelphia, Pennsylvania, 1958; Kimball Award, Conference of Public Health Laboratory Directors, 1959; Albert and Mary Lasker Basic Medical Research Award, 1964; Howard Taylor Ricketts Award, 1965; Paul Ehrlich-Ludwig Darmstaedter Prize, 1967, Horowitz Prize, Columbia University, 1973; Selman Waksman Award, National Academy of Sciences, 1974; Man of the Year, London, 1975; Targo d'oro, Villa San Giovanni, 1978; Italian-American of the Year, San Diego, California, 1978; Decorated Grand Officiale, Italian Republic, 1981; Mandel Gold Medal, Czechoslovak Academy of Sciences, 1982.

Citation: "For their discoveries concerning the interaction between tumour viruses and the genetic material of the cell" (with David Baltimore and Howard M. Temin).

Life Work: Dulbecco's field of investigation was tumor virus and tumor cells, especially the genetics of the Rous sarcoma virus and polyoma virus. He found that tumor cells are transformed by tumor viruses in such a way that they divide indefinitely, a process called cell transformation. They discovered that when normal cells divide and begin to encroach on neighboring tissue, a cellular regulatory system kicks in, signaling the cells to stop dividing. In tumor cells, this regulatory scheme is impaired.

Publications: *The Induction of Cancer by Viruses* (San Francisco: W. H. Freeman, 1967). *The Biology of Small DNA-Tumor Viruses* (New York: MSS Information Corp., 1974). *Induction of Host Systems, Integration and Excision* (Cambridge: Cambridge University Press, 1975). *Virology*, with Howard Ginsberg (Hagerstown, Md.: Harper and Row, 1980).

Bibliography: *Biographical Encyclopedia of Scientists* (New York: Facts on File, 1981), p. 219. *New Scientist* (October 23, 1975): 219–20. *New York Times* Bibliographical Service, October 1975, pp. 1266–67. *Science* 190 (November 14, 1975): 650, 712–13. *Scienza, Vita e Aventura* (Paris: Plow, 1990).

TEMIN, HOWARD MARTIN

Prize: Physiology or Medicine, 1975. *Born:* December 10, 1934; Philadelphia, Pennsylvania. *Died:* February 9, 1994; Madison, Wisconsin. *Nationality:* American. *Education:* Swarthmore College, Pennsylvania, B.A., 1955; California Institute of Technology, Ph.D., 1959. *Career:* California Institute of Technology, Researcher, 1959–60; University of Wisconsin, Professor, 1960–94. *Other Awards:* Warren Triennial Prize, Massachusetts General Hospital, 1971; Special Commendation, Medical Society of Wisconsin, 1971; PAP Award, Papanicolaou Institute, 1972; Bertner Award, M. D. Anderson Hospital and Tumor Institute, 1972; U.S. Steel Foundation Award, 1972; Waksman Award, Theobald Smith Society, 1972; Griffuel Prize, Association of Developmental Recherche Cancer, Villejuif, France, 1972; Award in Enzyme Chemistry, American Chemical Society, 1973; Award for Distinguished Achievement, Modern Medicine, 1973; Gairdner Foundation International Award, 1974; Albert Lasker Award, 1974; Lucy Wortham James Award, Society of Surgical Oncologists, 1976; Alumni Distinguished Service Award, California Institute of Technology, 1976; Gruber Award, American Academy of Dermatology, 1981.

Citation: "For their discoveries concerning the interaction between tumour viruses and the genetic material of the cell" (with David Baltimore and Renato Dulbecco).

Life Work: Researching the Rous sarcoma virus, he found that certain viruses alter the genetic information encoded in the cells they attack. Temin proposed that cell transformation was caused by a viral gene that had become part of the cellular DNA. According to this proviral hypothesis, the genetic code of certain RNA tumor viruses could be copied into cellular DNA by an enzyme in the protein coat of the virus, thus enabling the genes of the invading virus to take control of the genes of the host cell. The enzyme was later discovered by Temin and Baltimore and called reverse transcriptase; the RNA viruses that possess a reverse transcriptase and form proviral genes are now called retroviruses. They are believed to be responsible for such diseases as AIDS, hepatitis, and some forms of cancer. Temin also investigated how genetic information in the provirus transforms a normal cell into a tumor cell.

Publications: "Participation of Eoxyribonucleic Acid (DNA) in Rous Sarcoma Virus Production," *Virology* 22 (1964): 486–94. "Carcinogenesis by Avian Sarcoma Viruses. III. The Differential Effect of Erum and Polyanions on Multiplication of Uninfected and Converted Cells," *Journal of the National Cancer Institute* 37 (1966): 167–75. *RNA-Directed DNA Synthesis* (San Francisco: W. H. Freeman, 1972). "RNA-Directed DNA synthesis and RNA Tumor Viruses," with D. Baltimore, *Advances in Virus Research* 17 (1972): 51–94.

Bibliography: *Biographical Encyclopedia of Scientists* (New York: Facts on File, 1981), pp. 776–77. *New Scientist* (October 23, 1975): 219–20. *New York Times* Biographical Service, February 11, 1994, p. 226. *Science* 190 (November 14, 1975): 650, 712–13.

BLUMBERG, BARUCH SAMUEL

Prize: Physiology or Medicine, 1976. *Born:* July 28, 1925; New York, New York. *Nationality:* American. *Education:* Union College, New York, B.S., 1946; Columbia University, New York, M.D., 1951; Oxford University, England, Ph.D., 1957. *Career:* National Institutes of Health, Maryland, Administrator, 1957–64; Institute for Cancer Research, Pennsylvania, Administrator, 1964–. *Other Awards:* Albion O. Berstein Award, Medical Society of the State of New York, 1969; Grand Scientific Award, Phi Lambda Kappa, 1972; Annual Award, Eastern Pennsylvania Branch of the American Society for Microbiology, 1972; Eppinger Prize, University of Freiburg, Germany, 1973; Passano Award, 1974; Distinguished Achievement Award, 1975; Gairdner Foundation International Award, 1975; Karl Landsteiner Memorial Award, American Association of Blood Banks, 1975; Scopus Award, American Friends of Hebrew University, 1977; Strittmatter Award, Philadelphia County Medical Society, 1980; Zubrow Award, 1986; McGovern Award, 1988; Bundell Award, 1989; Huxley Medal, 1989; Mudd Award, 1990.

Citation: "For their discoveries concerning new mechanisms for the origin and dissemination of infectious diseases" (with D. Carleton Gajdusek).

Life Work: Blumberg's field of investigation was ethnophysiology. His major discovery was the role of Australia antigen in hepatitis B. Researching patients who received a large number of transfusions, he isolated antibodies that reacted against a serum from an Australian aborigine. This was the first time hepatitis B virus had been isolated. He was able to obtain the immunizing antigen directly from the blood of human carriers of the disease.

Publications: *Conference on Genetic Polymorphisms and Geographic Variations in Disease. Proceedings* (New York: Grune & Stratton, 1962). *Australia Antigen and Hepatitis,* with others (Cleveland, Ohio: Chemical Rubber Co., 1972). *Primary Hepatocellular Carcinoma and Hepatitis B Virus* (Chicago: Yearbook Medical Publishers, 1982). *Hepatitis B: The Virus, the Disease, and the Vaccine,* with K. Eisenstein and I. Milman (New York: Plenum Press, 1984).

Bibliography: *Current Biography Yearbook* (New York: H. W. Wilson, 1977), pp. 72–74. *Science* 194 (November 26, 1976): 928–29.

GAJDUSEK, DANIEL CARLETON

Prize: Physiology or Medicine, 1976. *Born:* September 9, 1923; Yonkers, New York. *Nationality:* American. *Education:* University of Rochester, New York, B.S., 1943; Harvard University, Massachusetts, M.D., 1946. *Career:* Columbia Presbyterian Medical Center, New York, Physician, 1946–47; Pediatrics Children's Hospital, Ohio,

Physician, 1947–48; Harvard University, Massachusetts, Researcher, 1949–52; Walter Reed Army Institute of Research, Washington, D.C., Researcher, 1952–53; Institute Pasteur, Iran, Researcher, 1954–55; Walter and Eliza Hall Institute of Medical Research, Australia, Researcher, 1955–57; National Institutes of Health, Maryland, Administrator, 1958–. *Other Awards:* E. Meade Johnson Award, American Academy of Pediatrics, 1963; Superior Service Award, National Institutes of Health, 1970; Distinguished Service Award, Department of Health, Education and Welfare, 1975; Professor Lucian Dautrebande Prize, Belgium, 1976; Cotzias Prize, American Academy of Neurology, 1979.

Citation: "For their discoveries concerning new mechanisms for the origin and dissemination of infectious diseases" (with Baruch S. Blumberg).

Life Work: Gajdusek's field of investigation was the kuru, a fatal degenerative brain disease affecting the Fore people of Papua New Guinea. He found that it was transmitted by slow virus through the practice of ritual cannibalism. He also found that other degenerative brain disorders, like Creutzfeldt-Jakob disease, were caused by slow viruses. These diseases do not cause a pronounced immune response, characterized by inflammation, fever, and the production of antibodies and interferon. Unlike other known viruses, slow viruses are not destroyed by formaldehyde, ultraviolet light, or high temperature. Gajdusek concluded that slow viruses may represent an infectious protein that is remarkably similar to that causing Alzheimer's disease and senile dementia.

Publications: *Journals. Study of Child Growth and Development of Disease Patterns in Primitive Cultures* (Bethesda, Md.: National Institute of Neurological Diseases and Blindness, 1963). *Slow Latent and Temperate Virus Infections,* with C. Gibbs, Jr., and M. Alpers (Bethesda, Md.: National Institute of Health, 1965). *Genetic Studies in Relation to Kuru,* with others (Chicago: University of Chicago Press, 1972–75). *Kuru,* with J. Farquhar (New York: Raven Press, 1981).

Bibliography: *Current Biography Yearbook* (New York: H. W. Wilson, 1981), pp. 156–59. *Science* 194 (November 26, 1976): 928–29. A. Hammond, ed., *A Passion to Know* (New York: Scribner's, 1984), pp. 11–22.

GUILLEMIN, ROGER

Prize: Physiology or Medicine, 1977. *Born:* January 11, 1924; Dijon, France. *Nationality:* French; later U.S. citizen. *Education:* University of Dijon, France, B.A., 1941; University of Dijon, France, B.Sc., 1942; Faculty of Medicine, France, M.D., 1949; University of Montreal, Quebec, Canada, Ph.D., 1953. *Career:* Baylor University, Texas, Professor, 1953–70; Salk Institute, California, Professor, 1970–89; Whittier Institute, California, Researcher, 1989–. *Other Awards:* Bonneau and La Caze Awards, Académie des Sciences, 1957, 1960; Legion of Honor, France, 1974; Gairdner International Award, 1974; Lasker Foundation Award, 1975; Dickson Foundation Award,

1975; Dickson Prize, 1976; Passano Award, 1976; Schmitt Medal, 1977; National Medal of Science, USA, 1977; Barren Gold Medal, USA, 1979; Dale Medal, Society for Endocrinology, England, 1980.

Citation: "For their discoveries concerning the peptide hormone production of the brain" (with Andrew V. Schally).

Life Work: Guillemin's field of investigation was experimental endocrinology, especially hypothalamic hormones which regulate the pituitary gland. He isolated the hypothalamic hormone that secretes thyrotropin (or thyroid-stimulating hormone, TSF), also called thyrotropin-releasing factor (TRF), in 1968. It is a peptide containing three amino acids. The discovery marked the beginning of neuroendocrinology as a discipline. A second hormone, growth-hormone-releasing hormone (GRH), was isolated in the late 1960s. It is a peptide containing ten amino acids and causes the release of gonadotropins from the pituitary glands. Later he discovered a third hypothalamic hormone, somatostatin, a peptide containing fourteen amino acids. It inhibits the release of growth hormone from the pituitary gland.

Publications: "Humoral Hypothalamic Control of the Anterior Pituitary. A Study which Combined Tissue Cultures," with Barry Rosenberg, *Endocrinology* 57 (1955): 599. "Hypothalamic Control of the Anterior Pituitary, Study with Tissue Culture Techniques," *Federation Proceedings* 14 (1955): 211. "The Adenohypophysis and Its Hypothalamic Control," *Annual Review of Physiology* 29 (1967): 313. *The Hormones of the Hypothalamus*, with R. Burgus (San Francisco: W. H. Freeman Co., 1972). "Control of Adenohypophysial Functions by Peptides of the Central Nervous System," *The Harvey Lectures* 71 (1975–76). "Purification, Isolation, and Primary Structure of the Hypothalamic Luteinizing Hormone-releasing Factor of Bovine Origin—A Historical Account," *American Journal of Obstetrics and Gynecology* 129 (1977): 214. *The Brain as an Endocrine Organ* (Cambridge: Massachusetts Institute of Technology Press, 1978). *Hypothalamic Control of Pituitary Functions: The Growth Hormone Releasing Factor* (Liverpool: Liverpool University Press, 1985).

Bibliography: *The Nobel Duel* (New York: Doubleday, 1981). *Pioneers in Neuroendocrinology II* (New York: Plenum Press, 1978), p. 351. *Science* 198 (November 11, 1977): 594–95.

SCHALLY, ANDREW VICTOR

Prize: Physiology or Medicine, 1977. *Born:* November 30, 1926; Wilno, Poland. *Nationality:* Polish; later Canadian and U.S. citizen. *Education:* McGill University, Quebec, Canada, B.Sc., 1955; McGill University, Quebec, Canada, Ph.D., 1957. *Career:* Baylor University, Texas, Professor, 1957–62; VA Hospital, New Orleans, Louisiana, Administrator, 1962–; Tulane University, New Orleans, Louisiana, Professor, 1962–. *Other Awards:* Director's Award, VA Hospital, New Orleans, Louisiana, 1968; Van Meter Prize, American Thyroid Association, 1969; Ayerst-Squibb Award,

Endocrine Society, 1970; William S. Middleton Award, VA Hospital, New Orleans, Louisiana, 1970; Charles Mickle Award, University of Toronto, 1974; Gairdner International Award, 1974; Edward T. Tyler Award, 1975; Borden Award, Association of Medical Colleges and Borden Company Foundation, 1975; Lasker Award, 1975; Laude Award, 1975; Award, Spanish Pharmaceutical Society, 1977; Medal of Scientific Merit, Federal University of Ceara, Brazil, 1977; First Diploma of Merit of St. Luke, Foundation of Social Pioneers, Rio de Janeiro, 1977.

Citation: "For their discoveries concerning the peptide hormone production of the brain" (with Roger Guillemin).

Life Work: Schally's field of investigation was hypothalamic hormones that regulate the secretions of the pituitary glands. In 1955 Schally provided the first direct experimental evidence of such hormones when he isolated corticotropin-releasing factor (CRF), now known as corticotropin-releasing hormones (CRH). In 1966 he isolated the hypothalamic hormone that causes the release of thyroptropin from the pituitary gland, called the thyroptropin-releasing hormone, or TRH. It is a peptide containing three amino acids. In the late 1960s he isolated the hypothalamic hormone that causes the release of gonadotropins from the pituitary gland. A peptide containing ten amino acids, it is now known as growth-hormone-releasing hormone (GRH).

Publications: "The Release of Cortico-tropin by Anterior Pituitary Tissue in Vitro," with M. Saffran, *Canadian Journal of Biochemistry and Physiology* 33 (1955): 408. "Stimulation of the Release of Corticotropin from the Adenohypophysis by a Neurohypophysial Factor," with M. Saffran, *Canadian Journal of Biochemistry and Physiology* 57 (1955): 439. "Isolation of Thyrotropin Releasing Factor (TRF) from Porcine Hypothalamus," with others, *Biochemical and Biophysical Research Communications* 25 (1966): 165. "Purification of Thyrotropic Hormone Releasing Factor from Bovine Hypothalamus," with others, *Endocrinology* 78 (1966): 726. "The Amino Acid Sequence of a Peptide with Growth Hormone Releasing Activity Isolated from Porcine Hypothalamus," with others, *Journal of Biological Chemistry* 246 (1971): 6647. *The Hypothalamus and Pituitary in Health and Disease*, with W. Locke (Springfield, Ill.: Thomas 1972).

Bibliography: *The Nobel Duel* (New York: Doubleday, 1981). *Pioneers in Neuroendocrinology II* (New York: Plenum Press, 1978), p. 351. *Science* 198 (November 11, 1977): 594–95.

YALOW, ROSALYN SUSSMAN

Prize: Physiology or Medicine, 1977. *Born:* July 19, 1921; New York, New York. *Nationality:* American. *Education:* Hunter College, New York, A.B., 1941; University of Illinois, M.S., 1942; University of Illinois, Ph.D., 1945. *Career:* Hunter College, New York, Professor, 1946–50; VA Hospital, New York, Researcher and Administrator, 1950–80; Montefiore Medical Center, New York, Administrator, 1980–86; Mount Sinai School of Medicine, New York, Professor, 1986–. *Other Awards:* William S. Middleton Medical Research Award, Veterans Administration, 1960; Eli Lilly Award, American Diabetes Association, 1961; Federal Woman's Award, 1961; Van Slyke Award, American Association of Clinical Chemists, 1968; Award, American College of Physicians, 1971; Dickson Prize, University of Pittsburgh, Pennsylvania, 1971; Howard Taylor Ricketts Award, University of Chicago, Illinois, 1971; Gairdner Foundation International Award, 1971; Commemorative Medallion, American Diabetes Association, 1972; Koch Award, Endocrine Society, 1972; Bernstein Award, Medical Society of the State of New York, 1974; Boehringer-Manheim Corporation Award, American Association of Clinical Chemists, 1975; Science Achievement Award, American Medical Association, 1975; Exceptional Service Award, Veterans Administration, 1975; A. Cressy Morrison Award, New York Academy of Sciences, 1975; Distinguished Achievement Award, Modern Medicine, 1976; Lasker Award, 1976; La Madonnina International Prize, Milan, 1977; Golden Plate Award, American Academy Achievement, 1977; G. von Hevesy Medal, 1978; Rosalyn S. Yalow Research and Development Award, American Diabetes Association, 1978; Banting Medal, 1978; Torch of Learning Award, American Friends of Hebrew University, 1978; Virchow Gold Medal, Virchow-Pirquet Medical Society, 1978; Gratum Genus Humanum Gold Medal, World Federation of Nuclear Medicine or Biology, 1978; Jubilee Medal, College of New Rochelle, 1978; Exceptional Service Award, Veterans Administration, 1978; Sarasota Medical Award, 1979; Gold Medal, Phi Lambda Kappa, 1980; Theobald Smith Award, 1982; John and Samuel Bard Award, Bard College, 1982; Distinguished Research Award, Dallas Association of Retarded Citizens, 1982; National Medal of Science, 1988; Sachar Medallion, 1989.

Citation: "For the development of radioimmunoassays of peptide hormones."

Life Work: Yalow is principally associated with radioimmunoassay (RIA), a technique she developed. She used this technique to measure the disappearance rate of insulin from plasma of diabetics tagging it with radioactive iodine and counting with a radiation counter. She found the rate of insulin disappearance from the plasma unexpectedly low. She concluded that diabetics produce antibodies to the foreign insulin molecule that inactivates the insulin. Later, she used radioimmunoassay to detect drugs in bodily tissues or fluids, in blood banks to screen blood donors, for the early detection of cancer and leukemia, and to measure the levels of neurotransmitters.

Publications: *Peptide Hormones*, with S. A. Berson (New York: American Elsevier, 1973). *Methods in Radioimmunoassay of Peptide Hormones* (New York: American Elsevier, 1976). *Basic Research and Clinical Medicine*, with others (New York: McGraw-Hill, 1981). *Radioimmunoassay* (New York: Van Nostrand-Reinhold, 1984).

Bibliography: *Current Biography Yearbook* (New York: H. W. Wilson, 1978), pp. 458–60. "Madame Curie from the Bronx," *New York Times Magazine*, April 9, 1978, pp. 29–31.

ARBER, WERNER

Prize: Physiology or Medicine, 1978. *Born:* June 3, 1929; Granichen, Switzerland. *Nationality:* Swiss. *Education:* University of Geneva, Switzerland, Ph.D., 1958. *Career:* University of Southern California, Researcher, 1958–59; University of Geneva, Switzerland, Professor, 1960–70; University of Basel, Switzerland, Professor, 1970–.

Citation: "For the discovery of restriction enzymes and their application to problems of molecular genetics" (with Daniel Nathans and Hamilton O. Smith).

Life Work: Arber's field of investigation was bacterial genetics, especially, host-cell induced variation/restriction or modification, a process in which the bacteriophage DNA is cleaved or cut into its component parts by the action of a restriction endonuclease enzyme acting in concert with a methylase enzyme. The bacterial cell's restriction endonuclease recognizes a certain nucleotide sequence on the bacteriophage DNA and cleaves it at several sites, rendering it inactive. Meanwhile, the methylase enzyme recognizes the identical nucleotide sequence in the DNA of the bacterial, or host, cell methylates it and protects it from enzymatic cleavage by its own endonuclease. This two-enzyme system is called a restriction-modification system. Arber found two types of restriction endonucleases: type I, which cleaves the DNA at random sites, and type II, which is specific for the cleavage site and which would permit precise gene splicing.

Publications: "Biological Specificities of Deoxyribonucleic Acid," *Pathol. Microbiol.* 25 (1962): 668–81. "Host-Controlled Restriction and Modification of Bacteriophage," *Symp. Soc. Gen. Microbiol.* 18 (1968): 295–314. "DNA Modification and Restriction," *Prog. Nucleic Acid Res. Mol. Biol.* 14 (1974): 1–37. *Genetic Manipulation: Impact on Men and Society* (New York: Cambridge University Press, 1984).

Bibliography: *Asimov's Biographical Encyclopedia of Science and Technology* (Garden City, N.Y.: Doubleday, 1984), pp. 888–89. *Science* 202 (December 8, 1978): 1069–71.

NATHANS, DANIEL

Prize: Physiology or Medicine, 1978. *Born:* October 30, 1928; Wilmington, Delaware. *Died:* November 16, 1999; Wilmington, Delaware. *Nationality:* American. *Education:* University of Delaware, B.S., 1950; Washington University, Missouri M.D., 1954. *Career:* Columbia Presbyterian Medical Center, New York, Physician, 1954–59; Rockefeller University, New York, Professor, 1959–62; Johns Hopkins University, Maryland, Professor and Administrator, 1962–80; Howard Hughes Medical Institute, California, Researcher, 1980–. *Other Awards:* National Medal of Science, 1993.

Citation: "For the discovery of restriction enzymes and their application to problems of molecular genetics" (with Werner Arber and Hamilton O. Smith).

Life Work: Nathans's field of investigation was the replication of bacteriophages, especially the regulation of the replication process and the location of genes on the DNA and RNA molecules. He studied animal viruses in detail, concentrating on simian virus 40, which causes tumors in monkeys. When Smith, a colleague, reported that he had isolated and purified a site-specific restriction endonuclease in *Haemophilus influenzae*, Nathans found it possible to use restriction enzymes to dissect the genomes of DNA tumor viruses. His efforts yielded the first genetic map of a DNA molecule. He made a map of the cleavage sites, identified the location and function of specific genes, made a detailed map of the DNA molecule including the sites of origin and termination of the replication process, and identified the template for messenger RNA and the location of the genes that direct the synthesis of the protein coat of the virus.

Publications: "Purification of a Supernatant Factor that Stimulates Amino Acid Transfer from Soluble Ribonucleic Acid to Protein," *Annals of the New York Academy of Sciences* 88 (1960): 718–21. "Cell-free Protein Synthesis Directed by Coliphage MS2 RNA: Synthesis of Intact Viral Coat Protein and Other Products," *Journal of Molecular Biology* 13 (1965): 521–31. "Natural RNA Coding of Bacterial Protein Synthesis," *Methods of Enzymology* 12 (1968): 787–91. "Restriction Endonucleases in the Analysis and Restructuring of DNA Molecules," with H.O. Smith, *Annual Review of Biochemistry* 44 (1975): 273–93.

Bibliography: *Biographical Encyclopedia of Scientists* (New York: Facts on File, 1981), pp. 584–85. *Science* 202 (December 8, 1978): 1069–71.

SMITH, HAMILTON OTHANEL

Prize: Physiology or Medicine, 1978. *Born:* August 23, 1931; New York, New York. *Nationality:* American. *Education:* University of California, A.B., 1952; Johns Hopkins University, Maryland, M.D., 1956. *Career:* Barnes Hospital, Missouri, Physician, 1956–57; U.S. Navy, 1957–59; Henry Ford Hospital, Michigan, Physician, 1959–62; University of Michigan, Researcher, 1962–67; Johns Hopkins University, Maryland, Professor, 1967–. *Other Awards:* Guggenheim Fellow, 1975–76.

Citation: "For the discovery of restriction enzymes and their application to problems of molecular genetics" (with Werner Arber and Daniel Nathans).

Life Work: Smith's field of investigation was the mechanism of bacterial cell destruction by bacteriophage particles. He studied the enzymology of restriction-modification systems in the bacteria *Hemophilus influenzae* and identified a site-specific endonuclease enzyme. He also determined the specific DNA nucleotide sequence recognized by the enzyme and its site of cleavage. On the basis of this discovery it became possible to analyze the genetic structure of DNA molecules.

Publications: "A Restriction Enzyme from Hemophilus Influenzae: I. Purification and General Properties," with K. W. Wilcox, *Journal of Molecular Biology* 51 (1970): 379.

"A Restriction Enzyme from Hemophilus Influenzae: II. Base Sequence of the Recognition Site," *Journal of Molecular Biology* 51 (1970): 393. "Restriction Endonucleases in the Analysis and Restructuring of DNA Molecules," with D. Nathans, *Annual Review of Biochemistry* 44 (1975): 273–93.

Bibliography: *Biographical Encyclopedia of Scientists* (New York: Facts on File, 1981), pp. 737–38. *Science* 202 (December 8, 1978): 1069–71.

CORMACK, ALLAN MacLEOD

Prize: Physiology or Medicine, 1979. *Born:* February 23, 1924; Johannesburg, South Africa. *Died:* May 7, 1998; Winchester, Massachusetts. *Nationality:* South African; later U.S. citizen. *Education:* University of Cape Town, South Africa, B.Sc., 1944; University of Cape Town, South Africa, M.Sc., 1945. *Career:* University of Cape Town, Rondebosch, South Africa, Professor, 1946–56; Harvard University, Massachusetts, Researcher, 1956–57; Tufts University, Massachusetts, Professor, 1957–. *Other Awards:* Ballou Medal, Tufts University, 1978; Honorable Mention, Swedish Radiological Society, 1979; Medal of Merit, University of Cape Town, South Africa, 1980; Hogg Medal, 1981; National Medal of Science, 1990.

Citation: "For the development of computer assisted tomography" (with Godfrey Hounsfield).

Life Work: Cormack's field of investigation was radiation, especially the absorption of X rays by different body tissues. Cormack developed a mathematical procedure for analyzing X-ray data. He tested his mathematical model with trials involving the use of cobalt 60 gamma rays. The rays were collimated into a thin, pencil-like beam in line, with a Geiger counter as a detector on the opposite side. The results were displayed as graphs (rather than as photographs) that together constituted a tomogram. This led to the development of CAT. Cormack's method permitted reconstruction of the interior details of a body on the basis of different X-ray absorption by different regions.

Publications: "Representation of a Function by Its Line Integrals, with Some Radiological Applications," *Journal of Applied Physics* 34 (September 1963): 2722–27. "Representation of a Function by Its Line Integrals, with Some Radiological Applications II, *Journal of Applied Physics* 35 (October 1964): 2908–13. "Small-Angle Scattering of 143-mev Polarized Protons," with J. N. Palmieri and D. J. Steinberg, *Nuclear Physics* 56 (1964): 46–64. "Measurement of Cross Sections with Neutrons as Targets," with M. W. Shapiro and A. M. Koehler, *Physical Review* 138 (1965): 823–30.

Bibliography: *Physics Today* 32 (December 1979): 19–20. *Science* 206 (November 30, 1979): 1060–62. *Son of the Angel* (Boston: B. Benacerraf, 1990).

HOUNSFIELD, GODFREY NEWBOLD

Prize: Physiology or Medicine, 1979. *Born:* August 28, 1919; Newark, England. *Nationality:* British. *Education:* City and Guilds College, England, Radio Communications Qualification, 1938; Faraday House Electrical Engineering College, England, Degree in Electrical and Mechanical Engineering, 1951. *Career:* Thorn EMI Limited, Middlesex, England, Researcher and Administrator, 1951–. *Other Awards:* MacRobert Award, 1972; Barclay Prize, British Institute of Radiology, 1974; Willhelm Exner Medal, Austrian Industrial Association, 1974; Ziedses des Plantes Medal, Physikalisch-Medizinische Gesellschaft, Wurzburg, Germany, 1974; Prince Philip Medal Award, City and Guilds of London Institute, 1975; ANS Radiation Award, Georgia Institute of Technology, 1975; Lasker Award, 1975; Duddell Bronze Medal, Institute of Physics, 1976; Golden Plate Award, American Academy of Achievement, 1976; Churchill Gold Medal, 1976; Gairdner Foundation Award, 1976; Reginald Mitchell Gold Medal, Stoke-on-Trent Association of Engineers, 1976; Ambrogino d'Oro Award, City of Milan, 1980; Deutsche Roentgen Plakette, Deutsche Roentgen Museum, 1980.

Citation: "For the development of computer assisted tomography" (with Allan Cormack).

Life Work: Hounsfield's field of investigation was the X-ray absorption patterns of biological tissues. Independently of Cormack, he worked on a computer-assisted tomography (CAT) system. CAT scanners represented a significant advance for making images of biological tissues. It revealed internal details of soft tissues and facilitated treatment by locating abnormalities such as tumors with greater precision. It also permitted accurate measurement of the X-ray absorption properties of body tissues. According to Hounsfield, a CAT scan is one hundred times more efficient than an X ray because it uses all the information it gathers whereas an X-ray record only about 1 percent.

Publications: "Magnetic Films for Information Storage," with P. H. Brown, *British Patent 1083673*, September 20, 1967. "Computerized Transverse Axial Scanning (Tomography)," *British Journal of Radiology* 46 (1973): 1016.

Bibliography: *Current Biography Yearbook* (New York: H. W. Wilson, 1980), pp. 153–55. *Physics Today* 32 (December 1979): 19–20. *Science* 206 (November 30, 1979): 1060–62.

BENACERRAF, BARUJ

Prize: Physiology or Medicine, 1980. *Born:* October 29, 1920; Caracas, Venezuela. *Nationality:* Venezuelan; later U.S. citizen. *Education:* Lycée Janson, France, baccalaureat, 1940; Columbia University, New York, B.S., 1942; Medical College of Virginia, M.D., 1945. *Career:* Queens General Hospital, New York, Physician, 1945–46;

United States Army, 1946–48; Columbia University, New York, Researcher, 1948–50; Centre National de Recherche Scientifiques, France, Administrator, 1950–56; New York University, Professor, 1956–68; National Institutes of Health, Maryland, Administrator, 1968–70; Harvard University, Massachusetts, Professor and Administrator, 1970–91. *Other Awards:* Rabbi Shai Schacknai Prize, Hebrew University of Jerusalem, 1974; T. Duckett Jones Memorial Award, Helen Jay Whitney Foundation, 1976; Waterford Award, 1980; National Medal of Science, 1990.

Citation: "For their discoveries concerning genetically determined structures on the cell surface that regulate immunological reactions" (with Jean Dausset and George D. Snell).

Life Work: Benacerraf's field of investigation was immune responses, the body's response against foreign substances or antigens. He found that the ability to respond to certain antigens is determined genetically. He called the involved factors the immune response (Ir). The genes were located inside the major histocompatibilty complex (MHC), also called transplantation genes because differences between donor and host antigens lead to the rejection of transplanted organs. In 1972 he discovered the Ir region restriction, a phenomenon involving two types of white blood cells designated B and T cells, which play a central role in the ability of the immune system to recognize and respond to specific substances of invading organisms. B cells produce antibodies to attack foreign antigens whereas T cells respond directly to other cells and kill cancerous or virus-infected cells and destroy bacteria. MHC includes both Ir genes (class II molecules) and transplantation genes (class I genes). This discovery was of great significance for the understanding of cell recognition, immune response, and graft rejection.

Publications: "Studies on Hypersensitivity. III. The Relation between Delayed Reactivity to the Picryl Group of Conjugates and Contact Sensitivity," with P. G. H. Gell, *Immunology* 2 (1959): 219–29. "Studies on Hypersensitivity. IV. The Relation between Contact and Delayed Sensitivity: A Study on the Specificity of Cellular Immune Reactions," with P. G. H. Gell, *Journal of Experimental Medicine* 113 (1961): 571–85. "Antigenicity of Altered Autologous Proteins, a Mechanism of Autoimmune Reactions," *Annals of the New York Academy of Sciences* 124 (1965): 126–32. *Textbook of Immunology* (Baltimore: Williams and Wilkins, 1979). *Immunogenetics and Immune Regulation* (New York: Masson Publications, 1982).

Bibliography: *New York Times* Biographical Service, October 1980, pp. 1358–59. *Science* 210 (November 7, 1980): 621–23.

DAUSSET, JEAN BAPTISTE GABRIEL JOACHIM

Prize: Physiology or Medicine, 1980. *Born:* October 19, 1916; Toulouse, France. *Nationality:* French. *Education:* University of Paris, France, M.D., 1943. *Career:* National Blood Transfusion Center, France, Administrator, 1946–63; University of Paris, France, Professor, 1958–77; Collège de France, Professor, 1977–87. *Other*

Awards: Grand Prix Scientifique, Ville de Paris, 1970; Stratton Lecture Award, International Hematology Society, 1970; Karl Landsteiner Award, American Association of Blood Banks, 1971; Gairdner Foundation Prize, 1977; Koch Foundation Prize, 1978; Wolf Foundation Prize, 1978; Honda Prize, 1987.

Citation: "For their discoveries concerning genetically determined structures on the cell surface that regulate immunological reactions" (with Baruj Benacerraf and George D. Snell).

Life Work: Dausset's field of investigation was immunohematology, especially abnormal transfusion reactions. He found a number of variants of the white blood cell antigen. He called these variants MAC. Anti-MAC bodies are formed when a MAC-negative person receives blood from a MAC-positive person. The MAC antigen is one of the factors whereby the body can distinguish its own components from those of another. Most of these antigens form part of a single system, the major histocompatibility complex (MHC). Human MHC consists of several genes called the human lymphocyte-antigen (HLA) group, each of which occurs in dozens of allelic forms. MHC holds the key to the immune system as a whole.

Publications: *Immuno-Hematologie Biologique et Clinique* (Paris: Flammarion, 1956). *Tissue Typing* (New York: S. Karger, 1966). *Advances in Transplantation* (New York: Williams and Wilkins, 1968). *Human Transplantation* (Orlando, Fla.: Grune and Stratton, 1971). *Histocompatibility Testing* (New York: Williams and Wilkins, 1973). *Histocompatibility*, with G. Snell and S. Nathanson (San Diego, Calif.: Academic Press, 1976). *Immunology*, with M. Fourgereau (New York: Academic Press, 1980). *A Modern Illustration of Experimental Medicine in Action*, with Felix Rapaport (New York: Elsevier/North-Holland, 1980).

Bibliography: *Current Biography Yearbook* (New York: H. W. Wilson, 1981), pp. 108–11. *Science* 210 (November 7, 1980): 621–23.

SNELL, GEORGE DAVIS

Prize: Physiology or Medicine, 1980. *Born:* December 13, 1903; Bradford, Massachusetts. *Died:* June 6, 1996; Bar Harbor, Maine. *Nationality:* American. *Education:* Dartmouth College, New Hampshire, B.S., 1926; Harvard University, Massachusetts, M.S., 1928; Harvard University, Massachusetts, Sc.D., 1930. *Career:* Dartmouth College, New Hampshire, Professor, 1929–30; Brown University, Rhode Island, Professor, 1930–31; University of Texas, Researcher, 1931–33; Washington University, Missouri, Professor, 1933–35; Jackson Laboratory, Bar Harbor, Maine, Researcher, 1935–69. *Other Awards:* Bertner Foundation Award, 1962; Griffin Award, Animal Care Panel, 1962; Gregor Mendel Award, Czechoslavak Academy of Sciences, 1967; Gairdner Foundation Award, 1976; Wolf Prize, 1978; Award, National Institute for Arthritis and Infectious Disease, National Cancer Institute, 1978.

PHYSIOLOGY OR MEDICINE | **1981**

Citation: "For their discoveries concerning genetically determined structures on the cell surface that regulate immunological reactions" (with Baruj Benacerraf and Jean Dausset).

Life Work: Snell's field of investigation was transplantation genetics and radiation induced mutations. He was especially interested in histocompatibility or tissue compatibility in genes, later called H–2. Comparing histocompatibility genes in mice, he identified a group of about ten loci that controlled graft resistance of which the H–2 was the most important. This locus was renamed major histocompatibility complex (MHC), later called a supergene. The MHC system provides an extraordinarily sensitive surveillance system to detect cells with changed membranes and to kill cells that are alienated from their community.

Publications: *The Biology of the Laboratory Mouse* (Philadelphia: Blakiston Co., 1941). *Cell Surface Antigens: Studies in Mammals Other Than Man*, with others (New York: MSS Information Corporation, 1973). *Genetic and Biological Aspects of Histocompatibility Antigens*, with others (Copenhagen: Munksgaard, 1973). *Histocompatibility*, with J. Dausset and S. Nathanson (New York: Academic Press, 1976).

Bibliography: *Current Biography Yearbook* (New York: H. W. Wilson, 1986), pp. 533–36. *Science* 210 (November 7, 1980): 621–23.

HUBEL, DAVID HUNTER

Prize: Physiology or Medicine, 1981. *Born:* February 27, 1926; Windsor, Ontario, Canada. *Nationality:* Canadian; later U.S. citizen. *Education:* McGill University, Quebec, Canada, B.Sc., 1947; McGill University, Quebec, Canada, M.D., 1951. *Career:* Montreal Neurological Institute, Canada, Physician, 1952–54; Johns Hopkins University, Maryland, Physician, 1954–59; Harvard University, Massachusetts, Professor, 1959–. *Other Awards:* Trustees Research to Prevent Blindness Award, 1971; Lewis S. Rosentiel Award, Brandeis University, Massachusetts, 1972; Friedenwald Award, Association for Research in Vision and Ophthalmology, 1975; Karl Spencer Lashley Prize, American Philosophical Society, 1977; Louisa Gross Horowitz Prize, Columbia University, New York, 1978; Dickson Prize, University of Pittsburgh, Pennsylvania, 1979; Ledlie Prize, Harvard University, Massachusetts, 1980; Kayser Award, 1989.

Citation: "For their discoveries concerning information processing in the visual system" (with Torsten Wiesel).

Life Work: Hubel's field of investigation was the neurophysiology of vision. He and Wiesel investigated the receptive fields of other nerve cells in the visual nervous system, especially those in the visual cortex of the brain. They found that whereas the retinal cells respond to circular images, the nerve cells in the visual cortex respond to linear patterns. They devised an experiment in which they placed a microelectrode in the visual cortex of live cats and monkeys and recorded the spontaneous nervous activity of the cell. They discovered that the visual cortex of the brain is organized into periodical vertical subdivisions, which they called ocular dominance columns and orientation columns. The former combines the neural input from the two eyes and the latter transforms the circular receptive fields of retinal and geniculate nerves into linear receptive fields. They classified cortical nerve cells into simple, complex, and hypercomplex groups that perform their transformations through a process of increasing or progressive convergence. This principle explained how the visual cortex is able to generate large images from the many fragments of neural information transmitted from the retina.

Publications: "Receptive Fields of Single Neurones in the Cat's Striate Cortex," with T. N. Wiesel, *Journal of Physiology* 148 (1959): 574–91. "Receptive Fields, Binocular Interaction and Functional Architecture in the Cat's Visual Cortex," with T. N. Wiesel, *Journal of Physiology* 160 (1962): 106–54. "Receptive Fields and Functional Architecture in Two Nonstriate Visual Areas (18 and 19) of the Cat," with T. N. Wiesel, *Journal of Neurophysiology* 28 (1965): 229–89. "Receptive Fields and Functional Architecture of Monkey Striate Cortex, " with T. N. Wiesel, *Journal of Physiology* 195 (1968): 215–43. "The Visual Cortex of Normal and Deprived Monkeys," *American Scientist* 67 (1979): 532–43.

Bibliography: *New York Times* Biographical Service, October 1981, p. 1362. *Science* 214 (October 30, 1981): 518–20.

SPERRY, ROGER WOLCOTT

Prize: Physiology or Medicine, 1981. *Born:* August 20, 1913; Hartford, Connecticut. *Died:* April 17, 1994; Pasadena, California. *Nationality:* American. *Education:* Oberlin College, Ohio, B.A., 1935; Oberlin College, Ohio, M.A., 1937; University of Chicago, Illinois, Ph.D., 1941. *Career:* Harvard University, Massachusetts, Researcher, 1941–46; University of Chicago, Illinois, Professor, 1946–53; California Institute of Technology, Professor, 1954–84. *Other Awards:* Oberlin College Alumni Citation, 1954; Howard Crosby Warren Medal, Society for Experimental Psychology, 1969; Distinguished Scientist/Contribution Award, American Psychological Association, 1971; California Scientist of the Year, 1972; William Thomas Wakeman Research Award, National Paraplegic Foundation, 1972; Passano Foundation Award, 1972; Claude Bernard Science Journalism Award, 1975; Karl Lashley Award, American Philosophical Society, 1976; Albert Lasker Award, 1979; Ralph Gerard Prize, 1979; Wolf Foundation Prize, 1979.

Citation: "For his discoveries concerning the functional specialization of the cerebral hemispheres."

Life Work: Sperry's field of investigation was cognition and the brain, especially how the brain functions in such areas as memory, language, and the perception of spatial relationships. He was interested in the operation, called commissurotomy, that separates two hemispheres of the brain. He found that the nerve connections between the hemisphere in the anterior commissure and corpus callosum are essential to an integrated sense of awareness. He established that the left and right hemispheres exhibited different cognitive capacities, but both hemispheres were capable of higher cognitive functions. Sperry developed new testing procedures that allowed an assessment of the independent cognitive performance of each cerebral hemisphere. These tests demonstrated that the left or dominant cerebral hemisphere processes neural information sequentially, logically and analytically. It excels in understanding temporal and symbolic relationships as well as performing verbal operations, mathematical calculations, and abstract thinking. The right cerebral hemisphere processes neural information intuitively and simultaneously, interprets visual and spatial relationships, as well as patterns and auditory impressions, such as music and comprehends complex relationships.

Publications: "Neurology and the Mind-Brain Problem," *American Scientist* 40 (1952): 291. "On the Neural Basis of the Conditioned Response," *British Journal of Animal Behavior* 3 (1955): 41. "Cerebral Organization and Behavior," *Science* 133 (1961): 1749. "Chemoaffinity in the Orderly Growth of Nerve Fiber Patterns of Connection," *Proceedings of the National Academy of Sciences U.S.A.* 50 (1963): 703. "Mental Unity Following Surgical Disconnection of the Cerebral Hemispheres," *Harvey Lectures* 62 (1968): 293–322. *Science and Moral Priority* (New York: Columbia University Press, 1983).

Bibliography: *Current Biography Yearbook* (New York: H. W. Wilson, 1986), pp. 53–56. *New York Times* Biographical Service, April 10, 1994, p. 561. *Science* 214 (October 30, 1981): 517–18.

WIESEL, TORSTEN N.

Prize: Physiology or Medicine, 1981. *Born:* June 3, 1924; Uppsala, Sweden. *Nationality:* Swedish; later U.S. citizen. *Education:* Karolinska Institute, Sweden, M.D., 1954. *Career:* Karolinska Institute, Sweden, Professor, 1954–55; John Hopkins University, Maryland, Professor, 1955–59; Harvard University, Massachusetts, Professor, 1959–83; Rockefeller University, New York, Professor, 1983–. *Other Awards:* Jules Stein Award, Trustees for Prevention of Blindness, 1971; Lewis S. Rosenstiel Prize, Brandeis University, Massachusetts, 1972; Friedenwald Award, Trustees of Association for Research in Vision and Ophthalmology, 1975; Lashley Prize, American Philosophical Society, 1977; Louisa Gross Horowitz Prize, Columbia University, New York, 1978; Dickson Prize, University of Pittsburgh, Pennsylvania, 1979; Ledlie Prize, Harvard University, 1980.

Citation: "For their discoveries concerning information processing in the visual system" (with David H. Hubel).

Life Work: Wiesel's field of investigation was ophthalmological physiology. Working with Hubel, he studied the receptive fields of nerve cells in the visual cortex of the brain. They found that whereas retinal cells responded to circular images, the nerve cells in the visual cortex responded to linear images. Investigating the visual cortex of live cats and monkeys, they found that it is organized into periodic vertical subdivisions, called *ocular* *dominance columns* and *orientation columns*. The former combine the neural input from the two eyes while the latter transforms the circular receptive fields of retinal and genic ulate nerve cells into linear receptive fields. These transformations are accomplished by a hierarchy of nerve cells that function according to the principle of increasing or progressive convergence. This principle explains how the visual cortex is able to generate large images from many small bits of neural information from the retina.

Publications: "Receptive Fields of Single Neurons in the Cat's Striate Cortex," with D. H. Hubel, *Journal of Physiology* 148 (1959): 574–91. "Receptive Fields, Binocular Interaction and Functional Architecture in the Cat's Visual Cortex," with D. H. Hubel, *Journal of Physiology* 160 (1962): 106–54. "Receptive Fields and Functional Architecture in Two Nonstriate Visual Areas (18 and 19) of the Cat," with D. H. Hubel, *Journal of Neurophysiology* 28 (1965): 229–89. "Receptive Fields and Functional Architecture of Monkey Striate Cortex," with D. H. Hubel, *Journal of Physiology* 195 (1968): 215–43. "Anatomical Demonstration of Orientation Columns in Macaque Monkey," with D. H. Hubel and M. P. Stryker, *Journal of Comparative Neurology* 177 (1978): 361–80.

Bibliography: *New York Times* Biographical Service, October 1981, p. 1451. *Science* 214 (October 30, 1981): 518–20.

BERGSTRÖM, SUNE

Prize: Physiology or Medicine, 1982. *Born:* January 10, 1916; Stockholm, Sweden. *Nationality:* Swedish. *Education:* Karolinska Institute, Sweden, D. Med. Sci., 1944; Karolinska Institute, Sweden, M.D., 1944. *Career:* Columbia University, New York, Researcher, 1940–41; Squibb Institute, New Jersey, Researcher, 1941–42; Nobel Institute, Stockholm, Sweden, Researcher, 1942–46; Basel University, Switzerland, Researcher, 1946–47; University of Lund, Sweden, Professor, 1947–58; Karolinska Institute, Sweden, Professor and Administrator, 1958–80. *Other Awards:* Louisa Gross Horowitz Prize, Columbia University, New York, 1975; Lasker Award, 1977.

Citation: "For their discoveries concerning prostaglandins and related biologically active substances" (with Bengt Samuelsson and John R. Vane).

Life Work: Bergström's field of investigation was prostaglandins, active substances obtained from the prostate gland and seminal vesicles. He isolated and purified small amounts of six prostaglandin compounds and produced the first description of their chemical structure. He also determined how prostaglandins are formed from arachidonic acid. He also conducted special studies in prostaglandin E and F. The former are vasodilators that relax smooth muscles in the walls of blood vessels, lower blood pressure and protect the lining of the stomach from the formation of ulcers and from the toxic side effects of aspirin and other anti-inflammatory drugs. The latter are vasconstrictors that stimulate the contraction of smooth muscles in the walls of blood pressure and also stimulate the contraction of the muscle of the uterus and thus induce abortion.

Publications: *Prostaglandins: Proceedings of the Second Nobel Symposium, Stockholm, June 1966*, with Bengt Samuelsson (New York: Interscience Publishers, 1967). *Third Conference on Prostaglandins in Fertility Control, January 17–20, 1972*, with K. Green and B. Samuelsson (Stockholm: Karolinska Institutet, 1972). *Report from the Meeting of the Prostaglandin Task Force Steering Committee, Chapel Hill, June 8–10, 1972, Stockholm, October 2–3, 1972, Geneva, February 26–28, 1973*, with John R. Vane (Stockholm: Karolinska Institutet, 1973). *Prostacyclin*, with John R. Vane (New York: Raven Press, 1979).

Bibliography: *New Scientist* 96 (November 14, 1982): 82–83. *Science* 218 (November 19, 1982): 765–68.

SAMUELSSON, BENGT INGEMAR

Prize: Physiology or Medicine, 1982. *Born:* May 21, 1934; Halmstedt, Sweden. *Nationality:* Swedish. *Education:* Karolinska Institute, Sweden, D. Med. Sci., 1960; Karolinska Institute, Sweden, M.D., 1961. *Career:* Karolinska Institute, Sweden, Professor and Administrator, 1961–. *Other Awards:* A. Jahres Award, Oslo University, 1970; Louisa Gross Horowitz Prize, Columbia University, 1975; Lasker Award, 1977; White Award, 1990.

Citation: "For their discoveries concerning prostaglandins and related biologically active substances" (with Sune Bergström and John R. Vane).

Life Work: Samuelsson's field of investigation was prostaglandins, which he found are derived from arachidonic acid. Prostaglandins E and F have many applications in clinical medicine. He investigated compounds called endoperoxides. He discovered that in one of the platelets one of the endoperoxides is converted into compounds called thromboxanes. Later, he discovered that in white blood cells, arachidonic acid is converted into compounds called leukotrienes, which control the symptoms of asthma and anaphylaxis. One of the leukotrienes increase the permeability of blood vessels to fluid and causes white blood cells to adhere to injured or inflamed tissue, where they engulf and dispose of tissue debris.

Publications: *Prostaglandins: Proceedings of the Second Nobel Symposium, Stockholm, June 1966*, with S. Bergström (New York: Interscience Publishers, 1967). *Third Conference on Prostaglandins in Fertility Control, January 17–20, 1972*, with K. Green and S. Bergström (Stockholm: Karolinska Institutet, 1972).

Bibliography: *New Scientist* 96 (November 14, 1982): 82–83. *Science* 218 (November 19, 1982): 765–68.

VANE, JOHN ROBERT

Prize: Physiology or Medicine, 1982. *Born:* March 29, 1927; Tardebigg, Worcestershire, England. *Nationality:* British. *Education:* University of Birmingham, England, B.Sc., 1946; Oxford University, England, B.Sc., 1949; Oxford University, England, D.Phil., 1953. *Career:* Yale University, Connecticut, Professor, 1953–55; University of London, England, Professor, 1955–73; Wellcome Laboratories, England, Researcher and Administrator, 1973–85; St. Bartholomew's Hospital Medical College, London, Board of Directors, 1986–. *Other Awards:* Lasker Award, 1977; Baly Medal, Royal College of Physicians, 1977; Peter Debye Prize, University of Maastricht, Netherlands, 1980; Feldberg Foundation Prize, 1980; Ciba Geigy Drew Award, Drew University, New Jersey, 1980; Dale Medal, Society of Endocrinology, 1981; Galen Medal, Apothecaries' Society, 1983; Biological Council Medal, 1983; Louis Pasteur Foundation Prize, California, 1984; Royal Medal, 1989.

Citation: "For their discoveries concerning prostaglandins and related biologically active substances" (with Sune Bergström and Bengt Samuelsson).

Life Work: Vane's field of investigation was prostaglandins. He demonstrated that certain prostaglandins and thromboxanes become biologically inactive after passing through the lungs once and are effective only locally at the site of their release. Prostaglandin E is a vasodilator, while prostaglandin F and thromboxane are vasoconstrictors. He found that aspirin inhibits the formation of prostaglandins and thromboxane. He discovered cells of the blood vessel tissue synthesize a different type of prostaglandin, called prostaglandin X (now prostacylin), which inhibits clotting and causes vasodilation. Thromboxane A and prostacylin constitute a kind of homeostatic system, keeping opposing forces in balance.

Publications: *Prostaglandin Synthetase Inhibitors—Their Effects on Physiological Functions and Pathological States,* with H. Robinson (New York: Raven Press, 1974). *Metabolic Functions of the Lung,* with Y. S. Bakhle (New York: Dekker, 1977). *Inflammation,* with S. H. Ferreira (New York: Springer Verlag, 1978). *Anti-Inflammatory Drugs* (New York: Springer Verlag, 1979). *Prostacyclin,* with S. Bergström (New York: Raven Press, 1979). *Interactions Between Platelets and Vessel Walls,* with G. V. R. Bonn (Great Neck, N.Y.: Scholium International, 1981). *Prostacyclin in Health and Disease* (Edinburgh: Royal College of Physicians, 1982).

Bibliography: *Current Biography Yearbook* (New York: H. W. Wilson, 1986), pp. 575–78. *New Scientist* 96 (November 14, 1982): 82–83. *Science* 218 (November 19, 1982): 765–68.

McCLINTOCK, BARBARA

Prize: Physiology or Medicine, 1983. *Born:* June 16, 1902; Hartford, Connecticut. *Died:* September 2, 1992; Long Island, New York. *Nationality:* American. *Education:* Cornell University, New York, B.S., 1923; Cornell University, New York, M.A., 1925; Cornell University, New York, Ph.D., 1927. *Career:* Cornell University, New York, Researcher, 1924–31; California Institute of Technology, Researcher, 1931–33; University of Freiburg, Germany, Researcher, 1933–34; Cornell University, New York, Researcher, 1934–36; University of Missouri, Professor, 1936–41; Carnegie Institution of Washington at Cold Spring Harbor Laboratory, New York, Researcher, 1941–85. *Other Awards:* Kimber Award, National Academy of Sciences, 1967; National Medal of Science, 1970; Rosenstiel Award, 1978; Lasker Award, 1978; Wolf Foundation Prize, Israel, 1981; Horowitz Prize, Columbia University, 1982.

Citation: "For her discovery of mobile genetic elements."

Life Work: McClintock's field of investigation was morphology of maize chromosomes and the exchange of genetic information and material during chromosomal crossing over in the early stages of meiosis. She discovered the phenomenon called genetic transposition, in which the genes involved are called transposable or jumping genes. Two transposable genes were involved—a dissociator gene (Ds) and an activator gene (Ac). If the Ds gene moved to a chromosomal site next to a structural gene, the Ds gene suppressed the phenotypical expression of the structural gene, but only if the Ac gene occupied a site near the other two genes. One of the transposable genes was a suppressor gene and the other was a desuppressor of the suppressor. The influence of her theories on genetic regulation was far-reaching.

Publications: "A Correlation of Cytological and Genetical Crossing Over in Zea Mays," with H. Creighton, *Proceedings of the National Academy of Sciences* 17 (August 1931): 492–97. "The Relation of a Particular Chromosomal Element to the Development of the Nucleoli in Zea Mays," *A Zellforsch. U. Mikr. Anat* 21 (1934): 294–328. "Mutable Loci in Maize," *Carnegie Institution of Washington Yearbook* 48 (1949): 142–43.

Bibliography: *Current Biography Yearbook* (New York: H. W. Wilson, 1984), pp. 262–65. E. Keller, *A Feeling for the Organism: The Life and Work of Barbara McClintock* (San Francisco: Freeman, 1983). M. Kittredge, *Barbara McClintock* (New York: Chelsea House Publishers, 1991). *Biographical Memoirs of the Fellows of the Royal Society* (London: Royal Society, 1994), vol. 40, p. 265.

JERNE, NIELS KAJ

Prize: Physiology or Medicine, 1984. *Born:* December 23, 1911; London, England. *Died:* October 7, 1994; Pont du Gard, France. *Nationality:* British; later Swedish and

Swiss citizen. *Education:* University of Copenhagen, Denmark, doctorate in medicine, 1951. *Career:* Danish State Serum Institute, Researcher, 1943–56; California Institute of Technology, Researcher, 1954–55; World Health Organization, Geneva, Switzerland, Chief Medical Officer, 1956–62; University of Pittsburgh, Pennsylvania, Administrator, 1962–66; Paul Ehrlich Institute, Frankfurt, Germany, Director, 1966–69; Basel Institute for Immunology, Switzerland, Director, 1969–80. *Other Awards:* Marcel Benorst Prize, Berne, Switzerland, 1979; Paul Ehrlich Prize, Frankfurt, Germany, 1982.

Citation: "For theories concerning the specificity in development and control of the immune system and the discovery of the principle for production of monoclonal antibodies" (with Georges J. F. Köhler and César Milstein).

Life Work: Jerne's field of investigation was antibodies as components of a dynamic immune system. He suggested a theory of selective antibody production according to which as the immune system developed, antibodies were being selected and progressively modified. When an antibody happens to bind to an antigen, the resultant combination is recognized by white blood cells, which then make additional copies of the bound antibody. His most significant contribution to immunology was his network theory, introduced in 1974, explaining how the body's immune system musters its forces to combat disease and then recedes into inactivity when no longer needed. He noted that there are many more types of antibodies than there are proteins and that the response to an invader is not merely a matter of increasing the production of a specific antibody, but rather one of the organized response of a complex, self-regulating system to a disturbance.

Publications: "Immunological Speculation," *Annual Review of Microbiology* 14 (1960): 341–58. "Antibody Formation and Immunological Memory," *Macromolecular Behavior* (1966): 151–57. "Regulation of Antibody Synthesis," *Transplant.* Organum Geweben, Int. Symp., Bad Hamburg v.d. H., Ger. (1966): 81–89. "The Immune System," *Scientific American* 229 (July 1973): 52–60.

Bibliography: *New Scientist* 104 (October 18, 1984): 3–5. *Science* 226 (November 30, 1984): 1025–28. *New York Times* Biographical Service, October 8, 1994, p. 1537.

KÖHLER, GEORGES JEAN FRANZ

Prize: Physiology or Medicine, 1984. *Born:* April 17, 1946; Munich, Germany. *Died:* March 1, 1995; Freiburg, Germany. *Nationality:* German. *Education:* University of Freiburg, Germany, doctorate, 1974. *Career:* Cambridge University, England, Researcher, 1974–76; Basel Institute for Immunology, Switzerland, Researcher, 1977–84; Max Planck Institute for Immune Biology, Germany, Director, 1985–1997.

Citation: "For theories concerning the specificity in development and control of the immune system and the discovery of the principle for production of monoclonal antibodies" (with Niels K. Jerne and César Milstein).

PHYSIOLOGY OR MEDICINE | 1984

Life Work: Köhler's field of investigation was mutations in myeloma cells. Generally, myeloma cells produce identical antibodies. However, these cancers appear randomly. Köhler produced a hybrid myeloma (or hybridoma) by immunizing a mouse against a known antigen, extracting the antibody-producing cells from the mouse's spleen and fusing them with myeloma cells. He also developed a way to isolate hybridomas as clones descended from a single fusion. They were identical monoclonal antibodies that are much superior to conventional antiserums. A batch of monoclonal antibodies is automatically standardized and all the antibodies in the sample are identical. An especially important group of monoclonal antibodies react only to cancer cells. They can be used to transport toxic materials directly to tumors, destroying the cancers without disturbing other cells.

Publications: "Continuous Culture of Fused Cells Secreting Antibody of Predefined Specificity," with C. Milstein, *Nature (London)* 256 (1975): 495–97. "Immunoglobulin Production by Lymphocyte Hybridomas," with H. Hengartner and M. J. Shulman, *European Journal of Immunology* 8 (1978): 82–88. "Immunoglobulin Chain Loss in Hybridoma Lines," *Proceedings of the National Academy of Sciences USA* 77 (1980): 2197–99. "The Technique of Hybridoma Production," *Immunological Methods* 2 (1981): 285–98.

Bibliography: *New York Times* Biographical Service, October 16, 1984, p. 1339. *Science* 226 (November 30, 1984): 1025–28.

MILSTEIN, CÉSAR

Prize: Physiology or Medicine, 1984. *Born:* October 8, 1927; Bahia Blanca, Argentina. *Nationality:* Argentinian; later British citizen. *Education:* University of Buenos Aires, Argentina, Licenciado en Ciencias Quimicas, 1952; University of Buenos Aires, Argentina, Doctor en Quimica, 1957; Cambridge University, England, Ph.D., 1960. *Career:* National Institute of Biology, Buenos Aires, Argentina, Researcher, 1961–63; Cambridge University, England, Researcher and Administrator, 1963–. *Other Awards:* Silver Jubilee Medal, 1977; Ciba Medal, Biochemistry Society, 1978; Rosenstiel Medal, 1979; Avery-Landsteiner Preis, 1979; Rosenberg Prize, 1979; Mattia Award, 1979; Louisa Gross Horowitz Prize, Columbia University, New York, 1980; Koch Preis, 1980; Wolf Prize, 1980; Wellcome Foundation Medal, 1980; Jimenez Diaz Medal, 1981; William Bate Hardy Prize, Cambridge Philosophical Society, England, 1981; Sloan Prize, General Motors Cancer Research Foundation, 1981; Gairdner Award, 1981; Royal Medal, Royal Society, 1982; Albert Lasker Award, 1984; Dale Medal, England, 1984; Copley Medal, 1989.

Citation: "For theories concerning the specificity in development and control of the immune system and the discovery of the principle for production of monoclonal antibodies" (with Niels K. Jerne and Georges J. F. Köhler).

Life Work: Milstein's field of investigation was antibodies, protein bodies produced by the immune system to bind to and inactivate foreign bodies or antigens. Working with

Köhler, he employed a technique devised by R. G. H. Cotton, who fused two different myeloma cells to produce a hybrid in which both proteins from the parent myelomas were present. The result, a hybrid myeloma or hybridoma, had the antibody producing ability of its normal parent but grew forever like its cancerous myeloma parent. Hybridomas can be isolated as clones descended from a single fusion. They are identical monoclonal antibodies. This discovery formed the basis of large commercial trade in monoclonal antibodies for diagnostic tests and hybridoma-based controlled vaccines and cancer therapies.

Publications: "Expansion and Contraction in the Evolution of Immunoglobulin Gene Pools," with J. Svasti, *Progr. Immunol., Int. Congr. Immunol., 1st* (1971): 33–45. "Clonal Variants of Myeloma Cells," with others, *Prog. Immunol., Proc. Intern Congr. Immunol., 2nd* 1 (1974): 173–82. "Continuous Cultures of Fused Cells Secreting Antibody of Predefined Specificity," with G. Köhler, *Nature (London)* 256 (1975): 495–97. "Immunoglobulin Genes in a Mouse Myeloma and in Mutant Clones," with others, *Miami Winter Symposium* 9 (1975): 131–52.

Bibliography: *New York Times* Biographical Service, October 16, 1984, p. 1361. *Science* 226 (November 30, 1984): 1025–28.

BROWN, MICHAEL STUART

Prize: Physiology or Medicine, 1985. *Born:* April 13, 1941; New York, New York. *Nationality:* American. *Education:* University of Pennsylvania, B.A., 1962; University of Pennsylvania, M.D., 1966. *Career:* Massachusetts General Hospital, Boston, Physician, 1966–68; National Institutes of Health, Maryland, Researcher, 1968–71; University of Texas Health Science Center, Dallas, Professor, 1971–. *Other Awards:* Pfizer Award, American Chemical Society, 1976; Passano Award, 1978; Lousbery Award, National Academy of Sciences, USA, 1979; Lita Annenberg Hazen Award, 1982, Horwitz Prize, Columbia University, New York, 1984; Lasker Award, 1985; National Medal of Science, 1988.

Citation: "For their discoveries concerning the regulation of cholesterol metabolism" (with Joseph L. Goldstein).

Life Work: Brown's field of investigation was cholesterol, especially hypercholesterolemia. Brown and Goldstein isolated the enzyme that controls the rate at which cholesterol is synthesized. Hypercholesterolemia patients have defective binding of low-density lipoproteins (LDL, or bad cholesterol). This led to the discovery of receptors for the LDL molecule on cell surfaces. In normal cells, as the level of LDL in the blood rises, the LDL molecules bind to cell-surface receptors and turn off cholesterol synthesis by a negative feedback loop. Since the cells from patients with hypercholesterolemia do not bind to the LDL, the cells keep on making LDL as though more were needed. The apoprotein portion of the LDL is bound to a specific receptor on the cell surface in a process called receptor-mediated endocytosis. The binding occurs in coated pits on the cell membrane that are subsequently folded into vesicles that pinch off and carry the LDL into the interior of the cell. When the LDL is released, it signals the enzyme responsible for making more cholesterol to stop and triggers the enzyme responsible for the storage. In hypercholesterolemia patients, the LDL receptors are unable to bind to LDL or are unable to deliver the proper signals.

Publications: "Binding and Degradation of Low Density Lipoproteins by Cultured Human Fibroblasts: Comparison of Cells from a Normal Subject and from a Patient with Homozygous Familial Hypercholesterolemia," with J. L. Goldstein, *Journal of Biological Chemistry* 249 (1974): 5153–62. "Development of a Cell Culture System for Study of the Basic Defect in Familial Hypercholesterolemia," with J. L. Goldstein, in *Atherosclerosis III: Proceedings of the Third International Symposium* (Berlin: Springer-Verlag, 1974), pp. 422–25. "Expression of the Familial Hypercholesterolemia Gene in Heterozygotes: Model for a Dominant Disorder in Man," with J. L. Goldstein, *Transactions of the Association of American Physicians* 87 (1974): 120–31. "Familial Hypercholesterolemia: A Genetic Regulatory Defect in Cholesterol Metabolism," with J. L. Goldstein, *American Journal of Medicine* 58 (1975): 147–50.

Bibliography: F. Magill, *Nobel Prize Winners: Physiology or Medicine* (Pasadena, Calif.: Salem Press, 1991), pp. 1480–91. *New York Times*, October 15, 1985, pp. C 1, 3. *Science* 231 (January 10, 1986): 126–29.

GOLDSTEIN, JOSEPH LEONARD

Prize: Physiology or Medicine, 1985. *Born:* April 18, 1940; Sumter, South Carolina. *Nationality:* American. *Education:* Washington and Lee University, Virginia, B.S., 1962; Southwestern Medical School, University of Texas, M.D., 1966. *Career:* Massachusetts General Hospital, Boston, Physician, 1966–68; National Institutes of Health, Maryland, Researcher, 1968–70; University of Washington, Seattle, Researcher, 1970–72; University of Texas Health Science Center, Dallas, Professor, 1972–. *Other Awards:* Heinrich-Wieland Prize, 1974; Pfizer Award, American Chemical Society, 1976; Passano Award, 1978; Lounsbery Award, National Academy of Sciences, USA, 1979; Gairdner Foundation Award, 1981; Award, New York Academy of Sciences, 1981; Lita Annenberg Hazen Award, 1982; Horowitz Award, Columbia University, New York, 1984; V. D. Mattia Award, 1984; Lasker Award, 1985; National Medal of Science, 1988.

Citation: "For their discoveries concerning the regulation of cholesterol metabolism" (with Michael S. Brown).

Life Work: Goldstein's field of investigation was cholesterol. Working with Brown, he discovered that cell surfaces have specific receptors for the LDL cholesterol complex. These receptors cluster in cell-surface pits coated with the protein clathrin. In a process called receptor mediated endocytosis, protective coverings in the cell membrane engulf and pinch off to form vesicles to carry it off into the interior of the cell. The receptor then separates from the LDL and returns to the cell surface. After LDL is released further production of cholesterol is inhibited and the enzyme responsible for storing cholesterol is activated. Hypercholesterolemia patients have abnormal LDL receptors that fail to remove enough LDL from the blood because of defective synthesis of the receptor, defective binding of LDL, inadequate transport of the receptor within the cell or the failure of the surface receptor to migrate to the coated pits.

Publications: "Familial Hypercholesterolemia: Identification of a Defect in the Regulation of 3-hydroxy–3-methylglutaryl Coenzyme A Reductase Activity Associated with Overproduction of Cholesterol," with M. S. Brown, *Proceedings National Academy of Sciences USA* 70 (1973): 2804–2808. "Expression of the Familial Hypercholesterolemia Gene in Heterozygotes: Mechanism for a Dominant Disorder in Man," with M. S. Brown, *Science* 185 (1974): 61–63. "Homozygous Familial Hypercholesterolemia: Specificity of the Biochemical Defect in Cultured Cells and Feasibility of Prenatal Detection," with M. J. E. Harrod and M. S. Brown, *American Journal of Human Genetics* 26 (1974): 199–206. "Familial Hypercholesterolemia: Biochemical, Genetic, and Pathophysiological Considerations," with M. S. Brown, *Advances in Internal Medicine* 20 (1975): 273–96.

Bibliography: *Current Biography Yearbook* (New York: H. W. Wilson, 1987), pp. 208–11. F. Magill, *Nobel Prize Winners: Physiology or Medicine* (Pasadena, Calif.: Salem Press, 1991), pp. 1480–91. *New York Times,* October 15, 1985, pp. C 1, 3. *Science* 231 (January 10, 1986): 126–29.

COHEN, STANLEY

Prize: Physiology or Medicine, 1986. *Born:* November 17, 1922; Brooklyn, New York. *Nationality:* American. *Education:* Brooklyn College, New York, B.A., 1943; Oberlin College, Ohio, M.A., 1945; University of Michigan, Ph.D., 1948. *Career:* University of Colorado, Professor, 1948–52; Washington University, Missouri, Professor, 1952–59; Vanderbilt University, Tennessee, Professor, 1959–. *Other Awards:* William Thomson Wakeman Award, 1977; Earl Sutherland Research Prize, 1977; Albion O. Bernstein Award, 1978; H. P. Robertson Memorial Award, 1981; Lewis S. Rosentiel Award, 1982; Alfred P. Sloan Award, 1982; Louisa Gross Horwitz Prize, 1983; Lila Gruber Memorial Cancer Research Award, 1983; Bertner Award, 1983; Gairdner Foundation International Award, 1985; Fred Conrad Koch Award, 1986; National Medal of Science, 1986; Albert Lasker Award, 1986; Franklin Medal, 1987; Albert A. Michaelson Award, 1987.

Citation: "For their discoveries of growth factors" (with Rita Levi-Montalcini).

Life Work: Cohen's field of investigation was the biochemistry of life processes. With Levi-Montalcini, he studied the nerve growth factor (NGF), a substance taken from certain tumors in mice that induced dramatic growth in parts of the nervous systems of chick embryos. NGF was later discovered in snake venom and the salivary gland of adult male mice. The chemical form of NGF was analyzed and found to consist of a chain of 118 amino acids. Two such chains join together to become biologically active. Continuing his research into NGF, he discovered the existence of a second agent in salivary gland extract, the epidermal growth factor (EGF) that stimulated the growth of epithelial cells in the skin and cornea. Cohen isolated and purified EGF and determined its sequence of 53 amino acids. In 1975 he isolated human EGF from the urine of pregnant women. EGF stimulates the healing of wounds in the skin and is effective in skin transplantation.

Publications: "Nerve Growth-stimulating Factor Isolated from Sarcomas 37 and 180," *Proceedings of the National Academy of Science. United States.* 40 (1954): 1014–18. "A Nerve Growth-stimulating Factor Isolated from Snake Venom," *Proceedings of the National Academy of Science. United States* 42 (1956): 571–74. "Purification and Properties of a Nerve Growth-promoting Factor Isolated from Mouse Sarcoma 180," *Cancer Research* 17 (1957): 15–20. "Isolation of a Mouse Submaxillary Gland Protein Accelerating Incisor Eruption and Eyelid Opening in the New-Born Animal," *Journal of Biological Chemistry* 237 (1962): 1555–62. "Isolation and Biological Effects of an Epidermal Growth-Stimulating Protein," *National Cancer Institute Monograph* 13 (1964): 13–27.

Bibliography: F. Magill, *Nobel Prize Winners: Physiology or Medicine* (Pasadena, Calif.: Salem Press, 1991), pp. 1495–1503. *New York Times*, October 14, 1986, pp. A1, C3. *Science* 234 (1986): 543–44.

LEVI-MONTALCINI, RITA

Prize: Physiology or Medicine, 1986. *Born:* April 22, 1909; Turin, Italy. *Nationality:* Italian; later U.S. citizen. *Education:* University of Turin, Italy, M.D., 1936. *Career:* University of Turin, Italy, Researcher, 1936–38, 1945–47; Washington University, St. Louis, Missouri, Professor, 1947–77; Institute of Cell Biology, Italy, Researcher, 1977–81. *Other Awards:* William Wakeman Award, 1974; Lewis Rosenstiel Award, 1982; Louisa Horwitz Prize, 1983; Albert Lasker Award, 1986.

Citation: "For their discoveries of growth factors" (with Stanley Cohen).

Life Work: Levi-Montalcini's field of investigation was the nerve growth factor (NGF), a concept that she developed after experiments in which mouse tumors grafted onto chick embryos grew rapidly into tumors. Working with Stanley Cohen, she established that NGF is a protein found also in snake venom and the salivary gland of male mice. They produced NGF antibodies which inhibited the action of NGF and also destroyed the sympathetic nerve tissues. It was the first of many growth factors that have been discovered since then. NGF is used to repair damaged nerves.

Publications: "The Nerve Growth Factor," *Scientific American* 240 (1979): 68–77. *Molecular Aspects of Neurobiology* (New York: Springer-Verlag, 1986). "The Nerve-Growth Factor 35 Years Later," *Science* 237 (1987): 1154–61.

Bibliography: "The Heart and Mind of a Genius," *Vogue* 177 (1987): 480. *In Praise of Imperfection: My Life and Work* (New York: Basic Books, 1988). "Interview—Rita Levi-Montalcini." *Omni* 10 (1988): 70–72.

TONEGAWA, SUSUMU

Prize: Physiology or Medicine, 1987. *Born:* September 5, 1939; Nagoya, Japan. *Nationality:* Japanese; later U.S. resident. *Education:* Kyoto Imperial University, Japan, B.S., 1963; University of California, San Diego, Ph.D., 1968. *Career:* Basel Institute for Immunology, Switzerland, Researcher, 1971–81; Massachusetts Institute of Technology, Professor, 1981–. *Other Awards:* Cloetta Prize, 1978; Avery Landsteiner Prize, 1981; Louisa Gross Horwitz Prize, 1982; Gairdner Award, 1983; Bunka Kunsho Order of Culture, Japan, 1984; Robert Koch Prize, 1986; Bristol-Myers Award, 1986; Lasker Award, 1987.

Citation: "For his discovery of the genetic principle for generation of antibody diversity."

Life Work: Tonegawa's fields of investigation were molecular biology and immunology. He tackled the problem of antibody diversity, for which there were two competing explanations. The germ line theory held that the specific genetic blueprint for every possible antibody was part of the genetic code. The somatic mutation theory held that the diversification of antibodies takes place in the cells. Each antibody is made up of two polypeptides, or two long chains of amino acids, one light and the other heavy. Each chain could be divided into a constant, or C region, which is the same for all antibodies of a given general class and a variable, or V region, that is distinct for each individual antibody. Tonegawa used restriction enzymes to break up two samples of DNA, one from embryonic mouse cells and one from antibody producing cells of an adult mouse. He found that a particular segment of DNA from the adult mouse corresponded to two separate segments of DNA in the mouse embryo representing two different genes, V and C. It was found that the segment of DNA identified as light chain V gene was not a complete gene but a gene segment that only coded for part of the length of the V region. The remainder of the V region was coded for by a separate segment of DNA labeled J (for joining) segment. The heavy chain V regions require a third gene segment called D (for diversity) in addition to V and J. Mutations and combinations of V, J, and D segments could generate up to 10 billion different kinds of antibodies.

Publications: "Genetic Transcription Directed by the b_2 Region of Lambda Bacteriophage," *Proceedings of the National Academy of Science. United States* 61 (1968): 1320–27. "Evidence for Somatic Generation of Antibody Diversity," *Proceedings of the National Academy of Science. United States* 71 (1974): 4027–31. "The Molecules of the Immune System," *Scientific American* 253 (1985): 122–31. "Antibody and T-Cell Receptors," *Journal of the American Medical Association* 259 (1988): 1854–57.

Bibliography: F. Magill, *Nobel Prize Winners: Physiology or Medicine* (Pasadena, Calif.: Salem Press, 1991), pp. 1519–26. *New York Times*, October 13, 1987, p. C1. *Science* 238 (1987): 484–85.

BLACK, SIR JAMES W.

Prize: Physiology or Medicine, 1988. *Born:* June 14, 1924; Uddingston, Scotland. *Nationality:* Scottish. *Education:* University of St. Andrews, Scotland, M.D., 1946. *Career:* University of St. Andrews, Scotland, Professor, 1946–47; University of Malaya, Professor, 1947–50; University of Glasgow, Scotland, Professor, 1950–58; Imperial Chemical Industries, England, Researcher, 1958–64; Smith, Kline and French, England, Researcher, 1964–73; University College, England, Professor, 1973–77; Wellcome Research Lab, England, Researcher, 1977–84; King's College Hospital Medical School, England, Professor, 1984–. *Other Awards:* Mullard Award, Royal Society, 1978; Knighthood, 1981.

Citation: "For their discoveries of important principles for drug treatment" (with Gertrude B. Elion and George H. Hitchings Jr.).

Life Work: Black's field of investigation was beta-blockers, drugs that would specifically interfere with beta-receptors. His researches led to the discovery of a number of important beta-blocker drugs: proethalol and propranolol (Inderal). He next turned his attention to treatment of ulcer, for which he developed H2 blockers, such as guanyl-histamine, burimamide, and cimetidine (Tagamet). Black has been called the greatest and most important pharmacologist of our time.

Publications: "A New Adrenergic Betareceptor Antagonist," *Lancet* (1964): 1080. "Definition and Antagonism of Histamine H2-Receptors," *Nature* 236 (1972): 385–90. "An Analysis of the Depressor Responses to Histamine in the Cat and Dog: Involvement of Both H1- and H2-Receptors," *British Journal Pharmacology* 54 (1975): 319–24. *The Medicine You Take* (London: Fontana, 1978).

Bibliography: *Journal of the American College of Cardiology* 13 (March 1989): 769. *New York Times*, October 18, 1988, pp. A1, C17. *Science* 242 (1988): 516–17.

ELION, GERTRUDE BELLE

Prize: Physiology or Medicine, 1988. *Born:* January 23, 1918: New York, New York. *Died:* February 21, 1999; Chapel Hill, North Carolina. *Nationality:* American. *Education:* Hunter College, New York, A.B., 1937; New York University, M.S., 1941. *Career:* New York City, Teacher, 1941–42; Quaker Maid Company, New York, Researcher, 1942–43; Johnson and Johnson, New Jersey, Researcher, 1943–44; Wellcome Company, North Carolina, Researcher, 1944–83. *Other Awards:* Garvan Medal, 1968; President's Medal, Hunter College, New York, 1970; Judd Award, 1983; Cain Award, 1984; Bertner Award, 1989; Medal of Honor, 1990; National Medal of Science, 1991.

Citation: "For their discoveries of important principles for drug treatment" (with James Black and George H. Hitchings Jr.).

Life Work: Elion's field of investigation was nucleic acid antimetabolite, chemicals that are similar enough to a parasite's necessary nutrients to disrupt its metabolism. In 1951 Elion discovered a compound, 6-mercaptopurine (6-MP) that was soon recognized as the most effective treatment against leukemia. 6-MP was also able to suppress the overall activity of the immune system and so is used during transplants. Elion and Hitchings discovered a more potent immunosuppressant in azathioprine (Imuran). Her search for new drugs also led to allopurinol (Zyloprim), the most effective remedy against gout, acyclovir (Zovirax) used in the treatment of infections of herpes, chicken pox and shingles, and azidothymidine (AZT), the first drug used to treat AIDS.

Publications: "Detection of Agents which Interfere with the Immune Response," *Proceedings for the Society for Experimental Biology and Medicine* 107 (1961): 796–99. "A Summary of Investigations with 6[(1-methyl–4-nitro-r-imidazolyl) thio] Purine," *Cancer Chemotherapy Report* 14 (1961): 93–98. "The Purine Path to Chemotherapy," *Science* 244 (1989): 41–47.

Bibliography: *Current Biography Yearbook* (New York: H. W. Wilson, 1995), p. 14. *New York Times*, October 18, 1988, pp. A1, C17. *Science* 242 (1988): 516–17. S. St. Pierre, *Gertrude Elion* (Vero Beach, Fla.: Rourke Enterprises, 1993).

HITCHINGS, GEORGE HERBERT, JR.

Prize: Physiology or Medicine, 1988. *Born:* April 18, 1905; Hoquiam, Washington. *Died:* February 27, 1998; Chapel Hill, North Carolina. *Nationality:* American. *Education:* University of Washington, B.S., 1927; University of Washington, M.S., 1928; Harvard University, Massachusetts, Ph.D., 1933. *Career:* Harvard University, Massachusetts, Professor, 1933–39; Western Reserve University, Ohio, Professor, 1939–42; Burroughs-Wellcome, North Carolina, Researcher, 1942–75. *Other Awards:* Gairdner Award, 1968; Gregor Mendel Medal, 1968; Passano Award, 1969; de Villier Award, 1969; Purkinje Medal, 1971; Cameron Prize, 1972; Medicinal Chemistry Award, 1972; Bertner Federation Award, 1974; Mullard Award, 1976; Papanicalaou Award, 1979; C. Chester Stock Medal, 1981; Oscar B. Hunter Award, 1984; Alfred Burger Award, 1984; Lekow Medal, Poland, 1988; Albert Schweitzer Prize, 1989.

Citation: "For their discoveries of important principles for drug treatment" (with James Black and Gertrude B. Elion).

Life Work: Hitchings's field of investigation was purine chemistry as the basis for the study of nucleic acids. He was convinced that since parasitic tissues generally depend for survival on a more rapid growth than that of the host tissues, nucleic acid antimetabolites should be good medicines. His first success came in 1949 with the compound pyrimethamine (Daraprim), used to treat malaria. They soon produced another DHFR (dihydrofolate reductase, an enzyme producing nucleic acid)-blocking chemical, trimethoprim, or cotrimoxazolre (Septrin or Bactrim). In 1951 Hitchings and Elion found a compound for the treatment of leukemia called 6-mercaptopurine

(6-MP). Efforts to imporve 6-MP further led to the formulation of azathioprine (Imuran) used to prevent the immunological rejection of transplanted tissues and allopurinol (Zyloprim) used in the treatment of gout. Among the other drugs that he developed during this period was acyclovir (Zovirax), the first effective antiviral agent to treat herpes.

Publications: "Pyrimethamine: The Use of an Antimetabolite in the Chemotherapy of Malaria and Other Infections," *Clinical Pharmacology and Therapeutics* 1 (1960): 570–89. "Suppression of the Immune Response by Drugs in Combination," *Proceedings for the Society for Experimental Biological Medicine* 111 (1962): 334–37. "Chemical Suppression of the Immune Response," *Pharmacology Review* 15 (1963): 365–405.

Bibliography: *New York Times*, October 18, 1988, pp. A1, C17. *New York Times Magazine*, January 29, 1989, p. 28. *Science* 242 (1988): 516–17.

BISHOP, JOHN MICHAEL

Prize: Physiology or Medicine, 1989. *Born:* February 22, 1936; York, Pennsylvania. *Nationality:* American. *Education:* Gettysburg College, Pennsylvania, B.A., 1957; Harvard University, Massachusetts, M.D., 1962. *Career:* Massachusetts General Hospital, Resident, 1962–64; National Institutes of Health, Maryland, Researcher, 1964–68; University of California, San Francisco, Professor, 1968–. *Other Awards:* Biomedical Research Award, American Association of Medical Colleges, 1981; Lasker Award, 1982; Armand Hammer Award, 1984; General Motors Foundation Award, 1984; Gairdner Foundation Award, 1984; Medal of Honor, American Cancer Society, 1985.

Citation: "For their discovery of the cellular origin of retroviral oncogenes" (with Harold E. Varmus).

Life Work: Bishop's field of investigation was molecular biology. The discovery of reverse transcriptase by Baltimore led him to research the replication of retroviruses. The virus's ability to cause cancers was determined by a certain Rous sarcoma virus (RSV) gene named src; genes with this property are called oncogenes. However, an RSV mutant was found in which the src gene was left out or deleted. Bishop and Harold Varmus speculated that by matching up (hybridizing) DNA from normal type (src) virus with RNA from src virus, they could isolate the src gene. They used an src probe and found that src-like genes were present not only in RSV but also in normal chicken DNA. They found src in birds, chickens, and mammals. These findings led to the discovery that the cancer-causing gene was not from a viral infection but was a normal cellular gene carried by the host and may have some normal and necessary function in animal cells.

Publications: "DNA related to the Transforming Gene(s) of Avian Sarcoma Viruses is Present in Normal Avian DNA," *Nature* 260 (March 11, 1976): 170–73. "Oncogenes," *Scientific American* 246 (March, 1982): 80–91. "Amplification of N-myc in

Untreated Human Neuroblastomas Correlates with Advance Disease State," *Science* 224 (June 8, 1984): 1121–24. "The Molecular Genetics of Cancer," *Science* 235 (January 16, 1987): 305–12.

Bibliography: *Chemical and Engineering News* 67 (October 16, 1989): 6–8. *Scientific American* 261 (December 1989): 34–36.

VARMUS, HAROLD ELIOT

Prize: Physiology or Medicine, 1989. *Born:* December 13, 1939; Oceanside, New York. *Nationality:* American. *Education:* Amherst College, Massachusetts, B.A., 1961; Harvard University, Massachusetts, M.A., 1962; Columbia University, New York, M.D., 1966. *Career:* Presbyterian Hospital, New York, Resident, 1966–68; National Institutes of Health, Maryland, Researcher, 1968–70; University of California, San Francisco, Professor, 1970–93; National Institutes of Health, Maryland, Director, 1993–. *Other Awards:* Lasker Award, 1982; Passano Award, 1983; Alfred Sloan Award, 1984; Armand Hammer Prize, 1984; Shubitz Prize, 1984.

Citation: "For their discovery of the cellular origin of retroviral oncogenes" (with J. Michael Bishop).

Life Work: Varmus's field of investigation was oncological viruses. The starting point of his research was the src (for sarcoma), an RSV gene that determined the virus's ability to cause cancers. Varmus and J. Michael Bishop isolated the src gene but found that src genes are located in normal chickens and even birds and mammals. These findings led to the conclusion that the cancer-causing gene was not from a viral infection but was a normal cellular gene carried by the host. Varmus and Bishop proposed that cellular oncogenes are present in all animals and have a necessary and normal function.

Publications: "DNA Related to the Transforming Gene(s) of Avian Sarcoma Viruses is Present in Normal Avian DNA," *Nature* 260 (March 11, 1976): 170–73. "Amplification of N-myc in Untreated Human Neuroblastomas Correlates with Advanced Disease State," *Science* 224 (June 8, 1984): 1121–25. "Oncogenes and Transcriptional Control," *Science* 238 (December 4, 1987): 1337–40.

Bibliography: *Chemical and Engineering News* 67 (October 16, 1989): 6–8. *Scientific American* 261 (December 1989): 34–36.

MURRAY, JOSEPH E.

Prize: Physiology or Medicine, 1990. *Born:* April 1, 1919; Milford, Massachusetts. *Nationality:* American. *Education:* Holy Cross College, Massachusetts, A.B., 1940;

Harvard University, Massachusetts, M.D., 1943. *Career:* Medical Practice, 1943–; Children's Hospital Medical Center, Massachusetts, Surgeon, 1972–85; Harvard Medical School, Massachusetts, Professor, 1970–. *Other Awards:* Gold Medal, International Society of Surgeons, 1963; Sabin Award, 1994.

Citation: "For their discoveries concerning Organ and Cell Transplantation in the Treatment of Human Disease" (with E. Donnall Thomas).

Life Work: Murray's field of investigation was transplant rejection. Murray's research focused on ways to suppress or inactivate the recipient's immune system so that he or she would tolerate a transplant. He found the answer in the drug 6-MP, which is used to treat leukemia, followed later by azathioprine (Imuran). Murray and his colleagues performed the first human kidney transplant using azathioprine in 1961. Surgeons soon learnt to transplant other organs, such as the liver, heart, pancreas, and lungs.

Publications: "Organ Transplantation: Status and a Look into the Future," *New York Journal of Medicine* 61 (October 1, 1961): 3245–48. "Organ Transplantation—The Kidney and the Skin," *Southern Medical Journal* 55 (September 1962): 890–93. "Prolonged Survival of Human-Kidney Homografts by Immunosuppressive Drug Therapy," *New England Journal of Medicine* 268 (June 13, 1963): 1315–23.

Bibliography: F. Magill, *Nobel Prize Winners: Physiology or Medicine* (Pasadena, Calif.: Salem Press, 1991), pp. 588–97. *New York Times*, October 9, 1990; p. A1.

THOMAS, EDWARD DONNALL

Prize: Physiology or Medicine, 1990. *Born:* March 15, 1920; Mart, Texas. *Nationality:* American. *Education:* University of Texas, B.A., 1941; University of Texas, M.A., 1943; Harvard University, Massachusetts, M.D., 1946. *Career:* Medical practice, 1946–; Harvard Medical School, Massachusetts, Professor 1953–55; Columbia University, New York, Professor, 1955–63; University of Washington, Professor, 1963–. *Other Awards:* McIntyre Award, 1975; Levine Award, 1979; Kettering Prize, 1981; de Villiers Award, 1983; Landsteiner Award, 1987; Fox Award, 1990; Gairdner Foundation Award, 1990; National Medal of Science, 1990; Kober Medal, 1992.

Citation: "For their discoveries concerning Organ and Cell Transplantation in the Treatment of Human Disease" (with Joseph E. Murray).

Life Work: Thomas's field of investigation was graft-versus-host-disease (GVHD), in which transplanted bone marrow was rejected by the rest of a patient's immune system. In 1969 Thomas and his team transplanted matched bone marrow into an adult leukemia patient. He developed complete procedures for such a treatment, including radiation and chemotherapy to cripple the immune system so the graft would not be rejected, tissue typing to ensure a compatible graft, and immunosuppressive drugs to control GVHD.

Bibliography: F. Magill, *Nobel Prize Winners: Physiology or Medicine* (Pasadena, Calif.: Salem Press, 1991), pp. 588–97. *New York Times,* October 9, 1990, p. A1.

NEHER, ERWIN

Prize: Physiology or Medicine, 1991. *Born:* March 20, 1944; Landsberg, Germany. *Nationality:* German. *Education:* University of Wisconsin, M.S., 1967: Institute of Technology, Germany, Ph.D., 1970. *Career:* Max Planck Institut für Psychiatrie, Germany, Researcher, 1970–76; Max Planck Institut fur Biophysikalische Chemie, Germany, Researcher, 1976–.

Citation: "For their discoveries concerning the function of single ion channels in cells" (with Bert Sakmann).

Life Work: Neher and Sakmann solved one of the most urgent problems in membrane biophysics: that of isolating a single ion channel and studying its individual properties. Ion channels are large protein molecules with a closable hole in the middle. When the hole is open, the ions can slip through the cell membrane and when it is closed, the channel is not penetrable. The most common tool for studying ion channel was the voltage clamp, which froze the electric field of a portion of the cell membrane at any level so that the flow of selected ions can be measured at a given point at any time. However, voltage clamps had many drawbacks, principally the background noise created by some ion channels leaking through the cell membrane by way of pores. Neher and Sakmann solved this problem with patch clamping using hollow glass tubes or pipettes with ultrafine tips only a few microns in diameter. When pressed against a cell membrane, the pipette forms a strong seal with very high electrical resistance. Patch clamping lets scientists study many diseases involving defective regulation of ion channels, including diabetes, cystic fibrosis, and epilepsy.

Publications: "Single-channel Currents Recorded from Membrane of Denervated Frog Muscle Fibres," with B. Sakmann, *Nature* 260 (1976): 799. "Noise Analysis of Drug-Induced Voltage Clamp Currents in Denervated Frog Muscle Fibers," with B. Sakmann, *J. Physiol. (London)* 258 (1976): 705–29. *Single Channel Recording,* with B. Sakmann (New York: Plenum Press, 1983).

Bibliography: *Chemical and Engineering News* 69 (October 14, 1991): 4. *Science* 254 (October 18, 1991): 380.

SAKMANN, BERT

Prize: Physiology or Medicine, 1991. *Born:* June 12, 1942; Stuttgart, Germany. *Nationality:* German. *Education:* University of Munich, Germany, B.A., 1967; University of Göttingen, Germany, M.D., 1974. *Career:* Max Planck Institut für Psychiatrie, Munich, Germany, Researcher, 1969–70; University College, England, Researcher, 1970–72; Max Planck Institut für Biophysikalische Chemie, Göttingen, Germany, Researcher, 1972–89; Max Planck Institut, Heidelberg, Germany, Researcher, 1989–.

Citation: "For their discoveries concerning the function of single ion channels in cells" (with Erwin Neher).

Life Work: Sakmann and Neher invented the patch clamping technique which made it possible to voltage clamps in the measurement of ion channels. *See* Neher, Erwin, p. 379.

Publications: "Single-channel Currents Recorded from Membrane of Denervated Frog Muscle Fibres." *Nature* 260 (1976): 799 (with E. Neher); "Noise Analysis of Drug-Induced Voltage Clamp Currents in Denervated Frog Muscle Fibers." *J. Physiol. (London)* 258 (1976): 705–29 (with E. Neher); *Single Channel Recording* (New York: Plenum Press, 1983 (with E. Neher).

Bibliography: *Chemical and Engineering News* 69 (October 14, 1991): 4. *Science* 254 (October 18, 1991): 380.

FISCHER, EDMOND HENRI

Prize: Physiology or Medicine, 1992. *Born:* April 6, 1920; Shanghai, China. *Nationality:* French; came to U.S. in 1953. *Education:* University of Geneva, Switzerland, licensure, 1943; diploma, 1944; Ph.D., 1947. *Career:* University of Geneva, Switzerland, Docent, 1950–53; University of Washinton, Professor, 1953–90. *Other Awards:* Passano Foundation Award, 1988; Beering Award, 1991.

Citation: "For their discoveries concerning reversible protein phosphorylation as a biological regulatory mechanism" (with Edwin J. Krebs).

Life Work: Fischer's field of investigation was adenosine monophosphate and glycogen phosphorylase. Working with Krebs, he found that muscle phosphorylase was regulated by phosphorylation-dephosphorylation. The process of reversible protein phosphorylation controls how chemical reactions within cells are turned on and off. This in turn regulates most of the biochemical processes of life. Proteins have a defined three-dimensional structure that dictates molecular interactions. An enzyme's ability to act on other proteins depends on an elaborate lock and key mechanism by which the enzyme and the protein upon which it acts fit together perfectly and each has the ability to act only on specific molecules. The enzyme is activated by a phosphate molecule and deactivated when the phosphate molecule is removed. The former activity, called phosphorylation is carried on by enzymes called protein kinases and the latter process called dephosphorylation is carried on by enzymes called phosphatases. The entire process is called protein phosphorylation.

Publications: "Phosphorylase Activity of Skeletal-muscle Extracts," with E. Krebs, *J. Biol. Chem.* 216 (1955): 113–20. "Conversion of Phosphorylase b to Phosphorylase a in Muscle Extracts," with E. Krebs, *J. Biol. Chem.* 216 (1955): 121–32. "Phosphorylase b-to-a Converting Enzyme of Rabbit Skeletal Muscle," with E. Krebs, *Biochem. Et Biophys. Acta* 20 (1956): 150–7.

Bibliography: *Chemical and Engineering News* 70 (October 19, 1992): 6. *Science* 258 (October 23, 1992): 542.

KREBS, EDWIN GERHARD

Prize: Physiology or Medicine, 1992. ***Born:*** June 6, 1918; Lansing, Iowa. ***Nationality:*** American. ***Education:*** University of Illinois, A.B., 1940; Washington University, Missouri M.D., 1943. ***Career:*** Washington University of St. Louis, Missouri, Researcher, 1946–48; University of California, Davis, Professor, 1968–76; University of Washington, Professor 1976–. ***Other Awards:*** Gairdner Foundation Award, 1978; Thorn Award, 1983; American Heart Association Award, 1987; 3M Award, 1989; Lasker Award, 1989; Horwitz Award, 1989; Ciba-Geigy-Drew Award, 1991; Beering Award, 1991; Welch Award, 1991.

Citation: "For their discoveries concerning reversible protein phosphorylation as a biological regulatory mechanism" (with Edmond H. Fischer).

Life Work: Krebs concentrated his research on phosphorylation. Working with Fischer, they studied the activation of the inactive phosphorylase enzyme by the addition of a phosphate from the compound adenosine triphosphate (ATP) to the protein and its inactivation upon the removal of the phosphate. They discovered that protein kinase was the enzyme responsible for the activation and phosphate was responsible for the inactivation. A small amount of protein kinase has a tremendous impact on a wide array of human functions because of a cascade effect creating a mechanism that is more like a dimmer than an on-off switch.

Publications: "Phosphorylase Activity of Skeletal-muscle Extracts," with E. Fischer, *J. Biol. Chem.* 216 (1955): 113–120. "Conversion of Phosphorylase b to Phosphorylase a in Muscle Extracts," with E. Fischer, *J. Biol. Chem.* 216 (1955): 121–32. "Phosphorylase b-to-a Converting Enzyme of Rabbit Skeletal Muscle," with E. Fischer, *Biochim. et Biophys. Acta* 20 (1956): 150–7.

Bibliography: *Chemical and Engineering News* 70 (October 19, 1992): 6. *Science* 258 (October 23, 1992): 542.

ROBERTS, RICHARD JOHN

Prize: Physiology or Medicine, 1993. *Born:* September 6, 1943; Derby, England. *Nationality:* English; later U.S. citizen. *Education:* Sheffield University, England, B.S. 1965; Ph.D. 1968. *Career:* Cold Spring Harbor Laboratory, New York, Researcher, 1972–92; New England Biolabs, Massachusetts, Researcher, 1992–.

Citation: "For their discoveries of split genes" (with Phillip A. Sharp).

Life Work: Roberts's field of investigation was DNA and RNA. He concentrated on Adenonvirus–2 DNA and mapped it. He determined the initiation and termination signals for Adenovirus–2 mRNA by sequencing the 5'-end of an mRNA, mapping its location on a restriction fragment, and then sequencing the upstream region. This was the promoter. He discovered the mRNA caps and developed an assay for capped oligonucleotides. He found that all late mRNAs began with the same capped oligonucleotide which was not coded on the DNA next to the main body of the mRNA. His experiments further proved the split structure for Adenovirus–2 mRNA and analyzed the sequences involving RNA splicing. Proof of the existence of split genes has been of fundamental importance in biology.

Publications: "Restriction Endonucleases," *CRC Crit. Rev. Biochem.* 4 (1976): 123–64. "The Role of Restriction Endonucleases in Genetic Engineering," *Miles Int. Symp. Ser.* 10 (1977): 21–32. "The Spliced Messenger RNAs of Adenovirus–2," *Proce. FEBS Meet.* 51 (1978): 245–53.

Bibliography: *Chemical and Engineering News* 71 (October 18, 1993): 7. *New Scientist* 14 (October 16, 1993): 4.

SHARP, PHILLIP ALLEN

Prize: Physiology or Medicine, 1993. *Born:* June 6, 1944; Falmouth, Kentucky. *Nationality:* American. *Education:* Union College, Kentucky, B.A., 1966; University of Illinois, Ph.D. 1969. *Career:* Cold Spring Harbor Laboratory, New York, Researcher, 1972–74; Massachusetts Institute of Technology, Professor, 1974–. *Other Awards:* Eli Lilly Award, 1980; Ricketts Award, 1985; Sloan Prize, 1986; Gairdner Foundation Award, 1986; Horwitz Prize, 1988; Lasker Award, 1988; Dickson Prize, 1990.

Citation: "For their discoveries of split genes" (with Richard J. Roberts).

Life Work: Sharp's early work on molecular and cell biology of tumors led to a study of adenoviruses. At MIT, Sharp discovered that genes in humans, unlike the genes of simpler organisms, could be arranged in a discontinuous pattern on several DNA segments. Such genes are called split genes. This discovery led to the genetic process of splicing and allowed scientists to gain a better understanding of certain cancers and hereditary diseases.

Publications: "Speculations on RNA Splicing," *Cell* 23 (1981): 643–46. "Adenovirus Late Transcriptional Unit," *Perspect. Virol.* 11 (1981): 9–30. *DNA Tumor Viruses* (Cold Spring Harbor, N.Y.: Cold Spring Harbor Laboratory, 1986).

Bibliography: *Chemical and Engineering News* 71 (October 18, 1993): 7. *New Scientist* 14 (October 16, 1993): 4.

GILMAN, ALFRED GOODMAN

Prize: Physiology or Medicine, 1994. *Born:* July 1, 1941; New Haven, Connecticut. *Nationality:* American. *Education:* Yale University, Connecticut, B.S., 1962; Case Western Reserve University, Ohio, M.D., Ph.D., 1969. *Career:* National Institutes of Health, Maryland, Researcher, 1969–71; University of Virginia, Professor, 1971–81; University of Texas Southwestern Medical Center, Professor, 1981–. *Other Awards:* Paulsson Award, 1982; Gairdner Foundation Award, 1984; Lasker Award, 1989; Passano Award, 1990; Waterford Award, 1990; American Heart Association Prize, 1990; Beering Award, 1990; Drew Award, 1991.

Citation: "For their discovery of G-proteins and the role of these proteins in signal transduction in cells" (with Martin Rodbell).

Life Work: Gilman's field of investigation was cellular signaling, or how cells within the human body receive and communicate outside stimuli. According to the conventional theory, the body produces, in response to outside stimuli, adrenaline that reaches the liver where receptors convey the message to the enzyme inside the cell. When so notified, the enzyme signals the liver cell to release glucose. Martin Rodbell proposed that a receptor, after it receives the adrenaline, changes shape and causes the molecule next to the receptor to change shape as well. It acts as a transducer or a clinical messenger. Working independently of Rodbell, Gilman found a protein that, when injected into mutated cells, restored normal transduction function. He called it *G-protein* because it binds with a nucleotide known as guanosine triphosphate (GTP). It acts as a biological traffic light that processes external signals such as neurotransmitters, light and small, and converts them into specific cellular responses in seconds. There are more than three hundred receptors that communicate with the nearly twenty known G-proteins. G-proteins have increased our understanding of certain diseases that have their roots in faulty transduction of signals.

Publications: "Resolution, Characterization, and Partial Purification of Components of Catecholamine sensitive Adenylate Cyclase," *NIH Publication* NIH–80–2017 (1980): 157–72. "Guanine Nucleotide-binding Regulatory Proteins and Dual Control of Adenylate Cyclase," *J. Clin. Invest.* 93 (1984): 1–4. "G Proteins and Dual Control of Adenylate Cyclase," *Cell* 36 (1984): 577–79.

Bibliography: *Chemical and Engineering News* 72 (October 17, 1994): 4. *New York Times* Biographical Service, 1994, p. 1562.

RODBELL, MARTIN

Prize: Physiology or Medicine, 1994. *Born:* December 21, 1925; Baltimore, Maryland. *Died:* December 7, 1998; Chapel Hill, North Carolina. *Nationality:* American. *Education:* Johns Hopkins University, Maryland, B.A., 1949; University of Washington, Ph.D., 1954. *Career:* National Institutes of Health, Maryland, Researcher, 1956–1994. *Other Awards:* Jacobeus Award, 1973; Health and Human Services Superior Service Award, 1974; Gairdner Foundation Award, 1984; Lounsberry Award, 1987.

Citation: "For their discovery of G-proteins and the role of these proteins in signal transduction in cells" (with Alfred G. Gilman).

Life Work: Rodbell originated the concept of transducers which informs the informational transaction between receptor and enzyme. Signal transduction now defines transactions between all types of receptors and cellular regulatory processes. Rodbell found that there are at least two types of transducers, one for stimulation and the other for inhibition of adenyl cyclase, and that these transducers are separate proteins from receptors and enzyme. He formulated the disaggregation theory to explain the concerted actions of hormones and GTP on receptors and transducers (called G-proteins). He also introduced the concept that there are multiple types of G-proteins to transduce the actions of hundreds of signals on their receptors. Since 1980, Rodbell has concentrated his research on the multimeric or poylmeric structures of G-proteins that play a prominent role in the coupling between receptors and a wide variety of effector systems, such as ion transporters, phospholipases and phosphodiesterases.

Publications: "Cell Surface Receptor Sites," *Curr. Top. Biochem.* (1972): 187–218. "Problem of Identifying the Glucagon Receptor," *Fed. Proc., FASEB* 32 (1973): 1854–58. "Molecular Mechanisms of Hormone Receptors," *Neurosci. Res. Program Bull.* 11 (1973): 211–15, 271–94.

Bibliography: *Chemical and Engineering News* 72 (October 17, 1994): 4. *New York Times* Biographical Service, 1994, p. 1562.

LEWIS, EDWARD B.

Prize: Physiology or Medicine, 1995. *Born:* May 20, 1918; Wilkes-Barre, Pennsylvania. *Nationality:* American. *Education:* University of Minnesota, B.A., 1939; California Institute of Technology, Ph.D., 1942. *Career:* California Institute of Technology, Professor, 1946–88. *Other Awards:* Gairdner Foundation Award, 1987;

Rosenstiel Award, 1987; Wolf Foundation Prize, 1989; Wolf Foundation Prize, 1989; Rosenstiel Award, 1990; National Medal of Science, 1990; Lasker Award, 1991; Horwitz Prize, 1992.

Citation: "For their discoveries concerning the genetic control of early embryonic development" (with Christiane Nüsslein-Volhard and Eric F. Wieschaus).

Life Work: Lewis's field of investigation was the gene system that regulates the development of specific regions of the body. His work first led to a new study of genetic development and to an understanding of the way in which life forms are controlled by a set of master regulatory genes that causes homeotic mutations. These mutations occur because a missing section of the body is replaced by a duplicate. He concluded that the genes of the body are segmented and ordered even at the embryo stage. Each section in the body is controlled by a specific group of genes arranged in the same order on the chromosomes as the body segments they controlled. Lewis's work has been instrumental in providing a better understanding of congenital malformations.

Publications: "The Relation to Repeats to Position Effect in Drosophila," *Genetics* 30 (1945): 137–66. "Germinal and somatic Reversion of the Ivory Mutant in Drosophila," *Genetics* 44 (1959): 522–31. "Clusters of Master Control Genes Regulate the Development of Higher Organisms," *JAMA* 267 (1992): 1524–31.

Bibliography: *New York Times*, October 10, 1995, p. B5.

NÜSSLEIN-VOLHARD, CHRISTIANE

Prize: Physiology or Medicine, 1995. ***Born:*** October 20, 1942; Magdeburg, Germany. *Nationality:* German. *Education:* University of Tübingen, Germany, Ph.D., 1972. *Career:* Max Planck Institute, Germany, Researcher, 1972–75; Biozentrum Basel, Switzerland, Researcher, 1975–76; University of Freiburg, Germany, Researcher, 1976–77; European Molecular Biology Laboratory, Germany, Researcher, 1978–80; Max Planck Institute, Germany, Professor, 1980–. *Other Awards:* Leibnitz Prize, 1982; Vogat Prize, 1987; Rosensteil Medal, 1988; Lasker Prize, 1990.

Citation: "For their discoveries concerning the genetic control of early embryonic development" (with Edward B. Lewis and Eric F. Wieschaus).

Life Work: Nüsslein-Volhard followed upon the work of Lewis, hoping to discover all the genes that determine embryo development. She and Weischaus bred forty thousand fruit fly families, each with a single defect, in an effort to assess which of its twenty thousand genes were significant to development and which essential. They found that 5,000 genes were significant and 137 were essential. They discovered that mutant flies could be classified into four categories: gap, pair-rule, even-skipped, and segment polarity. Gap genes divide the embryo into general regions. Pair-rule and even-skipped genes segment these regions, and segment polarity genes order anterior-posterior arrangements in each segment.

Publications: "Mutations Affecting Segment Number and Polarity in Drosophila," with E. Wieschaus, *Nature* 287 (1980): 795–801. "Determination of the Embryonic Axes of Drosophila," *Dev. Suppl.* (1991): 1–10. "The Formation of the Embryonic Axes in Drosophila," *Cancer* 71 (1993): 3189–93.

Bibliography: *New York Times*, October 10, 1995, p. B5.

WIESCHAUS, ERIC F.

Prize: Physiology or Medicine, 1995. *Born:* June 8, 1947; South Bend, Indiana. *Nationality:* American. *Education:* University of Notre Dame, Indiana, B.S., 1969; Yale University, Connecticut, Ph.D., 1974. *Career:* University of Zürich, Switzerland, Researcher, 1975–78; European Molecular Biology Laboratory, Germany, Researcher, 1978–81; Princeton University, New Jersey, Professor, 1981–.

Citation: "For their discoveries concerning the genetic control of early embryonic development" (with Edward B. Lewis and Christiane Nüsslein-Vohlard).

Life Work: Working with Nüsslein-Volhard, Wieschaus extended Lewis's work by identifying the role of genes in the development of the embryo. They determined which genes played significant and essential roles and the number of genes involved in the process and also classified the genes in four distinct categories: gap, pair-rule, even-skipped, and segment polarity.

Publications: "The Development and Function of the Female Germ Line in Drosophila," *Dev. Biol.* 68 (1979): 29–46. "Mutations Affecting Segment Number and Polarity in Drosophila," with C. Nüsslein-Volhard, *Nature* 287 (1980): 795–801. "Ortho Dentical Activity is Required for the Development of Medial Structures in the Larval and Adult Epidermis of Drosophila," *Development* 115 (1992): 801–11.

Bibliography: *New York Times*, October 10, 1995, p. B5.

DOHERTY, PETER C.

Prize: Physiology or Medicine, 1996. *Born:* October 15, 1940; Queensland, Australia. *Nationality:* Australian. *Education:* University of Queensland, B.A., 1962, M.A., 1966; University of Edinburgh, Ph.D. 1970. *Career:* Brisbane Animal Research Institute, 1963–67; Moredun Research Institute, Edinburgh, 1967–71; John Curtin School of Medical Research, Canberra, 1972–75; Wistar Institute, Philadelphia, 1975–82; John Curtin School of Medical Research, Canberra, 1982–88; Department of Immunology, St. Jude's Children's Research Hospital, Memphis, Tennessee, 1988–1992; University of Tennessee College of Medicine, 1992–. *Other Awards:* Paul

Ehrlich Prize, 1983; Gairdner Foundation International Award, 1986; Albert Lasker Medical Research Award, 1995.

Citation: "For their discoveries concerning the specificity of the cell mediated immune defence" (with Rolf M. Zinkernagel).

Life Work: Working with mice, Doherty and Zinkernagel found that T cells recognize and kill only if they are from the same strain of mice; they ignore all others. They concluded that T cells attack an infected cell only after it recognizes two key factors: a set of molecules known as major histocompatibility antigens (MHC) that indicate that the cell is indeed a part of the self, and a fragment of the virus itself indicating that the virus is infected. MHCs are an integral part of the body's two-step process in recognizing infected cells. This discovery has considerable potential in the treatment of diseases related to the immune system, such as AIDS.

Publications: "Restrictions of In Vitro T Cell Mediated Cytotoxicity in Lymphocytic Choriomeningitis Within a Syngenic and Semiallogenic System," with R. M. Zinkernagel, *Nature* 248 (1974): 121–27. "Immunological Surveillance Against Altered Self Components by Sensitized T Lymphocytes in Lymphocytic Choriomeingitis," with R. M. Zinkernagel, *Nature* 251 (1974): 243–49. "A Biological Role for the Major Histocompatibility Antigens, with R. H. Zinkernagel, *Lancet* (1975): 74–77.

Bibliography: *Lancet* 356 (July 8, 2000): 172. *New York Times,* October 8, 1996, p. C6.

ZINKERNAGEL, ROLF M.

Prize: Physiology or Medicine, 1996. *Born:* January 6, 1944; Basel, Switzerland. *Nationality:* Swiss. *Education:* University of Basel, Ph.D., 1968; University of Lausanne, M.D., 1970. *Career:* Institute of Biochemistry, Professor, 1971–73; John Curtin School of Medical Research, Professor, 1973–75; University of California, La Jolla, Professor, 1975–77; University of California, San Diego, Professor, 1977–79; Department of Pathology, University of Zürich, Professor, 1979–. *Other Awards:* Cloetta Stiftung Award, 1981; Gartner Foundation International Award, 1981; Jung Stiftung Award, 1982; Paul Ehrlich Prize, 1983; Mack Forster Prize, 1985; Christoforo Colombo Award, 1992; Albert Lasker Medical Research Award, 1995.

Citation: "For their discoveries concerning the specificity of the cell mediated immune defence" (with Peter C. Doherty).

Life Work: Zinkernagel and Doherty investigated the recognition mechanisms in the cellular immune systems, especially those involved in the killing of virus-infected cells by T lymphocytes. Because the T cells recognize only the infected cells and kill them if they come from the same strain, they found that T lymphocytes were looking for two indicators: a protein called major histocompatibility antigen that exists on the surface of every cell in the body and tells the immune system that the cell is part of th self, and a protein fragment from the infecting virus that signals the cell's infection. The discovery had many medical applications, especially in the development of new vaccines against viruses.

Publications: "Restriction of in Vitro T Cell-Mediated Cytotoxicity in Lymphocytic Choriomeningitis within a Syngenic and Semi-allogenic System," with P. C. Doherty, *Nature* 248 (1974): 701–702. "Immunological Surveillance against Altered Self-Components by Sensitized T Lymphocytes in Lymphocytic Choriomeningitis," with P. C. Doherty, *Nature* 251 (1974): 547–48. "Cytotoxic T Cells Learn Specificity for Self-H2 during Differentiation in the Thymus," *Nature* (January 19, 1978): 251–53. "The Discovery of MHC Restriction," with P. C. Doherty, *Immunology Today* (January 1997): 14–17.

Bibliography: *Lancet* 356 (July 8, 2000): 172. *New York Times,* October 8, 1996, p. C6.

PRUSINER, STANLEY BEN

Prize: Physiology or Medicine, 1997. *Born:* May 28, 1942; Des Moines, Iowa. *Nationality:* American. *Education:* University of California, Santa Barbara, Ph.D., 1965. *Career:* Professor, University of Pennsylvania, MD, 1968. *Other Awards:* Potamkin Prize for Alzheimer's Disease Research, 1991; Distinguished Achievements in Neurosciences Research Award, Bristol-Myers-Squibb, 1991; Medical Research Award, Met Life Foundation, 1992; Christopher Columbus Dicovery Award, NIH and Medical Society, Genoa, Italy, 1992; Charles A. Dana Award for Pioneering Acievements in Health, 1992; Dickson Prize for Outstanding Contributions to Medicine, University of Pittsburgh, 1992; Max Planck Research Award, Alexander von Humboldt Foundation and Max Planck Society, 1992; Gairdner Foundation International Award, 1993; Presidential Award, 1993; Albert Lasker Award for Basic Medical Research, 1994; Calendonian Research Foundation Prize, Royal Society of Edinburgh, 1995; Paul Ehrlich and Ludwig Darmstaedter Award, Germany, 1995; Paul Hoch Award, American Psychopathological Association, 1995; Wolf Prize in Medicine, 1996; ICN Virology Prize, 1996; Victor and Clara Soriano Award, World Federation of Neurology, 1996; Pasarow Foundation Prize in Neurosciences, 1996; Charles Leopold Mayer Prize, French Academy of Sciences, 1996; Keio International Prize for Medical Research, 1996; Baxter Award, American Association of Medical Colleges, 1996; Louisa Gross Horwitz Prize, Columbia University, 1997; K. J. Zulch Prize, Gertrude Reemtsma Foundation, 1997; Benjamin Franklin Medal, Franklin Institute, 1998; Jubilee Medal, Swedish Medical Society, 1998.

Citation: "For his discovery of Prions—a new biological principle of infection."

Life Work: In 1972, inspired by a patient who died from Creutzfeldt-Jakob disease (CJD), Prusiner began to investigate the causative agent of that disease. In 1982 he and his colleagues found a protein unique to the brains of scrapie-infested hamsters. This protein was later identified and named prion. Pruisner demonstrated that prions are normally present in healthy animals and humans but appear in an altered form in diseased brains. The prion's amino acid chain can fold into two distinct forms with different three-dimensional structures. One is a tightly coiled, unstable, normal form that does not cause disease. The other is an unwound, more stable, abnormal form, which causes CJD and other diseases by a catalytic process in which it, on contact with the normal protein, causes the latter to change its structure and become abnormal. In a chain reaction, more of the abnormal protein is produced and, after months or years, it finally accumulates to levels that damage the brain.

Publications: *The Enzymes of Glutamine Metabolism,* with Earl R. Stadtman (New York: Academic Press, 1973). *Slow Transmissible Diseases of the Nervous System,* with William J. Hadlow (New York: Academic Press, 1979). *Prions: Novel Infectious Pathogens Causing Scrapie and Creutzfeldt-Jakob Disease,* with Michael P. McKinley (San Diego: Academic Press, 1987). *Prion Biology and Diseases* (Cold Spring Harbor, N.Y.: Cold Spring Harbor Laboratory Press, 1999).

Bibliography: *Current Biography Yearbook* (New York: H. W. Wilson, 1997), pp. 440–44. *New York Times,* October 7, 1997, p. A1. Gary Taubes, "The Name of the Game Is Fame: But Is It Science?" *Discover* (December 1986): 44–56.

FURCHGOTT, ROBERT FRANCIS

Prize: Physiology or Medicine, 1998. *Born:* June 4, 1916; Charleston, South Carolina. *Nationality:* American. *Education:* Northwestern University, Evanston, Ill., Ph.D., 1940. *Career:* Medical School, Washington University, Professor, 1949–56; State University of New York, Brooklyn, Professor and chairman of department, 1956–88; Health Science Center, State University of New York, Brooklyn, Distinguished Professor, 1988–90; State University of New York, Brooklyn, Emeritus Professor of Pharmacology, 1990–. *Other Awards:* Goodman and Gilman Award, American Society of Pharmacology and Experimental Therapeutics, 1990; Achievement Award, American Heart Association, 1990; Bristol Myers Squibb Award for Achievement in Cardiovascular Research, 1991; Medal, New York Academy of Medicine, 1992.

Citation: "For their discoveries concerning nitric oxide as a signalling molecule in the cardiovascular system" (with Louis J. Ignarro and Ferid Murad).

Life Work: Furchgott's field of investigation was pharmacology and biochemistry of cardiac and smooth muscle, adrenergic mechanisms, vasodilation, endothelium-dependent relaxation of blood vessels, and nitric oxide in biology. Nitric oxide is well known as a common air pollutant formed from the burning of nitrogen. Within the human body, nitric acid has many different activities. In the circulatory system, nitric oxide induces vasodilation, inhibits platelet aggregation, smooth cell proliferation and migration, and maintains endothelial call barrier function. Its other functions include neurotransmission and antimicrobial activity. In 1977, Furchgott found that endothelial cells, which line the interior of blood vessels, produce an unknown signal molecule that induces relaxation of vascular smooth muscle cells. In 1986, Furchgott and Ignarro proposed that endothelium-derived relaxing factor (EDRF) and nitric acid are the same molecule. Further research has proved that nitric oxide has many more functions and plays a role in memory formation, tumor suppression, and immunity. Its therapeutic applications include bronchodilation and vasodilation to increase blood flow.

Publications: "The Role of Endothelium in the Responses of Vascular Smooth Muscle to Drugs," *Annual Review of Pharmacology and Toxicology* 24 (1984): 175–97. "Evidence for Endothelium-Dependent Vasodilation of Resistance Vessels by Acetylcholine," *Blood Vessels* 24, no. 3 (1987): 145–49. "Endothelium-Derived Relaxing Factor: Discovery, Early Studies, and Identification as Nitric Oxide," *Biusci Reports* 19, no. 4 (1999): 235–51.

Bibliography: *Lancet* 356 (July 22, 2000): 346. *New York Times*, October 13, 1998, p. A14.

IGNARRO, LOUIS J.

Prize: Physiology or Medicine, 1998. *Birth:* May 31, 1941; Brooklyn, New York. *Nationality:* American. *Education:* Columbia University, New York, B.A., 1962; University of Minnesota, Ph.D., 1996. *Career:* Medical School, Tulane University, Professor of Pharmacology, 1979–86; School of Medicine, University of California, Professor of Pharmacology, 1986–91; University of California, Dean of Research, 1991–. *Other Awards:* Research Award, Pharmaceutical Manufacturers Association Foundation, 1973; Research Award, Edward G. Schleider Foundation, 1973; Merck Research Award, 1974; Lilly Research Award, 1978; Smith, Kline and French Award, 1979.

Citation: "For their discoveries concerning nitric oxide as a signalling molecule in the cardiovascular system" (with Robert F. Furchgott and Ferid Murad).

Life Work: Ignarro's fields of investigation were inflammation and arthritis, cyclic nucleotides, bioregulation of human cell function, hormonal control mechanisms, free radicals and enzyme activation, nitric oxide metabolics, and regulation of vascular and platelet function. This finding fueled a boom in research on nitric oxide. Later research showed that NO is manufactured by many different kinds of cells and has a role in regulating a variety of body functions. The discovery was the key to the development of the drug Viagra, and has medical applications in the treatment of heart disease, shock, cancer, lung diseases and intestinal disorders.

Publications: "Endothelium-Derived Relaxing Factor Produced and Released from Artery and Vein Is Nitric Acid," *Proceedings of the National Academy of Sciences* 84 (December 1987): 9265–69. "Endothelium-Derived Relaxing Factor and Nitric Oxide Possess identical Pharmacologic Properties As Relaxants of Bovine Arterial and Venous Smooth Muscle," *Journal of Pharmacology and Experimental Therapy* 246 (July 1988): 218–26. *Nitric Oxide: Biochemistry, Molecular Biology and Therapeutic Implications* (Orlando, Fla.: Academic Press, 1995).

Bibliography: *Lancet* 356 (July 22, 2000): 346. *New York Times*, October 13, 1998, p. A14.

MURAD, FERID

Prize: Physiology or Medicine, 1998. *Birth:* September 14, 1936; Whiting, Indiana. *Nationality:* American. *Education:* DePauw University, B.S., 1958; Western Research University, M.D. and Ph.D., 1965. *Career:* School of Medicine, University of Virginia, Professor, 1975–81; Stanford University, Director, Clinical Research Center, 1971–81; Stanford University, Director, Division of Clinical Pharmacology, 1973–81; Stanford University, Medicine and Pharmacology, Professor, 1981–88; Abbot Laboratories, Vice President, 1990–. *Other Awards:* CIBA Award, 1988.

Citation: "For their discoveries concerning nitric oxide as a signalling molecule in the cardiovascular system" (with Robert F. Furchgott and Louis J. Ignarro).

Life Work: Murad's fields of investigation were cyclic adenosine monophosphate and cyclic guanosine monophosphate metabolism, endocrinology, and clinical pharmacology. Murad and his colleagues showed that NO acts as a signaling molecule in the cardiovascular system and their work uncovered an entirely new mechanism by which blood vessels in the body relax and widen. NO is a simple molecule, very different from the complex neurotransmitters and other signaling molecules that regulate biological events, and it is the only gas that does so. NO plays a role in memory formation, tumor suppression, and immunity and has significant potential in the treatment of many other diseases.

Publications: *Pharmacological Basis of Therapeutics* (Orlando, Fla.: Academic Press, 1985). *Cyclic GMP* (Orlando, Fla.: Academic Press, 1994). *Nitric Oxide: Biochemistry Molecular Biology, and Therapeutic Implications* (Orlando, Fla.: Academic Press, 1995).

Bibliography: *Lancet* 356 (July 22, 2000): 346. *New York Times*, October 13, 1998, p. A14.

BLOBEL, GÜNTER

Prize: Physiology or Medicine, 1999. *Birth:* May 21, 1936; Waltersdorf, Silesia, Germany. *Nationality:* German; later U.S. citizen. *Education:* Eberhard-Karl University, Tübingen, Germany, Ph.D. 1960; University of Wisconsin, Ph.D., 1967. *Career:* Professor, Cell Biology, Rockefeller University, New York, 1976–; Howard Hughes Medical Institute, Professor, 1986–. *Other Awards:* U. S. Steel Award in Molecular Biology, National Academy of Sciences, 1978; Warburg Medal, German Biochemical Society, 1983; Richard Mattia Award, Roche Institute of Molecular Biology, 1984; Wilson

Medal, American Society of Cellular Biology, 1986; Louisa Gross Horwitz Prize, 1988; Waterford Bio-Med Science Award, 1989.

Citation: "For the discovery that proteins have intrinsic signals that govern their transport and localization in the cell."

Life Work: Blobel's field of investigation was cell biology. In the 1970s Blobel discovered that newly synthesized proteins, destined to be transported out of the cell, have an intrinsic signal that directs them to and across the membrane of the endoplasmic reticulum, one of the cell's organelles, and then on to specific other compartments of the cell. He suggested that the protein traverses the membrane of the endoplasmic reticulum through a channel and detailed the molecular mechanisms underlying these processes. Proteins are long, folded, chainlike molecules made up of building blocks called amino acids. Either at one end of the protein or within it are particular sequences of amino acids that act as signals. These signals direct the protein to its compartment and membrane destination. The signal sequence is often removed by an enzyme called signal peptidase. Signal sequence-mediated targeting and protein translocation across the membrane occur through two mechanisms: The signal sequence is first recognized by a soluble signal recognition factor which in turn binds to a receptor in the target membrane. After its release from this targeting complex, the signal sequence binds to a receptor that opens a protein channel, allowing translocation across the membrane. After translocation, the channel closes. In another mechanism, protein is trafficked in and out of the nucleus. Proteins dock on fibers that project from the nuclear pore complexes. These complexes contain a central tube that serves as a conduit for the translocation of proteins. The same topography-based or topogenic signaling system exists in all other higher forms of life, including yeast, plant, and animal cells. Diseases, especially hereditary diseases and immune system disorders, occur because of errors in topogenic signals. Blobel's research made it possible to develop laboratory procedures to alter cells to churn out drugs such as insulin and human growth hormone.

Publications: "Gene Gating: A Hypothesis," *Proceedings of the National Academy of Sciences* 82 (1985): B527–29. "KAP104p: A Karyopherin Involved in the Nuclear Transport of Messenger RNA Binding Proteins," with J. D. Aitchison and M. P. Rout, *Science* 274 (1996): 624–27. "Nuclear Protein Import: Ran-GTP Dissociates the Karyopherin Alpha Beta Heterodimer by Displacing Alpha from an Overlapping Binding Site on Beta," with J. Moroianu and A. Radu, *Proceedings of the National Academy of Sciences* 93 (1996): 7059–67.

Bibliography: *New York Times*, October 12, 1999, p. B1. *Science News* (October 16, 1999): 1363. *Scientific American* 282 (May 2000): 38–40.

CARLSSON, ARVID

Prize: Physiology or Medicine, 2000. *Born:* January 25, 1923, Uppsala, Sweden. *Nationality:* Swedish. *Education:* University of Lund, Sweden, M.D., 1951. *Career:*

Goteborg University, Sweden, Professor of Pharmacology, 1959–1989. *Other Awards:* Anders Jahre Medical Prize, 1974; Stanley R. Dean Lecture and Prize, 1975; Anna-Monika Prize, 1975; Wolf Prize in Medicine, 1979; Bjorkenska Priset, University of Uppsala, 1981; Gairdner Foundation Award, 1982; Hilda and Alfred Eriksson Prize, Royal Swedish Academy of Science, 1985; Bristol-Myers Award, 1989; Paul Hoch Prize, 1990; Fred Springer Award, 1990; William K. Warren Schizophrenia Research Award, 1991; Open Mind Award in Psychiatry, 1992; Julius Axelrod Medal, 1992; Japan Prize, 1994; Lieber Prize, 1994; Research Prize of the Lundbeck Foundation, 1995; Robert J. and Clare Pasarow Foundation Award, 1995; Kraepelin-Medaille in Gold, 1997; Antonio Feltrinelli International Award, 1999.

Citation: "For their discoveries concerning signal transduction in the nervous system" (with Paul Greengard and Eric R. Kandel).

Life Work: Carlsson's work showed that dopamine is a neurotransmitter in the brain and lack of this chemical causes Parkinson's and other diseases. He also showed that both the chemical deficiency and its clinical symptoms can be reversed by L-DOPA, a dopamine precursor that is converted into the neurotransmitter in the brain. In a series of experiments in the 1950s Carlsson showed that dopamine was concentrated in parts of the brain controlling movement. He noted that reserpine, a natural alkaloid used to treat schizophrenia, depleted dopamine in the presynaptic neurons and reduced the capacity for voluntary movement. Overall, his work revealed how important dopamine balance is in the brain: too much of it results in psychosis and too little causes motor disorders. His work laid the foundation for such drugs as Prozac and L-Dopa. His research also laid the groundwork for the development of a family of drugs called selective serotonin reuptake inhibitors. These drugs, including Prozac, are used in treating depression.

Publication: "Birth of Neuropsychopharmacology—Impact on Brain Research," *Brain Research Bulletin* 50 (November/December 1999): 363.

Bibliography: *Lancet* 32 (October 7, 2000): 16. *Nature* 15 (October 12, 2000): 22. *New York Times*, October 10, 2000, p. 31; *Denver Post*, October 10, 2000, p. 18.

GREENGARD, PAUL

Prize: Physiology or Medicine; 2000. *Born:* December 11, 1925; New York, New York. *Nationality:* American. *Education:* Johns Hopkins University, Ph.D., 1953. *Career:* Geigy Research Laboratories, Director, Biochemistry, Ardsley, New York, 1959–67; Albert Einstein College of Medicine, New York, Visiting Associate Professor and Professor of Pharmacology, 1961–70; Yale University School of Medicine, Professor of Pharmacology and Psychiatry, New Haven, 1968–83; Rockefeller University, New York, Professor and Head, Laboratory of Molecular and Cellular Neuroscience, 1983–. *Other Awards:* Dickson Prize and Medal in Science, 1977; CIBA-Geigy Drew Award, 1979; New York Academy of Sciences Award in Biological and Medical Sciences, 1980; Pfizer Biomedical Research Award, 1986; 3M Life Sciences Award of the Federation of American Societies for Experimental Biology, 1987; Mental Health Research Achievement Award, National Mental Health Association, 1987; Robert and Adele Blank Award Lecture, New York University, 1988; Bristol-Myers Award, 1989; National Academy of Sciences Award, 1991; Goodman and Gilman Award, 1992; Karl Spencer Lashley Prize, 1993; Ralph W. Gerard Prize, 1994; Thudichum Medal, Biochemical Society, 1996; Lieber Prize, 1996; Charles A. Dana Award, 1997; Metropolitan Life Foundation Award, 1998; Ellison Medical Foundation Award, 1999.

Citation: "For their discoveries concerning signal transduction in the nervous system" (with Arvid Carlsson and Eric R. Kandel).

Life Work: Greengard took Carlsson's work and worked on the principal cell type of the dopamine-making region of the brain, known as the medium-spiny projection neuron because, unlike the cerebral cortex, where many different types of neuron work side by side, the corpus striatum has almost pure medium-spiny neurons. He followed dopamine's path through the brain and uncovered a chain reaction that occurs in a neuron after dopamine reaches it. Greengard found that it set off a cascade of changes, as dopamine made its way through each neuron. Signal transduction, the field Greengard discovered, describes the cascade of molecular events needed for a signal to pass through the synapses. In a series of experiments in the 1960s Greengard showed what happens after dopamine binds to receptors on the surface of postsynaptic neurons. It was known that when some hormones bind to the receptors there is an increase in the level of the second-level messenger, cyclic AMP. This activates enzymes known as kinases, which adds phosphate groups to various proteins, modifying their functions. This provokes a complicated cascade of phosphorylation and dephosphorylation events. In particular, a protein called DARPP-32 plays a fundamental role in regulating the phosphorylation states of many of the proteins in dopamine signaling pathways. Greengard also investigated the interactions among different pathways and demonstrated how several classes of common antipsychotic, hallucinogenic and antidepressant drugs interfere with chemical reactions and transmission of electrical signals in the brain.

Publications: *Advances in Cyclic Nucleotide and Protein Phosphorylation Research*, with Alan G. Robinson (Ann Arbor, Mich.: Books on Demand, 1984). *Advances in Second Messenger and Phospoprotein Reserach* (Ann Arbor, Mich.: Books on Demand, 1988). *Cyclin Nucleotides: Phosphorylated Proteins and Neuronal Function* (Ann Arbor, Mich.: Books on Demand, 1989). *Role of Cyclic AMP in Cell Function* (Ann Arbor, Mich.: Books on Demand, 1990).

Bibliography: *New York Times*, October 10, 2000, p. A22.

KANDEL, ERIC R.

Prize: Medicine or Physiology, 2000. ***Born:*** November 7, 1929; Vienna, Austria. *Nationality:* Austrian; later U.S. citizen. ***Education:*** Harvard University, M.A., 1952,

New York University School of Medicine, M.D., 1956. *Career:* New York University School of Medicine, Professor, 1974–83; Center for Neurobiology and Behavior, Columbia University College of Physicians and Surgeons, Founding Director, 1974–83; Howard Hughes Medical Institute, Columbia University, Senior Investigator, 1984–. *Other Awards:* Lester N. Hofheimer Prize, 1977; Lucy G. Moses Prize, 1977; Karl SpencerLashley Prize, 1981; Dickson Prize, 1982; Albert Lasker Medical Research Award, 1983; Lewis S. Rosensteil Award, 1984; Howard Crosby Warren Medal, 1984; American Association of Medical Colleges Award, 1985; Gairdner International Award for Outstanding Achievements in Medical Science, 1987; National Medal of Science, 1988; Distinguished Service Award of the American Psychiatric Association, 1988; Robert J. and Claire Pasarow Foundation Award, 1989; Bristol-Myers-Squibb Award, 1991; Warren Triennial Prize, 1992; Jean-Louis Signoret Prize, 1992; Harvey Prize, 1993; F. O. Schmitt Medal and Prize, 1993; Stevens Triennial Prize, 1995; New York Academy of Medicine Award, 1996; Gerard Prize, 1997; Charles A. Dana Award for Pioneering Achievement in Health, 1997; Wolf Prize, 1999.

Citation: "For their discoveries concerning signal transduction in the nervous system" (with Arvid Carlsson and Paul Greengard).

Life Work: Kandel, only the second psychiatrist to win the Nobel Prize, worked with the invertebrate Aplysia, a sea slug, famous for its large neurons, which are easy to study. With the sea slug, Kandel pinpointed the biochemical changes that occur during memory formation. The Aplysia does not have much to remember, but it does have a reflex to protect its gills. Kandel found that an increase in neurotransmitter release at synapses connecting the sensory nerve cells to those that activate the muscles involved in the reflex amplified this reflex for days or weeks. Kandel showed that changes in synaptic function are essential for learning and memory. He elucidated the cellular basis of short- and long-term memory and the mechanism known as long-term potentiation, which correlates synaptic efficiency to changes in behavior. His work forms an important foundation of the phenomenon known as brain plasticity: the recognition that the brain is a dynamic organ that changes constantly as it learns and stores information. Short-term memory is controlled by the phosphorylation of proteins called ion channels at the synapses, which are actually storage sites for memories. These channels let specific ions, such as sodium, into and out of cells. Long-term memory is produced by more permanent changes in these proteins. He also identified serotonin, cyclic AMP (cAMP), cAMP-dependent protein kinase, and cAMP response element binding protein (CREB) as key proteins in a signaling cascade involved in the acquisition of short-term memory and the conversion of short-term memory into long-term memory. He has elucidated the molecular pathways involved in both implicit memory (such as that relating to procedures and skills) and explicit memory (which involves conscious recall of information).

Publications: "Control of Memory Formation through Regulated Expression of a CaMKII Trensgene," *Nature* 27 (1996): 142–47. "The Long and Short of Long-Term Memory," *Nature* 13 (1986): 212–21. *Behavioral Apology of Aplysia: A Contribution to the Comparative Study of Opisthobranch Molluces* (New York: W. H. Freeman, 1995). *Essentials of Neural Science* (Stamford, Conn.: Appleton and Lange, 1995). *Handbook* *of Physiology: The Nervous System* (New York: Oxford University Press, 1988). *Principles of Neural Science* (Stamford, Conn.: Appleton and Lange, 1991).

Bibliography: *Denver Post,* October 10, 2000, p. 18. *Economist* 16 (October 14, 2000): 34–35. *Lancet* 32 (October 7, 2000): 16. *Nature* (October 12, 2000): 22. *New York Times,* October 10, 2000, p. 31. *Science* 18 (October 20, 2000): 83–85.

INDEX
BY NAME

INDEX BY NAME

INDEX BY NATION

INDEX BY NATION

VENEZUELA

YUGOSLAVIA

INDEX BY
SCIENTIFIC
WORK